AUGGIE BOHN
BEEBE DRIVE
CUTCHOGUE
516-734-60

AIRCRAFT PROFILES

AIRCRAFT IN PROFILE

VOLUME 4

PROFILE Nos. 73-96

GENERAL EDITOR
MARTIN C. WINDROW

DOUBLEDAY AND COMPANY, INC.
Garden City, New York
1968

Uniform with this Volume

Aircraft in Profile, Vol. 1 (Nos. 1–24)
Aircraft in Profile, Vol. 2 (Nos. 25–48)
Aircraft in Profile, Vol. 3 (Nos. 49–72)
Classic Cars in Profile, Vol. 1 (Nos. 1–24)
Classic Cars in Profile, Vol. 2 (Nos. 25–48)
Classic Cars in Profile, Vol. 3 (Nos. 49–72)
Classic Cars in Profile, Vol. 4 (Nos. 73–96)

Printed in England

First Published in Great Britain (1967) *by*
PROFILE PUBLICATIONS LIMITED

FOREWORD

The military aeroplane is always associated with violence, and perhaps this is the reason for the many thousands of words lauding their exploits, while the more docile, but far more productive, civil airliner tends to be forgotten by aviation historians.

The Junkers Ju 87 *has certainly left its mark on history and if we are to believe all that has been written, destruction followed in its path whenever its ugly silhouette appeared in the sky. But strip away the propaganda and mysticism and it is revealed as a first rate attack aircraft which, provided opposition was negligible, created havoc amongst troops and civilians alike.*

*Another more sedate, but far more destructive military machine was the Boeing B-*17 *Fortress, exponent of the "Precision Bombing" school of thought. Originally advanced by General Douhert, Precision Bombing rested on the theory that a fast, well-armed bomber flying at high altitude could fight its way in daylight through and over defending interceptors and destroy targets at will. Schweinfurt and Regensburg provided the acid test and it was not until the long-range Mustang and Thunderbolt became available that the Fortress came into its own.*

Those of us who study aviation history may remember the exploits of the Short Empire Boats which laid the foundations of long-range air travel in the 1930*'s. They could carry twenty-four passengers, plus mail or freight, in spacious comfort, and the cabin proportions made flying a pleasure. Had not the Second World War interrupted production and development, the flying boat as conceived by Shorts, might have made a major impact on civil aviation. In the event the entire British aircraft industry was devoted towards landplane development and by the end of hostilities the flying boat had been left behind in performance.*

*Finally, no history of aviation could be written without mentioning that most magical of all civil transports, the Douglas DC-*3 *which, as the Dakota provided the backbone of the Allied transport fleets in World War Two.*

*More DC-*3*'s were constructed than any other transport and this record is likely to remain unchallenged for the foreseeable future. The aircraft founded the fortunes of the Douglas Aircraft Company and today, thirty-three years after the prototype flew for the first time in December* 1935, *a large number of DC-*3*'s are still in active service. It was well named "The workhorse of the Air".*

CONTENTS

ACKNOWLEDGEMENTS

The Authors, Artists, Editor and Publishers wish to acknowledge the kind assistance given by many learned bodies, societies, companies, clubs, libraries, museums and individuals during the course of preparation of the various Profiles presented in this volume. Particular mention should be made of the following:

Mr. Harold Andrews
Sgr. G. Apostolo
M. E. C. Armees
Mr. R. G. Ashford
Mr. G Baumwart
Mr R. Besecker
Mr. R. Boden
Mr. R. C. Bowyer
Mr. John W. Caler
Mr. Charles W. Cain
Mr. Ed Carlson
Mr. J. Chatterton
Mr. E. F. Cheesman
Mr. Logan Combs
Mr. W. J. Connell
Mr. H. F. Cowley
Mr. J. B. Cynk
Mr. Grant Daly
Mr. Jay Frank Dial
Mr. Fred C. Dickey, Jr.
Mr. D. E. Dolan
Mr. F. C. Dobson
Mr. M. F. Eacock
Mr. Lee Enich
Mr. Roger E. Freeman
Mr. L. H. Gregson
Mr. Peter M. Grosz
Col. William Guier
Joseph G. Handelman, D.D.S.
Mr. R. W. Harrison
Mr. E. C. Hine (of the Imperial War Museum)
Mr. Alex Imrie
Mr. Walter Jeffries
Mr. W. Klepacki
Sqd. Lrdr. F. Kornicki
Herr Egon Krueger
Mr. William T. Larkins
Mr. G. J. Letzer
Mr. B. Male
Mr. E. G. Marsh
Mr. R. R. Martin
Mr. James Mathiesen
Lt-Col. M. E. McGuinn, U.S. Army
Mr. David W. Menard
Col. Cesare Milani
Mr. K. M. Molson
Maj. R. E. Nicoll
M. Jean Noel
Herr Heinz Nowarra
Herr Hans Obert
Mr. M. Olmstead
Mr. Douglas D. Olsen
Mr. Malcolm Passingham
Mr. F. Pawlowicz
Mr. Cyril Peckham, F.R.P.S.
Mr. Stephen Peltz
Mr. Ian Primmer
Mr. J. Roberts
Mr. Bruce Robertson
Mr. R. C. Seeley
Lt.-Col. E. M. Sommerich, U.S.A.F.
Mr. C. C. Stewart
Mr. John W. R. Taylor, F.R.Hist.S., A.R.Ae.S.
Mr. James Tenety
Mr. William T. Thomas
Mr. Charles D. Thompson
Mr. Zdenek Titz
Mr. Paul Trither
Mr. Jack Walton
Mr. R. Waugh
Mr. G. H. Whowell
Mr. Gordon S. Williams
Mr. Derek P. Woodhall
Mr. H. H. Wynne
Mr. Frank Yeoman
The Admiralty
H.M. Ministry of Defence
The Air Historical Branch (Air Ministry)
The Royal Aeronautical Society
The Royal Air Force
The Royal Australian Air Force
The Royal Canadian Air Force
The Australian War Memorial
Aviation Belge Militaire
The Royal Netherlands Air Force
The Royal Netherlands Navy
The South African Air Force
The United States Air Force
The United States Army
The United States Army Signal Corps
The United States Marine Corps
The United States Navy
The United States National Archives
The United States Bureau of Aeronautics
The United States National Aviation and Space Administration
American Airlines
British Aircraft Corporation
British European Airways Corporation
The Boeing Airplane Company
Curtiss Aircraft Corporation
Douglas Aircraft Co., Inc.
Ford Motor Co.
Foto-Dolling
Grumman Aircraft Engineering Corporation
Gruppe 66
Hawker Siddeley Aviation Ltd.
Imperial War Museum
K.L.M.
Ling-Temco-Vought Inc.
La Museé de l'Air
S.A.E. Nieuport
Orenda
Pan American Airways Corp.
Republic Aviation Corp.
Short Bros. & Harland Ltd.
Skrzydlata Polska
Smithsonian Institute
Swedish Air Lines
Swissair
United Air Lines
"The Aeroplane"
"Aeromodeller"
"Air Pictorial"
"Airview" (Tokyo)
"Flight International"
Texas Aviation Historical Society Inc.

PROFILE PUBLICATIONS

The Sopwith Triplane

NUMBER 73
TWO SHILLINGS

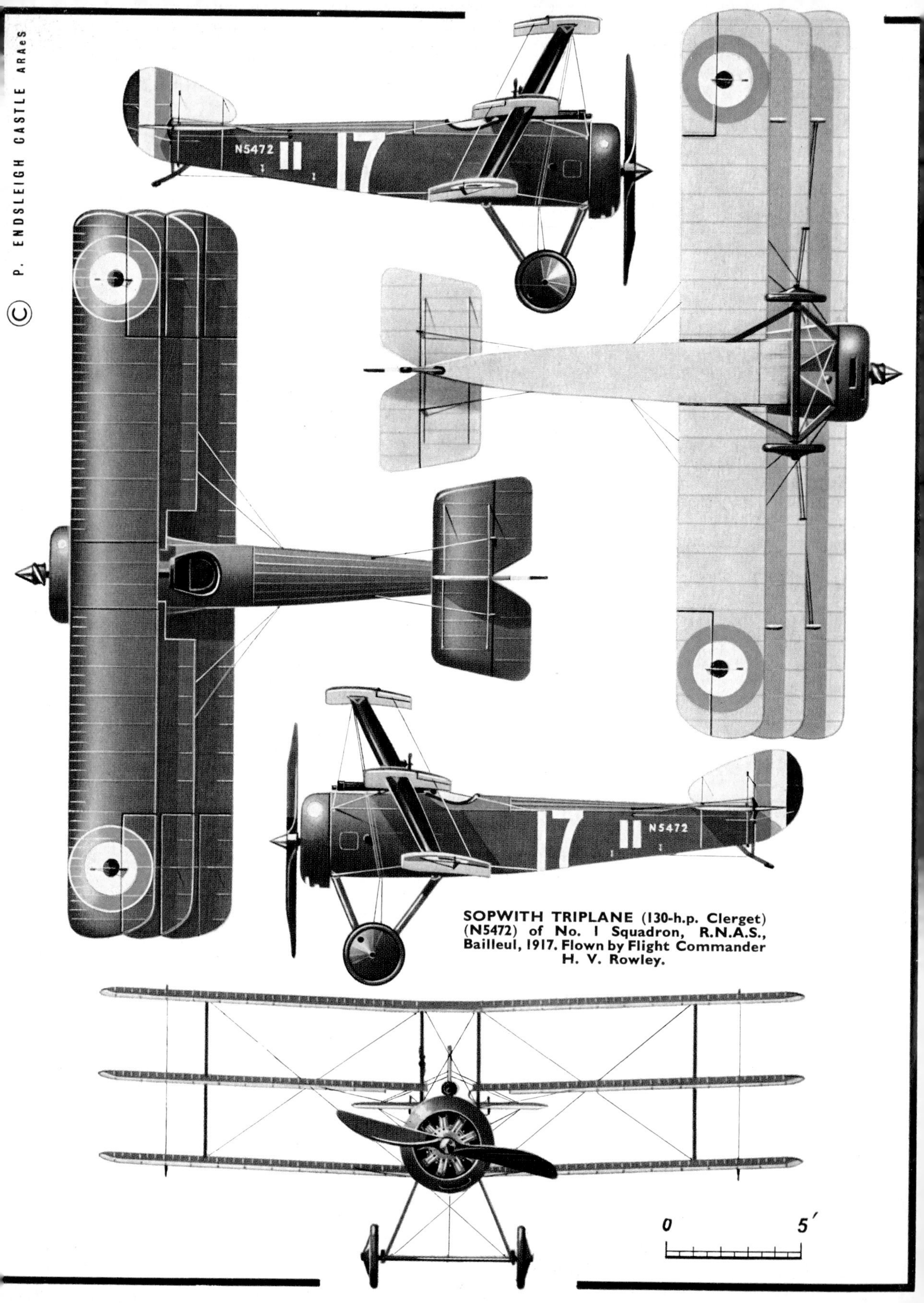

SOPWITH TRIPLANE (130-h.p. Clerget) (N5472) of No. 1 Squadron, R.N.A.S., Bailleul, 1917. Flown by Flight Commander H. V. Rowley.

This well-known photograph depicts the triplanes of No. 1 Naval Squadron at Bailleul about June 1917.

The Sopwith Triplane

by J. M. Bruce

In the Sopwith Pup Herbert Smith designed one of the world's great aeroplanes. Not only was it a redoubtable fighter in its day but it was aesthetically appealing and in its flying qualities probably unsurpassed by any aircraft built since that time. The Pup was wholly conventional, yet its successor was, aerodynamically, a startling new conception of a fighting aircraft.

The new single-seat fighter that was passed by the Sopwith experimental department on 28th May 1916 was a triplane. It was contemporary with the three-seat Sopwith LRTTr triplane, and it is possible that the three-seater's wing configuration may have partly inspired Smith to fit triplane wings to an aircraft that was otherwise very similar to the Pup. The single-seat triplane proved to be as graceful and manœuvrable as the three-seater was elephantine and ponderous.

Despite its wing arrangement the Sopwith triplane was a remarkably simple aircraft. Its fuselage was structurally similar to that of the Pup but differed in several details. A bold feature was the use of single, broad-chord interplane struts that were continuous from the top wing to the bottom. The centre-section struts were similar and, being attached to the top and bottom longerons of the fuselage, served as spacers in the side frames. At their mid-points, just above the upper longerons, they carried the attachment fixtures for the centre wings. The fuselage was designed to accommodate the 110-h.p. Clerget 9Z rotary engine.

The wings were of precisely the same span as those of the Pup and only 21 sq. ft. less in area. With the middle wing level with the pilot's eyes and the chord of each mainplane no more than 3 ft. 3 in., the pilot's view was not seriously impaired by the triplane configuration. The narrow chord and short span had aerodynamic advantages that enhanced the triplane's manœuvrability. Each wing had two spars fifteen inches apart; the spars of the top wing were solid but those of the middle and bottom wings were spindled out between the compression members. Ailerons were fitted to all three wings.

The first prototype under construction in the Sopwith works. In the background is the big three-seat triplane, the LRTTr.

The bracing of the mainplanes looked almost dangerous in its simplicity. The top and bottom wings were braced as a biplane structure, with one close-set pair of flying wires and a single landing wire on each side. Additionally, the middle and bottom wings were stayed fore-and-aft to the fuselage longerons. Long securing pins anchored all three wings to their attachment points.

The entire tail assembly was identical with that of the Pup but the triplane had the refinement of an adjustable tailplane; its actuating wheel was mounted on the starboard centre-section strut where it passed through the cockpit.

Test flying of the prototype was done by Harry Hawker at Brooklands. Such was his confidence in this radical new fighter that he looped it three minutes after its first take-off. At that time the triplane had no armament and the top centre section was covered with transparent material. It then bore no official serial number but under Admiralty Contract No. C.P. 117520/16 it acquired the identity *N500*.

A single Vickers gun was soon mounted centrally in front of the cockpit, as on the Pup, and *N500* was delivered to the R.N.A.S. The triplane reached France in mid-June 1916. It was sent to Furnes, the base of "A" Squadron, R.N.A.S., and was in action fifteen minutes after its arrival there, having been sent up to intercept an enemy aircraft.

The sensation created by the Pup was repeated by the triplane. Its manœuvrability was exemplary and its rate of climb was, for mid-1916, phenomenal. At a time when unconventional aircraft were regarded with suspicion by Service pilots the triplane won instant approval from the pilots of "A" Squadron. This compliment to its qualities must have been unique.

Even the Admiralty and War Office had no doubts, for the type was ordered in quantity for both the R.N.A.S. and R.F.C. Contracts were awarded to the Sopwith company, Clayton & Shuttleworth Ltd., and Oakley & Co. Ltd. The serial numbers *A9000–A9099* and *A9813–A9978* were allocated for triplanes,

Above and below: *The first prototype shortly after its completion, when its Vickers gun had been installed.*

apparently for the R.F.C.; the former batch was ordered from Sopwith, the latter from Clayton & Shuttleworth. For the R.N.A.S. *N5420–N5494* were ordered from Sopwith, *N5350–N5389* from Clayton & Shuttleworth, and *N5910–N5934* from Oakley.

A second Sopwith-built prototype, *N504*, was flying by 26th August 1916. This aircraft was powered by a 130-h.p. Clerget 9B engine, which re-emphasised the extraordinary climbing performance of the triplane, for it maintained a rate of climb of 1,000 ft./min. right up to 13,000 ft. It seems likely that *N504* was the triplane that climbed to a height of 22,000 ft. in September 1916. By the twenty-second of that month it was at Eastchurch. On that date it was flown by Squadron Commander Harry Busteed, who recorded that he had reached a speed of 116 m.p.h. at ground level. Busteed flew *N504* from Eastchurch to Dunkerque on 14th November 1916.

September 1916 saw the appearance on the Western Front of the Albatros D I, closely followed by the Albatros D II. These new German fighters were soon recognised as highly effective weapons that posed a serious threat to Allied air supremacy. Major-General H. M. Trenchard immediately foresaw that the German air service would become progressively more aggressive; on 29th September he gave the War Office advance notice of his intention to send, via Sir Douglas Haig, a request for substantial increases in the numbers of fighting squadrons attached to each army.

On the following day Haig wrote:

"I have the honour to request that the immediate attention of the Army Council may be given to the urgent necessity for a very early increase in the numbers and efficiency of the fighting aeroplanes at my disposal. Throughout the last three months the Royal Flying Corps in France has maintained such a measure of superiority over the enemy in the air that it has been enabled to render services of incalculable value. The result is that the enemy has made extraordinary efforts to increase the number, and develop the speed and power, of his fighting machines. He has unfortunately succeeded in doing so and it is necessary to realise clearly, and at once, that we shall undoubtedly lose our superiority in the air if I am not provided at an early date with improved means of retaining it. Within the last few days the enemy has brought into action on the Somme front a considerable number of fighting aeroplanes which are faster, handier, and capable of attaining a greater height than any at my disposal with the exception of one squadron of single-seater 'Nieuports', one of 'F.E. Rolls-Royce', and one of 'Sopwiths', the last mentioned being inferior to the enemy's new machines in some respects though superior in others. All other fighting machines at my disposal are decidedly inferior. The result of the advent of the enemy's improved machines has been a marked increase in the casualties suffered by the Royal Flying Corps, and though I do not anticipate losing our present predominance in the air for the next three or four months, the situation after that threatens to be very serious unless adequate steps to deal with it are taken at once. I have directed the G.O.C. Royal Flying Corps in France to put forward a statement of our estimated requirements."

Haig's letter arrived at a time when relations between the Air Board and the Admiralty were strained following the Admiralty's request for Treasury permission to purchase independently aircraft and aero-engines to the value of about £3,000,000. At that time the Air Board was responsible for organising and co-ordinating the supply of material and preventing competition between the Admiralty and the War Office, and the Board's displeasure, not merely at the Admiralty's request but at the Treasury's consent thereto, was understandable.

The Air Board did not discuss Haig's letter until 11th December 1916, but Trenchard attended the meeting to press forcefully for the strengthening of the R.F.C. He asked for the attachment to the R.F.C. of four fully-equipped R.N.A.S. squadrons and, as a means of providing two D.H.4, two Bristol Fighter

N500 *at R.N.A.S. Station Chingford, 1916.*
(Photo: Major R. E. Nicoll)

and one Spad squadrons, the transfer from the Admiralty of 100 Rolls-Royce and 50 Hispano-Suiza engines.

Like the Sopwith triplane the Spad VII had been ordered for both the R.N.A.S. and the R.F.C. The Admiralty offered, instead of 50 Hispano-Suiza engines, 60 complete Spads; but this was superseded in February 1917 by an agreement that provided for the R.F.C. to take over all 120 Spads then on order for the R.N.A.S. in exchange for all Sopwith triplanes ordered for the R.F.C.

A new triplane, fresh from the factory. (Photo: K. M. Molson)

Thus it was that the Sopwith triplane was used operationally only by the R.N.A.S. What has never been adequately explained is why the contracts for triplanes were so drastically reduced. Possibly by the time the R.N.A.S./R.F.C. agreement was reached the more conventional and better-armed F.1 Camel was regarded as more promising than the triplane and available production facilities were devoted to the Camel at the expense of the triplane. Only twenty more triplanes (*N6290–N6309*) were built by Sopwith; Clayton & Shuttleworth supplied only a further six, which had twin Vickers guns and were numbered *N533–N538*. It is uncertain whether these were the odd six from the 166 ordered from the firm for the R.F.C. or an experimental batch ordered by the Admiralty direct.

Deliveries of production triplanes had begun late in 1916. The first Sopwith-built production aircraft, *N5420*, was sent to Clayton & Shuttleworth, who in turn delivered their own first triplane, *N5350*, on 2nd December 1916.

The fourth Sopwith-built machine, *N5423*, was fitted with wings of 3 ft. 6 in. chord; these increased the wing area to 257 sq. ft. This triplane was at Eastchurch on 11th December 1916, and its official trials were conducted during that month. The broader wings made no appreciable difference to the aircraft's performance, consequently the original surfaces of 3 ft. 3 in. chord were retained as standard on all other triplanes.

At least one was fitted with a 110-h.p. Le Rhône engine. On test this aircraft proved to have a slightly better climbing performance than the Clerget-powered triplane but, in general, overall performance with the Le Rhône was not significantly different and the engine was not adopted as a standard power unit. Most of the triplanes that saw operational use had the 130-h.p. Clerget 9B.

N500 *after a mishap at Dunkerque. On at least one other occasion this triplane ended up in a similar position but was rather more extensively damaged.*

N500 *shortly after its arrival at St. Pol.* (Photo: E. F. Cheesman)

On the Western Front the Sopwith triplane was flown by R.N.A.S. Squadrons Nos. 1, 8, 9, 10, 11 and 12. By mid-February 1917 Naval squadrons Nos. 1 and 8 had been fully equipped with triplanes; both were attached to the R.F.C., No. 1 on 15th February, No. 8 on 28th March. No. 10 (Naval) Squadron, another triplane unit, was attached to the R.F.C. in mid-May 1917.

The triplane had not been in service long when a modification was introduced. In February 1917 an order was issued to the effect that a new, smaller tailplane and elevators were to be fitted, and all units were to replace the original Pup-type surfaces with the new components as they became available. The revised tail surfaces were shorter in span by 2 ft. 1 in. and had a total area of 23·6 sq. ft. This modification improved the triplane's control response considerably and enabled the aircraft to be dived vertically with greater ease.

The Design Flight of the R.N.A.S. station Eastchurch tested *N5440* fitted with the new tailplane and elevators (the aircraft was at Eastchurch as early as 31st January 1917) and reported:

"The decrease in horizontal tail area has resulted in making the machine much more handy. The fore-and-aft

A royal visit to the Sopwith works. King George V and Queen Mary inspecting triplanes and Pups, being built side by side. Second from the left in the group is Mr. (now Sir) Thomas Sopwith.

stability is not so good but there is sufficient control to get the machine out of any position possible whilst fighting. In effect it is considered that the alteration has improved the machine from a war point of view."

Operational squadrons do not seem to have hastened to fit the new tailplanes, possibly because supplies may have taken some time to reach France. Some aircraft still had the original surfaces in June 1917.

On its wider introduction to the R.N.A.S. the triplane became the subject of rumours about its structural strength, doubtless inspired by the economical interplane bracing. The rumours had no foundation in fact (though clearly the risk of both flying wires being severed by a bullet or shell splinter was obvious), and the aircraft had delightful flying qualities that won the admiration of the men who flew it. It was fully aerobatic and, during its brief operational career, it proved to be a formidable fighter in the hands of pilots like Flt. Comdr. R. S. Dallas, Flt. Lt. R. A. Little and Flt. Lt. Raymond Collishaw.

On the evening of 7th April 1917 Little attacked, single-handed, a formation of eleven enemy fighters. Although he did not shoot down any of the enemy on that occasion Little outclassed and outmanœuvred them. Two weeks later Dallas and Flt. Sub-Lt. T. G. Culling attacked a mixed formation of fourteen two-seaters and single-seat fighters and, in a running fight that lasted forty-five minutes, shot down three German aircraft, broke up the formation, and finally drove the remainder back behind the enemy lines.

On 1st April 1917 Flt. Sub-Lt. Raymond Collishaw joined No. 10 Squadron R.N.A.S. He had already won several combat victories with No. 3 Squadron R.N.A.S., and opened his score with No. 10 on 1st May, when he shot down an enemy aircraft that

It has been suggested that the reversed roundel colours and rudder stripes on this triplane appear to be so because panchromatic film had been used by the photographer. It seems more likely, however, that the colours were in fact reversed and that this aircraft was one of the four that were sent to the French Government. (Photo: Imperial War Museum Q67487)

crashed near Cortemarck. Two weeks later Naval Ten was attached to the R.F.C. On 1st June 1917 Collishaw shot down an Albatros single-seater in flames; this was the first of his sixteen victories (eleven destroyed, five out of control) in that month; all were won on a Sopwith triplane.

With Collishaw in Naval Ten were several brother Canadians: Flt. Sub-Lts. W. M. Alexander, G. E. Nash, E. V. Reid and J. E. Sharman. During June 1917 they flew triplanes named *Black Maria* (*N5492*, Collishaw), *Black Prince* (*N5487*, Alexander), *Black Roger* (probably *N5483*, Reid), *Black Sheep* (probably *N5376*, Nash) and *Black Death* (probably *N6307*, Sharman). This quintet came to be known as the Black Flight; the engine cowlings, metal fuselage panels and wheel covers of their triplanes were painted black. The Black Flight's existence was short and it is doubtful whether all five members actually flew together on more than a few occasions. Reid and Sharman joined "B" Flight (the Black Flight) of Naval Ten on 4th June; Nash was brought down and taken prisoner on 25th June; Sharman was transferred to "C" Flight on 30th June but flew with Collishaw on at least two later dates before his death on 22nd July; Reid was killed on 28th July. The Germans subsequently claimed to have brought down Collishaw's *N5492* in July 1917; its unnamed pilot on that occasion was killed.

Nevertheless, these five gallant Canadians between them shot down many enemy aircraft in the summer of 1917 and provided ample proof of the Sopwith triplane's qualities as a fighting aircraft.

The triplane itself was one of the very few aircraft of its time that were withdrawn without being outclassed. Its two main disadvantages seemed to be that even minor damage necessitated a disproportionate amount of repair work, and that it was more difficult to rig than a biplane. The second reason is difficult to accept, in view of the triplane's simple structure, but the former seems to be corroborated by the remarkable number of triplanes that saw service with several squadrons. This suggests that frequent visits to Aeroplane Repair Depots were required, with subsequent re-allocation to different units. A further reason for the triplane's withdrawal must have been the difficulty of maintaining the squadrons from the small number of completed aircraft.

Photographed in France, this triplane also had reversed colours in its roundels and rudder stripes. As it is surrounded entirely by French personnel it seems possible that it is here seen in French service. (Photo: Jean Nöel)

N5364 *photographed at Farnborough. This triplane is known to have been there on 15th May 1917, and this photograph was probably made at about that time.*

During its brief operational career the Sopwith triplane made a deep impression on the enemy. Its extraordinary rate of climb and great manœuvrability made it an elusive opponent and it was more than a match for the Albatros D III and D V. In April 1917 Manfred von Richthofen reported that the Sopwith triplane was the best Allied fighter at that time, and his opinion was echoed by General von Hoeppner, the *Kogenluft*, in an unusually candid interview reported in neutral newspapers in May 1917.

Several Sopwith triplanes were captured and tested at Adlershof, the first in June and July 1917; it had the early, large tailplane; a later captured specimen had the later tailplane. These aircraft must have provided ample proof that there was nothing structurally remarkable about the triplane, yet the *Flugzeugmeisterei* remained sufficiently impressed to send a

A captured triplane in German markings, apparently at Adlershof. The fin and airscrew were not standard components; the latter was almost certainly German. This aircraft was tested by the Germans in June and July 1917 and still had the original large tailplane.

N5430, *the triplane that was transferred to the R.F.C., photographed at Orfordness. It was fitted with an Aldis optical sight.* (Photo: "Aeromodeller")

Apparently one of the six triplanes built by Clayton and Shuttleworth with twin Vickers guns. (Photo: Imperial War Museum Q60483)

circular to all German manufacturers inviting them to examine the Sopwith at Adlershof; at the same time the *IdFlieg* encouraged them to design triplane fighters. Further discussion of the German developments is given in *Profile* No. 55, *The Fokker Dr.I.* Much as the functional Platz-designed Fok. Dr.I differed from the graceful Sopwith, one thing is certain: the Fokker would never have existed if its Sopwith predecessor had not convinced German fighter pilots and the German authorities that the triplane configuration contained in itself assurance of success for a fighter aircraft.

Replacement of the Sopwith triplane by the Camel began in the summer of 1917. Naval Eight and Naval Nine began to re-equip in July, Naval Ten at the end of August, when three of its triplanes were transferred to Naval One to bring that squadron's strength up to its full establishment of eighteen aircraft. Naval One's attachment to the R.F.C. ended on 2nd November 1917. The squadron continued to fly its triplanes for a few weeks; one of the last successful combats with the elegant Sopwith occurred on 12th November, when Flt. Lt. S. M. Kinkead and Flt. Sub-Lt. J. H. Forman attacked and destroyed an enemy fighter near Dixmude.

Of the contractors for the triplane, Oakley & Co. Ltd., had no previous experience of aircraft construction, and this is doubtless why they did not start to deliver until the autumn of 1917. As the replacement of the triplane was then well advanced the Oakley contract was terminated when only three aircraft had been completed. The third and last, *N5912*, was delivered on 19th October 1917 and is the only surviving Sopwith triplane of war-time construction, though it lost several of its original components during W.W.II. It was flown at the 1936 R.A.F. Display at Hendon, where its climbing performance, undiminished by the years, came as a revelation to many who saw it.

It was intended that the Oakley-built triplanes should have twin Vickers' guns like *N533–N538*, and it is perhaps a pity that some of the Oakley triplanes did not reach the front. It seems that the only two-gun triplanes to see operational use were *N533*, which was with Naval Ten in July and August 1917, and *N534*, which was on the strength of Naval One for a time. *N535* was flown at R.N.A.S. Manston.

In British service only one triplane, *N5431*, saw service outside France. This aircraft was sent to No. 2 Wing, R.N.A.S., at Mudros in the Aegean, presumably for operational evaluation in that theatre of war, for it was at Mudros as early as March 1917. In that month "E" Squadron, R.N.A.S., was formed. It was to provide the R.N.A.S. component of a joint R.F.C./R.N.A.S. fighting squadron at Hadzi Junas created to oppose *Kampfgeschwader I*, a German bombing unit that had arrived at Hudova in February 1917. The equipment of "E" Squadron consisted of four Sopwith 1½-Strutters and *N5431*, which was flown by Flt. Lt. J. W. Alcock (later pilot of the Vickers Vimy that made the first non-stop transatlantic flight). Unfortunately the triplane crashed badly at Salonika on 26th March 1917 and was therefore never used by "E" Squadron. The remains were taken back to Mudros and the aircraft was rebuilt. On 30th September 1917 a triplane from Mudros, flown by Flt. Lt. H. T. Mellings, shot down an enemy seaplane. The Sopwith was almost certainly the rebuilt *N5431*.

Alcock himself employed a number of Sopwith triplane components, possibly from the original

N5431, *the solitary triplane of No. 2 Wing, R.N.A.S., at Salonika, March 1917.*

A late survivor of the type was this triplane, marked "94", seen at Redcar during winter 1918–19. (Photo: Frank Yeoman)

Another two-gun triplane, this aircraft had a Lewis gun in addition to its standard single Vickers.

N5431, in a unique single-seat fighter that he built at Mudros. This aircraft embodied Pup and Camel parts also, and Alcock called his creation the Sopwith Mouse; it was also known as the Alcock A.1. Alcock was taken prisoner before his aircraft was completed; it was not flown until mid-October 1917.

Four Sopwith triplanes, *N5384*, *N5385*, *N5386* and *N5388*, were transferred to the French Government, *N5385* and *N5388* having the 110-h.p. Clerget. Four triplanes lent to France and subsequently returned to the R.N.A.S. by the French authorities had the serial numbers *N524* and *N541–N543*. It is uncertain whether there was any connection between these two groups of four aircraft, but it is possible that *N5384–N5386* may have been renumbered *N541–N543* on their return from French service. The Germans claimed to have brought down *N5388* in September 1917; and *N524* was used by No. 11 Squadron, R.N.A.S., at Hondschoote, where it was flown by Flt. Sub-Lt. A. R. Brown who, some six months later, played a leading part in the combat in which Manfred von Richthofen died.

On 4th May 1917, triplane *N5486* was dispatched from the R.N.A.S. White City depot to Russia. It saw service with the Imperial Russian Air Service and, in the winter of 1917–18, was still in service and was fitted with skis. Its fate is unknown.

An example of the type, *N5458*, was sent to the U.S.A., where it was exhibited in December 1917. This veteran had seen service with R.N.A.S. Squadrons Nos. 8 and 10; in the latter unit it had been flown by Flt. Sub-Lt. D. F. Fitzgibbon, a member of "B" Flight.

After withdrawal of the triplane from operational use it continued in service for a time for training and experimental purposes. On 7th February 1918 *N5453*, *N5462* and *N5468* were still on the strength of "C" Flight of No. 12 Squadron, R.N.A.S., at Dunkerque and were reported to be serviceable. As late as 1st October 1918 *N5430* visited Farnborough from Orfordness. This triplane had been transferred to the R.F.C. and was apparently at the armament experimental unit at Orfordness for some time.

The first triplane, *N500*, had a long career, for it survived until 17th December 1917, when it was written off at Dunkerque after what the R.N.A.S. was pleased to regard as fair wear and tear. It had survived several crashes and little of its original structure can have remained.

A belated modification of the triplane was called for in 1918 by R.A.F. Technical Order M.108 (42622/18), which required a compression strut to be fitted spanwise between the centre-section struts just above the gun. This was intended to prevent deformation of the centre-section struts which would, in certain conditions, bend inwards during aerobatics. The modification was probably a measure of the enthusiasm with which the triplane was flown at training units.

Before the Clerget-powered triplane had entered service, the Sopwith company had built two proto-

The wreckage of N5431 *beside the ditch that was evidently its undoing, 26th March 1917.* Above: *The rebuilt* N5431 *at Mudros.*

N5486, *with ski undercarriage, which served with the Imperial Russian Air Service in 1917–18.*

N509 *with some Sopwith employees at Brooklands.*

types of another fighting triplane powered by the Hispano-Suiza engine. These were numbered *N509* and *N510*, the former having a 150-h.p. Hispano-Suiza, the latter a 200-h.p. geared engine. The Hispano-Suiza triplane seemed to owe more to the Sopwith 1½-Strutter than to the Pup and was heavier-looking and less attractive than the Clerget-powered aircraft. The same system of plank-type interplane struts and bracing was used, but the wings were of 4 ft. 3 in. chord.

In December 1916 *N510* was destroyed in a crash at Eastchurch, apparently as a result of tail flutter. *N509* was also there at that time and also seemed to suffer from tail flutter: Harry Busteed flew it on 21st November 1916 on a "tail vibration test" and again for the same reason on 23rd November and 2nd January 1917. The Hispano-Suiza triplane was not developed, but *N509* survived until 29th October 1917, when it was written off at Manston after fair wear and tear. The Sopwith Hispano-Suiza triplanes provide an interesting comparison with the Fokker V.6 (see *Profile* No. 55).

At the time of writing (December 1965) a new Sopwith triplane is nearing completion in the workshop of Carl Swanson at Sycamore, Illinois, U.S.A. This authentic aircraft is destined for the Canadian War Museum.

PRODUCTION

At least 147 and possibly 150 Clerget triplanes were built under war-time contracts. Only two Hispano-Suiza triplanes were built by the Sopwith company with the serial numbers *N509* and *N510*.
Sopwith Aviation Co. Ltd., Canbury Park Road, Kingston-on-Thames: N500, N504, N524, N5420–N5494, N6290–N6309.
Clayton & Shuttleworth Ltd., Lincoln: N533–N538, N5350–N5389.
Oakley & Co. Ltd., Ilford: N5910–N5934 (*N5913–N5934* were not completed).
The serial numbers *N541–N543* were allotted to Sopwith triplanes that were lent to the French Government and subsequently returned to the R.N.A.S.
Service Use: Western Front—R.N.A.S. Squadrons Nos. 1, 8, 9, 10,

N509, *the 150-h.p. Hispano-Suiza triplane.* (Photo: Imperial War Museum Q67508)

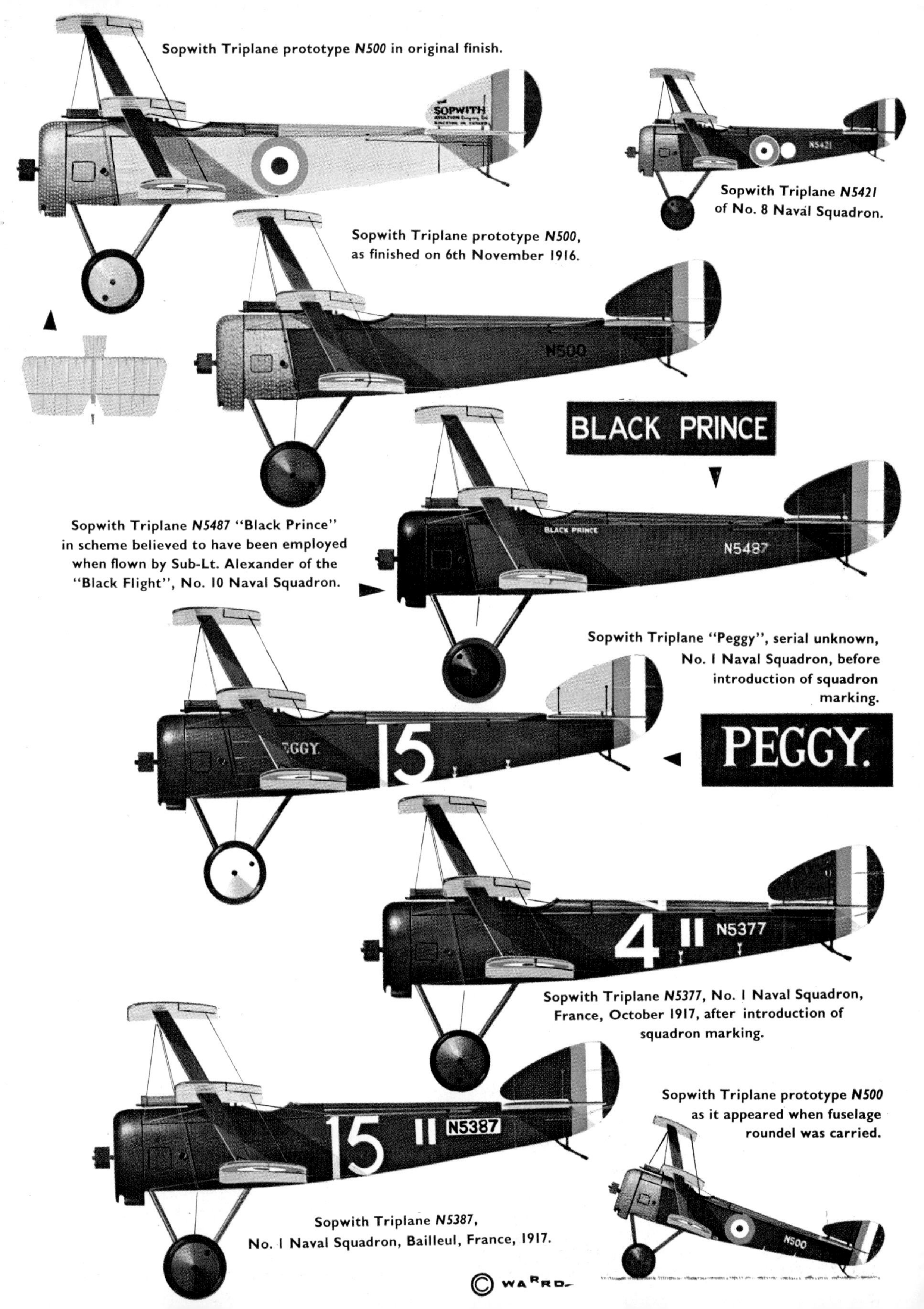

Sopwith Triplane prototype *N500* in original finish.

Sopwith Triplane *N5421* of No. 8 Naval Squadron.

Sopwith Triplane prototype *N500*, as finished on 6th November 1916.

Sopwith Triplane *N5487* "Black Prince" in scheme believed to have been employed when flown by Sub-Lt. Alexander of the "Black Flight", No. 10 Naval Squadron.

Sopwith Triplane "Peggy", serial unknown, No. 1 Naval Squadron, before introduction of squadron marking.

Sopwith Triplane *N5377*, No. 1 Naval Squadron, France, October 1917, after introduction of squadron marking.

Sopwith Triplane prototype *N500* as it appeared when fuselage roundel was carried.

Sopwith Triplane *N5387*, No. 1 Naval Squadron, Bailleul, France, 1917.

N510, *the second (200-h.p.) Hispano-Suiza triplane, also photographed at Brooklands.*

11 and 12. *Aegean*—No. 2 Wing, R.N.A.S., Mudros; "E" Squadron, R.N.A.S.
Examples of triplanes used by R.N.A.S. squadrons:
No. 1 Sqn.—N534, N5364, N5373, N5428, N5451, N5473, N6300, N6308.
No. 8 Sqn.—N5434, N5442, N5449, N5460, N5469, N6290, N6295, N6301.
No. 9 Sqn.—N5374, N5378, N5459 (previously with No. 1), *N5462* (later with No. 12), *N5475* (previously with No. 1), *N5484* (previously with No. 1, later with No. 12), *N5489, N5490* (previously with Nos. 1 and 10).
No. 10 Sqn.—N533, N5354, N5366, N5381, N5429, N5478, N6302, N6306.
No. 11 Sqn.—N500, N524, N5351.
No. 12 Sqn.—N5361, N5453 (previously with No. 1), *N5462* (previously with No. 9), *N5468* (previously with No. 8), *N5484* (previously with Nos. 1 and 9).
No. 2 Wing, R.N.A.S., Mudros—N5431.

SPECIFICATION

Power: 110-h.p. Clerget 9Z, 130-h.p. Clerget 9B, 110-h.p. Le Rhône 9J.

Dimensions: Span 26 ft. 6 in.; length 18 ft. 10 in.; height 10 ft. 6 in.; chord (standard) 3 ft. 3 in.; gap (each) 3 ft.; stagger (total) 3 ft.; dihedral 2 deg. 30 min.; incidence 2 deg.; span of tail originally 10 ft. 1 in., later 8 ft.; wheel track 5 ft. 6 in.; airscrew diameter (Lang) 8 ft. 11·9 in., (A.D.555) 8 ft. 6 in.

Areas: Wings (standard) 231 sq. ft.; ailerons each 5·66 sq. ft., total 34 sq. ft.; tailplane originally 23 sq. ft., later 14 sq. ft.; elevators originally 11·8 sq. ft., later 9·6 sq. ft.; fin 3·5 sq. ft.; rudder 4·5 sq. ft.

Armament: One fixed 0·303-in. Vickers machine gun with Scarff-Dibovski interrupter mechanism and 500 rounds. Six triplanes built by Clayton & Shuttleworth and those ordered from Oakley & Co. had two Vickers guns.

WEIGHTS AND PERFORMANCE

Aircraft	*N504*	C.F.S. test report, Dec. 1916 (130-h.p. triplane)	*N5423* with wings of 3 ft. 6 in. chord	*N5440* with small tailplane	Triplane with 110-h.p. Le Rhône	*N5350* with A.D.555 airscrew	*N5350* with Lang 1½-Strutter airscrew	*N5350* with Lang 7922 airscrew
Weights (lb.):								
Empty ...	1,135	1,101	993	1,168	1,095	1,178	1,178	1,178
Military load	—	80	58	58	—	—	—	—
Pilot ...	—	180	180	—	—	—	—	—
Fuel and oil	—	180	184	—	—	—	—	—
Loaded ...	1,502	1,541	1,415	1,538	1,451	1,548	1,548	1,548
Max. speed (m.p.h.) at:								
Ground level	—	—	—	—	121	—	—	—
1,000 ft. ...	—	—	—	115	—	—	—	—
3,000 ft. ...	122	—	—	114	—	—	—	—
6,500 ft. ...	119	113	116	114	111·5	—	—	—
10,000 ft. ...	119	107·5	114	117	108·5	100·5	99	104·5
15,000 ft. ...	—	98	105	—	—	—	—	—
Climb to:	m. s.	m. s.	m. s.	m. s.	m. s.	m. s.	m. s.	m. s.
6,000 ft. ...	— —	5 50	5 40	4 54	— —	6 8	5 25	5 58
6,500 ft. ...	— —	— —	6 20	— —	5 16	— —	— —	— —
10,000 ft. ...	9 25	11 50	10 36	10 12	9 20	12 28	11 0	12 27
13,000 ft. ...	13 0	22 20	15 0	15 42	— —	18 35	17 0	19 22
15,000 ft. ...	— —	— —	19 0	— —	— —	— —	24 0	— —

PROFILE PUBLICATIONS

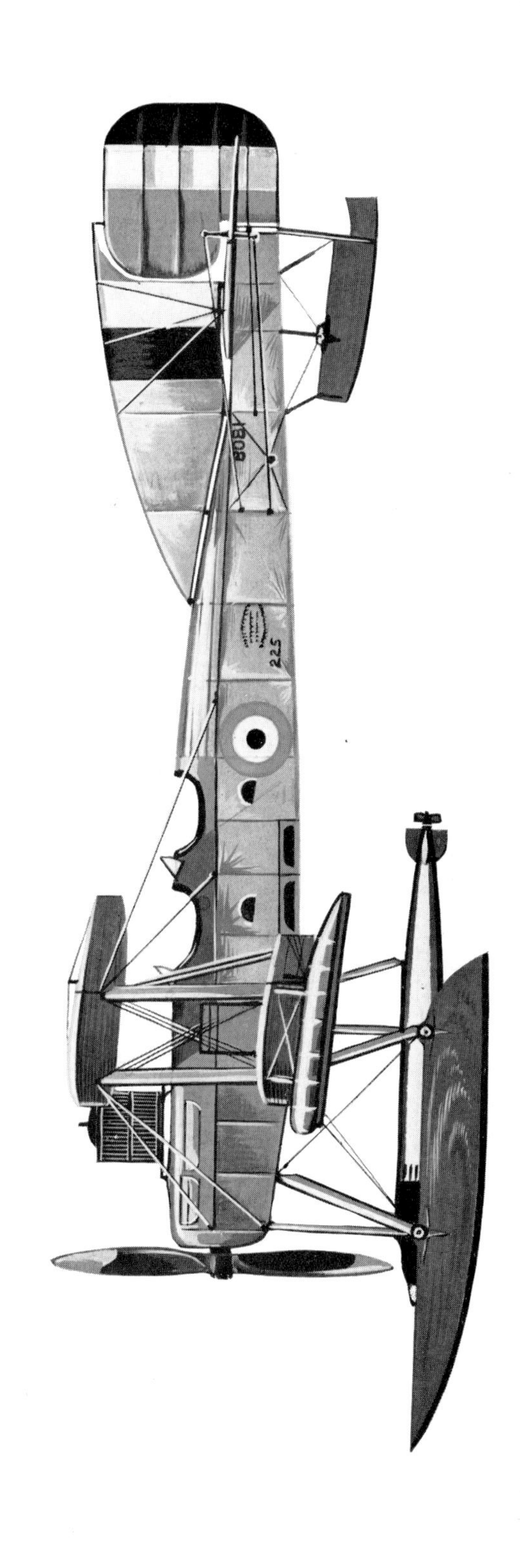

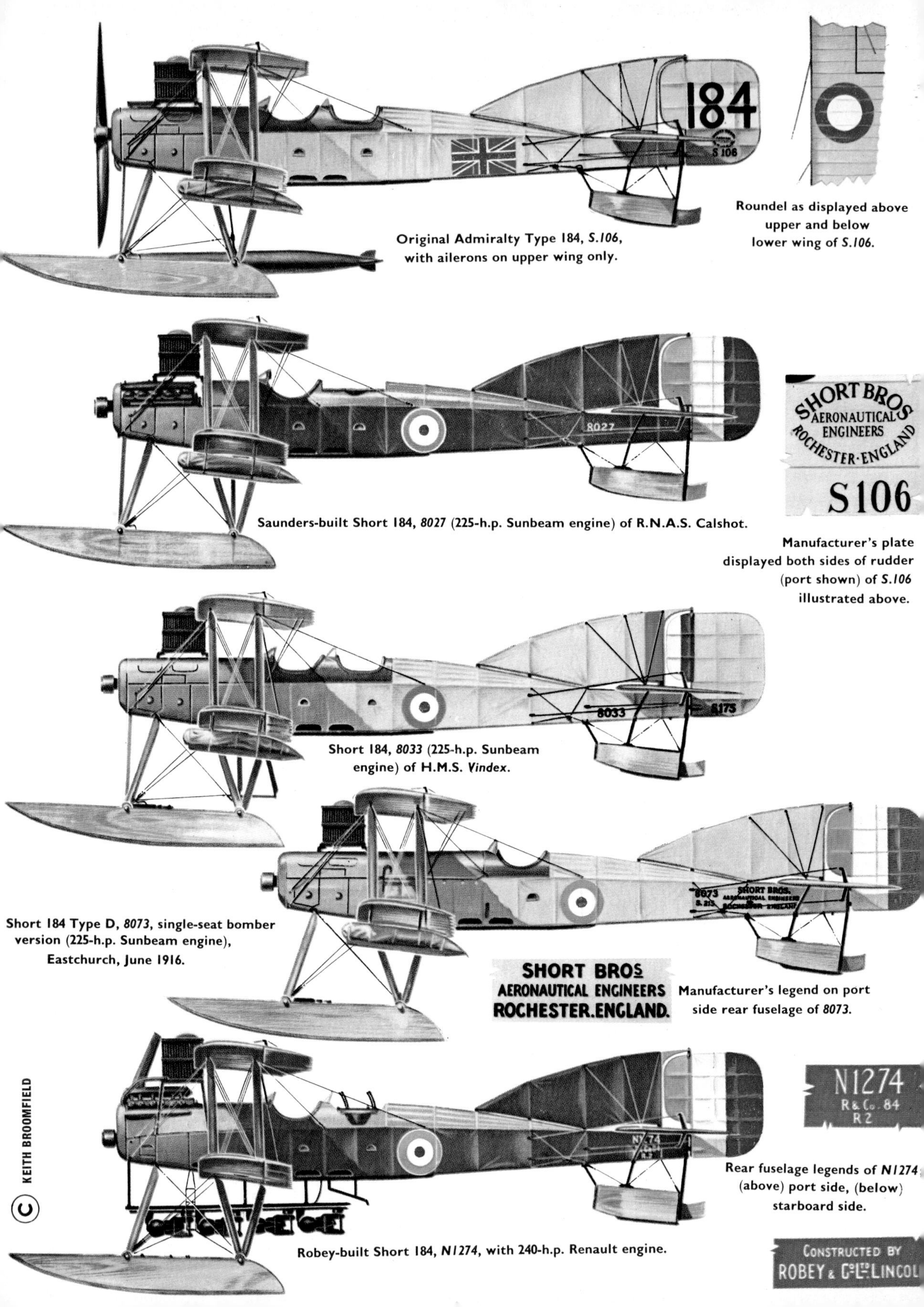

Original Admiralty Type 184, *S.106*, with ailerons on upper wing only.

Roundel as displayed above upper and below lower wing of *S.106*.

Saunders-built Short 184, *8027* (225-h.p. Sunbeam engine) of R.N.A.S. Calshot.

Manufacturer's plate displayed both sides of rudder (port shown) of *S.106* illustrated above.

Short 184, *8033* (225-h.p. Sunbeam engine) of H.M.S. *Vindex*.

Short 184 Type D, *8073*, single-seat bomber version (225-h.p. Sunbeam engine), Eastchurch, June 1916.

Manufacturer's legend on port side rear fuselage of *8073*.

Rear fuselage legends of *N1274* (above) port side, (below) starboard side.

Robey-built Short 184, *N1274*, with 240-h.p. Renault engine.

The Short 184

by J. M. Bruce

Short Improved 184 N1147 *here displays the revised aileron control system. This aircraft has a Maori I or II (the cowling panels have been removed), the original wing-tip floats, and the lengthened tail-float struts.*

It is difficult, more than fifty years after the event, to determine who was the first to make a successful drop of a torpedo from an aircraft. It has been said that this was first done in 1911 by Capitano Alessandro Guidoni, flying a Farman from which he released a 352-lb. torpedo. Guidoni's own account of early Italian experiments is very different, however. In his book *Aviazone—Idroaviazone* he states quite clearly that the idea of a torpedo-carrying seaplane was first proposed to the Italian navy by a lawyer, Pateras Pescara, in 1912, and that Guidoni's experiments with the Farman in that year were confined to proving the feasibility of dropping weights of up to 80 kg. (176 lb.) from the aircraft.

A remarkable monoplane designed by Pateras Pescara had to wait until 1914 for its two 160-h.p. Gnôme engines, and it was some time during that year that Guidoni successfully dropped a dummy torpedo weighing 375 kg. (825 lb.) from the aircraft. Unfortunately, Guidoni did not record the precise date, but claimed that his was "the first torpedo drop ever attempted and accomplished".

In the basic idea of dropping a torpedo from an aircraft the Royal Navy preceded the Italians by a year. Early in 1911 the subject was discussed by Captain Murray F. Sueter, Lt. Neville Usborne, Lt. L'Estrange Malone and Lt. D. H. Hyde-Thomson. The idea was developed by Hyde-Thomson in a paper that was submitted to the Admiralty by Captain Sueter, who used the opportunity to request that Hyde-Thomson be attached to what was then the Naval Wing of the R.F.C. to develop his proposals.

It seems that Hyde-Thomson's ideas were worked out and given specific form by an Admiralty draughtsman named Bowden, and Mr. (now Sir) T. O. M. Sopwith was then asked by Captain Sueter to build an aircraft incorporating the device.

After feasibility trials with a non-flying twin-float hydroplane that incorporated aerofoil centre sections, presumably for structural reasons only, Sopwith built in 1913 a very large seaplane powered by a 200-h.p. Salmson engine. With this aircraft a 14-inch torpedo was successfully lifted late in 1913. For reasons that seem not to have been recorded, however, no drop was made from the Sopwith torpedo carrier. The first drop from a British aircraft was made on 28th July 1914 by Squadron Commander A. M. Longmore (now Air Chief Marshal Sir Arthur Longmore, G.C.B., D.S.O.), flying a Short seaplane powered by a 160-h.p. fourteen-cylinder Gnôme engine; the missile was a 14-inch torpedo of some 900 lb. The aircraft was of a type that had not been specifically designed for torpedo dropping, and the installation of the release mechanism necessitated modifications that were designed by Horace Short in a matter of hours. Doubtless the mechanism itself was based on British Patent No. 6938 dated 19th March 1914, in which Captain Sueter and Lt. Hyde-Thomson had set down their designs for torpedo-carrying seaplanes.

In his book *Airmen or Noahs* Rear-Admiral Sueter wrote:

> "Just before the war, I showed this machine [Longmore's 160-h.p. Short] to Mr. Churchill and Lord Fisher. . . . The latter was very much interested, and impressed upon Mr. Churchill and myself that we should develop these machines.
>
> After the war broke out, we required all Mr. Sopwith's efforts and those of his factory to produce high performance machines, then just beginning to show some promise. But Hyde-Thomson and myself were quite determined to succeed with a torpedo machine. So I sent for that fine pioneer seaplane constructor, the late Mr. Horace Short. When I explained my requirements to him and the great weight that had to be lifted with a 225-h.p. Sunbeam engine, in addition to pilot and petrol, Horace Short looked at me with a determined grin and said: 'Well, if you particularly wish this done, I will produce a seaplane that will satisfy you'; and he did."

The product of Horace Short's promise was a large, unlovely two-seat seaplane powered by a 225-h.p. Sunbeam Mohawk engine. To provide the lifting

The first Short 184 being launched, with torpedo in place, at Rochester. At this time the rudder bore the works number S.106 and the ailerons had not been fitted with their rubber return springs. (Photo: Flight 014)

No. 184 *airborne with torpedo, pilot and observer. The rubber cords attached to the aileron control horns can be seen; the roundels on the upper wing consisted of a red outer ring and large white centre, the official R.N.A.S. national marking of early 1915.*
(Photo: H. F. Cowley)

surface needed to get a torpedo, two souls and a worthwhile load of fuel airborne, three-bay wings more than 63 ft. in span were fitted. With shipboard operation in view these were arranged to fold, employing the folding mechanism devised by Horace Short in 1912.

The airframe of the 225-h.p. Short seaplane was made of the conventional materials of the time and followed earlier Short practice in most respects. Wood predominated, but the interplane and undercarriage struts were of faired steel tubing, and the trailing edges of the mainplanes were of wire; this produced the characteristic scalloped appearance under the pull of the doped fabric. The main floats were wooden pontoon-type structures, 16 ft. long and 2 ft. 10 in. in beam; their basic framework of ash, silver spruce and Canadian elm was covered with $\frac{1}{8}$-in. plywood on the sides and top, while the bottom planking was $\frac{3}{16}$-in. to $\frac{1}{4}$-in. thick. At each attachment point spools of rubber cord provided a measure of shock absorption. The tail float had a three-ply hull with metal sheathing of the underside; it supported the water rudder. It was mounted pivotally at about its mid-point on two steel-tube struts and was sprung fore-and-aft by rubber cord. As the stern of the float had appreciable vertical movement the shaft of the water rudder was telescopic. Under each lower wing tip was a small float consisting of a series of steel rings covered with balloon fabric, the whole being inflated through a Dunlop valve in the nose. A wooden keel and small horizontal fin surface of three-ply were fitted to the underside of the float.

Numbered *184*, the first seaplane of the new type was completed at Rochester early in 1915. It was launched with a 14-inch torpedo in position between the main floats. Ailerons were fitted to the upper wing only and were of the single-acting type. Appropriate movement of the control wheel depressed the aileron on one side only; there was no spanwise balance cable connecting the ailerons; each was independently restored to the normal position by the spring action of two lengths of rubber cord pulling on control horns on the upper side of the aileron.

The official serial number *185* was allotted for a second prototype, which apparently was completed soon after No. *184*. Trials of the aircraft confirmed its ability to lift its designed load, and a small production batch of ten, *841–850*, were ordered. In accordance with the Admiralty's system of aircraft nomenclature the seaplane was officially designated Short 184 type, but in the R.N.A.S. it was usually known as the Short Two-two-five. This unofficial name was derived from the horse-power of its Sunbeam engine and continued in use long after the 225-h.p. Sunbeam had been superseded by other power units.

Batches of ten Wight 840 and Sopwith 860 seaplanes (respectively *831–840* and *851–860* were ordered at the same time as the Short 184s. All three types had the 225-h.p. Sunbeam Mohawk, and it seems likely that some comparative evaluation must have been contemplated. A few more Wights and Sopwiths were built, but clearly it was decided to standardise the Short 184. A further group of contracts for a total of 153 aircraft were given in mid-1915 to Shorts (*8031–8105*), Mann Egerton (*8344–8355*), Phœnix Dynamo (*8368–8379*), Sage (*8380–8391*), Saunders (*8001–8030*) and Westland (*8356–8367*). Of the additional contractors only Saunders had had experience of aircraft manufacture; nevertheless the first Sage-built Short 184 was completed late in September 1915 and delivered in November.

As there were no production drawings immediately available for distribution these were made "from life". Each of the contractors provided a draughtsman who, working from an actual Short 184, produced drawings of a group of components. Each firm then made enough sets of its draughtsman's drawings to send copies to the other contractors; in this way each firm received a full set of drawings.

The production Short 184s were substantially similar to the prototype. Initially, at least, the 225-h.p. Sunbeam Mohawk was the standard engine, and arched inter-float cross-bars with provision for torpedo crutches were fitted. A major innovation on the production aircraft was the provision of ailerons on the lower wings. Spanwise balance cables were still not fitted, and the revised aileron system would have won the approval of Mr. Heath Robinson. Cables from the control horns on the upper ailerons were taken forward and passed over upright pulleys mounted externally on the front spar; these cables were then led vertically downwards through the upper wing an inch or two ahead of and parallel to the interplane struts, passed through the lower wing, and then ran aft over pulleys under that wing to the control horns on the lower ailerons. Lengths of rubber cord attached to the upper surface of the lower ailerons were anchored to the tops of the two outer rear interplane struts on either side. The control cables from the pilot's wheel were led out along the

Details of the torpedo slinging gear on a single-seat Short 184 *at Felixstowe.*

upper surface of the lower mainplane, over pulleys at the lower ends of the two outer rear interplane struts, thence up to the underside of the upper ailerons. The inter-aileron cable ensured that depression of the upper surface produced a corresponding movement of the lower; conversely, the righting pull of the rubber cords acted directly on the lower ailerons and via the cable and pulleys on the upper.

It was a somewhat disquieting feature of this aileron system that, as the activated aileron was depressed the control cable to the opposite surface went slack. This engendered in Short pilots a fear that the slack cable would jump its pulleys.

The Short-built 184s of the batch *841–850* were mostly delivered by July 1915. As noted above, Sage deliveries began in November 1915. Mann Egerton 184s started to come along in December; deliveries from Westland and Phœnix started in, respectively, January and February 1916.

Before the production 184s appeared the two prototypes were on their way to war aboard the *Ben-my-Chree*, a former cross-channel ship that had been taken over by the Admiralty and converted into a seaplane carrier. The *Ben-my-Chree*, commanded by Squadron Commander C. J. L'Estrange Malone, sailed from England on 21st May 1915 and arrived at Iero Bay, Mitylene, on 12th June. According to A.P. 1344 (*History of the Development of Torpedo Aircraft*) the carrier went to the Dardanelles "with the unofficial intention of torpedoing the *Goeben* and the *Breslau*".

The Shorts had to be content with smaller fry than the two German cruisers then lying at Constantinople, but their early torpedo attacks were remarkably successful, in terms of direct hits. On 12th August 1915 Flight Commander C. H. K. Edmonds scored a hit at 350 yards range on a 5,000-ton Turkish supply ship off Injeh Burnu. At the time Edmonds did not know that his victim had been immobilised four days earlier by the submarine E.14. This did not diminish the significance of his achievement, which he repeated on 17th August when he torpedoed a Turkish supply ship bringing stores and reinforcements to Ak Bashi Liman. Both Shorts were out that day: the other, piloted by Flight Lt. G. B. Dacre, torpedoed a large steam tug in False Bay.

Worthy though these exploits were, they exposed the shortcomings of the seaplanes. On 12th August Edmonds had flown his Short solo with fuel for only forty-five minutes; even so, he was unable to coax his aircraft higher than 800 ft. The operational limitations of these early torpedo-carrying aircraft are made plain in *The War in the Air*, Vol. II (page 65):

> "Unhappily, the torpedo-loaded Short seaplane could only be made to get off the water and fly under ideal conditions. A calm sea with a slight breeze was essential and the engine had to be running perfectly. Further, the weight of the torpedo so restricted the amount of petrol which could be carried that a flight of much more than three-quarters of an hour was not possible. So it came about that while a number of torpedo attacks from the air were attempted, only three were successfully concluded."

Thus it was that the Short 184 made no more operational torpedo attacks. Some were used in later torpedo experiments at Felixstowe; one such was No. *8349* which, on 28th May 1916, was flown carrying a 14-inch torpedo with the object of determining the aircraft's radius of action. The text of the report is interesting:

> "Difficult to get on her step—once there, got off easily at 46 knots (2,200 revolutions), climbed to 600 feet fairly well, then shut down to 2,050 revolutions and just flew level at 49 knots. Tried at 48 knots and became very soggy. After 1½ hours flying throttled down to 1,975 revolutions; landed owing to breakage of rubber water connection."

The aircraft had by then used 61 of the 84 gallons of fuel it was carrying and had been airborne for a total of 4 hr. 5 min. Poor though its performance may seem half a century later, the report concluded by stating that the test result was "Very satisfactory, and a great improvement on all previous attempts at torpedo carrying". One of Felixstowe's torpedo-trials Shorts was a single-seater, the rear cockpit having been faired over.

As the production Short 184s became available they

No. 8040 fell intact into German hands and was tested in German markings. In this photograph the rubber return springs attached to the lower ailerons can be seen as oblique lines leading up to the upper ends of the two outboard rear interplane struts. This aircraft had the 225-h.p. Sunbeam Mohawk engine. (Photo: Peter L. Gray)

A German photograph of the Mohawk installation in a captured Short 184, possibly No. 8040. *As noted on the photograph, the radiator had been removed and its recess in the leading edge of the centre section can be seen.*

This rare photograph depicts the Short 184 that was modified by Cdr. C. R. Samson. Note the shortened lower wing, reduced fin area, king-post bracing of the upper-wing extensions, and the small ski-like replacements for the wing-tip floats. The aircraft retained the arched float cross-bars of the original design.

were issued to R.N.A.S. seaplane stations round the coasts of the United Kingdom and to the various seaplane-carriers then in use. Several went to the East Indies and Egypt Seaplane Squadron in the eastern Mediterranean; the squadron consisted of the seaplane carriers *Ben-my-Chree*, *Anne* and *Raven II*, later augmented by *Empress*. Shorts used by the squadron included *8004*, *8018*, *8021*, *8022*, *8080* and *8091*. Commander C. R. Samson, who took over command of this unit on 10th May 1916, quickly found that the climate imposed limitations on the use of the Shorts. In his book *Fights and Flights* he wrote:

"I knew that our only chance of being able to fly with the Shorts was to try to get off very early in the morning or late in the afternoon, as the severe heat would inevitably not only boil all our cooling water away, but probably affect our lift.

As it was, we had a terrible time getting the Shorts off the water under the existing conditions, and being unable to ascend beyond about 1,500 ft. we soon began to lose our water whilst flying.

On several trips it was touch-and-go whether we would get back before the engine seized up through this cause."

Samson also recorded that on 8th June his Short 184 had required a take-off run of two miles. He went on to give this graphic picture of the conditions under which the Shorts of the East Indies and Egypt Seaplane Squadron operated:

"I must inform my readers that we generally carried the 16-lb. bombs loose in the passenger's seat. I leave to the imagination the job the observer used to have. He was in a restricted space with a Lewis gun hitting him in the neck every time he moved, nursing a camera on his knees, with three or four 16-lb. bombs somewhere loose at his feet. Somewhere handy he had to have a pair of binoculars, writing-pad, map, and pencil. Added to this he had to attempt to understand what an excited and, in his view, imbecile pilot wanted him to do. Of course, he couldn't often hear what the pilot said amid the noise of the engine and general turmoil of fight.

I may add as a finishing touch to complete this actual picture of real life, that the 16-lb. bombs had a safety device, consisting of a revolving fan retained by a pin. Once you removed the pin, the fan had a nasty habit of revolving. When it had completed about three revolutions the bomb was liable to explode on the slightest provocation. It will thus be seen that the observer's life was a hectic one.

The pilot, on the other hand, on one of the old Shorts in hot climates had no joy-ride. He had generally a really hard time. First coaxing, or most probably forcing, the seaplane off the water, he then had a tough job trying to make the machine climb in the gradually increasing heat of the atmosphere with the water in the radiator on the verge of boiling. He had to keep the engine at practically full revolutions the whole time to have sufficient power to maintain his meagre altitude, and to have some sort of control in the fierce *remous* that constantly were encountered. At the same time he had to seize every chance, when he gained a few hundred feet, to throttle down."

No. 8359, *the Short 184 that flew during the Battle of Jutland, on display at the Crystal Palace after the Armistice. By the time this photograph was made the aircraft had a 240-h.p. Sunbeam Gurkha in place of its original Mohawk; the stack-type exhaust was not always fitted to the Gurkha.*

(Photo: Flight International)

Determined to obtain better performance, Samson made extensive modifications to one of his 184s. He reduced the span, fitted two bays only of interplane struts and braced the upper extensions by cables and king-posts. He also reduced the fin area and replaced the wing-tip floats by flat plates. Samson claimed that his "Experimental Short" was 6 knots faster than the standard 184 and had a better climbing performance. The aircraft survived until March 1917, when it sank following float failure.

In more temperate climates the Short 184 gave good, if unspectacular, service, and efforts were made to extend the type's usefulness. With their torpedo-carrying capability abandoned, the 184s were used increasingly for reconnaissance and bombing duties. On 25th March 1916 three Shorts and two Sopwith Baby seaplanes of H.M.S. *Vindex* set out to bomb an enemy airship base believed to be at Hoyer. The bomb load of each Short was three 65-lb. bombs. Engine trouble brought down two of the Shorts and one of the Sopwiths; the Short that returned was No. *8346*, flown by Flt. Lt. H. F. Towler.

When the Grand Fleet and Battle Cruiser Fleet put to sea on 30th May 1916 to meet the German fleet in what was to become known as the Battle of Jutland, they should have been accompanied by H.M.S. *Campania* with her ten seaplanes, three of which were Shorts. But *Campania* did not receive her stationing

Short 184 Type B built by Mann, Egerton & Co. Ltd. On this variant the upper wing was of constant chord and revised ailerons were fitted.

and timing signal when the Fleets sailed, consequently the only carrier with the British force was the *Engadine* with her two Shorts and two Baby Sopwiths. One of the Shorts, the Westland-built *8359*, flown by Flt. Lt. F. J. Rutland with Assistant Paymaster G. S. Trewin as his observer, made the only reconnaissance flight of the battle from 3.8 p.m. to 3.48 p.m. on 31st May. A few observations were wirelessed back by the seaplane before a broken petrol pipe terminated the flight. The aircraft was later preserved in the Imperial War Museum but was seriously damaged by bombing during the 1939–45 war.

Production had again been expanded and modifications of the basic design were beginning to appear. An early general modification was the replacement of the wire-cable interplane bracing by Rafwires, which were of streamline section. Technical Memorandum No. 79 dated 15th September 1916 announced that "Fifty sets of streamline wires and the necessary fittings for fitting to Short 225-h.p. Tractor Seaplanes have been ordered to existing machines at present equipped with cable".

Twenty 184s (*9041–9060*) were ordered from Robey & Co. of Lincoln, a second batch (*9065–9084*) from Sage. Ten modified aircraft numbered *9085–9094* were ordered from Mann Egerton & Co.; these had shortened lower wings and cable-and-kingpost bracing of the extensions of the upper mainplanes. This variant was known as Type B: certainly Mann Egerton & Co. regarded it as their own Type B (their Type A was the standard Short 184), but it may well have been the Short 184 Type B also, for one official reference suggests that the Type B configuration was first applied to the Short-built 184 No. *8070*. As torpedo carrying was no longer a duty of the Short 184, all later aircraft had straight cross-bars between the floats.

The Type B seaplanes were specifically mentioned in an Admiralty instruction dated 1st February 1917, which stated that several cases of failure of compression ribs had occurred in "Short Seaplanes 184, Types A and B", and ordered the fitting of additional struts as opportunity offered. The Type B seaplanes *9085–9094*, however, were not to be flown until new inner front interplane struts were fitted; these were to be of steel tubing of the same external diameter as the original struts but of 17-gauge steel instead of 20-gauge.

The Short 184 Type D was a single-seat bomber version of the design. The official designation of this sub-type was "Short 184 single type". It was flown from what was ordinarily the rear cockpit; the space normally occupied by the front cockpit provided internal stowage for nine 65-lb. bombs. Several examples of the Type D were built: *8073*, *8103* and *9048* are known. On one occasion when it was rumoured that the German High Sea Fleet had put to sea a Short 184 Type D with eight bombs aboard, flown by Flt. Lt. S. T. Freeman, set out from R.N.A.S. Dover in company with other assorted aircraft. Another Type D was used by the R.N.A.S. Station, Dunkerque, in October 1916; and the four Dunkerque Shorts that bombed Ostend and Zeebrugge on 9th November probably included some Type D single-seaters.

Alternative engines were fitted. No. *8104* had a 250-h.p. Rolls-Royce engine, its installation being remarkably bulky and ugly. This Short was at the Isle of Grain early in December 1916. The excellent Rolls-Royce engine was somewhat scarce, however, and it was not adopted as a standard power unit for the Short 184.

Many Shorts had the 240-h.p. Sunbeam Gurkha* which, like the 225-h.p. Mohawk, was a V-12 side-valve engine. The Gurkha had the same stroke (150 mm.) as the Mohawk but its bore (100 mm.) was greater by 10 mm. and it had two inlet and two exhaust valves per cylinder, whereas the Mohawk had only one of each. Many Short 184s that had been

**The names Mohawk and Gurkha were little used in the R.N.A.S., despite their appearance in an official* Data Chart of Engines in R.N.A.S. *dated November 1917. In practice these engines were referred to simply by their power rating, as were the later Maori I and II. Not until the Maori III came into use was the engine name employed in the R.N.A.S.*

This Type D is No. 9048, *built by Robey and powered by a 240-h.p. Sunbeam Gurkha driving a four-blade airscrew. Like No.* 8359, *it had a stack-type exhaust pipe.*

The Short-built 184 No. 8073 *was a Type D, the single-seat bomber version of the aircraft. It had a 225-h.p. Mohawk engine, and straight cross-bars were fitted between the floats.*

No. 8104 with 250-h.p. Rolls-Royce engine, photographed at the Isle of Grain in December 1916.

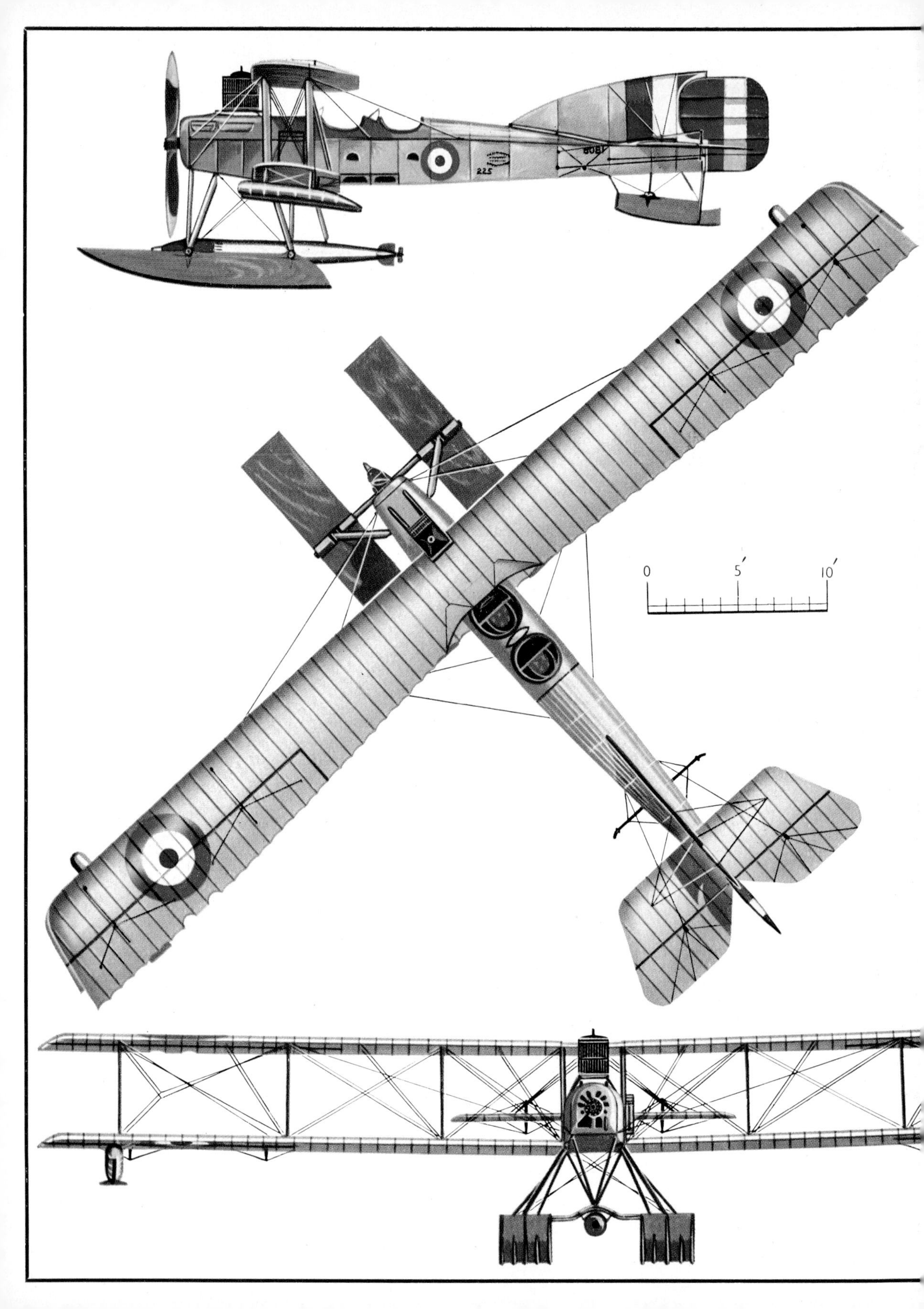
0
5′
10′

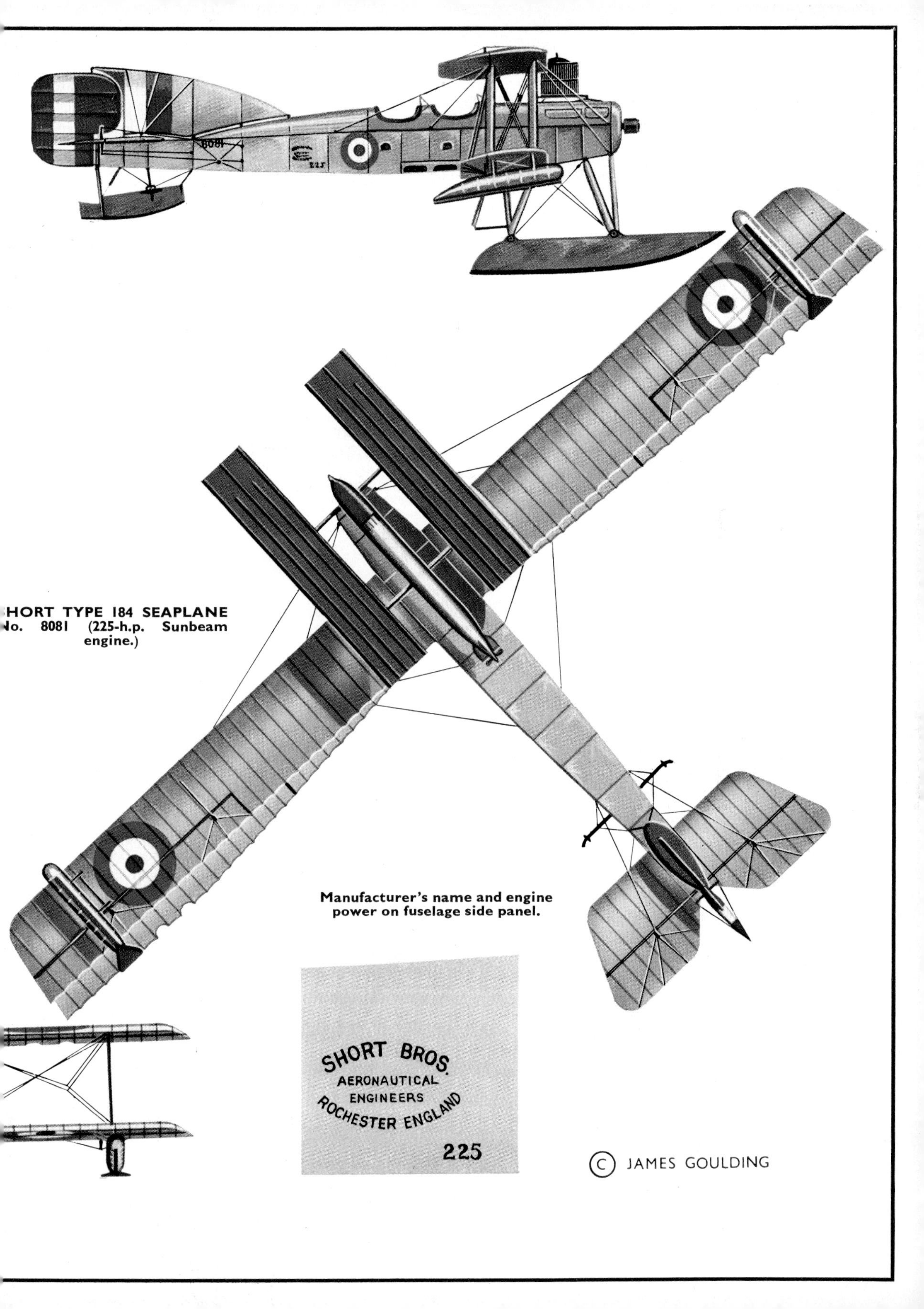

HORT TYPE 184 SEAPLANE
No. 8081 (225-h.p. Sunbeam engine.)

Manufacturer's name and engine power on fuselage side panel.

© JAMES GOULDING

Sage-built Short Improved 184 powered by the 240-h.p. Renault engine with the original installation that embodied two flank-mounted radiators. This aircraft also has the later type of wing-tip floats.

built with the 225-h.p. engine were later fitted with the Gurkha.

Another engine of the same nominal h.p. as the Gurkha was fitted to many Short 184s. This was the 240-h.p. Renault, a V-12 with a bore of 125 mm. and stroke of 150 mm., distinguishable from the Sunbeams by its right-hand airscrew. The original installation had two flank-mounted radiators, and appeared on the Short-built aircraft of the batch *N1080–N1099* and on some contractor-built 184s also. This installation was not successful. A "home-made" modification was devised at R.N.A.S. Dover and proved to be more effective; apparently this consisted of replacing the twin radiators with a single radiator of the box-like shape that characterised the Sunbeam-powered 184. Flt. Lt. S. T. Freeman of R.N.A.S. Dover was sent round all Short 184 contractors to instruct them in the Dover installation, and it seems that all subsequent Renault-powered Shorts embodied it.

This important modification was probably the origin of the designation Short 184 Dover type. However, Flt. Cdr. A. H. Sandwell has recorded:

> "Dover was the repair depot for the Short seaplanes used at Dunkerque, and so many improvements were introduced from time to time that eventually the machines came to be known as 'Dover-type Shorts'."

The Renault engine enjoyed a better reputation than the Sunbeams. To quote again from Sandwell's reminiscences (which were published in *Canadian Aviation* in 1936–37):

> "Although we [of R.N.A.S. Dundee] later acquired boats, most of our patrolling was done in Short seaplanes, about half of which were powered with 260-h.p. Sunbeams and the balance with a French-built copy of a captured 240-h.p. German Mercedes engine.* There was great competition for the 'Renault-Merks' among the pilots; since with these slow-revving and reliable engines, they considered that they had an almost 100 per cent chance of arriving home under their own power. Their faith in the Sunbeams was by no means so great."

**The 240-h.p. Renault was frequently referred to as the Renault-Mercedes.*

Left: *The installation of the 240-h.p. Sunbeam Gurkha in No. 8014 did not differ externally from that of the 225-h.p. engine. The aircraft is seen at Grain on 9th December 1916, fitted with the underslung bomb rail with racks for four bombs.* (Photo: Imperial War Museum MH2869.) Right: *The Dover-type Renault installation with central elevated radiator, here exemplified on Short 184* N1616 *built by Saunders.*

Left: *The standard installation of the Maori I and II was characterised by a central, near-vertical exhaust stack. Some aircraft, like the Robey-built* N2833 *seen here, had four-blade airscrews. This Short 184 displays the deep indentations of the upper-aileron trailing edges that were made on some aircraft. These were made in the rib spaces that rested against the tailplane bracing wires when the wings were folded and were intended to minimise chafing. Other details to note on* N2833 *(an original 184) are the Scarff ring mounting on the rear cockpit and the fairlead for the trailing aerial just above the rear end of the bomb rail. This Short was on the strength of Cherbourg seaplane station from September to December 1918.* (Photo: Imperial War Museum Q68223.) Right: *Short 184 with Sunbeam Maori III engine, distinguished by its twin outside exhaust manifolds. This photograph was made at Killingholme.*

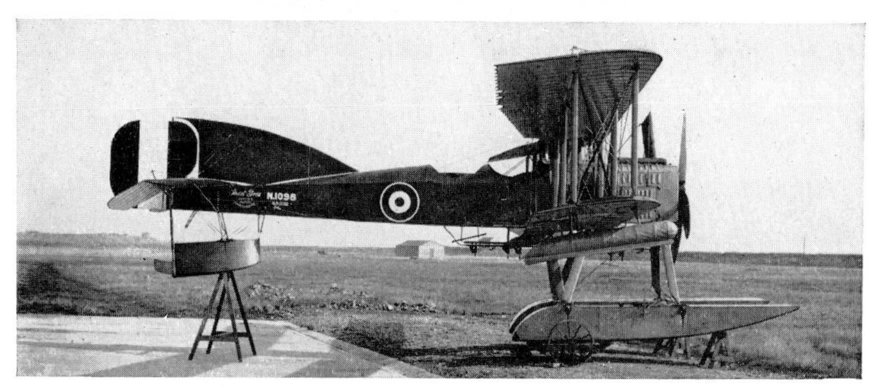

N1098 *at the Isle of Grain, October 1917, with square frontal radiator on its Maori engine. This aircraft, although not originally built as an Improved 184, had the revised aileron system at the time when this photograph was made; it also had the longer tail-float struts.*

No. 8052 *with two 65-lb. bombs under each lower wing. This was an early attempt to fit bomb racks to the Short 184 but was abandoned in favour of the under-fuselage bomb rail. This Short still had arched float cross-bars when this photograph was made.*

Shorts of the late production batches were fitted with Sunbeam Maori engines. An official report dated 25th July 1917 suggests that one of the earliest installations of a Maori engine was made in the Robey-built Short *N1260*. By that date the aircraft had completed ten hours' flying, fitted with engine No. 436, and no trouble had been experienced. The Maori, like its Sunbeam predecessors, was a V-12; its cylinders had the same bore as those of the Gurkha but stroke was only 135 mm.; the Maori had four magnetos to the Gurkha's two. The Maori I and II had their exhaust valves on the inboard side of the cylinders, consequently a single central exhaust stack was fitted. The Maori III had only two H.C.7 carburettors as opposed to the four Claudel-Hobson C.Z.S. (38 mm.) of the Maori II; in the Maori III the compression ratio reverted to 5·2 to 1 (5·3 to 1 in the Mk. II) and an improved lubrication system was fitted. But the Maori III could be distinguished infallibly by its twin exhaust stacks, for its exhaust valves were on the outsides of the cylinders.

At least one Short 184 that had a Maori I or II (*N1098*) was fitted with a frontal radiator in place of the elevated box-like affair that was standard. No doubt this improved the pilot's view somewhat, but it was not so successful as the more primitive installation. The Shorts often had to taxi long distances before take-off and after landing, and at such times the

No. 8076 *at the Isle of Grain with Whitehouse gun mounting on the rear cockpit and four 100-lb. bombs. This aircraft had a 260-h.p. Maori I or II driving a two-blade airscrew.*

original form of radiator was much more effective than the frontal surface. *N1098* was at the Isle of Grain in October 1917.

It is difficult to be specific as to which type of engine was fitted to any individual Short 184 at any particular time. Changes, doubtless dictated by engine availability, were apparently made during manufacture and in service, and one cannot be certain that the engines attributed to various batches of Short 184s were in fact fitted or, if fitted, retained.

The airframe and its appurtenances underwent various modifications as time went on. The rear cockpit was modified to take a mounting for a movable Lewis gun. To some aircraft a Whitehouse mounting was fitted, but later Shorts had a Scarff No. 2 mounting as standard. The Whitehouse mounting apparently gave the gun considerable flexibility: in March 1917 it was recommended that Shorts having this mounting should be fitted with a sliding panel 13 in. by $25\frac{1}{4}$ in. in the fuselage floor to allow the observer to fire downwards under the tail float.

With the need to use the Short 184 as a bomber came the need for bomb racks. The Seaplane Test Depot, Isle of Grain, tested No. *8052* with racks for two 65-lb. bombs under each lower wing, but this arrangement was abandoned, probably for structural reasons, in favour of an untidy-looking rail slung under the fuselage, with accommodation for four 100-lb. bombs. In operational service alternative combinations of other bombs were carried.

Also flown at Grain was No. *8105*, which had a greatly heightened undercarriage; its tail float was also carried on lengthened struts. This aircraft was at Grain on 6th November 1916. Its ungainly undercarriage did not find favour. No. *8105* was later on the strength of R.N.A.S. Station Great Yarmouth.

A stage in the evolution of the bomb rail. As this Short still had the arched cross-bars it was possible to anchor the forward end of the bomb rail to the front V-strut; aircraft with the straight cross-bars had to be fitted with a small V-strut to hold the forward end of the bomb rail. On this aircraft the bomb load appears to consist of three 100-lb. and one 112-lb. bombs.

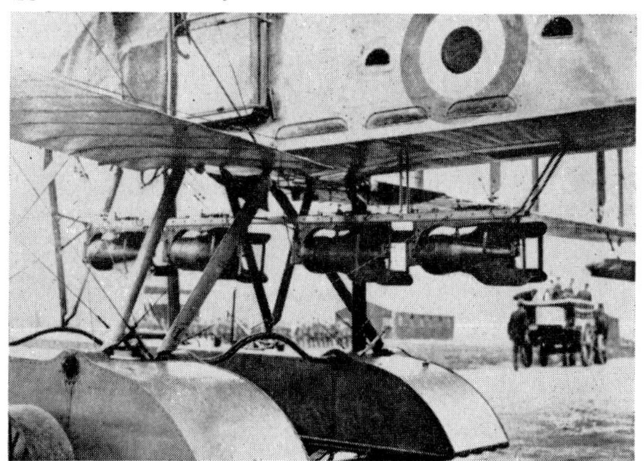

Dated 6th November 1916, this photograph depicts No. 8105 fitted with lengthened float struts and a four-blade airscrew. The struts supporting the tail float were also lengthened, and the aircraft retained arched cross-bars.

Later aircraft had enlarged wing-tip floats of more refined appearance and construction than the original inflatable floats. Some 184s had the tail float mounted on longer struts; this modification decreased the angle of the aircraft on the water and presumably helped to shorten the take-off run.

In the production batches numbered in the N series some aircraft were designated Short Improved 184. These were distinguished from the original 184 type by having aileron balance cables in place of the return springs, consequently the depression of the aileron on one side produced a corresponding upward movement of the control on the other. Upper and lower ailerons were interconnected by cables. Official listings indicate that the first ten aircraft of the batch *N1080–N1099* were Improved 184s, the remainder being of the original form; other known Improved 184s were *N1130–N1134* and *N1140–N1149*; some aircraft of later batches also had the modified aileron system. At least thirty aircraft (*N1240–N1259* and *N1260–N1269*) were described as Short Intermediate 184s but the significance of this designation has yet to be determined. Of these, *N1242* at least had the revised aileron arrangement.

In 1917 attempts were made to improve on the main floats. The Saunders company built enlarged floats, 18 ft. 11 in. long and 3 ft. in beam; as on the standard (16 ft. by 2 ft. 10 in.) float the sides and top were planked with ⅛-in. three-ply, the bottom with $\frac{3}{16}$-in. to ¼-in. ply; the weight was 248 lb. as against 220 lb. for a standard Saunders-built float. These may have been the floats that were fitted to *N1086*: certainly that Short's floats were longer than standard.

Linton Hope, a well-known yacht designer of the pre-war period, served in the Air Department of the Admiralty during the war. He designed several flying-boat hulls and seaplane floats, all of characteristic circular or near-circular cross section and all of elegant lines and proportions. For the Short 184 he designed a float 19 ft. in length and 2 ft. 6 in. in beam (3 ft. across the planing bottom); this was a single-step float weighing 208 lb. The timbers were spaced 1½ in. apart; the sides and top were planked with ⅛-in. mahogany, the planing bottom with ⅛-in. to $\frac{1}{16}$-in. mahogany. A pair of these floats were fitted to *N1081*, which had started life with standard pontoon-type floats. The Linton Hope float was not adopted for the Short 184, however.

This front view of N1631 *shows how the absence of a spanwise balance cable allowed the ailerons on both sides to be depressed. This photograph also shows that the large radiator was much less substantial than it looked when seen at other angles: the camera here is looking straight through the vertical tubes and the radiator is scarcely visible.*

Short Improved 184 N1086 *with the original Short-designed Renault installation and lengthened floats, photographed at the Isle of Grain on 1st May 1917.*

In November 1917 No. *8076* was tested at the Isle of Grain with Martin automatic stabilisers on its upper wing tips. The wing was partly cut away to accommodate the device which, contrary to earlier belief, appeared to function independently of the ailerons. The Martin stabiliser was also tested on a Norman Thompson N.T.4a flying boat. It was apparently not regarded as sufficiently successful to warrant further development.

The R.N.A.S. was interested in the Davis gun, a recoil-less shell-firing weapon of American origin, and made protracted efforts to find a means of using it. One installation was made in a Short 184; the gun was arranged to fire over the upper wing. Some of the trials of this Davis-gun Short were flown by Flt. Lt. W. G. Moore, D.S.C. The Davis gun was a monstrously unwieldy weapon, however, and the R.N.A.S. wisely abandoned it.

Short 184s were flown from the decks of the carriers H.M.S. *Furious* and H.M.S. *Campania*. Wheeled dollies were fitted under the floats to permit take-off. At first these dollies were jettisoned from the seaplane once it was airborne, but subsequently they were arranged to run in a groove on the carrier's deck and were arrested and retained when the seaplane became airborne. The first take-off made by a Short 184 from the deck of *Campania* was accomplished on 3rd June 1916.

The Short 184 gave faithful service in most theatres of war until hostilities ended. In home waters the Shorts began anti-submarine patrols in 1916, and at the end of November a Short from Portland (Flt. Lt. J. R. Ross, Air Mechanic J. Redman) tracked down a U-boat off the Casquets and contributed to its destruction by a Q-ship. On two occasions, 28th November 1916 and 25th May 1917, engine failure resulted in Short 184 crews being taken prisoner by the U-boats they had been stalking.

Short 184s sighted and bombed a considerable number of U-boats in the North Sea and the Mediterranean but positive success seemed to elude them. One occasion when the target was at least damaged occurred on 19th December 1917, when *N1606* of R.N.A.S. Newlyn (Flt. Sub-Lt. Hughes, Observer Sub-Lt. Spaight) dropped two 100-lb. bombs on a submerged U-boat 10 miles W.S.W. of the Lizard.

Left: *This view of the cockpits of* N1086 *suggests that one reason for reverting to the single central radiator for the Renault engine may have been to improve the pilot's view for landing.* Middle: *There was no truly standard cockpit layout for Short 184s, as these illustrations show. This is the dashboard of* 8076, *the Short-built Maori-powered 184 that appears in other illustrations.* Right: *The pilot's dashboard on* N1081, *Short-built Improved 184 with 240-h.p. Renault engine.*

Left: *Yet another layout of instruments in* N1260, *the Robey-built 184 that had an early installation of a Sunbeam Maori engine.* Right: *Dashboard of a Short 184 equipped for night flying.*

These exploded 8 yards apart on either side of the U-boat; large quantities of oil and bubbles came to the surface.

Official records show that during the period 1st May to 12th November 1918 two-seat seaplanes, the great majority of which were Short 184s, flew a total of 17,558 hours on anti-submarine patrols, averaging 35 patrols daily; 33 hostile submarines were sighted and 25 of them were attacked. The daily average number of aircraft on station strength was 176, but of these only 66 were, on average, serviceable. This poor proportion hints at the difficulties of operating seaplanes with wooden floats in British waters.

In the air the Short 184 was not the most manageable of aircraft. Flt. Cdr. A. H. Sandwell, writing in 1936, had this to say about flying the aircraft and attacking U-boats:

"It was a physical impossibility to fly a Short at much more than 75 miles an hour. If you tried to dive it steeply it would start taking the control away from you at, say, 65 m.p.h., and would have flattened itself out before it picked up another ten miles an hour. No pilot was strong enough to hold the wheel forward so that it would continue to dive, and if he had been he would probably have broken the control wires, or the horns on the elevators or the elevators themselves. Consequently, even if you had the height to spare, you could not get anywhere in a hurry on a Short by 'stuffing its nose down' as you could with most land machines.

Now the state of visibility over the North Sea is such that one could rarely spot a submarine on the surface very far away; two miles being perhaps a good average. The sub. could, of course, see you as soon as, if not sooner than, you saw it. The subs. used to come up at night, or in the early morning, and open up their hatches so that they could run the Diesel engines and recharge their batteries. There were often a few people on deck and it would take them from one minute to a minute and a half to submerge when surprised by a seaplane patrol . . . it was usually impossible for a Short to reach a submarine two miles away in a minute and a half, even if you had the height to spare and could coax 75 m.p.h. out of it. Unlike the English Channel, where the bottom can often be seen to a depth of 100 feet or so, the water in the North Sea is thick and muddy, and a submarine once submerged was gone for good."

In spite of his criticisms of its operational short-

Short 184 fuselage structure at the cockpits. The L-shaped fitting on the perforated plywood panel at extreme left was the pivoting mounting for the wind-driven generator. The mounting is here seen in the stowed position; it could be turned outboard through 90 deg. to bring the generator face on to the slipstream (the generator is not fitted here).

No. 8076 at the Isle of Grain, fitted with Martin stabilisers on the upper wings, 5th November 1917.

One of the five Short 184s that came on to the British civil register, G-EBBN *was originally* N9118; *it was powered by a Maori III.*

comings, Sandwell liked the Short 184 well enough as an aircraft to describe it as:

> ". . . the pilot's dream for putting in hours—docile, stable, obedient, and thoroughly deserving its affectionate nickname 'Home from Home'."

In the Eastern Mediterranean the Shorts of the *Ben-my-Chree* spotted for the guns of the monitors *M.15*, *M.23* and *M.31* and the sloop *Espiègle* in 1916. Short 184s from the carrier *Empress* bombed the railway and Turkish supplies at Tul Karm on 23rd June 1916, thus playing a small but important part in the events that led to the fall of Jerusalem.

Some four months earlier five 225-h.p. Short 184s had arrived in Mesopotamia for the use of the R.N.A.S. detachment. Operating from the River Tigris at Ora, three of these Shorts took part in the air-lift of food and supplies to the beleaguered garrison of Kut-al-Imara in April 1916.

A belated attempt to use a Short 184 as a torpedo aircraft came to naught in January 1918. When the German cruiser *Goeben* lay aground near Nagara one of *Ark Royal*'s Shorts was fitted with a torpedo in the hope that the enemy ship might be sunk. The Short, thus loaded, refused to leave the water. *Ark Royal*'s men succeeded in fitting a Short with a 300-lb. depth charge or an 18-in. warhead, and on 27th January Flt. Cdr. Malet dropped a warhead on the spot where the *Goeben* was believed to be. Visibility was poor, and Malet could not see that his quarry had gone, having managed to get away the previous day.

No other country used the Short 184 operationally during the war. Nos. *8083* and *8084* had been transferred to the French Government, presumably for evaluation, but nothing more was heard of them. No. *8057* was given to Japan and undoubtedly inspired the design of at least two of the Yokosho Rogo-Kogata seaplanes: these aircraft displayed many design characteristics of the Short 184.

A late experimental engine installation was that of a 300-h.p. Sunbeam Manitou in *N9135* in 1918, but no development ensued. The Manitou was dimensionally little different from the Maori, but the bore was increased to 110 mm.; like the Maori, it had outside exhausts.

The standard Maori-powered Short remained in service with the R.A.F. for some time after the Armistice, making mine-spotting patrols over British coastal waters. At least four (*N9290–N9293*) went to North Russia in 1919 but seem to have done nothing noteworthy there.

Other countries using Short 184s in the post-war period included Chile, Esthonia, Greece and Japan. The Chilean aircraft apparently had Maori III engines, and some of those used by Esthonia had Rolls-Royce Eagles. The Esthonian Shorts included *N9130* which, in the service of that country, was numbered 39.

Five Short 184s had a brief civilian existence for seaside pleasure flights. In 1919, *N2986* and *N2998* became respectively *G-EAJT* and *G-EALC* and apparently survived for about a year in the service of the Eastbourne Aviation Co. They were modified to carry four passengers, as were *N9096* and *N9118* in 1922, when they became *G-EBBM* and *G-EBBN* and were operated by the Seaplane and Pleasure Trip Co., Ltd. Last of the civil 184s was Manchester Airways' *G-EBGP* (ex-*N2996*), registered on 1st June 1923.

The Short 184 was one of the war's great workhorses. Its prosaic appearance matched the unspectacular nature of its duties; it served in one form or another from the spring of 1915 until the Armistice and beyond; it was still in production at the end of the war and deliveries continued at least until the end of December 1918. In that month 315 Short 184s were in commission and current orders for 259 were still outstanding. By the standards of 1914–18 this was a not undistinguished record.

SPECIFICATION

Power: 225-h.p. Sunbeam Mohawk, 240-h.p. Sunbeam Gurkha, 260-h.p. Sunbeam Maori I, II or III, 240-h.p. Renault, 250-h.p. Rolls-Royce (Eagle), 300-h.p. Sunbeam Manitou.

Dimensions: Span 63 ft. 6¼ in. (folded 16 ft. 4¾ in.); length 40 ft. 7½ in. (folded 44 ft. 2 in.); height (airscrew vertical) 13 ft. 6 in.; chord, upper (max.) 6 ft. 6 in., lower 5 ft.; gap 5 ft. 6 in.; stagger nil; dihedral 1 deg. 45 min.; incidence 5 deg.; span of tail 16 ft. 4¾ in.; airscrew diameter (A.D. No. S.93 for Mohawk engine and A.D. 572 R.H. for Renault) 3,280 mm. (10 ft. 9⅛ in.), (A.D. No. 501M for Gurkha engine) 3,200 mm. (10 ft. 6 in.). Wing area about 680 sq. ft.

Armament: One 0·303-in. Lewis machine gun on movable mounting on rear cockpit; on some Short 184s this was a Whitehouse mounting, but the Scarff No. 2 Ring Mounting was standardised for later aircraft. Three 97-round drums of ammunition were the standard provision. One 14-in. torpedo or bomb load that could consist of one of the following combinations of bombs: one 520-lb.; one 500-lb.; four 112-lb.; four 100-lb.; three 65-lb. and several 16-lb.; one 264-lb. and one 100-lb.; one 300-lb. depth charge; one 18-in. warhead.

PRODUCTION

Under wartime contracts a total of 1,095 Short 184s, Improved 184s and Intermediate 184s were ordered, and it seems likely that about 900 were delivered. On 31st October 1918 the R.A.F. had on charge only 312 Short 184s, of which all but thirty had the Sunbeam Maori engine.

Short Brothers, Rochester—184, 185, 841–850, 8031–8105, N1080–N1099, N1580–N1589.

Brush Electrical Engineering Co. Ltd., Loughborough—N1660–N1689, N2600–N2659, N2790–N2819, N9060–N9099, N9260–N9289, N9350–N9399 (cancelled).

Mann, Egerton & Co. Ltd., Prince of Wales Road, Norwich—8344–8355, 9085–9094 (Type B).

Phoenix Dynamo Manufacturing Co. Ltd., Bradford—8368–8379, N1630–N1659, N1740–N1759.

Robey & Co. Ltd., Lincoln—9041–9060, N1220–N1229, N1260–N1279, N1820–N1839, N2820–N2849, N2900–N2949, N9000–N9059, N9140–N9169, N9290–N9349.

Frederick Sage & Co. Ltd., Peterborough—8380–8391, 9065–9084, N1130–N1139, N1230–N1239, N1590–N1599, N1780–N1799.

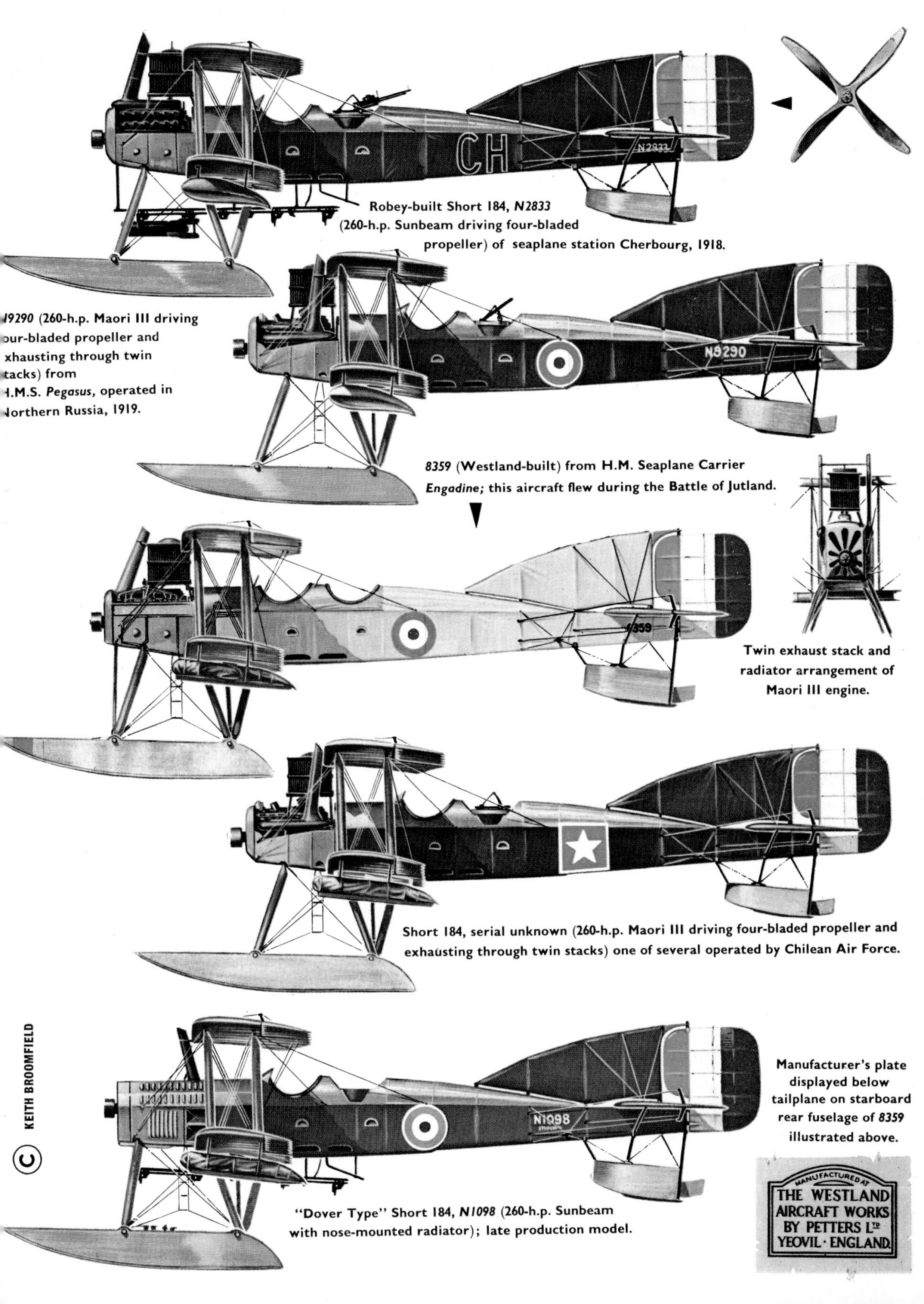

Robey-built Short 184, *N2833* (260-h.p. Sunbeam driving four-bladed propeller) of seaplane station Cherbourg, 1918.

N9290 (260-h.p. Maori III driving four-bladed propeller and exhausting through twin stacks) from H.M.S. *Pegasus,* operated in Northern Russia, 1919.

8359 (Westland-built) from H.M. Seaplane Carrier *Engadine;* this aircraft flew during the Battle of Jutland.

Twin exhaust stack and radiator arrangement of Maori III engine.

Short 184, serial unknown (260-h.p. Maori III driving four-bladed propeller and exhausting through twin stacks) one of several operated by Chilean Air Force.

Manufacturer's plate displayed below tailplane on starboard rear fuselage of *8359* illustrated above.

"Dover Type" Short 184, *N1098* (260-h.p. Sunbeam with nose-mounted radiator); late production model.

A Short 184 at the moment of leaving its captive dolly on the flight deck of H.M.S. Furious, *15th July 1917. The dolly has been arrested at the forward end of the channel along the deck centre line.*

This Short 184 airframe was used in trials of the early catapult fitted to H.M.S. Slinger. *With its fuselage fabric stripped and sacks of ballast lashed into the engine bay, it was launched at a weight of 5,000 lb. on 1st October 1917, its speed at the moment of release being 30 m.p.h. In these trials a pair of Short 184 floats, loaded with sand to a total weight of two tons, were also launched; their speed was 40 m.p.h. These trials paved the way for the successful catapult launch of the Fairey seaplane* N9 *on 14th May 1918.*

S. E. Saunders Ltd., East Cowes, Isle of Wight—8001–8030, N1140–N1149, N1600–N1624, N1760–N1774.
Supermarine Aviation Works Ltd., Woolston, Southampton—N9170–N9199.
Westland Aircraft Works, Yeovil, Somerset—8356–8367.
J. Samuel White & Co. Ltd., Cowes, Isle of Wight—N1240–N1259, N2950–N2999, N9100–N9139, N9400–N9449 (cancelled).

Service use

R.N.A.S. Seaplane Stations, United Kingdom—Bembridge, Calshot, Cattewater, Dartmouth, Dover, Dundee, Felixstowe, Fishguard, Great Yarmouth, Hornsea, Killingholme, Houton Bay, Lee-on-Solent, Newhaven, Newlyn, Pembroke, Plymouth, Portland, Prawle Point, Scilly (Tresco), Scapa Flow, Seaton Carew, South Shields, Strath Beg, Torquay, Westgate, Westward Ho.
France—Cherbourg, Dunkerque. *Gibraltar.*
Italy—Otranto, Santa Maria di Leuca, Taranto.
Malta—Calafrana (also used by the Torpedo School, Malta).
Aegean—Mudros, Suda Bay, Syra.
Egypt—Alexandria, Port Said.
Mesopotamia—R.N.A.S. Detachment, Basra and Ora.
North Russia—Aircraft carrier H.M.S. *Pegasus* with North Russian Expeditionary Force at Archangel.
Seaplane Carriers—Anne, Ark Royal, Ben-my-Chree, Campania, City of Oxford, Empress, Engadine, Furious, Nairana, Pegasus, Raven II, Riviera, Vindex.
Light Cruisers—Arethusa, Aurora.

Examples of Short 184s used by operational units

Bembridge—N1611, N1613.
Calshot—8365, N1621, N2975, N9018, N9091, N9176.
Cattewater—N1099, N1142, N1624, N1796, N2836, N2959.
Dartmouth—N1588, N1678.
Dover—8003, 8038, 9067.
Dundee—N1276, N1661, N1831.
Felixstowe—8066 (also used by Great Yarmouth), *8349.*
Fishguard—N1086, N1242, N1683, N2795, N2830, N2908.
Great Yarmouth—8368, 8378, 8389, N1250, N1599, N1675.
Killingholme—8068, 8391, N1655, N1829, N2902.
Houton Bay—N1645, N2652.
Lee-on-Solent—N1640, N2984, N9071, N9106, N9142, N9181.
Newhaven—8348, N1244, N1246 (also used by Great Yarmouth), *N2827* (also used by Calshot).
Newlyn—N1255, N1607, N1616, N1618, N1767, N2958.
Plymouth—N1601.
Portland—N1259, N1794, N2965.
Scilly (Tresco)—N1622, N2828, N2955, N2963.
Torquay—N2962.
Westgate—N1229, N2938, N2939, N2977.
Cherbourg—N1793, N2805, N2900, N2981, N9021, N9170.
Dunkerque—8013, 9042, 9050, 9057.
Otranto—N1833.
Calafrana—9053, N1096, N1097, N1823.
Mudros—N1234.
R.N.A.S. Detachment, Basra—8047.
East Indies & Egypt Seaplane Sqn.—8080, N1668 (also *Ark Royal*).
(See also carriers *Anne, Ben-my-Chree, Empress* and *Raven II.*)

Examples of Short 184s used from seaplane carriers

Ark Royal—N1747, N1750, N2813, N2931, N2933, N2934.
Ben-my-Chree—184, 185.
Empress—8018, 8021, 8022, 8091, N1091, N1582.
Engadine—8050, 8065, 9073, N2822, N2944, N9000.
Manxman—N1788.
Pegasus—N9290–N9293 (1919).
Raven II—8004 (also used from *Empress*).
Riviera—N2929, N2930, N2943, N2948.
Vindex—8033, 8346, N1232.

WEIGHTS AND PERFORMANCE

Aircraft	—	*8014*	*8076*	*N1090*	*N1135*	Type D
Engine	Mohawk	Gurkha	Maori	Renault	Renault	Gurkha
Load	—	4 ×65-lb. bombs	4 ×100-lb. bombs	—	—	9 ×65-lb. bombs
Weights (lb.):						
Empty	—	3,634	3,479	3,798	3,514	3,620
Military load	—	325	512	668	650	673
Crew	—	360	360	360	360	180
Fuel and oil	—	690	637	734	666	690
Loaded	5,100	5,009	4,988	5,560	5,190	5,163
Max. speed (m.p.h.):						
At sea level	—	74	—	—	—	70
At 2,000 ft.	75	—	84	80	85	—
At 6,500 ft.	—	75	83	70	78	77
At 10,000 ft.	—	—	80·5	—	—	—
Climb to:	m. s.	m. s.	m. s.	m. s.	m. s.	m. s.
2,000 ft.	— —	— —	6 15	8 15	9 20	— —
6,500 ft.	— —	39 0	26 15	42 30	51 30	40 30
Service ceiling (ft.) ...	—	—	8,700	5,700	5,000	—
Endurance (hours) ...	—	—	—	4½	5	—

PROFILE
PUBLICATIONS

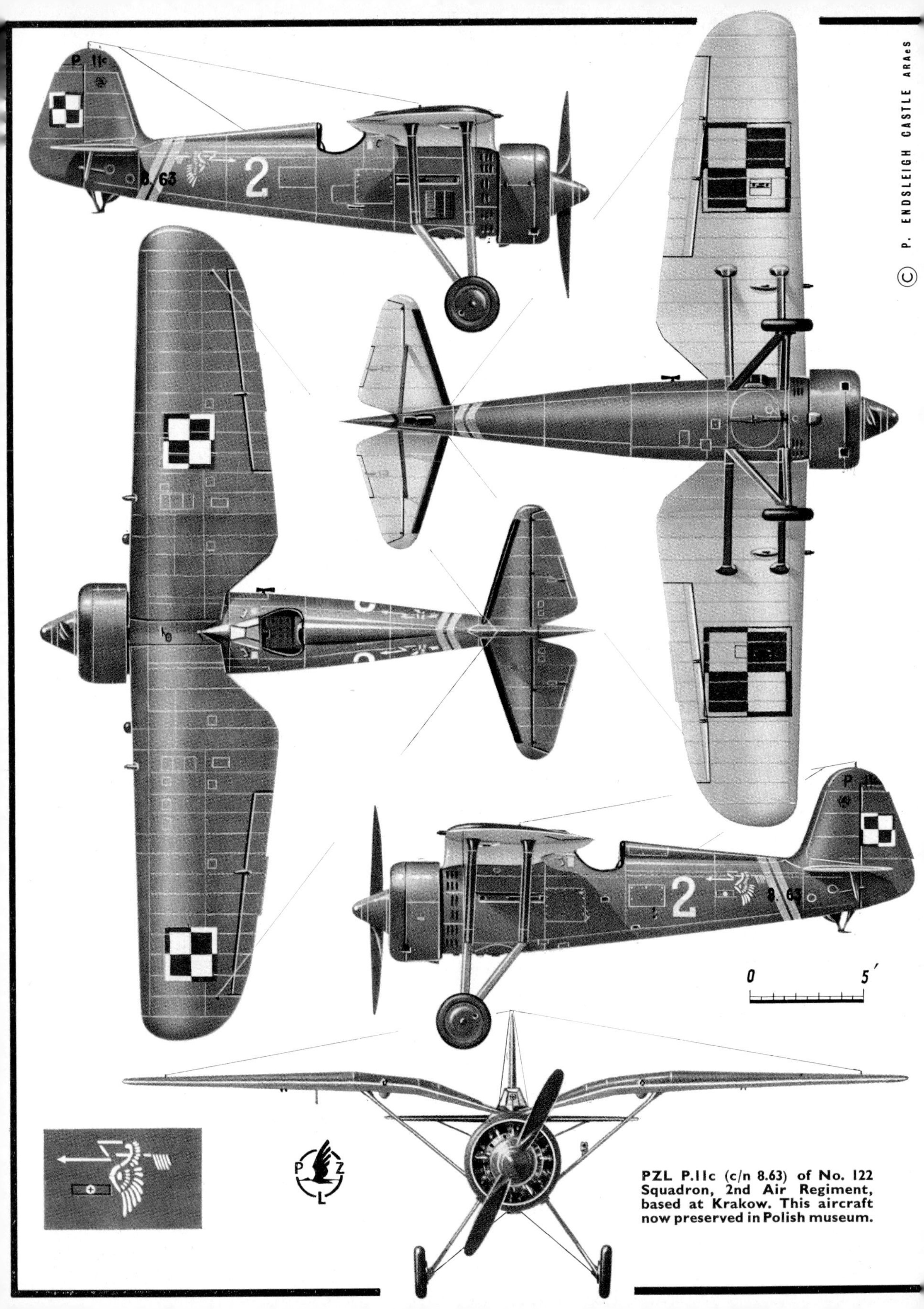

PZL P.11c (c/n 8.63) of No. 122 Squadron, 2nd Air Regiment, based at Krakow. This aircraft now preserved in Polish museum.

The P.Z.L. P-11

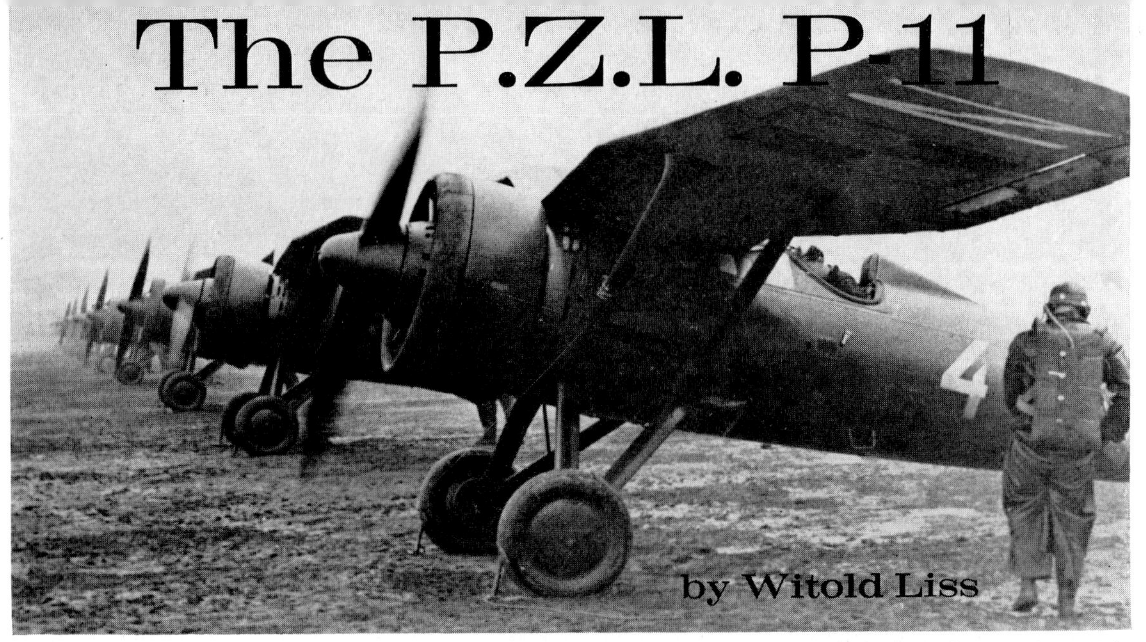

by Witold Liss

P.Z.L.s of the 1st Air Regiment photographed at Warsaw in 1939. The machine in the foreground is a P-11a, the remainder P-11c's.
(Photo: J. B. Cynk)

The reasons for an aircraft being particularly remembered by the historian and enthusiast are many and varied; but the most frequent include unusual beauty or peculiarity of appearance, particular achievement in service, or the marking of some historic point in design progress. The Spitfire had beauty; the P-51 gained immortality through its widespread and successful service; the Me 262 is remembered as the world's first jet fighter in squadron service. The P.Z.L. P-11 *Jedenastka* represents a mixture of qualities which won it a special place in the hearts of the Polish nation, and all others who traced the agony and the triumphs of that tortured country during the Second World War. It would not be easy to name an aircraft which at its birth represented a greater step forward in design, and yet was so nearly obsolete in the days of its greatest test; or an aircraft of more beauty which despite the great odds against it performed its work so well, and won such affection from its pilots. To her pilots the little gull-winged P-11 was essentially feminine; "She—the Eleventh"; and they remember her as they would remember a woman.

THE P-SERIES FIGHTERS

All the P-series fighters were designed by Ing. Zygmunt Pulawski, born in Lublin in 1901, and a graduate of the *Politechnika Warsawska* Technical University. In 1924, the Aviation Department of the Polish War Ministry proposed a contest for the best combat aircraft design; Pulawski entered and tying in third place was enabled to go to France for further technical education. On his return he passed through the Polish military pilots' school and later joined the P.Z.L. (*Panstwowe Zaklady Lotnicze*, State Aircraft Factory) in Warsaw.

The Polish aircraft industry was given an excellent incentive to progress when in 1928 the Skoda works Polish branch began production of aircraft engines; up to that date the industry had produced almost exclusively foreign machines of wooden structure under licence. The first all-metal design built in Poland was the French Vibault 70 fighter, which had some influence on Pulawski when he came to design his P-series. Although displaying features of the "French school", his machines introduced several original innovations, notably the highly characteristic wing design, and the general concept of the aerodynamically-clean monoplane, which was a significant step, appearing as it did at a time when the major aviation powers of the world were still wedded to the idea of strutted biplanes. Pulawski's "Polish Wing" consisted of a gull configuration with two parallel struts, the aerofoil being thinnest at the fuselage join and thickest at the "break". The angle of the inboard sections closely followed that of the cylinders of the Vee-pattern engine. The advantages of the gull layout were obviously headed by the unobstructed forward vision it afforded. When later models in the series, from the P-6 to the P-24, were fitted with radial engines, this necessitated an immediate lowering of the thrust line and in fact represented a distortion of Pulawski's idea.

The experimental P-8 never reached production, but this illustration is interesting in that it gives an impression of the original type of engine installation conceived by Pulawski.
(Photo: via the author)

Left, top to bottom: *The P-11 was first examined by the aeronautical world at large in December 1932 during the Paris Salon. It excited favourable comment and great interest at a time when most of the major powers still retained confidence in the strutted biplane as a first-line fighter.* (Photos: via G. Cattaneo)

The Polish Wing consisted of a two-spar duralumin structure with ribs riveted to spars and skin, the latter being made up of finely corrugated Vibault duralumin sheeting. The slotted ailerons were of metal construction, fabric covered. The wing aerofoil was the Polish Bartel BM 37 IIa, with an inboard thickness of 6·5%, reaching 16% at the junction of wing and strut and 8% at the tip. The Hispano Suiza V liquid-cooled engine of 600 h.p. was selected for the P-1; and the first prototype flew in September 1929. The design was fully vindicated when in 1930 it won first place in the Bucharest competition against such aircraft as the Bristol Bulldog and the Dewoitine D.27. Unfortunately, the Polish War Ministry raised objections to the Hispano powerplant on economic and practical grounds; and as a result all P-series machines powered by in-line engines remained in the prototype stage.

The first radial-engined variant, powered by a 500-h.p. Bristol Jupiter VI FH cowled in a Townend ring, was designated P-6. Engine overheating problems rendered the P-6 rather troublesome in service, and several changes were made which eventually resulted in the appearance of the P-7, the most significant forerunner of the later models. Tragically, Pulawski was killed on 21st March 1931 due to control malfunction during a test flight of a light amphibian of his own design. The death of this brilliant pilot and designer was a great loss to the Polish aviation industry; but work on the P-series continued under the direction of Ing. Wsiewolod Jakimiuk, later designer of the SE 5000 Baroudeur, the DHC Chipmunk and the DHC Beaver. As the head of P.Z.L.'s fighter team, Jakimiuk finished the P-7 project; this was the first of the series to see serial production. It was a development of the P-6 powered by a 585-h.p. Bristol Jupiter VII F; some 150 machines were produced, remaining in service with the Polish Air Forces until 1939, and some 30 aircraft were still in squadron service during the Polish campaign of that autumn.

THE P-11 APPEARS

The first prototype of the next (and for Polish units, final) model in the P-series, the P-11/1, flew for the first time in September 1931, and it immediately became obvious that for its time this fighter was a world-beater. The prototype was powered by a Gnôme-Rhône (Bristol) Jupiter, similar to those used in the P-7. The P-11/2 and /3 were powered with Bristol Mercury engines (P-11/2 fitted with a G-R Mistral K.9 in 1932). The fourth and fifth machines were similar to the P-11/3, and the P-11/6 was the production prototype, with an exhaust collector ring. All prototypes were tested with several different pro-

The third and production prototype of the P-11, which participated in the 1932 National Air Races in the United States.
(Photo: J. B. Cynk)

pellers, and the final configuration of the P-11/6 was retained for the initial production batch of 30 P-11a's. This batch was completed in one year—1934—and all aircraft were fitted with the Bristol Mercury IV S2 built by the Polish Skoda works.

In December 1932 the P-11/2 was exhibited at the *Salon International d'Aeronautique* in Paris, where it had excited much favourable comment as a revolutionary modern design. In July 1932 the P-11/3 had been sent to the International Contest at Zürich. In a speed contest for single-seat fighters round a 367-km. triangle, Jerzy Bajan, the Challenge pilot, placed the P-11/3 second to the Hawker Fury flown by the Jugoslavian Captain Sintic. The Fury recorded a speed of 318 km./h. against the P.Z.L.'s 310 km./h.; however, the Polish Aero Club authorities protested at the addition of lead ethyl to Sintic's fuel. In Zürich the P-11 came up against its old adversaries, the Bulldog, D.27 and also the Fokker D.XVI. One of the later prototypes took part in the U.S. National Air Races in 1932, and won the admiration of many interested spectators.

The P-11a was introduced to service units in 1935 and almost immediately Roumania, concluding negotiations in hand since 1931, placed an order for one batch. Fifty machines were produced in slightly modified form and designated P-11b (see below "The P-11 Abroad").

During this period the P-11/3 underwent various tests to determine the best airscrew, those tested including the Chauvier, Bristol, Ratier and Letoviszomanski, the last-mentioned being eventually adopted for the further developments of the P-11. A side-effect of this programme was valuable information gained regarding power unit selection for the P-24.

After completing the P-11a order the P.Z.L. plant at Paluch Okecie, Warsaw, immediately undertook production of a new version, the P-11c. The first examples quickly passed service acceptance tests and reached the fighter units during 1935. By 1936 monthly output of P-11c's reached 25 machines, and continued until 1936–37. The full production order was for 175 machines; and after the completion of delivery in 1937 the type gave place on the production lines to the P-24. During 1936, however, some trouble occurred over the production of fuel tanks. Made by a private sub-contractor, these tanks were assembled with riveted joint-lines covered with a resin sealer. This type of seam proved very sensitive to vibration, however, and was therefore replaced by a welded joint.

P-11/3 at the 1932 Zürich Meeting.
(Photo: courtesy of Skrzydlata Polska)

This close-up of the tail of a damaged P-11a of No. 113 Squadron, 1st Air Regiment ("Owls" Squadron) shows to advantage the flatter silhouette of the P-11a's tail and the squadron emblem.
(Photo: J. B. Cynk)

P-11c during construction. (Photo: via the author)

This proved a disastrous change; the welded joints began to fail early in the aircraft's service life, and eventually the acceptance commission began to reject deliveries of machines with this type of installation. Extensive experiments with various types of seam led eventually to a satisfactory welding technique,

A P-11c (foreground) and P-11a's of No. 113 Squadron.
(Photo: J. B. Cynk)

Standard production P-11c, with four-gun armament.
(Photo: J. B. Cynk)

Line-up of the 1st Air Regiment's P-11c's at Warsaw Air Base in summer, 1939.
(Photo: J. B. Cynk)

P-11c of the Commanding Officer of Fighter Dyon III/6, comprising Nos. 161 and 162 Squadrons of the 6th Air Regiment.
(Photo: via Sqdn. Ldr. F. Kornicki)

and the problem was completely overcome at the cost of some delay in service deliveries.

The story of the P-24 does not fall within the scope of this work, and will be covered in a future *Profile*; however, it is pertinent to record here the story of the *Kobuz* project. Due to the inability of the War Ministry to obtain delivery of the MS 406, Hurricane or Spitfire during 1938, and the hold-ups in the P.Z.L. 50 *Jastrzab* programme, the original P-11 airframe was stressed and tested for a new engine, the P.Z.L. (Bristol) Mercury VIII of 840 h.p. The new variant, named *Kobuz*, was ordered from the P.W.S. Biala Podlaska works in July 1939. The type was planned for an armament of four 7·7 mm. Wz.36 machine guns and was expected to retain the P-11's excellent manœuvrability while achieving a higher speed. First machines were scheduled for completion in May–June 1940; according to some reports the prototype was completed and flown in August 1939; but the War put paid to this project, and the Polish Air Forces faced the swarms of enemy still mounted in P-11a's and P-11c's.

THE P-11 DESCRIBED

All versions of the P-11 were built with very similar techniques, and the following description of the P-11c, as the major production variant, may be taken as representative. The aircraft was an all-metal shoulder-wing monoplane with fixed undercarriage. Powerplants used were the P.Z.L. (Bristol) Skoda Mercury V S2 of 560 h.p. and later the Mercury VI S2 of 645 h.p. driving a wooden two-blade fixed-pitch airscrew produced by the firm Szomanski. Armament varied from two to four 7·7 mm. Vickers (later Polish 7·7 mm. Wzor 37) machine guns. The fuselage, of all-metal construction with duralumin skinning, had the engine bay forward with an engine bearer in the form of a duralumin ring strengthened by L-shaped frames; the engine itself was mounted on rubber vibration absorbers of the "Lord" type. The fuel installation comprised the main jettisonable 213-litre tank placed in a fuselage bay aft of the firewall, and an additional 11-litre gravity tank in the port wing, all joined by fuel lines and Le Bosec-type fuel cocks. The oil tank, of 27-litre capacity, was placed near the oil cooler on the aft face of the firewall. The wings were of two-spar all-metal construction, the double-T section main spars being skinned with corrugated duralumin sheets of Vibault patent, riveted to spars and ribs with Daude-type rivets. Tail surfaces and ailerons were of similar design. The wing/fuselage joint was a steel component fixed to duralumin bearers on the upper part of the first and second fuselage frames; each wing was also supported by two parallel struts of duralumin with streamlined cross-section, the forward struts being additionally strengthened with duralumin plate. Single struts supported the horizontal tail surfaces. The undercarriage was of the "scissors" configuration, an original P.Z.L. patent, consisting of two V-struts streamlined with tin-plate, and two Avia-type oleo pneumatic shock absorbers were attached to the first fuselage frame; both undercarriage legs were braced with steel wire. The tail skid was fitted with a similar Avia shock absorber.

Apart from the Wz.37 guns, manufactured by the Warsaw National Armaments Factory (P.W.U.) a camera gun and four bomb-racks each capable of

P-11c's of No. 142 "Wild Ducks" Squadron, 4th Air Regiment, in flight in the summer of 1939. The machines with white-painted fin tips were the aircraft of Flight Commanders.
(Photo: J. B. Cynk)

Detached K.O.P. (Border Protection Corps) Flight from No. 161 Squadron stationed at Sarny for firing practice in the spring of 1939. Note upper wing markings denoting service with the K.O.P.; the squadron's "Turkey" emblem was applied later in the year to the fuselage sides. (Photo: via Sqdn. Ldr. F. Kornicki)

carrying one 12·5-kg. bomb were fitted. In four-gun machines, two guns were mounted in the wings, one just outboard of each wing "break", to fire obliquely upwards at a 3° angle; the other two guns were mounted in side fuselage bays, with barrels exposed, firing inside the nose-skinning and Townend ring. Only the fuselage guns were synchronised; wing guns carried 300 r.p.g., fuselage guns 500 r.p.g., all ammunition in steel-link belts loaded in the sequence armour-piercing/incendiary/explosive/armour-piercing, etc.

The open cockpit was protected by a plexiglass windshield, and equipped with a complex of Polish navigational and engine control instruments and a German Züru compass. Safety equipment comprised three "knock-out" flame dampers, one Salva Ra flame damper, a fuel-tank jettisoning device and Siebe-Gorman Mk. VIII oxygen equipment. Theoretically all P-11c's should have been radio-equipped but in practice only about one in three were. All machines carried a flare pistol and twelve cartridges, but the majority of pilots used the classic communication techniques of wing-rocking and hand signals. Additional engine equipment comprised the Viet 200 starter with Bth ASZ-type starter switches.

The P-11a differed mainly in power plant—the 9-cylinder air-cooled radial Skoda Mercury IV S2 of 500 h.p. with supercharger. Armament comprised two 7·7-mm. guns in fuselage bays with 700 r.p.g., and the most visually characteristic difference was the lower, flat-topped fin and rudder assembly. The engine in the P-11a was mounted 100 mm. higher, the pilot's seat 50 mm. lower and 300 mm. farther forward. The dihedral of the inboard wing sections was slightly less than in the P-11c; all these differences had slight effects on the performance figures. The Roumanian Air Force P-11b corresponded closely to the P-11a, and the P-11f to the P-11c, with slight armament and installations differences.

THE P-11 ABROAD

The *Jedenastka* was produced in two countries only, Poland and Roumania, and served only with these two air forces. During 1936 the Spanish Republican Government entered negotiations to buy a batch of P-11s, and the sale of an initial batch of 15 machines was almost finalised when a Polish diplomatic note of 29th July 1936 put a stop to the discussions.

The first batch of aircraft ordered by Roumania consisted of 50 machines, and to fill this order P.Z.L. developed the P-11b, which was, as stated above, a modified P-11a with the Roumanian-built Gnôme-Rhône K.9 Krse engine of 595 h.p. and Roumanian instruments. The first deliveries took place in 1934, and negotiations for licence production in Roumania opened the same year. These discussions did not in fact reach a conclusion until the entire P-11b order had been completed, and it was the modified P-11c designated P-11f that was built in Roumania. In 1934 a group of technicians led by Ing. Timesencu came to the P.Z.L. plant from the Roumanian I.A.R. concern (*Industria Aeronautica Romana*) to study construction techniques, and after some six months they returned home to supervise the programme; no members of the Roumanian industry had any experience in the construction of all-metal aircraft. However, many problems arose, and despite considerable assistance from P.Z.L. (in the early stages taking the form of deliveries

The emblem of No. 161 "Turkeys" Squadron. (Photo: via Sqdn. Ldr. F. Kornicki)

A P-11c of the "Fighting Cocks" in flight. (Photo: J. B. Cynk)

A flight of No. 121 Squadron P-11c's running-up. (Photo: J. B. Cynk)

of half-completed wings and entire fuselages) production was extremely slow. During the period 1935–37 I.A.R. built only 120 P-11s and P-24s, with a yearly production of about 40 P-11f's. Various small systems changes were made in Roumania; all P-11f models were four-gun aircraft, and special low-pressure tyres were fitted for use from unprepared airstrips.

After September 1939 numerous Polish workers from the P.Z.L. plant were evacuated to Roumania to avoid the German onslaught; Poles formed several teams in I.A.R. especially in the technical control divisions, and played a large part in the production of the P-24. Although the entire strength of Roumanian P-11s never exceeded 120 machines, they equipped five fighter squadrons and were still in service when Germany and Roumania allied against the U.S.S.R. in 1941. Several types of aircraft of Polish origin served with the R.R.A.F., the P-37, P-23 and P-43 as well as the P-11. It was only through experience gained while producing the P-11 and P-24 under licence that I.A.R. was able to produce the first indigenous fighter monoplane, the I.A.R. 80. No less than 26 Polish technicians held key posts in I.A.R. at this time, and after the cessation of P-24 production the tail assembly and aft fuselage of this design was used, unchanged, on the I.A.R. 80. All Polish workers were made welcome by I.A.R. and later the company helped them to leave Roumania to escape purges by the SS and SD.

It has been rumoured that some captured P-7s and P-11s were test-flown by the Germans during the last months of 1939. No evidence can be found to support this claim, however; the only known cases of use by the Germans are the rough re-assembly of parts of wrecked machines for purposes of staging mock "kill" photographs for the propaganda services. However, these were by no means perfect replicas and the modern researcher can identify the fakes without difficulty.

DEFIANCE AND ANNIHILATION

The organisation of the Polish Air Forces changed several times in the pre-war years to accommodate the varying rôles it was called upon to perform; but after the late 1920s the strength of the service was

Details of the P-11c: (left) *Wing strut attachment point, showing empty cartridge ejector chute for wing gun, and corrugated skin effect;* (below) *Fuselage gun installation, with cover plate swung open.* (Photos: via the author)

Details of the P-11c: (above) *Cowling (note jettisonable fuel tank visible on underside of fuselage);* (right) *Main undercarriage gear.* Photos: via the author.

divided into Air Regiments composed of units of various types of machines. Each of the six regiments included a fighter force of two or three squadrons; on 1st September 1939 the fighter force had 158 first line fighters, 128 P-11s and 30 P-7s. The 1st Air Regiment was based on Warsaw, the 2nd at Krakow, the 3rd at Poznan, the 4th at Torun, the 5th in the Wilno/Lida area, and the 6th at Lwow. Until the beginning of hostilities the fighter units were rigidly attached to the regimental organisations, but during the brief fighting they were detached in order to give the maximum support to ground forces. The units were numbered according to the following sequence. Fighter and bomber squadrons carried a three figure designation, reconnaissance units a two figure code. The first figure referred to the type of unit, "1" denoting fighters, "2" denoting bombers. The second figure denoted the regiment, and the third the squadron within the regiment. Thus 124 Fighter Squadron was the designation of the 4th fighter squadron of the 2nd Air Regiment at Krakow. Virtually all squadrons had a colourful emblem painted on the fuselage side corresponding to the popular name of the unit, e.g. "Owls", "Wild Ducks", etc. After about the 6th September 1939, these markings were usually over-painted with the standard olive shade, as were wing upper-surface insignia.

During the ominous spring months of 1939, the fighter squadrons were re-grouped in the following manner. A central fighter establishment, the *Brygada Poscigowa* or Pursuit Brigade, was formed of five squadrons, Nos. 111, 112, 113, 114, and 123, based around Warsaw for the defence of the capital and to

Cockpit of the P-11c. (Photos: J. B. Cynk)

The P-11c's Mercury engine bursts into life. (Photo: J. B. Cynk)

P-11c, serial 8.63, *of the 2nd Air Regiment's No. 122 Squadron, based at Krakow. This machine, no longer airworthy, is preserved in Poland as a museum exhibit.* (Photo: F. Pawlowicz)

serve as a reserve pool for the C-in-C of the P.A.F. Squadrons drawn from the 2nd, 3rd, 4th, 5th and 6th Regiments were assigned as fighter cover to various ground formations; 121 and 122 to Army Krakow, 161 and 162 to Army Lodz, 131 and 132 to Army Poznan, 141 and 142 to Army Pomorze, and 152 to Army Modlin.

Operations had started in the summer of 1939 for the *Jedenastka*; German Dornier reconnaissance aircraft had begun to violate Polish airspace on photo-recce missions, and after warning fire from anti-aircraft batteries failed to deter them the fighters were ordered to intercept and force them to land. This was not in fact such an easy task as it may have appeared from the Staff offices of the War Ministry. The P-11 was a brilliant "pilot's aircraft" and had been a formidable weapon in 1934; but by 1939 was frankly obsolescent and no match for even a Dornier in performance. With a top level speed of 380 km./h. and an 8,000-m. ceiling, the P-11 was inadequate for intercepting Dorniers of the *Fernaufklärer Gruppen* which had a 20-km./h. speed advantage and a ceiling of 9,000 to 10,000 m. Combat experience at the outbreak of open hostilities showed that with the

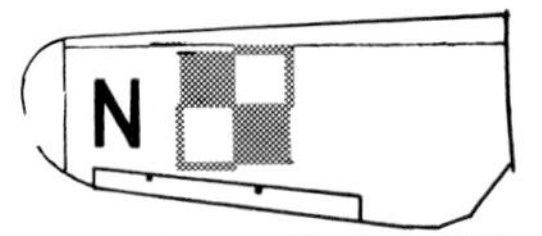

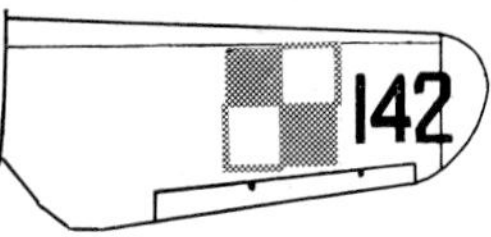

Underwing detail of a/c "3" No. 111 "Kosciuszko" Squadron. "N142" *radio call sign in black. National insignia red only on pale blue undersurface.*

exception of the Hs 126 and Ju 87, German machines could avoid action at will. The high numbers of kills achieved by Polish fighter pilots may be put down to their high determination and fighting spirit, and also to the fact that the *Luftwaffe*, confident of the superiority of their aircraft, seldom sought to avoid combat.

The cat-and-mouse interception attempts of the summer months ended abruptly immediately after 4.45 a.m. on the morning of 1st September. Great numbers of German aircraft appeared; there were 10 *Luftwaffe* machines, including three fighters, for every Polish fighter available. The Bf 109E had a 150-km./h. speed advantage and a 2,000-m. higher ceiling than the P-11, and they were no longer bothering to avoid combat. The first German aircraft to be shot down during the entire Second World War was a Ju 87 destroyed near Olkusz at 5.30 a.m. by Lt. W. Gnys of the 2nd Air Regiment; and the first Allied pilot to score two kills in one sortie was Lt. Gedymin of the 3rd Air Regiment. During the 1st, 2nd and 3rd September, 46 P-11s and P-7s were lost; but a fair proportion were repaired and returned to their units. In the same period 60 *Luftwaffe* machines were shot down. Even the P-7s scored some successes, a great tribute to the pilots of these obsolete fighters. On the 3rd September, P-11s made the first attack on a German armoured column, with small results and heavy losses.

During the fighting the P-11 proved itself most versatile, performing tactical reconnaissance and liaison sorties as well as fighter missions, and carrying a passenger on at least one occasion. However, the quantity and quality of German types committed to the campaign was too great for this brave but hopeless resistance to be prolonged more than a matter of days. Contrary to many reports, the main losses suffered by the fighter units were not caused by destruction on the ground. The entire Polish fighter force was exhausted

Roumanian P-11b's, powered by the K.9 engine. Note early Roumanian Air Force roundel markings under wing-tips. (Photo: via the author)

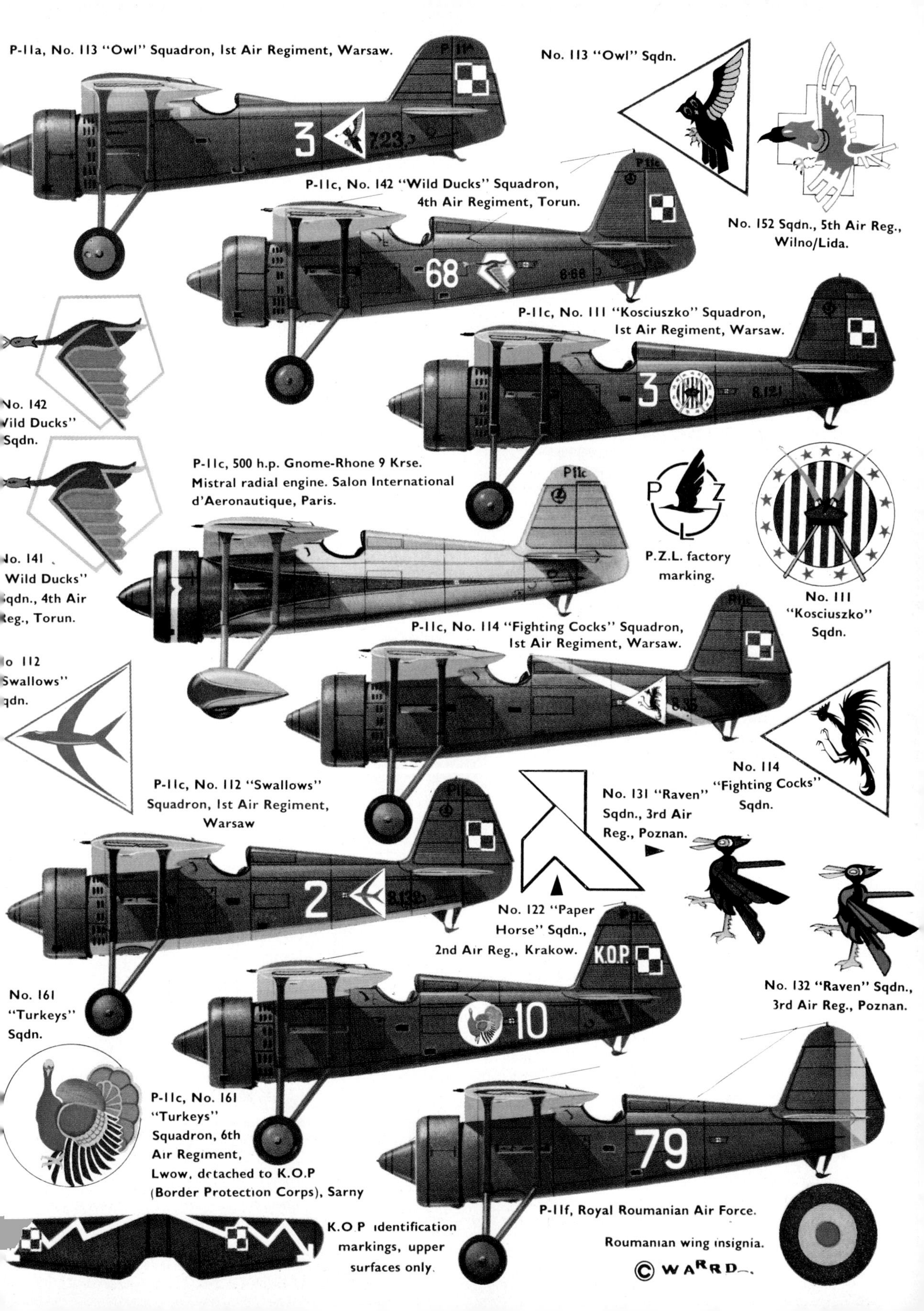
P-11a, No. 113 "Owl" Squadron, 1st Air Regiment, Warsaw.
No. 113 "Owl" Sqdn.
No. 152 Sqdn., 5th Air Reg., Wilno/Lida.
P-11c, No. 142 "Wild Ducks" Squadron, 4th Air Regiment, Torun.
P-11c, No. 111 "Kosciuszko" Squadron, 1st Air Regiment, Warsaw.
No. 142 "Wild Ducks" Sqdn.
P-11c, 500 h.p. Gnome-Rhone 9 Krse. Mistral radial engine. Salon International d'Aeronautique, Paris.
P.Z.L. factory marking.
No. 141 "Wild Ducks" Sqdn., 4th Air Reg., Torun.
No. 111 "Kosciuszko" Sqdn.
P-11c, No. 114 "Fighting Cocks" Squadron, 1st Air Regiment, Warsaw.
No. 112 "Swallows" Sqdn.
No. 114 "Fighting Cocks" Sqdn.
No. 131 "Raven" Sqdn., 3rd Air Reg., Poznan.
P-11c, No. 112 "Swallows" Squadron, 1st Air Regiment, Warsaw
No. 122 "Paper Horse" Sqdn., 2nd Air Reg., Krakow.
No. 161 "Turkeys" Sqdn.
No. 132 "Raven" Sqdn., 3rd Air Reg., Poznan.
P-11c, No. 161 "Turkeys" Squadron, 6th Air Regiment, Lwow, detached to K.O.P (Border Protection Corps), Sarny
K.O.P identification markings, upper surfaces only.
P-11f, Royal Roumanian Air Force.
Roumanian wing insignia.
© WARRD

A flight of No. 121 Squadron P-11c's in the air. (Photo: J. B. Cynk)

One of the few P-11's destroyed on the ground, in this case by a bombing raid during maintenance. (Photo: via the author)

in action. Of 166 fighters of all types, 116 were destroyed in combat, including eight by Polish and three by German ground fire. Fifty or so were evacuated to Roumania. Pilot losses were 12 killed, 15 wounded, and seven missing—giving the surprisingly low figure of 15% losses. This is all the more heartening when one recalls the distasteful fact that as early as 2nd September cases were recorded of German airmen attempting to kill adversaries who were descending by parachute; Lt. Szyszko of 142 Sqdn. was seriously wounded by gunfire from three Bf 109s on that date while hanging from his parachute. German losses during this campaign were 129 aircraft destroyed in the air, an impressive figure when the great superiority of *Luftwaffe* equipment is taken into consideration. Poles are known to have rammed as a last resort on several occasions; a notable example is Lt.-Col. Pamula of 114 Sqdn., who shot down one Ju 87, one He 111, and when attacked by Bf 109 escort fighters rammed one and baled out without injury.

The P-11 was in her day a revolutionary aircraft, and even in the twilight of her career put up a resistance against overwhelming odds which will always be remembered by an admiring world. Pilots who first joined battle mounted in the *Jedenastka* outlived her, and went on to fight on all fronts in aircraft better matched to those of the enemy, until they contributed at last to the victory they had earned so well.

The author would like to acknowledge the assistance afforded during the preparation of this Profile *by the Skrzydlata Polska, and his indebtedness to the researches of A. Kurowski (Lotnictwo Polskie W 1939 Roku) and S. Skalski (Czarne Krzyze Nad Polska).*

Units equipped with P-series fighters during the Polish campaign of September 1939.

	Squadron No.	Type	Quantity
1st A.R.	111	P-11	11
	112	P-11	11
	113	P-11	11
	114	P-11	11
2nd A.R.	121	P-11	10
	122	P-11	10
	123	P-7	10
3rd A.R.	131	P-11	10
	132	P-11	10
4th A.R.	141	P-11	11
	142	P-11	11
5th A.R.	151	P-7	10
	152	P-11	11
6th A.R.	161	P-11	12
	162	P-7	10

SPECIFICATIONS

	P-11c	P-11f
Span	10·719 m. (30·2 ft.)	10·719 m. (30·2 ft.)
Length ...	7·55 m. (25·19 ft.)	7·55 m. (25·19 ft.)
Wing area		
Weight:		
Empty ...	1,147·5 kg. (2,530 lb.)	1,108 kg. (2,440 lb.)
Fuel ...	272 kg. (600 lb.)	272 kg. (600 lb.)
Pilot and parachute	88 kg. (194 lb.)	88 kg. (194 lb.)
Loaded ...	1,590 kg. (3,500 lb.)	1,586 kg. (3,490 lb.)
Static stress coefficient...	16	16
Top speed at:		
Sea level	300 km./h. (186 m.p.h.)	280 km./h. (173 m.p.h.)
5,000 m. (0,000 ft.)	390 km./h. (242 m.p.h.)	360 km./h. (223 m.p.h.)
Climb to:		
16,400 ft. ...	6 min.	6½ min.
24,400 ft. ...	13 min.	13¾ min.
Service ceiling	8,000 m. (24,400 ft.)	7,500 m. (22,800 ft.)
Absolute ceiling ...	11,000 m. (33,600 ft.)	10,500 m. (32,000 ft.)
Landing speed	98 km./h. (61·5 m.p.h.)	98 km./h. (61·5 m.p.h.)
Landing roll ...	343 m. (1,050 ft.) in 18·7 sec.	
Take-off roll ...	99 m. (302 ft.) in 6·5 sec.	
Engine ...	Licence-built Bristol Mercury VI S2	Licence-built Gnôme-Rhône 9 Krse.

A faked German propaganda photograph of a P-11 "destroyed in combat". Note unconvincing damage and strange "tail-plane". (Photo: via the author)

PROFILE PUBLICATIONS

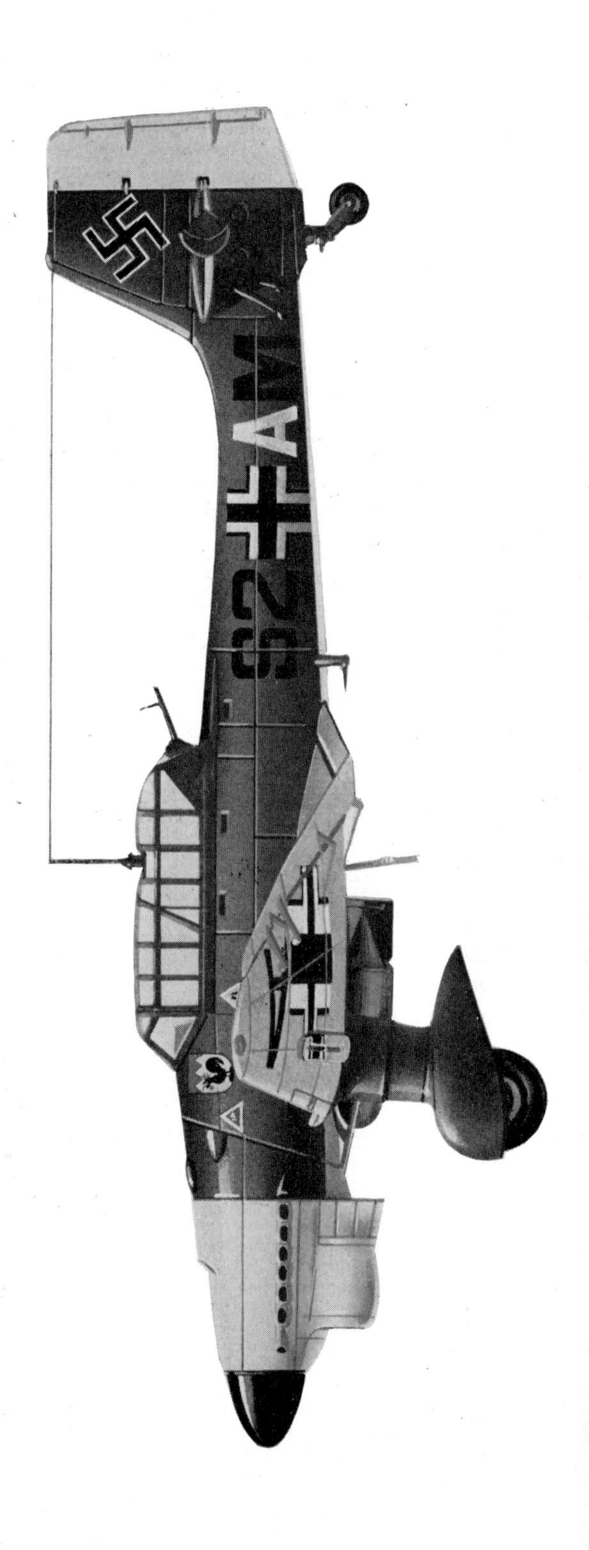

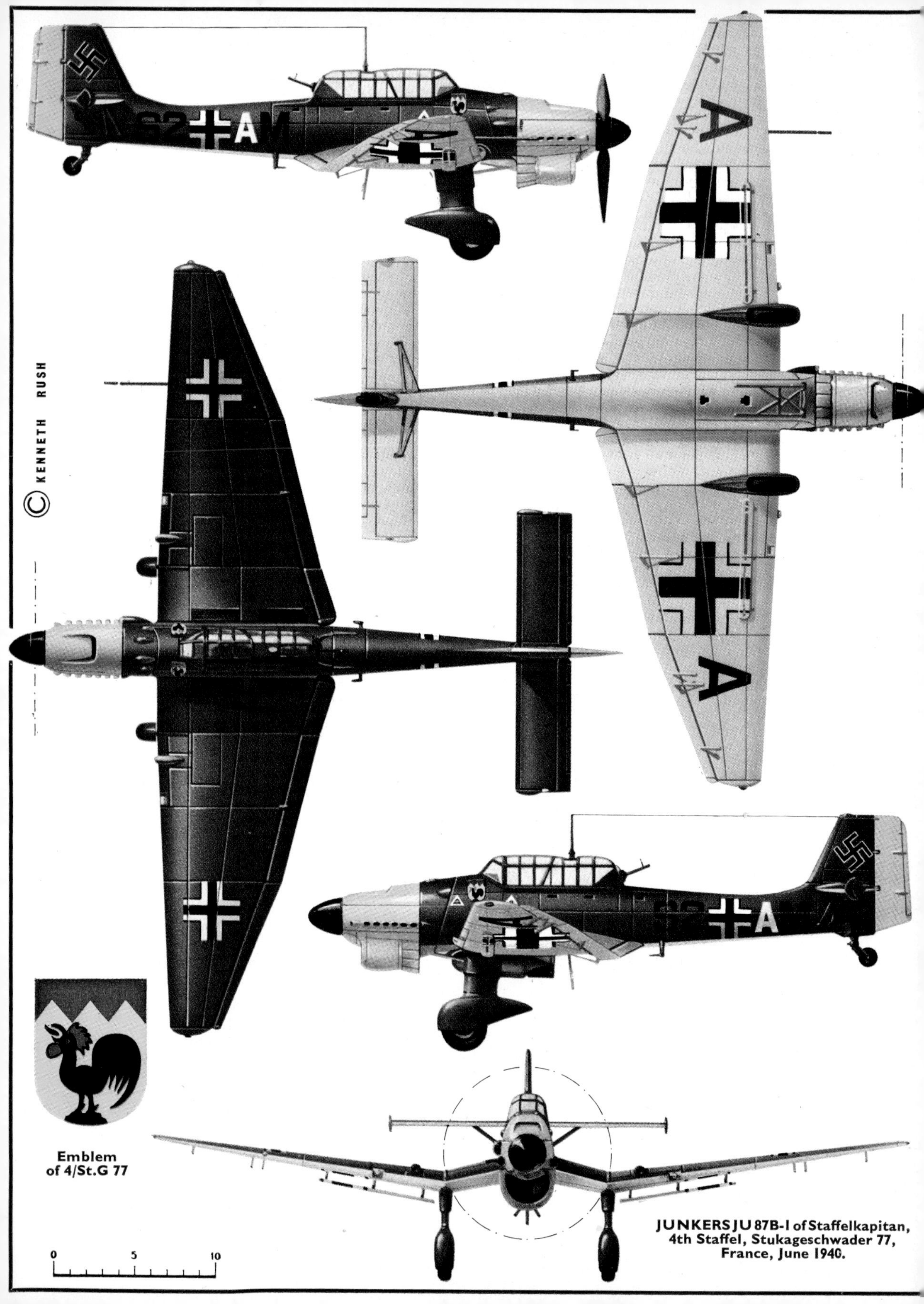

JUNKERS JU 87B-1 of Staffelkapitan, 4th Staffel, Stukageschwader 77, France, June 1940.

The Stuka in its classic rôle—a near-vertical dive, with sirens howling and bombs dropping away in a tight cluster.

The Junkers Ju 87A & B

by J. Richard Smith

The Junkers Ju 87 was hailed by the German propaganda machine as being the supreme weapon, and it seemed that its phenomenal successes in the Polish and French campaigns were to justify these claims. During these it was allowed to roam freely over enemy territory, creating havoc amongst troops and civilians alike as its ugly, cranked-wing silhouette and screaming sirens demoralised its opponents. As the most effective attack bomber of the opening months of W.W.II the Ju 87 was to become synonymous with the word "Stuka", an abbreviation of the German word *Sturzkampfflugzeug* or dive bomber. However, when it did at last encounter really effective fighter opposition, as at Dunkirk and in the Battle of Britain, it was decimated. Slow, unwieldy, and having but one puny machine gun to defend its rear, the all too numerous inadequacies of the machine were at last revealed.

The progenitor of the Ju 87 was the Swedish-built Junkers K.47 which made its first flight in 1928. Powered by a 480-h.p. Bristol Jupiter radial engine, the aircraft was classed as a two-seat interceptor, but was fitted with special wing bomb racks outboard of the airscrew arc and can be considered to be the forerunner of the Stuka. Ernst Udet (one of the architects of the new German Air Force), became enthusiastic as to the capabilities of the dive bomber after seeing a demonstration by Curtiss Helldivers at Cleveland, Ohio, on 27th September 1933 and a contract was placed for the construction of a German dive bomber.

Four companies produced projects, the Ju 87 designed by Dipl. Ing. Pohlmann being the Junkers entry. The first prototype, the Ju 87 V1, appeared in 1935, possessed twin fins and rudders and was powered by a 640-h.p. Rolls-Royce Kestrel V engine with fixed pitch airscrew. The machine crashed due to tail flutter, but was replaced shortly afterwards by the Ju 87 V2 which differed from its forerunner in having a 610-h.p. Junkers Jumo 210 A engine with controllable pitch propeller. Before this machine could take to the air, however, it was fitted with a new square fin and rudder with which it was hoped to cure the flutter trouble.

The Ju 87 V2, and generally similar V3 (D-UKYQ) were fitted with special dive brakes under the wings outboard of the undercarriage. In June 1936, the four competing designs performed at the newly founded *Erprobungstelle* (Experimental Station) at Rechlin for a production contract. The Ju 87 was pitted against the Arado Ar 81, the Blohm und Voss Ha 137 and the Heinkel He 118. The Junkers and Heinkel designs soon proved their superiority over the other two machines, but it was not until the He 118 was crashed by Ernst Udet (owing to his unfamiliarity with the airscrew pitch control) that the Ju 87 was chosen.

By the late autumn of 1936 the fourth prototype, the Ju 87 V4 (D-UBIP) was flying, this employing larger and more angular vertical tail surfaces, improved visibility due to a lowered engine centre line, and a single 7·9 mm. MG 17 machine gun in the starboard wing. This aircraft was the forerunner of the Ju 87 A-0 pre-production variant of which ten were laid down in the summer of 1936. The Ju 87 A-0 differed from the fourth prototype solely in having a straight leading edge taper to simplify production, and was followed by the generally similar Ju 87 A-1 production model. Deliveries of the Ju 87 A-1 commenced during the spring of 1937. It was powered by a 635-h.p. Junkers Jumo 210 Da twelve cylinder engine which gave it a maximum speed of 199 m.p.h. at 12,000 ft. The Ju 87 A-2 was similar to the A-1, but employed a different airscrew with broader blades.

SERVICE IN SPAIN

During the summer of 1937, the first Ju 87 As entered service with *Stukageschwader 163 "Immelmann"*, a recently established unit and somewhat of an élite formation. St.G 163 was entrusted with the operational evaluation of the new dive bomber, developing suitable tactics for the machine. In December 1937, a flight of three Ju 87 A-1s, known as the "*Jolanthe Kette*", was detached from St.G 163 and sent to Spain as part of the Condor Legion. The three aircraft first saw action at Teruel, north-west of Valencia, and subsequently supported the Spanish Nationalists' drive towards the Mediterranean coast, destroying Republican communications. Later, they took part in the offensive in Catalona and the fighting on the Ebro front, crews from St.G 163 being constantly changed in order to provide operational experience to as many as possible.

Although only three Ju 87 A-1s were delivered to Spain they were remarkably successful, the National-

The first prototype, showing twin tail and undercarriage "trousers".

Below: *Rolls-Royce Kestrel V engine of the Ju 87V1, with distinctive radiator.*

The V4 displays the early wing taper.

A moment of relaxation during the French campaign; aircrew and Ju 87 Bs of 10 Staffel, Lehrgeschwader *1. This operational training unit was redesignated as 1/St.G 5 in February 1942.* (Photo: R. Ward collection)

ists having air superiority which enabled the dive bombers to operate freely. It was found that bombs could be accurately placed on roads, bridges and shipping targets; communications destroyed and enemy troops effectively cut-off in the mountainous Spanish countryside. In early 1939 several Ju 87 B-1s were sent to Spain to supplement the earlier variant. These took part in the bombing of shipping in the Spanish ports of Barcelona, Tarragona and Valencia, successfully sinking many enemy vessels and destroying much of the dock area. The legend of the Stuka was born.

PRODUCTION OF THE Ju 87 B

During the summer of 1938, the Ju 87 B succeeded the A series on the production lines. Ten Ju 87 B-0 pre-production aircraft were built, the aircraft employing the 900-h.p. Junkers Jumo 211 A engine. In addition, the Ju 87 B series differed from earlier models in having an entirely re-designed cockpit canopy, enlarged vertical tail surfaces, "spats" in place of "trousers", and an additional 7·9 mm. MG 17 machine gun in the port wing. Length was increased by eight inches, empty and loaded weights were also increased and the machine normally carried a 1,100-lb. bomb under the fuselage or one 550-lb. and four 110-lb. bombs, the latter on underwing racks. The ten pre-production machines were followed by the generally similar Ju 87 B-1 of which four variants were produced. These were the standard Ju 87 B-1/U1, the B-1/U2 with alternative radio equipment, the B-1/U3 with additional armour and armoured glass for the gunner and the B-1/U4, which was similar to the U3, but with provision for a ski undercarriage. The Ju 87 B-1/Trop was similar, but had tropical filters and desert survival equipment.

In 1940 the Ju 87 B-1 was replaced in production by the Ju 87 B-2. This differed in being powered by a 1,100-h.p. Junkers Jumo 211 Da engine with hydraulically operated radiator cooling gills and modified undercarriage legs. The aircraft, which was the first

"*Black men*" (Luftwaffe *slang for ground crew) bombing up the Ju 87 A-1s of St.G 163* "Immelmann" *early in 1938.*

The Ju 87 A saw service with the Condor Legion in Spain, and limited use as a dive-bombing trainer in the early stages of W.W.II.

Below: *A* kette *of Ju 87 B-1s in flight, 1939.* (Photo: R. Ward collection)

really large production variant, could carry a 2,200-lb. bomb load in some circumstances. The Ju 87 B-2/U1, U2, U3 and U4 and B-2/Trop were similar modifications to those of the B-1 mentioned earlier, but pertaining to the B-2.

The Ju 87 C was a special conversion of the Ju 87 B-1 intended for operations from the *Kriegsmarine's* aircraft carrier *Graf Zeppelin* which was then under construction. The Ju 87 C-0 was stressed for catapulting, had an arrester hook, and was provided with electrically operated folding outer wing panels. Only a few Ju 87 C-0 and production C-1s were completed, and with the suspension of the aircraft carrier programme most machines were re-converted to B-1 standard. A unit was formed in December 1938 to operate the Ju 87 C from the *Graf Zeppelin*, designated *4.(Stuka)Staffel/Trägergruppe 186.* The unit was equipped with standard Ju 87 As and Bs however, and although increased to full *Gruppe* strength on 16th September 1939, the unit never received the Ju 87 C.

One Ju 87 C-0 was fitted with an 88 mm. recoilless gun at Treuburg in 1944. The weapon was housed in the forward fuselage, firing through the airscrew disc, but the aircraft was damaged when the compensating charges failed to ignite.

The final production variant of the Ju 87 based on the B series was the Ju 87 R, the "R" indicating *Reichweite* or range. This was a long-range modification of the Ju 87 B with larger fuel cells in the wing and provision for underwing drop tanks beneath the wings. The Ju 87 R-1 had a range of 875 miles as compared with 342 miles of the Ju 87 B-1. Other variants were the Ju 87 R-2, R-3 and R-4 which differed only in minor equipment.

Several experimental variants of the Ju 87 B were produced including an aircraft fitted with a 1,475-h.p. Daimler-Benz DB 605 engine. Diving trials were carried out in 1942, but the DB 605 engine was in great demand at that time and the project was abandoned.

Fighter units did not have a monopoly of colourful markings in the Luftwaffe, *as evidenced by these two photographs. The shark's teeth appeared on an unidentified Ju 87 B-1 in 1939, the red and white snake on a B-2/Trop of II/St.G 2 in North Africa, 1941.* (Photos: R. Ward collection and *Der Adler*)

Ju 87 Bs of I/St.G 2 "Immelmann" *over France, 1940. At this time the Stuka was still thought to be an invincible weapon of* Blitzkrieg, *but the theory was soon to be shattered over the southern counties of England.* (Photo: R. Ward collection)

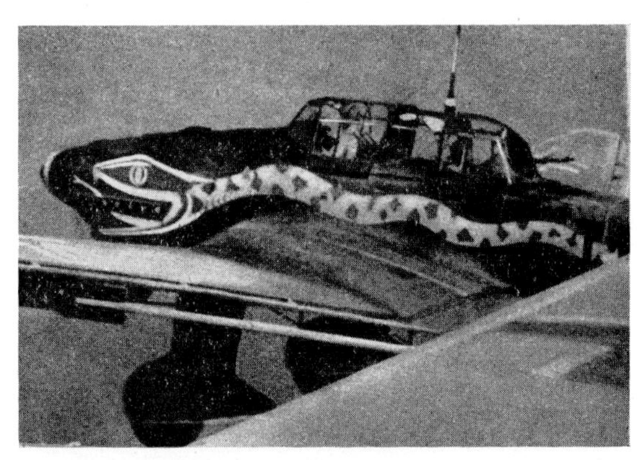

The Ju 87 R was basically a B-model with enlarged wing fuel cells and underwing tanks. They were employed extensively by the Stukaverbande, *as range was almost doubled.*

The most advanced project based on the Ju 87 was the Ju 187 which was proposed in 1940. It was to have employed more streamlined contours, a retractable undercarriage, a Jumo 213 engine and remotely controlled defensive armament. With the failure of its progenitor the Ju 187 was abandoned.

"STUKA" CONSTRUCTION

The fuselage of the Ju 87 was of oval section built in two halves with the smooth metal skin flush riveted to Z-section frames and open-section stringers. The crew of pilot and radio operator/air gunner were seated back-to-back under a continuous glazed canopy with a sliding section for access. The crew were protected by 5 mm. armour plate, the pilot having a 50 mm. armoured glass windscreen. The wing was a two-spar structure with closely spaced ribs with stressed skin covering, the centre section being built integrally with the fuselage. The trailing edge of the wing was hinged on the Junkers "double wing" principle, the outer sections forming the ailerons, the inner the landing flaps. Hydraulically operated dive brakes were mounted under the outer wing sections, close to the undercarriage legs, these turning through 90°. The bomb was mounted on an arm which swung forwards and downwards to clear the airscrew during the dive which the pilot angled by a system of lines painted on the cabin which he lined up with the horizon.

THE Ju 87 IN W.W.II

At a quarter to five on the morning of 1st September 1939 German forces with strong air support invaded Poland. The Luftwaffe's *Stukaverbande* had completely re-equipped with the Ju 87 B by this time, and nine Stuka *Gruppen* plus one *Staffel* were operational for the attack. These units were: I./St.G 1, I, II and III./St.G 2, III./St.G 51, I./St.G 76, I and II./St.G 77, IV.(*Stuka*)/LG 1 and 4.(*Stuka*)/186, the total having a strength of 366 aircraft. In addition to the Ju 87 B, each *Stabskette* (headquarters flight) was equipped with a small number (usually three) Dornier Do 17s to guide the Stukas on to the target, the twin-engined bombers remaining aloft whilst the Ju 87s peeled off for the attack. The majority of the *Stukagruppen* were employed to support the *Wehrmacht's* 3rd, 4th, 8th, 10th and 14th armies as they thrust into Poland. For the first time the notorious "Blitzkrieg" tactics were employed in which the dive bombers formed what was virtually long range artillery, knocking out strong points as they were encountered by the *Panzer* Divisions. The war against Poland culminated in the destruction of Warsaw in which the Ju 87 played no small part.

Without effective opposition the dive bomber shattered all opposition, much to the delight of its protagonists. During the winter of 1939–40 *Luftwaffe* activity was restricted to the minimum, but on 9th April 1940 German forces invaded Denmark and Norway the assault being known as Operation *Weserubung*. Only one dive bomber *Gruppe*, I./St.G 1 with Ju 87 Rs, took part in the operation. Denmark fell on the first day and many of the major towns in southern Norway were captured; 2./St.G 1 moving from Kiel to Stavanger on the 10th. I./St.G 1 carried out various attacks on Norwegian strong points, one such notable being the bombing of Vigra radio station on 15th April when a Ju 87 rammed one of the aerials putting the transmitter out of action.

Before the campaign in Norway was complete, Hitler launched his assault on the Low Countries and France, nine Stuka *Gruppen* with 320 Ju 87 B and 38 Ju 87 Rs taking part. The dive bombing forces were

Two contrasting colour schemes displayed by Stukas captured in North Africa. The spotted Ju 87 B-2/Trop operated with 3/St.G 1 and carries the codes A 5+H L and that unit's "crow" emblem. The unusual striped scheme is seen here on a machine of 5/St.G 2 "Immelmann". (Photos: Imperial War Museum)

A Hungarian Air Force training machine, summer 1942. (Photo: G. Cattaneo)

under the control of *VIII Fliegerkorps* commanded by *General Feldmarschall* Wolfram von Richtofen. Most Dutch and Belgian Air Force aircraft were destroyed on the ground following surprise attacks on their airfields, and the *l'Armee de l'Air* with obsolescent machines was largely ineffectual. With virtually no effective opposition the Ju 87 was again hailed as the wonder weapon, as it attacked troop concentrations and strongpoints and co-operated closely with the *Panzer* Divisions as they thrust deep into France. By the end of the first week of the assault Dutch forces had surrendered, but not before the *Luftwaffe* virtually destroyed the ancient port of Rotterdam. The German propaganda machine hailed this as another feat of the Stuka, but it was in fact carried out by Heinkel He 111P bombers from KG 54.

On 26th May 1940 the troops of the British Expeditionary Force began to evacuate from the encircled port of Dunkirk. The *Luftwaffe* was entrusted with the task of smashing the evacuation, but for the first time they met effective aerial opposition in the shape of Hurricanes and Spitfires of R.A.F. Fighter Command. The initiative lay with the *Luftwaffe*, making it difficult for the British fighter squadrons to maintain continuous cover over the bridgehead. Some Ju 87s appeared between R.A.F. patrols and bombed the beaches, although little damage was caused as the soft sand absorbed the bomb explosions. When R.A.F. fighters were in position the Ju 87s, although heavily escorted by Bf 109 Es, suffered severe losses and the Stuka's supremacy was challenged for the first time. By 4th June the evacuation had been successfully completed and on 6th July, the *Luftwaffe* re-grouped, many units being re-designated to bring *Geschwader*

Left: *The Stuka contributed considerably to the Allied defeats in the Balkan campaign. The mountainous countryside rendered such favourite targets as roads and bridges of vital importance.* Right: *The headquarters flight of III/St.G 2 in flight over Russia. The machine in the left foreground is flown by the* Gruppe *C.O., Hans Ulrich Rudel.* (Photos: R. Ward collection)

Left: *Stukas and bomb sledges on an airstrip in the Balkans, summer 1941.* Right: *Probably the best-known Stuka unit was III/St.G 2* "Immelmann", *commanded for many months by the legendary Hans Ulrich Rudel. Here a snow-camouflaged B-2 of that unit returns to base from a sortie over the Soviet lines in the winter of 1941.* (Photos: R. Ward collection)

Stuka pilot, 1940. Note sliding rear canopy section.

up to full strength of three *Gruppen.* Amongst the *Stukaverbande*, III./St.G 51 became II./St.G 1, I.(*Stuka*)/186 became III./St.G 1 and I./St.G 76 became III./St.G 77.

Early in July 1940 the *Luftwaffe* began making tentative attacks on British coastal shipping, a special force comprising fighters from JG 26 and JG 53, bombers from KG 2 and sixty dive bombers, assembling under the command of Obst. Johannes Fink. The Stuka operated with fighter cover, but as at Dunkirk they found they were not going to have things all their own way. These operations were a prelude to the major assault in which it was hoped to destroy the R.A.F. and prepare the way for "Operation Sealion"—the invasion of the British Isles. On 20th July, 316 Ju 87s were operational with *Luftflotten* 2 and 3, the majority operating under the control of *VIII Fliegerkorps.*

The first really major dive bombing operations against British shipping took place on 8th August, when three separate attacks were made on a convoy. Although escorted by Bf 109 E fighters, Ju 87 losses were severe, at least one formation being scattered before it could reach the target. Five days later a force of Stukas from *VIII Fliegerkorps* set out to bomb Middle Wallop airfield, but none reached the target owing to the massive destruction wreaked by No. 609 Squadron's Spitfires—the day being dubbed the "glorious 13th" in the squadron records. On 15th, forty Ju 87s with heavy fighter escort attacked Hawkinge and Lympne airfields, and although intercepted by No. 54 Squadron's Spitfires, they severely damaged the latter. The following day St.G 2 attacked Tangmere airfield suffering severe losses in the process. Two days later St.G 77 dive bombed the Poling radar station, losing twelve aircraft for their pains. This was the final blow for the dive bomber forces, and *VIII Fliegerkorps* was withdrawn to the Pas de Calais area on 29th August to take part in the proposed invasion, if and when it came. The three remaining *Stukagruppen*, II./St.G 1, II./St.G 2 and the recently formed I./St.G 3 made an abortive raid on 30th August 1940, but this was virtually the last time the aircraft was seen over the British Isles.

MIDDLE EAST AND RUSSIA

Early in January 1941, I./St.G 1 and II./St.G 2 and the *Stab* flight of St.G 3 were transferred to Trapani in Sicily with the aim of making a surprise attack on the Gibraltar–Malta–Alexandria convoys. On 10th January II./St.G 2 under Maj. Enneccerus attacked a British convoy escorted by a cruiser and the aircraft carrier H.M.S. *Illustrious. Illustrious* was hit by four 1,100-lb. bombs and was all but sunk, but managed to reach Valetta harbour in Malta. A few days later I./St.G 1 under Hptm. Werner Hozzel attacked the aircraft carrier in the harbour, 2./St.G 1 losing all its pilots except the *Staffelkapitän.* Four hits were made on the carrier, but again her armoured deck saved her from a watery grave.

On 6th April 1941, German forces invaded Yugoslavia and Greece, *Luftwaffe* forces operating under the control of *Luftflotte 4.* Two dive bomber *Gruppen* transferred from France (I and III./St.G 2) and one from North Africa took part in the attack. The campaign opened with large scale attacks on Belgrade, and Yugoslavia soon fell. The *Luftwaffe* then switched its attentions to the invasion of Greece, and Athens fell on 27th April.

The early completion of the Balkans campaign prompted Germany to attack Crete on 20th May 1941. The main assault was carried out by DFS 230 gliders towed by Ju 52/3m transports, but St.G 2's Ju 87 Bs participated in attacks on Royal Navy cruisers and destroyers. Flying with 1./St.G 2 was a young pilot who later was to become almost legendary within the *Luftwaffe.* His name was Hans Ulrich Rudel, who

Right: *Ground crew strain to turn the engine crank handle of a B-1 model.*

A gaudy B-2 on a Balkan airfield.

Above: *Two Ju 87 B-2s of II/St.G 1 over Russia, winter 1941. The machine in the background retains the code (6G) of III/St.G 51, redesignated as II/St.G 1 in July 1940.* (Photo: R. Ward collection)

Left: *A pre-war B-1 beginning to pull out of its dive as the bomb drops away.*

at the end of the war reached the rank of *Oberst* (Colonel) and became the only person to be awarded the Knight's Cross with Golden Oak Leaves. The campaign in Crete was successfully completed although both the *Luftwaffe* and the *Wehrmacht* suffered severe losses.

The 22nd June 1941 was the date set for "Operation Barbarossa", the attack over a 1,000-mile front on the Soviet Union. Three Army Groups were supported by four Air Fleets; *Luftflotte 5* in Northern Norway, *Luftflotte 1* in Northern Russia, *Luftflotte 2* in Central Russia and *Luftflotte 4* in Southern Russia and the Crimea. The dive bomber forces of *VIII Fliegerkorps* comprised eight *Stukagruppen*; *Stab*, II and III./St.G 1, *Stab* I and III./St.G 2, *Stab* I, II, and III./St.G 77 and IV.(*Stuka*)/LG 1 with a total of 334 Ju 87 Bs. The Soviet Air Force had suffered severe casualties, and the ugly Junkers dive bomber was again able to roam freely over enemy territory being rapidly transferred from one sector of the front to another. On 23rd September 1941, I and III./St.G 2 based at Tyrkowo attacked the Russian battleships *October Revolution* and *Marat* at Kronstadt. The *Marat* was sunk by a 2,200-lb. bomb dropped at a 90° angle by Rudel, but the other vessel escaped with light damage.

In December 1941, *Luftflotte 2* transferred to the Mediterranean with the object of finally "neutralising" the island fortress of Malta and driving British forces out of Africa. At its disposal were Ju 87 Bs from Stab, I, II and III./St.G 3 plus the *Ergänzungs* (training and replacement) *Gruppe* of St.G 1. The dive bomber forces operated mainly in North Africa, contributing to the capture of Bir Hakim in early June 1942. By this time however, the *Luftwaffe* in the Middle East was suffering from lack of fuel, sorties being substantially reduced by August 1942. St.G 3 had, like the other *Stukageschwader*, begun to re-equip with the much improved Ju 87 D which does not come within the scope of this work.

The final unit to equip with the Ju 87 B was I *Gruppe*/St.G 5 which was formed from IV.(*Stuka*)/LG 1 in February 1942. The unit was based in Northern Norway and Finland and commanded by Maj. Karl Stepp. The main function of the *Gruppe* was to attack the Murmansk railway which was the only link between that northern port and the south, and was used to bring urgently needed supplies from Britain and America to the Soviet Union.

FOREIGN SERVICE

Before the end of 1940 it was decided to supply the Ju 87 B to several of Germany's allies. Roumania and Hungary received the Ju 87 B-2, whilst the Italian Air Force was equipped with the Ju 87 B-1/Trop. It was widely thought that the Ju 87 B-1/Trop was in fact built under licence by the Breda concern under the designation Ba 201. The Ba 201 was an entirely different design, no Ju 87s being constructed in Italy, those serving with the *Regia Aeronautica* being German built.

The Ju 87 B was operated by the *Regia Aeronautica*'s 960 and 970 *Gruppi Bombardamento* and the 208ma, 238ma and 239ma *Squadriglia*. The 209ma Sq. used them in Sicily late in 1940. Hungarian aircraft were operated by that Air Force's 102/1 Dive Bomber Squadron which often co-operated closely with St.G 77 on the Eastern Front.

LUFTWAFFE UNITS AND MARKINGS

The basic *Luftwaffe* unit was the *Geschwader* or wing which had a nominal strength of 100–150 aircraft depending on availability and serviceability of air-

This Ju 87 B-1 was probably photographed over Poland in 1939. The starboard undercarriage leg has been shot off, and the port leg apparently jettisoned. Close examination of the original negative fails to reveal evidence of re-touching.

Left to right: *Gunner's position in Ju 87 A; MG 15 gun position of a Ju 87 B-1; Ju 87 B-1 instrument panel.*

craft. Each Stuka *Geschwader* or dive bomber wing was usually sub-divided into three *Gruppen* each normally comprising three *Staffeln*. The *Geschwader* and *Staffeln* were identified by an Arabic numeral, *Gruppen* being distinguished by a Roman figure. For example *Stukageschwader* 77 was made up of a *Geschwader Stab* (headquarters flight) and three *Gruppen*—I, II and III./St.G 77. Each *Gruppe* comprised in turn a *Gruppe Stab* and three *Staffeln*—II *Gruppe* having for example the 4th, 5th and 6th *Staffeln*.

All *Luftwaffe Geschwader* and *Gruppen*, with the exception of the single-engined fighter units, employed a four symbol code system painted on the fuselage sides and occasionally repeated underwing. The first two symbols positioned forward of the fuselage *Balkankreuz* (cross) always comprised a number/letter combination, and identified the *Geschwader*. The letter positioned directly to the right of the *Balkankreuz* (often painted in the *Staffel* colour) was the individual aircraft identification, and the last letter indicated the *Staffel*.

JUNKERS Ju 87 A-1 SPECIFICATION

Powerplant: One 635-h.p. Junkers Jumo 210 Da twelve cylinder inverted Vee liquid cooled in-line engine.
Dimensions: Span 45 ft. $3\frac{1}{4}$ in. *Length* 35 ft. $5\frac{1}{8}$ in. *Height* 12 ft. $9\frac{1}{2}$ in. *Wing area* 343·3 sq. ft.
Weights: Empty 5,104 lb. *Loaded* 7,495 lb.
Performance: Maximum speed 199 m.p.h. at 12,000 ft. *Maximum range* 620 miles.
Armament: One fixed 7·9 mm. MG 17 machine gun in starboard wing and one movable 7·9 mm. MG 15 on mounting in rear cockpit. *Maximum bomb load* (i.e. with one crew member) 1,100 lb.

JUNKERS Ju 87 B-1

Powerplant: One 900-h.p. Junkers Jumo 211 A-1 twelve cylinder inverted Vee liquid cooled in-line engine.
Dimensions: Span 45 ft. $3\frac{1}{4}$ in. *Length* 36 ft. 1 in. *Height* 13 ft. $10\frac{1}{2}$ in. *Wing area* 343·3 sq. ft.
Weights: Empty 6,051 lb. *Loaded* 9,336 lb.
Performance: Maximum speed 217 m.p.h. at 16,405 ft., 186 m.p.h. at sea level. *Landing speed* 68 m.p.h. *Climb* 12 minutes to 13,500 ft. *Service ceiling* 26,248 ft. *Range* 342 miles at 18,045 ft.
Armament: Two fixed 7·9 mm. MG 17 machine guns in wings firing forward, one movable 7·9 mm. MG 15 on mounting in rear cockpit. *Maximum bomb load* one 1,100-lb. and four 110-lb. bombs.

JUNKERS Ju 87 B-2

Powerplant: One 1,100-h.p. Junkers Jumo 211 Da twelve cylinder inverted Vee liquid cooled in-line engine.
Dimensions: As Ju 87 B-1.
Weights: Empty 6,085 lb. *Loaded* 9,370 lb.
Performance: Maximum speed 232 m.p.h. at 13,500 ft. *Cruising speed* 175 m.p.h. at 15,000 ft. *Range* 370 miles with a 1,100-lb. bomb load.
Armament: As Ju 87 B-1.

CODE LETTER ALLOCATIONS

Letter	Sub-unit	Colour
A	Geschwader Stab	Blue
B	I Gruppe Stab	Green
C	II Gruppe Stab	Green
D	III Gruppe Stab	Green
E	IV Gruppe Stab	Green
F	V Gruppe Stab	Green
H	1 Staffel I Gruppe	White
K	2 Staffel I Gruppe	Red
L	3 Staffel I Gruppe	Yellow
M	4 Staffel II Gruppe	White
N	5 Staffel II Gruppe	Red
P	6 Staffel II Gruppe	Yellow
R	7 Staffel III Gruppe	White
S	8 Staffel III Gruppe	Red
T	9 Staffel III Gruppe	Yellow
U	10 Staffel IV Gruppe	White
V	11 Staffel IV Gruppe	Red
W	12 Staffel IV Gruppe	Yellow
X	13 Staffel V Gruppe	White
Y	14 Staffel V Gruppe	Red
Z	15 Staffel V Gruppe	Yellow

LUFTWAFFE UNITS OPERATING THE Ju 87 B

Unit	Code	Commanders and Notes
St.G 1	A 5	Gen. Maj. Walter Hagen RK-EL (July 1940 to November 1942). I *Gruppe* established before the war; operations in Poland and France. II and III *Gruppen* formed on 6th July 1940 from III./St.G 51 and I.(*Stuka*)/186 respectively. Took part in the Battle of Britain, I./St.G 1 to N. Africa, later joining the other two *Gruppen* in Russia. Became SG 1 in October 1943.
St.G 2	T 6	Obst. Oskar Dinort RK-EL (1939 to April 1942). Obst. Paul-Werner Hozzel RK (April 1942 to November 1942). Named "*Immelmann*", I, II and III *Gruppen* being formed pre-war from

Machine of 3/St.G 2 with SC 500 and PC 500 bombs on the main crutch.

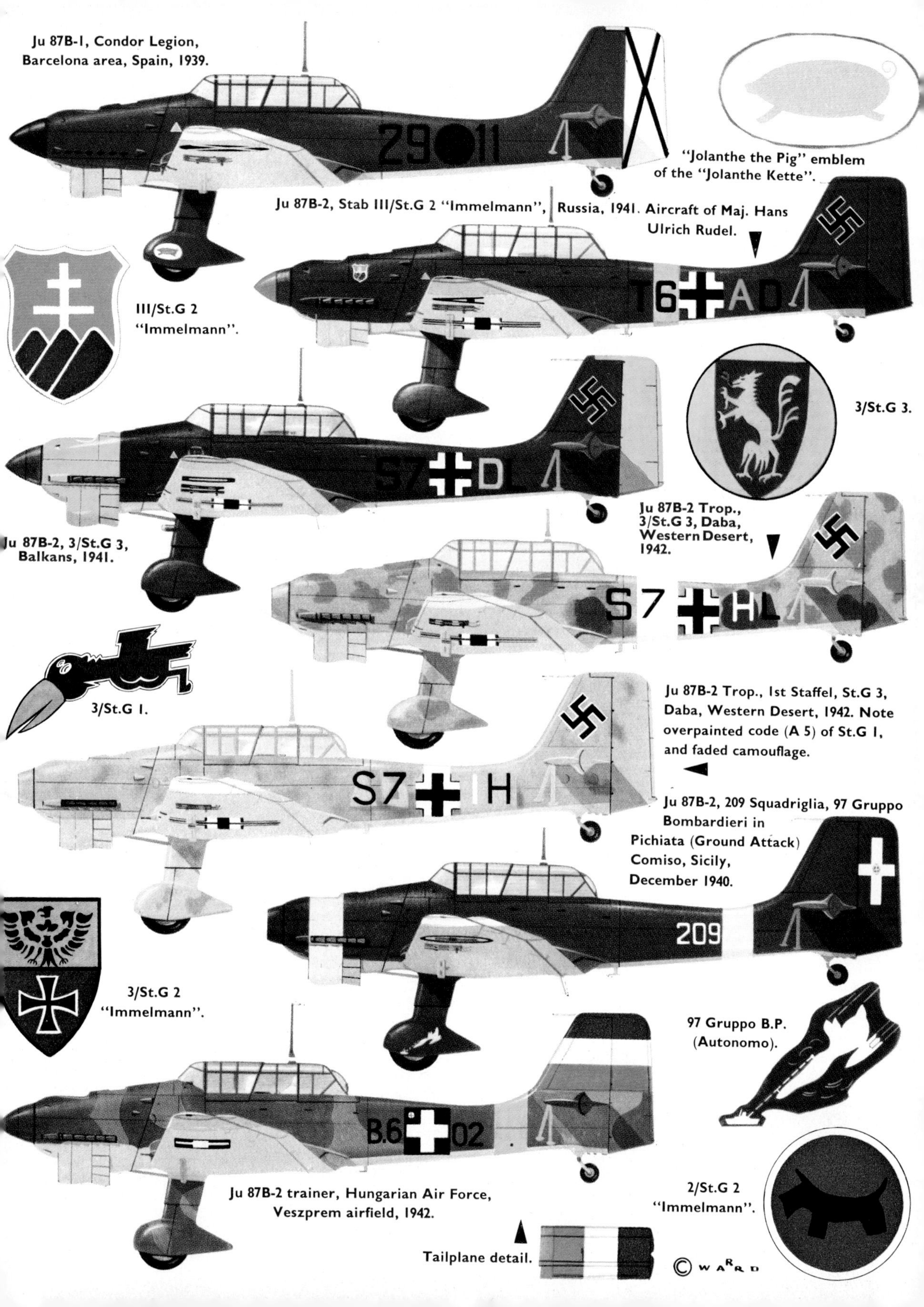

Ju 87B-1, Condor Legion, Barcelona area, Spain, 1939.

"Jolanthe the Pig" emblem of the "Jolanthe Kette".

Ju 87B-2, Stab III/St.G 2 "Immelmann", Russia, 1941. Aircraft of Maj. Hans Ulrich Rudel.

III/St.G 2 "Immelmann".

3/St.G 3.

Ju 87B-2, 3/St.G 3, Balkans, 1941.

Ju 87B-2 Trop., 3/St.G 3, Daba, Western Desert, 1942.

3/St.G 1.

Ju 87B-2 Trop., 1st Staffel, St.G 3, Daba, Western Desert, 1942. Note overpainted code (A 5) of St.G 1, and faded camouflage.

Ju 87B-2, 209 Squadriglia, 97 Gruppo Bombardieri in Pichiata (Ground Attack) Comiso, Sicily, December 1940.

3/St.G 2 "Immelmann".

97 Gruppo B.P. (Autonomo).

Ju 87B-2 trainer, Hungarian Air Force, Veszprem airfield, 1942.

2/St.G 2 "Immelmann".

Tailplane detail.

A B-2 over the Mediterranean.

		St.G 163. Operations in Poland, France, the Low Countries, the Battle of Britain. II./St.G 2 to N. Africa, I and III *Gruppen* taking part in the assault on the Balkans and Russia. By early 1942 all *Gruppen* were operating on the Eastern Front, the *Geschwader* being re-designated SG 2 in October 1943.
St.G 3	S 7	Obst. Walter Sigel RK-EL (1940 to 1942). I *Gruppe* formed during the summer of 1940, two further *Gruppen* being added later. Battle of Britain, later to N. Africa, replacing all other *Stukagruppen* by early 1942. Became SG 3 in October 1943.
St.G 5	J 9	Maj. Karl Heinz Stepp RK-EL (February 1942 to October 1943). I *Gruppe* only formed from IV.(*Stuka*)/LG I in February 1942. Operated in N. Russia and Finland, becoming I./SG 5 in October 1943.
St.G 51	6 G	Hptm. Anton Keil (1939 to July 1940). III *Gruppe* only formed before the war. Took part in the assaults on France and the Low Countries, becoming II./St.G I on 6th July 1940.
St.G 76	F I	Hptm. Karl Bode (1939 to 1940), Hptm. Friedrich Karl von Dalwigk zu Lichtenfels (1940 to July 1940). I *Gruppe* only formed pre-war from elements of KG 76. Took part in the invasion of Poland and France, becoming III./St.G 77 on 6th July 1940.
St.G 77	S 2	Obst. Günther Schwarzkopff RK (1939 to May 1940), Obstlt. Graf von Schönborn RK (May 1940 to summer 1942), Maj. Alfons Orthofer RK (summer 1942 to October 1942). I and II *Gruppen* formed pre-war, operating in Poland, the Low Countries and France. III./St.G 77 formed from I./St.G 76 on 6th July 1940, all *Gruppen* taking part in the Battle of Britain and the assault on Russia. Became SG 77 in October 1943.
LG I	L I	Hptm. von Brauchitsch (1939 to February 1942). IV.(*Stuka*)*Gruppe* only (the other four *Gruppen* being bomber or heavy fighter formations) formed pre-war. Operated in Poland, France, Battle of Britain and Russia, being re-designated I./St.G 5 in February 1942.
Träg.Gr 186		Hptm. Helmut Malcke (September 1939 to July 1940). I.(*Stuka*)*Gruppe* only (the other *Gruppe* being a fighter formation). Formed in December 1938 as 4.(*Stuka*)/186, being increased to *Gruppe* strength on 16th September 1939. Became III./St.G I on 6th July 1940.

Jumo 211 Da powerplant of a Ju 87 B-2 with cowling removed. Note also contoured armour back-shield in cockpit.
(Photo: R Ward collection.)

Note: *"RK" denotes holder of the Ritterkreuz or Knight's Cross. "EL" indicates that he was also awarded the Eichenlaub or Oak Leaves.*

Author and publishers wish to acknowledge their indebtedness to the officials of "Gruppe 66" for invaluable assistance during the preparation of this Profile.

Pilot's position in the Ju 87A.

© Profile Publications Ltd., P.O. Box 26, 1a North Street, Leatherhead, Surrey. Printed by Hills & Lacy Ltd., London and Watford.

PROFILE PUBLICATIONS

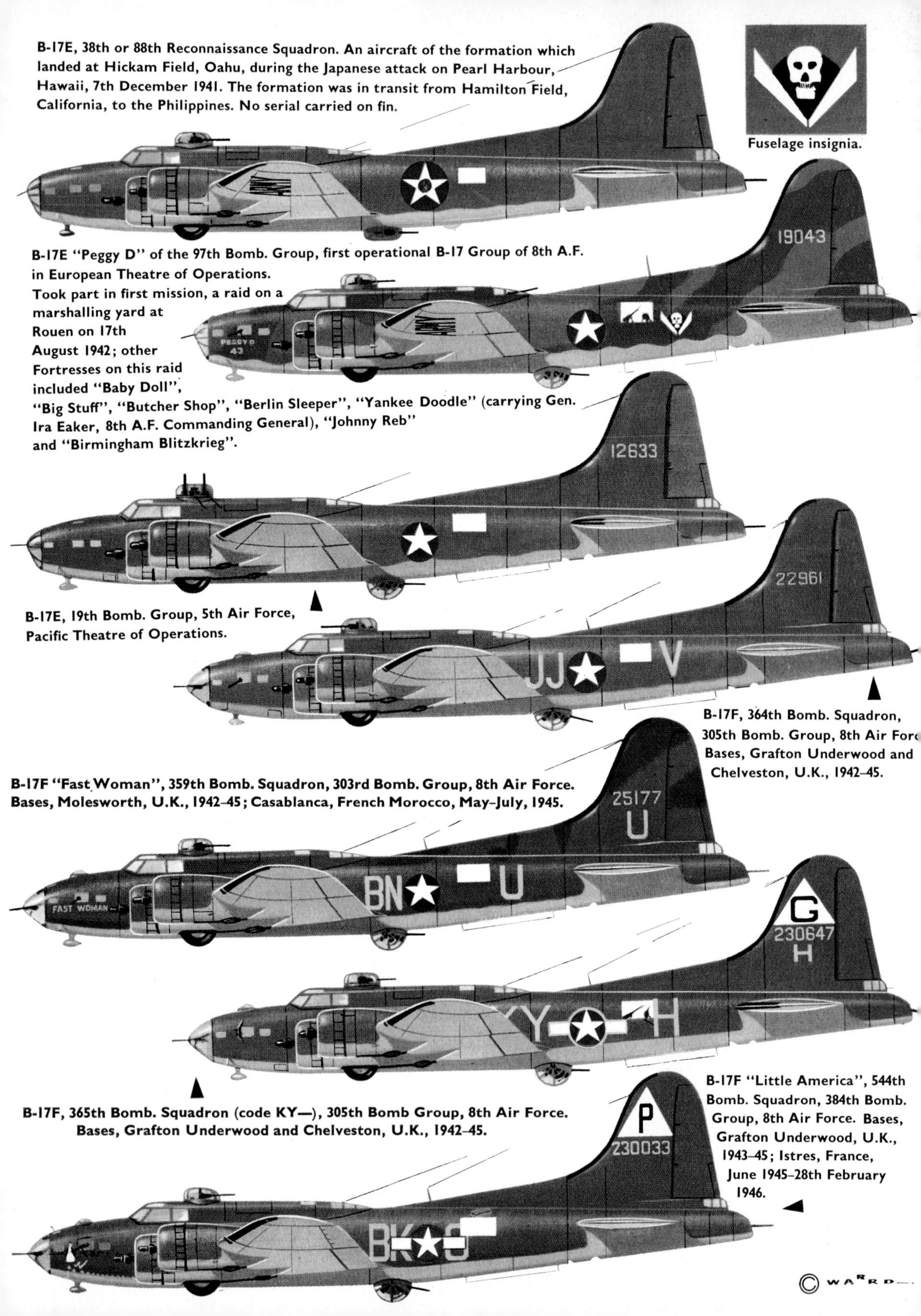

B-17E, 38th or 88th Reconnaissance Squadron. An aircraft of the formation which landed at Hickam Field, Oahu, during the Japanese attack on Pearl Harbour, Hawaii, 7th December 1941. The formation was in transit from Hamilton Field, California, to the Philippines. No serial carried on fin.

B-17E "Peggy D" of the 97th Bomb. Group, first operational B-17 Group of 8th A.F. in European Theatre of Operations. Took part in first mission, a raid on a marshalling yard at Rouen on 17th August 1942; other Fortresses on this raid included "Baby Doll", "Big Stuff", "Butcher Shop", "Berlin Sleeper", "Yankee Doodle" (carrying Gen. Ira Eaker, 8th A.F. Commanding General), "Johnny Reb" and "Birmingham Blitzkrieg".

B-17E, 19th Bomb. Group, 5th Air Force, Pacific Theatre of Operations.

B-17F, 364th Bomb. Squadron, 305th Bomb. Group, 8th Air Force. Bases, Grafton Underwood and Chelveston, U.K., 1942–45.

B-17F "Fast Woman", 359th Bomb. Squadron, 303rd Bomb. Group, 8th Air Force. Bases, Molesworth, U.K., 1942–45; Casablanca, French Morocco, May–July, 1945.

B-17F, 365th Bomb. Squadron (code KY—), 305th Bomb Group, 8th Air Force. Bases, Grafton Underwood and Chelveston, U.K., 1942–45.

B-17F "Little America", 544th Bomb. Squadron, 384th Bomb. Group, 8th Air Force. Bases, Grafton Underwood, U.K., 1943–45; Istres, France, June 1945–28th February 1946.

The Boeing B-17E & F Flying Fortress

by Charles D. Thompson

The Boeing B-17 aircraft series was a strange mixture of brilliant design work, dogmatic misuse, aerodynamic honesty, adaptability, myth, bravery, and luck, seasoned by wartime propaganda into a soufflé greatness. As is the case with all "pilot's aeroplanes", her docility endeared her to her crews and tended to overshadow her faults; but despite her many design and tactical faults, the B-17 emerged as truly a giant among aircraft, in every sense of the word.

Any aeroplane is only as good as the men who build her. The B-17 was fortunate indeed in her creators, the Boeing Company, who as one of America's pioneer aviation concerns had produced some thirty-nine different designs in the company's eighteen-year life prior to the B-17's debut in 1934. Many were notable trend-setters, and some were revolutionary. Among these earlier designs had been the PW-9 and FB-series fighters for the U.S. Army and Navy; the U.S. Post Office's Model 40; the elegant little F4B/P-12 fighter series; the revolutionary B-9 high speed bomber; the classic P-26; and the B-17's ancestor, the XB-15. With such a comprehensive list of forebears, the B-17 had to be good; Boeing's name had been a synonym for quality for nearly two decades.

Conceived as a defensive weapon comparable to a flying coastal artillery battery, the B-17 was to be called upon to test a rather dogmatic offensive theory of unescorted daylight precision bombing. Originally advanced by the Italian General Douhet, this theory rested essentially on the proposition that a fast, well-armed bomber flying at very high altitude could fight its way in broad daylight through and over any number of defending interceptors to destroy targets at will. (The name "Flying Fortress" did not arise from the aircraft's fabled invulnerability, but rather from the original defensive conception, so quickly forgotten when American tacticians subscribed to Douhet's theory.) The B-17 seemed tailor-made to be the instrument of this new concept of strategic bombardment; and she became the symbol, and at first the only concrete expression, of daylight precision bombing.

It was on 28th June 1935 that the prototype, *X13372*, was rolled out for the first time; on 28th July she made her first flight, and from that date until her untimely end two months later the prototype participated in many test flights. An attempted take-off with gust locks engaged ended the career of *X13372* at Wright Field and cost test pilots Hill and Tower their lives. There were only a few points of difference between *X13372* and the thirteen XB-17s constructed for service tests and assigned to the 2nd Bomb. Group for evaluation. Long-range navigation was a major aspect of this programme, and in this field the early Fortresses recorded several remarkable performances. They won the 1938 Mackay Trophy for a formation flight between Langley Field and South America. The one structural test airframe, designated B-17A, set a load/speed record for 1,000 km., and a load/altitude record.

A 1937 contract called for a batch of thirty-nine machines with more powerful engines providing even higher speed and altitude figures; and although the first B-17B was not delivered until July 1939, it immediately set a new transcontinental speed record. The B-17C requirement called for further engine refinements and cleaned-up gun emplacements. The -C variant was the fastest of all previous *or subsequent* B-17 models; and England's need for combat aircraft caused the diversion of large numbers of B-17Cs to the Royal Air Force, under the designation Fortress I, the first arriving in March 1941. R.A.F. Bomber Command and Coastal Command began operations with the type in June 1941, and for a short time the Fortress seemed to have her own way in the cold substratosphere over Europe; but it was soon made painfully apparent that the *Luftwaffe* had high altitude capability as well. Mechanical problems appeared daily, and after many attempts to improve the situation, the R.A.F. dropped the Fortress from first-line operations altogether. Reports of these problems filtered back to Boeing; vulnerability to gunfire, a tendency to burn easily, icing problems, oxygen

Heading photograph shows the "Memphis Belle", B-17F-10-BO serial number 41-24485, photographed before her return to the U.S.A. after completing twenty-five operational missions from England. Despite numerous hits from flak and fighter cannon-fire, only one crew member, the tail gunner, was wounded during the tour. The "Belle" was the subject of the sixth War Bond Drive, and her last mission was filmed in colour as a feature documentary. Note blotching effect of Medium Green on Olive Drab paint scheme. (Photo: U.S.A.F.)

B-17F-30-BO "Delta Rebel" of the 322nd B.S., 91st B.G. en route for the Reich. This was the Fortress in which the late actor Clark Gable flew a mission as observer. (Photo: U.S.A.F.)

system failures, crew fatigue from high altitude operations, and a subsequent general distrust of the type. Boeing's efforts to rectify these problems resulted in the B-17D, with self-sealing fuel tanks, additional armour, engine nacelle cowl flaps, and two extra ·30 calibre machine guns.

All remaining -C models were brought up to -D standard, but the first few days after the attack on Pearl Harbour saw many lost to enemy action and attrition. The surviving B-17Ds were evacuated to Australia and the Java area for regrouping; many were the subjects of a field modification which provided a ·50 calibre machine gun in the tail cone to supplement rear armament. However, further complaints from units in the Pacific theatre, when examined in conjunction with R.A.F. reports, made it painfully obvious that more than modifications were needed to make a realistic combat aircraft out of the B-17. Something drastic had to be done to both the aircraft and the mission concept; the first requirement was met quickly, the second, unfortunately, not for many months.

This photo of the B-17E "Avenger" shows to good effect the greenhouse nose peculiar to this variant. (Photo: U.S.A.F.)

B-17E "Goonie" of the 7th B.G., Pacific Theatre, 1942. The battle star on the nose is marked "Midway". (Photo: U.S.A.F.)

THE FORTRESS REDESIGNED

The first version of the ultimate series was the B-17E, which was more of a 30% re-design than a new variant. A new empennage and rear fuselage were the most obvious changes; also provided were two-gun power turrets in dorsal and ventral positions, a new twin-gun tail position, ·50 calibre guns in all positions except the nose, extensive armour plating, simplified waist emplacements, and numerous smaller internal improvements. Production was initiated without interruption, the first B-17E serving as the prototype and flying on 5th September 1941. (Although production lines were being set up at this time by Vega and Douglas, they were to produce no E-models.)

The B-17E was first delivered to combat units of the 7th Air Force in early February 1942, and the type made its first combat raid on 2nd April over the Andaman Islands. Shipping attacks were carried out by units of the 5th Air Force (from Australia) and the 7th Air Force (from India) in the Philippines some ten days later; and the B-17E was also active during the Battles of Midway and the Coral Sea.

The first 8th Air Force units arrived in Great Britain on 12th May 1942 to "set up house" and to prepare for the coming campaign of unescorted daylight precision bombing. Despite warnings from the combat-experienced R.A.F. authorities, the 8th Air Force Staff began training. The first raid was launched by eighteen B-17Es of the 97th Bomb. Group on 17th August, against Rouen. Twelve machines made the actual assault, the remaining six performing a diversionary sweep up the coast. Subsequent attacks on coastal targets were more in the nature of operational training flights than serious attempts to damage the enemy, and were not forcefully challenged by the *Luftwaffe*. The 8th A.F. Staff grew more secure in its convictions.

On 20th September 1942 the famous General Jimmy Doolittle formed the nucleus of the 12th Air Force in England, and early in October the 97th, 99th, 301st and 2nd Bomb. Groups were transferred to the new formation. The 8th A.F.'s "muscle" was needed for the North African campaign of November.

THE B-17F JOINS BATTLE

The last B-17E rolled off the line on 28th May 1942, and only two days later the first production model of a new version was rolled out, tested and delivered. Although it incorporated over 400 changes from its predecessor's specification, the -F variant could be distinguished externally from the -E only by its single-piece blown transparent nose. The changes, however, were extremely important. A new ball turret, external bomb racks, paddle-blade propellers, an improved oxygen system, carburettor intake dust filters, stronger landing gear, dual brake system, more photographic equipment, an electronic link between the autopilot and the Norden bombsight, additional ball-and-socket machine gun mounts in the nose; all these combined with Wright R1820–97 engines in place of R1820–60s, added fuel capacity and an improved gross weight and payload performance to make the -F model a considerably more sophisticated fighting aeroplane. No prototype of the -F was built, the first production model being processed in one day, as stated above. The Vega and Douglas lines were put into operation and in the next fifteen months 2,400 B-17Fs were produced.

The initial assault by American forces on the German homeland was a raid on the 27th January 1943 against the port of Wilhelmshaven, carried out by a force of B-17Fs drawn from the 91st, 303rd, 305th and 306th Bomb. Groups; simultaneously, two lonely B-17Fs made a nuisance raid on Emden. "Milk Runs" were the order for February, due to bad weather; but March came in like a lamb, and with it the legendary P-47 Thunderbolt. The "Jug" made its debut in a fighter sweep off Holland; at last, effective there-and-back escort for the bombers was possible.

The 18th March saw first use of Automatic Flight Control over Vegesak. The *Luftwaffe* put up a determined resistance to the raid, but at this stage a certain lack of co-ordination dulled the edge of their attacks; a state of affairs which was not to last, as the 8th A.F. would learn to their cost. Other notable raids in this period were upon the Renault works at Billancourt, the Focke-Wulf plant at Bremen, Kiel, Antwerp, Courtrai, Ijmuiden, Heroya, Trondheim, and Kassel.

These seven months of operations were but a prologue; for in August, in co-operation with R.A.F. Bomber Command, the 8th A.F. was to embark upon a task which almost ended unescorted daylight raids. On 17th August, in a simultaneous daylight attack upon the ball-bearing and aircraft industries at Schweinfurt and Regensburg, the 8th A.F. lost sixty aircraft to enemy action, with further heavy losses in immediate strength through combat damage and attrition. The Regensburg force proceeded to North African bases, and after licking its wounds returned to England via the Focke-Wulf works at Bordeaux. Losses from this raid brought the week's losses to over

Clark Gable poses with the crew of "Delta Rebel".
(Photo: W. J. Connell collection)

The pilot of "Delta Rebel No. 2" awards his aircraft the D.F.C.
(Photo: W. J. Connell collection)

100 B-17s; another week of comparable casualties, and the 8th Air Force would have ceased to exist. The *Luftwaffe* had found the formula.

Attacks in September were, of necessity, weak, and the 8th A.F. picked its targets carefully. Bad-weather "through-the-overcast" techniques were used under conditions so bad that interceptors could not operate. Night attacks were made on Billancourt, Chartres, and the Paris area. By October, sufficient replacements of crews and aircraft were available to mount once more an all-out offensive. "Big Week" saw attacks on Anklam, Marienburg and Gdynia in Poland; and the climax of the week was a continuation on 14th October of the 8th A.F.'s "private war" against Schweinfurt, in what was probably the most bloody and savage air battle in history. Sixty Fortresses fell to flak and to the guns of the recklessly brave *Luftwaffe*

A 5th B.G. B-17E on SeaSearch duties over the Pacific. (Photo: U.S.A.F.)

Messerschmitt's eye-view of a B-17F radio-operator's ·50 cal. gun in the O-type mounting. (Photo: W. J. Connell collection)

Navigator's eye-view of the single ·50 cal. gun in the nose of a B-17F. In this case the installation appears to be a factory-supplied kit rather than a field modification. Note shrouded Norden bombsight. (Photo: W. J. Connell collection)

fighter pilots. An untold number were damaged so badly as to be permanently removed from service. The 305th B.G. based at Chelveston lost thirteen out of the sixteen aircraft dispatched. Total losses for the week, combined with the time needed to repair the 200 damaged machines, morale factors and the demands of replacement training cost the 8th A.F. almost two full months before in-strength attacks were again possible. By this time the battered -F model was being phased out of first-line operations in favour of the B-17G, and relegated to various second-line duties such as training. As the -G began to take the strain, the P-51 Mustang became available in sufficient quantities to make its presence felt. A new era in the European air war was dawning.

COMBAT SUMMARY

In retrospect, it is greatly to the credit of the 8th Air Force crews that in spite of extreme losses the B-17Fs were never turned back from a raid. They made many determined attempts to vindicate the tacticians' theory of the unescorted day bomber's relative invulnerability; but even with the heaviest defensive battery ever provided for a bomber the B-17F was unable to gain the necessary air superiority over Germany. Failure may appear to be the lot of the B-17E and -F; but in all justice it must be stated that it was not the aircraft which failed the theory, but rather the theory which demanded more than any contemporary aircraft could have delivered. There were solid technical reasons for the B-17's vulnerability. Its tendency to take fire was never cured, and even its great inherent strength could not withstand the flames. The much-publicised defensive weakness in the nose when subjected to frontal attack by fighters was not so great a factor as some writers would have one believe. The ventral, or ball turret could be brought to bear on attacks from low front; the dorsal turret upon level or high frontal attacks; and the nose guns (up to five in number and of heavy calibre) while limited in individual arcs of fire, should have provided sufficient concentrated firepower. The startling truth is that it was not defensive power that was lacking, but protection; of the Fortress's twenty-seven pieces of heavy armour plate and numerous flak curtains, *not one* was positioned to protect the crew from frontal attack. When hit from the front by machine gun and light or heavy cannon fire, the crew of the B-17 was, effectively speaking, naked.

"*Delta Rebel*" *in flight over England. Note Medium Green blotching on control surfaces.* (Photo: W. J. Connell collection)

THE PACIFIC THEATRE

Only five Bombardment Groups employing the B-17 drew assignment in the Pacific Theatre. After using B-17s during the Philippine and Java operations, the 7th B.G. moved to India and retrained on B-24s. The 19th B.G. took a serious beating at Clark Field on the 8th December 1941, and after hastily regrouping found operations over the Philippines too costly to continue. The Group's ground personnel were transferred to the ground forces and most were killed or wounded, while the air echelon evacuated to Australia where they participated in the Netherlands Indies, Java and Coral Sea operations before returning to the Z.I. late in 1942. The 5th B.G. carried out Sea-Search duties from Hawaii, and were transferred thence to the S.W. Pacific in time to participate in the drive from the Solomons back to the Philippines, using both B-17s and B-24s.

The 11th and 43rd B.G.'s careers closely paralleled that of the 5th, but they retrained completely on B-24s early in 1943. This trend was due to the B-24's better speed and bomb-load at medium altitudes; also, the losses in Europe were reaching such magnitude that the production was needed for replacements and training in that theatre.

THE MEDITERRANEAN THEATRE

The brunt of the theatre's bombing operations was borne by the B-24 Liberator, although a few B-17 Groups were employed. The four B.G.s spirited away from the 8th A.F. participated in the Tunisian Bizerta and Kasserine Pass battles. The 68th Reconnaissance Group used B-17Fs equipped with electronic counter-measure apparatus alongside their tactical fighter complement. When the war moved northwards, the 12th A.F. B-17s took part in the 28th June raid on Messina, the 5th and 8th September Naples raids, the operations against the *Wehrmacht* counter-attack at Salerno between 13th and 18th September, and the 24th October raid on Wiener Neustadt. By the end of the year the 15th A.F. establishment consisted primarily of B-17G types.

THE FORTRESS DESCRIBED

There are many ways to judge a bomber aircraft: speed, bomb load/range factors, defensive ability, ability to absorb combat damage, aerodynamic honesty, versatility, handling ease, speed and ease of maintenance and battle damage repair; and in all these respects the B-17E and -F ranked high. Pilots liked the Fortress; they trusted her, for she was completely predictable. Landing speed at normal landing weight was low, an amazing 73 m.p.h.; and two-engine landings were possible without too much drama. Formation flying is never easy, but the Fort took to it much more willingly than the B-24 or even the B-29 Superfortress. Anybody who has had the privilege of seeing a B-17 do a "buzz job" will testify to the apparent lightness of handling. A brief tour of the internal layout of the B-17 reveals the rather Spartan conditions under which Fortress crews existed. The bombardier's "greenhouse" offered magnificent visibility and was reasonably warm; a crawl back past the navigator's position and upwards leads to the flight deck, with side-by-side seats for pilot and co-pilot. Directly behind them and above is the top turret, usually manned by the flight engineer; the miniscule "bicycle seat" must have been uncomfortable in the extreme to a big man in flying gear, but the turret does provide excellent all-round vision. Moving aft from the turret one has to negotiate a door apparently designed with Greek gods in mind—a V-shaped aperture, none too large in the first place. This affords albeit awkward access to the bomb-bay, which is traversed by a narrow catwalk with precarious rope grab-handles. The aft exit door is conventional in shape, but small; it leads to the radio room, the only place in a Fort where a six-footer can stand erect,

(continued on page 10)

Battle damage 1: this Fortress returned to base safely after a burning wing tank had destroyed 30% of the wing root. (Photo: W. J. Connell collection)

Battle damage 2: this B-17F-65-BO of the 91st B.G. came home with her fin wrecked by Luftwaffe *aerial bombing. The practice of dropping bombs to break up Fortress formations is believed to have been pioneered in August 1943 by the* Staffelkapitän *of the crack* 5th Staffel, Jagdgeschwader 1, *Oblt. Heinz Knocke.* (Photo: W. J. Connell collection)

Battle damage 3: a bomb from a Fortress in a higher-flying Group knocked the starboard stabiliser and elevator off this B-17 over the target. She was repaired and put back into service. Note tail gunner's hatch. (Photo: W. J. Connell collection)

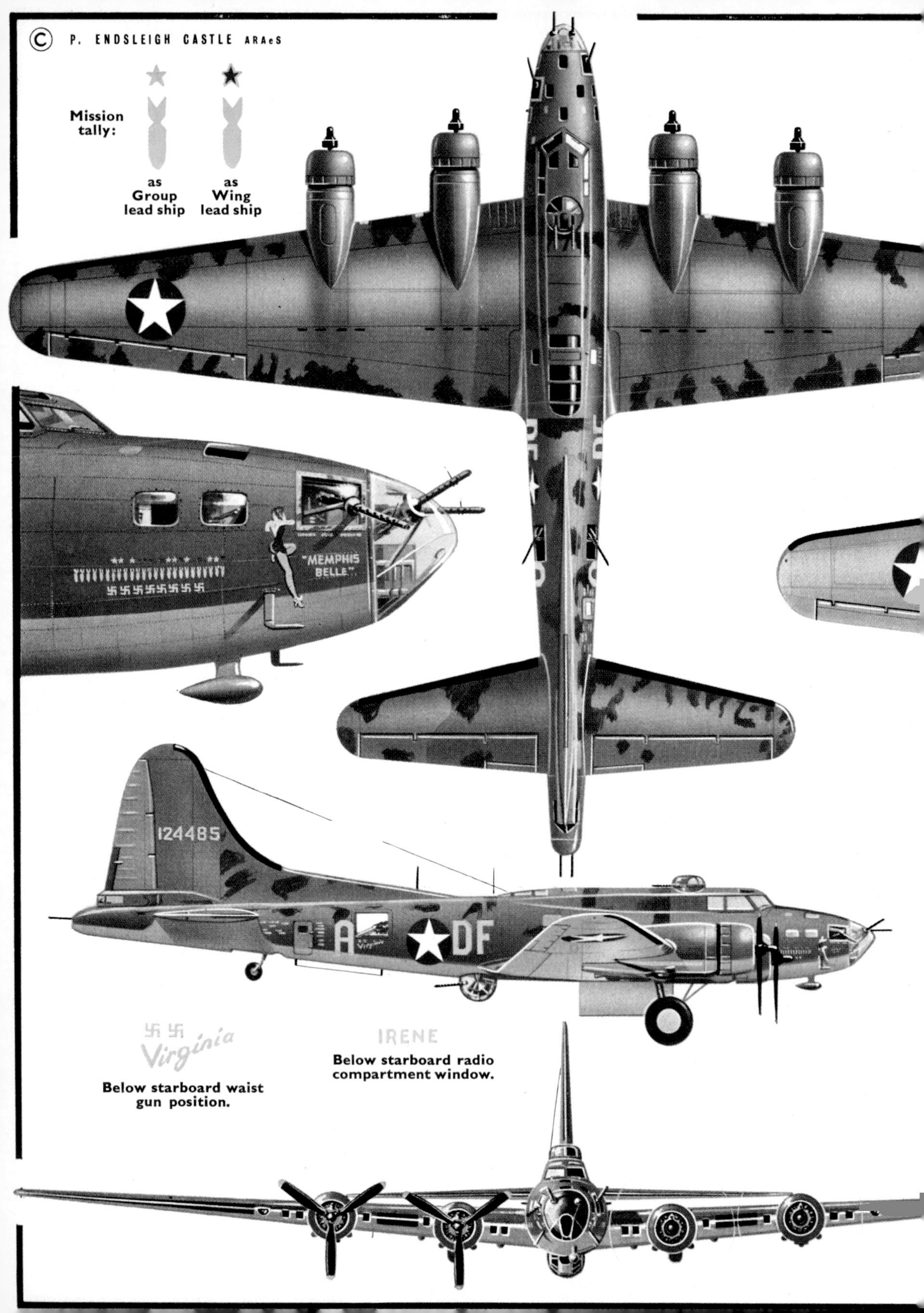
© P. ENDSLEIGH CASTLE ARAeS
Mission tally:
as Group lead ship
as Wing lead ship
"MEMPHIS BELLE"
124485
A
DF
Virginia
IRENE
Below starboard radio compartment window.
Below starboard waist gun position.

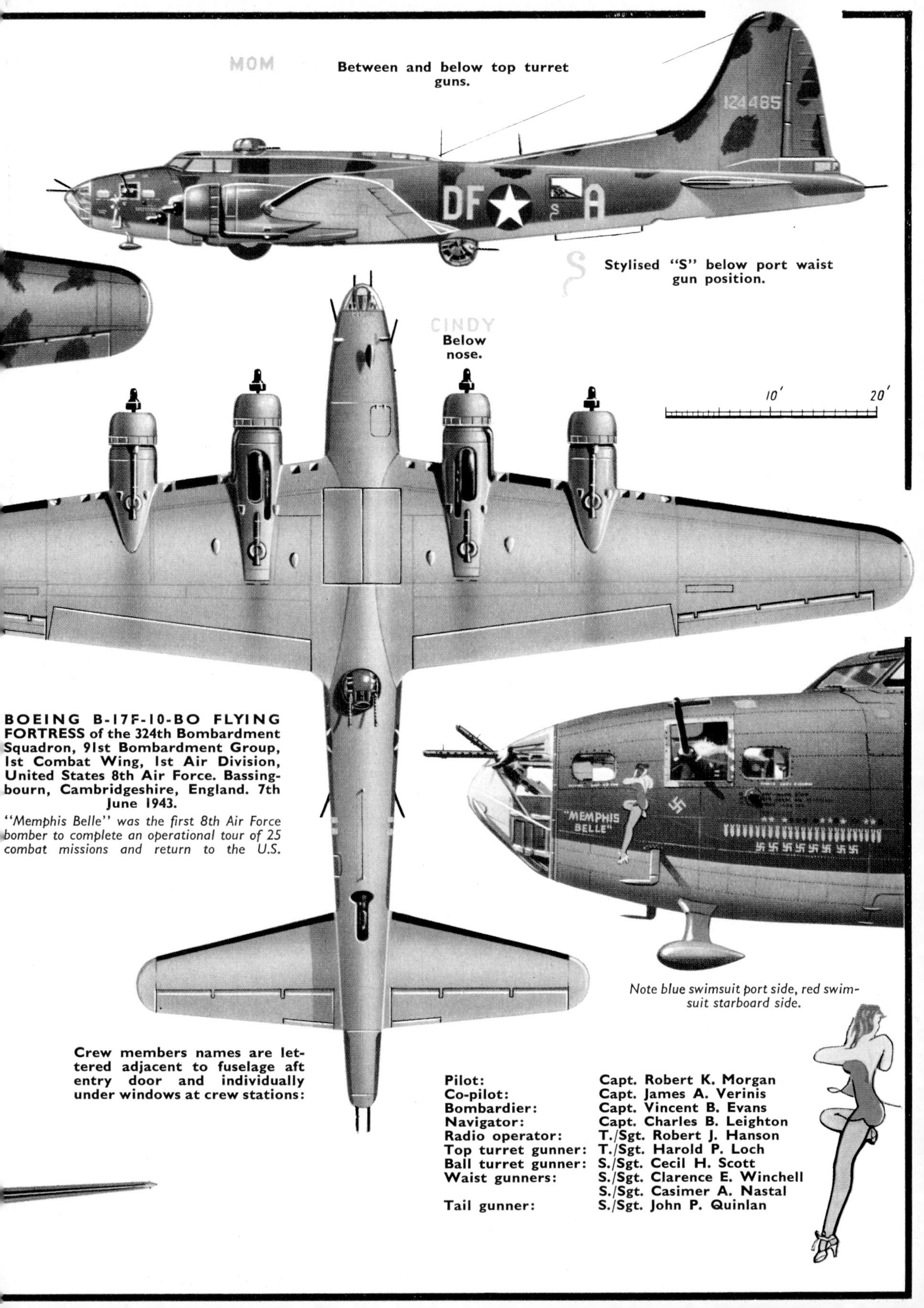

BOEING B-17F-10-BO FLYING FORTRESS of the 324th Bombardment Squadron, 91st Bombardment Group, 1st Combat Wing, 1st Air Division, United States 8th Air Force. Bassingbourn, Cambridgeshire, England. 7th June 1943.

"Memphis Belle" was the first 8th Air Force bomber to complete an operational tour of 25 combat missions and return to the U.S.

Crew members names are lettered adjacent to fuselage aft entry door and individually under windows at crew stations:

Pilot:	**Capt. Robert K. Morgan**
Co-pilot:	**Capt. James A. Verinis**
Bombardier:	**Capt. Vincent B. Evans**
Navigator:	**Capt. Charles B. Leighton**
Radio operator:	**T./Sgt. Robert J. Hanson**
Top turret gunner:	**T./Sgt. Harold P. Loch**
Ball turret gunner:	**S./Sgt. Cecil H. Scott**
Waist gunners:	**S./Sgt. Clarence E. Winchell**
	S./Sgt. Casimer A. Nastal
Tail gunner:	**S./Sgt. John P. Quinlan**

B-17F-80-BOs serials 42-30018, /15 and /25 in formation with B-17F-85-BO serial 42-30032 of the 532nd B.S., 381st BG., 8th Air Force. (Photo: U.S.A.F.)

brightly lit through the big skylight/gun hatch. Through the rear door lies the tail section, with the big ball turret hanging in its gimbals; a narrow catwalk leads down the centre of the fuselage to the waist-gun windows, with two smaller walk-ways higher on the cabin sides for the waist gunners. With the top hatch open, the radio room was breezy; but the temperature in the tail section, with its yawning side-ports, made the provision of points for electrically heated flying suits an absolute necessity. High-altitude operations in winter were a waist-gunner's nightmare, with hurricane winds clawing through the gun-ports. Leaving the waist, one moves aft down a rapidly-tapering fuselage, and a kneeling posture is necessary to negotiate the tail wheel well cover safely. A further short crawl ends in the tail gunner's position; a tiny plexiglass cage, where perhaps the most vital gunner in a Fort's crew fought a cramped war from a bicycle seat and padded knee supports. All the draught from the waist positions seems to sweep through into the tail position, and the endurance of the kneeling warriors on long, cold trips over Germany is worth a moment's admiring memory. The mildest comment one can make on crew comfort is that the farther one moves from "officers' country", the colder it gets!

There are three ways to enter a B-17; the nose hatch, located lower left; the main door just forward of the right horizontal stabiliser; and the tail gunner's escape hatch under the right elevator. In Hollywood epics the hero always enters by the nose hatch, jumping from the ground and performing an indescribable wriggle to enter feet first. If the reader had ever tried this manœuvre in forty pounds of leather and fleece flying clothing, he would follow the example of most Fort crews and enter by the main door. It is said that by the twenty-fifth mission of a

Left: *"Sugar", a late model B-17F, displays the cheek positions usually associated with the B-17G.* Right: *"The Eagle's Wrath", a B-17F-20-BO, serial 41-24524, of the 91st B.G., with twin nose guns. The armour plate covering the bombardier's optical-flat panel is a pointed reminder of the B-17's vulnerability to head-on attack, one of the main reasons for the failure of the Unescorted Daylight Precision Bombing theory.* (Photos: W. J. Connell collection)

Left: *"I Got Spurs", a B-17F-10-BO of the 3rd Reconn. Group, 12th Air Force, based in North Africa; Group Commander was Col. Elliot Roosevelt. Note "dimple" nose transparency and Tri-Metrogon window under nose.* (Photo: U.S.A.F.). Right: *The famous "Piccadilly Commando"; note lack of guns in nose transparency.* (Photo: W. J. Connell collection)

tour, the tail gunner was so shrunken and withered by the constant cold blast that he could enter his hatch with ease; but it was as well to ensure that no one was checking out elevator movement at the crucial moment.

The last "people-hatch" is the armoured, hinged plate that forms the seat back of the ball turret, and serves as an emergency exit for this foetal gladiator. It could be used as an entrance door only if the gunner wished to stay in the turret during take-off, and with a ground-clearance of only fifteen inches, that took a brave man. The door was only inside the ship when the guns pointed vertically down, a position not possible on the ground.

The B-17, for all its size, was neither luxurious nor roomy. One could stand in the centre and touch both sides in any part of the aircraft. Unlike its successor the B-29, the Fortress sacrificed comfort for efficiency; but it could at least be claimed that no one ever suffered from lack of ventilation in the rear sections.

A B-17F-70-BO of the 422nd B.S., 305th B.G., coded XK-O. Note twin nose guns and Group tail marking. (Photo: U.S.A.F.)

STRUCTURE OF THE B-17

Fuselage A conventional semi-monocoque all-metal structure of basically circular configuration consisting of four main assemblies bolted together. Major assemblies made up of nine sub-assemblies riveted together into stressed elements. A series of vertical frames and bulkheads with longitudinal stringers and stressed skin provided an exceptionally strong structural unit.

Wings Eighteen sub-assemblies made up an extremely efficient lifting surface with a low weight/strength ratio. Truss-type main spars were capped with sheet metal and gusseted girders. Sections between spars covered with corrugated aluminium sheet and stressed skin riveted to corrugated areas and to the truss-type ribs. The entire structure gave a wing with an exceptional ability to absorb damage without loss of structural integrity. Ailerons were of all-metal structure with fabric covering; the split flaps were of all-metal construction.

Empennage All-metal pressed flanged ribs and stringers covered with riveted aluminium sheeting. Control surfaces all-metal with fabric covering.

Landing Gear Single-strut oleo assembly formed rear portion of drag strut, and wheel combination electrically retracted to bring assembly forward and upward into inboard nacelles. Tyres remained partially exposed to slipstream. Tail wheel oleo shock equipped, fully retractable electrically.

VARIATIONS ON A THEME

XB-38—B-17E (41-2401) with Allison V-1710-89 liquid-cooled engines; not produced.

YB-40—B-17F-B0 conversion intended as heavily-armed escort; two additional power turrets in chin and dorsal positions, twin waist gun mounts, additional ammunition rather than bomb load. Saw limited operational service, but as YB-40 was slower than the standard B-17F this necessitated formation slowdown, and plan was dropped.

BQ-7—Converted war-weary B-17Es and B-17Fs stripped of armament and all unnecessary equipment. Packed with explosives, these machines were radio controlled on to targets. Several attacks carried out, but control problems caused alarm and the project, designated Castor, was discontinued.

C-108—B-17E-B0s (41-2593 and 41-2595), B-17F-VE (42-6036) and B-17F-B0 (42-30190) were converted for evaluation in VIP, Cargo and Tanker rôles. Gen. Douglas MacArthur used a V.I.P. conversion retaining nose and tail guns.

F-9—B-17F aircraft converted and manufactured to fulfil duties of long-range reconnaissance. Six-inch Tri-Metrogon, 12 in. vertical, 24 in. split vertical, and 6 in. oblique camera positions were possible in three versions, the F-9, F-9A and F-9C.

CAMOUFLAGE AND MARKINGS

With B-17E and -F production covering only a year, and operational use being limited to U.S.A.A.C. and R.A.F. units, only two basic schemes apply for the

B-17F-10-BO "Adorable" of the 369th B.S., 306th B.G., after a wheels-up landing. Note yellow surround on cocarde. Swastika flashes show that the ball turret gunner has three confirmed kills, the top turret and starboard waist gunners one each.
(Photo: W. J. Connell collection)

This unusual sequence graphically demonstrates the "repairability" of the Fortress. Top left *shows "Eight Ball", a B-17F-25-DL (DO) of the 91st B.G., serial 42-3138, with nose damage from a runaway propeller. The area to be replaced is marked off with masking tape.* Top right *shows the section removed, with the replacement nose from "Sweet Pea 1st" ready.* Bottom left *shows the section in place.* Bottom right *shows job almost complete.* (Photos: W. J. Connell collection)

former and one for the latter. Basic scheme as delivered consisted of Olive Drab (Shade 41) on all upper surfaces and Neutral Grey (Shade 43) on all under surfaces with the two shades meeting in a four-inch overspray blending. June 1943 saw the addition of Medium Green (Shade 42) specified for use on leading and trailing edges of all flying surfaces in blotches not exceeding 20% of the surface, but not on fuselage surface. However, several E.T.O. Groups applied Medium Green on the fuselage in the form of irregular stripes ending either at the under surface blend or at the wing root.

Markings consisted of cocardes on the fuselage sides midway between the wing trailing edge and the horizontal stabiliser leading edge. Wing cocardes were placed above the port wing and below the starboard wing. Some groups used a yellow surround on the fuselage cocardes. Production covered the specified use of three cocarde styles: blue field with white star; blue field with white star and horizontal bars bordered in red; and blue field with white star and horizontal bars bordered in blue.

Radio call numbers were marked in yellow characters measuring 8 × 12 in. or larger. Many E.T.O.-based Groups used formation code letters in the British style consisting of two letters or one letter and one number serving as a unit designation, with a single letter identifying the individual aircraft. Formation codes were applied in yellow or white paint, three to five feet high. Individual aircraft in combat areas were often emblazoned with names and artwork covering (or uncovering) a broad range of styles, some so bawdy that on one occasion orders were given to "cover up". Petty and Vargas styles were most popular, followed by anti-Nazi and patriotic themes and cartoon characters. Some of the better-known examples are *Southern Comfort*, *Bat Outa Hell*, *Quitchurbitchin'*, *Lady Halitosis*, *Impatient Virgin*, *Wabbit Twacks*, *King Malfunction*, *Berlin Sleeper*, and *Chugalug Lulu*.

R.A.F. Fortresses were used primarily by Coastal Command and were camouflaged in the Temperate Sea scheme of dark slate grey/extra dark sea grey on all plan view surfaces with white under surfaces and fuselage sides. National markings followed standard British practice of the period.

R.A.F. UNITS EQUIPPED WITH B-17E & -F (FORTRESS II & IIA)

Unit	Squadron Code
Coastal Command	
59 Sqdn.	TR
86 Sqdn.	XQ
206 Sqdn.	VX & 2V
220 Sqdn.	ZZ
251 Sqdn. (Met.)	AD
517 Sqdn. (Met.)	X9
519 Sqdn. (Met.)	Z9
521 Sqdn. (Met.)	50
Bomber Command	
214 Sqdn.	BU
223 Sqdn.	6G

With the exception of 223 Sqdn., which saw service in the

B-17E of 97th B.G. displays striped camouflage after that unit's transfer to the 12th A.F. in N. Africa in support of Operation Torch. (Photo: Imperial War Museum)

Mediterranean Theatre, all above units operated from the British Isles.

B-17E & -F SERIALS

B-17 E-BO

Military Serials	Manufacturer's Serials
41-2393–41-2669	2204–2480
41-9011–41-9245	2493–2717

B-17-F: Boeing Production

Military Serial	Type and Block	Boeing Serial
41-24340–24389	B-17F-1-BO	3025–3074
41-24390–24439	B-17F-5-BO	3075–3124
41-24440–24489	B-17F-10-BO	3125–3174
41-24490–24503	B-17F-15-BO	3175–3188
41-24504–24539	B-17F-20-BO	3189–3224
41-24540–24584	B-17F-25-BO	3225–3269
41-24585–24639	B-17F-27-BO	3270–3324
42-5050–5078	B-17F-30-BO	3589–3617
42-5079–4159	B-17F-35-BO	3618–3688

Nose emblems varied from the extremely simple ("Cased Ace"), through the vulgar ("Down and Go!"), the beautiful ("Elusive Elcy"), and the original ("Dame Satan") to the frankly weird ("The Witche's Tit"). The last-mentioned was a B-17F-50-BO, serial 42-5382 of the 91st B.G. (Photos: W. J. Connell collection)

B-17E (Fortress II) of No. 1435 Fligh , Coastal Command, R.A.F. The R.A.F's major use of the type was on maritime patrol missions. (Photos: Imperial War Museum)

42-5150–5249	B-17F-40-BO	3689–3788
42-5250–5349	B-17F-45-BO	3789–3888
42-5350–5484	B-17F-50-BO	3890–4023
42-29467–29531	B-17F-55-BO	4581–4645
42-29532–28631	B-17F-60-BO	4646–4745
42-29632–29731	B-17F-65-BO	4746–4845
42-29732–29831	B-17F-70-BO	4846–4945
42-29832–29931	B-17F-75-BO	4946–5045
42-29932–30031	B-!7F-80-BO	5046–5145
42-30032–30131	B-17F-85-BO	5146–5245
42-30132–30231	B-17F-90-BO	5246–5345
42-30232–30331	B-17F-95-BO	5346–5445
42-30332–30431	B-17F-100-BO	5446–5545
42-30432–30531	B-17F-105-BO	5546–5645
42-30532–30616	B-17F-110-BO	5646–5730
42-30617–30731	B-17F-115-BO	5731–5845
42-30732–30831	B-17F-120-BO	5846–5945
42-30832–30931	B-17F-125-BO	5946–6045
42-30932–31031	B-17F-130-BO	6046–6145

Douglas Production

42-2964–2966	B-17F-1-DL	42-3284–3338	B-17F-45-DL
42-2967–2878	B-17F-5-DL	42-3339–3393	B-17F-50-DL
42-2979–3003	B-17F-10-DL	42-3394–3422	B-17F-55-DL
42-3004–3038	B-17F-15-DL	42-3423–3448	B-17F-60-DL
42-3039–3073	B-17F-20-DL	42-3449–3482	B-17F-65-DL
42-3074–3148	B-17F-25-DL	42-3493–3503	B-17F-70-DL
42-3149–3188	B-17F-30-DL	42-3504–3562	B-17F-75-DL
42-3189–3228	B-17F-35-DL	42-37714–37715	B-17F-80-DL
42-3229–3283	B-17F-40-DL	42-37717–37720	B-17F-85-DL

Vega Production

42-5705–5709	B-17F-1-VE	42-5855–5904	B-17F-30-VE
42-5710–5724	B-17F-5-VE	42-5905–5954	B-17F-35-VE
42-5725–5744	B-17F-10-VE	42-5955–6029	B-17F-40-VE
42-5745–5764	B-17F-15-VE	42-6030–6104	B-17F-45-VE
42-5765–5804	B-17F-20-VE	42-6105–6204	B-17F-50-VE
42-5805–5854	B-17F-25-VE		

A B-17F-25-VE, serial 42-5809, coded LF-D, Squadron and Group unknown. The tail wheel of this Fortress apparently collapsed on landing; note severe damage from cannon and machine gun fire. Bull emblem on tail is captioned Wunhunglo; Ruth *appears by tail gun position,* Ola *under top turret on port side, and* Strato Sam *figure on both sides of fuselage.* Strato Sam's *"balloon" reads: "The boys on this ship sure have a lot to learn about shooting dice!"* (Photo: W. J. Connell collection)

TABLE OF SPECIFICATIONS

B-17F Aeroplane (B-17E specifications shown in parentheses when differing from -F).

Official Description: "Ten-Place Landplane Monoplane, Long Range High Altitude Low Wing Bomber".

Manufacturer's Model Designation: 299-0.

Military Designation: B-17F (B-17E).

Popular Name: Boeing Flying Fortress.

Total Produced: 2,300 (512).

Period of Production: 30th May 1942–2nd September 1943. (5th September 1941–28th May 1942).

First Flight: 30th May 1942 (5th September 1941).

DIMENSIONS AND SPECIFICATIONS

Wing: Span 103 ft. 9·38 in. Area 1,420 gross, 1,277·5 net. Root chord 228 in. Tip chord 106·7 in. Incidence 3½ degrees. Dihedral 4½ degrees. Sweepback 8 degrees 9 minutes. Airfoil NACA 0018 root, NACA 0010 tip. Wing loading 28·3 lb. per sq. ft.

Fuselage: Length 74 ft. 8·9 in. (73 ft. 1·52 in.). Height 19 ft. 2·44 in.

Landing Gear: Tread 21 ft. 1·52 in. Wheel 55 in. diameter. Tail wheel 26 in. solid core.

Powerplant: Type: 4 Wright R1820–97 (R1920–65). Power rating: 1,200 b.h.p. at take-off, 1,000 b.h.p. maximum at 25,000 ft., 2,300 r.p.m.

Propeller: 4 Hamilton Standard Hydramatic, 3 blade of 11 ft. 7 in. diameter.

Fuel Capacity: Normal 2,520 U.S. gallons (2,490 gallons), maximum 3,612 U.S. gallons with Tokyo tanks.

Oil Storage: 147·6 U.S. gallons (180 gallons).

Performance: Speed: Top 325 m.p.h. at 25,000 ft. (318 m.p.h.). Cruise 160 m.p.h. at 5,000 ft. Landing 73 m.p.h. (70 m.p.h.). Range: Maximum 4,420 miles on 3,612 gallons at 5,000 ft. (maximum 3,300 miles on 2,492 gallons at 5,000 ft.).

Weight: Design empty 35,728 lb. (33,279 lb.). Design gross 40,260 lb. (40,260 lb.). Maximum gross 48,720 lb. (48,726 lb.).

Bomb Load: Design bomb load maximums: 26 M30 100-lb. GP (20), or 16 M31 300-lb. GP (14), or 12 M43 500-lb. GP (8), or 8 M44 1,000-lb. GP (4), or 4 M34 2,000-lb. GP (2).

Specified Defensive Armament

Nose Position: 6 Type K-1 ball-and-socket ·30 calibre mounts located in windows and nose. 1 M-2 ·30 calibre Browning machine gun with 5,100 rd. ammo. boxes.

Dorsal Position: 1 Sperry No. 645473E power turret with 2 ·50 calibre M-2 Browning machine guns. 500 rds. per gun. 1 type K-2 ball-and-socket ·50 calibre mount in radio compartment with M-2 ·50 calibre Browning machine gun. 5,100 rd. ammo. boxes.

Ventral Position: 1 Sperry No. 645849-J power turret with 2 ·50 calibre M-2 Browning machine guns. 500 rds. per gun.

Waist Position: 1 ·50 calibre M-2 Browning machine gun in each of the 2 waist windows. 400 rds. per gun.

Tail Position: 2 ·50 calibre M-2 Browning machine guns. 500 rds. per gun. Equipped with remote sight.

B-17F with external bomb racks in place on a test flight over Mt. Rainier, near Seattle, Washington. (Photo: Boeing)

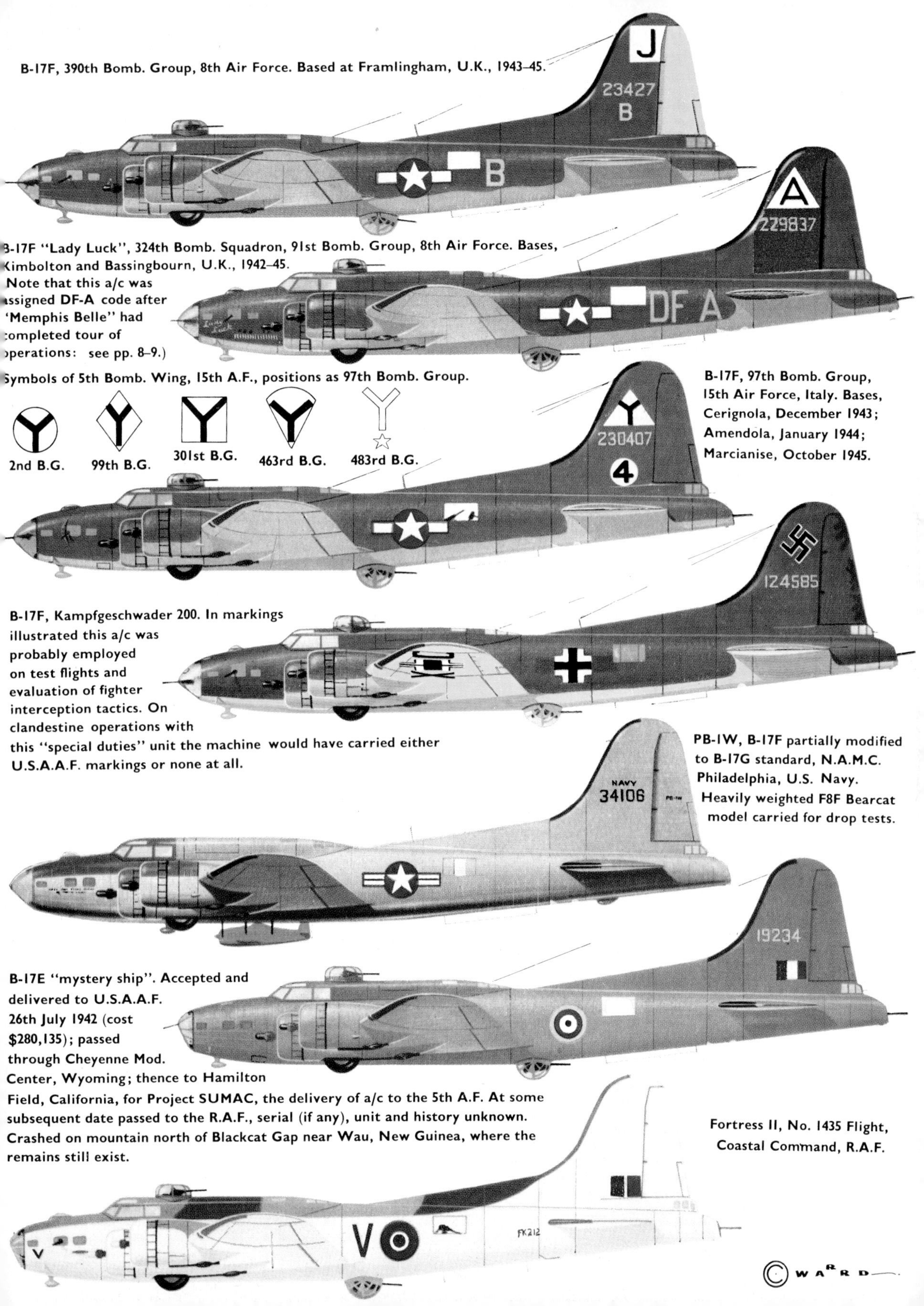

B-17F, 390th Bomb. Group, 8th Air Force. Based at Framlingham, U.K., 1943–45.

B-17F "Lady Luck", 324th Bomb. Squadron, 91st Bomb. Group, 8th Air Force. Bases, Kimbolton and Bassingbourn, U.K., 1942–45. Note that this a/c was assigned DF-A code after "Memphis Belle" had completed tour of operations: see pp. 8–9.)

B-17F, 97th Bomb. Group, 15th Air Force, Italy. Bases, Cerignola, December 1943; Amendola, January 1944; Marcianise, October 1945.

B-17F, Kampfgeschwader 200. In markings illustrated this a/c was probably employed on test flights and evaluation of fighter interception tactics. On clandestine operations with this "special duties" unit the machine would have carried either U.S.A.A.F. markings or none at all.

PB-1W, B-17F partially modified to B-17G standard, N.A.M.C. Philadelphia, U.S. Navy. Heavily weighted F8F Bearcat model carried for drop tests.

B-17E "mystery ship". Accepted and delivered to U.S.A.A.F. 26th July 1942 (cost $280,135); passed through Cheyenne Mod. Center, Wyoming; thence to Hamilton Field, California, for Project SUMAC, the delivery of a/c to the 5th A.F. At some subsequent date passed to the R.A.F., serial (if any), unit and history unknown. Crashed on mountain north of Blackcat Gap near Wau, New Guinea, where the remains still exist.

Fortress II, No. 1435 Flight, Coastal Command, R.A.F.

A late model B-17F "Bomb Boogie" of the 401st B.S., 91st B.G. with modified cheek gun position which allows ·50 to fire directly forward. (Photo: U.S.A.F.)

U.S.A.A.C. UNITS EQUIPPED WITH B-17 AIRCRAFT

Abbreviations: BG=Bomb. Group; BS=Bomb. Squadron; SA=Search-Attack Unit; PS=Photo Squadron; RS, RG=Reconnaissance Squadron, Group; ETO=European Theatre of Operations; PTO=Pacific Theatre of Operations; MTO=Mediterranean Theatre of Operations; CBI=China, Burma, India Theatre; ZI=Zone of the Interior, i.e., United States of America. Sqdn. formation codes, where known and verified, are in parentheses for ETO sqdn. Identification symbols are Group tail, etc., markings.

Group	Squadrons		Theatre
1st SAG	2nd, 3rd, 4th SAS		ZI
2nd BG	20th, 49th, 96th, 429th BS		MTO
5th BG	23rd, 31st, 72nd, 394th BS		PTO
5th RG	21st, 22nd, 23rd, 24th RS		MTO
6th BG	3rd, 25th, 74th, 395th, 397th BS		ZI
7th BG	9th, 11th, 22nd, 88th BS		PTO/ CBI
9th BG(SA)	1st, 5th, 99th, 430th BS		ZI
9th RG	No sqdns. assigned		ZI
11th BG	26th, 42nd, 98th, 431st BS		PTO
11th PG	1st, 3rd, 19th PS		PTO
19th BG	14th, 28th, 30th, 40th, 93rd BS		PTO
29th BG	6th, 29th, 52nd BS		ZI
34th BG	4th, 7th, 18th, 391st BS		ZI
39th BG	6th, 61st, 62nd BS		ZI
40th BG	29th, 44th, 45th, 74th BS		ZI
43rd BG	63rd, 64th, 65th, 403rd BS		PTO
68th RG	16th, 111th, 122nd, 125th, 127th, 154th RS		MTO
88th BG	316th, 317th, 318th, 399th BS		ZI
91st BG	322nd BS (OR) 323rd BS (LG) 324th BS (DF) 401st BS (LL)	△ A	ETO
92nd BG	325th BS (JW) 326th BS (NV) 327th BS (PY) 407th BS (UX)	△ B	ETO
94th BG	331st BS (GL) 332nd BS (QE) 333rd BS (TS) 410th BS (XM)	□ A	ETO
95th BG	334th BS (BG) 335th BS (ET) 336th BS (OE) 412th BS (QW)	□ B	ETO
96th BG	337th BS (AW) 338th BS (BX) 339th BS (MZ) 413th BS (QJ)	□ C	ETO
97th BG	340th, 341st, 342nd, 414th BS		ETO/ MTO
99th BG	346th, 347th, 348th, 416th BS		ETO/ MTO
100th BG	349th, 350th, 351st, 418th BS		ETO/ MTO
301st BG	32nd, 352nd, 353rd, 354th, 419th BS		ETO/ MTO
303rd BG	358th BS (VK) 359th BS (BN) 360th BS (GN) 427th BS (PU)	△ C	ETO
304th BG	361st, 362nd, 363rd, 421st BS		ZI
305th BG	364th BS (JJ) 365th BS (KY) 366th BS (WF) 422nd BS (XK)	△ G	ETO
306th BG	367th BS (BO) 368th BS (GY) 369th BS (RD) 423rd BS (WW)	△ H	ETO
307th BG	370th, 371st, 372nd, 424th BS		ETO
331st BG	461st, 462nd, 463rd, 464th BS		ZI
333rd BG	466th, 467th, 468th, 469th BS		ZI
346th BG	502nd, 503rd, 504th, 505th BS		ZI
351st BG	408th BS (DS) 409th BS (RQ) 410th BS (TU) 411th BS (YB)	△ J	ETO
379th BG	524th BS (FO) 525th BS (FR) 526th BS (LP) 527th BS (WA)	△ K	ETO
381st BG	532nd BS (VE) 533rd BS (VP) 534th BS (GD) 535th BS (MS)	△ L	ETO
383rd BG	540th, 541st, 542nd, 543rd BS		ZI
384th BG	544th BS (BK) 545th BS (JD) 546th BS (SO) 547th BS (SU)	△ P	ETO
385th BG	548th, 549th, 550th, 551st BS		ETO
388th BG	560th BS 561st BS 562nd BS 563rd BS	□ H	ETO
390th BG	568th BS (BI) 569th BS (CC) 570th BS (DI) 571st BS (FC)	□ J	ETO
393rd BG	580th, 581st, 582nd, 583rd BS		ZI
395th BG	588th, 589th, 590th, 591st BS		ZI
396th BG	592nd, 593rd, 594th, 595th BS		ZI
398th BG	600th BS (K8) 601st BS (N7) 602nd BS (N8) 603rd BS (30)	△ W	ETO
401st BG	612th BS (IN) 613th BS (IW) 614th BS (IY) 615th BS (SC)	△ S	ETO
444th BG	676th, 677th, 678th, 679th BS		ZI
447th BG	708th BS 709th BS 710th BS 711th BS	□ K	ETO
452nd BG	728th BS 729th BS 730th BS 731st BS	□ L	ETO
457th BG	748th BS 749th BS 750th BS 751st BS	△ U	ETO
463rd BG	772nd, 773rd, 774th, 775th BS		MTO
469th BG	796th, 797th, 798th, 799th BS		ZI
482nd BG	812th, 813th, 814th BS		ETO
483rd BG	815th, 816th, 817th, 818th BS		MTO
486th BG	832nd BS (H8) 833rd BS (2S) 834th BS (3R) 835th BS (4N)	□ W	ETO
487th BG	836th BS (RS) 837th BS (3C) 838th BS (3G) 839th BS (4F)	□ P	ETO
488th BG	840th, 841st, 842nd, 843rd BS		ETO
493rd BG	860th, 861st, 862nd, 863rd BS		ETO
504th BG	393rd, 398th, 421st, 507th BS		ZI
505th BG	482nd, 483rd, 484th, 485th BS		ZI

PROFILE PUBLICATIONS

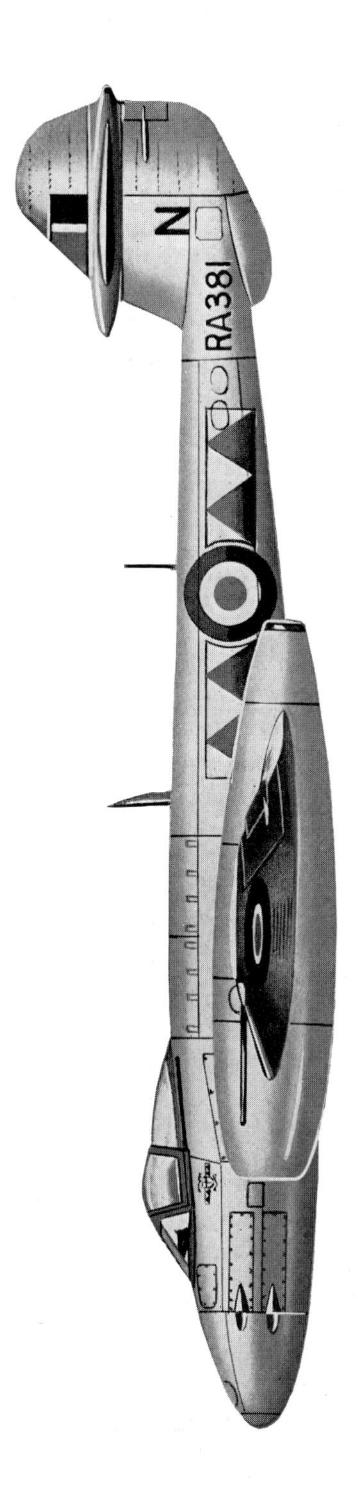

This particular Meteor, in common with several other aircraft of the Squadron, is shown carrying mixed styles of the national marking. The wing roundels and fin stripes are of the 1939–45 War period, and the fuselage roundels are of the post-war period.

No. 600 Squadron was unique in having two official badges. The second badge was authorised by King George VI at the beginning of 1951. When carried on the Squadron's Meteor aircraft, the badge was flanked by smaller additions of the Squadron marking.

Port (left-hand) view shows the aircraft without the 180-gal. drop-tank.

GLOSTER METEOR F. Mk. 4, RA381, of No. 600, "City of London" Squadron, Royal Auxiliary Air Force. April, 1951.

The Gloster Meteor F.IV

by J. J. Partridge

Meteor F. Mk. 4 of No. 275 "Burma" Squadron in the all-silver finish, circa 1948–50. The squadron aircraft later carried 275's green and yellow check marking on either side of the fuselage roundel. (Photo: Ministry of Defence)

The Gloster Meteor F. Mk. 4 was the first fully operational jet fighter to result from the F9/40 specification issued five years earlier. The eight prototypes had proved that the infant jet engine could carry a military load and had enabled a wide range of engines to be flight tested. The small batch of Mk. 1s had, to a large extent, continued this work but had also seen operational service against the V.1 flying bombs, being one of the only aircraft of that period to have the necessary speed to catch them at their operational height. The Mk. 2 which was to have been the production version of the Halford-engined prototypes was never built. The Mk. 3 was the logical development of the Mk. 1 with a few refinements such as the improved canopy and airbrakes, but the first production batch still had the Welland reverse-flow engine. However the development of the Rolls-Royce R.B.37 or Derwent 1 straight-flow engine was pushed forward to power the Mk. 3 and this showed a real improvement both in specific consumption and in total thrust.

This increase in thrust was able to push the airframe to the edge of compressibility troubles. Investigation showed that these were largely caused by disturbed flow around the nacelles and tunnel tests indicated that lengthening the nacelles would go a long way towards curing the troubles. Accordingly the last thirty Mk. 3s were fitted with the lengthened nacelle fitted to all the subsequent Marks.

In the meantime, Rolls-Royce had been developing the Nene engine which, while it followed the same general layout as the Derwent, was physically much larger and embodied many new features. It was the power unit specified for the Gloster E1/44 and the Supermarine E10/44 which was finally produced as the Attacker. The engine was much too large to fit comfortably into a Meteor despite the fact that a Mk. 4 did fly with Nenes, at a much later date, as a short take-off research machine. Rolls-Royce were convinced that the Nene layout was a good one and set about producing a scaled-down version. This was developed in a surprisingly short space of time and appeared as the Derwent 5 with a static thrust of 3,500 lb.

The installation of these engines was the basic modification which created the Meteor 4 and, while this massive increase in thrust produced the most spectacular results, it was by no means the only improvement introduced in the Mk. 4. It was the first Mark to have a fully operational pressure cabin, a very real necessity to an aeroplane with a time of 8 minutes to 40,000 ft. Underwing tanks were added to give an increased ferrying range. Pioneer work was done carrying bombs and rockets under the outer wings, paving the way for the ground attack Mk. 8s used in Korea. The gear tab ailerons were much appreciated by the pilots who found a marked improvement in handling throughout the speed range.

An unfortunate accident early in the life of the Mk. 4 gave rise to its most distinctive recognition feature, its clipped wings. An aircraft flown by Gloster test pilot Moss broke up in the air when the pilot appeared to misjudge a dive and became forced into a very rapid pull out. It was afterwards decided to cut 5 ft. 10 in. off the span to improve the stress factors in the centre section spars. This had to be done retrospectively on some aircraft which had been manufactured, before delivery to the Service.

This then was the final shaping of Britain's first "600+" fighter and although many minor modifications were embodied during its long and outstanding Service career, none was to produce any major change.

DESCRIPTION

The F9/40 was a war-time concept, designed to be built in sub-assembly units in as many widely dis-

"Ground start" with the aid of a trolley. The air intake guard is fitted for safety during ground running, replacing the earlier fixed mesh. (Photo: "Flight")

Meteor F. Mk. 4s of No. 222 Squadron. Squadron letters soon disappeared when many units applied their personal markings, such as those shown on the F. Mk. 4s in the illustration below. (Photo: "Flight")

No. 600 "City of London" Squadron with unit markings on fuselage. Note differences in roundels. (Photo: "Flight")

persed factories as possible. This structural breakdown remained unchanged in the Mk. 4 and made it one of the most easily transported, repaired or salvaged aeroplanes ever to go into service.

The fuselage was divided into three major units—nose, centre and rear. The basis of the front fuselage structure was two vertical webs and three solid bulkheads. The nose-wheel bulkhead carried the tubular structure from which the nose-wheel unit was mounted and formed the front wall of the pressure cabin. The seat bulkhead formed the rear wall while the front spar bulkhead completed the rear end of the front fuselage. Between the nose-wheel and seat bulkheads, the main diaphragms and the top skin were of heavy gauge light alloy to absorb the loads imposed by the 3 lb. sq. in. cabin differential pressure. The windscreen consisted of three bullet-proof panels set in a light alloy frame. The sliding hood was operated by a hand winding gear and could be jettisoned completely in an emergency. Both hood and windscreen were of dry air sandwich construction. The canopy lines were completed by a transparent rear fairing attached to the top magazine bay door which completed the top fuselage contour aft of the cabin and provided access to the ammunition tanks for the four 20 mm. Hispano guns. The latter were mounted between the main diaphragms and the outer skin and were accessible through large gun doors. The original F9/40 design had made provision for six guns, the other two being under the cabin floor. However these two guns proved to be so inaccessible that in certain jammed conditions, they would have had to be removed while still containing live rounds. Needless to say they were only fitted in one of the F9/40 prototypes, and then only fired on the ground.

The front fuselage was joined to the centre fuselage at four longeron joints, these members collecting the loads at the top and bottom of each main diaphragm. The centre fuselage was an integral part of the centre section and enclosed the fuel tank. The front and rear spar bulkheads formed the fore-and-aft boundaries of the bay, the structure between consisting of four tank bearers extended at each side to take the side skins and top longerons. The top was completed by two quickly detachable tank doors.

The rear fuselage, which was also attached at the four longerons, was of semi-monocoque construction with hoop Z section frames and top-hat section stringers. The last two frames were extended upwards to form the lower fin posts and to provide attachment for the tailplane and the upper fin.

The main plane was a two-spar, stressed-skin structure divided into two outer planes and a centre section. In the latter, the spars were spaced by six major ribs interspaced with lighter skin ribs. The engine nacelles were built up between the inner and outer engine ribs at each side and were each based on two main frames attached to the spars. Between these two ribs the rear spar was increased in depth so that the jet pipe could pass through it, both the webs and booms being of steel in this area. The nacelles gave splendid access to the power unit, the complete top half between the spars being detachable, in addition to the entire nose forward of the front spar. The undercarriage bays were formed inboard of the nacelles and between the spars, while behind the rear spar the tail ribs incorporated the top and bottom air brakes and the flaps.

The outer wings, which were attached by pin joints at the front and rear spars, had pressed and lattice-type ribs. The wing tips were detachable. The ailerons were internally mass-balanced and had geared tabs.

The components of the tail unit were of all-metal, stressed-skin construction. The high position of the

In the field with the Meteor 4. Above: *high-speed refuelling of a Norwegian Mk. 4.* Below: *armourers change the four 20-mm. cannon.* (Photos: Ministry of Defence)

Side, rear and underside flying view of a typical Meteor F. Mk. 4 powered by Rolls-Royce Derwent 5 turbo-jets. E.E.592 *was a type G.41F Gloster-built aircraft.* (Photos: Ministry of Defence)

tailplane split the rudder into two halves which were joined by a tubular spar. The two elevators were joined in a similar manner, all these units being fitted with trim tabs.

The hydraulically-operated alighting gear was somewhat unusual. All three units were on the Dowty lever suspension principle which had been pioneered on the Gloster E28/39. They provided a robust yet compact unit essential to the low ground clearance associated with jet aircraft. The system had another advantage in that it could easily incorporate a leg-shortening device which greatly reduced the space occupied by the main legs when retracted. This was achieved by pivoting the shock absorber at a lower point than the top casting, so that as the unit was retracted, the shock absorber acted as a tie strut pulling the wheel fork in closer to the top casting. The units retracted sideways and were each enclosed by two doors. The nose-wheel retracted rearwards and was enclosed by three doors. It was fully castoring and incorporated a self-centring device. Since retractable undercarriages were then still considered a bit of a hazard, in addition to the normal electrical indicators, the nose-wheel was provided with a mechanical down lock indicator in the form of a red painted rod which stuck up through the top skin in front of the windscreen when the down lock was fully engaged. Such a device was not considered necessary for the main wheels as the pilot could look back and see that they were at least down (if not locked).

The controls, apart from the rudder pedals, were conventional consisting of the normal spade grip control column which was connected to the elevators and ailerons by torque shafts, rods, chains and cables. Each rudder pedal was mounted on a separate roller unit moving in its own fore-and-aft guide. This was necessary because the cover which enclosed the nose-wheel in the retracted position occupied the space in which the normal rudder bar pivot would be mounted. After some initial trouble caused by the floor flexing under pressure, the system operated very well. The trimming tabs on the rudder and elevators were controlled from conventional hand wheels in the cabin. The rudder tab gearbox was offset from the hinge line so that the tab also operated as a balance tab.

Each engine was mounted between an inner and an outer engine rib, the trunnion at each side of the engine fitting inside a spherical bush which in turn fitted in a mounting block to give a high degree of self-alignment. Only one bush was pinned to its trunnion thus checking side float without preventing expansion and contraction due to temperature changes. The rear of the engine was steadied by four struts in diamond pattern, from the turbine casing to the sides of the nacelle.

An extension shaft from each engine wheel case extended forward through the front spar to drive a Rotol auxiliaries gearbox, the port gearbox driving a KX generator, a Heywood air compressor and a vacuum pump while the starboard box drove the Dowty Live-Line hydraulic pump and the second vacuum pump.

Fuel was normally carried in the two-cell, self-sealing tank in the centre fuselage and a drop tank under the fuselage. Fuel from the latter was transferred by air pressure into the main tank, the flow being controlled by a float valve in each cell. An electric low-pressure pump drew fuel through an inverted flight trap in each half and delivered it through a low pressure cock to its respective engine, the front half feeding the port engine and the rear half the starboard. A balance cock could be opened to

The small frontal area and clean lines of the Mk. 4 show up well in this head-on view. It also illustrates the good grouping and positioning of the four 20-mm. guns and shows the cine camera vision tube in the nose.

make all the fuel available to one engine if desired; in fact, flying on one engine was recommended for maximum endurance. Later in the aircraft's life, wing tanks were introduced for ferrying only. On one occasion an aircraft was modified in a hurry so that it could be ferried to the Continent. Unfortunately the inward vent valves were omitted in the rush. The wing tanks were used first and were shut off after they had emptied at about 30,000 ft. During the subsequent descent no air could enter the tanks to equalise the increasing ambient pressure. When the aircraft landed it was carrying two wing tanks that looked as if they had just been under a steam roller!

The hydraulic system operated the flaps, airbrakes and undercarriage, a large accumulator being provided to smooth the flow and act as a power reservoir in case of pump failure. A hand pump would operate all services very slowly.

Compressed air to operate the main wheel brakes and cock the guns was provided by a Heywood compressor charging an air bottle in the rear fuselage. The compressor was an innovation on the Mk. 4, previous Marks having two ground-charged bottles. A relic of the nose-wheel brake was the brake torque strut, long since non-functional but left to operate the nose-wheel door retraction mechanism.

Since in 1945 electrically-operated gyro instruments were some way in the future, a cumbersome vacuum system, consisting of two engine-driven pumps and their oil separators, was fitted to operate the blind flying instruments.

The pressure cabin system was unique in its day, being the only one to take its pressurising air directly from the engine compressor casings, the pipes from the two engines joining at the duplex non-return valve to prevent cross feeding. From this point a single pipe, which incorporated a control valve and a constant flow valve, ran to the cabin. A Westland (later to become Normalair) control valve under the cabin floor prevented any build up of cabin pressure below 7,000 ft.; above this height the escaping air was progressively restricted until the full cabin differential of 3 lb. sq. in. was achieved at 24,000 ft. This system also provided the heating with no temperature control. It worked well enough but looks a little primitive alongside today's sophisticated refrigeration and heating systems with fully automatic controls.

The main armament consisted of four 20-mm. Hispano Mk. II guns fed with ammunition via Mk. I or Mk. V belt feed mechanisms, cases and links being ejected through chutes in the bottom skin. Firing was by Dunlop electrical sear release units, controlled from a selective gun button which gave the pilot the choice of top pair, low pair or all four guns. The Mk. II gyro-gunsight was fitted with a recording camera and was ranged from a twist grip on the throttle levers. A G.45.B cine-camera was mounted in the fuselage nose.

The electrical system which operated the normal heating, lighting and instrument services was powered by one 1,500 watt, 24-volt generator, Type KX, charging two 12-volt accumulators in series. Towards the end of the production run, a modification to install twin 02 generators was raised but was fitted to only a handful of aircraft.

A T.R.1143, or later a T.R.1464, two-way V.H.F. radio was fitted with the added provision for beam approach. Radar identification was given by an R.3121 1FF installation.

Neville Duke, "Bill" Waterton and Teddy Donaldson discuss tactics for the 1946 attempt on the World Air Speed Record.

E.E.530 *with wide-span wings was used as a trainer for the second attempt by the Meteor on the World Air Speed Record. As originally delivered to the High Speed Flight, R.A.F., it was fitted with a normal transparent canopy. The metal rear canopy was fitted at a later stage.* (Photo: "Flight")

Other equipment included oxygen, gun heating and windscreen de-icing.

The Meteor had been faced with an acute C.G. problem ever since the two lower guns had had to be abandoned in the F9/40 stage. The tail heavy moment got worse and worse as more modifications were added, necessitating more and more ballast in the nose. The heavier engines and jet pipes in the Mk. 4 represented the penultimate straw and forced the Meteor 4 to carry no less than 1,095 lb. of ballast in the most adverse case. This was all in the form of lead and was dispersed as follows:

Fixed in the nose-wheel bulkhead ..	100 lb.
Fixed in the nacelle leading edges ..	250 lb.
Fixed on the main webs	275 lb.
Removable on the nose-wheel mounting	470 lb.

It was not until the Meteor Mk. 8 that the situation was relieved by an extra 30 in. of fuselage inserted between the front spar bulkhead and the frost fuselage so that the increased moment arm of the pilot and guns practically eliminated the need for ballast.

FLYING THE METEOR 4

The Meteor Mk. 4 was a simple aircraft to handle both on the ground and in the air. The controls were well harmonised and provided good handling qualities right up to the service ceiling. The clipped wings and gear tab ailerons improved the rate of roll, while the tendency to snake was noticeably less than on earlier marks.

With such enormous power and a very clean aircraft, it was extremely easy to exceed the limiting Mach No. of 0·8 even in level flight. To lose height quickly, it was essential to use the airbrakes which would be opened at any speed, a blow-back valve preventing undue strain. The deceleration was swift, 0·8G at 400 m.p.h.!

An excellent safety feature was the aircraft's tendency to pitch up gently at the edge of compressibility, providing a warning and correction at the same time.

At very high Mach numbers, the unpowered controls were almost solid, so that there was little fear of high stresses being imposed by violent manœuvres.

The single-engine performance was outstanding—over 400 m.p.h. at sea level with no serious deterioration in control.

The approach was made at 125–130 m.p.h. with flaps and air brakes down. Full lateral and fore-and-aft control was maintained right down to the stall at about 105 m.p.h.

THE RECORD BREAKERS

The two aircraft which might be considered Mk. 4 prototypes were produced in 1945. These were two Mk. 3s, *E.E.454* and *455*, fitted with prototype Derwent 5 engines to attack the World Speed Record, at that time still standing at the pre-war figure of 469 m.p.h. On 7th November, Group Captain Wilson, flying *E.E.454* raised the record to 606 m.p.h., while Eric Greenwood flying *E.E.455* (sometimes known as the "Yellow Peril" from its overall yellow finish) could only manage 603 m.p.h.

A new record must better the existing one by at least 1% or in this case just over 6 m.p.h. As this was thought to be within the reach of the Lockheed Shooting Star, preparations for a new British attempt were put in hand in the summer of 1946 when the R.A.F. High Speed Flight was formed at Tangmere on 14th June. After training on standard Mk. 4 aircraft, two Mk. 4s especially prepared for the record

Above, top: E.E.455 *"Britannia" or the "Yellow Peril", achieved 603 m.p.h. when attempting the Air Speed Record in 1945.* Above, bottom: R.A.476 *broke the Turnhouse, Scotland–Bovingdon, Hertfordshire record.* Below: E.E.549 *which broke the World Air Speed Record in 1946 with a speed of 616 m.p.h. The Meteor now stands outside R.A.F. Innsworth.* (Photos: the author)

The Egyptian Air Force operated the F. Mk. 4 and T.7 Trainer, examples of which are shown in flight over Gloucestershire. A total of twelve Mk. 4s and six T.7s were delivered. (Photo: Hawker Siddeley Aviation Ltd.)

attempt were delivered in August. These were serial numbered *E.E.549* and *E.E.550*. The guns had been removed and the gun ports faired over, the air brakes were locked down and generally all cracks and dents were filled. A 43-gallon fuel tank was installed in the magazine bay and two tanks of thirteen gallons each were fitted, one in each gun bay. An extra 563 lb. of ballast was necessary to compensate for the guns, giving the aircraft an all-up weight of 14,075 lb. in record-breaking trim. Special metal canopies with small transparent windows replaced the normal perspex hoods as the latter suffered from softening and distortion caused by the temperature rise induced by skin friction when flying at high speed at low altitudes.

Before the record attempt on 7th September, both aircraft had special Derwent 5 engines, rated at 4,200 lb. thrust for short periods, substituted for the 3,500 lb. thrust engines. The weather was far from ideal with low cloud and drizzle accompanied by a low air temperature. Group Captain Donaldson took off first in *E.E.549* at 5.45 p.m. and landed fourteen minutes later having raised the record to 616 m.p.h. Squadron Leader Waterton took off later in *E.E.550* but his average was only 614 m.p.h.

E.E.549 was displayed at the Paris Aero Show in November and on its return trip, set up a new Paris–London Record of 520 m.p.h. Since no special preparation had been made for this flight, Glosters thought that the record could be improved. Accordingly on 19th January 1947, *E.E.549*, again flown by Waterton, flashed over the timing point at Le Bourget and twenty minutes, eleven seconds later passed a similar point at Croydon having raised the record to 618·4 m.p.h.

Happily *E.E.549* has been preserved and now stands at the gate of R.A.F. Innsworth, Gloucestershire, only some four miles from the factory where it was built.

After an abortive attempt on 4th February, a Meteor 4 (*V.T.103*) raised the World's 100 kilometre closed circuit record to 542·9 m.p.h. on 6th February 1948, flying on a triangular course from Moreton Valance aerodrome.

During the demonstration tour of Europe in 1947, Coates Preedy set up a new Brussels to Copenhagen record of 630 m.p.h. in the privately owned Gloster Meteor *G-AIDC*.

MK. 4 VARIANTS

As had been the case with the earlier marks of Meteor, the Mk. 4 was much in demand as a test aircraft. Axial flow engines were reaching an advanced stage of development and it was natural that the Meteor was chosen to test them in flight.

Two such engines were the Metropolitan Vickers F2/4 Beryl and the Rolls-Royce R.A.2 and 3 Avons. Both these engines were far too long to mount between the spars of the Meteor centre section and too large to be entirely underslung in the same manner as the M.V.F1. The problem was solved by fitting a curved section to both front and rear spars in the nacelles so that the engines could be underslung and still leave sufficient ground clearance when the longer type undercarriage units (similar to those used on the F1 F9/40) were used. This modification was applied to *R.A.490* to mount the Beryls and *R.A.491* for the Avons. Both had fantastic rates of climb, *R.A.491* with *R.A.3* clocking 2·7 min. to 40,000 ft. (12,190 m.) and 3·65 min. to 50,000 ft. (15,250 m.).

Later *R.A.490* was converted by Westland Aircraft in 1954 to take two Nene engines fitted with jet deflectors. As the engines had to be mounted forward of the front spar to allow the deflected jet to operate in the region of the centre of gravity, very large nacelles were necessary, extending some 8 ft. forward of the spars. A Mk. 8 tail unit and full span wings were fitted to give a span of 44 ft. 4 in. (13.51 m.). The trials were technically successful, a minimum indicated air speed of 65 knots (115 km. h.) being achieved but the installation was complicated. The Service had to wait another twelve years for the Hawker Siddeley Kestrel before it got its first jet-deflected aircraft.

The Royal Netherlands Air Force took delivery of a total of sixty-five Meteor F. Mk. 4s and they served from 1948 until 1962. (Photo: Ministry of Defence)

Belgium took delivery of the first of forty-eight Meteor 4s in April 1949, the last arriving the following September. The Mk. 4s were in service for five years before being replaced by the Mk. 8.

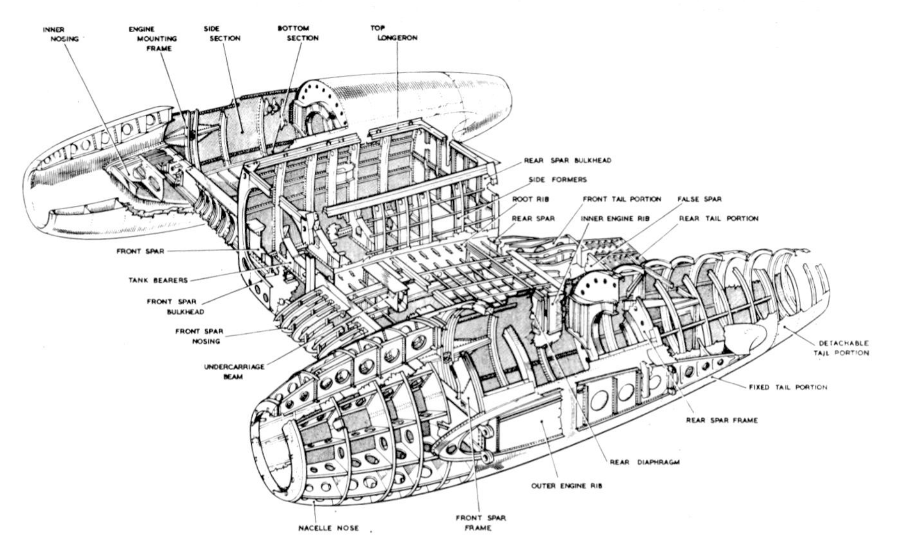

Structural heart of the Meteor F. Mk. 4 was the centre-section incorporating engine nacelles and undercarriage mounting.

R.A.491 was also subsequently modified to take a pair of French Atar engines. Among many other modifications a Mk. 8 front fuselage was fitted.

Reheat was also under intensive development at this time, *R.A.435* and *V.T.196* both being modified to take reheat tail pipes for the Derwent Mk. 5 and Mk. 8 respectively. The system increased the thrust of a Derwent by 25% but at a cost of a 900 g.p.h. fuel consumption.

Flight Refuelling Ltd. were bringing their technique of air-to-air refuelling to perfection and two Meteor Mk. 4s, *R.A.438* and *V.Z.389*, were each fitted with a probe on the fuselage nose, connected to the main fuel tanks. The first fuel load was transferred on 2nd April 1950. The same method is still used by the R.A.F. today.

A trial installation on *R.A.382* was to influence the shape of subsequent marks of Meteor. The quantity of ballast necessary on the Mk. 4 was so high that it was decided to insert an extra 30 in. of fuselage at the front spar bulkhead joint, thus increasing the moment of the front fuselage. The modification was a success but some attendant troubles caused by the larger C.G. shift due to using ammunition was not finally cured until the E1/44 tail unit was fitted.

Following the successful trials of the Martin Baker ejection seat in the two-seater Meteor 3, *E.E.416*, it was decided to fit ejector seats to Meteor aircraft as standard equipment and the aircraft chosen for the trial installation was a Mk. 4, *V.T.150*. This entailed moving the windscreen forward, fitting a completely new one-piece hood, cutting out the centre of the seat bulkhead and sloping it back, fitting a retractable gyro gunsight and many smaller modifications to instruments and controls. The man-hours involved and the complexity of the work soon made it clear that it was unrealistic to modify existing aircraft, even though at least one foreign government had been sold some seats by an over-enthusiastic seat salesman. It was decided that these modifications, together with the installation of Derwent Mk. 8 engines, would be the basis of the Meteor F. Mk. 8 which would supersede the Mk. 4 in preference to the more sophisticated Mk. 6. *V.T.150* was further modified to take the E1/44 tail unit and the 30 in. front fuselage extension, so becoming a true Mk. 8 prototype.

Another variation pioneered by the Mk. 4 was the photographic reconnaissance rôle, *V.T.347* being converted to take two F36 vertical cameras in the rear fuselage and an F24 oblique camera on a mounting in the fuselage nose which was fitted with three optically flat windows. Thus the oblique camera could be set on the ground to operate straight ahead or to either beam. This version carried the normal armament and was known as the Meteor P.R. Mk. 5. Unfortunately it went to pieces in the air during a very fast run over Moreton Valance aerodrome on its first flight on 13th July 1949. The pilot, Rodney Dryland, was killed. However the installations were successful and were built into the F.R.9 and the P.R.10.

Rolls-Royce Derwent 5 engines equipped with afterburners were installed in RA435. *Note "eyelids" protruding from the engine exhaust.* (Photo: Ministry of Defence)

Another RA-*serialled Meteor to be used as an engine test-bed was* 490, *shown with Metro-Vick Beryl axial-flow engines. These were later replaced by non-standard Rolls-Royce Nenes fitted with jet deflection units. As a STOL aircraft the Meteor was the forebear of the Hawker Siddeley Kestrel. The airframe was drastically modified; major modifications being the F. Mk. 8 tail assembly and the end-plate fins on the tailplane.* (Photo: Hawker Siddeley Aviation Ltd.)

G-AIDC was not really a variant but a private aeroplane built by the Gloster Aircraft Company to use as a demonstration machine on overseas sales tours. It was painted all scarlet with a white flash and registration letters. Its career came to an end when being flown by a Belgian pilot. One leg extended at 550 m.p.h. and the aircraft went into a series of wild upward rolls. The pilot regained control but the weakened leg collapsed on landing and the aircraft was damaged beyond repair.

IN R.A.F. SERVICE

The first Mk. 4s off the production line were finished in the standard day-fighter scheme of dark green and dark sea-grey on upper surfaces and medium sea-grey on under surfaces. It was a gloss dope finished with wax polish, but at about the same time, camouflage was abandoned by the R.A.F. and before delivery all Mk. 4s were finished with silver dope, cut and polished to a high gloss. The Meteor never left the factory without dope of some kind being applied. In later years fewer undercoats were applied and filling was not so thorough in the interests of weight saving and reducing man-hours.

A total of 465 aircraft were built for the R.A.F. in the following batches.

Built by Gloster Aircraft Co. at Gloucester: E.E.517–554, E.E.568–599, R.A.365–398, R.A.413–457, R.A. 473–493, V.T.102–150, V.T.168–199, V.T.213–247, V.T.256–294, V.T.303–347, V.W.255–304, V.W.308–315, V.W.780–791, V.Z.437.

Built by Sir W. G. Armstrong Whitworth Aircraft at Coventry: V.Z.386–419, V.Z.427–429, V.Z.436.

Between 1947 and 1952 the following squadrons were, at some period, equipped with Mk. 4s: 1, 41, 43, 56, 63, 66, 74, 92, 222, 245, 257, 263, 266, 500, 504, 600, 610, 611, 615 and 616.

THE METEOR 4 OVERSEAS

At the end of the war in 1945, Great Britain possessed the most highly developed jet fighter, in the form of the Meteor 4. The British Government and the Gloster Aircraft Company were quick to realise the export potential and an intensive sales drive was soon under way.

The first export contracts were placed by the Argentine Government in May 1947 for 100 aircraft, serial numbered 1·001 to 1·100. The first 50 were to have been R.A.F. aircraft and the second 50 were specially built. The aircraft were shipped in their sub-assembly units to be assembled by Gloster personnel in the Argentine, the last aircraft being delivered in September 1948. The finish was all silver with national markings. At first the serial numbers were painted in black on the nose but were later transferred to the rear fuselage. Also black anti-dazzle panels were subsequently added on the decking in front of the windscreen.

During the revolution of 1955, the Meteors were used by both Government and Rebel Forces in action, which resulted in the loss of at least two aircraft. The Meteor proved to be a reliable machine however and in 1961 at least half the original number were still flying.

Close on the heels of the Argentine order came an order from the Royal Netherlands Air Force in June 1947, for the first five of a total of 60 aircraft. Serial

At the end of a long career, albeit not exciting, a large number of Mk. 4s were converted to drones. As such they were designated the Meteor U Mk. 15. Illustration shows two manned U.15s under the control of a Firefly drone over Malta.
(Photo: via Paul Trither)

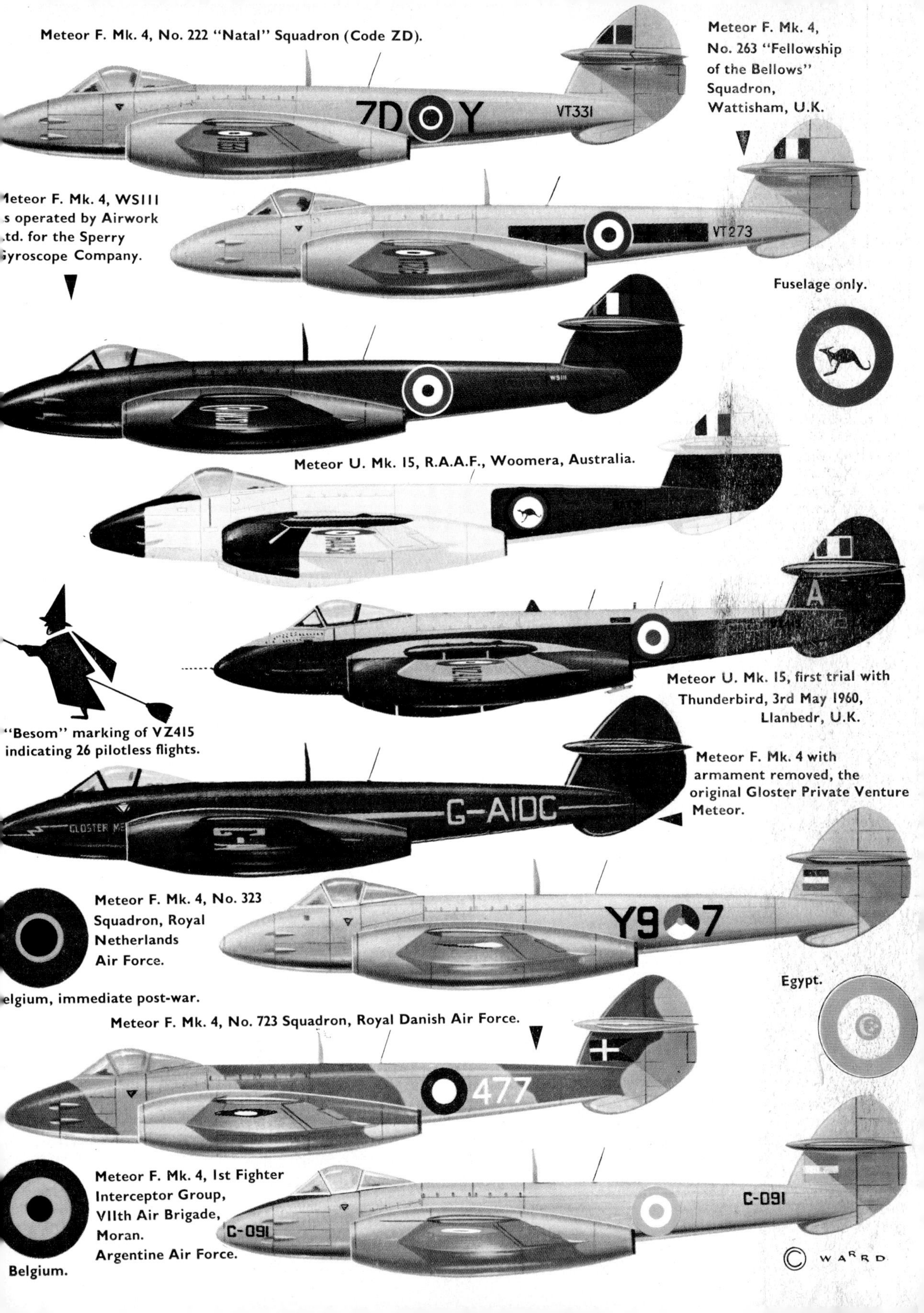

Meteor F. Mk. 4, No. 222 "Natal" Squadron (Code ZD).
7D Y
VT331
Meteor F. Mk. 4, No. 263 "Fellowship of the Bellows" Squadron, Wattisham, U.K.
Meteor F. Mk. 4, WS111 s operated by Airwork Ltd. for the Sperry Gyroscope Company.
VT273
Fuselage only.
WS111
Meteor U. Mk. 15, R.A.A.F., Woomera, Australia.
A
Meteor U. Mk. 15, first trial with Thunderbird, 3rd May 1960, Llanbedr, U.K.
"Besom" marking of VZ415 indicating 26 pilotless flights.
G-AIDC
GLOSTER ME
Meteor F. Mk. 4 with armament removed, the original Gloster Private Venture Meteor.
Meteor F. Mk. 4, No. 323 Squadron, Royal Netherlands Air Force.
Y9 7
Egypt.
elgium, immediate post-war.
Meteor F. Mk. 4, No. 723 Squadron, Royal Danish Air Force.
477
Meteor F. Mk. 4, 1st Fighter Interceptor Group, VIIth Air Brigade, Moran. Argentine Air Force.
C-091
C-091
Belgium.
© WARD

The prototype Meteor F. Mk. 8 was VT150, *originally produced as an F. Mk. 4. Modification of the Mk. 4 airframe included a new tail assembly and a 30-inch fuselage extension.* (Photo: Hawker Siddeley Aviation Ltd.)

numbers ran from I.21 to I.81. The aircraft were in standard silver finish with black squadron letters and numbers fore-and-aft of the national insignia on the fuselage sides. Squadrons 322, 323, 326 and 327 were equipped with Mk. 4s.

In 1949, Belgium purchased 48 aircraft, serial numbered E.F.1 to E.F.48. These were issued to 349 and 350 squadrons. The finish on delivery was all silver with black serial numbers on the rear fuselage. The roundels had a narrow yellow ring.

Subsequently the aircraft were camouflaged with white squadron letters. The aircraft finally became obsolete in 1957.

Later in 1949, Denmark ordered 20 Meteor 4s, serial numbered D.461 to D.480. Unlike any other Meteor 4s, the Danish aircraft were finished in green and grey camouflage with white serial numbers behind the fuselage roundels. The unit operating the aircraft was first known as the Third Air Flotilla of the Naval Air Service, but later as 723 squadron of the Royal Danish Air Force.

After the British Government's arms embargo was lifted, Glosters delivered the first of 12 Meteor 4s to Egypt in October 1949. Serial numbers ran from 1401 to 1412 and the aircraft were finished in silver dope.

France purchased two Meteor 4s for development work. The first was formerly *E.E.523* but was re-registered *F-WEPQ* before delivery. The second was *R.A.491*, the original Avon test-bed, which was converted to take Atar engines.

Meteor 4s of No. 66 carry out a mock stern attack on an R.A.F. Lincoln bomber. (Photo: Ministry of Defence)

Flight tests with 1,000-lb. bombs were carried out on E.E.519. *Carriage of 98-lb. rocket projectiles was also flight tested on this aircraft.* (Photo: Hawker Siddeley Aviation Ltd.)

SPECIFICATION

Dimensions: Wing span 37 ft. 2 in. (11·33 m.); overall length 41 ft. (12·5 m.); height over rudder 13 ft. (3·3 m.); height over cabin 8 ft. 7 in. (2·6 m.); height over wing tip 5 ft. (1·52 m.); wheel track 10 ft. 5 in. (3·23 m.); wheel base 13 ft. 4 in. (4·06 m.). *Main Plane:* Area, gross 350 sq. ft. (32·5 sq. m.); aspect ratio 3·9; aerofoil centre section E.C.1240; aerofoil outer section root E.C.1240; aerofoil outer section tip E.C.1040; incidence 1 deg.; dihedral centre section 0 deg. 52½ min.; dihedral outer section 6 deg.; aileron area total 28 sq. ft. (2·6 sq. m.); flaps area total 18 sq. ft. (1·67 sq. m.) airbrakes area total 13·5 sq. ft. (1·25 sq. m.). *Tail Unit:* Tailplane, span 15 ft. 8 in. (4·76 m.); area 61 sq. ft. (5·67 sq. m.); incidence 1 deg.; elevator area total 26·6 sq. ft. (2·47 sq. m.); fin area total 14·3 sq. ft. (1·33 sq. m.); rudder area total 19 sq. ft. (1·77 sq. m.).
Tank Capacities: Fuel, internal tank 325 Imperial gall. (1,480 litres), fuselage drop tank 180 Imperial gall. (818 litres), underwing tanks 2 × 100 Imperial gall. (910 litres). *Oil,* engine tanks 2 × 22 pints (25 litres).
Weights: Weight empty 10,050 lb. (4,562 kg.); military load 2,792 lb. (1,265 kg.); loaded weight (full internal fuel) 15,000 lb. (6,800 kg.); loaded weight (with fuselage drop tank) 16,750 lb. (7,600 kg.); loaded weight (with fuselage and wing tanks) 18,000 lb. (8,440 kg.); gross wing loading at 15,000 lb. 41·4 lb. sq. ft. (202 kg. sq. m.).
Performance: Maximum level speed: Sea level 585 m.p.h. (940 km.h.); 10,000 ft. (3,050 m.) 585 m.p.h. (940 km.h.); 20,000 ft. (6,100 m.) 570 m.p.h. (915 km.h.); 30,000 ft. (9,150 m.) 540 m.p.h. (870 km.h.); 40,000 ft. (12,190 m.) 490 m.p.h. (790 km.h.). *Maximum cruising speed:* Sea level 540 m.p.h. (870 km.h.); 30,000 ft. (9,150 m.) 530 m.p.h. (855 km.h.). *Maximum rate of climb:* Sea level 7,500 ft./min. (2,280 m./min.); 10,000 ft. (3,050 m.) 6,100 ft./min. (1,860 m./min.); 20,000 ft. (6,100 m.) 4,750 ft./min. (1,440 m./min.); 30,000 ft. (9,150 m.) 3,300 ft./min. (1,010 m./min.); 40,000 ft. (12,190 m.) 1,650 ft./min. (490 m./min.). Time to 30,000 ft. (9,150 m.) 5 min.; time to 40,000 ft. (12,190 m.) 8 min.; absolute ceiling 49,000 ft. (14,900 m.). *Range at 30,000 ft. (9,150 m.):* With full internal fuel 420 miles (670 km.); with full internal and fuselage drop tank 680 miles (1,100 km.); with full internal and fuselage and wing tanks 1,000 miles (1,610 km.). *Landing speed:* 125 m.p.h. (200 km.h.). *Stalling speed:* Flaps and alighting gear up 120 m.p.h. (195 km.h.); flaps and alighting gear down 105 m.p.h. (165 km.h.). Take-off distance to clear 50 ft. (15·25 m.) 834 yds. (760 m.). Landing distance from 50 ft. (15·25 m.) 1,000 yds. (910 m.).

PROFILE PUBLICATIONS

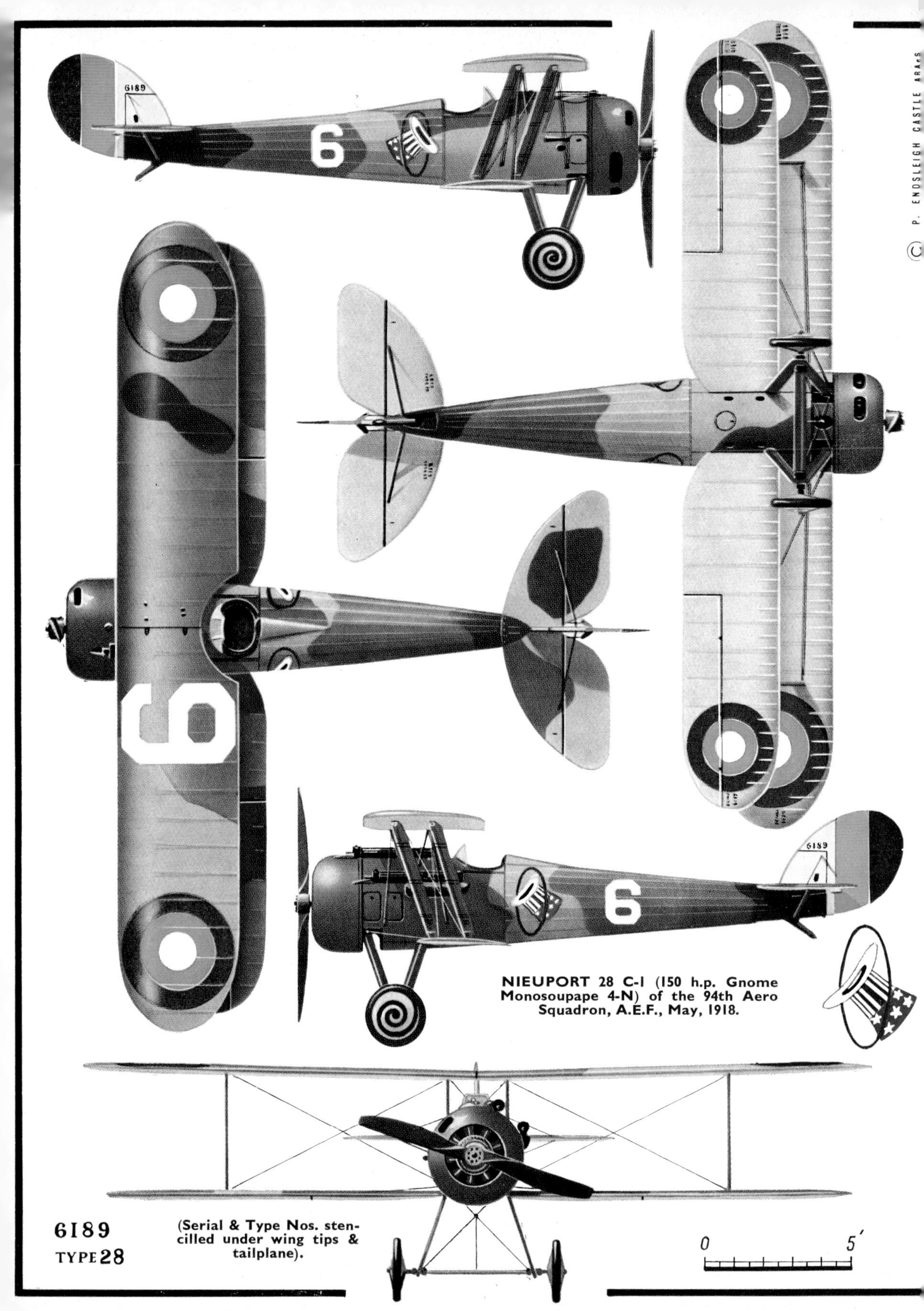

NIEUPORT 28 C-I (150 h.p. Gnome Monosoupape 4-N) of the 94th Aero Squadron, A.E.F., May, 1918.

6189
TYPE 28

(Serial & Type Nos. stencilled under wing tips & tailplane).

The Nieuport N.28C-I

by Peter M. Bowers

Production Nieuports of the 95th Aero Squadron, A.E.F., showing the upper wing raised above the fuselage while retaining the dihedral, and the initial application of American white-centre roundels to the underside of the upper wing. Since these machines had no brakes or steerable tailskids and the engines could not be throttled, it was necessary for mechanics to guide them during taxiing by holding on the wing struts. (Photo: U.S. Army Signal Corps)

The French Nieuport 28, properly designated N28C-1, is unique in aviation history for having achieved a considerable degree of fame that it didn't really deserve. The design, one of the long and famous line of Nieuport single-seaters, had been rejected as first-line equipment by the French Air Service. However, because of its availability in the absence of more suitable equipment, the 28 was supplied to the first pursuit squadrons of the American Expeditionary Forces early in 1918 and was therefore the first fighting plane to carry American colours into combat.

EVOLUTION OF THE DESIGN

The Nieuport 28, with its preceding and following models, is an excellent example of the step-by-step evolution of a single basic design to its point of ultimate development and then its transition into a new model to meet changing requirements. The first Nieuport to win fame as a fighter was the diminutive Model 11, a distinctive 80-h.p. sesquiplane. Both wings were nearly the same span, but the single-spar lower wing had less than half the chord of the upper and was therefore barely half a wing. This made the design a "Sesquiplane", or "1½ Winger", rather than a proper biplane. This basic configuration was retained for all production Nieuport models through the 27. There were minor variations in powerplant, seating, and wing area as determined by the mission of the particular model. The little Model 11 had only 13 square metres of wing area (140 sq. ft.) while some of the larger observation and trainer designs such as the Model 15 had 30 square metres (322 sq. ft.). Some-

Above, left: *The most famous fighting ancestor of the Nieuport 28—the Model 17.* (Photo: Signal Corps, U.S. Army). Right: *The beginning of the Nieuport 28—a modified Model 24 with 160-h.p. Gnôme engine and centre section struts altered to permit mounting of single Vickers machine gun outboard of the struts. New tail shape had appeared on Model 23.* (Photo: Nieuport)

Left: *Further evolution of the Model 28—a modified 24 with enlarged two-spar lower wing that increased the total wing area to eighteen square metres from the fifteen of the standard Model 24.* Right: *Original prototype of the Nieuport 28 with single machine gun and unique one-piece interplane struts.* (Photos: Nieuport)

Prototype Nieuport 28 showing absence of dihedral on upper wing. (Photo: Nieuport)

times the different models, especially at training schools, were referred to by their areas, as "15-Metre Nieuport" for the Model 21 trainer. Since they were also referred to by their actual model numbers, some confusion existed since there was a "23-Metre" model and a Model 23 in service at the same place and time.

The basic design philosophy of the Nieuport firm *Société Anonyme des Etablissements Nieuport* was to achieve maximum manœuvrability with relatively low power through use of light and simple construction. Consequently, the air-cooled rotary engine was used in all but a few two-seat observation designs that had power requirements beyond what could be delivered by the relatively low-powered rotaries. The concept of lightness extended even to the armament. Nieuport fighters were normally armed with a single machine gun long after other manufacturers had standardised on two.

The major changes between the Model 11 of 1915 and the following V-strut fighter model, the 16, was the substitution of a 110-h.p. Le Rhône for the original 80-h.p. version. The greater weight of the new engine was a distinct handicap to the lightweight 11/16 airframe, which had been named "Bebe" because of its relative size. The next model, the 17 (detailed in *Profile* No. 49), used the same 110-h.p. engine but was built to higher load factors. To retain the light wing loading necessary for maximum manœuvrability, the wing area was increased to 14·75 square metres (158 sq. ft.). This was frequently referred to as a "15-Metre Nieuport" in the schools along with the following 21, 23, 24, and 27 models. The lines of the 17 were improved by use of a completely circular cowling around the engine which was faired smoothly into the sides of the fuselage. The Model 21 was the 17 airframe fitted with the 80-h.p. Le Rhône for advanced training purposes. Some had the open bottom cowling of the 11/16 while others had the closed version of the 17.

Three major changes that marked the beginning of the 28 design appeared on the Model 23. Wings, cowling, and undercarriage were identical to those of the 17/21, but the fuselage streamlining was improved by the addition of plywood formers and wooden longitudinal stringers that rounded it out. An entirely new shape was adopted for the horizontal stabiliser and elevators, and the traditional one-piece Nieuport rudder was replaced by a rudder of entirely new shape that was fitted to a vertical fin. The main purpose of this feature was to give the pilot better "feel" of the rudder function in flight. The models 24 and 27 were

Modified Nieuport 28 prototype, still with single-unit interplane struts but dihedral added to top wing by shortening centre section struts and bringing wing down to fuselage. (Photo: Nieuport)

Nieuport 28 of 94th Pursuit Squadron forced down in enemy territory. Compare rudder striping with later models. Below: *A different view of the same machine. Apparently the Germans made a very hasty assembly for inspection purposes after bringing the machine to the rear area for the top wing is rigged with no dihedral while the lower wing droops.* (Photos: Official German)

outwardly identical to the 23, differing mainly in minor powerplant and equipment details. The exploits of the famous Charles Nungesser gave the 23 and 24 a measure of combat fame, but the major use of the 23, 24, and 27 was in the training schools. The British did use the 24 in combat, and even manufactured the design in England. The "24 bis" was a trainer from the start and used the older 17/21 tail surfaces on an otherwise standard 24 airframe. The 27 saw squadron service with both the French and Italians.

ENTER THE MODEL 28

Even before the 24s and 27s entered service, it was obvious that the basic V-strut sesquiplane design had reached the limit of its capabilities. One of the most obvious needs in a follow-on model was for increased wing area, since increased speed and rate of climb could best be obtained by using more powerful, and therefore heavier, powerplants. The first break with the sesquiplane tradition came with the installation of a larger two-spar lower wing on an experimental variant of a standard Model 24 that had been fitted with a new 160-h.p. Gnôme rotary engine. This increased the wing area to 18 sq. m. (193 sq. ft.). However, other changes were also needed to produce a good 160-h.p. fighter, so an entirely new prototype was built.

Early production Nieuport 28, serial number 6125, *in French markings and camouflage.* (Photo: Nieuport). Below: *Nieuport 28 of the 94th Pursuit Squadron on its back following a forced landing caused by engine failure, 18th April 1918. Note location of the squadron insignia.* (Photo: U.S. Army Signal Corps)

Late production Nieuport 28, serial number 6215, *showing correct form of U.S. tail striping.* (Photo: U.S. National Archives)

THE PROTOTYPE

The model that eventually became the 28 followed the same basic construction as its predecessors, a wire-braced four-longeron wood fuselage with fabric covering, wood frame wings and tail, and aluminium-tube undercarriage. The tail surfaces were identical to those of the 23/24/27 and the deep-chord cowling matched that of the experimental 24 variant. The fuselage was almost four feet longer than that of the V-strutters, and the longitudinal stringers carried the rounded cross-section clear under the fuselage instead of leaving a flat bottom. Since the fuselage was the same depth as before, it had a considerably slimmer look. Instead of metal turtledeck and side panels in the nose-cockpit area, a material rather like fibreboard was used. In thinner gauge, this same material was used to cover the tail surfaces. The major design change was in the wings, both of which were now two-spar type, with the chord of the lower nearly matching that of the upper. Both were fitted with graceful elliptical wing tip bows in contrast to the angular raked tips of the V-strutters. Total area was 20 sq. m. (215 sq. ft.). The original version of the prototype had no dihedral on either wing. The interplane struts were not individual pieces but formed a single "box" or parallelogram that eliminated the need for incidence and stagger wires and supposedly simplified the setting-up of the machine. As on earlier models, the upper wing was built in two sections that joined over the fuselage centre-line at a point inboard of the centre-section struts. Testing soon determined that dihedral was necessary, so some was added to the upper wing by shortening the centre-section struts and leaving the outer box struts the same size. This dihedral was retained on production models, but the entire upper wing was raised by lengthening all struts in order to improve the pilot's forward visibility and also make room for an additional machine gun.

POWERPLANT

The powerplant was the new nine-cylinder Gnôme 9-N rotary engine of 160–170 "questionable horsepower", the first Gnôme used on a production Nieuport since the early versions of the Model 10 two-seater used the 80-h.p. version in 1914. The reliability of the Gnôme, whatever the model, was never outstanding, and the corresponding Le Rhône model was preferred. Some of the chronic troubles were supposed to have been taken care of in the 160-h.p. model, which featured dual ignition. Since rotary engines were not fitted with the standard carburettors of the fixed models and could not be throttled down, both the Le Rhônes and the Gnômes had a "Blip Switch", a cut-off button on the control stick, that enabled the pilot to switch the engine off for brief intervals when it was desired to reduce power, as for landing. The Le Rhônes could be throttled to a degree, from their wide-open speed of some 1,250

Photo taken 5th May 1918. 95th Aero Squadron, Toul, France. (Photo: U.S. Army Signal Corps)

r.p.m. down to about 900 r.p.m. This low speed was enough to keep a light machine like the Nieuport flying, hence the need for the "on-off" operation for landing. The Gnôme, on the other hand, could not even be throttled to this degree. In addition to the single "on-off" switch, it had additional buttons on the control stick that enabled the pilot to cut out one or more cylinders for continuous running at lower power. To prevent flooding, fouling of the spark plugs, and the danger of fire in the cowling from unburned fuel, it was necessary to switch all cylinders back on at frequent intervals. This practice produced a very distinctive sound.

The late model Gnômes, starting with the single-ignition nine-cylinder 100-h.p. model, were known as "Monosoupapes". This meant that each cylinder was fitted with only one valve instead of the traditional two. Earlier models had the exhaust valve in the cylinder head but the intake valve was in the top of the piston, where it worked automatically as a result of differing pressures in the cylinder and in the crank-case into which the air-fuel mixture had been drawn somewhat in the manner of the well-known two-stroke-cycle engine. This feature had been trouble-some, so the intake valve was eliminated on the "Monosoupape" models. The fuel was passed into the cylinder through bypass ports similar to those of the two-stroke engines. All Gnômes were wasteful of fuel because of the passage of a certain amount of fuel mixture into the cylinder on the non-firing part of the cycle. Discharge of this unburned mixture into the cowling created a serious fire hazard.

ARMAMENT

In its original form, the new model (not yet called 28) carried only a single Vickers ·303 machine gun out-board of the left centre-section struts. This was soon seen to be inadequate, so when the upper wing was raised on the production models, a second Vickers was placed on top of the fuselage and a bit to the left of the centre-line. Some model plans show a third gun outside of the struts on the right side, but this is erronious. While the standard guns were the British Vickers, some of the American squadrons used the American Marlin for short periods. Nieuport 28s used for balloon-strafing missions were sometimes fitted with a single 11-mm. Vickers in the inboard location. Such guns were usually armed with incen-diary ammunition.

DESIGNATION AND SERIAL NUMBERS

As with other Nieuport experimental designs, the prototype 28 did not carry a standard designation when it was first designed and built. While there may have been a company designation for each production or experimental model, the well-known numbers associated with the Nieuports and contemporary French aircraft designs are those assigned by the French Air Force in sequence of acceptance from the various manufacturers. Although logical, the number "28" did not actually identify the 28th design accepted

Left: *An unarmed training squadron Nieuport 28 of the A.E.F. with the letters HELLO JOE painted along the length of the fuselage.* Right: *Another unarmed and uncamouflaged trainer with a painted serpent encircling the fuselage and the name of THEDA BARA, the leading film "vamp" of the period, lettered between the wings. Tail stripes painted out, but U.S. roundel still under upper wing.* (Photo: courtesy Col. Wm. Guier)

U.S. Navy Nieuport 28 with flotation gear, star insignia, and reduced-size tail stripes. (Photo: U.S. Navy)

from Nieuport. Nieuport's own Model 10 was in service before the official system was adopted, so the official system started there.

The manufacturer was identified by a letter in the official system, "N" in the case of the Nieuports. This was to be painted in a fairly large size in black near the top of the white rudder stripe, and was to be followed by the model and type designation either adjacent to or below it. Nieuport was rather non-conformist, and generally skipped the model-type data, using only the serial number below the "N". The proper designation should be 28C-1, the 28 indicating the sequence of model procurement, the type letter "C" designating a "Chasse" (Pursuit) airplane, and the figure "1" that it was a single-seater. Nieuport sometimes used the model number on the rudder, but called it a "type" number and placed it near the bottom, as "Type 28". However, this lettering was widely used over the rest of the airplane in conjunction with the serial number. This was largely because the jigs and tooling of the time did not make for good interchangeability of major components. Parts were hand-fitted to each machine, and the ailerons of one might, but probably would not, fit another. Each removable component, therefore, carried both the Nieuport "Type" number and the serial number. For the 28, this was on the underside of each upper wing near the tip, in approximately the same location under the lower wing but with the numbers on the wing directly adjacent to those on the aileron, under the horizontal stabiliser and one elevator in adjacent positions, and on each side of the fuselage just beneath the leading edge of the horizontal stabiliser. These figures appeared in the following form:

6125
TYPE 28

The serial number indicated the sequence of procurement by the French Air Force from a particular manufacturer, not total aircraft procurement as in the case of U.S. and British systems. In the case of Nieuports, it was not a useful guide to sequence of models or to distinguish, say, late model 17s with rounded fuselages from the Model "24 bis". The prototype Model 28, after acceptance, carried serial number *4434*. A Model 23 flown by Nungesser carried serial number *5324*, a Model 24 carried *4445*, a 27 carried *6100*, and a late-production 21 trainer carried *7000*. The earliest known serial for a production 28 is *6125* and the earliest seen on an A.E.F. machine is *6189*. While the American services had their own serial numbering systems it was not applied to aircraft obtained from the Allies during the war. Even these Nieuport 28s taken to the United States by the Army after the Armistice continued to use the original French-assigned numbers. However, these turned over to the U.S. Navy were given new Navy serial numbers, *5794* through *5805*, for the 12 machines transferred.

MARKINGS AND COLOURING

The prototype and some production 28s were painted in the characteristic Nieuport silver-grey, but the

Left: *Beginning of the end—little trace of the original Model 28 remains in this experimental Nieuport powered with a 180-h.p. Gnôme fitted with a laminated wood fuselage that was soon to be seen on the production Model 29.* Right: *Further departure from the 28—a modified 28 fuselage fitted with wings of increased area, revised dihedral arrangement, and an 11-cylinder 200-h.p. Clerget rotary engine.* (Photos: Nieuport)

A post-war civilian conversion with an 80-h.p. Le Rhône engine. Although carrying French registration, this must have been an A.E.F. left-over because the "Lift Here" placards on the fuselage are in English. (Photo: SAFARA)

combat models used the standard French upper surface and side camouflage pattern of greens and browns with the undersurfaces of wings and tail clear-doped. The Nieuport V-strutters, along with a few other French near-sesquiplane designs, carried standard French roundels on the underside of the upper wing as well as on the top, and duplicated the undersurface application on the narrow-chord bottom wing. This practice became a Nieuport habit, for when new designs with wide-chord lower wings came along roundels were still carried under the upper wingtips. Early deliveries to the A.E.F. carried the American white-centre circles under the upper wing, but the practice was discontinued at American request. When Nieuports, V-strut models included, were re-covered or repainted at American bases, the roundels were not re-applied to the underside of the upper wing. Neither the French nor the Americans used roundels on the side of the fuselage in standard practice.

The earlier Nieuport models, without fixed vertical fin, applied the rudder stripes to the full width of the rudder. For the French and British, this put the red at the trailing edge. When the vertical fin was added on Model 23, old habits died hard and the stripes were again applied over the full width of the entire vertical surface. When the Americans adopted a new circular marking to replace the white star of 1917, they picked the old Russian marking, which had a red outer circle, a blue, and then a white centre. Russia had just been knocked out of the war, so this marking was available. Since the other Allies had their tail striping in the same sequence of colours as their wing and fuselage roundels, the French factories made a rather logical mistake in applying tail stripes to the original American orders. They put the tail stripes on in the order of red, blue, and white, starting at the trailing edge, when the new American striping order was actually blue, white, and red, starting at the rear. This rudder stripe reversal had been made to distinguish the American machines from the French and British, both of which started with red at the trailing edge of the rudder. The first two Squadrons of A.E.F. Nieuports went into action with this marking and the error was not corrected until later deliveries were made to the training schools.

Individual aircraft in the American squadrons were marked with large block numbers on each side of the fuselage and on the upper and lower wings. Application of the wing numbers was not consistent, sometimes being on the left wing and sometimes on the

Left: *U.S. Navy Nieuport 28 on gun turret of the battleship* Arizona. *Such use of airplanes, tried by French and British as well as U.S. Navies, was short-lived.* Right: *Top view of silver-painted Nieuport 28 on battleship* Arizona. *The original wartime roundels show through the post-war star-in-circle markings on the wings. Tail stripes on this particular model are still in the original Nieuport width.* (Photos: U.S. Navy)

right, but the fuselage number was always aft of the squadron insignia. Two squadrons went into action without squadron insignia, which consisted of an Indian head for the 27th Squadron, an American "Hat-in-the-Ring" for the 94th, a kicking Army mule for the 95th, and a Scotty dog for the 147th. Squadron insignia was not authorised for pursuit squadrons until a particular squadron had won three victories or else had been given a specific citation for distinguished service by higher authority. On the Nieuports, the squadron insignia was carried on the fabric just aft of the cockpit.

The Nieuport 28s taken to the United States in 1919 were mostly repainted in the standard U.S. Army olive drab all over, the white stars replaced the roundels on the wings, and the tail striping was switched back to red at the trailing edge and reduced in size to cover only the rudder. The Navy machines likewise changed to the star and reversed tail stripes, but were repainted in the over-all light grey that was standard Navy colouring at the time. Photos indicate that at least one of the Navy-painted Nieuports carried the full-width rudder stripes for a while.

The next production Nieuport—the Model 29. Laminated wood veneer fuselage had been tested on an earlier experimental model. The only Model 28 design feature carried over to this 300-h.p. model was the dihedral on the upper wing. (Photo: P. M. Bowers' collection)

Clipped-wing I-strut civil Nieuport 28 used in the 1931 film "Dawn Patrol". (Photo: R. R. Martin)

PRODUCTION

Although ordered into production by the French, the 28 did not prove to be a desirable combat type in spite of its performance gain over earlier models. Other designs, notably the Spad XIII (*Profile* No. 17) proved more suitable, and if it had not been for the extreme need of the A.E.F., Nieuport would have found itself out of the fighter plane business as far as its own designs were concerned. Some 297 28s were delivered to the Americans so that their pursuit squadrons could take to the air. The Spad was the better machine, but all production was committed to the French at the time. Even Nieuport, after completing Model 28 deliveries to the A.E.F., retooled its fighter line and delivered 700 Spad XIIIs.

Nieuport 28 with further modifications used in the film "Lost Squadron". Rudder area has been reduced and shallow-chord cowling from a Thomas-Morse S-4C has replaced the deep-chord cowling, although the Gnôme engine has been retained. Marlin machine gun is improperly located. (Photo: P.M. Bowers' collection)

COMBAT USE

The entry of the A.E.F. into combat with its Nieuport 28s was anything but spectacular. Four squadrons of the First Pursuit Group used the 28—the 27th, 94th, 95th, and the 147th. The first to reach the front were the 94th and the 95th, which shared an aerodrome at Villeneuve. The 95th arrived first, at the end of

Non-flying Nieuports in the 1937 remake of "Dawn Patrol" Errol Flynn seated in the first machine, which has full-span wings and steel-tube N-struts. David Niven in the second, with clipped wings and N-struts. Next are two clipped-wing I-strut 28s and then three Thomas-Morse S-4Cs. Lettering on tail of Flynn's machine copied from a Nieuport 24E-1 (E: Entrainment, or trainer) and then misread, for the full designation appears as "Nie 24EL" instead of E-1. Marlin guns above the wing are strictly Hollywood hokum. (Photo: courtesy Walter Jeffries)

February 1918, and made its first patrol over the lines on 15th March. The planes had been delivered without guns, hence the delay in starting operations. Finally, in desperation, Major Raoul Lufbery, veteran of the Lafayette *Escadrille*, led an unarmed patrol to the lines on 15th March. This was strictly in the interest of squadron morale and to show that the Air Service, A.E.F., was finally ready for action. However, just at this time, someone discovered that the personnel of the 95th had not received any gunnery training, so the squadron was sent back to gunnery school and did not return to the front until 2nd May.

The 94th fared somewhat better. Although galled by the fact that the 95th had been the first to reach the front, the 94th made the first combat patrol and drew first blood. Like the 95th, it had received airplanes without guns and had made its first unarmed patrol on 6th March. The guns arrived on 13th April, but the squadron had received orders to transfer to Toul, so did not fly armed patrols from Villeneuve. The first armed patrol was made from Toul on 14th April 1918. Captain Peterson led a flight of three Nieuport 28s, the others piloted by Lt. Edward V. Rickenbacker and Lt. Reed Chambers. Foggy weather caused Peterson to turn back immediately after take-off. Rickenbacker and Chambers did not notice his departure (so they said) and continued the patrol alone but made no contact with the enemy. Just after this patrol returned to the aerodrome, two German single seaters, apparently lost in the poor visibility, appeared over the field. The two pilots of the second patrol, Lt. Alan Winslow and Lt. Douglas Campbell, jumped into their waiting Nieuports and gave chase. Winslow scored the first victory for the A.E.F. by shooting down a Pfalz DIII in flames while Campbell, who was also destined to become America's first Ace, forced an Albatros DVa to crash-land minutes later.

While a great morale-builder, this victory did no particular credit to the Nieuport 28. The Germans were the victims of surprise more than anything else, and even if there had been a dog-fight, the Pfalz and Albatros were both 1917 models that were becoming second-class equipment at the time. In addition to being outclassed as a fighter by the new German Fokker DVII (*Profile* No. 25) that reached the front shortly after the Americans, the Nieuport 28 had other shortcomings. Aside from the troublesome Gnôme engine, the 28 had a tendency to shed its upper wing fabric during an extended dive. Sometimes this took all the ribs ahead of the front spar with it. Lt. Jimmy Meissner was the first to encounter the problem. During a fight with two Albatros DVa's on 2nd May, he managed to shoot one down after chasing it through a long dive. During his pull-up, he noticed the fabric stripping off the left upper wing and starting to repeat the process on the right wing. He nursed the crippled machine back across the lines and crash-landed it in the American forward area. The same thing happened to him again during a loop in a dogfight at 4,000 ft., but this time he managed to fly the machine all the way home. The same characteristic was responsible for the capture of Lt. James Norman Hall, a former Lafayette *Escadrille* pilot attached to the 94th squadron. (He later became a world-famous author, not only of W.W.I flying books but the notable "Mutiny on the Bounty".) Loss of fabric during a dive forced him to crash-land in German territory. The Nieuport flipped on to its back and Hall was a prisoner for the duration. Eddie Rickenbacker, too, who was to become America's Ace-of-Aces, flew a Nieuport 28 home sans upper wing fabric. By the time a suitable fix was developed, the Nieuport was being replaced by the Spad XIII. This was on 17th July 1918. Much as they had cursed the Nieuports, the Americans were not overjoyed with the Spads. While they would hold together under any treatment that could be given them, they did not have the manœuvrability of the Nieuports and the geared Hispano-Suiza engine was almost as great a

Clipped-wing Nieuport 28 with I-*struts currently owned and flown by Tallmantz Aviation of Santa Ana, California. Indian head insignia is supposed to represent Lafayette Escadrille (which did not use 28s) and tail stripes are confined to rudder only.*
(Photo: Lee Enich)

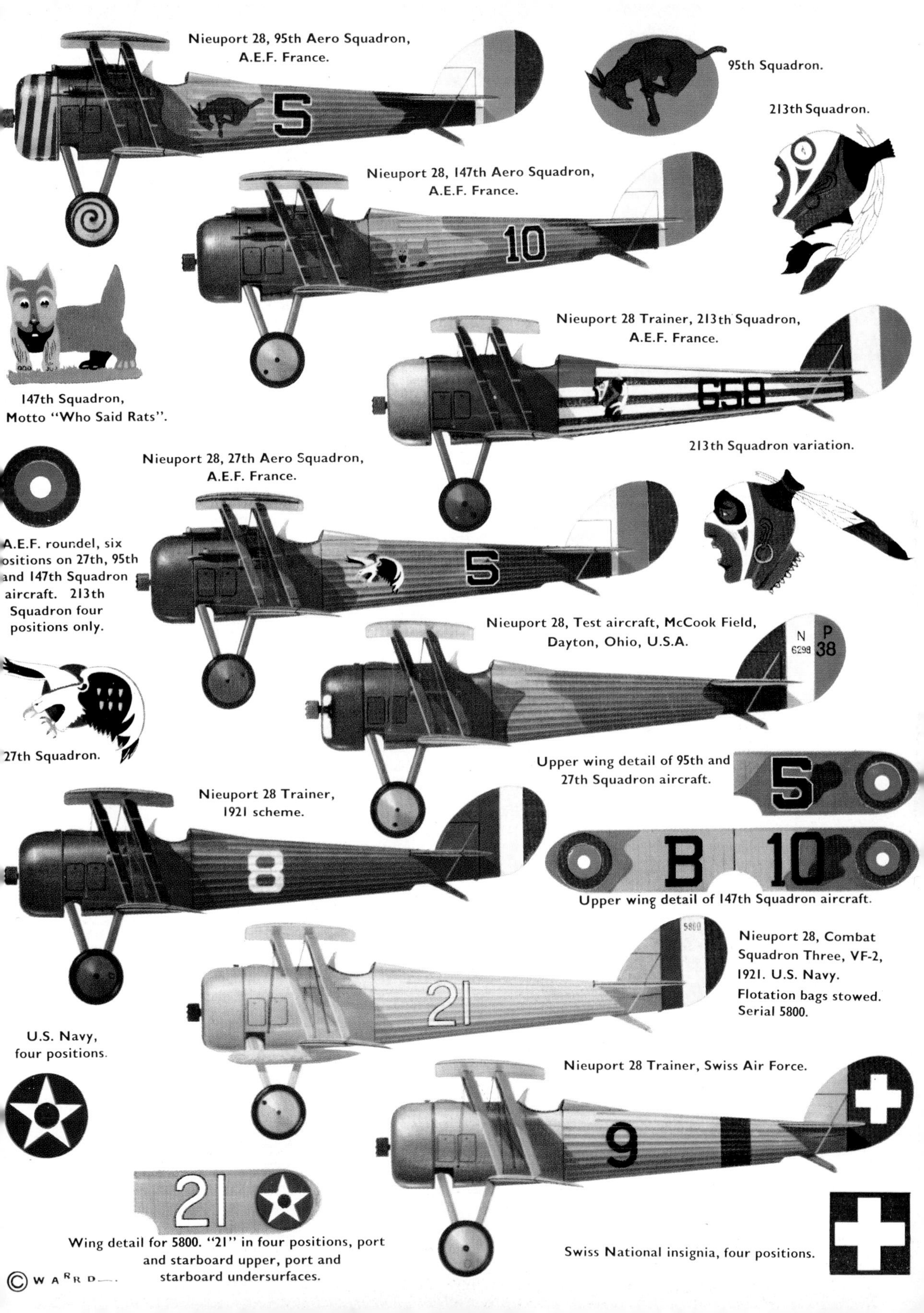
Nieuport 28, 95th Aero Squadron, A.E.F. France.
95th Squadron.
213th Squadron.
Nieuport 28, 147th Aero Squadron, A.E.F. France.
147th Squadron, Motto "Who Said Rats".
Nieuport 28 Trainer, 213th Squadron, A.E.F. France.
213th Squadron variation.
Nieuport 28, 27th Aero Squadron, A.E.F. France.
A.E.F. roundel, six positions on 27th, 95th and 147th Squadron aircraft. 213th Squadron four positions only.
Nieuport 28, Test aircraft, McCook Field, Dayton, Ohio, U.S.A.
27th Squadron.
Upper wing detail of 95th and 27th Squadron aircraft.
Nieuport 28 Trainer, 1921 scheme.
Upper wing detail of 147th Squadron aircraft.
Nieuport 28, Combat Squadron Three, VF-2, 1921. U.S. Navy. Flotation bags stowed. Serial 5800.
U.S. Navy, four positions.
Nieuport 28 Trainer, Swiss Air Force.
Wing detail for 5800. "21" in four positions, port and starboard upper, port and starboard undersurfaces.
Swiss National insignia, four positions.
© WARD

Restored Nieuport 28 with standard wings and struts owned and flown by Cole Palen of Old Rhinebeck, New York. Markings are authentic, but machine is not camouflaged. Note how far propeller hub projects ahead of shallow-chord Thomas -Morse cowling.
(Photo: E. M. Sommerich collection)

source of trouble as the Monosoupape Gnôme had been.

In spite of maintaining a favourable ratio of victories to losses, the American squadrons suffered some notable losses. Lt. Quentin Roosevelt of the 95th, son of former president Theodore Roosevelt, fell to the guns of a Fokker DVII on 14th July 1918, and Lufbery himself, with 18 confirmed victories and probably as many more scored deep in enemy territory where they were unconfirmed, was shot down right over the Toul Aerodrome on 19th May. He had taken off to engage a German two-seater. In the combat, his machine was hit and set afire. In spite of his oft-proclaimed intention to try and ride a "flamer" down, he chose to jump at low altitude when it became obvious that he could not land his blazing machine.

POSTWAR USE

Twelve of the 50 or more Nieuport 28's brought to the U.S. in 1919 were turned over to the U.S. Navy, which put them to a most unique use—they were flown from platforms built over the forward turret guns of battleships. Their light weight and quick acceleration suited them for this mission. Because of the possibility of a water landing, some of these machines were fitted with hydrovanes ahead of the undercarriage to keep them from nosing over and with flotation gear that could be inflated by compressed air after landing to keep them afloat. The Army models saw short service as trainers and were then scrapped.

A few, however, found their way into the hands of civilian owners and began a new career. Some were apparently used for racing, for their wing spans were decreased by five feet and the parallel wing struts were replaced by a single L-strut. By the late 1920's, air-war movies were becoming increasingly popular, and many W.W.I vintage aircraft were taken to Hollywood to perform before the cameras. Unfortunately, many were deliberately destroyed in crash scenes. At least five of the Nieuport 28's, including three clipped-wing L-strut models, one clipped-wing model with steel-tube N-struts, and a full span model also with N-struts, appeared in numerous pictures. The last film in which this many appeared together was the original production of "Dawn Patrol", made in 1931. Four of the five appeared in the remake of 1937, but were used only in ground scenes, the flying scenes involving actual old airplanes being re-runs of the 1931 footage.

One Nieuport remains in Hollywood in flyable condition, the clipped-wing N-strut model, owned by Tallmantz Aviation at Orange County Airport, Santa Ana, California. Two of the clipped-wing I-strutters in "Basket Case" condition are also owned by the firm. The long-wing version was traded to Cole Palen of Old Rhinebeck, New York, for other machines needed in the 1957 movie "Spirit of St. Louis". Mr. Palen has since restored this 28 to flyable condition and has reverted to the original parallel wood struts. One unmodified model, formerly on display in the Jarret Museum of W.W.I history but now in "Basket Case" condition, is owned by Mr. Ned Kensinger, who hopes eventually to restore it. One other Nieuport 28 is rumoured to exist in the United States, but no others are known outside of that country.

NIEUPORT 28 SPECIFICATIONS

Wing span (upper and lower) ...	26 ft. 3 in.
Length	20 ft. 4 in.
Wing area... ...	215 sq. ft.
Empty weight ...	1,172 lb.
Gross weight ...	1,625 lb.
Stagger	23 in.
Dihedral	1 deg. 10 min.
Powerplant ...	Gnôme 9-N, 165-h.p. at 1,380 r.p.m.
Wing loading ...	7·6 lb. per sq. ft.
Fuel capacity ...	30 U.S. gallons
Oil capacity ...	5 U.S. gallons
Top speed... ...	122 m.p.h.
Landing speed ...	53·7 m.p.h.
Rate of climb ...	5,000 ft. in 4·5 min. 10,000 ft. in 11·5 min.
Endurance... ...	1 hr. 30 min.
Service ceiling ...	17,000 ft.
Standard armament	Two ·303 Vickers M.G.

PRINTED IN ENGLAND © Profile Publications Ltd., P.O. Box 26, 1a North Street, Leatherhead, Surrey, England.
Printed by Hills & Lacy Ltd., London and Watford, England. U.S. 2nd Class Mailing Rates applied for.

PROFILE
PUBLICATIONS

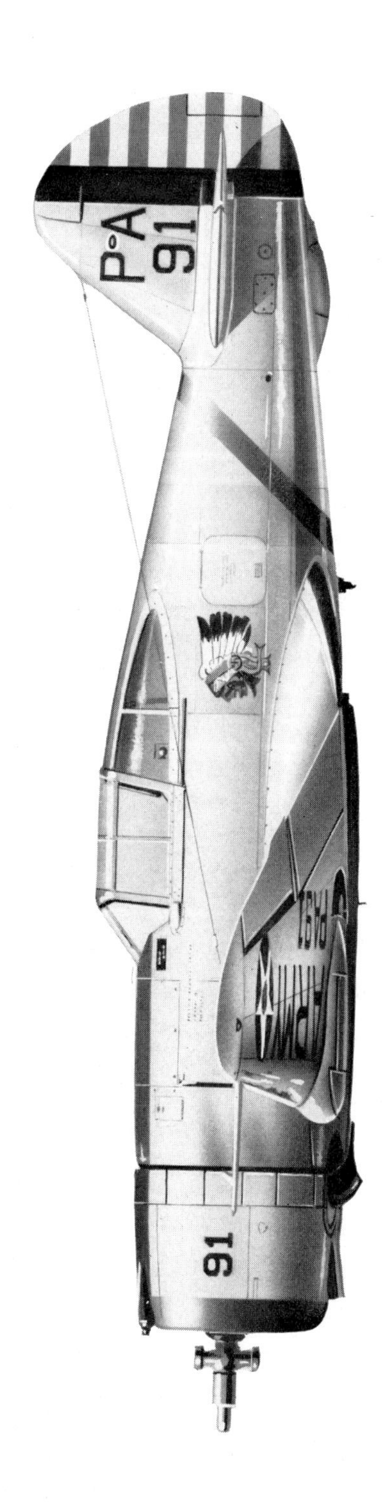

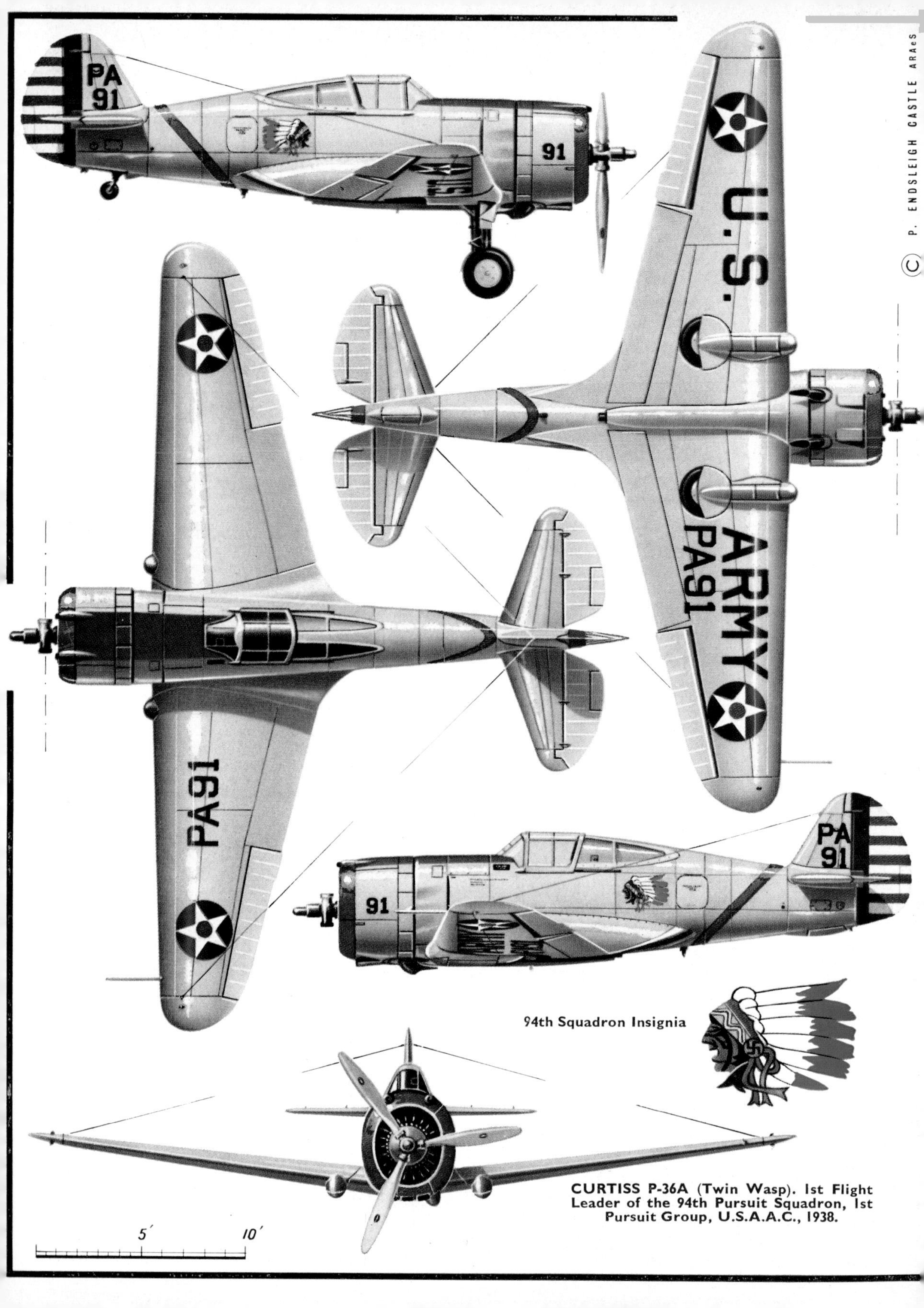

CURTISS P-36A (Twin Wasp). 1st Flight Leader of the 94th Pursuit Squadron, 1st Pursuit Group, U.S.A.A.C., 1938.

The Curtiss Hawk 75

by Peter M. Bowers

Y1P-36, one of three service-test Curtiss 75s ordered as a result of the design competition. The arrowhead insignia on the fuselage is the emblem of Wright Field, the Air Corps Test Centre. (Photo: U.S.A.F.)

The Curtiss Model 75, known to the U.S. Army Air Corps as the P-36 and to the R.A.F. as the "Mohawk", was the first of the "Modern" single-seat fighters to enter U.S. military service. In accordance with the Air Corps policy of the time, it was developed simultaneously with a similar model, the Seversky P-35. While both were great advances over their immediate predecessor, the Boeing P-26 (*Profile* No. 14), they were obsolescent by the time the U.S. entered W.W.II. P-35s were the main defensive force in the Philippines while P-36s fought the Japanese at Pearl Harbour. Those models still in U.S. service after the opening months of U.S. involvement were relegated to training duties while those that had been delivered to other nations were likewise withdrawn from active combat areas, except in the case of Finland, by the end of 1942.

However, the exported Curtiss 75s saw wide military service in all theatres of the war and probably served in more different air forces than any other pre-W.W.II design. The fortunes of war put the Hawk 75 in a unique situation—significant numbers were used by both sides at various times during the war.

ORIGIN OF THE DESIGN

By 1930 it had become apparent that the traditional fighter biplane had nearly reached the limit of its development. Such refinements as enclosed cockpit and retractable undercarriage could do little to prolong its life in the rapidly advancing age of the speedy monoplane. The United States was the first to put fighter monoplanes into full-scale military service. Curtiss and Boeing both developed experimental prototypes for evaluation, but only the Boeing, designated the P-26, was adopted. This was strictly a transitional design, and had many features that placed it simultaneously in both the "Old" and the "New" design eras. However, the P-26 gave the Air Corps experience with the new fighter monoplane and a clearer picture of just what its design requirements were. These resulted in the establishment of a design competition, to be held in 1935. Eventually, four competitors were to appear—Curtiss, with an entirely new Model 75; Seversky, with a fighter version of the famous two-seat amphibian of 1933; Chance Vought, with the V-141, an improved version of the Northrop Model 3A that it had purchased from Northrop; and Consolidated, with a single-seat conversion of the then standard PB-2A two-seat fighter.

The first Hawk 75A-1 built for France, photographed during the initial test-flying period when the only markings carried were French tail stripes. Apart from modified armament and a commercial powerplant, the export 75A series was similar to the U.S. Army Air Corps P-36A. (Photo: Curtiss-Wright)

The Curtiss design was not only new as far as the Air Corps was concerned, it was new for Curtiss. None of its major features were to be found in earlier company products. Even the powerplant was new. This was a 14-cylinder twin-row air-cooled Wright radial of 1,670 cubic inch displacement producing 900 h.p. The aircraft structure was all metal with metal skin on all but the movable control surfaces, which were fabric covered. Portions of the outer wing structure were sealed to provide flotation in case of forced landing in water. Hydraulically-actuated split flaps were fitted to the trailing edge of the wing. The Curtiss 75's undercarriage was unique among the competitors. The single strut under each wing rotated aft hydraulically to place the wheel inside the wing, but at the same time, pivoted about its axis to turn the wheel ninety degrees so that it would lay flat in the thinner aft portion of the wing. The Seversky rotated the strut aft in the same manner but did not pivot it, so half of the wheel projected into the airstream. The Vought and Consolidated designs retracted the wheel inward towards the fuselage so that the wheels lay flat. Vought later adopted the Curtiss system for the SB2U

The original form of the Curtiss 75 prototype as entered in the Air Corps design competition of May 1935, with the twin-row Wright R-1690 powerplant. (Photo: Curtiss-Wright)

"Chesapeake" and F4U "Corsair". Actually, although not used by that manufacturer, the "Swing-aft-and-pivot" undercarriage had been developed by Boeing, which received a royalty for all installations used by other manufacturers.

The armament of the Curtiss, and the other competitors, followed the U.S. standard that had prevailed since shortly after W.W.I—a single ·30 calibre and a single ·50 calibre machine gun synchronised to fire through the propeller. New European designs then in the development stages featured far greater firepower, but the U.S. held to the same standard for several more years.

The Curtiss 75 was the only competitor ready on the contest date of May 1935. The Seversky was not ready in time and was granted a delay to August, much to Curtiss' chagrin. Preliminary testing by the Air Corps revealed many shortcomings in each design that were cause for rejection as a service fighter, so a postponement was granted to allow each manufacturer to make improvements. Both changed engines; the Seversky replaced its 850-h.p. 9-cylinder Wright "Cyclone" radial with a 14-cylinder twin-row Pratt & Whitney R-1830 "Twin Wasp" of the same power while Curtiss replaced the experimental Wright R-1670 with virtually the same Wright "Cyclone" that Seversky had abandoned. In its final version, the Curtiss 75 prototype was known as Model 75B. The other competitors were on hand for the final judging, and the winner was the Seversky. A production order was placed for seventy-seven production versions under the designation of P-35. A few months later, Curtiss was given a Service Test order for three "Twin Wasp"-powered versions of the 75B under the designation of Y1P-36. While there had been an experimental prototype, there never was an actual XP-36 designation because the machine was company-owned and did not carry a military designation.

CURTISS MODEL 75 DEVELOPMENT

Some confusion has prevailed over the years as to the proper designation of the Curtiss Model 75 and its many variations. This resulted from different organisations within the company handling the designations a bit differently. In company advertising of the period, the fixed-undercarriage export models were mostly referred to as "Model 75" while the export models with retractable undercarriage similar to the prototype and the production P-36 were known as "Model 75A". Actually, 75A was an intermediate designation used before the final configuration of the prototype appeared in the form of the 75B. There were many other sub-designations assigned by the engineering department and used for detailed identification within the factory. The entire 75 series is detailed in the following paragraphs, which also cover the service histories of each sub-model.

MODEL 75. First prototype. Design initiated in 1934, with actual construction beginning in November. Flight testing began in May 1935. This was a company-owned machine and did not carry military markings. The civil registration number was X-17Y,

The 75 prototype in its final form, March 1936; the twin-row engine replaced by a single-row Wright "Cyclone", and slight recesses in the fuselage aft of the pilot's head to give a degree of rear vision. (Photo: Curtiss-Wright)

Curtiss Model 75E, one of three tested by the Air Corps as Y1P-36. The machine illustrated, serial 37-68, *has been fitted with an experimental four-blade Curtiss electric propeller.* (Photo: U.S.A.F.)

which, by coincidence, immediately preceded that of the Seversky design, which carried X-18Y. The designation "Hawk 75" was used by the sales and publicity departments when referring to the simplified fixed-undercarriage versions of the design.

MODEL 75A. Intermediate designation of the prototype during the Air Corps competition but best known as the principal designation of the export versions of the retractable-undercarriage design. These export models had the basic model number preceded by the prefix "H" as follows:

H75A-1. 100 equivalents of the standard Air Corps P-36A ordered by France in May 1938, but using the 1,050-h.p. P. & W. R-830-SC-3G "Twin Wasp" engine. Detail differences were the fitting of two 7·5-mm. Browning machine guns in the nose and an additional 7·5-mm. gun in each outer wing panel. Instrumentation was in the metric system and some of the furnishing and equipment were to French, rather than U.S., standards, including a reverse-acting throttle. As delivered from the factory, the H75A-1s were finished in natural metal with French roundels on wings only and the standard French stripes on the rudder. The manufacturer, model designation, and serial number were spelled out in black on each side of the rudder as follows:

CURTISS
H75-C1
No. 77

The C-1 was the standard French abbreviation for a *Chasse*, or pursuit, machine while the figure 1 indicated it to be a single seater. The number 77 identified the seventy-seventh machine of that model built for the Armée de l'Air.

The first victories of the French over German aircraft in W.W.II were won by H75A-1s over the Western Front on 8th September 1939. However, the "Hawks" were outmatched by the standard German fighter of the time, the Messerschmitt Bf-109E. After the collapse of French resistance, those "Hawks" which had not escaped to unoccupied French territory, North Africa, or England were taken over by the Luftwaffe. Unsuitable for anything but training by Western European standards, some found their way back to combat areas following sale to Finland. A few H74A-1s that came under British control were taken

Left: *Hawk H75A-2 of* l'Armée de l'Air*; compare wide rudder stripes with those on the aircraft illustrated at the foot of page 3, where the stripes were kept aft of the rudder hinge line.* (Photo: courtesy Charles W. Cain.) Right: *A Cyclone-powered H75A-4 taken over by the* Luftwaffe *for training use after the fall of France in 1940.* (Photo: courtesy H. J. Nowarra)

Left: *A Cyclone-powered H75A-4 taken into the Royal Air Force as "Mohawk IV". Cyclone variants could be identified by the larger diameter, narrower-chord cowling, and the absence of "blisters" over the nose gun muzzles.* (Photo: Crown Copyright.) Right: *An H75A in the markings adopted by the Finnish Air Force subsequent to 4th September 1944. Germany sold thirty-six "Twin-Wasp"-powered H75A-1s, -2s and -3s from France and eight H75A-6s from Norway to Finland for use against the Russians.* (Photo: courtesy Charles W. Cain)

P-36A of the 94th Pursuit Squadron, First Pursuit Group. The squadron is identified by the insignia, the Group by the letters on the tail. The aft-sloping fuselage stripe identifies the leader of "C" Flight. (Photo: U.S.A.F.)

into the R.A.F. as "Mohawk Is".

H75A-2. An additional 100 "Hawks" on 1938 French orders, similar to the -1 except for the use of a 1,050-h.p. P. & W. R-1830-S1C3G engine, which made it more like the Air Corps' P-36A. The armament was increased by an additional 7·5-mm. Browning in each wing, matching the firepower of the experimental XP-36D. French serial numbering of the -2s continued from where it had ended at the last -1, and again initial delivery was in natural metal finish. The combat record of the -2 was the same as the -1, with those impressed into the R.A.F. after evacuation from France becoming Mohawk IIs.

H75A-3. A further 135 "Hawks" identical to the -2s except for an improved 1,200-h.p. P. & W. R-1830-SC3G engine. Since deliveries were under way at the time of the French capitulation, many were undelivered. Some that were en route at the time were diverted to French possessions. Some merely rotted away where they were unloaded while others were evacuated from the West Indies to Morocco, where they were refurbished and used for training by the Free French forces. Those still in the factory when France fell were delivered to England as Mohawk IIIs.

The Mohawk IIIs were refitted with British equipment, including ·303 calibre Browning machine guns. Since they were inferior to the Hurricanes and Spitfires then in service, they were used for reserve duties prior to being shipped to India early in 1942. Earlier, a number had been sent to South Africa while others went to Portugal.

H75A-4. The final French order was for 395 -4s powered with the 1,200-h.p. "Cyclone" R-1820-G205A and equipped and armed as the -2s and -3s. Those taken over by the R.A.F. became Mohawk IV and were treated the same as the IIIs. A single "Cyclone" Hawk, not actually an H75A-4, was built in India by the Hindustan Aircraft Company as the first of forty-eight to be built under licence from Curtiss. When the programme was discontinued, the single pilot model was impressed into the R.A.F.

H75A-5. Curtiss built only one "Cyclone"-powered H75A-5. This machine was supplied as a pilot model to the Chinese Government along with materials kits for an unspecified number of similar machines. Considering the conditions in wartime China, it is not surprising that nothing has been heard of the accomplishments of the H75A-5.

H75A-6. Twenty-four "Twin Wasp" Hawks armed with four 7·9 mm. Brownings ordered by Norway. Deliveries were interrupted by the German invasion. Some of the delivered machines were taken over by the *Luftwaffe* and eight were eventually sold to Finland. Others still in the United States were diverted to Free Norwegian forces in Canada for use as trainers.

H75A-7. Twenty "Cyclone" - powered "Hawks" ordered by the Netherlands were diverted to the Netherlands East Indies after German occupation of the home country and saw combat against the Japanese.

H75A-8. Thirty-six additional "Hawks" ordered by Norway, differing from the -6s in having two 12·7-mm.

Y1P-36 37-68 *with the first co-axial propeller to be fitted to an American aeroplane.* (Photo: U.S.A.F.)

Below: *P-36A with revised tail designator of the 1940–41 period; the 51st aircraft in the 56th Pursuit Group.* (Photo: the author)

Curtiss Model 75H, first demonstrator of a simplified export version marketed as the "Hawk 75". This Cyclone-powered demonstrator was bought by China and presented to General Claire Chennault by Madame Chiang Kai Shek. (Photo: Curtiss-Wright)

nose guns and "Cyclone" engines. Six were delivered to the Norwegians in Canada while the remaining thirty were impressed into the U.S. Army Air Corps and given the designation of P-36G (serial numbers *42-38305/38322*, *42-108995/109006*). All but two of these were sent to Peru on Lend-Lease.

H75A-9. Ten "Cyclone"-powered "Hawks" similar to 75A-4s were delivered to Iran (formerly Persia). British forces occupied the country before the machines were uncrated and set up. They were re-shipped to India and impressed into the R.A.F. as Mohawks.

MODEL 75B. Final "Cyclone"-powered version of the prototype as flown in the final stages of the Air Corps' fighter competition in April 1936, still in civil markings. After the competition, this machine continued to be used by the Curtiss company for test and demonstration.

MODEL 75E. No C or D variants were built, the designations being assigned to studies. Model 75E was the factory designation for the three service-test Y1P-36 models. Except for the P. & W. R-1830-13 "Twin Wasp" engine, these were essentially the same as the 75B. Minor refinements were noticeable in the form of a retractable tail wheel and transparent panels at each side of the pilot's headrest to permit a degree

Left: *Curtiss Model 75I, ordered by the Air Corps as XP-37 to evaluate the new Allison V-1710 engine in a contemporary fighter design.* (Photo: Curtiss-Wright.) Right: *YP-37* 38-484, *one of thirteen ordered to service-test the Allison-engined version of the Curtiss Model 75. The designator letters on the tail indicate the 141st aircraft in the 10th Air Base Squadron at Chanute Field, Illinois, the Air Corps Service-Test Centre.* (Photo: the author)

P-36A 38-180 *assigned to Wright Field for test work; a rigid landing gear fitted with streamlined metal skis has been installed.* (Photo: U.S.A.F.)

of rearward visibility. Following completion of the service testing, which began in February 1937, the Y1P-36s were redesignated plain P-36. Army serial numbers were *37-68* to *37-70*.

MODEL 75H. In 1937 Curtiss produced a simplified and lighter export version of the 75B that was fitted with a rigid undercarriage. Two demonstrators were built under the designation of 75H. The first one, registered *NR-1276*, carried Chinese markings and was bought by the Chinese Government. This was eventually presented to General Clair Chennault, formerly of the U.S. Army Air Corps, who was reorganising the Chinese Air Force before achieving his later fame as leader of the "Flying Tigers" and the 14th U.S. Air Force. The second demonstrator, registered *NR-1276*, carried Argentine markings and was sold to that country. Both carried a standard armament of one ·50 calibre and one ·30 calibre nose gun and a single ·30 calibre in each wing panel. Bomb racks were fitted under each wing panel for combinations totalling 300 pounds of bombs.

MODEL 75I. A major change in the 75 series was initiated with this model. The Air Corps had expressed interest in the streamlining advantages offered by liquid-cooled V-12 engines, and asked for designs built around the new Allison V-1710 powerplant. The first of these to appear was the XP-37 (serial number *37-375*), which Curtiss produced quickly by adapting the existing Model 75 to the new powerplant. Because of the longer nose combined with greater weight, it was considered necessary to move the pilot aft some distance to maintain proper balance. The 1,150 h.p. Allison V-1710-11 was turbo-supercharged to deliver 1,000 h.p. at 20,000 feet, where the top speed was 340 m.p.h. Armament remained the Air Corps' standard of one ·50 calibre and one ·30 calibre machine gun. Although an all-metal machine, the XP-37 differed from its contemporaries in being finished all over with silver paint.

Following initial evaluation of the XP-37, which was delivered on 1st April 1937, the Air Corps ordered thirteen service test versions as YP-37 (serial numbers *38-472* to *38-484*). These were somewhat heavier than the prototype, had the pilot moved forward slightly, and were finished in natural metal. Powerplant was the V-1710-21 Allison, delivering 1,000 h.p. for take-off and 880 h.p. at 25,000 feet, where the top speed was 331 m.p.h. Delivery was made in June 1939, but no

Left: *P-36B, a temporary designation assigned to P-36A* 38-20 *while being used as a test-bed for a 1,100-h.p. R-1830-25 engine.* Right: *The single XP-36D was created by installing ·30 calibre machine guns in each wing panel of P-36A* 38-174. *Note segmented colouring on cowling of an aeroplane used by a Group Headquarters Squadron.* (Photos: U.S.A.F.)

Left: *The XP-36 was P-36A* 38-172 *fitted with 23-mm. Madsen cannon under the wings. Markings are for Group Headquarters Squadron of the Eightieth Pursuit Group, aircraft No. 10.* Right: *Hawk 75M, production version of the 75H demonstrator; the first of 112 Hawk 75Ms, production versions of the 75H demonstrator sold to China. Note enlarged rear-view panels behind the cockpit.* (Photos: Curtiss-Wright)

Above: *A P-36C, probably of the 27th Pursuit Squadron, with the experimental camouflage of the 1939 War Games. The external underwing ammunition box for the ·30 calibre wing guns is clearly visible.* (Photo: courtesy Gordon S. Williams.) Below: *Another P-36C with a different War Games camouflage pattern; these schemes were applied with washable paint and could easily be removed.* (Photo: courtesy William T. Larkins)

further interest was shown in the design because a later Allison-powered adaption of the 75 known as the XP-40 held greater promise as a suitable fighter.

MODELS 75J AND K. These were studies for 75s powered with a turbo-supercharged "Twin Wasp" and a new 1,200-h.p. Pratt & Whitney "Twin Hornet" but were not built.

MODEL 75L. As a result of testing the three Y1P-36s, the Air Corps placed an order for 210 improved P-36As in July 1937. The first production machines were delivered in April 1938. The only outward recognition feature that distinguished them from the Y1P-36 was the addition of cowl flaps. The fourth and tenth airframes were held at the factory for conversion to new experimental prototypes and only 178 were delivered as P-36A. The last thirty were completed as P-36C. Others delivered as P-36A were modified in service and given new designations. The military designations of all Model 75Ls are listed below:

P-36A. 210 ordered, with Army serial numbers *38-1* to *38-210*. P-36As were the main fighter defence of the Hawaiian Islands at the time of the Pearl Harbour attack in December 1941 and were the first Air Corps fighters to shoot down Japanese aircraft. In the process of being replaced by P-40s at the time, the surviving P-36As were relegated to training rôles. One survives today in the Air Force Museum at Wright-Patterson Air Force Base near Dayton, Ohio.

P-36B. The twentieth P-36A, *38-20*, was fitted temporarily with a 1,100-h.p. R-1830-25 engine in November 1938. This increased power and the better altitude capability of the engine gave the machine, redesignated P-36B, a top speed of 313 m.p.h. The P-36B was actually an engine test-bed rather than a development model of the aeroplane, and was soon reconverted to a standard P-36A.

P-36C. The eighty-fifth P-36A, *38-85*, was fitted with an additional ·30 calibre machine gun in each outer wing panel. Ammunition was carried in an external box fitted to the underside of the wing. The additional armament proved to be desirable, so the last thirty machines on the P-36A order, *38-181* to *38-210*, were completed as P-36C. These differed from the prototype in being fitted with the 1,200-h.p. R-1830-17 engine.

XP-36D. The 174th P-36A, *38-174*, was withdrawn from squadron service early in 1939, redesignated XP-36D, and fitted with improved wing armament consisting of four ·30 calibre machine guns with ammunition carried internally in the manner of the later H75A-2. The nose armament was changed to two ·50 calibre guns.

XP-36E. The 147th P-36A, *38-147*, was fitted with new outer wing panels containing four ·30 calibre guns each. The nose ·50 calibre gun was retained but was rendered inoperable.

XP-36F. The 172nd P-36A, *38-172*, retained the standard nose armament of the P-36A but carried a single 23-mm. Madsen automatic cannon under each wing.

MODEL 75M. 112 production versions of the Model 75H fixed-undercarriage demonstrator delivered to the Republic of China. While virtually obsolete by the standards of the major powers, the 75Ms were the highest performance machines seen in China up to that time and were a bit beyond the capabilities of the average Chinese pilot of the time.

H-75R was the designation of a company-owned version of the standard P-36A fitted with a turbo-supercharger mounted between the engine and the wing. (Photo: U.S.A.F.)

The majority were destroyed in training accidents without ever encountering a Japanese aeroplane.

MODEL 75N. Thailand (formerly Siam) purchased twenty-five Model 75Ns, similar to the Chinese 75M except for one additional ·30 calibre gun in each wing. These saw combat in two wars, the Thai invasion of Indo-China in January 1941 and the brief defence of Thailand against the Japanese in December of the same year.

MODEL 75O. Thirty "Cyclone"-powered fixed-undercarriage Model 75Os with six ·30 calibre wing guns were sold to Argentina in 1938. A manufacturing licence was granted and 200 of the model were built by the Argentine Government in 1940.

MODEL 75P. The tenth P-36A, *38-10*, was retained at the factory to serve as the prototype for still another Allison-powered version of the Model 75. Designated XP-40, this was more nearly a re-engined P-36A than the XP-37 had been since it was not necessary to move the cockpit aft. The weight change was compensated for by locating the radiator behind the wing in the manner of the later North American P-51. Powerplant was the Allison V-1710-19, delivering 1,160 h.p. for take-off and 1,000 h.p. at 10,000 feet without need for a turbo-supercharger. Delivered in October 1938 the XP-40 had a top speed of 342 m.p.h. at 12,200 feet. Armament was still the standard ·30 and ·50 calibre set of nose guns. After undergoing considerable refinement and a notable relocation of the radiator to the nose, the P-40 design went into production as the Curtiss Model 81 (see *Profile* No. 35).

MODEL 75R. A company-owned demonstrator generally similar to a P-36A and painted in Air Corps markings was fitted with a turbo-supercharger and submitted to the Army for test under the designation of Model 75R. The supercharger was installed beneath the nose just aft of the engine cowling while the inter-cooler was mounted under the trailing edge of the wing. The complications of this installation ruled out supercharged versions of the P-36 and the demonstrator was returned to Curtiss. It was subsequently fitted with a Wright "Cyclone" and continued as a demonstrator in civil markings with the registration *NX-22028*.

MODEL 75S. The fourth P-36A, *38-4*, was retained at the factory to be fitted with an experimental version of the "Twin Wasp" that was developed to determine if the streamlining advantages of the liquid-cooled "Vee" engine could be imparted to the air-cooled radial. The nose portion of the 1,050 h.p. P. & W. R-1830-31 engine was extended considerably and the propeller was fitted with an exceptionally large spinner. Cooling air was taken in through an airscoop below the spinner in a position matching that of the radiator on a liquid-cooled engine. Tested in March 1939 this strategem increased the top speed of the XP-42, as the Air Corps had named the Model 75S, to only 315 m.p.h., not enough to justify the develop-

Curtiss assigned the designation of 75P to the Allison-powered conversion of P-36A 38-10 *that was delivered to the Air Corps as XP-40.* (Photo: U.S.A.F.)

The fourth P-36A was retained at the factory for conversion to XP-42 (Curtiss Model 75S) with long-nose P. & W. "Twin Wasp" engine. Washable camouflage was added when the XP-42 participated in the 1939 War Games. (Photo: U.S.A.F.)

Below: *The XP-42 was used for other engine testing after the long-nose idea was abandoned. Tail designation letters identify 10th aeroplane of the Materiel Division at Wright Field. Note Wright Field arrowhead insignia.* (Photo: N.A.S.A.)

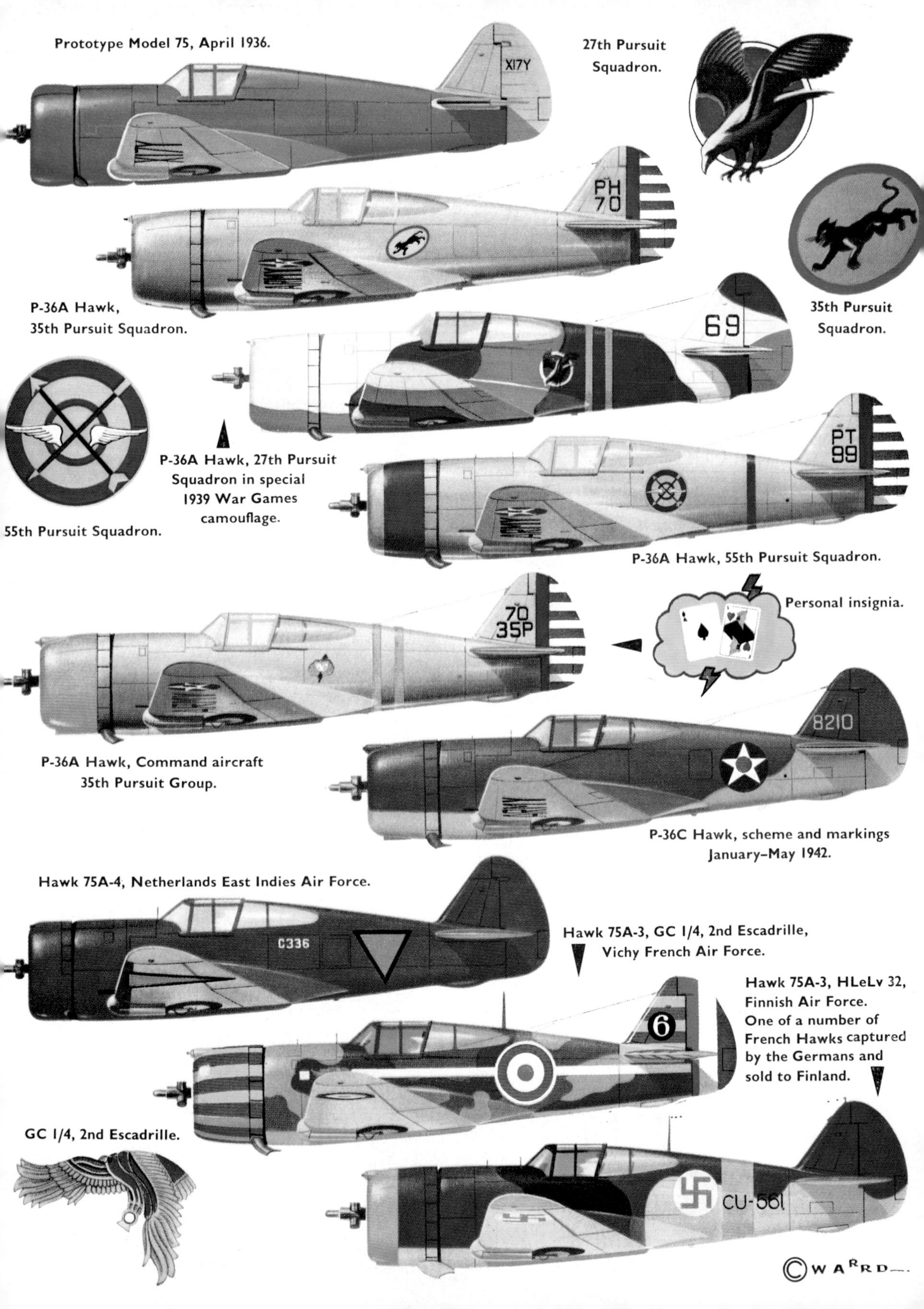

Prototype Model 75, April 1936.

27th Pursuit Squadron.

P-36A Hawk, 35th Pursuit Squadron.

35th Pursuit Squadron.

55th Pursuit Squadron.

P-36A Hawk, 27th Pursuit Squadron in special 1939 War Games camouflage.

P-36A Hawk, 55th Pursuit Squadron.

Personal insignia.

P-36A Hawk, Command aircraft 35th Pursuit Group.

P-36C Hawk, scheme and markings January–May 1942.

Hawk 75A-4, Netherlands East Indies Air Force.

Hawk 75A-3, GC I/4, 2nd Escadrille, Vichy French Air Force.

Hawk 75A-3, HLeLv 32, Finnish Air Force. One of a number of French Hawks captured by the Germans and sold to Finland.

GC I/4, 2nd Escadrille.

P-36A, leader of the 77th Pursuit Squadron of the 35th Pursuit Group. Command stripes and engine cowling painted in yellow, the squadron identifying colour. (Photo: the author)

ment of a new engine. When used later as a test-bed for "Twin Wasp" engines of more conservative dimensions, the XP-42 showed a top speed of 343 m.p.h.

COLOURING AND MARKINGS

The prototype, although a civilian aeroplane, was painted in the standard Air Corps blue and yellow of the period but carried civil markings. By the time the Y1P-36s were delivered, the Air Corps had standardised on natural finish for all-metal machines. Those parts still covered with fabric, notably the movable control surfaces, were silver-doped. For the War Games of 1939, special experimental camouflage was applied to the participating P-36s in washable paint that covered all but the squadron insignia and the aeroplane number. This camouflage was extremely colourful, and included yellow, orange and white in addition to greens and browns. There was no uniformity—each machine had a different pattern.

Standard Air Corps olive drab warpaint was added to the top and side surfaces and undersides were painted grey starting in March 1941. When this warpaint was added, the colourful Army tail stripes were deleted, the stars on the upper right and lower left wings were deleted, and a star was added to each side of the fuselage.

By the time the P-36As entered service in 1938, operating units and individual aircraft of the G.H.Q. (General Headquarters) Air Force were identified by a combination of black block figures eight inches high on the vertical fin and across the upper surface of the left wing known as the designator. On the left wing undersurface, the lettering was reduced in size to squeeze it between the 24-inch letters of ARMY and the leading edge of the wing. The combination of the letters PA above the numeral 91 indicated that the machine was the ninety-first in the First (letter A, first in the alphabet) Pursuit Group (letter P-for-Pursuit). The number was usually repeated on the side of the engine cowling. The 20th Pursuit Group was identified by the letters PT, which took a little finger-counting to determine that "T" was the twentieth letter of the alphabet. This system was in use through 1938 and 1939. In 1940 it was revised for easier reading. The machine number was put at the top of the combination on the fin and the group designation was changed to use the actual group number first, then the type letter. The PT of the 20th Pursuit Group then became 20P. When warpaint was adopted, this lettering remained black, but was changed to yellow after Pearl Harbour.

Under both designator systems, the different squadrons within the group were identified by squadron insignia on each side of the fuselage aft of the cockpit and by the application of a distinctive squadron colour to the engine cowling. Aircraft assigned to the group's Headquarters Squadron had the cowling divided into segments, with one colour for each regular squadron (usually three) within the group. Squadron Commanders were identified by two vertical five-inch stripes around the fuselage forward of the tail. The leader of "A" Flight within the squadron had a single vertical stripe, and the leaders of "B" and "C" Flights had single stripes sloping forward and aft, respectively. All these "Command" stripes were in the squadron colour. This striping system was abandoned on all U.S. combat aircraft outside the U.S.A. following Pearl Harbour and was not re-adopted for overseas service until after the war. For the P-36s, therefore, it effectively ended in December 1941.

SPECIFICATIONS

	HAWK 75 (Export Hawk 75M)	HAWK 75A (Model 75L, Army P-36A)
Wing span	37 ft. 4 in.	37 ft. 4 in.
Length	28 ft. 7 in.	28 ft. 6 in.
Wing area	236 sq. ft.	236 sq. ft.
Empty weight	3,975 lb.	4,567 lb.
Gross weight	5,305 lb.	5,470 lb.
Undercarriage	Fixed	Retractable
Powerplant	Wright "Cyclone" GR-1820-G3 875 h.p.	P. & W. R-1830-13 or 17, 1,050 h.p. at 10,000 ft.
Maximum speed	280 m.p.h. at 10,700 ft.	313 m.p.h. at 10,000 ft.
Rate of climb	2,340 ft. per min.	4·8 min. to 15,000 ft.
Service ceiling	31,800 ft.	33,000 ft.
Range	1,210 miles (extra fuel). 547 miles (normal) at 10,700 ft. at 240 m.p.h.	825 miles at 270 m.p.h. at 10,000 ft.
Armament	one ·50, one ·30 calibre m.g., or one ·50 and three ·30; 300 lb. bombs	one ·50, one ·30 calibre m.g.; no bombs

P-36A, aeroplane No. 9 of the 51st Pursuit Group carrying the olive drab and grey warpaint adopted for U.S. combat aircraft in March 1941. Tail stripes eliminated and stars added to side of fuselage. (Photo: the author.)

PRINTED IN ENGLAND © Profile Publications Ltd., P.O. Box 26, 1a North Street, Leatherhead, Surrey, England.
Printed by Hills & Lacy Ltd., London and Watford, England. U.S. 2nd Class Mailing Rates applied for.

PROFILE PUBLICATIONS

The Hawker Typhoon

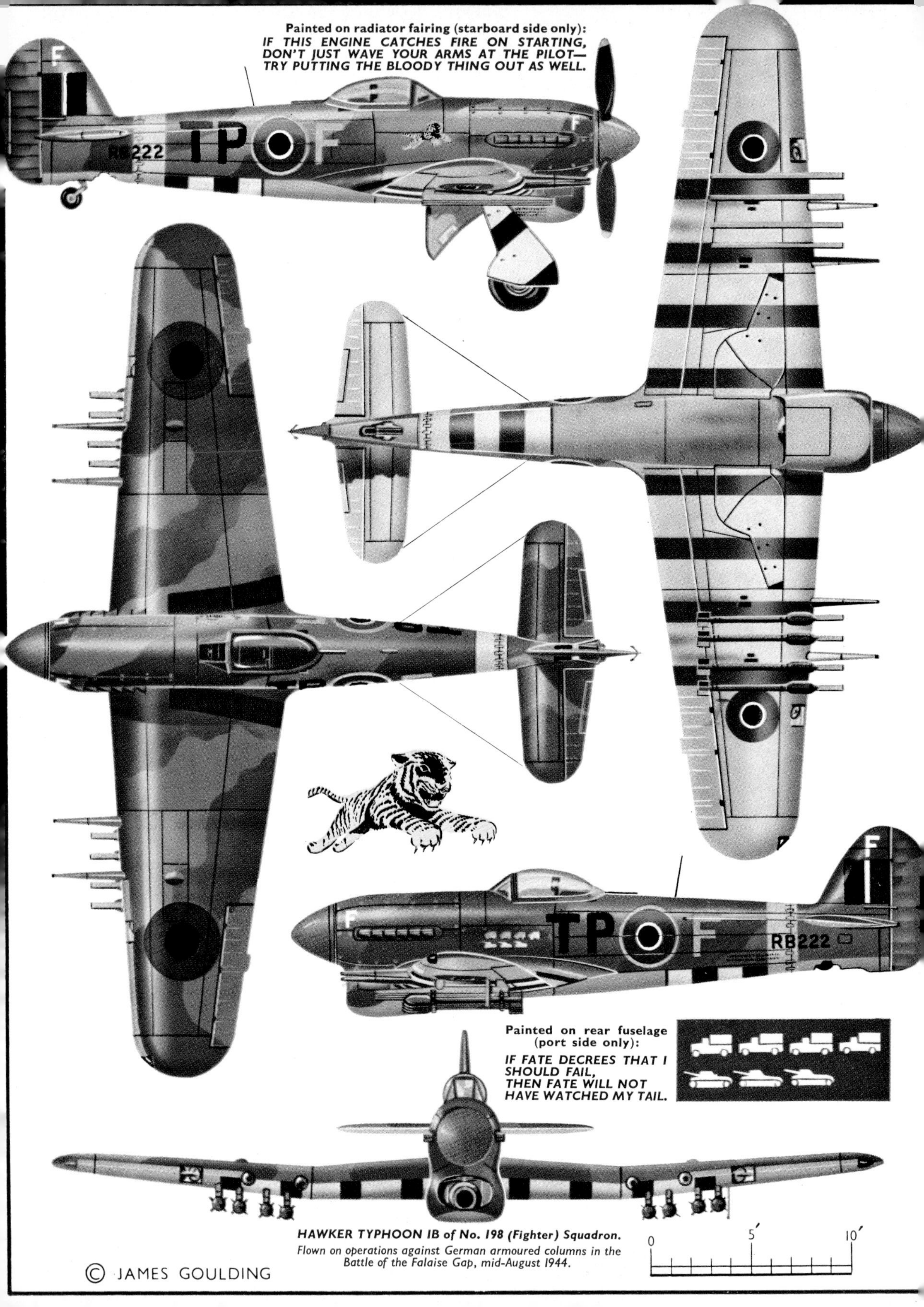

HAWKER TYPHOON IB of No. 198 (Fighter) Squadron.

Flown on operations against German armoured columns in the Battle of the Falaise Gap, mid-August 1944.

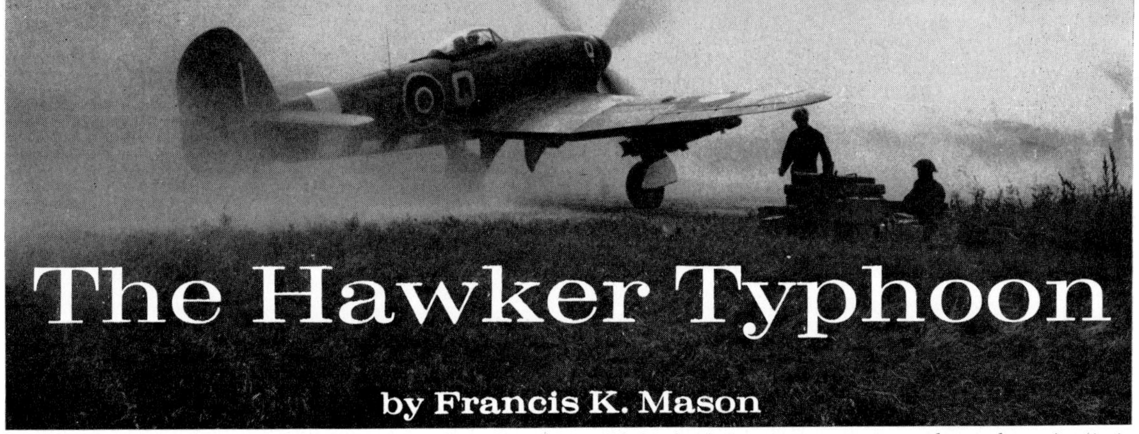

The Hawker Typhoon

by Francis K. Mason

In their historic environment, rocket-equipped Typhoon IBs of No. 198 (Fighter) Squadron taxying on a dusty advanced strip in Normandy shortly after D-Day, 1944. (Photo: Imperial War Museum, Neg. No. CL472)

"She certainly sorted the men from the boys." Never was an epitaph more aptly applied to an aircraft than to the Hawker Typhoon. The design had been conceived in peacetime (at a time when Air Staff planners were not quite sure for what they were planning), was hurried through its early development, test flown during times of dire political stress and national emergency and introduced into service *before* full Service clearance had been achieved either for the aircraft as a fighting machine, or for the engine as a reliable combat powerplant. In other words, from the outbreak of war in 1939 the Typhoon and its Sabre engine were regarded by non-responsible (as distinct from irresponsible) bureaucrats as of first tactical priority, while others, more *au fait* with the technical state of the art, sought in vain to administer a more realistic development programme. That the bureaucrats succeeded is surely evidenced by the unprecedented spate of failures in the early Service days of the aircraft. That the aircraft came to occupy a key place in the arsenal supporting history's greatest invasion nevertheless justified the faith placed in it by its sponsors, its designers and, in the last resort, its pilots.

* * *

The year 1937 found British Operational Requirement staffs in something of a quandary. Already well advanced were the metropolitan defence fighters, the Spitfire and Hurricane, while an ill-found theory had started the Defiant escort fighter on its dismal path. A so-called heavy fighter, the Westland Whirlwind, had been conceived to provide surface attack.

Superficially, therefore, the fighter spectrum appeared complete. News of German activity in the heavy fighter field (hinted at by Intelligence reports of the Messerschmitt Bf 110's first flight) suggested that the new *Luftwaffe* included in its tactical plans the escort of strategic bombers by formidable long range fighters. Whereas Spitfires and Hurricanes were designed to combat fast bombers and lightly-armoured fighters, no interceptor existed to match a heavily-armoured, well-armed long-range fighter.

Already plans were advanced for the large-scale production of Oerlikon and Hispano 20-mm. guns for use in aircraft, but as yet no powerplant existed that could carry these into the air at high speed. The 12-cylinder Rolls-Royce Peregrine was scheduled for the Whirlwind, and as part of the research plan to find the formula for powerful engines Rolls-Royce were planning to produce a 24-cylinder X-type engine by virtually mounting one Peregrine atop another. Napier, on the other hand, was achieving some success with the H-type Dagger and this provided the basis of a new 24-cylinder sleeve-valve engine—an H-type engine on its side.

As these two engines, the Rolls-Royce Vulture and Napier Sabre, came to promise very high power outputs, so the Air Staff evolved a new fighter Specification around them, F.18/37.

Meanwhile at Hawker Aircraft Ltd., Sydney Camm was seeing his Hurricane production line maturing and by the close of 1937 the first deliveries were made to the R.A.F. Thus early was he anxious to commence development of a Hurricane replacement and his project designers set-to to tender alternative designs to F.18/37. By March 1938 these had been accepted in principle and a contract for four prototypes was issued to Hawker—two to be powered by the Sabre and two by the Vulture. Official armament proposals at the time were still somewhat flexible owing to the fact that air testing of the 20-mm. guns had not taken place in a single engine aircraft, and it was decided to arm the prototypes with the alternative armament of twelve Browning 0·303-in. machine guns.

Two views of the first F.18/37 Typhoon prototype, P5212. *Principal features that identified this aircraft were the small fin and rudder, short span wings, low pressure tyres without wheel doors, triple exhaust stubs and absence of armament. Colour scheme in February 1940 was mid blue-grey upper surfaces, and black and white underwing and tailplane surfaces. Red and blue roundels appeared on upper wing surfaces only.* (Photos: Ministry of Defence, Neg. No. 10280C, and Imperial War Museum, Neg. No. MH4961)

Two early photos of the second Typhoon prototype, P5216. *That on the left, taken at Boscombe Down, shows the 12-gun wing to advantage as well as the hinged door flaps attached to the leg fairings. Note also the tailwheel doors.* Right: *A later photo taken at Langley after the tailwheel doors had been removed.*
(Photos: Imperial War Museum, Neg. No. MH4962, and Hawker Siddeley Aviation Ltd.)

The Munich crisis was the first of many events to threaten the smooth progress of Camm's new fighter. As the certainty of war grew, so did the necessity to arm Fighter Command with established fighters, and all priorities were accorded to the Hurricane and Spitfire. Napiers were perhaps more fortunate than Rolls-Royce in that their only production engine, the Dagger, occupied little of their production facilities, and they were thus less prevented from activating their new project. Nevertheless their experience with the Sabre prototype in the ill-fated Heston-Napier racer must have provided an indication of the volume of work that required to be completed before the Sabre was ready for service in a fighter.

(As this *Profile* is concerned only with the fortunes of the Typhoon, it is only necessary here to record that the Vulture-powered Tornado prototypes achieved their first flights on 6th October 1939 and 5th December 1940 respectively, but that difficulties with the Vulture engine led to the eventual abandonment of that design after only a handful of Tornados had been built.)

TESTING THE TYPHOON

Shrouded in the utmost secrecy, the prototype Typhoon, *P5212*, commenced manufacture in the old Hawker factory in Canbury Park Road, Kingston. It was first flown by Philip Lucas on 24th February 1940 but owing to a lack of directional stability it was returned to Kingston for enlargement of the fin and rudder, and it was during this period that a German bomb—one of a stick aimed at the nearby railway line to London—fell outside the Experimental Shops and narrowly missed causing serious damage to the valuable new prototype.

Shortly afterwards, during the course of a test flight, *P5212* suffered structural failure of the monocoque on the starboard side of the fuselage just aft of the cockpit. The stressed skin failed and damage occurred to the primary structure; however Philip Lucas, who would have been justified in abandoning the aircraft, nursed the Typhoon back to his airfield and landed safely. He was subsequently awarded the George Medal.

It has been thought likely that the failure occurred as the result of the larger tail unit being fitted, without re-stressing of the fuselage structure, and, although an immediate remedy was applied, the inherent weakness was to re-appear with dire results later.

During its early flights *P5212* remained unarmed though provision was made for twelve Browning guns. A good deal of trouble was encountered with the Sabre I in this prototype, occasional starting fires and overheating in the air being traced to the exhaust system. As the second prototype passed through the Experimental Shop a number of improvements were included. When *P5216* first flew on 3rd May 1941 it carried the twelve-gun armament, but shortly after this was replaced by the four-cannon battery. D-doors, originally fitted to the undercarriage leg fairing, were replaced by doors mounted on the centre-line of the fuselage.

Production of the Typhoon was scheduled to be undertaken both by Hawker and by the Gloster Aircraft Company at Hucclecote, near Gloucester, and as assembly lines were beginning to take shape early in 1941 the bulk of the prototype testing fell upon but one aircraft—*P5212*, the only example yet completed.

This one aircraft, between frequent groundings for engine inspections (the Sabre I was only cleared for ten hours' flying between inspections), performed all gun-firing trials on the 12-gun installation, initial performance and handling trials, carbon monoxide contamination trials, spinning clearance and initial Service evaluation. The programme, spread over six months, occupied forty-seven flying hours only, and was almost completed before *P5212* was joined by *P5216*. Much of the time was spent at Boscombe Down where critical Service pilots frequently expressed doubts about the Typhoon's potential value as an interceptor.

Not unnaturally such sentiments inevitably reached the ears of senior Air Ministry officials, and thence those of others whose vested interests might have influenced the conduct of British fighter production as a whole. Rumours reached Hawker that the Typhoon's days were numbered, rumours that seemed not ill-founded when snags and delays began to be met with the Chatellerault ammunition feed mechanism for the 20-mm. guns.

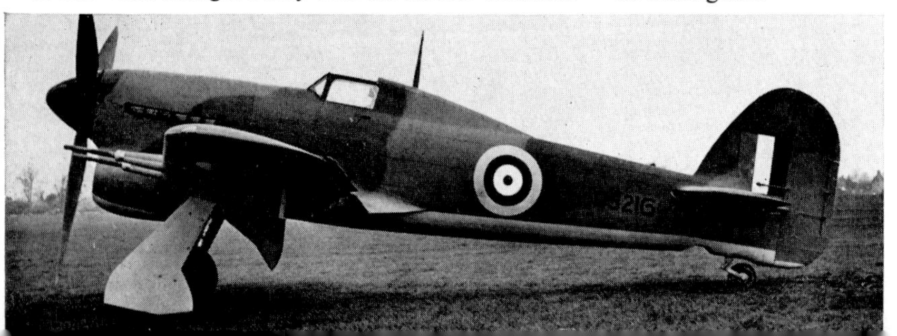

P5216 *after it had been brought up to the initial production standard. Centrally - hinged mainwheel doors have been fitted, as has the four-cannon armament. Standard "dark earth and spinach" camouflage has been applied, but the absence of the "circled-P" is curious.* (Photo: Hawker Siddeley Aviation Ltd., Neg. No. TYG5)

First Gloster-built Typhoon to be fitted with rear-vision hood. The photo, taken during assembly at Hucclecote, also shows the engine and radiator installation, whereas the other picture was taken during evaluation by Hawker pilots at Langley.
(Photos: F. K. Mason collection and Hawker Siddeley Aviation Ltd., Neg. No. TYG9)

It was, however, undoubtedly the Focke-Wulf Fw 190 that saved the Typhoon, for this outstanding German fighter gained ascendancy over the Spitfire V during 1941 and demonstrated that it could out-manœuvre any R.A.F. aircraft that might venture over the Channel—and this was exactly what Fighter Command's principal actions in 1941 constituted.

Far from thus being shelved, the Typhoon's development was accelerated. Both prototypes were delivered to Boscombe Down for intensive evaluation, and the first Gloster-built Typhoon was flown by Michael Daunt on 27th May 1941.

THE EVENTFUL BAPTISM

The circumstances surrounding the Typhoon's entry into the R.A.F. can only be described as macabre. Had such events occurred in peacetime they would most certainly have been the subject of searching questions in Parliament; but this was war, and the enemy possessed an aircraft—the Focke-Wulf Fw 190A—that not only outclassed the Spitfire V and Hurricane II but posed a serious barrier to Britain's determination to win air superiority over France and the Low Countries. The Typhoon's original antagonist, the Messerschmitt Bf 110, had all but vanished as an effective offensive weapon and the appearance of the Fw 190 presented not only a dangerous threat to R.A.F. medium and heavy bombers but real danger to morale by hit-and-run raids on Southern England.

The first Typhoons were delivered to the A.F.D.U., Nos. 56 and 601 Squadrons at Duxford and its forward satellite at Matlaske, Norfolk. The aircraft were a motley mixture of Mark IAs and IBs, some with fully transparent cockpit enclosures, others with "solid" rear cockpit fairings. The engines were initially cleared for only 25 hours between major overhauls, but few reached that total. Intake fires on the ground were frequent, as were engine failures on the climb. There was also a number of unexplained structural failures for which no eye witness could account. Naturally working-up was prolonged by combat limitations and losses, but when in November 1941 the Wing was moved south under Sqdn. Ldr. R. P. Beamont to Manston and Biggin Hill to combat the sneak-raiding Focke-Wulfs, the nature of the Typhoon's major weakness was exposed—and as a result the whole matter of persevering with the aircraft at all was seriously questioned at high level.

For in one of the relatively few instances when Typhoon pilots were brought to a perfect combat position with a height advantage from which to pounce on the enemy aircraft, the entire tail units of two aircraft were seen to break away during their dive recovery.

Lengthy structural testing in war is seldom possible and the speed with which the R.A.F. had introduced the Typhoon had precluded all but the most cursory tests. Philip Lucas' experience of failure had been confined to the monocoque immediately aft of the cockpit; the new failure occurred locally at the rear fuselage joint so that a local remedy was considered adequate—and so it proved—by the simple expedient of riveting fish plates all round the joint. Yet it is a fact born out by surviving records that of the initial 142 Typhoons delivered to the R.A.F., no less than 135 suffered serious accidents—either attributable to engine or airframe failures—without enemy action being involved.

The first Typhoon squadrons had to contend with another hazard, not previously fully understood and certainly never previously encountered at such a high level. This was the seepage of carbon monoxide into the cockpit, caused by the deterioration of bulkhead seals around the non-integral firewall. After a number of unexplained disappearances on operations, an ex-Squadron aircraft was minutely inspected and a partial remedy effected. However, the Typhoon was always regarded as potentially hazardous in this respect and it became standard practice to use oxygen breathing from the moment the engine started.

On the production side, further delays were being encountered in the delivery of Hispano guns to Gloster and Hawker, it being suspected that there was reluctance to apportion valuable stocks to an aircraft whose future was by no means assured (when other cannon-armed aircraft had already become firmly established). The result was that most of the first Service aircraft were armed with 12 Brownings, and it soon was evident that against ground targets the Typhoon was impotent.

Gradually, however, maintenance and flying experience was achieved; civilian working parties toiled side by side with Service personnel, and test pilots visited the fighter stations to dispel a feeling that every

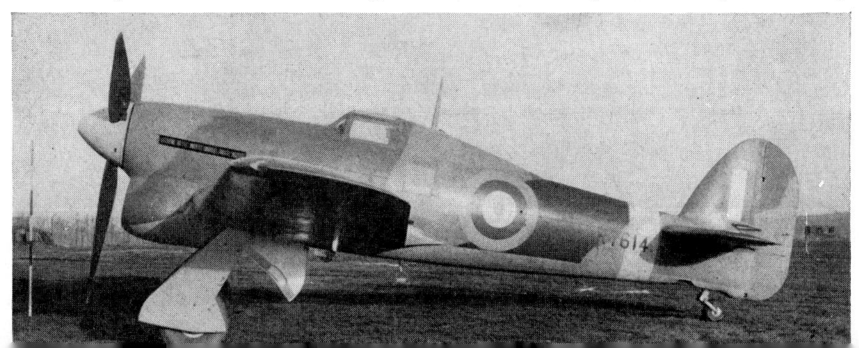

The only known photo of a hand-tooled Gloster-built Typhoon IA showing the similarity with the prototype P5216. R7614 *is shown here at Boscombe Down early in 1941 for performance trials.* (Photo: F. K. Mason collection)

Typhoon IB, R8224, *was used for investigation into recognition schemes to eliminate confusion with the Focke-Wulf Fw 190A. The white nose was tried in an effort to so modify the Typhoon's appearance as to leave no superficial resemblance. After various alternative schemes had been discarded, reliance was placed on the now-familiar black and white stripes under the wings.*
(Photo: Ministry of Defence, Neg. No. 12062B)

Typhoon IB, R8762, *used at Boscombe Down for performance trials with drop tanks. The aircraft displays evidence of early anticipation of tail failure in the use of a butt strap applied round the rear transport joint (on the white band)—an interim expedient pending development of the official "fish plate" method.*
(Photo: Ministry of Defence, Neg. No. 14227)

One of many Typhoon accidents, this Mark IA of No. 56 (Fighter) Squadron suffered engine failure and undershot the runway at Matlaske, Norfolk, in attempting a forced landing.
(Photo: Ministry of Defence, Neg. No. 567G (Duxford))

Cockpit of an early Typhoon IB. Elimination of the "car door" entry on later aircraft led to some tidying up of the port side of the cockpit. (Photo: Ministry of Defence, Neg. No. 10484F)

Typhoon was a rogue aircraft. And it must be mentioned that several test pilots lost their lives. For instance, Gerry Sayer, who had been Gloster's Chief Test Pilot since 1934, was posted missing after a flight in a Typhoon, and Hawker's own K. G. Seth-Smith crashed near Windsor while testing hoods.

During the winter of 1941–42 a third Duxford-based Squadron, No. 266, became operational on the type and was followed shortly after by No. 182 at Martlesham Heath and No. 1 at Acklington.

By March 1942 Typhoon IBs had been in action against Fw 190As at low altitude with adequate success to show that below 10,000 feet there was scarcely another aircraft to match them, while at tree-top level they had proved the scourge of the tip-and-run Focke-Wulfs. But catch a Typhoon at 20,000 feet and it fell easy prey to any current first line enemy fighter. The lesson was obvious. Except for Metropolitan defence against the sneak raider, the Typhoon had failed as an interceptor, the fault lying as much in accelerated engine development as in the abbreviated aerodynamic development. Once again the Typhoon's future came under scrutiny: was it worth applying production facilities and special flying training to an aircraft for so limited a task—when variations of the Spitfire IX might well achieve better results with less industrial and military disruption?

It was the very weakness in the Typhoon's interceptor qualities that brought about the fundamental and successful change in its operational rôle, that of ground attack. For the thick wing and high wing loading that had placed the aircraft at a disadvantage at altitude now bestowed the qualities required by a load-carrying low flying fighter that might be required to survive tremendous punishment from light *flak* as well as provide a steady aiming platform in turbulent conditions.

Thus from the beginning of 1942 relatively large numbers of Typhoons were earmarked for weapon clearance trials at Boscombe Down, with back-up work being applied by Glosters and Hawker. After 44-gallon drop tank clearance trials had been completed, clearance for 500-lb. bombs was a simple next step, followed by light bomb clusters, smoke canisters, mines and finally rocket projectiles. At one time no fewer than 23 Typhoons were being tested at Boscombe Down. Encouraged by the power of the 4-cannon armament, Hawker had designed and built

The late Flt. Lt. P. E. G. (Gerry) Sayer, Chief Test Pilot of Gloster Aircraft Co. Ltd., who lost his life while flying a Typhoon. In the instance of his death, there was no evidence of structural failure of the aircraft, and the pilot of another Typhoon accompanying him at the same time also failed to return. No trace was ever found of aircraft or pilots.
(Photo: Flight International, Neg. No. 16444S)

The Typhoon IB night fighter, of which only one was built, was not considered successful owing to longitudinal dynamic instability; nor was the aircraft suitable for long range night operations, the wing tanks being used to accommodate the A.I. Mk. IV radar. Colour scheme was "middle stone" (which was extended to cover the undersurfaces) and "extra dark sea green". Trials were conducted during the winter of 1942–43.
(Photo: Hawker Siddeley Aviation Ltd.)

a set of wings mounting a 6-cannon battery and although these were fitted to a Typhoon they were never flown.

Furthermore, in an attempt to improve the high altitude performance of the Typhoon, *P5216* was flown with a wing span increased to 44 ft. 2 in., but when this was abandoned the wings were reduced to 39 ft. 6 in. in an effort to further improve the low altitude performance. And although the rate of roll was considerably enhanced the aircraft displayed a marked reluctance to leave the ground at all when carrying full ammunition *or* two 500-lb. bombs.

ROCKETS

It was during the course of this clearance to deliver an increased broadside that the rocket projectile came to be considered. Already a trial installation of six rockets had been successfully concluded in a Hurricane at Boscombe Down, and the projectiles were in late 1942 being produced in large numbers—destined for Mosquitoes, Beaufighters, Hurricanes and Swordfish.

In themselves the British 3-in. rocket projectiles—called initially U.P.s ("unrotated projectiles") for security reasons—were grotesque in their simplicity: a length of 3-in. cast iron pipe containing the propellant charge, a 60-lb. H.E. warhead screwed on the front and four cruciform rectangular fins at the rear. In an effort to maintain some degree of stability the charge was ignited at the forward end and exhausted through a central longitudinal orifice. Nevertheless the R.P.s were characterised by a considerable gravity drop after launching and demanded constant practice and long experience to hit a tank or other small moving targets. Theoretically a vertical dive was the best expedient . . . but pulling out . . . !

All told, a dozen Typhoons were employed in the rocket trials which were conducted from Boscombe Down, Wittering, Duxford and Farnborough, the missiles being fired over the Pendine Sands and at Leysdown on the Isle of Sheppey. On one occasion, when firing concrete-filled warheads in shallow dives over the latter range, two ricocheting missiles from one Typhoon hit and passed clean through the wings of the aircraft ahead—without fatal results.

Throughout 1943 Typhoon squadrons were withdrawn in rotation from operations for modifications to enable eight rocket-launching rails to be attached under the wings of the aircraft, and to give the pilots some opportunity to fire practice rounds. By and

Two views of one of the tropical Typhoons. Just visible is the ventral air exit fairing between the central wheel doors. Colour scheme was sand and dark green upper surfaces and pale blue undersurfaces. Two other Typhoons, R8925 *and* R8889, *were also equipped for tropical trials and all were shipped to Khartoum early in 1943.*
(Photos: Hawker Siddeley Aviation Ltd., Neg. Nos. TYG36 and 1127)

Below: *Comparative views showing the older "car door" canopy assembly and the later single-piece sliding hood. It was while performing hood development tests in* R7692 *that K. G. Seth-Smith, the Hawker test pilot, lost his life in a crash at Thorpe, near Windsor, in August 1942.*
(Photos: F. K. Mason collection)

Cleaning up the Typhoon. A programme was initiated in 1942 to increase the performance by attention to detail; pictures of R8809 *show the change in hood shape, elimination of external rear view mirror, adoption of whip aerial, fairing of cannon barrels and addition of exhaust manifold plinth.* (Photos: Hawker Siddeley Aviation Ltd., Neg. Nos. TYG4 and TYG37)

large, however, there were ample targets of the operational variety, and in Operation Channel Stop daily sweeps by rocket-firing Typhoons wrought tremendous havoc among E-Boats, coastal trawlers, *flak* vessels, blockade runners and minelayers in the English Channel, and enemy airfields, railways, road vehicles and bridges in France and the Low Countries.

By 1944 the Typhoon had been mastered. Still very much a handful, it now represented a considerable portion of the Allied close-support inventory located in Southern England, poised ready to support the inevitable invasion of Europe. Now, with the Tempest coming into service as an interceptor, Typhoons were withdrawn from defence commitments and the new Tactical Air Force included twenty-two squadrons of the deadly support fighter.

Technically the aircraft had been cleaned up considerably. All now had Chatellerault cannon-feed mechanism and the Sabre IIB or IIC engine. All Typhoon IAs had long since been withdrawn, and the gun barrels of the Typhoon IBs were now faired; car doors were being replaced by single-piece sliding hoods, and Rotol and D.H. four-blade propellers appeared. The maximum speed had risen from 404 to 412 m.p.h., and numerous pilots dived Typhoons at speeds well in excess of 500 m.p.h. without parting company with their tail units!

One malady persisted until the last days of the Typhoon. Ground fires were common and often resulted in the total loss of the aircraft. Over-priming on starting, kick-back and backfiring sometimes led to otherwise easily controlled fires, but on the Typhoon the position of the large radiator caused a discontinuity in the firewall in the vicinity of the fuel trunk lines, and pilots were quick to vacate their cockpits at the first sign of smoke entering their confines in the region of their feet! During 1944 and 1945 twenty-eight Typhoons were totally destroyed in engine-starting fires.

THE INVASION

As D-Day approached, Typhoons switched their attacks to shore installations all along the French Channel coast. The "No-Ball" sites, radar installations and gun emplacements were harried and often damaged. As a prelude to the actual landings, Typhoons of Nos. 198 and 609 Squadrons on 2nd June 1944 destroyed the vital radar installation at Dieppe/Caudecôte with bombs and gunfire, and as part of the preliminary air assault twenty-six Typhoons of Nos. 174, 175 and 245 Squadrons eliminated the Jobourg radar station which would have covered the actual landing areas. The astonishing element of surprise achieved on D-Day has seldom been adequately attributed to this attack—yet its success must have been a key factor in the Allies' ability to gain a foothold on the mainland. Certainly the *Luftwaffe* was deprived of all local fighter control over the landings.

Following the "right hook" advance by American armoured divisions, there followed the classic investment of heavy German forces in Normandy, almost contained within a pocket whose only escape aperture lay at Falaise. By then most of the Typhoon squadrons were operating from airstrips on the mainland and were conveniently positioned to afford minute-to-minute support. As the German infantry and armour strived desperately to extricate themselves through the Falaise Gap, the Allied fighter-bombers dealt fearsome carnage, first blocking roads and destroying bridges and then decimating the paralysed enemy forces. At the mercy of no fewer than ten Typhoon squadrons allocated to this operation alone, it was of little wonder that survivors were anxious to surrender rather than face further inferno in the blast of the terrifying rocket salvoes.

In the open battle, however, a new close support technique had been evolved, known as "Cab Rank".

One of the first Squadrons to receive the Typhoon was No. 609 (West Riding). The aircraft seen here at Biggin Hill in 1943 carried a score tally of 18 locomotives and the name "Mavis" on the fuselage and a dark red and white spinner of "A" Flight. (Photo: Imperial War Museum, Neg. No. CH9822)

Squadron Commander's aircraft of No. 197 (Fighter) Squadron. (Photo: Imperial War Museum, Neg. No. CH11592)

Interim-standard Typhoon IB fighter, JP853, *of No. 486 Squadron, R.N.Z.A.F.* (Photo: Imperial War Museum)

Typhoon IB line-up of No. 193 (Fighter) Squadron. Photo believed taken at Manston late in 1943. (Photo: Imperial War Museum)

The Typhoons would maintain a standing patrol at about 10,000 feet over the battle area until enemy resistance could be pin-pointed. An R.A.F. liaison officer, often stationed in a leading armoured vehicle, would then call his fighters down by radio, directing the pilots on to the aggravating target.

By October 1944 the Typhoon squadrons had reached bases close to the Dutch frontier and it was on the 24th of that month that Nos. 193, 197, 257, 263 and 266 Squadrons of No. 84 Group staged one of the brilliant "set pieces" that occasionally characterised the North European campaign. Led by Group Captain D. E. Gillam, three waves of Typhoons attacked the Headquarters of the German Fifteenth Army in the ancient city of Dordrecht. Planned to the minutest detail, the attack was entirely successful and resulted in the destruction of the Headquarters building and the deaths of two enemy generals and more than seventy other Staff officers.

The advance continued and by the New Year Typhoons were operating from Dutch airfields. On New Year's day they suffered severe losses in the *Luftwaffe's* forlorn and desperate—yet brilliantly conceived—surprise attack, Operation Hermann. All manner of enemy fighters and fighter-bombers streaked over Allied airfields straffing every possible target of opportunity. Typhoon-equipped Nos. 438 and 439 Squadrons of the R.C.A.F. were caught taxying out for a dawn take-off when the enemy appeared. Almost every aircraft in the two squadrons was damaged or destroyed; pilots with no chance of take-off promptly dived for cover, while one or two who struggled into the air were promptly shot down.

Nevertheless the Typhoon came to be regarded as the yardstick by which future close support specifications were evaluated for some years. When the War in Europe ended, the Typhoon was speedily replaced by the Tempest, and most aircraft were reduced to scrap (few being allocated to training units owing to many Tempests being surplus to the post-war R.A.F.'s requirements).

A total of 3,330 Typhoons were built, almost all by Gloster Aircraft Co. Ltd. A surprisingly small number of experimental variants was developed and included a night fighter, a tropical version (which underwent clearance trials at Khartoum), and an aircraft with an annular radiator. The constant uncertainty as to the Typhoon's capacity to overcome progressive faults and limitations, together with the early arrival of the Hawker Tempest, prevented more exotic development of this, surely one of the most outstanding—if notorious—of all close support fighters.

For many months No. 183 (Fighter) Squadron flew Typhoons on fighter-bomber strikes. These two pictures are interesting in that both aircraft are carrying the same code letters; that above, R8884, *was one of the first Typhoons modified to carry underwing bombs (note old canopy and unfaired cannon).* JR128 *displays faired exhaust stacks, faired cannon, sliding canopy, whip aerial and 3-blade propeller.*
(Photo: Hawker Siddeley Aviation Ltd., Neg. No. TYF1)

FLYING THE TYPHOON

To pilots accustomed to the low wing loading and sensitivity of the Spitfire IX, the Typhoon was undoubtedly a fearsome experience! Perhaps one of the most animated reminiscences of a pilot's first encounter with the aircraft was written in Pierre Clostermann's *The Big Show**:

"I tightened my straps, released the brakes, carefully aligned myself on the white line down the middle of the concrete and slowly opened the throttle, with my left foot hard down on the rudder bar.

I had been warned that Typhoons swung, but surely not as much as this! And the brute gathered speed like a rocket! I corrected as much as I could with the brakes, but even then I found myself drifting dangerously to the right.

Halfway down the runway my right wheel was practically on the grass. If I came off the concrete I would gracefully flip on my back . . . To hell with it, I tore her off the ground.

This plane just had no lateral stability at all. I still went on drifting to starboard and, with those miserable ailerons that only 'bit' at speeds higher than 100 m.p.h. I daren't lower my port wing too much. . . . I retracted my undercart but forgot to put the brakes on. A terrific vibration which shook the whole plane from stem to stern reminded me that my wheels had gone into the cavities in the wings still revolving at full speed. . . .

In the end I got my hand in a bit and felt better. There was a tendency to skid in the turns, but it wasn't too bad.

Just a wee dive to see what happened. Phew! With its seven tons, the thing's acceleration downhill was simply fantastic. I realised with satisfaction that as far as speed was concerned this was much better than a Spitfire. What would it be like in a Tempest?

Half an hour quickly passed and I began to summon courage for the landing. First a circuit at full throttle at 420 m.p.h. to clear those plugs again. But after that I couldn't seem to reduce speed enough

*The Big Show, *Pierre Clostermann, translated by Oliver Berthoud (Chatto & Windus, London).*

Scourge of the Normandy battlefields were the rocket-armed Typhoons. Eight 3-in. rockets were carried in addition to the standard 4-cannon armament.

to lower my undercart with safety, even though I throttled back, swishtailed violently, and lowered my radiator. . . . In desperation I did a vertical climb, without the engine; this took me up about 3,000 feet but it reduced my speed to about 200 m.p.h. At this low speed the machine was horribly unstable, and letting down the undercart had an unexpected effect on the centre of gravity.

Cautiously . . . I made my approach, lowered the flaps, and everything went off fine until I tried to level out—those thick wings seemed to have plenty of lift, but they were treacherous. I had just begun to ease the stick back when the whole contraption stalled and dropped like a stone. Then it bounced back a good 30 feet with its nose in the air, amidst an appalling din.

I opened up like mad to break the fall, wrestling at the same time with the ailerons so as not to land on my back.

Eventually, after bucking two or three times like a mustang, my Typhoon finally calmed down and rolled drunkenly down the runway, which now looked distinctly short. However, I managed to stop before ramming the scenery, in a cloud of smoke and oil. A strong smell of burnt rubber rose from my poor tyres, which had stood up valiantly to seven tons landing on them at 120 m.p.h. . . ."

PRODUCTION AND SERVICE ALLOCATION

Hawker F.18/37 prototypes. Two aircraft, *P5212* and *P5216*, ordered under Contract No. 815124/38 and built under Works Order No. 5232 dated 3/3/38. *P5212* powered by Napier Sabre I No. 95007 (later 95018), ff. 24/2/40 with provision for 12 machine guns. *P5216* powered by Sabre I No. 95023 (later 95018 from *P5212*, ff. 3/5/41 armed with four 20-mm. Hispano Mk. I guns. *P5216* flown on 9/11/41 with production cockpit canopy and extended wing tips.

Hawker Typhoon (Centaurus). One aircraft, *LA594*, ordered under Contract No. 21392/41, commenced but not completed. Centaurus II engine proposed. Referred to as Typhoon II, later developed into Tempest II.

Hawker Typhoon IA and IB. Production batch of 15 aircraft built by Hawker Aircraft Ltd., Langley, Bucks. *R8198–R8200, R8222–R8231*. Most aircraft with 12-gun wings.

Hawker Typhoon IA and IB. Contract for 250 aircraft placed with Hawker Aircraft Ltd., but sub-contracted to Gloster Aircraft Co., Hucclecote, Glos. Most aircraft with 4-cannon wings. Car-type cockpit doors, Sabre I and II. *R7576–R7599, R7613–R7655, R7672–R7721, R7738–R7775, R7792–R7829, R7845–R7890, R7913–R7923.*

Hawker Typhoon IB. Second sub-contract for 250 aircraft placed with Gloster. Sabre II. *R8630–R8633, R8680–R8722, R8737–R8781, R8799–R8845, R8861–R8900, R8923–R8947, R8966–R8981.*

Hawker Typhoon IB. First contract for 700 aircraft placed with Gloster. Sabre II, Deliveries commenced 20/9/42; average production rate 22 aircraft per week. *DN241–DN278, DN293–DN341, DN355–DN389, DN404–DN453, DN467–DN513, DN529–DN562, DN576–DN623, EJ900–EJ934, EJ946–EJ995, EK112–EK154, EK167–EK196, EK208–EK252, EK266–EK301, EK321–EK348, EK364–EK413, EK425–EK456, EK472–EK512, EK535–EK543.*

Two views of a Typhoon F.R.IB, EK427. *Armed with the outboard cannon only, these aircraft were equipped to carry a forward-facing camera in the starboard inboard gun bay, an oblique camera in the port wing and one or two vertical cameras in the fuselage. About sixty such aircraft were thus modified.* (Photos: Ministry of Defence, and Imperial War Museum)

Hawker Typhoon IB. Second contract for 698 aircraft placed with Gloster. Sabre II. Deliveries commenced 5/4/43. Many aircraft later modified with sliding hoods. Average rate of production 17 aircraft per week. *JP361–JP408, JP425–JP447, JP480–JP516, JP532–JP552, JP576–JP614, JP648–JP689, JP723–JP756, JP786–JP802, JP836–JP861, JP897–JP941, JP961–JP976, JR125–JR152, JR183–JR223, JR237–JR266, JR289–JR338, JR360–JR392, JR426–JR449, JR492–JR535.*

Hawker Typhoon IB. Third contract for 800 aircraft placed with Gloster. Sabre II. Deliveries commenced 8/12/43. Most aircraft fitted with sliding hoods; some aircraft with four blade propellers. Average rate of production 29 aircraft per week. *MM951–MM995, MN113–MN156, MN169–MN213, MN229–MN269, MN282–MN325, MN339–MN381, MN396–MN436, MN449–MN496, MN513–MN556, MN569–MN608, MN632–MN667, MN680–MN720, MN735–MN779, MN791–MN823, MN851–MN896, MN912–MN956, MN968–MN999, MP113–MP158, MP172–MP203.*

Hawker Typhoon IB. Fourth contract for 255 aircraft placed with Gloster. Sabre II. Deliveries commenced 6/3/44. (Most aircraft delivered with Sabre IIB and IIC driving 4-blade propellers.) Average rate of production 5 aircraft per week. *RB192–RB235, RB248–RB289, RB303–RB347, RB361–RB408, RB423–RB459, RB474–RB512.*

Hawker Typhoon IB. Fifth contract for 300 aircraft placed with Gloster during 1944. Sabre IIC. Deliveries commenced 5/1/45; last aircraft delivered 13/11/45. Average rate of production 7 aircraft per week. *SW386–SW428, SW443–SW478, SW493–SW537, SW551–SW596, SW620–SW668, SW681–SW716, SW728–SW772.*

Representative aircraft in R.A.F. service:

No. 1 (Fighter) Sqdn., Acklington and Tangmere: *R7919, R7921, R7922, R8630, R8631, R8634, R8690, R8708, R8862, R8981, EJ974* ("T"), *EJ992* ("M"), *JP337* ("A"), *JP685* ("O"), *JP738* ("N"), *JR126* ("H"), *MN115* ("Q"), *MN124* ("F"), *MN252* ("M"), *MN513* ("N"), *RB352* ("L").

No. 3 (Fighter) Sqdn.: *JP741* ("U"), *JR446, JR448, JR497.*

No. 33 (Fighter) Sqdn.: *EJ930* ("P"), *EJ987* ("M"), *EK187* ("K"), *EK495* ("L"), *MN515* ("A"), *MN779* ("P").

No. 56 (Fighter) Sqdn., Duxford, Matlaske, Snailwell: *R8220–R8223, R8231* ("Z"), *R7583* ("W"), *R7584* ("S"), *R7586* ("P"), *R7587* ("D"), *R7588* ("N"), *R7591* ("T"), *R7593* ("A"), *R7594* ("B"), *R7596* ("M"), *R7598* ("O"), *R7599* ("L"), *R7615* ("J"), *R7616* ("F"), *R7619* ("O"),

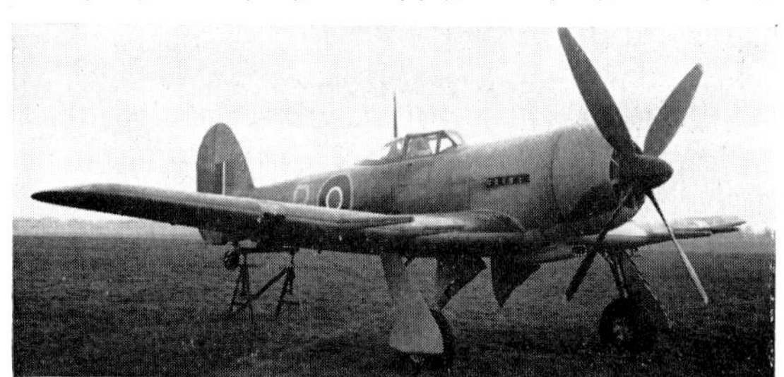

One of the interesting installations carried out on the Typhoon was that of the annular radiator with Sabre II and IV engines in R8694. *By and large this was a successful experiment but disruption to production lines forestalled any interest by the Air Ministry. Top speed was quoted by Napiers at 452 m.p.h.*

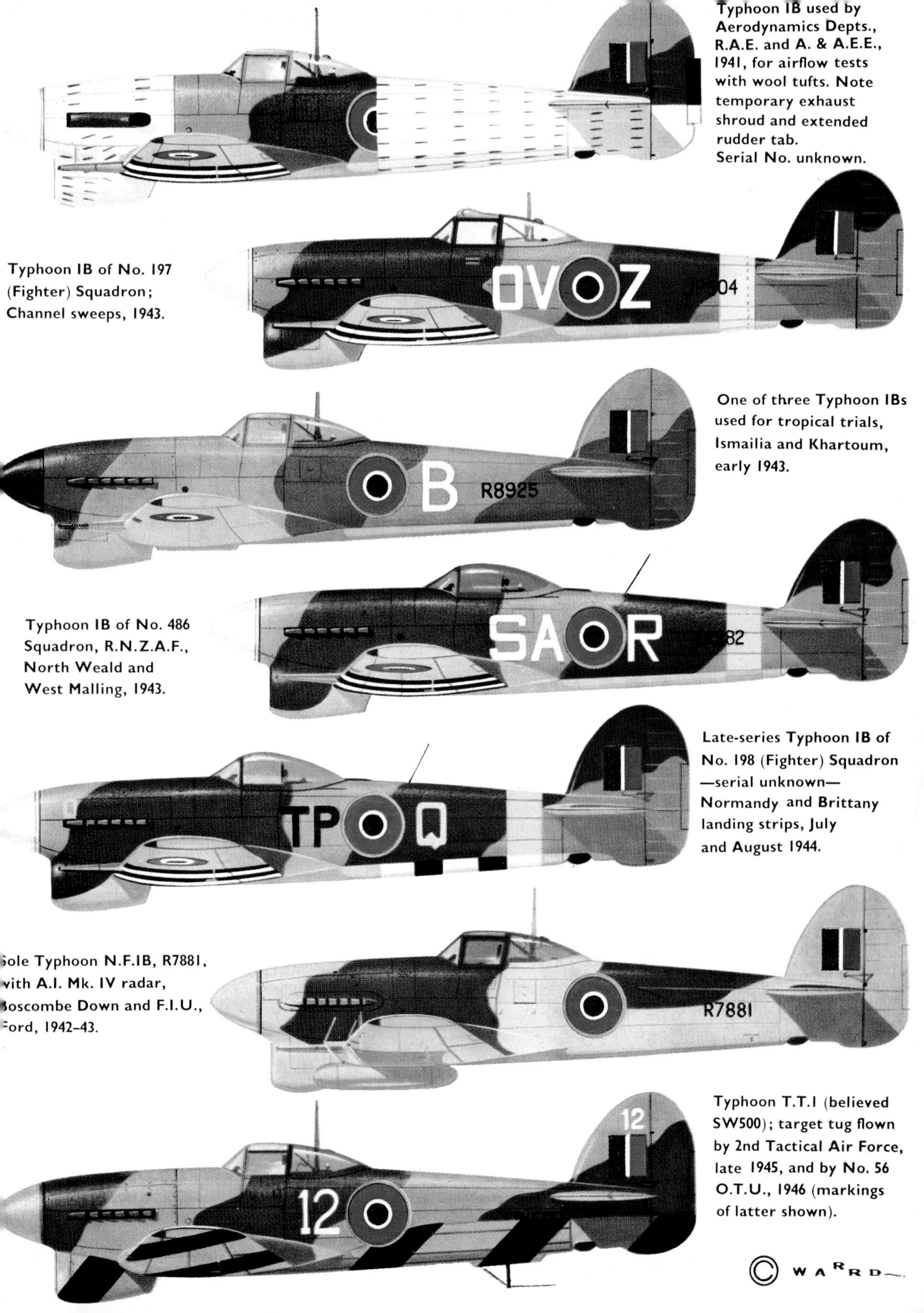

Typhoon IB used by Aerodynamics Depts., R.A.E. and A. & A.E.E., 1941, for airflow tests with wool tufts. Note temporary exhaust shroud and extended rudder tab. Serial No. unknown.

Typhoon IB of No. 197 (Fighter) Squadron; Channel sweeps, 1943.

One of three Typhoon IBs used for tropical trials, Ismailia and Khartoum, early 1943.

Typhoon IB of No. 486 Squadron, R.N.Z.A.F., North Weald and West Malling, 1943.

Late-series Typhoon IB of No. 198 (Fighter) Squadron —serial unknown— Normandy and Brittany landing strips, July and August 1944.

Sole Typhoon N.F.IB, R7881, with A.I. Mk. IV radar, Boscombe Down and F.I.U., Ford, 1942–43.

Typhoon T.T.1 (believed SW500); target tug flown by 2nd Tactical Air Force, late 1945, and by No. 56 O.T.U., 1946 (markings of latter shown).

Final production standard shown by Typhoon IB, SW537, *delivered to the R.A.F. just before the end of the European war in 1945. Napier Sabre IIC driving four-blade D.H. propeller, faired cannon, exhaust plinth, sliding canopy and whip aerial all characterised the last production batch.* (Photo: Hawker Siddeley Aviation Ltd., Neg. No. TYP11)

R7621 ("H"), *R7622* ("Q"), *R7629* ("P"), *R7633* ("C"), *R7679* ("L"), *R7711* ("M"), *R7713* ("Z"), *R8884* ("L"), *R8869* ("T"), *R8973* ("B"), *DN317* ("C"), *EJ962* ("R"), *EK181* ("X"), *EK269* ("K"), *EK326* ("E"), *JP446* ("U"), *JP681* ("F"), *JP682* ("L"), *JP728* ("G"), *JP749* ("V"), *JR262* ("J"), *MM992* ("B"), *MN182* ("C"), *MN198* ("D"), *MN206* ("J").
No. 137 (Fighter) Sqdn.: *DN492* ("W"), *JR261* ("Z"), *MN455* ("A"), *MN533* ("E"), *MN584* ("W").
No. 164 (Fighter) Sqdn.: *DN432* ("F"), *EK115* ("L"), *EK379* ("J"), *JP367* ("J"), *JP437* ("J").
No. 168 (Fighter) Sqdn.: *EK384, EK413, EK432, JP515, JP920, JR308, JR332, JR444, JR508, MN265, MN366, MN369, MN999, RB427, RB499.*
No. 175 (Fighter) Sqdn.: *EK153* ("S"), *EK447* ("B"), *EK455* ("B"), *JP394* ("E"), *JP753* ("S"), *JR308* ("D"), *JR501* ("R"), *MN204* ("Y"), *MN606* ("T").
No. 181 (Fighter) Sqdn., Duxford: *R8772, R8802, R8826–R8830, R8831* ("U"), *R8835, R8865, R8873, R8877, R8879, R8896, R8929, DN337, DN358* ("B"), *EK184* ("U"), *EK221* ("Q"), *EK280* ("G"), *JP604* ("W"), *JP917* ("O"), *JP920* ("E"), *JR212* ("K"), *JR294* ("C"), *JR297* ("B"), *JR381* ("Z"), *MN199* ("F"), *MN304* ("N"), *MN992* ("E"), *RB341* ("R").
No. 182 (Fighter) Sqdn., Martlesham Heath: *R8221, R7624* ("D"), *R8833* ("A"), *R8834* ("M"), *R8836* ("B"), *R8840* ("L"), *R8862* ("C"), *R8924* ("E"), *R8928* ("H"), *DN261* ("L"), *DN319* ("X"), *EK388* ("F"), *JP395* ("H"), *JP397* ("S"), *JP920* ("P"), *JR220* ("X"), *JR255* ("Y"), *JR293* ("C"), *JR528* ("J"), *MN995* ("A").
No. 183 (Fighter) Sqdn.: *JP790* ("C"), *JR128* ("L"), *JR209* ("G"), *JR263* ("Z"), *MN260* ("H"), *MN454* ("L"), *MN549* ("A").
No. 184 (Fighter) Sqdn.: *DN471, JP367, JR337* ("Z"), *MN301* ("Y"), *MN485* ("G").
No. 189 (Fighter) Sqdn., Digby: *R8939.*
No. 193 (Fighter) Sqdn.: *MN716* ("B"), *MN886* ("E"), *MN902* ("X"), *RB227* ("P").
No. 195 (Fighter) Sqdn., Hutton Cranswick: *R8938.*
No. 197 (Fighter) Sqdn.: *DN494* ("N"), *EJ928* ("A"), *EK505* ("D"), *JP504* ("Z"), *JR318* ("L"), *MN326* ("A"), *MN752* ("C").
No. 245 (Fighter) Sqdn.: *JP660* ("S"), *MN182* ("C"), *MN267* ("V"), *MN371* ("J").
No. 247 (Fighter) Sqdn., Duxford: *R8687, R8809, R8894, R8968, DN252* ("N"), *DN278* ("D"), *EJ911* ("J"), *EK190* ("X"), *JP578* ("Z"), *JP661* ("P"), *JR205* ("B"), *JR207* ("L"), *JR208* ("C"), *JR326* ("T"), *MN975* ("A"), *MN299* ("H"), *MN979* ("S").
No. 257 (Fighter) Sqdn., High Ercall and Exeter: *R8631–R8633, R8636–R8639, R8650–R8655, R8646* (delivered 24/7/42, crashed 29/7/42), *EJ926* ("L"), *EK172* ("T"), *MN645* ("F"), *MP116, MP124.*
No. 263 (Fighter) Sqdn., Exeter: *R8923* ("U"), *R8927* ("V"), *JR442* ("D"), *JR532* ("H"), *MN139* ("R"), *MN187* ("A"), *MN295* ("S"), *MN407* ("T"), *MN883* ("J"), *RB300* ("M"), *SW419* ("C"), *SW570, SW586, SW588.*
No. 266 (Fighter) Sqdn., Duxford, Wittering and Warmwell: *R7626* ("W"), *R7627* ("L"), *R7634* ("D"), *R7635* ("V"), *R7649* ("O"), *R7676* ("Q"), *R7921* ("K"), *R8937* (crashed at Exeter, 8/4/43), *DN296* ("K"), *EK448* ("A"), *JP853* ("K"), *MN353* ("J"), *MN683* ("R"), *MN712* ("Z"), *RB451* ("U").
No. 438 Sqdn., R.C.A.F.: *DN619* ("G"), *EK383* ("N"), *EK481* ("H"), *JR135* ("J"), *MM959* ("B"), *MN283* ("L"), *MN626* ("A"), *RB391* ("Y"), *SW398* ("E"), *SW414* ("G").
No. 439 Sqdn., R.C.A.F., Dunsfold: *R8926* ("B"), *R8977* ("D"), *EK219* ("X"), *JR299* ("S"), *JR362* ("F"), *JR444* ("J"), *JR506* ("X"), *MN427* ("Y"), *MN464* ("N"), *MN516* ("W"), *RB257* ("S"), *RB441* ("Z"), *SW423* ("J"), *SW460* ("D").
No. 440 Sqdn., R.C.A.F.: *JR432* ("A"), *MN428* ("B"), *RB377* ("Z"), *SW428* ("S").
No. 486 Sqdn., R.N.Z.A.F., Wittering, North Weald and West Malling: *R8684* ("B"), *R8707* ("V"), *R8713* ("T"), *R8746* ("P"), *EJ973* ("B"), *EK511* ("T").
No. 609 (West Riding) Sqdn., A.A.F., Duxford, Biggin Hill and Manston: *R7688* ("K"), *R7873* ("T"), *R8810, R8888, DN406* ("F"), *EK225* ("H"), *JP851* ("Q"), *JR379* ("L"), *MN701* ("Z"), *MN868* ("W"), *SW501, SW504, SW536, SW566.*
Operational Training Units. No. 54: *MN753* ("R"). No. 55: *DN442, EJ990, EK232, JP578* ("P"), *JR185* ("H"), *MN266* ("W"), *RB481, SW627* ("X"). No. 56: *EK173, JP970* ("F"), *JR149* ("V"), *MN240* ("J"), *SW474* ("K"), *SW523* ("D"). No. 59: *EK221* ("M"), *JR371* ("J"), *MN804* ("E"), *SW531* ("A"), *SW636* ("T").
Random examples of Typhoon accidents: *R7646* (crashed at Cranwell during stability trials, 4/5/42); *R8705* (crashed during test flight, 15/8/42); *R8720* and *R8756* (collided in bad weather); *DN323* (forced landed after engine failure, 31/12/42); *R8769* (crashed during delivery to R.A.F., 19/9/42); *MN173* (extensively damaged in fire during engine starting, 1944); *MP136* (fire in the air; aircraft exploded during dive bomb attack, 22/10/44); *JP551* (aircraft destroyed in fire during engine starting, 24/1/45); *RB404* (ditto, 31/1/45); *SW456* (fire in the air, pilot safe, 16/3/45).
Other Notes: R8198, R8222, R8225, R7576, R7618, R7672, DN340, EK122, JR333, MN551, RB306, SW555 (retained for prolonged trials by H.A.L. & G.A.C.); *R7638* (Rotol propeller trials); *R7578, R7618, R7638, R7712* (engine trials at Napiers, Luton); *R7684* (No. 17 O.T.U., 1943); *R7771* (Sabre IIA with mixed-matrix radiator; trials at Luton); *R7846, R8925, DN323* (tropical radiators; trials at Khartoum); *R7850* (Napier engine test bed); *R7881* (radar-equipped night fighter); *R8693* (R.A.E. camouflage and other paint schemes); *JR210* (rogue aircraft extensively tested by experimental establishments; painted *TR210* in error); *MN148* (A.F.D.U.); *RB306* (trials with cluster bombs, 1945).

SPECIFICATION	1st Prototype P5212	Typhoon IA R7576	Typhoon IB R8762	Typhoon IB DN348	Typhoon IB SW555
Date of performance report	6/6/40	17/8/41	26/11/42	9/7/43	13/10/45
Powerplant	2,020 h.p. Napier Sabre I and 3-blade D.H. propeller	2,100 h.p. Napier Sabre I and 3-blade D.H. propeller	2,180 h.p. Napier Sabre IIA and 3-blade Rotol propeller	2,200 h.p. Napier Sabre IIB and 3-blade D.H. propeller	2,260 h.p. Napier Sabre IIC and 4-blade Rotol propeller
Dimensions:					
Wing span	41 ft. 4 in.	41 ft. 7 in.	41 ft. 7 in.	41 ft. 7 in.	41 ft. 7 in.
Length	31 ft. 6 in.	31 ft. 10 in.	31 ft. 10 in.	31 ft. 10 in.	31 ft. 11½ in.
Height (tail down)	15 ft. 1 in.	14 ft. 10 in.	14 ft. 11 in.	14 ft. 10 in.	15 ft. 4 in.
Weights:					
Empty	7,109 lb.	7,630 lb.	8,280 lb.	8,690 lb.	8,840 lb.
Loaded (clean)	10,990 lb.	11,502 lb.	11,700 lb.	11,777 lb.	11,850 lb.
Loaded (overload)	—	—	—	12,905 lb.	13,980 lb. (U.S. 1,000-lb. bombs)
Performance:					
Max. speeds (at usual operating altitudes)	408 m.p.h. at 18,000 ft. and 396 m.p.h. at sea level	406 m.p.h. at 16,600 ft. and 398 m.p.h. at sea level	404 m.p.h. at 10,000 ft. and 398 m.p.h. at sea level	409 m.p.h. at 10,000 ft. and 406 m.p.h. at sea level	413·5 m.p.h. at 11,500 ft. and 412 m.p.h. at sea level
Time to height	5 min. 55 sec. to 15,000 ft.	6 min. 30 sec. to 15,000 ft.	6 min. 20 sec. to 15,000 ft.	5 min. 55 sec. to 15,000 ft.	5 min. 50 sec. to 15,000 ft.
Range with max. fuel	405 miles	380 miles	374 miles	910 miles with two 44-gal. drop tanks	510 miles with two 500-lb. bombs
Armament	Nil	12 0·303-in Brownings	4 20-mm. Hispano Mk. I	4 20-mm. Hispano Mk. I	4 20-mm. Hispano Mk. I*
Other data	Car door	Car door	Car door	Car door	Sliding hood

PRINTED IN ENGLAND © Profile Publications Ltd., P.O. Box 26, 1a North Street, Leatherhead, Surrey, England.
Printed by Hills & Lacy Ltd., London and Watford, England. U.S. 2nd Class Mailing Rates applied for.

PROFILE PUBLICATIONS

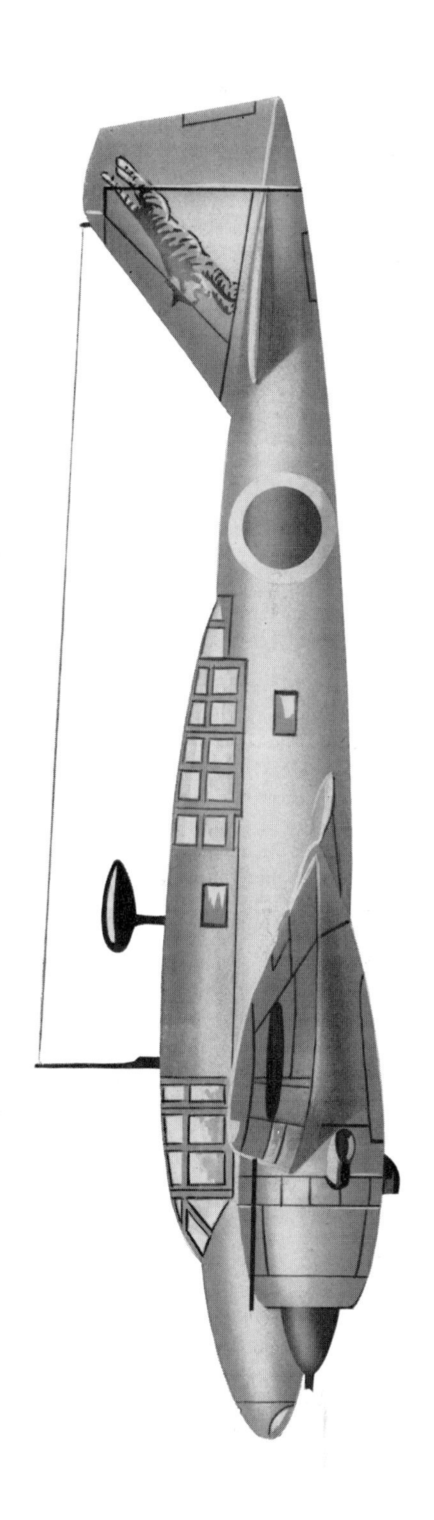

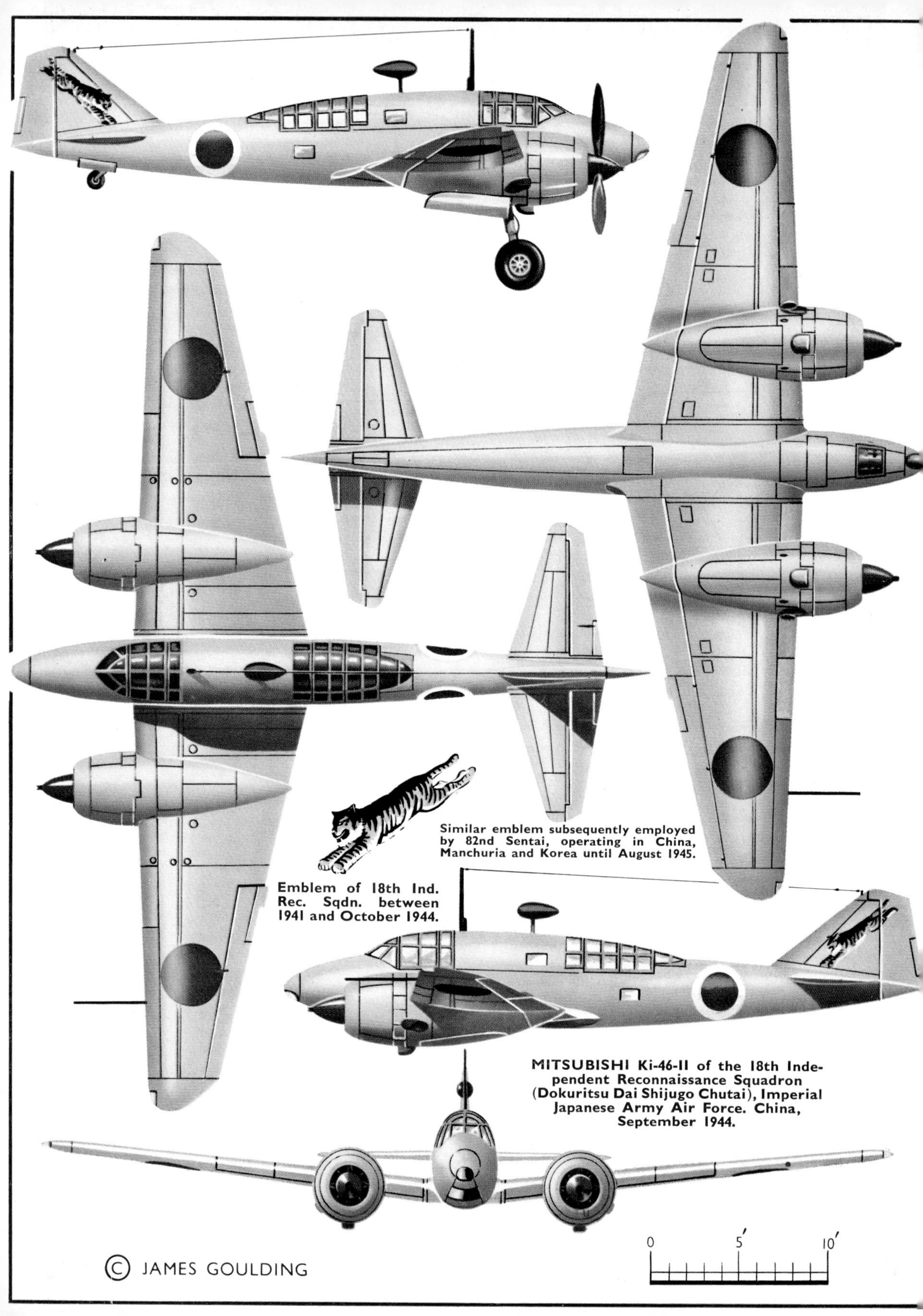
Similar emblem subsequently employed by 82nd Sentai, operating in China, Manchuria and Korea until August 1945.
Emblem of 18th Ind. Rec. Sqdn. between 1941 and October 1944.
MITSUBISHI Ki-46-II of the 18th Independent Reconnaissance Squadron (Dokuritsu Dai Shijugo Chutai), Imperial Japanese Army Air Force. China, September 1944.
0
5′
10′
© JAMES GOULDING

The Mitsubishi Ki-46

by René J. Francillon, Ph.D.

An Army Type 100 Model 2 Command Reconnaissance aircraft of the 2nd Chutai, 81st Sentai, in flight over China. (Photo: courtesy *Aireview*)

Due to the vast distances separating Japanese airfields from the bases of its potential enemies, the Japanese Army Air Force had a standing requirement for a fast long-range reconnaissance aircraft. In the mid-thirties, this requirement had been met by a single-engined monoplane with trousered undercarriage, the Army Type 97 Command Reconnaissance Plane or Mitsubishi Ki-15, later named "Babs" by the Allies, which, initiated in December 1935, became operational in May 1937. The outstanding performance of this aircraft was revealed to the Western world when, between 6th and 9th April 1937, at the occasion of the Coronation of H.M. King George VI, the second prototype was flown from Tachikawa to London covering 9,542 miles in 94 hours 17 minutes 56 seconds, the actual flying time being 51 hours 17 minutes 23 seconds and the average speed being 101·2 m.p.h. (according to the *Fédération Aéronautique Internationale* which homologated this record). This aircraft, registered J-BAAI and named *Kamikaze* (Divine Wind), had been bought by *Asahi Shimbum*, one of the leading Japanese newspapers, which entrusted it to Masaaki Iinuma, pilot, and Kenji Tsukagoshi, flight mechanic and navigator. Although the range performance of the Ki-15-I was quite outstanding (1,500 miles) its maximum speed of 298 m.p.h. was obviously too low if the aircraft was to avoid interception by the modern monoplanes then entering service with the air forces of the Western Powers.

While the Ki-15 was undergoing flight trials and initial service operations, Major Fujita and Engs. Ando and Tanaka of the Technical Branch of the JAAF Headquarters were already studying the requirements for a future Ki-15 replacement. Towards the end of 1937, having defined the problems to be solved, they were authorised to approach the staff of Mitsubishi Jukogyo K.K. (Mitsubishi Heavy Industries Co.), which was responsible for the aeronautical activities of the powerful Mitsubishi Zaibatsu (Combine), to initiate the project. On 12th December 1937, a specification for a high-speed, long-range, reconnaissance aircraft known as the Ki-46 was issued to Mitsubishi. The JAAF wanted an aircraft able to collect intelligence data and photographs without being detected, as it was intended to use this aircraft during peacetime for unauthorised overflights of potential enemy territory. Actually, the war broke out too soon for this aircraft to be operated as such but it was to be used extensively throughout the 1941–45 conflict. The JAAF specified that the aircraft was to cruise for six hours at a speed of 250 m.p.h. between 13,125 ft. and 19,685 ft. and to have a maximum speed of 373 m.p.h. at 13,125 ft. It was to be powered by one or two 790-h.p. Kawasaki Ha-20b, 950-h.p. Nakajima Ha-25, or 850-h.p. Mitsubishi Ha-26 engines and the defensive armament was limited to one 7·7-mm. Type 89 flexible machine gun with 216 rounds in the rear cockpit. All other usual requirements were waived to help Mitsubishi meet the stringent speed and range specifications.

Earlier in the same year Mitsubishi, Nakajima and Kawasaki had been instructed by JAAF Headquarters to initiate design studies for twin-engined, two-seat, long-range fighters, these projects being respectively assigned the designations Ki-39, Ki-37 and Ki-38. Mitsubishi's engineering staff being fully committed to other pressing projects, the Ki-39 did not progress further than the initial design stage and the JAAF Headquarters allowed the Company to withdraw from this competition. While working on the Ki-39, Mitsubishi had studied the possibility of adapting this design for long-range missions, the project being known as the Ki-40, but further studies were suspended at the time of the Ki-39's cancellation. However, the work done on the Ki-39 and the Ki-40 was to serve as a basis for the Ki-46 design study.

Captured Ki-46-II in the markings of the Technical Air Intelligence Centre. (Photo: via the author)

The challenge facing Tomio Kubo, who had been assigned the responsibility of leading Mitsubishi's design team, was tremendous, especially in regard to the maximum speed specified, which was to exceed that of the early Hurricane I, then just entering service, by some 55 m.p.h. and that of the Curtiss P-36A, about to be delivered to the squadrons of the U.S. Army Air Corps, by 60 m.p.h. Although no liquid-cooled engine of suitable power was then available in Japan, Tomio Kubo was initially in favour of using this type of engine as opposed to the radial with its larger diameter and associated drag. However, as there was little or no prospect of obtaining a satisfactory liquid-cooled engine in the time available, it was decided to use the 15-cylinder radial Mitsubishi Ha-26 as it had the smallest diameter of the three types of engines recommended by the JAAF. To find a solution to the drag problem Tomio Kubo called upon facilities of the Aeronautical Research Institute of the University of Tokyo which conducted extensive wind tunnel tests. As a result of these tests close-fitting cowlings, minimising drag and improving the pilot's side vision while ensuring satisfactory engine cooling, were adopted. At the same time a thinner wing section than had been originally planned was selected and the fuselage diameter was kept to a minimum. To locate a large fuel tank in the fuselage close to the aircraft centre of gravity it was found necessary to separate the two crew members, the pilot being seated over the wing leading-edge whilst the radio-operator/gunner sat over the trailing-edge under a separate canopy. The Aeronautical Research Institute also recommended the use of constant speed propellers and conducted some studies of the retractable landing gear.

Ki-46-II of the 55th Dokuritsu Dai Shijugo Chutai. (Photo: via the author)

Rear view of the same machine. (Photo: via the author)

The Australian Army discovered this Army Type 100 Model 2 of the 76th Dokoritsu Dai Shijugo Chutai at Gasmata, New Britain. (Photo: Australian War Memorial)

FLIGHT TRIALS BEGIN

The first prototype Ki-46 was completed at Mitsubishi's Nagoya aircraft plant in early November 1939, and the aircraft was transported to Kakumugahara airfield where flight testing began later in the month with Major Fujita, who had been the moving force behind the programme, at the controls. The aircraft was powered by two 875-h.p. 14-cylinder Mitsubishi Ha-26-I engines, each with a single-speed supercharger, driving constant-speed, three-blade propellers. Provision was made for one 7·7-mm. Type 89 flexible machine gun with 216 rounds of ammunition manned by the radio-operator. Early in the flight test programme the aircraft attained a maximum speed of 335·5 m.p.h. at 13,125 ft. and few teething troubles were encountered. Even though the maximum speed was some 40 m.p.h. below that specified, JAAF Headquarters was still satisfied as the aircraft was faster than the A6M2 (331 m.p.h. at 14,930 ft.) and the Ki-43-I (308 m.p.h. at 13,125 ft.) then undergoing flight test evaluation. However, the JAAF was aware that the performance of the Ki-46 was insufficient to assure freedom of interception by Western fighters, such as the Spitfire IIA with its maximum speed of 370 m.p.h., and it instructed Mitsubishi to explore the possibilities of adapting more powerful engines to the Ki-46 airframe. Fortunately, Mitsubishi had under development an advanced version of the Ha-26, the Ha-102, which had the same overall diameter and was expected to develop 1,050 h.p. at take-off rating and 950 h.p. at 19,000 ft.

Pending availability of the Mitsubishi Ha-102 engine the Ki-46 was placed in production with the Type 99 Model 1, the production version of the Ha-26-I, as the Army Type 100 Model 1 Command Reconnaissance Plane (Ki-46-I). These aircraft, which were identical to the prototypes, were used for pilot training and intensive service evaluation, most aircraft

Undercarriage and engine details visible on a captured 55th D.D.S.C. machine. (Photo: via the author)

A Ki-46-II during flight test evaluation by the T.A.I.C. (Photo: via the author)

being delivered to the *Shimoshizu Rikugun Hikogakuko* (Shimoshizu Army Flying School). During the production of these aircraft it became apparent that during the design phase the emphasis had been placed on meeting the stringent performance requirements at the expense of ease in production and maintenance. Pilots also complained about the slow response of ailerons and the lack of effectiveness of rudder control, but these were minor shortcomings as the Ki-46 was not intended for combat, its speed and altitude performances protecting it from interception by enemy fighters.

MAJOR PRODUCTION MODEL

In March 1941, the first Ki-46 powered by two 1,080-h.p. Mitsubishi Ha-102 with a two-speed, two-stage supercharger was readied for flight test evaluation. Immediately the aircraft met the most sanguine expectations of the JAAF Headquarters as it exceeded slightly the maximum speed initially specified, attaining 375 m.p.h. at 19,000 ft. Production aircraft, known as Army Type 100 Model 2 Command Reconnaissance Plane (Ki-46-II), were already rolling off Mitsubishi's assembly lines at Nagoya and were rushed to operational units. In July 1941, the 50th, 70th, 74th, and 76th Dokuritsu Dai Shijugo Chutais (Independent Squadrons) in Manchuria and the 51st Dokuritsu Dai Shijugo Chutai in China were activated and were equipped mainly with Ki-46-IIs as well as a few Ki-46-Is. These units were followed by the 18th Dokuritsu Dai Shijugo Chutai and the 81st Sentai (Group), also operating in China. As the Chinese Air Force was virtually annihilated at that time the Ki-46s went about their business undisturbed, their performances overshadowing those of the Ki-15-Is and Ki-15-IIs, which previously equipped the China-Manchuria based Command Reconnaissance units.

When the war broke out the Ki-46 units were split in small elements to cover a vast area encompassing China, the Philippines, Thailand, Burma, India, Malaya and the Dutch East Indies. These units were constantly on the move reconnoitring territories under Allied control ahead of the fast-advancing Japanese forces. As the Allies lacked radar equipment in the South-west Pacific and CBI theatres, the Ki-46-IIs were seldom intercepted by Allied fighters, which did not have the speed or the climbing rate necessary to catch the nimble Japanese aircraft. The Japanese Navy Air Force was one of the first to pay tribute to the magnificent Army Type 100 Command Reconnaissance Plane by negotiating with the JAAF the delivery of a small number of Ki-46s. At that time the land-based reconnaissance units of the JNAF were flying the obsolescent Navy Type 98 Reconnaissance Plane (Mitsubishi C5M1 & 2 "Babs"), a naval version of the Ki-15, which lacked the performance necessary to avoid interception by Allied fighters. Some of the JNAF Ki-46-IIs, flying from Timor Island, were active over Northern Australia. In late 1942, the Ki-46 received from the Allies the code name "Dinah".

In the light of combat experience some weaknesses of the design, most of which had been already uncovered during service trials, became more apparent. Vapour locks occurred frequently in hot and humid weather and tests were specially conducted in Formosa during June 1940, using a Ki-46-I, and June 1941 with a Ki-46-II. As a result of these tests the fuel lines around the engines were modified to improve cooling and the fuel was changed from 87 octane petrol to 92 octane petrol. Oil was also found to overheat during the long climb to cruising altitude but no remedy was found and the pilots were instructed to choose the most favourable climbing speed as, due to the type of operations in which the aircraft was engaged, there

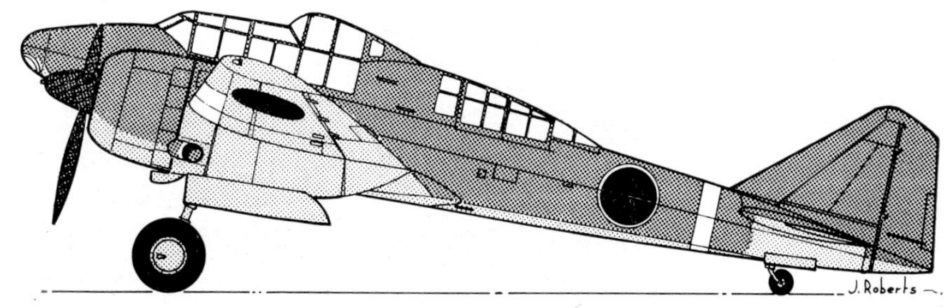

Ki-46-II-KAI (Army Type 100 operations trainer)

Right and below: *Three views of a Model 3 abandoned in China. Note bullet damage, also that the leading edge fuel tank has been removed from the port wing.*
(Photos: via the author)

was no need for a fast climb such as required from a fighter aircraft. Oxygen supply was another source of difficulty, especially during missions flown at maximum range. Furthermore, with a wing loading high by Japanese standards, ranging from 21 lb./sq. ft. at zero fuel weight to 37·1 lb./sq. ft. at maximum gross take-off weight, the Ki-46-II had a high sinking rate and the undercarriage often failed on landing. The trouble was traced to the undercarriage auxiliary rear strut which bent under heavy stress; a stronger strut was adopted but on occasions the undercarriage still collapsed. However, these problems were too minor to seriously affect the operational use of the Ki-46. A measure of the Ki-46's success is given by the fact that, contrary to its usual policy to constantly adopt new aircraft types rather than to improve operational aircraft in its inventory, the JAAF kept the aircraft in production throughout the war; of the two Ki-46 replacements which were studied during the war one, the Tachikawa Ki-70 "Clara", failing to show an improvement over its predecessor and being overweight, was abandoned, while the second, the Mitsubishi Ki-95, remained a project on its manufacturer's drawing boards. It should also be noted that during the war 1,742 Ki-46s were built as compared to 698 P.R. Mosquitoes, many of the latter converted from bomber or fighter versions of this aircraft, and 1,334 Lockheed F-4s and F-5s, which were converted from the P-38 Lightning for photo-reconnaissance work. The Germans were also sufficiently impressed by the performance of the Ki-46-II to negotiate under the Japanese-German Technical Exchange Programme the acquisition of a manufacturing licence, but the deal failed to materialise.

A three-seat radio navigation trainer characterised by a stepped-up cockpit behind the pilot's seat was produced in 1943 as the Army Type 100 Operation Trainer (Ki-46-II KAI), all Ki-46-II KAIs being converted from standard Ki-46-IIs and none being built as such.

IMPROVING THE PERFORMANCE

In May 1942, the JAAF Headquarters, anticipating that the Allies would soon have at their disposal fast-climbing fighters such as the P-38F and F4U-1 which, guided by Ground Interception Radar, would be capable of intercepting the Ki-46-II, instructed Mitsubishi to further improve it. The JAAF specified that flight duration was to be increased by one hour, maximum speed raised to 404 m.p.h. and that the aircraft was to be powered by two 1,500-h.p. Mitsubishi Ha-112-II, while the landing gear was to be reinforced to cope with the increase in weight.

To achieve the specified flight duration Mitsubishi entirely redesigned the fuel system, and fuel capacity was increased from 365 Imp. gallons to 417 Imp. gallons contained in two unprotected fuselage tanks,

Front view of a Ki-46-IVa with wing leading-edge identification band and air intakes offset to port. (Photo: via the author)

Port side view of the Ki-46-IV reveals turbo-supercharger installation at the rear of the engine nacelle. (Photo: courtesy *Aireview*)

one ahead and one behind the pilot, and five unprotected tanks in each wing. A ventral drop tank containing 101·2 Imp. gallons was also fitted. Although the pilot was seated between two unprotected fuel tanks he was given the token protection of 13 mm. back and head armour plate. To save some weight the flexible machine gun, which had been so far provided more for psychological purposes than as an effective means of defence, was dispensed with on the Ki-46-III. Some redesign of the engine cowling was necessary to accommodate the Mitsubishi Ha-112-II which, although being a direct development of the Ha-102 fitted with a direct fuel injection system, had a diameter increase of four-tenths of an inch; and the already streamlined fuselage was further improved by the use of a new canopy over the pilot's seat without the step between the nose and the top of the fuselage.

Following flight testing of two prototypes, which had begun in December 1942, the Ki-46-III was adopted for mass production as the Army Type 100 Model 3 Command Reconnaissance Plane, coming off the assembly lines at Nagoya parallel with the earlier Ki-46-II until the complete phasing out of the Model 2 during 1944. However, Ki-46-III production was transferred in early 1945 to Toyama, Toyama Prefecture, following the almost complete destruction of Mitsubishi's Nagoya plant by a severe earthquake in December 1944 combined with massive raids by B-29s of the U.S. 20th Air Force. Prior to this event a slightly improved version of the Ki-46-III, characterised by the replacement of the single exhaust pipe on the outboard of each engine by individual exhaust stacks providing some thrust augmentation, had been introduced. A slight increase in range and maximum speed (+7 m.p.h.) was registered as a result of this modification.

Upon its initial introduction in operational squadrons the Ki-46-III was received enthusiastically by its pilots due to its maximum speed of 391 m.p.h. at 19,685 ft. and its markedly improved performances between 26,000 ft. and 32,800 ft. over the earlier Ki-46-II. At first the pilots' enthusiasm was not shared by the maintenance crews, who experienced difficulties with the novel fuel injection system of the Ha-112-II engines, this problem being finally solved by appropriate training given to the ground crews by roving field teams sent out by Mitsubishi. Ki-46-IIIs, often operating alongside Ki-46-IIs, covered the entire South-west Pacific and CBI theatres of operations where they enjoyed a relative, though rapidly disappearing, freedom from interception. Amongst the final major tasks undertaken by the Army Type 100 Model

A Ki-46-IVa in front of the Mitsubishi aircraft plant at Nagoya. (Photo: via the author)

Although the strengthening of the undercarriage was one of the requirements of the Ki-46-III development, the Model 3 still suffered chronic weakness of the landing gear struts.
(Photo: via the author)

An operational "Dinah", probably photographed in China.
(Photo: R. Ward collection)

3 Command Reconnaissance Plane were regular reconnaissance flights by aircraft based at Shimoshizu near Tokyo which, with a fuelling stop at Iwo-Jima, kept a constant watch over the B-29 bases in the Marianas. Allied pilots respected this enemy, which proved difficult to intercept even by high-performance fighters such as were available in 1944–45 but which, once overtaken, was an easy prey lacking all defensive armament and fire protection equipment.

FIGHTER DEVELOPMENT

Shortly before China-based B-29s of the U.S. XX Bomber Command initiated high-altitude daylight raids over Japan, the JAAF Headquarters became aware of the urgent need to develop an interceptor fighter with good performances at high altitude. The Army Aeronautical Research Institute at Tachikawa *(Rikugun Kokugijutsu Kenkyujo)* had, in June 1943, studied the possibility of adapting the Mitsubishi Ki-46-III, which was one of the few JAAF operational aircraft to have the required altitude performance, to this type of operation. In May 1944, the project was urgently revived and conversion lines were quickly set up at the *Tachikawa Dai-ichi Rikugun Kokosho* (First Army Air Arsenal at Tachikawa). The photographic equipment and forward fuselage fuel tank were replaced by two 20-mm. Ho-5 cannon with 200 r.p.g., the canopy was modified to resemble that of the Ki-46-II and a 37-mm. Ho-203 cannon with 200 rounds of ammunition was mounted in the centre fuselage firing forward and upward at an angle of 30°. The first aircraft of this model, known as the Army

A Ki-46-III Kai prepares for take-off; note nose battery.
(Photo: R. Ward collection)

Type 100 Air Defence Fighter (Ki-46-III KAI), was completed in October 1944. From November of that year aircraft of this type served in the defence of Japan, equipping two Sentais, five Dokuritsu Dai Shijugo Chutai and one Dokuritsu Hikotai. However, the aircraft was not very successful, being too vulnerable to the concentrated fire of the B-29s and lacking the climbing speed required of an interceptor.

Development of two additional fighter versions, dispensing with the 37-mm. cannon, were begun by Mitsubishi in March 1945. They were the Ki-46-IIIb or Army Type 100 Ground-Attack Aircraft, of which only a few were built, and the Ki-46-IIIc, with obliquely mounted 20-mm. Ho-5 cannons, which remained on the drawing boards.

Details of the Ki-46-III now preserved in the aircraft museum at R.A.F. Biggin Hill, Kent, U.K. (Photos: John Pitt)

Nose, showing forward camera position.

Starboard view of rear cockpit.

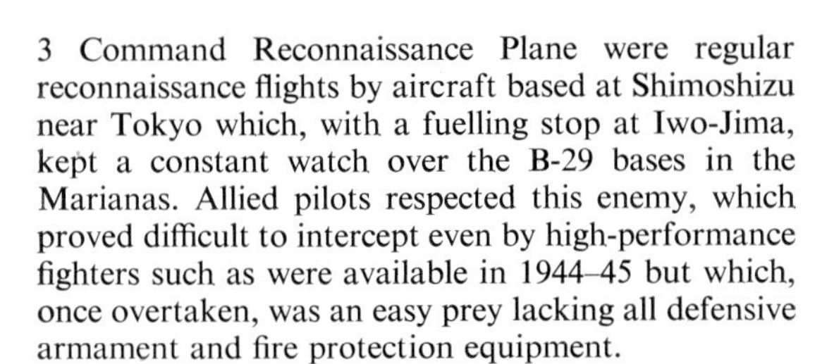

Port engine nacelle.

Starboard spinner.

TURBO-SUPERCHARGER ADAPTED

Following the failure of its intended replacement, the Tachikawa Ki-70, the weight and wing loading of which proved excessive (21,730 lb. and 46·9 lb./sq. ft. respectively), the Ki-46 had to be further developed to improve its capabilities of avoiding interception. Little could be done to improve the aerodynamic characteristics of the aircraft, and performance could only be improved by using engines of increased power, in particular at high altitude. Rather than selecting a new type of engine, which would have entailed a major redesign of the wings and nacelles, Mitsubishi decided to use a newer version of the Ha-112-II, the Ha-112-IIRu, fitted with an exhaust-driven turbo-supercharger, and rated at 1,500 h.p. on take-off at sea-level, but developing 1,250 h.p. up to 22,965 ft. and 1,100 h.p. at 33,465 ft. The turbo-superchargers were mounted in the lower rear portion of the nacelles and the intake air was methanol-cooled as the space available in the nacelles was too limited for using a normal intercooler. The front fuselage fuel tank was further enlarged bringing the total internal capacity to 435 Imp. gallons but no other change was introduced.

Four prototypes Ki-46-IVa were built in 1944–45 and flight tests commenced in February 1944. Performance at altitudes over 26,250 ft. was spectacularly improved, but the aircraft were a source of constant headache to the ground crews as the novel engines proved to be quite unreliable. On 28th February 1945, two of the prototypes demonstrated the capabilities of the Ki-46-IVa by covering the 1,430 miles separating Peking from Fussa (now Yokota AFB) in 3 hours 15 minutes, the aircraft flying at 32,800 ft. and averaging 435 m.p.h. However, the production of the turbo-supercharged Ha-112-IIRu was too slow to gain tempo and these engines were assigned in priority to power high-altitude interceptor fighters such as the Kawasaki Ki-100-II, Ki-102a and Ki-102c. Consequently the Ki-46-IVa never replaced the Ki-46-III on Mitsubishi's production lines and a fighter version, the Ki-46-IVb, with nose-mounted cannons remained on the drawing boards.

Thus ended the development of what was perhaps the most outstanding Japanese aircraft to serve its country during the Pacific war. Fortunately for historians, one of these aircraft, a Ki-46-III, has been preserved by the Royal Air Force at Biggin Hill, Kent, U.K.

Left to right: *Aft view of rear cockpit, also showing fine aerodynamic finish of the fuselage; rear cockpit interior, looking aft; ventral camera mounting and sliding belly hatch in rear cockpit.*

SERVICE DEPLOYMENT OF THE MITSUBISHI Ki-46

I. Army Type 100 Command Reconnaissance Plane.

Unit	Period	Theatres of Operation
Sentai		
2nd	1943–44	Manchuria, Philippines.
8th	1942–July 1943	—
10th	1943–45	New Guinea, Rabaul, Formosa, Japan.
15th	Jan. 1944–45	Philippines, New Guinea, French Indo-China (created by merger of the 50th, 51st and 55th Dokuritsu Dai Shijugo Chutais).
38th	April 1943–July 1945	Japan, Philippines, Formosa.
81st	Sept 1941–Aug. 1945	China, Indo-China, Malaya, Sumatra, Java, Burma.
82nd	Oct. 1944–Aug. 1945	China, Manchuria, Korea.
88th	Oct. 1944–Aug. 1945	—
Dokuritsu Dai Shijugo Chutai		
17th	July 1944–July 1945	Japan.
18th	1941–Oct. 1944	China, Indo-China.
19th	July 1944–June 1945	Japan.
50th	July 1941–Jan. 1944	Manchuria, Indo-China, Java, Sumatra, Malaya, Burma.
51st	July 1941–Jan. 1944	China, Formosa, Indo-China, Malaya, Thailand, Japan.
55th	Mar. 1942–Oct. 1944	Manchuria, China.
63rd	—	—
70th	July 1941–Aug. 1945	Manchuria, Formosa, Indo-China, Thailand, Burma, Java.
74th	July 1941–Mar. 1944	Manchuria, Formosa, Philippines, Java, New Guinea.
76th	July 1941–June 1943	Manchuria, Formosa, Philippines, New Britain, Solomon Islands, New Guinea.
81st	1941–Nov. 1944	—
85th	? –Jan. 1944	—
Dokuritsu Hikotai		
38th	July–Aug. 1945	Japan.
Shimoshizu Rikugun Hikogakuko (Shimoshizu Army Flying School).	1941–June 1944	Japan.
Tokorozawa Rikugun Koku Seibigakuko (Tokorozawa Army Air Maintenance School).	Mar. 1943–June 1944	Japan.

81st Group, 1st Squadron, white, red outline.

Ki-46-II, 81st Group, 2nd Squadron, Malaya, 1942. Overall pale green, yellow stripe on wing leading edge, white fuselage band, brown spinners, red fin marking outlined in white.

15th Group, white, red outline.

Ki-46-II, 76th Direct Command Squadron, Gasmata, New Britain, 1943. Overall pale grey, yellow stripe on wing leading edge, white fuselage band, red tail marking.

Shimoshizu Ar Flying School, 1941–June 194 Colours as Tokorozawa Sch aircraft (left).

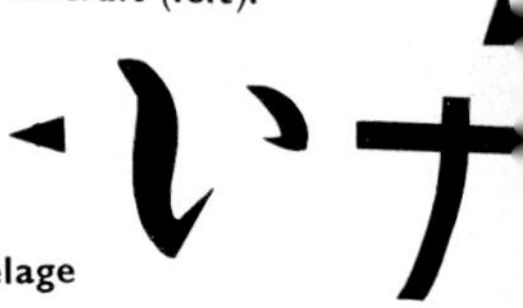

Ki-46-II, Tokorozawa Army Air Maintenance School, 1943–44. Overall bare metal, pale green rudder, black rudder markings, black anti-glare panel, two white fuselage bands, red spinners.

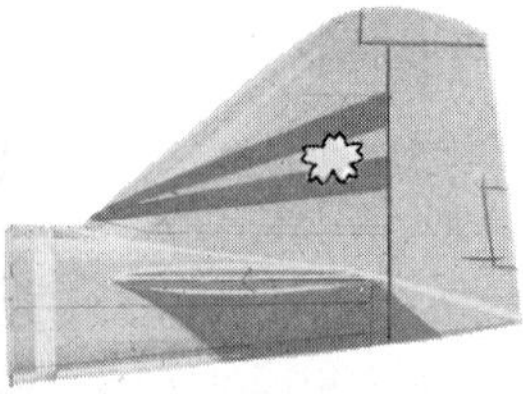

Ki-46-II, 15th Group, 3rd Squadron. Overall pale green, white emblem outlined in red, superimposed on yellow stripes.

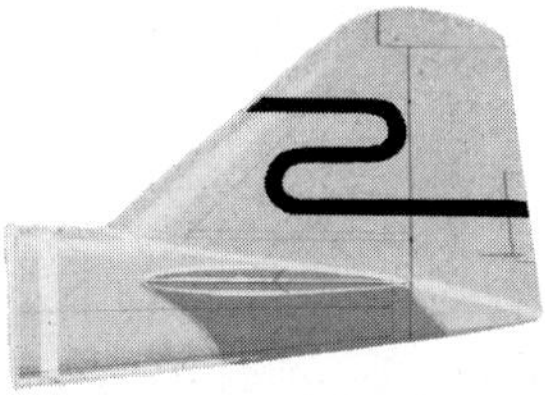

76th Direct Command Squadron; red marking on pale green.

74th Direct Command Squadron; yellow marking, as 76th.

70th Direct Command Squadron; white marking, as 76th.

17th Direct Command Squadron, 1944–45. Note yellow sta

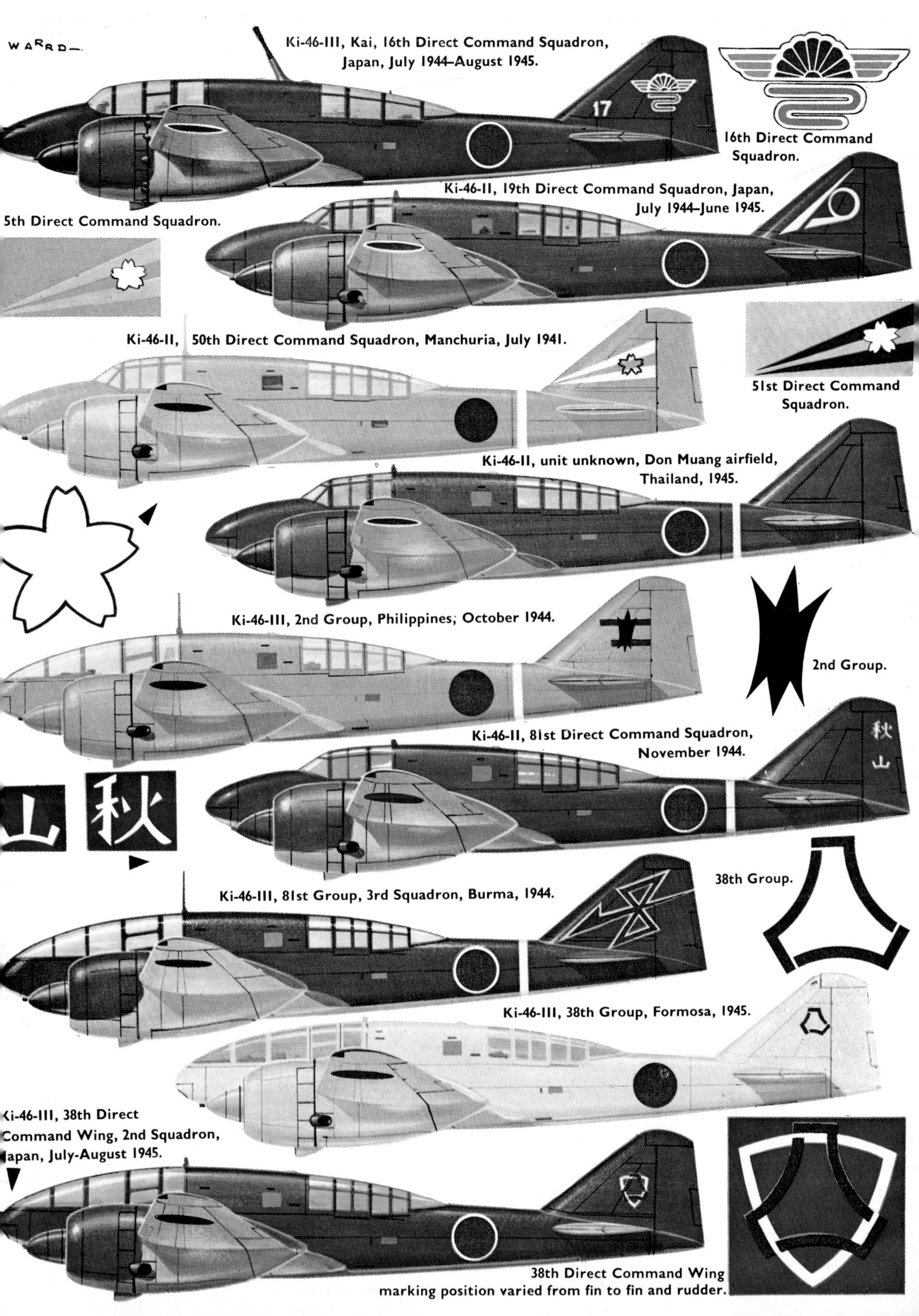
WARRD—
Ki-46-III, Kai, 16th Direct Command Squadron, Japan, July 1944–August 1945.
17
16th Direct Command Squadron.
Ki-46-II, 19th Direct Command Squadron, Japan, July 1944–June 1945.
5th Direct Command Squadron.
Ki-46-II, 50th Direct Command Squadron, Manchuria, July 1941.
51st Direct Command Squadron.
Ki-46-II, unit unknown, Don Muang airfield, Thailand, 1945.
Ki-46-III, 2nd Group, Philippines, October 1944.
2nd Group.
Ki-46-II, 81st Direct Command Squadron, November 1944.
秋
山
Ki-46-III, 81st Group, 3rd Squadron, Burma, 1944.
38th Group.
Ki-46-III, 38th Group, Formosa, 1945.
Ki-46-III, 38th Direct Command Wing, 2nd Squadron, Japan, July-August 1945.
38th Direct Command Wing marking position varied from fin to fin and rudder.

Army Type 100 Air Defence Fighter of the 16th Dokuritsu Hikotai. Note oblique-mounted 37-mm. Ho-203 cannon.
(Photo: courtesy *Aireview*)

2. Army Type 100 Air Defence Fighter.

Unit	Period	Theatres of Operation
Sentai		
28th	? –July 1945	Japan.
106th	Nov. 1944–May 1945	Japan.
Dokuritsu Dai Shijugo Chutai		
4th	—	Japan.
16th	July 1944–Aug. 1945	Japan.
81st	Nov. 1944–Feb. 1945	Manchuria.
82nd	Feb. 1945–July 1945	Japan.
83rd	Feb. 1945–July 1945	Japan.
Dokuritsu Hikotai		
16th	1945	Japan, Okinawa.

PRODUCTION

All Ki-46s were built by Mitsubishi Jukogyo K.K. at Nagoya and Toyama.

34	Ki-46 and Ki-46-I (1939–40).
1,093	Ki-46-II (1940–44).
2	Ki-46-III prototypes (1942).
609	Ki-46-III (including fighter conversions) (1942–45).
4	Ki-46-IV (1943–44).
1,742	

Or:

52	(1939–41).
118	(December 1941–March 1942).
282	(April 1942–March 1943).
603	(April 1943–March 1944).
551	(April 1944–March 1945).
136	(April 1945–August 1945).
1,742	

SPECIFICATIONS

	Ki-46-I	Ki-46-II	Ki-46-III	Ki-46-III Kai	Ki-46-IV
Span	48 ft. 2$\frac{3}{4}$ in.	48 ft. 2$\frac{3}{4}$ in.	48 ft. 2$\frac{3}{4}$ in.	48 ft. 2$\frac{3}{4}$ in.	48 ft. 2$\frac{3}{4}$ in.
Length	36 ft. 1$\frac{1}{16}$ in.	36 ft. 1$\frac{1}{16}$ in.	36 ft. 1$\frac{1}{16}$ in.	37 ft. 8$\frac{3}{16}$ in.	36 ft. 1$\frac{1}{16}$ in.
Height	12 ft. 8$\frac{3}{4}$ in.	12 ft. 8$\frac{3}{4}$ in.	12 ft. 8$\frac{3}{4}$ in.	12 ft. 8$\frac{3}{4}$ in.	12 ft. 8$\frac{3}{4}$ in.
Wing Area	344·4 sq. ft.	344·4 sq. ft.	344·4 sq. ft.	344·4 sq. ft.	344·4 sq. ft.
Empty Weight	7,449 lb.	7,194 lb.	8,446 lb.	—	8,840 lb.
Loaded Weight	10,631 lb.	11,133 lb.	12,619 lb.	13,730 lb.	13,007 lb.
Maximum Weight	—	12,787 lb.	14,330 lb.	—	14,330 lb.
Wing Loading*	30·9 lb./sq. ft.	32·3 lb./sq. ft.	36·6 lb./sq. ft.	39·9 lb./sq. ft.	37·8 lb./sq. ft.
Power Loading*	13·6 lb./h.p.	10·3 lb./h.p.	8·4 lb./h.p.	9·2 lb./h.p.	8·7 lb./h.p.
Fuel Capacity: (Internal) ...	327·8 Imp. gals.	364·5 Imp. gals.	416·9 Imp. gals.	—	434·9 Imp. gals.
(Drop Tank) ...	—	—	101·2 Imp. gals.	—	101·2 Imp. gals.
Engine	Ha-26-I	Ha-102	Ha-112-II	Ha-112-II	Ha-112-II Ru
Take-off Rating	780 h.p. at 2,540 r.p.m.	1,080 h.p. at 2,700 r.p.m.	1,500 h.p. at 2,600 r.p.m.	1,500 h.p. at 2,600 r.p.m.	1,500 h.p. at 2,600 r.p.m.
Military Power Rating	900 h.p. at 11,810 ft.	1,055 h.p. at 9,185 ft.	1,350 h.p. at 6,560 ft.	1,350 h.p. at 6,560 ft.	1,350 h.p. at 6,560 ft.
	—	950 h.p. at 19,030 ft.	1,250 h.p. at 19,030 ft.	1,250 h.p. at 19,030 ft.	1,250 h.p. at 24,280 ft.
Propeller: (No. of Blades) ...	3	3	3	3	3
(Diameter)... ...	9 ft. $\frac{1}{4}$ in.	9 ft. 8$\frac{1}{8}$ in.	9 ft. 8$\frac{1}{8}$ in.	9 ft. 8$\frac{1}{8}$ in.	9 ft. 8$\frac{1}{8}$ in.
Maximum Speed	335·5 m.p.h. at 13,350 ft.	375 m.p.h. at 19,030 ft.	391 m.p.h. at 19,685 ft	391 m.p.h. at 19,685 ft.	391 m.p.h. at 32,800 ft.
	—	—	—	—	394 m.p.h. at 23,625 ft.
Cruise Speed	—	264 m.p.h. at 13,125 ft.	—	—	280 m.p.h. at 13,125 ft.
Climbing Speed...	16,405 ft. in 7 min. 45 sec.	26,250 ft. in 17 min. 58 sec.	26,250 ft. in 20 min. 15 sec.	—	32,800 ft. in 16 min. 30 sec.
Service Ceiling	35,530 ft.	35,170 ft.	34,450 ft.	34,450 ft.	36,090 ft.
Range	1,305 m.	1,540 m.	2,485 m.	1,245 m. plus one hour combat	2,485 m.
Armament	1 7·7-mm. Type 89 (216 r.p.g.)	1 7·7-mm. Type 89 (216 r.p.g.)	—	2 20-mm. Ho-5 & 1 37-mm. Ho-203 (200 r.p.g.)	—

PRINTED IN ENGLAND © Profile Publications Ltd., P.O. Box 26, 1a North Street, Leatherhead, Surrey, England.
Printed by Hills & Lacy Ltd., London and Watford, England. U.S. 2nd Class Mailing Rates applied for.

PROFILE
PUBLICATIONS

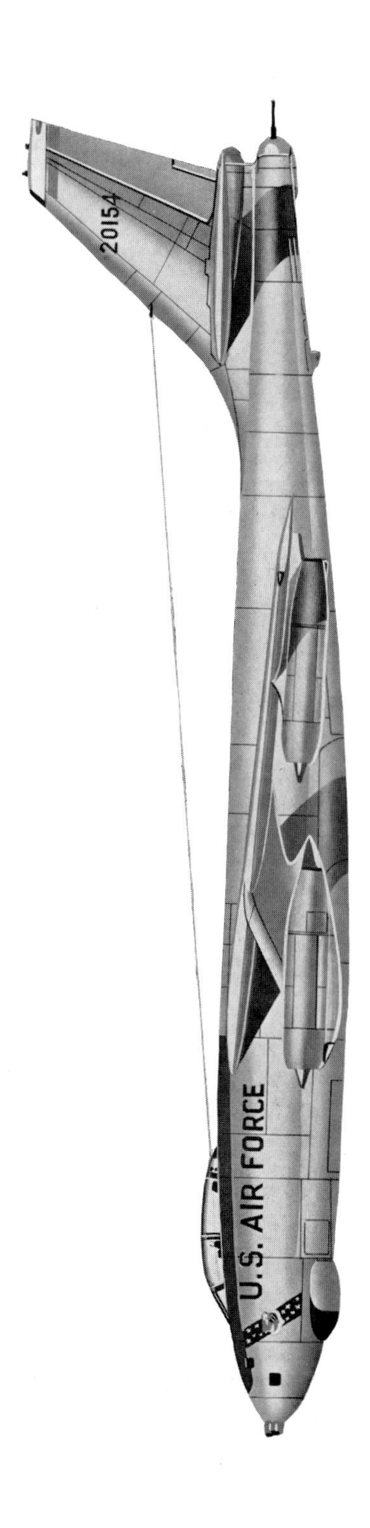

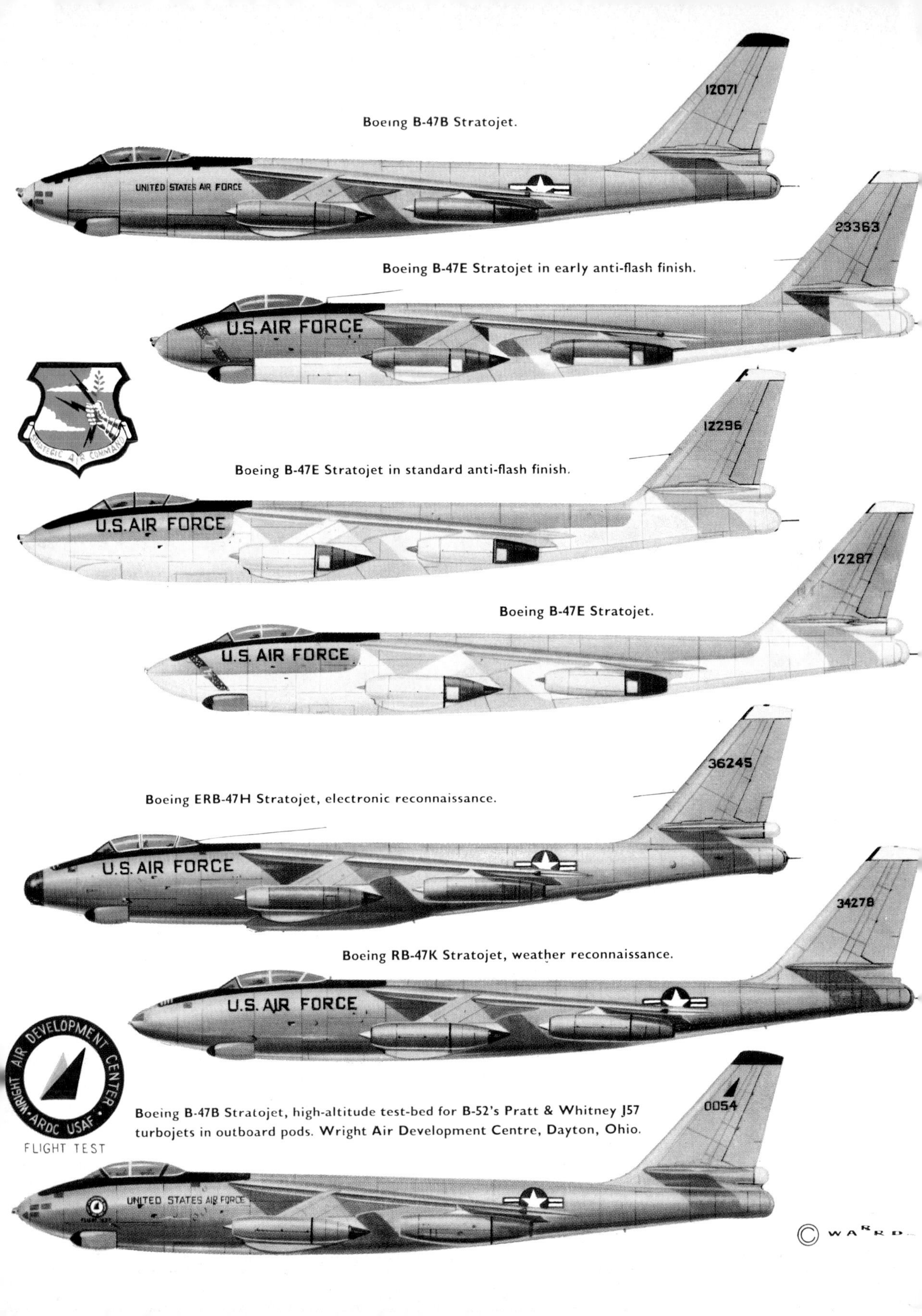

Boeing B-47B Stratojet.

Boeing B-47E Stratojet in early anti-flash finish.

Boeing B-47E Stratojet in standard anti-flash finish.

Boeing B-47E Stratojet.

Boeing ERB-47H Stratojet, electronic reconnaissance.

Boeing RB-47K Stratojet, weather reconnaissance.

Boeing B-47B Stratojet, high-altitude test-bed for B-52's Pratt & Whitney J57 turbojets in outboard pods. Wright Air Development Centre, Dayton, Ohio.

The Boeing B-47

by Peter M. Bowers

The second RB-47E flying with a standard B-47E clearly demonstrates the longer nose of the reconnaissance model. (Photo: Boeing)

December 17th 1947, saw the first flight of one of the world's truly revolutionary aeroplanes—the Boeing XB-47. It turned out to be revolutionary in many ways. Aerodynamically, it featured a swept-back wing, the first applied to any but a fighter-category aircraft, which, combined with the thrust of six jet engines and extremely clean aerodynamic design again brought the speed of the bomber up to that of the contemporary fighter. Boeing had accomplished this feat once before, when the B-9 monoplane bomber of 1931 outran the biplane fighters of its day. As had the B-9, the XB-47 exerted great influence on subsequent designs, both military and civil, and the present-day jet transports of America and Europe can trace their origins to the two prototypes of the B-47 and the 2,030 production models that followed them.

After the B-47 was ordered into large-scale production in 1948, the government-owned Boeing Plant II at Wichita, Kansas, was chosen for its manufacture since the Seattle plants were committed to the production of B-50s, C-97As, commercial "Stratocruisers", and the conversion of obsolescent B-29s to KB-29P aerial tankers. When production beyond the capability of the Wichita facility was desired at the time of the Korean war, Douglas and Lockheed were requested to manufacture B-47s in their own plants. The Lockheed versions, designated B-47-LM, were built in the former Bell plant at Marietta, Georgia, which had been used to manufacture Boeing-designed B-29s during W.W.II. The Douglas models, designated B-47-DT, were manufactured in Douglas' branch plant at Tulsa, Oklahoma, which had been built during W.W.II. The B-47s built by Boeing at Wichita were designated B-47-BW to distinguish them from Seattle-built Boeings, which used the suffix letters -BO.

ORIGIN OF THE DESIGN

The XB-47 (Boeing Model 450) was the result of design study contracts issued by the U.S. Army Air Force in 1943, calling for jet-propelled light bombers or fast long-range reconnaissance machines. Jet propulsion was beginning to prove itself in fighter-type aircraft at the time, and the extension of its advantages to larger designs was considered desirable. However, the war ended before any of the American jet designs, fighter or bomber, was able to go into action.

The XB-47 that took to the air in 1947 was not the first design that Boeing had developed to meet the specification although all had the same military designation. Many had been developed, evaluated, and rejected, with work starting anew along different lines. At first, the problem of adapting jet propulsion to a "big" aeroplane was regarded as a fairly simple one—the engines could be put in relatively conventional nacelles and hung on the wings as direct substitutes for the traditional piston engines. The studies soon proved the fallacy of this, and all manner of combinations were tried. From the aerodynamic and structural standpoints, six jet engines buried in the fuselage seemed to be the optimum design, and one paper design progressed quite far in this direction until the military rejected the feature on the grounds of vulnerability of the aircraft and its fuel system to damage from engine fire or a disintegrating turbine wheel. The final design used six engines in suspended nacelles, thirty-five-degree swept-back wing, a unique "Bicycle" landing gear, and was so fast that the only defensive armament considered necessary was a tail turret with two ·50 calibre machine guns.

The first XB-47 soon after roll-out from the Seattle factory in September 1947. Only the two prototypes were built in Seattle. (Photo: Boeing)

DESIGN DETAILS

Although the XB-47 presented a radical appearance when it first appeared, no single feature was radical or even new in itself. It was the combination of so many unorthodox features, previously confined to purely experimental or research types, that made the XB-47 distinctive. The principal features are described in the following paragraphs.

THE WING

The original wing chosen for the XB-47 was a straight design. Consideration was given to the use of sweep-back when Boeing engineers touring Germany in the wake of the Allied Armies found data in the German research centres that amplified information already on hand about the desirable characteristics of swept wings on high-speed aircraft. Following telegraphed orders from Europe, Boeing engineers adapted swept wings to the XB-47 design and tested them in the wind tunnel. The results justified a request to the Air Force for a major design change, which was approved.

The thirty-five-degree swept wing used on the XB-47 was not entirely new, but it was the first applied to a large aircraft. Previously, only two other designs had flown with such a wing; the propeller-driven Bell L-39, a pure research machine converted from a P-63 "King Cobra" fighter, and the North American XP-86, a single-jet fighter prototype that beat the XB-47 into the air by only a month. The function of the swept wing was to add speed to the aeroplane by delaying the formation of the shock waves that formed as the air passing over the wing approached the speed of sound. Various angles of sweep were effective for this purpose, but wind tunnel testing determined that the angle of thirty-five degrees was the optimum from a structural and aerodynamic standpoint.

Again for speed, the airfoil section was thin. Combined with the extremely high aspect ratio of eleven, far higher than anything ever before used on any standard aircraft but a sailplane, this gave still greater aerodynamic efficiency but introduced serious design problems in several directions. First, the resulting flexibility of the structure brought about control problems—critics maintained that conventional ailerons would serve as control tabs when moved, twisting the wing structure in the opposite direction and producing reversed control action. To offset this possibility, lateral control by means of spoilers was tried on the B-47 prototypes, but it proved to be unnecessary and the new bomber worked perfectly well with conventional ailerons. Second, the thin wing left no space for fuel tanks or the stowage of conventional landing gear. As a result, both of these items were stowed in the fuselage. For take-off and landing, Fowler flaps were fitted to the wing. These provided a means of actually increasing the wing area as well as increasing lift coefficient. They moved aft a considerable distance from their nested position in the underside of the wing as well as moving downward.

The first XB-47 demonstrates the steep take-off angle made possible by the eighteen internally-mounted JATO bottles.
(Photo: Boeing)

The No. 6 B-47A demonstrates the use of the thirty-two-foot diameter deceleration parachute. (Photo: Boeing)

The Fowler flap, named for its inventor, was first used on the Lockheed Model 14 transport of the immediate pre-W.W.II years and its famous military derivative, the "Hudson" bomber and contributed greatly to the success of Boeing's own B-29 "Superfortress" design of W.W.II.

LANDING GEAR

Since it couldn't be stowed in the wing, the landing gear of the XB-47 had to be accommodated in the fuselage, which brought up other design problems. It could not be allowed to intrude into the bomb bay, so it had to be located forward or aft of that area. The final result was that it appeared in both places, one two-wheel main unit being installed forward and one aft to form a "Bicycle" arrangement. This had appeared from time to time in various experimental designs from about 1911, but had never before gone into production. The most recent application had been made by the Glenn L. Martin Company to the XB-26H, an experimental conversion of a standard B-26 "Marauder" bomber used to test the design. Since the main weight-supporting wheels were on the aircraft centre-line, lateral stability was provided by outrigger wheels that were mounted under the inboard nacelles and retracted into them for flight. Each set of main wheels was so far from the centre of gravity of the machine that the normal "Rotation" method of take-off was impossible. Consequently, the design was arranged so that it rolled forward, took off, and landed at the same attitude.

POWERPLANT

The jet engines chosen for the XB-47 were General Electric J-35s, which were soon changed in 1949 to 5,200-lb. GE-J-47s. This is easy to remember—J-47s in the B-47. Early contemporary references stating that Allison engines were used in the prototypes are in error. When different manufacturers were put to building the same jet engine, the actual manufacturer, other than the designer, was made part of the designation. General Electric-designed J-47s, also built by G.E., were designated J-47-GE, followed by the dash number that indicated the series of the engine. The early J-35s produced 4,000 pounds of thrust each. Their location in the final XB-47 design was the result of much study and experiment. Engines buried in the fuselage were ruled out by the military and those

A Lockheed-built B-47E with the sixteen-foot diameter "Ribbon" approach parachute during landing. (Photo: Peter M. Bowers)

mounted to the wing in traditional nacelles were ruled out by Boeing's aerodynamicists as seriously compromising the efficiency of the wing. The use of external pods mounted on struts was finally chosen, and much testing was done in the wind tunnel to determine the optimum locations of the engines relative to the wing from the structural and aerodynamic standpoints. In the final design, two engines were paired in a double nacelle suspended from a single strut on each side of the fuselage while each outboard engine was mounted close under each wingtip. This was a really radical innovation, as designers of large multi-engine aircraft had previously tried to keep the engines as close to the aircraft centre-line as possible to ease the trim problems resulting from operation with one engine out.

Workers at the Boeing Wichita plant thought something was wrong when sets of B-47 inboard pods began to appear on the production line without provisions for the outrigger wheel on them. It turned out that the Air Force had directed that the pods be installed on the contemporary Consolidated-Vultee B-36 Intercontinental bomber. The first model so equipped was

The thirty-five-degree swept wing of an RB-47E provides marked contrast to the straight wing of the Boeing KC-97F tanker. (Photo: Boeing)

The No. 1 XB-47 shows the ground angle established by the tandem landing gear. (Photo: Gordon S. Williams)

the B-36D, and the feature was retained on all subsequent models.

B-47 inboard pods were also used by the Air Force to create the first American jet transport. Two were installed on a Chase G-20 all-metal assault glider, resulting in the XC-123A transport. The jets were not suited to the design, but the piston engines fitted to another G-20 which became the XC-123 were, and this version was placed in large-scale production by Fairchild as the C-123B.

JET-ASSISTED TAKE-OFF

The poor acceleration characteristics of the jet engine were responsible for some unconventional equipment features of the XB-47. With a gross weight nearly double that of the wartime B-29, the B-47 needed a very long take-off run. The jets put out more total power than did the B-29's piston engines, but it took a long time for this power to develop (one pound of jet thrust is equal to approximately one horsepower at a speed of 375 miles per hour; less below and more above). Since more power was needed at low speed, an ingenious system was developed whereby eighteen of the 1,000-lb. thrust solid-fuel rocket units developed during W.W.II to help boost heavily loaded flying boats off of the water were mounted in the fuselage behind the wing. Since the auxiliary-thrust units, soon named JATO for Jet-assisted Take-off, were mounted externally on the flying boats, they could be dropped after take-off. On the XB-47 and subsequent models into the early B-47Es, the discharged units had to be carried along as so much dead weight. The later Es, and earlier models that were updated through modification, were fitted with a total of thirty-three 1,000-lb. JATO units on an external rack that could be dropped after take-off.

The No. 1 B-47A showing the original long bomb bay. (Photo: Boeing)

Below: *B-47B dropping eight conventional 500-lb. bombs from short bomb bay. Note how quickly the doors return to the closed position.* (Photo: Boeing)

BRAKING AND DECELERATION PARACHUTES

The great weight and clean design of the B-47, coupled with the lack of reverse-thrust features on the jet engines, introduced further operating problems to the new design. During W.W.II, the crews of bombers with their braking systems shot out had slowed their landing runs by deploying personnel parachutes from the side gun positions. The Germans had also tested heavy-duty parachutes as an actual aircraft braking device during W.W.II, and the idea was developed and perfected on the B-47. A thirty-two-foot diameter "Ribbon" parachute was stowed in the bottom of the fuselage forward of the tail guns and was deployed immediately after touchdown to help slow the aircraft. It soon became customary to deploy the "Drag Chute" as it came to be called, while the B-47 was still a few feet in the air.

The poor acceleration characteristics of the early jets made a go-around following a refused landing a risky affair. In order to have the jet engines up to speed for such an emergency, a smaller sixteen-foot diameter "Ribbon" parachute was developed to serve as an air brake and bring the B-47 down to landing speed at the higher power setting. Called the "Deceleration Chute", this was deployed on the downwind leg of the landing pattern and remained open until after the landing was completed. If it became necessary to go around, the parachute was jettisoned by the

B-47B-II is B-47B modified to B-47E standard. Note how Fowler flaps increase wing area prior to assuming lowered position. (Photo: Gordon S. Williams)

pilot. Both chutes were jettisoned at the end of the runway before the B-47 taxied in and were recovered and repacked by the ground crews.

FUEL SYSTEM

Another undesirable characteristic of the jet engine was its terrific fuel consumption compared to the piston engine. This was a serious drawback for a powerplant to be used in a long-range machine such as a bomber. Even the enormous tankage of the B-47, 17,000 U.S. gallons (compared to 5,500 gallons for the B-29) was insufficient to give the B-47 the desired range. This was stowed in the upper portion of the fuselage above the bomb bay and for a considerable distance aft, creating a serious balance problem as fuel was used up. Consequently, various systems of in-flight re-fuelling (IFR) then under development were tried. The B-47Es and earlier modified models were equipped to use the Boeing-developed "Flying Boom" system, with the receptacle at the very nose of the B-47. The first tanker aircraft used to re-fuel production B-47s were propeller-driven Boeing KC-97s, but these were soon replaced by jet-propelled Boeing KC-135s.

ACCOMMODATION

For all its weight, the B-47 has a remarkably small crew—three men, who serve as pilot, co-pilot/tail gunner, and bombardier/navigator. All three are housed in a pressurised forward compartment forward of the wing and bomb bay, the pilot and co-pilot under a long fighter-like blown Plexiglass canopy and the bombardier in the conventional nose bombing station. In some special reconnaissance and electronics countermeasures variants, the bomb bay is converted to a crew station and additional personnel are carried there. Ejection seats are provided for the crew of the B-47E and on; the pilot and co-pilot eject upward and the bombardier ejects downward.

MILITARY FEATURES

The XB-47 was designed to carry both conventional bombs and the early forms of the atomic bomb in existence at the time it was built. Total bomb weight capacity was 20,000 pound, and the bomb bay was quite long to accommodate the large-sized ordnance. When the atomic bombs decreased in size, the bomb bay was made considerably smaller. Elaborate electronic gear is carried for navigation, counter-measures, and bomb and defensive gun-aiming. Initial

(continued on page 10)

Above: *A B-47B takes off.* (Photo: Boeing). Below: *B-47B used to test external JATO bottle racks as used on late B-47Es and converted B-47B-IIs.* (Photo: Douglas D. Olsen)

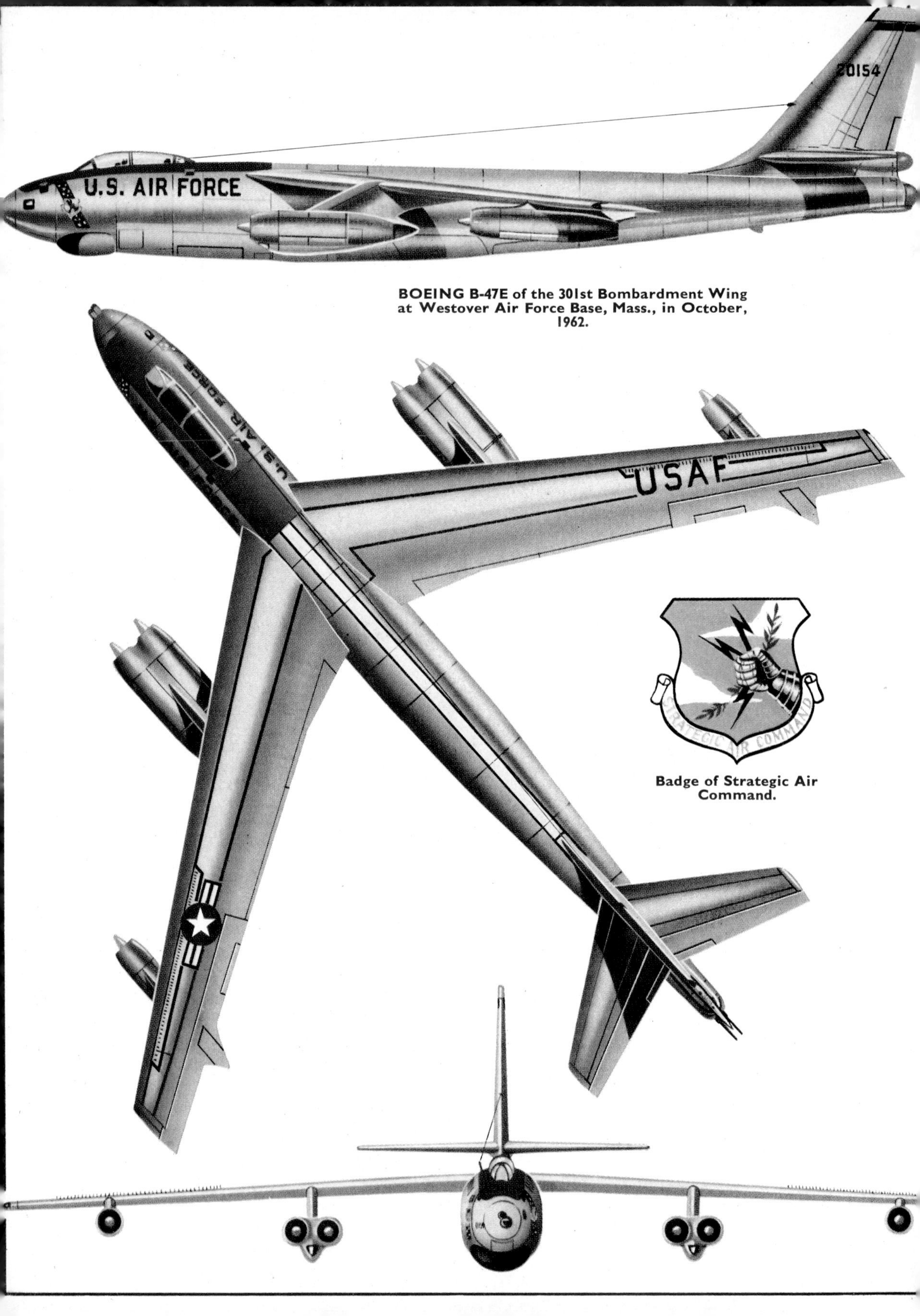

BOEING B-47E of the 301st Bombardment Wing at Westover Air Force Base, Mass., in October, 1962.

Badge of Strategic Air Command.

Badge of the 301st Bombardment Wing.

Typical section of "Star spangled" band.

A B-47B loaned to Canada for testing of the Canadian-built Orenda "Iroquois" 20,000-lb. thrust jet engine. The airframe was modified by Canadair, Ltd., and designated CL-52. (Photo: Orenda)

tail armament consisted of a pair of ·50 calibre machine guns in a turret remotely controlled from the cockpit. These could also be operated by an A-5 radar fire-control system that detected targets approaching from the rear, tracked them, and fired on them without any supervision from the crew. In the B-47E, the machine guns were replaced by 20-mm. cannon.

The B-47 was adapted to numerous duties for which it had not originally been designed. Conceived as a high-altitude strategic bomber, it was modified through extensive strengthening of the wing to be used in a low-level tactical lob-bombing rôle, where it would streak toward a pinpoint target at tree-top level, zoom upward, release its bomb when passing through the vertical position, complete the half-loop and half-roll of the classic Immelmann manœuvre, and streak away before the bomb came down. The first public demonstration of this tactic took place in 1957.

For those B-47s equipped to carry atomic bombs, a special colour scheme (also used on B-36s and B-52s) was developed. This is an all-white coating for the undersurfaces and the lower half of the fuselage. Its purpose is to reflect the heat and radiation of an atomic blast, thereby protecting the aircraft structure to a degree. The normal military markings and lettering are not applied to surfaces covered with the white reflective paint.

DESIGN DEVELOPMENT

The major B-47 models, from the XB-47s of 1947 to the final Es and their variants produced in 1956 by Boeing and Douglas and by Lockheed in early 1957, are detailed in the following paragraphs. Except for the RB-47E, only those models distinguished by the adoption of separate series letters are described (B-47A, B-47B, etc.). Special-purpose variants, such as QB-47 radio-controlled drones, TB trainers, and WB-47 weather-reconnaissance conversions, are too numerous to detail in a publication this size.

Top left: *A B-47B of Wright Air Development Centre fitted experimentally with 10,000-lb. thrust J-57 engines, the type used in early B-52s, in the outboard positions.* (Photo: Boeing)

Left: *A B-47B fitted with an early set of 1,780-gallon auxiliary tanks. The odd colouring is to help photographic studies of the drop tests.* (Photo: Boeing)

Right: *A WB-47B, converted from the bomber configuration, photographed in 1964 with special colouring.*
(Photo: Boeing)

Below, right: *An early B-47E takes off on a test flight. Markings on fuselage are to aid photo-theodolite readings.*
(Photo: Boeing)

XB-47. Two prototypes, the first being flown on 17th December 1947, and the second on 21st July 1948. Both of these aircraft, ordered in April 1946, were built in the Boeing plant at Seattle, Washington, the only B-47s to be built there. Since the design was so new, testing of the first prototype proceeded very cautiously. By the time the second was ready to fly, so much confidence was gained that its first take-off from Boeing Field was made with the JATO bottles. In 1949 the 4,000-lb.-thrust J-35 engines of the first prototype were replaced with 5,200-lb.-thrust J-47s. Air Force serial numbers were *46–65* and *46–66*.

B-47A. Ten production versions of the modified No. 1 prototype. Actually, these were test and training models for both the military and the manufacturers, and were never intended to be combat-ready equipment. The first B-47A flew on 25th June 1950. Serial numbers *49–1900* to *49–1909*.

B-47B. The first true production B-47, with armed versions being supplied to the squadrons of the Strategic Air Force (SAC). More powerful J-47-GE-11 engines of 5,800-lb. thrust were fitted. The first of 399 B-47Bs flew on 26th April 1951.

By the time the B-47B was being ordered, the U.S. Air Force decided that it needed B-47s in a greater quantity than the Boeing facilities could supply, so Lockheed and Douglas were signed up to produce the model in their own plants. The first B-47s turned out by these additional manufacturers were B-models, using parts supplied by Boeing. These aircraft were delivered with the Air Force serial numbers already assigned to Boeing. Air Force serial numbers for all the B-47s were: *49–2642* to *49–2646*; *50–1* to *50-82*; *51–2045* to *50–2356*.

The eight Lockheed-assembled B-47Bs had serial numbers *51–2197*, *2204*, *2210*, *2217*, *2224*, *2231*, *2237*, and *2243*. A ninth B-47B at Lockheed, *51–2145*, was used as a mock-up and was not flown. The ten Douglas-assembled B-47Bs had serial numbers *51–2141*, *2150*, *2155*, *2160*, *2165*, *2170*, *2175*, *2180*, *2185*, and *2190*.

B-47B-II. In 1954 the majority of SAC's B-47Bs

A B-47B-II in flight near the Boeing factory at Wichita, Kansas, in 1955. The white paint on the undersurfaces is to reduce the absorption of heat and radiation effects from nuclear blast. (Photo: Boeing)

Anti-atom flash white paint on B-47 B-IIs' undersurfaces. Note lack of national markings. (Photo: Boeing)

were returned to the Boeing Wichita plant for a modernisation programme that brought them up to B-47E standard. Outwardly, the converted Bs could be distinguished from the Es only by their serial numbers so extensive was the re-work. These changes did not actually make the Bs into Es, but the change was reflected in the aeroplane model designation, which became B-47B-II.

YB-47C. The eighty-eighth B-47B, *50–92*, was to have been converted to use four 10,090-lb. thrust Allison J-71 engines in place of the six J-47-GEs and was to have been redesignated YB-56. This machine was to have photo and electronic reconnaissance equipment in place of bombs, and the powerplant and equipment changes were considered sufficient to justify a completely new aircraft designation. However, since the airframe was still that of a B-47, the designation was changed to YB-47C. The project was cancelled before completion and the four-jet version never materialised.

XB-47D. Two B-47Bs, *51–2046* and *51–2103*, were selected for conversion to XB-47D. This was not an attempt to develop an improved bomber—the machines were strictly flying test-beds for the new Wright YT-49-W-1 turbo-prop engines, which pro-

Early B-47E with in-flight refuelling receptacle in nose opened. (Photo: Boeing)

duced 9,710 equivalent shaft horsepower. These were the most powerful propeller-engines to fly at the time, and a single unit was installed in place of each pair of inboard J-47s. The outboard J-47s were retained. The first XB-47D made its first flight in July, 1955.

B-47E. An extensively improved version of the B-47B, of which 931 were built by Boeing, 385 by Lockheed, and 274 by Douglas. Early units retained the internal JATO and the port side nose windows of the B-47B, but the later ones deleted the windows and replaced the eighteen internal JATO bottles with thirty-three external units on a single rack that could be jettisoned. Two radar-directed 20-mm. cannon replaced the earlier machine gun armament and the nose section was completely redesigned to provide ejection seating for the crew and provide for in-flight refuelling by the Flying Boom system. Because of the IFR capability, the built-in fuel capacity was reduced to 14,610 gallons including the two 1,780 U.S. gallon drop tanks. Later J-47-GE-25 engines, with a thrust of 6,000 lb., were installed. These had the additional feature of water injection, which raised the thrust to 7,200 lb. for take-off. The first B-47E flew on 30th January 1953.

The Air Force serial numbers for all B-47Es are presented here in sequence of assignment, with the actual manufacturer indicated in parentheses. To save space, a stroke is used to indicate "to", as 1/5 for 1 to 5, inclusive: *51–2357/2445*, *51–5214/5257*, *51–7019/7083* (Boeing), *51–15804/15812* (Lockheed), *51–15821/15853* (Boeing), *52–118/120*, *52–146/201* (Douglas), *52–202/393* (Lockheed), *52–*

Boeing-built B-47E with auxiliary fuel tanks and the star-spangled blue band of a Strategic Air Command aircraft painted on the nose. (Photo: Peter M. Bowers)

The first of two propeller-driven XB-47Ds on its first flight, August 1955. The XB-47Ds were B-47B airframes with Wright T-49 turbo-prop engines replacing each in-board pair of J-47 jets. (Photo: Boeing)

The four-bladed Curtiss turbo-electric propellers, each 15 feet in diameter and having "paddle-type" blades 24 inches wide, were used with the T-49s. Changes necessary to adapt the 600-mile-an-hour bombers for the test duties included removal of the original twin-jet inboard engine pods, modification of wing flaps to allow installation of the T-49s, and changes in instrumentation and controls for four engines rather than the normal six engines. (Photo: Boeing)

Lockheed-built B-47E-LM with both approach and decelerating parachutes still deployed near the end of the landing roll. (Photo: E. M. Sommerich)

B-47E taking off with the assistance of thirty-three externally-mounted JATO bottles. (Photo: Boeing)

YDB-47E carrying Bell GAM-63 "Rascal" missile. The white-painted area on the B-47 fuselage is to provide a good background for photos of the missile release during tests. (Photo: Boeing)

394/620 (Boeing), *52–3343/3373, 53–1819/1972* (Lockheed), *53–2028/2040, 53–2090/2170* (Douglas), *53–2261/2147, 53–4207/4244, 53–6193/6249* (Boeing).

RB-47E. While it was customary to add a special-mission prefix to standard models assigned to other than their basic mission, the RB-47Es were actually built for a different mission—long-range photo reconnaissance instead of bombing. However, no standard-type designation existed in the Air Force for such a mission at the time, so the supplemental designation was added to the B-for-Bomber designation. Up to 1948, when many Air Force types were redesignated, there had been an F-for-Photographic type, but most of the aircraft used in it were converted bombers (B-17s became F-9s and B-29s became F-13s). When the F designation was dropped, bombers converted to photo work became RBs. All of the 240 RB-47Es were built by Boeing, and could easily be distinguished from the standard bombers by their elongated noses and a return to the built-in JATO units. Up to eleven cameras, including night flash equipment, could be carried. The bombing equipment was deleted and the bombardier became the photographer

B-47E. Stress wrinkles can be seen under the wing leading-edge.

Above: *Colour study of a Strategic Air Command B-47E in flight.* Below: *The YB-47F fitted with IFR probe in 1952, to test the hose-and-drogue refuelling system.* (Photos: Boeing)

Below: *B-47 with four GAM-67 "Crossbows" mounted under wings.* (Photo: Boeing)

The RB-47Ks were started as RB-47Es but were redesignated prior to completion. (Photo: Boeing)

except in special versions where extra crew members were carried. Although the RB-47E could be refuelled in flight, the tankage was increased to a capacity of 18,405 U.S. gallons. Powerplants were the same as the standard B-47E. Air Force serial numbers *51–5258/5276*, *51–15821/15853*, *52–685/825*, *52–3374/3400*, *53–4245/4264*.

YB-47F. In 1952, one B-47B, *50–09*, was fitted with an IFR probe to test the suitability of the hose-and-drogue refuelling system for the B-47. The Flying Boom system proved more practical and was used for all subsequent B-47 and B-52 refuelling.

KB-47G. Another converted B-47B, *50–40*, used as the tanker for the YB-47F IFR experiments. The K prefix was assigned to the B-47G to indicate its status as a tanker.

RB-47H. Thirty-two Boeing-built B-47s were completed as RB-47H with first flight in June, 1955. These were used for electronic reconnaissance; detecting and locating surface radar stations. Normal crew was three, but three additional could be carried, some in the special equipment capsule in the bomb bay. U.S.A.F. serial numbers *53–4280/4309*, *6247*, *6248*.

B-47I. No "I" series letter was assigned, in keeping with U.S.A.F. policy of not using the letter "I" in designations because of possibility of confusion with the figure one.

YB-47J. A single standard bomber modified to serve as a test vehicle for the newly-developed MA-2 radar bombing-navigation system.

RB-47K. An additional fifteen RB-47Es were ordered for use in both weather and photo-reconnaissance missions, but because of differences in equipment details, these were redesignated RB-47K before completion. Serial numbers *53–4265/4279*.

EB-47L. In 1963, thirty-five obsolescent B-47Es were modified to become electronic communications aircraft that could serve as relay stations between other aircraft or between aircraft and ground communications stations.

CL-52. In 1956, the U.S.A.F. loaned a B-47B, *51–2059*, to the Royal Canadian Air Force as a test vehicle for the new 20,000-lb. thrust Orenda "Iroquois" jet engine. The R.C.A.F. turned the machine over to Canadair, Ltd., for modification. This company assigned its own model number of CL-52 to the project. The CL-52/B-47B was flown in R.C.A.F. markings but retained the last three digits of its U.S.A.F. serial number, which followed the prefix "X" to become the R.C.A.F. serial number.

© Peter M. Bowers, 1966

A QB-47E being guided to the ground controllers at the end of the runway by an airborne controller in the T-33 seen flying just off the right wingtip. (Photo: Boeing)

The YB-47F being refuelled from the KB-47G hose tanker. Both of these experimental machines were converted from B-47B airframes. (Photo: Boeing)

PRINTED IN ENGLAND © Profile Publications Ltd., P.O. Box 26, 1a North Street, Leatherhead, Surrey, England.
Printed by Hills & Lacy Ltd., London and Watford, England. U.S. 2nd Class Mailing Rates applied for.

PROFILE
PUBLICATIONS

The Short Empire Boats

TWO SHILLINGS

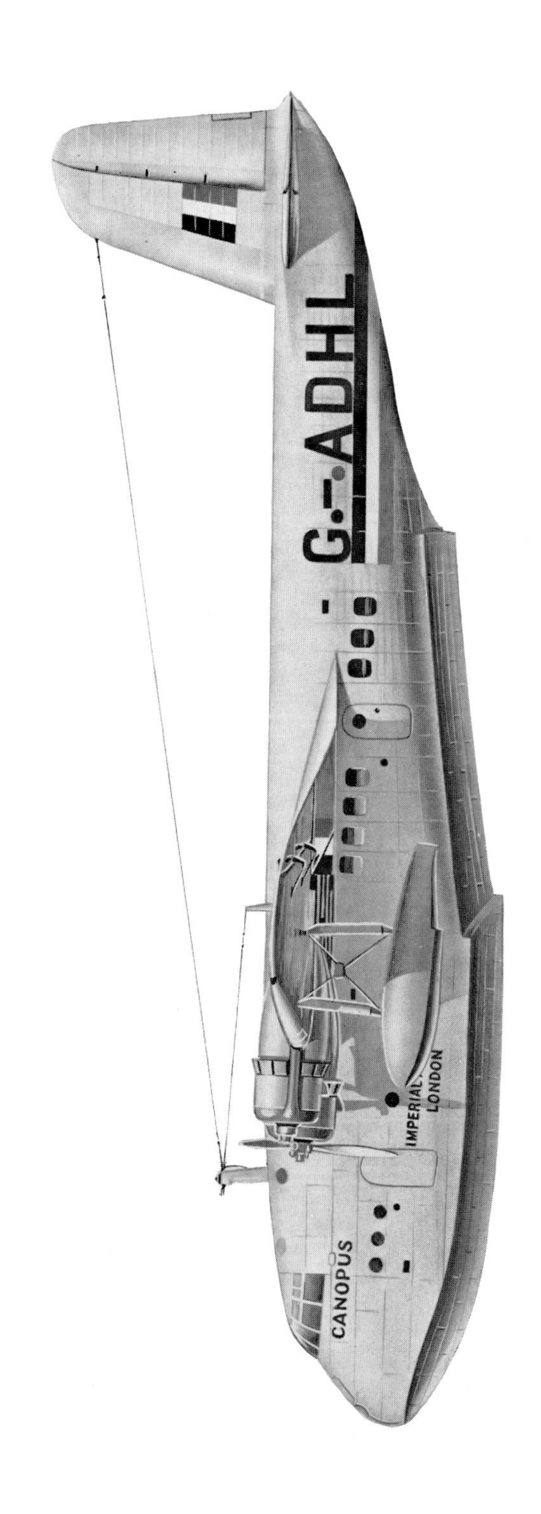

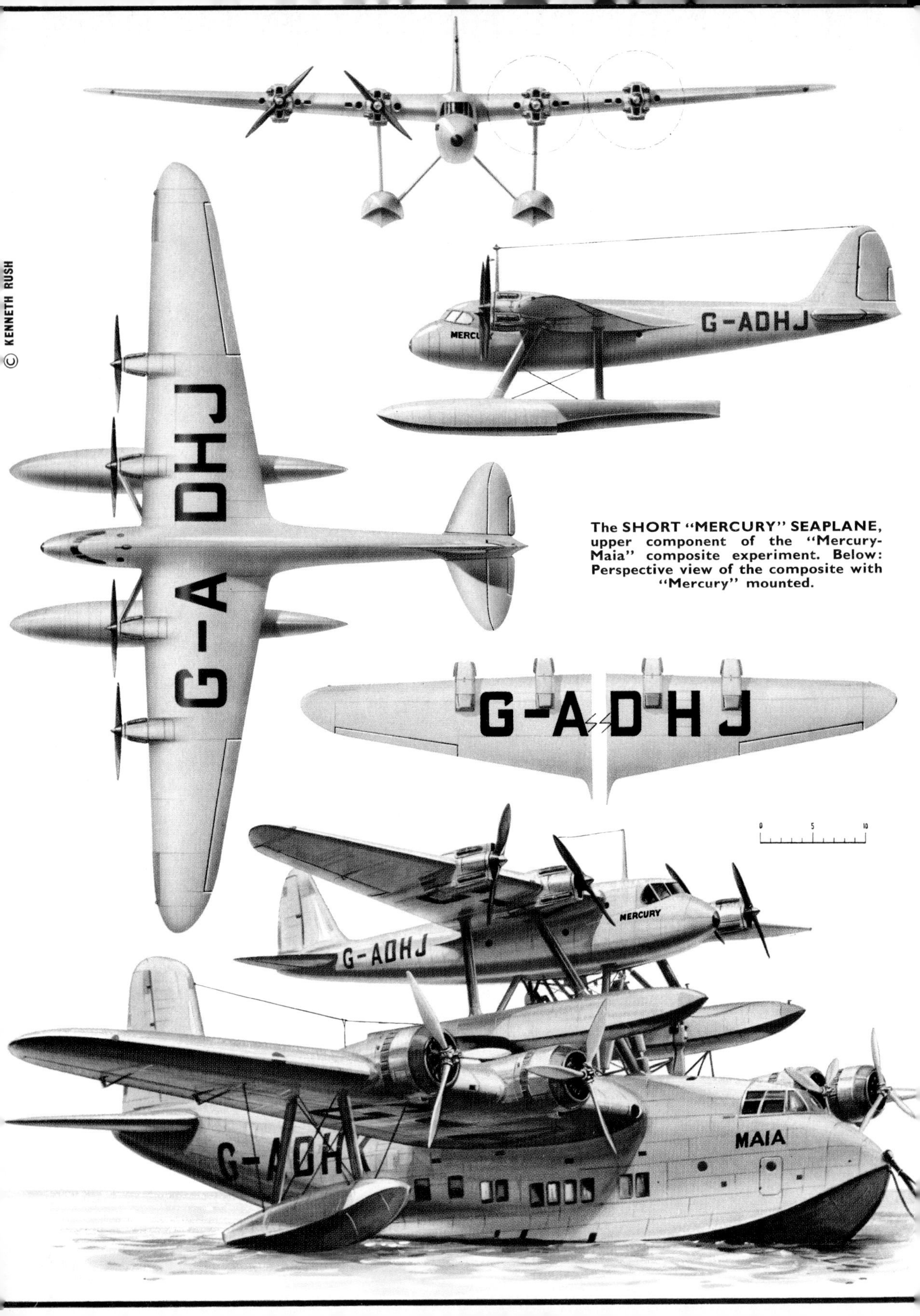

The SHORT "MERCURY" SEAPLANE, upper component of the "Mercury-Maia" composite experiment. Below: Perspective view of the composite with "Mercury" mounted.

The Short Empire Boats

by Geoffrey Norris

Cameronian, *the twenty-fourth "C" Class boat to be constructed.* (Photo: Short Bros. and Harland)

When, in 1935, it was announced that Imperial Airways had placed an order for twenty-eight flying boats of a new type that had not yet been designed, yet alone flown, and that these new boats would weigh eighteen tons apiece, the act was hailed as one of the world's boldest experiments in aviation. But there were others, however, who referred to the order as a gamble.

The reason for Imperial Airways' hurry was not difficult to see. World-wide air travel was booming and the company was anxious to get more than its fair share of future business for Britain. Major R. H. Mayo, Imperial Airways' Technical Adviser, had been collecting statistics for some time and from this research had built up a specification for an aircraft which could be used for passengers and freight throughout the world. It would carry twenty-four passengers in spacious comfort and still have ample room for air mail or freight; cruising speed would be 160 m.p.h. and normal range 700 miles—although there would have to be room to stretch this to some 2,000 miles to serve the North Atlantic route which the company hoped to open later. Because the flying boat was in vogue and because it was thought impossible to build a landplane of this size and weight with acceptable landing and take-off characteristics, a flying boat was required.

It was obvious that the order should go to Short Brothers of Rochester. The company had already built several series of large flying boats both for the R.A.F. and Imperial Airways and these had an enviable record for both performance and safety. Nevertheless, Shorts were reluctant to build such an advanced aircraft straight into production and asked for time to build a prototype. Imperial Airways insisted that there was no time for this and, as an order for twenty-eight aircraft each costing some £45,000 could not lightly be turned down, Oswald Short, chairman of the company bearing his name, signed the contract.

The man responsible to Short for the design of the Empire Boat was Arthur Gouge and his starting point was the cubic capacity which Imperial Airways had specified for each passenger. Preliminary calculations indicated an aircraft with the wing carried on a hump above the fuselage to provide the necessary clearance between propeller tip and water but it was then decided that there would be less drag if the fuselage depth could be increased up to the wing. This gave more volume than required but enabled the cantilever wing to be fitted into the fuselage in a manner that was both lighter and stronger than that possible with a hump.

Up to this time Short flying boats had been built with wide planing bottoms but, with a boat weighing eighteen tons, excessive water drag would inhibit take-off performance. Gouge therefore set out to design a new type of planing bottom and, after many experiments in Shorts' own water tank, succeeded in whittling the beam down to eighteen inches below that shown necessary by the first calculations.

As another aid to take-off and landing Gouge designed into the aircraft flaps patented by himself. The Gouge flaps fitted to the Empire Boats were designed to increase wing area with little or no increase in drag and without destroying the flow over the top of the aerofoil. Calculations, later borne out in operation, showed that the lift coefficient of the wing could be increased by 30% to reduce landing speed by 12 m.p.h. without any change in trim.

The basic aerodynamic design was built around the

Canopus *at rest on the Medway at Rochester.* (Photo: Short Bros. and Harland)

Above and below: Canopus, *first of the "C" Class boats. Top illustration shows* Canopus *on the slip-way ready for initial launching.* (Photos: Short Bros. and Harland)

Short Scion Senior which virtually served as a half-scale prototype for the Empire Boats. This development of the twin-engined Scion was a high cantilever wing cabin monoplane powered by four Pobjoy Niagara engines of 90 h.p. each. First flown in 1935, it was built in both landplane and floatplane versions, had a span of 55 ft., a length of 42 ft. and a wing area of 400 sq. ft. As a floatplane it had a maximum speed of 134 m.p.h. and cruised at 121 m.p.h. at 3,200 r.p.m. or 115 m.p.h. at 3,100 r.p.m. All-up-weight was 5,750 lb.

The final design of the S.23 Class Empire Boat showed its obvious relationship with the Scion Senior. The Empire Boat was a clean-looking high-wing monoplane spanning 114 ft., 88 ft. long and 31 ft. $9\frac{3}{4}$ in. high. Wing area was 1,500 sq. ft. The chosen powerplant was the Bristol Pegasus Xc engine which delivered 740 b.h.p. at 3,500 ft. Empty weight was 24,000 lb. and all-up-weight 40,500 lb. The useful load comprised 600 gallons of fuel weighing 4,560 lb.; 44 gallons of oil at 400 lb.; equipment, 3,340 lb.; payload and crew of five, 8,200 lb.

No machine of this size and complexity had been built before by the British aircraft industry and Shorts found many problems in construction which could only be overcome by developing new techniques. The mainplane spar booms, for instance, were machined from lengths of "T"-shaped Reynold's extrusions in Hiduminium R.R.56 alloy. These came in lengths of 22 ft. only and had to be joined end to end to make up one half spar boom. These sections then had to be machined to a constant taper from root to tip to an accuracy of within 0·005 in. and there was no machine

on the market capable of performing this task. Shorts accordingly built their own.

The wings were covered with flush-riveted Alclad and had Frise-type ailerons. The Gouge flaps were worked by screw jacks driven by a $\frac{1}{2}$-h.p. Rotax electric motor running at 6,000 r.p.m. geared down to turn the jacks at 500 r.p.m. and which lowered the flaps in 60 seconds and raised them in 90. The size of the wings made accommodation of fuel tanks simple and the normal medium-range Empire Boat carried fuel to Air Ministry spec. D.T.D. 230 in two 325-gallon cylindrical tanks placed between the inner and outer engines.

Sections of the wing leading edge on each side of the four nacelles folded down to serve as servicing platforms for the engines and the floats, which were carried on a pair of struts in tandem attached to the main spar, had a shock absorber carried between the bracing wires which allowed them to move backwards some four inches and thus prevent undue torsional loads being transmitted to the wing if sudden waves were struck at speed.

Cambria, *second of the long-range boats.* (Photo: Short Bros. and Harland)

Above and below: Clio *before and after conversion for long-range reconnaissance duties with Coastal Command during W.W.II. Note the dorsal radar aerials.* (Photos: Short Bros. and Harland)

Although the hull was radically new in shape its construction generally followed the practices evolved in previous Short boats and stringers were interrupted at formers instead of being notched to run continuously. The Empire Boats had stringers of "Z" section which were attached to the formers by plain angle brackets. The keel was built up on an "I" section girder and, with the two chines (the angle where the fuselage sides meet the planing bottom) formed a triangular section. Earlier Short boats such as the Kent Class and the Calcutta had been characterised by a sudden reduction in beam above the chines, the sides of the fuselage being faired into the chines by a planking of double or "S" curvature—a difficult form of construction involving considerable panel beating. In order to simplify construction—and to help achieve the necessary interior volume, this system was discontinued in the Empire Boats which had only a light curve sweeping the sides into the chines.

The 17-ft. deep hull made it possible to provide accommodation on two decks. The pilot and co-pilot sat in a spacious cockpit dignified with the word "bridge", with the radio operator facing rearwards behind the captain. Aft of this on the upper deck was a long compartment divided longitudinally to provide space for 3,000 lb. of freight and mail on the port side and the ship's clerk's office to starboard. The clerk had charge of a panel containing fuses and switches for all circuits and lighting inside the boat. He also had access to handles controlling the opening of the annular skirts of the cooling flaps for the four engines, fuel cocks and ventilation air intake controls. A step-ladder at the aft end of the clerk's office led to the galley in the lower deck. Behind the clerk's office, but not directly accessible from it was a storage space for bedding and other sundries.

A spacious marine compartment was located at the forward end of the lower deck and this carried an anchor, two drogues, a retractable mooring bollard and a boat hook. A retractable Harley lamp was mounted on a hinged panel off-set to port. Direct communication between the "bridge" and mooring compartment was by step-ladder. Aft of the mooring compartment was the forward passenger saloon with three seats along the port side facing inwards, two to starboard also facing inwards and another pair facing forwards. Behind this was a central corridor flanked on the port by toilets and to starboard by the galley. A mid-ship cabin aft of this accommodated three passengers by day and four at night and led on to the promenade cabin, a spacious compartment with seats

Centurion, *which crashed on Hooghly River, India, in June 1939.* (Photo: Short Bros. and Harland)

for eight or sleeping accommodation for four. On the port side there was a rail where passengers could lean and look out of the windows. An after-cabin at the rear, ending level with the after-step of the planing bottom, had six seats for daylight flying or bunks for four. Aft of this again was another freight and mail compartment extending well back into the after fuselage.

The flight deck was, for its day, very well equipped. Rudder, elevator trim and the flap-operating switch were carried above the windscreen between the two pilots. Engine starter switches were placed at the top of the central coaming and below this were the engine switches and auto-pilot panel. The throttle quadrant was normal but carried on each side two large "cut out levers". Large boats were often called on to do much taxiing after a flight and engines tended to overheat and continue firing after being switched off. The "cut out levers" cut the fuel at the jets to make the engines dead. Below the throttle and mixture controls were the switches for the auto-pilot and, at the base of the central console, the four switches for controlling the de Havilland variable-pitch propellers.

The flying instruments included a Hughes turn indicator, Sperry artificial horizon and directional gyro, a Kollsman sensitive altimeter, a liquid pitch indicator, a Hughes rate-of-climb indicator, a Marconi homing indicator and a special Smith's chronometer. Both pilots also had a Hughes P/4/11 compass.

The radio officer sitting behind the captain had Marconi sets for receiving and transmitting on 600–2,000 metres and in the 16–75-metre band. The sets were mounted in shock-proof supports and incorporated the direction-finding receiver. The loop for this was on a retractable mounting which had provision for turning the assembly athwartships so that it could be used for visual or aural homing.

The nine-cylinder, radial, air-cooled Pegasus Xc engines were the commercial version of the Pegasus X and were rated at 740 b.h.p. at 3,500 ft. 910 b.h.p. was available for take-off with the de Havilland v.p. propeller permitting the engine to turn at 2,475 r.p.m. Normal cruising output was 510 b.h.p. The 28·7 litre engine weighed 1,010 lb. and measured 55·3 in. in diameter. Rotax-Eclipse direct-cranking starters with hand-turning gear operated from 12 volts and turned the engines at some 25–30 r.p.m.

Canopus, the first of the Empire Boats, made her maiden flight on 4th July 1936, with Shorts' Chief Test Pilot, John Lankester Parker at the controls. She gave no trouble and Lankester Parker pronounced himself pleased with her performance. The new style of planing bottom proved its value when *Canopus* unstuck after a run lasting only seventeen seconds—

Above: Cabot, *which gave its name to the improved class of Empire Boat.* Below: Coorong, *last of the first order for twenty-eight "C" boats. Shot down off the Timor Sea in January 1942.* (Photos: Short Bros. and Harland)

Champion, *first of the improved Empire Boats.* (Photo: Imperial War Museum)

although on this occasion she was flown at something like 1½ tons below her maximum all-up-weight.

Performance figures proved by test flights showed a maximum speed of 200 m.p.h. at 5,500 ft., a maximum cruising speed of 165 m.p.h. using 510 b.h.p. per engine and a minimum flying speed of 73 m.p.h. Rate of climb at sea level using coarse pitch was 950 ft. per min., absolute ceiling was 20,000 ft. and normal still air range, 760 miles. Take-off time at maximum all-up-weight was twenty-one seconds.

The first flight on behalf of Imperial Airways was made on 17th September by Squadron Leader (later Air Commodore) H. G. Brackley, I.A.'s Air Superintendent, and the final proving and delivery flight to Marseilles for use on the Mediterranean route was made on Thursday, 22nd October. Bad weather delayed the boat's arrival at Marseilles until 25th October.

Caledonia, the second Empire Boat, had made her maiden flight on 15th September and was delivered to Imperial Airways on 4th December 1936. She was the first of the long-range boats and had three fuel tanks in each wing containing 380 gals., 325 gals. and 175 gals. each, plus another two tanks each containing 280 gals. fitted inside the wing torsion box at the top of the fuselage.

From September the Empire Boats were completed at a rate of rather more than one per month and delivery dates were never more than a few days after the first flight—sometimes an aircraft was handed over to Imperial Airways immediately after its first flight. *Coorong*, the last of the initial order of twenty-eight

(continued on page 10)

Above: Ao-tea-roa, *a* Cabot *class boat used on the New Zealand–Australia run with the registration ZK-AMA.* (Photo: Short Bros. and Harland). Below: Cleopatra, *last of the Empire "C" boats to be constructed.* (Photo: Imperial War Museum)

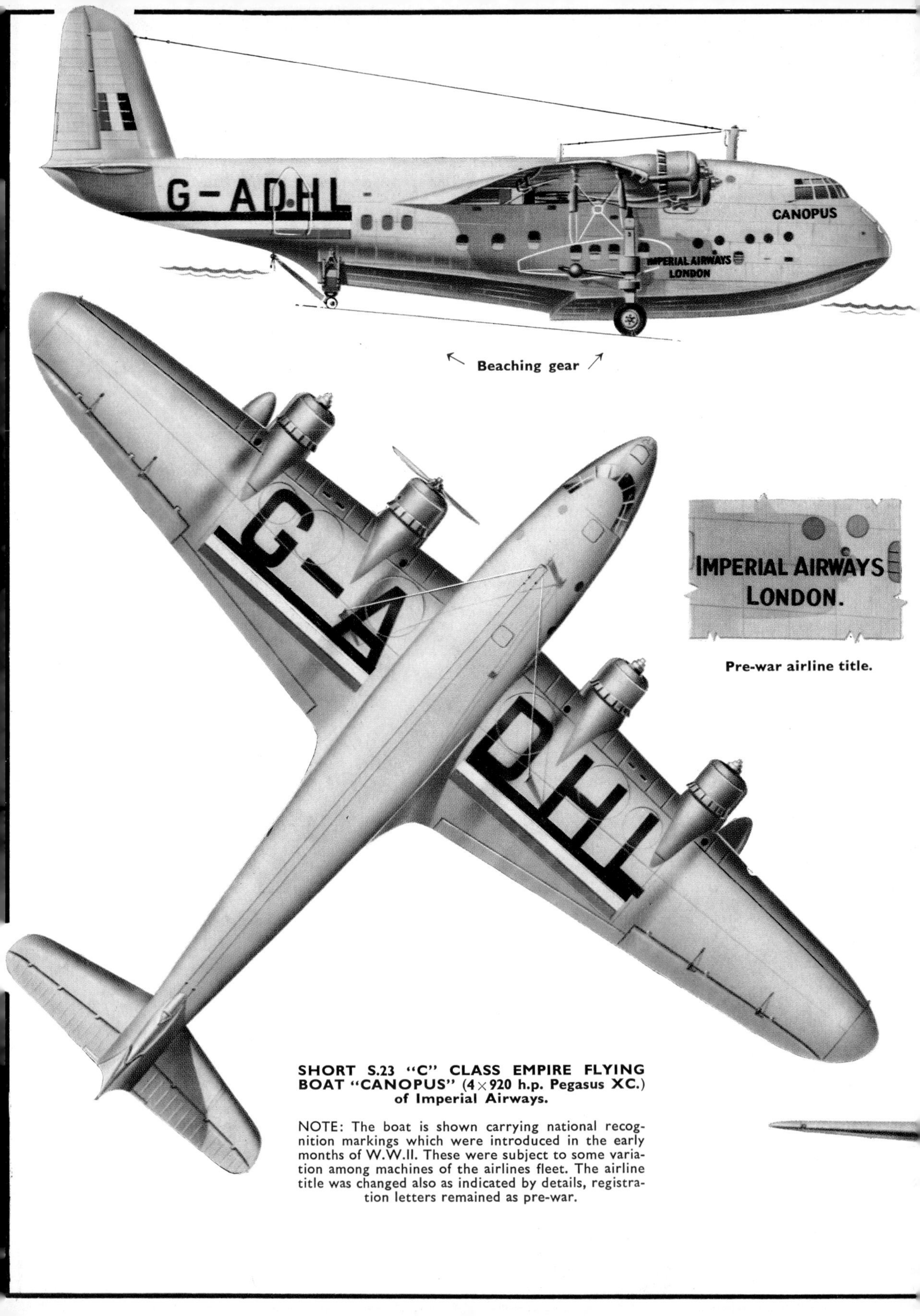

Pre-war airline title.

SHORT S.23 "C" CLASS EMPIRE FLYING BOAT "CANOPUS" (4×920 h.p. Pegasus XC.) of Imperial Airways.

NOTE: The boat is shown carrying national recognition markings which were introduced in the early months of W.W.II. These were subject to some variation among machines of the airlines fleet. The airline title was changed also as indicated by details, registration letters remained as pre-war.

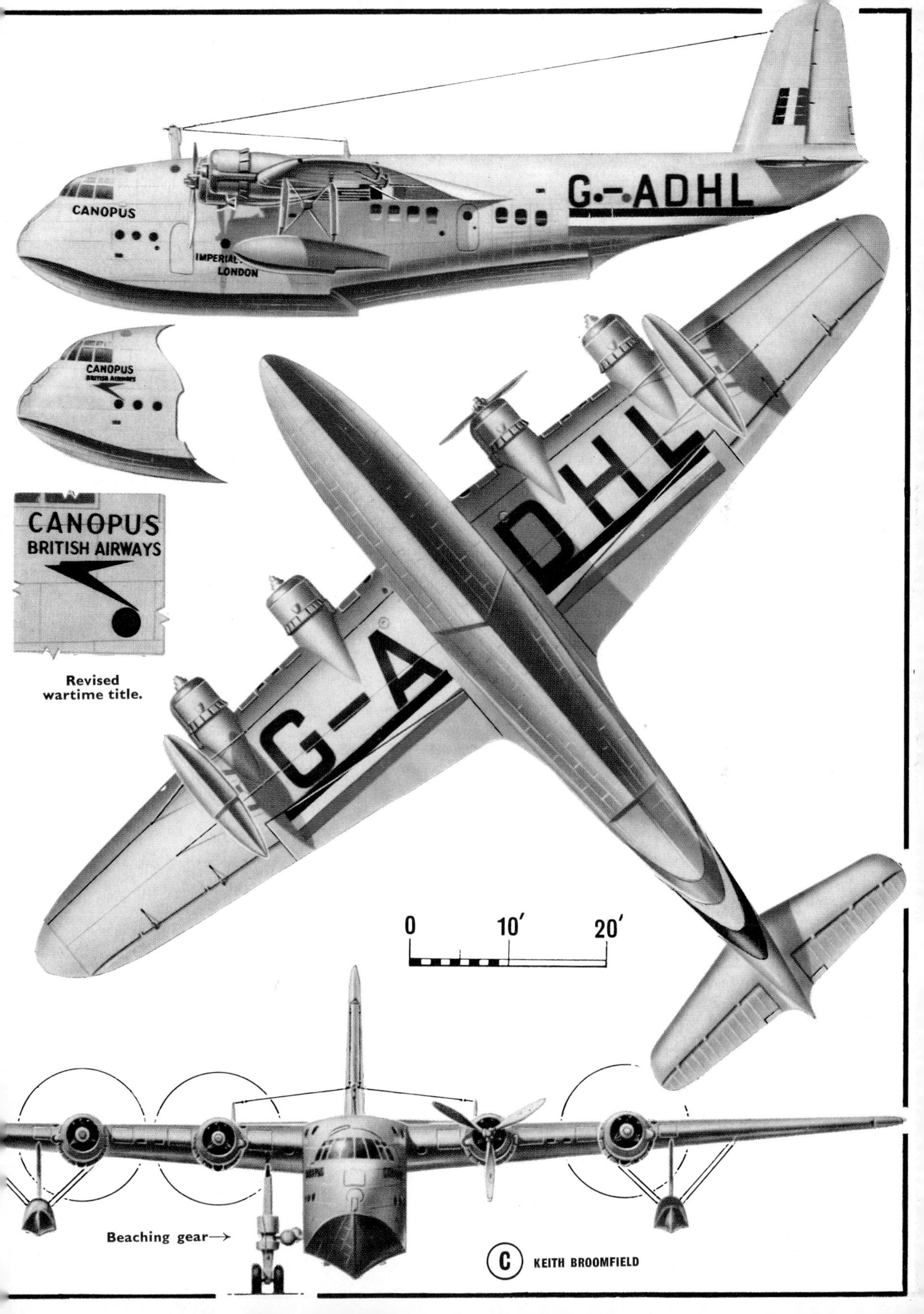

Revised wartime title.

Above, left and right: Canopus *cockpit looking aft and showing radio station, pilots' controls and greenhouse.* (Photos: Short Bros. and Harland)

Below, left and right: *Ship's clerk station on* Canopus; *radio operator's station on* Centaurus. (Photos: Short Bros. and Harland)

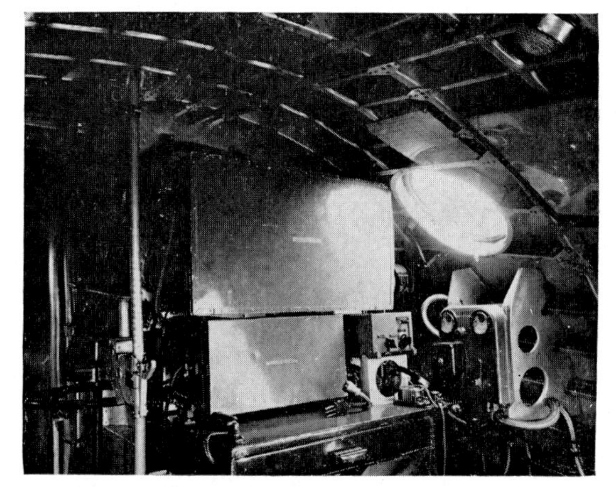

aircraft was delivered on 26th February 1938 and this boat, together with *Coogee* and *Corio* which preceded it on the production line, were taken out of the Imperial Airways order and delivered to Qantas Empire Airways.

These S.23 boats served their purpose admirably. They were seldom out of the news and rapidly built-up what must still rank as one of the most highly-developed air networks linking England with Africa, India and Australia. True enough there were crashes, *Cygnus*, *Capricornus*, *Courtier* and *Calpurnia* had been written off by the end of 1938, but in no case could the blame be placed on a fault inherent in the boats concerned.

The honour of making the first regular flight in a "C" Class boat fell to Captain H. W. C. Alger in *Castor*. The journey should have started on 6th February 1937 and the boat did, in fact, take off promptly at 11.45 a.m. from Hythe carrying eight passengers and more than a ton of freight and mail, including bullion. Unfortunately the plugs had become oiled up and, after circling Southampton for an hour, *Castor* landed again. Bad weather prevented take-off on the following day and Captain Alger and his passengers finally left for Alexandria on 8th February.

Ten days later the long-range boat *Caledonia*, flown by Captains W. N. Cumming and A. S. Wilcockson flew the 2,300 miles between Calshot and Alexandria non-stop at an average speed of 170 m.p.h. On 21st February Captain J. G. Powell took *Cambria*, another long-range boat, on a circuit of Britain flight covering 1,300 miles non-stop in 8 hr. 42 min., an average speed of 135 m.p.h.

The greatest achievement of 1937 was, however, the first Atlantic crossing by an Empire Boat which was made by *Caledonia* on 5th July with Captain Wilcockson at the controls. Flying a rhumb-line course *Caledonia* covered the 1,993 miles between Shannon and Botwood in 15 hr. 3 min. A Sikorsky Clipper III made the reverse crossing simultaneously on the slightly shorter great circle course and her time was 12 hr. 34 min. *Caledonia* was, however, to regain the honour for Britain. Simultaneous return crossings were made on 22nd July and *Caledonia's* time for the West–East journey was 12 hr. 7 min. against the Clipper III's 16 hr. 24 min. for the East–West crossing. After all allowances for wind differences and other variables, the Empire Boat was fastest overall.

Proof that Imperial Airways thought their original conception of the Empire Boat was correct and that Shorts had provided an excellent realisation came at the end of 1937 when the airline ordered another

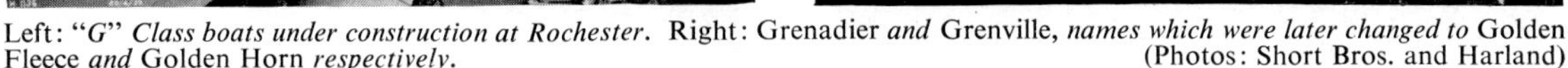

Left: *"G" Class boats under construction at Rochester.* Right: Grenadier *and* Grenville, *names which were later changed to* Golden Fleece *and* Golden Horn *respectively.* (Photos: Short Bros. and Harland)

eleven aircraft which brought the total up to thirty-nine and the largest single order for a British civil aircraft ever placed at that time. The first three boats of this new order were to complete the need for six for Qantas Empire Airways and *Carpenteria*, *Coolangatta* and *Cooee* were of the normal S.23 Class. The rest were built under the designation S.30 and, except for one boat, were re-engined with the Bristol Perseus XIIc which developed 890 h.p. against the 920 h.p. of the Pegasus used in the S.23 boats. Despite this drop in power, some strengthening in the fuselage and the use of heavier gauge sheeting on the fuselage and wings, the new boats had the same performance as those in the S.23 Class. These apparently magical advantages with less power were obtained because the new engines fitted into nacelles three inches less in diameter than those demanded by the Pegasus to give a significant decrease in drag. In addition these boats were cleared to take off at 46,000 lb. all-up-weight or to take on fuel up to 53,000 lb. all-up-weight if refuelled in the air—and these models were fitted with aerial refuelling equipment. Wing loading was increased from 30 lb. to 31 lb. per sq. in.

Champion was the first S.30 boat to be laid down but *Cabot*, the aircraft which retained Pegasus engines, was the first to be completed as it was not immediately fitted out but was used by Shorts for tests. Early in December 1938 *Cabot* made the first successful take-off at 46,000 lb. all-up-weight—a trouble-free flight by Lankester Parker from Rochester with a take-off time of only 21 secs. G-AFCY, G-AFCZ and G-AFDA, the last three boats of this additional order, were re-registered ZK-AMA, ZK-AMB and ZK-AMC and named *Ao-tea-roa*, *Australia* and *Awarua* respectively for use by Tasman Airways on the Sydney–Auckland route. *Australia* was placed back on the British register when BOAC was formed in April 1940 and given her original name, *Clare*.

One other S.30 boat was ordered during 1939 and G-AFKZ *Cathay* was delivered to Imperial Airways during its last days in March 1940. Another three boats ordered by I.A. in 1939 were built to the same basic construction as the others but were powered by Pegasus XI engines and cleared only up to 40,500 lb. all-up-weight. They were, therefore, virtually the same as the original S.23 boats but were built as the S.33 Class. Only two boats were completed and *Clifton* and *Cleopatra*, as they were named, were delivered direct to BOAC.

PICK-A-BACK EXPERIMENT

No mention of the Empire Boats would be complete without including what is still one of the most remarkable aerial experiments of all time. Major R. H. Mayo, who had played no small part in the conception of the Empire Boats, had long been of the opinion that both range and payload could be increased tremendously if an aircraft did not have to heed the demands of take-off and climb. Cobham had, of course, been pursuing the same line of thought with his aerial refuelling experiments but Mayo's thoughts were more revolutionary. He reasoned that a large aircraft could be designed to carry a smaller machine well on its way and then release it to fly alone to its destination, already at cruising height and with full tanks. This, coupled with the fact that the smaller aircraft could also start its journey at an all-up-weight unthinkable if it had to take-off by itself, meant that a compara-

Golden Hind *which had a Sunderland-type planing bottom fitted.* (Photo: Short Bros. and Harland)

Left and right: *Flight deck and ship's clerk bay.* (Photos: Short Bros. and Harland)

tively small aircraft could carry a very heavy load, or a medium load a great distance. Mayo's reasoning impressed both Imperial Airways and the Air Ministry and the latter placed an order with Shorts. Design work on the two aircraft needed was started before that on the S.23 boats but *Maia*, the larger of the two, was closely related to the Empire Boats. The most obvious difference was the superstructure to carry the upper component but, compared with normal S.23 boats, *Maia* was wider in the fuselage, had a more pronounced flare at the chines to give added water stability, more fin and rudder area and 250 sq. ft. more wing area. The outboard Pegasus engines were placed farther out to provide greater clearance for the floats of the upper aircraft.

Mercury, the upper component, was a four-engined, high-wing monoplane which also had an obvious affinity with the Scion Senior. Power was provided by Napier Rapier V engines each developing a maximum of 340 h.p. at 13,000 ft. Span was 73 ft. and all-up-weight 12,500 lb. when flying alone but increasing to 20,500 lb. when air-launched from *Maia*. These weights were later increased to 14,000 lb. and 20,800 lb. respectively when the engines were changed to Rapier VIs developing a maximum of 395 h.p.

Tests of the two aircraft continued individually during the latter part of 1937 with Lankester Parker being responsible for *Maia* and Harold Piper, another Shorts' test pilot, flying *Mercury*. Neither aircraft displayed any alarming symptoms although there was trouble with the telephone communication between the two aircraft when they were coupled and this was to lead to a slight delay in the crucial test for combined flying and release.

All eight engines were used during combined flight but the controls of *Mercury* were locked. The aerofoil designs of the two aircraft were such that *Mercury's* wings were carrying the major part of the air load at the speed and height chosen for separation. Safety locks prevented separation until this speed and height were reached and both pilots had an unlocking handle, both of which had to be pulled to cause release. The first test of this seemingly foolproof theory came on 6th February 1938. The first separation was carried out well over the Thames Estuary and away from the prying eyes of the Press, but there was no cause for worry. *Mercury* leapt upwards as planned and *Maia*, deprived of the lift of her smaller companion, went into a shallow dive.

The first attempt on the Atlantic came on 21st July 1938. Captain Wilcockson was at the controls of *Maia* and Captain D. C. T. Bennett, later of Pathfinder fame, piloted *Mercury* when the composite took off from Foynes on the west coast of Ireland. *Mercury*, which carried 600 lb. of freight and mail, arrived at Boucherville, Montreal, 20 hr. 20 min. later, having flown the 2,860-mile course at an average ground speed of 141 m.p.h. Average air speed was 177 m.p.h. Later that year, on 6th October, the same technique was used for *Mercury*, again flown by Bennett, to fly from Dundee, Scotland, to Orange River, South Africa, a distance of 6,045 miles, in 42 hr. 5 min.

Above and below: *Forward and rear beaching gear of* Canopus.
(Photos: Short Bros. and Harland)

So successful were the experiments with this pair that there was little doubt that they would have continued with landplane versions, but the war intervened. The scheme was to be resurrected, however, when a means was sought to provide aerial protection for Atlantic convoys. A Liberator/Hurricane composite was proposed and work was well-advanced at Hawkers but discontinued when other means of convoy protection became available.

BIGGER STILL

There was to be one other development of the Empire Boats and that was the S.26 or "G" Class. Three of these were ordered by Imperial Airways. Basically similar to the "C" Class but bigger in every way, they were designed to an all-up-weight of 73,500 lb., had a span of 134 ft. 4 in., and were powered by four Bristol Hercules IV engines. Maximum speed was 209 m.p.h. and cruising speed 175 m.p.h. at 5,000 ft. Outwardly they looked like normal "C"-Class boats but had a Sunderland-type planing bottom with its sharp, V-shaped step at the aft end, and a cleaner sweep to the lines at the forward end of the fuselage. Imperial Airways planned to use these boats on the North Atlantic route but war intervened. *Golden Hind* was the first of these boats and the other two were originally named *Grenadier* and *Grenville*, but these were re-christened before launching as *Golden Fleece* and *Golden Horn*. All three were impressed into R.A.F.

Cabot, *first "C" Class boat to take-off at an a.u.w. of 46,000 lb.*
(Photo: Short Bros. and Harland)

service and fitted with turrets before being used as V.I.P. transports. Neither *Golden Fleece* nor *Golden Horn* survived the war but *Golden Hind* soldiered on and was probably the longest lived of the Empire Boats. After the war she was used on routes to Australia and Africa by the Ministry of Aviation and sold to BOAC in 1948 when her Certificate of Airworthiness expired. The airline seemed in no hurry to put her into service and several other interested parties announced plans for getting her flying again, but nothing came of these. She was eventually

Golden Fleece *as a wartime V.I.P. transport. Right-hand illustration below shows the original turret before fairing (left) was fitted.*
(Photos: Short Bros. and Harland)

Mercury and Maia, *the "C" Class composite.*

damaged during a storm in 1954 and broken up soon after.

Many other Empire Boats played their part in the war, mainly as transports with BOAC or QEA. Two of them were returned to Short Brothers and Harland at Belfast at the beginning of 1941 and modified to incorporate gun turrets and an array of ASV aerials on the top and sides of the fuselage. *Clio* arrived at Belfast having flown 4,382 hr. 55 min. in her civilian rôle and was re-launched on 12th March 1941 as AX659. *Cordelia* flew 4,261 hours with airlines and became AX660 when she was re-launched at Belfast on 16th April.

S.23 CLASS

Dimensions: Span, 114 ft.; length, 88 ft.; height, 31 ft. 9¾ in.; wing area, 1,500 sq. ft.
Weights: Empty, 24,000 lb.; loaded, 40,500 lb.
Engines: Four Bristol Pegasus Xc each rated at 740 b h.p. at 3,500 ft.
Performance: Maximum speed 200 m.p.h. at 5,500 ft.; cruising speed at 510 b.h.p. per engine, 165 m.p.h. Normal still air range, 760 miles.

S.30 CLASS

Dimensions: As for S.23 Class.
Weights: Empty, 27,825 lb.; loaded, 46,000 lb.
Engines: Four Bristol Perseus XIIc rated at 700 b.h.p. at 3,500 ft.
Performance: Speeds as for S.23 Class. Normal still air range, 1,870 miles.

"G" CLASS

Dimensions: Span, 134 ft. 4 in.; length, 103 ft. 2 in.; height, 37 ft. 7 in.; wing area, 2,160 sq. ft.
Weights: Empty, 37,705 lb.; loaded, 73,500 lb.
Engines: Four Bristol Hercules IV rated at 1,030 h.p. at 3,000 ft.
Performance: Maximum speed, 209 m.p.h. at 4,500 ft.; cruising speed, 177 m.p.h. at 5,000 ft. Cruising range against 40 m.p.h. headwind, 2,500 miles.

MERCURY

Dimensions: Span, 73 ft.; length, 50 ft. 11½ in.; height, 20 ft. 3 in.; wing area, 611 sq. ft.
Weights: Empty, 10,000 lb.; loaded (for solo take-off), 12,500 lb.; loaded for air launch, 20,500 lb.
Engines: Four Napier Rapier V rated at 1,020 h.p. for maximum continuous cruise at 10,000 ft.
Performance: Maximum speed, 207 m.p.h. at 13,000 ft.; cruising speed, 180 m.p.h. at 10,000 ft. Still air range with solo take-off, 350 miles; still air range with air launch, 3,800 miles.

MAIA

Dimensions: Span, 114 ft.; length, 84 ft. 10¾ in.; height, 32 ft. 7½ in.; wing area, 1,750 sq. ft.
Weights: Empty, 2,400 lb.; loaded (solo) 38,000 lb.
Engines: As for S.23 Class.
Performance: Maximum speed, 200 m.p.h.; cruising speed, 165 m.p.h. at 5,000 ft. Still air range at cruising speed, 850 miles.

Unfortunately for the flying boat the war turned virtually the entire British aircraft industry towards landplane development and by 1945 the flying boat had been left behind in performance. Nevertheless, the Sandringhams and Hythes which provided flying boat services with BOAC and other airlines in the years immediately following the war owed their design directly to the Empire Boats and, in fact, their influence can be seen in every flying boat built since. This is no mean achievement for an aircraft which was designed, built and in service within eighteen months of an order being placed.

Perseus engine of Cabot. (Photo: Short Bros. and Harland)

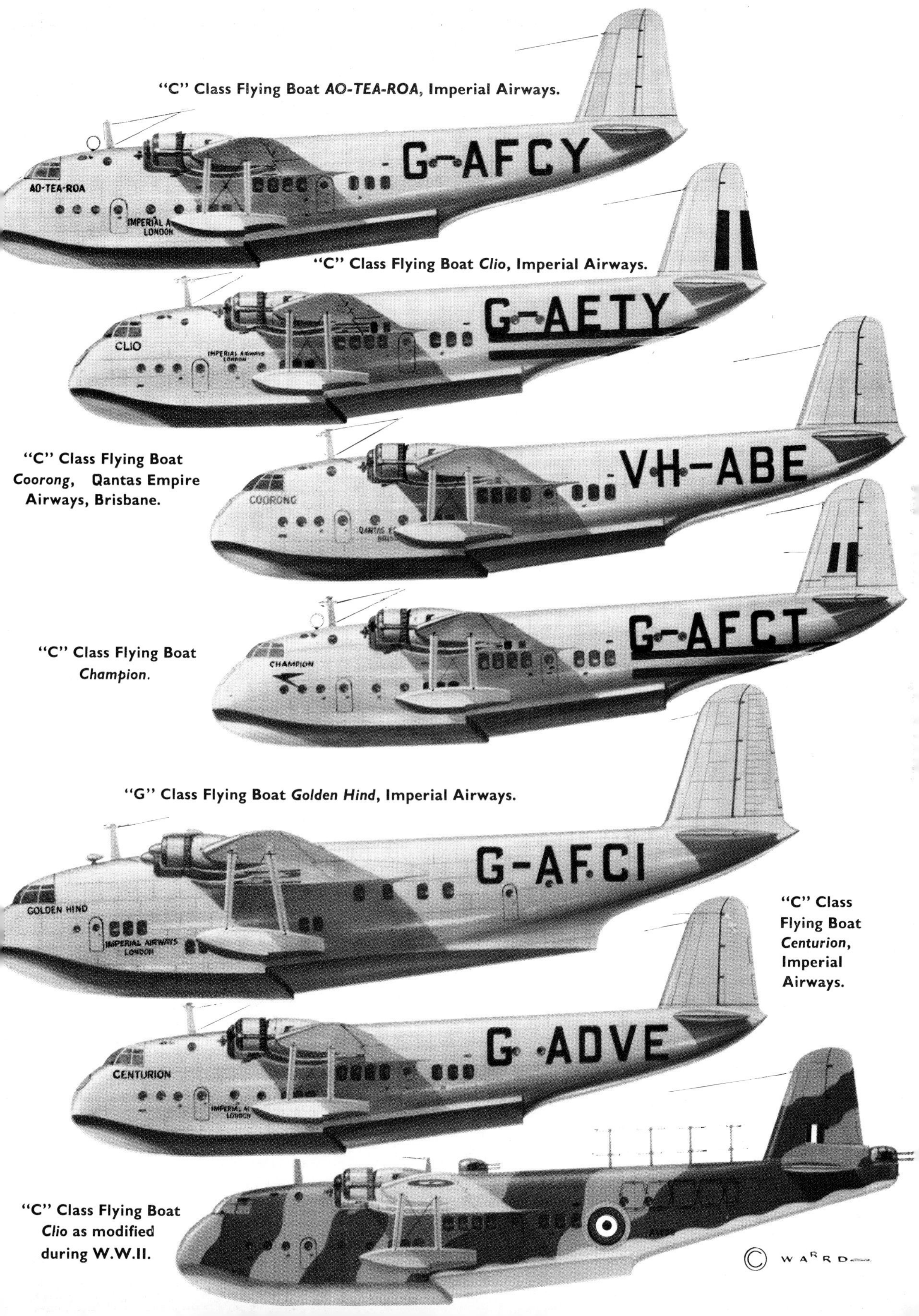

"C" Class Flying Boat *AO-TEA-ROA*, Imperial Airways.

"C" Class Flying Boat *Clio*, Imperial Airways.

"C" Class Flying Boat *Coorong*, Qantas Empire Airways, Brisbane.

"C" Class Flying Boat *Champion*.

"G" Class Flying Boat *Golden Hind*, Imperial Airways.

"C" Class Flying Boat *Centurion*, Imperial Airways.

"C" Class Flying Boat *Clio* as modified during W.W.II.

SHORT "C" CLASS FLYING BOATS

Serial	Registration	First Flight	Delivery	Name and Remarks
S.795	G-ADHL	4.7.36	22.10.36	*Canopus*. Passed to BOAC, April 1940.
S.796	G-ADHJ	2.9.37*	March, 1938	*Mercury*. Built for Air Ministry. Passed to BOAC April 1940. Reduced to produce at Rochester 21.8.41.
S.797	G-ADHK	11.8.37	March, 1938	*Maia*. Built for Air Ministry. Passed to BOAC April 1940. Destroyed in air raid 11.5.42.
S.804	G-ADHM	15.9.36	4.12.36	*Caledonia*. First long-range boat with extra tanks. Made first Atlantic crossing by Empire Boat. Passed to BOAC.
S.811	G-ADUT	18.11.36	7.12.36	*Centaurus*. Bermuda Boat. Surveyed Far East route to Australia and New Zealand. Commandeered by Australian Government, September 1939.
S.812	G-ADUU	30.11.36	10.12.36	*Cavalier*. Bermuda Boat. Dismantled and shipped to Bermuda. Made first New York–Bermuda run. Crashed in Atlantic 21.1.39.
S.813	G-ADUV	14.1.37	21.1.37	*Cambria*. Second long-range boat. Made circuit of Britain flight. Used by Cobham in air refuelling experiments. Passed to BOAC.
S.814	G-ADUW	22.12.36	2.1.37	*Castor*. Made first regular Southampton–Alexandria flight 6.2.37. Passed to BOAC.
S.815	G-ADUX	25.1.37	1.2.37	*Cassiopeia*. Passed to BOAC. Crashed at Sabang 22.12.41.
S.816	G-ADUY	15.2.37	16.2.37	*Capella*. Crashed March 1939.
S.817	G-ADUZ	3.3.37	3.3.37	*Cygnus*. Crashed at Brindisi 5.12.37.
S.818	G-ADVA	15.3.37	16.3.37	*Capricornus*. Crashed near Macon, France, 24.3.37.
S.819	G-ADVB	5.4.37	8.4.37	*Corsair*. Passed to BOAC.
S.820	G-ADVC	22.4.37	23.4.37	*Courtier*. Crashed near Athens 1.10.37.
S.821	G-ADVD	5.5.37	6.5.37	*Challenger*. Crashed on landing at Mozambique 1.5.39.
S.822	G-ADVE	28.5.37	29.5.37	*Centurion*. Crashed on Hooghly River, India, 12.6.39.
S.838	G-AETV	17.6.37	17.6.37	*Coriolanus*. Passed to BOAC.
S.839	G-AETW	27.6.37	30.6.37	*Calpurnia*. Crashed on landing on Lake Habbaniyah 27.11.38.
S.840	G-AETX	15.7.37	17.7.37	*Ceres*. Passed to BOAC.
S.841	G-AETY	28.7.37	30.7.37	*Clio*. Passed to BOAC. Impressed as AX659, served with 201 Squadron, crashed 22.8.41.
S.842	G-AETZ	13.8.37	16.8.37	*Circe*. Passed to BOAC. Shot down off Tjilaejap 28.2.42.
S.843	G-AEUA	27.8.37	27.8.37	*Calypso*. Passed to BOAC.
S.844	G-AEUB	11.9.37	13.9.37	*Camilla*. Passed to BOAC.
S.845	G-AEUC	24.9.37	29.9.37	*Corinna*. Passed to BOAC. Destroyed in air raid at Darwin 3.3.42.
S.846	G-AEUD	8.10.37	9.10.37	*Cordelia*. Passed to BOAC. Impressed as AX660, took part in depth charge trials with 119 Squadron. Released to BOAC 19.9.41. Broken up at Hythe 6.3.47.
S.847	G-AEUE	21.10.37	23.10.37	*Cameronian*. Passed to BOAC.
S.848	G-AEUF	5.11.37	6.11.37	*Corinthian*. Passed to BOAC. Crashed at Darwin, March 1942.
S.849	G-AEUG	1.1.38	3.1.38	*Coogee*. Used by QEA under registration VH-ABA.
S.850	G-AEUH	9.2.38	10.2.38	*Corio*. Used by QEA under registration VH-ABD. Commandeered by Australian Government, September 1939. Shot down by Jap fighter off Koepang 10.1.42.
S.851	G-AEVI	25.2.38	26.2.38	*Coorong*. Used by QEA as VH-ABE. Passed to BOAC. Shot down off Timor 30.1.42. Last of initial order of 28 aircraft by Imperial Airways.
S.876	G-AFBJ	25.11.37	3.12.37	*Carpentaria*. Passed to QEA as VH-ABA.
S.877	G-AFBK	17.12.37	18.12.37	*Coolangatta*. Passed to QEA as VH-ABB.
S.878	VH-ABF	28.3.38	31.3.38	*Cooee*. Used by QEA.
S.879	G-AFCT	22.10.38	28.10.38	*Champion*. First S.30 boat at increased all-up-weight but with Pegasus engines.
S.880	G-AFCU	8.12.38	27.7.39	*Cabot*. S.30 boat with Perseus engines. Made first take-off at 46,000 lb., December 1938. Passed to R.A.F., September 1939 as V3137. Destroyed at Bodo 5.5.40.
S.881	G-AFCV	14.12.38	13.7.39	*Caribou*. Long-range boat used for in-flight refuelling experiments. Passed to R.A.F. as V3138. Destroyed in air raid at Bodo 6.5.40.
S.882	G-AFCW	24.3.39	24.3.39	*Connemara*. Long-range boat. Burned out during refuelling at Hythe 19.6.39.
S.883	G-AFCX	27.3.39	27.3.39	*Clyde*. Long-range boat. Passed to BOAC. Wrecked in gale at Lisbon 14.2.41.
S.884	G-AFCY	20.4.39	21.4.39	*Ao-tea-roa*. Medium-range boat used on Sydney–Auckland route as ZK-AMA.
S.885	G-AFCZ	5.4.39	6.4.39	*Australia*. Medium-range boat used on Sydney–Auckland route as ZK-AMB. Passed to BOAC and renamed *Clare*. Lost off Bathurst 14.9.42.
S.886	G-AFDA	10.5.39	12.5.39	*Awarua*. Medium-range boat used on Sydney–Auckland route as ZK-AMC.
S.1003	G-AFKZ	21.2.40	8.3.40	*Cathay*. S.30 Boat with Pegasus engines.
S.1025	G-AFPZ	9.4.40	17.4.40	*Clifton*. S.33 Boat with Pegasus XI engines.
S.1026	G-AFRA	4.5.40	10.5.40	*Cleopatra*. S.33 Boat with Pegasus XI engines.
S.1027	G-AFRB	—	—	——. S.33 Boat not completed.

*Date of launch.

SHORT "G" CLASS FLYING BOATS

Serial	Registration	First Flight	Delivery	Name and Remarks
S.871	G-AFCI	14.7.39	24.9.39	*Golden Hind*. Passed to R.A.F. as X8275. Passed to BOAC 1948. Scrapped 1954.
S.872	G-AFCJ	8.7.40	14.8.1940	*Golden Fleece*. Delivered to R.A.F. as X8274. Used by "G" Flight and later 10 Squadron R.A.A.F. Sank off Cape Finisterre 20.6.41.
S.873	G-AFCK	21.1.40	16.5.40	*Golden Horn*. Delivered to R.A.F. as X8273. Crashed River Tagus, Lisbon, 9.1.43.

PRINTED IN ENGLAND © Profile Publications Ltd., P.O. Box 26, 1a North Street, Leatherhead, Surrey, England.
Printed by Hills & Lacy Ltd., London and Watford, England. U.S. 2nd Class Mailing Rates applied for.

PROFILE PUBLICATIONS

The R.E.8

NUMBER 85

TWO SHILLINGS

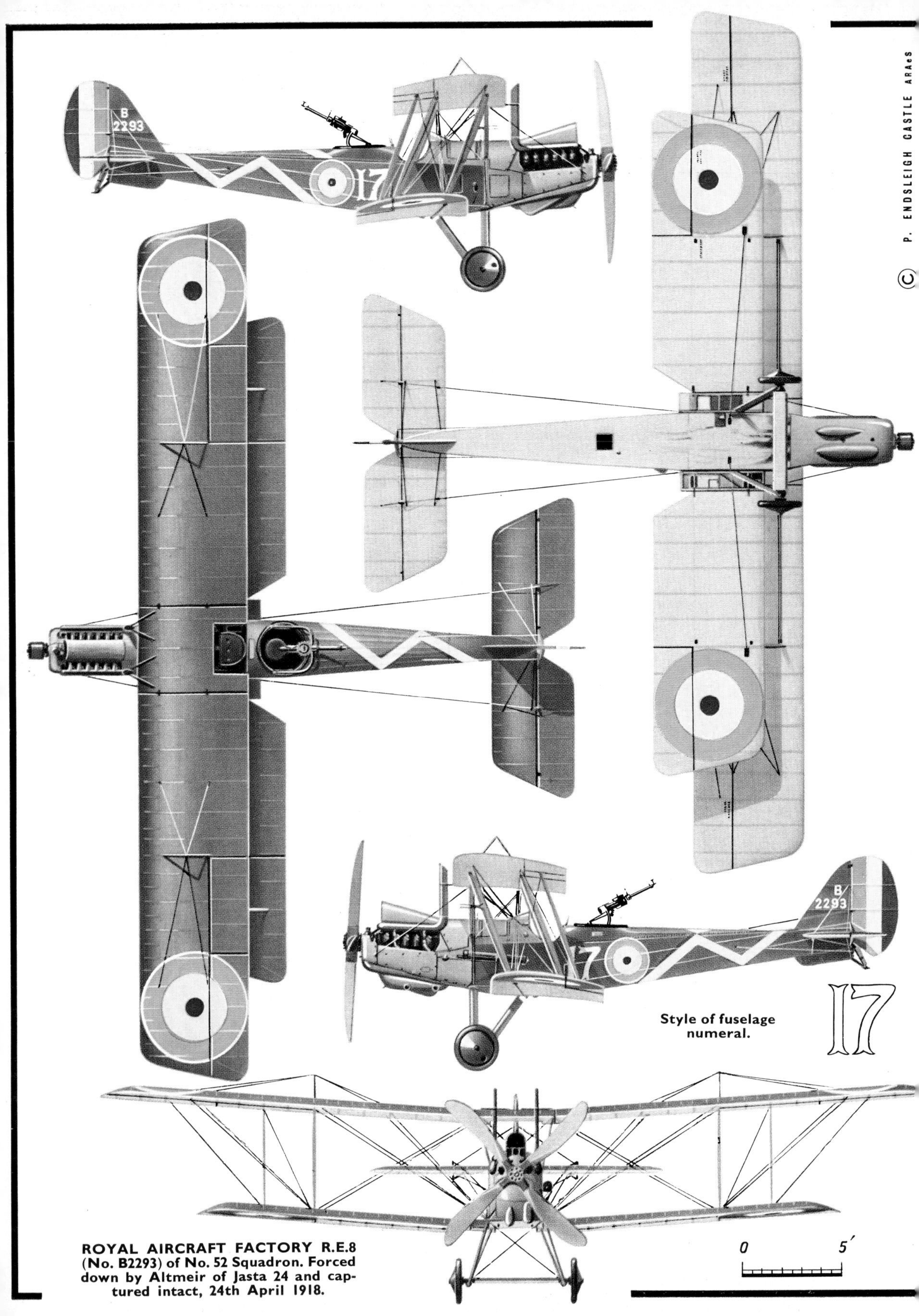

ROYAL AIRCRAFT FACTORY R.E.8 (No. B2293) of No. 52 Squadron. Forced down by Altmeir of Jasta 24 and captured intact, 24th April 1918.

The first prototype, 7996, photographed at Farnborough on 28th June 1916. (Photo: Crown copyright)

The eighth type in the Royal Aircraft Factory's Reconnaissance Experimental series was designed to meet an Expeditionary Force request, made in the autumn of 1915, for a replacement for the B.E.2c, 2d and 2e for corps reconnaissance and artillery spotting duties. It had been specified that the new type must be capable of defending itself. The B.E.s were inherently stable aircraft, this characteristic being an inheritance from the pre-war belief that military aeroplanes were flying observation posts and therefore had to be as stable as possible. By the autumn of 1915 it was beginning to be realised that inherent stability was a disadvantage, for it denied the reconnaissance aircraft the agility that was needed in order to elude the Fokker monoplanes.

It will probably never be known whether the operational disadvantages of inherent stability were made known to the design staff at Farnborough. If they were, the warning was ignored, for the R.E.8 embodied the Factory's ideas on stability and was far from tractable. Possibly it was felt that the terms of the Expeditionary Force specification had been met by placing the pilot in the front cockpit with a fixed forward-firing gun, the observer behind with a Lewis gun on a rotating mounting.

Early thoughts on the R.E.8 are depicted in an R.A.F. drawing dated 9th March 1916. This shows that the airframe was conceived as a conventional wire-braced, fabric-covered wooden structure with unequal-span wings; the aerofoil section was apparently to be R.A.F. 6. In the light of later events, one of the most significant features of this early drawing is its provision of a fin and rudder of generous area. The selected engine was the 140-h.p. R.A.F. 4a, an air-cooled V-12; and an adjustable tailplane was envisaged. Military equipment included a camera and a wireless transmitter, for which Morse keys were to be provided in both cockpits.

An interesting commentary on the state of the art of aircraft armament in early 1916 is provided by the fact that the original forward-gun installation was to consist of a Lewis gun mounted on the starboard inner side of the front cockpit and, for want of a British synchronising mechanims, steel deflector plates were to be fitted to the airscrew blades in the line of fire as in the Saulnier device pioneered in combat by Roland Garros (see *Profile* No. 38, pp. 4 and 5). As the gun was to be mounted relatively low down in the cockpit there was provision for a trigger lever on the upper longeron, connected by Bowden cable to the trigger on the gun. Apparently it was not considered remarkable that the pilot would have to fly left-handed while firing his gun. Five 47-round drums of ammunition were to be provided for each gun.

A mock-up of the R.E.8 was in existence by 8th April 1916 and work on two prototypes, to be numbered *7996* and *7997*, was put in hand. The first was submitted for its final pre-flight inspection on 16th June 1916; its engine at that time was an R.A.F. 4a made by the Siddeley-Deasy Motor Car Co., No. W.D.1635/S.D.202, driving a T.28008 airscrew. Perhaps the most interesting feature of the official records relating to this aircraft is that they indicate that the pilot's gun was a Lewis (No. 7632). The airscrew bore no deflector plates, however.

With Capt. F. W. Goodden at the controls, No. *7996* took off on its first flight at 8.30 p.m. on 17th June 1916 and landed ten minutes later. Goodden flew the aircraft on all its early flights. On 1st July the rear cockpit was occupied by Brigadier General W. Sefton Brancker, when Goodden flew him to Hounslow.

The second prototype, No. *7997*, underwent its final inspection on 28th June 1916; apparently it had a different airscrew of new design. The first recorded flight of this aircraft was made on 5th July, with Goodden as pilot. On 16th July No. *7997* was flown to France by Goodden with Capt. F. M. Green in the rear seat. Against the date 18th July 1916 Maurice Baring recorded:

> The R.E.8 is at the A.D. Its camera needs a larger case. The machine is to be kept a fortnight so that the gun-mounting and camera can be altered to what we want.*

By the time the prototypes were built the R.E.8 design has been extensively revised. The fuselage

**Flying Corps Headquarters 1914–1918*, page 161.

Royal Aircraft Factory drawing No. A9429, dated March 1916, showing the large vertical tail assembly originally designed for the R.E.8. The pilot's Lewis gun and the deflector plates on the airscrew can be seen. At this time it was intended to mount the gun upright on the starboard side of the cockpit; later the gun installation was modified, the weapon being fitted at an inward angle of 33 deg. from the vertical.
(Photo: Crown copyright)

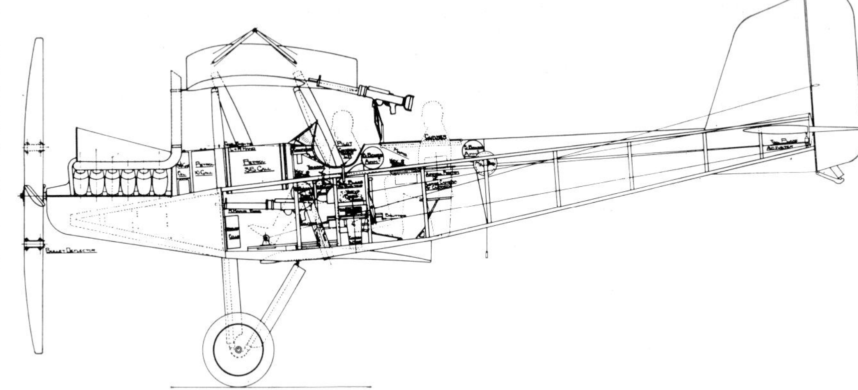

structure was modified in detail, the aerofoil section of the mainplanes had been changed to R.A.F. 14, and a completely re-designed fin and rudder were fitted. The new rudder was of slightly greater area than that of the original design but was of lower aspect ratio; the fin was about half the size. The tail skid was faired into the lower end of the rudder.

Why it was considered necessary thus to reduce the vertical tail area of the R.E.8 is one of the mysteries of the war period. It becomes even more incomprehensible when one remembers that it had been found necessary to fit an enlarged fin to the B.E.2e, that surface being subsequently adopted as standard for B.E.2c's, 8a's, 12s, 12a's and 12b's also. In the case of the R.E.8 the use of the small fin was to cause many accidents.

Several features that were typical of Royal Aircraft Factory designs appeared on the R.E.8. Its mainplanes and ailerons were virtually identical with those of the B.E.2e, apparently differing only in detail; the tailplane and elevators were standard B.E.2e components but had the refinement of an adjusting mechanism. The wings were heavily staggered and had pronounced dihedral; the engine drove a large four-blade airscrew, was surmounted by a large air scoop, and its exhaust manifolds terminated in two tall funnel-like stacks that led the efflux up above the centre section.

A peculiarity of the fuselage structure was the termination of the longerons at the points of attachment of the forward centre-section and undercarriage struts: the engine bearers were separate from and several inches closer together than the longerons.

The second prototype had returned to Farnborough in August 1916 and by the 31st of that month it had been modified in various ways, doubtless as a result of its sojourn in France. Its rudder, tailskid and tailplane adjusting gear had been modified; the Lewis gun (presumably the pilot's) had been removed, thus permitting the transfer from the port side of the cockpit to the starboard of the R.L. Tube (a chute with an electrical priming device; through it could be dropped 3·45-in. anti-aircraft incendiary bombs, smoke marker bombs, signal flares or parachute flares). The gunner's seat was lowered, and the centre section was covered with transparent Cellon.

By that time production had begun. A batch of fifty, *A66–A115*, was started at the Royal Aircraft Factory, but large-scale production was entrusted to other contractors. Contract No. 87/A/488, dated 25th

Left: *The first production R.E.8,* A66, *photographed at Orfordness; no fixed gun is visible in this photograph.* A66 *later crashed at Orfordness and was quite extensively damaged.* Right: A73 *with Vickers gun installed inside the fuselage. The firing port and the connecting rod of the Vickers-Challenger interrupter gear can be seen.* (Photo: Imperial War Museum Q55991)

Left: *On* A3186 *the area of the upper fin was slightly increased, but the underfin remained its original size.* Right: *Subject of the official performance test report quoted in the table on page 12,* A4716 *had the standard design of upper fins and underfins fitted to all operational R.E.8s until the end of the war.* (Photos: Imperial War Museum Q56852 and Q63817)

Built by Siddeley-Deasy, A3433 *had the original small fins but a Scarff ring-mounting had replaced the earlier type of rotating mounting.*

August 1916, called for 100 R.E.8s (*A3169–A3268*) to be built by the Austin Motor Co. Five days later, *A3405–A3504* were ordered from the Siddeley-Deasy company under Contract No. 87/A/486; this order was augmented on 6th September by 87/A/785, which was for *A3681–A3830*. By the end of September 1916 a further 850 had been ordered from the Austin, Daimler, Napier and Standard companies and the Coventry Ordnance Works.

The Royal Aircraft Factory built only 44 R.E.8s: there is no record of *A110–A115*, nor of the second R.A.F. batch *A3506–A3530*. This curtailment may have been attributable to the findings of the Burbidge Report. The first R.A.F.-built production R.E.8, *A66*, was inspected on 13th November 1916; *A67* and *A68* followed next day, *A69* on 18th September; then a full month elapsed before *A70–A73* were passed. Thereafter deliveries continued regularly until 17th January 1917, when *A109* underwent its pre-flight inspection.

These early production R.E.8s were similar to the prototypes, having the same small-area fin. The tail-skid was hinged to the stern-post separately from the rudder, which was modified in shape to clear the tail-skid. The Thornton-Pickard camera (of a type that had been specially designed for the R.E.8) was installed behind the observer's cockpit instead of under the pilot's seat, as was originally intended. A rotating mounting for the observer's Lewis gun, similar to that on the prototypes, was fitted to the Factory-built R.E.8s; but the first few at least seemed to have no visible provision of armament for the pilot. Surviving records show that a Vickers gun and interrupter gear had been installed in *7997* by 11th October 1916, but it is not certain that this was the first such installation.

Late in 1916 an installation of the Le Prieur gun sight was designed for the R.E.8. This device was an elaboration of the ring-and-bead sight, embodying a traversing bead sight, presumably to enable adjustment to be made to allow for deflection. The sight was to be mounted nine inches to starboard of the aircraft centre line. It was a large, clumsy device that was too complex to be adjusted in combat as was apparently intended, and would have been a source of facial injury to the pilot in the event of a crash. It was not developed.

When a Vickers gun was installed in the R.E.8 for the pilot, advantage was taken of the difference in width between the engine bearers and longerons to mount the gun inside the fuselage, on the port side. It fired through a long triangular slot in the metal panel that faired the engine cowling side panels to the fuselage sides. The gun was fitted with the Vickers-Challenger interrupter gear, a mechanical system in which a long connecting-rod ran along the outside of the fuselage.

This armament arrangement would have led to maintenance difficulties in the field and it was short-lived. By 5th November 1916, *A75*, *A76*, *A77*, *A78* and *A82* had their Vickers guns mounted on the outside of the fuselage; within the next three days a similar modification on *A73*, *A74*, *A79*, *A80* and *A81* had been inspected. The second prototype, *7997*, had

A3406 *fitted with the enlarged fin and balanced rudder designed for the R.E.8 but almost indistinguishable from the corresponding surfaces designed for the R.E.9 and R.T.1.*

The 12 sq. ft. fin fitted to A4598. *This photograph is dated 10th May 1917* (Photo: Crown copyright)

R.E.8s used by training units were frequently fitted with greatly enlarged fins. The profile of the curved leading edge varied somewhat, but the basis of these enlarged fins seems to have been the standard B.E.2e fin, the variation in contour depending on the length and shape of the piece of steel tubing used to take the leading edge up to the top of the R.E.8 rudder post. This R.E.8 also has a transparent cut-out in its centre section, and the wooden undercarriage V-struts that replaced the original faired steel-tubing components.

also been modified in this way by 13th December 1916.

Contractor-built R.E.8s began to appear in December 1916: on the 8th of that month, *A4306* was reported to be at Farnborough. The first Austin-built aircraft, *A3169*, was at Farnborough on 14th January 1917. Hence, the R.E.8s that were issued to No. 52 Squadron, R.F.C., must have come from the first eighteen or so built by the Royal Aircraft Factory, for the unit went to France on 16th November (*A85* was inspected on 16th November, *A84* on the 20th, but the latter aircraft was subsequently subjected to structural tests at Farnborough; *A86* onwards were inspected between 22nd November 1916 and 17th January 1917).

The R.E.8's operational début was disastrous. Doubtless the aircraft could be handled successfully enough by pilots of the calibre of Frank Goodden, but its idiosyncrasies were too much for many of the sketchily-trained young men of No. 52 Squadron. A series of accidents, several caused by spins, had such a damaging effect on squadron morale that in January 1917 the squadron exchanged its R.E.8s for the B.E.2e's of No. 34 Squadron. Presumably it was thought that No. 34's pilots were, by virtue of their greater experience, more likely to be able to cope with the R.E.8.

Both squadrons were in the Third (Corps) Wing. On the staff of the Wing at that time was Major J. A. Chamier, D.S.O., who had earlier commanded No. 34 Squadron. Early in 1917 he issued some notes on the R.E.8 for the guidance of pilots. The following extracts speak for themselves:

> This is a splendid flying machine but it is not a perambulator and requires at first a little care. . . .
>
> In the R.E.8 the chief thing to remember is that the machine gives very little indication of losing its speed until it suddenly shows an uncontrollable tendency to dive which cannot be corrected in time if you are near the ground.
>
> All the recent accidents in R.E.8s can be equally divided into two classes:
>
> (a) With the engine pulling.
> (b) With the engine off.
>
> (a) With the engine pulling the machine will not stall at 50 m.p.h., but it is not advisable to get the speed as low as this. The only accident which is likely to occur with the engine on is spinning, or more correctly swinging tail. This is caused by having too little bank for the

The cockpits of an R.E.8 fitted with the Constantinesco C.C. gear for its Vickers gun. The pilot's Aldis optical sight is mounted to starboard of his windscreen.
(Photo: Imperial War Museum Q67969)

The pilot's cockpit of an R.E.8 captured by the Germans. The pilot's morse transmitting key and the tail-trimming wheel can be seen to starboard.

The engine installation on the same aircraft. As the cowling panels have been removed from both sides of the fuselage the drive of the Vickers-Challenger interrupter gear can be seen on the port side.

Seen at Bickendorf in 1919, this R.E.8, H7139, *was one of many rebuilt by Aeroplane Repair Depots.* (Photo: Royal Aeronautical Society)

amount of rudder used. It can be stopped immediately by increasing the bank and taking off the rudder. . . .

You will find the rudder control in every case of spinning or swinging tail will become very stiff, and you may not be able to get it very central but you should aim (without putting on sufficient pressure to break anything) to do this.

(b) With the engine off the only thing to avoid is gliding too slowly. I have already told you that with the engine on the machine will not stall at 50 m.p.h., but at 65 m.p.h. or below, when gliding, the machine suddenly loses speed. This is particularly the case when making a turn to enter the aerodrome as the extra resistance caused by the rudder is sufficient to bring down the pace. . . .

One more point as regards losing speed. Observers must be cautioned that when an aeroplane is gliding down from work over the lines they must not stand up in order to look over the pilot's shoulder for the fun of the thing, as the extra head resistance caused may lead to the aeroplane falling below its critical gliding speed, and so bring about an accident.

Major Chamier's note was a sensible and necessary measure at the time, but something had to be done about the R.E.8 itself, for it was a bad and dangerous aeroplane in the conditions of early 1917. The situation was described thus in the official history:

> The early R.E.8's, especially in the hands of new pilots, had a marked tendency to spin, and there were fatal accidents, at home and overseas, before this tendency was checked by adjustments in the design. If a bad landing threw the aeroplane on its nose there was almost a certainty of fire. The engine was pushed back into the emergency and main petrol tanks, so that the whole of the spirit flowed over the engine, and in the fires which resulted many pilots and observers perished. The evil reputation of the R.E.8 spread throughout the Royal Flying Corps. . . . Under the direction of the deputy-controller of the technical department of the Air Board, a series of investigations and trials of the aeroplane were undertaken, and so numerous were the modifications in the design that the R.E.8 emerged almost as a new type. It outlived its bad reputation and survived to the end of the war as the standard aeroplane for the corps squadrons in France.†

It is rather too much of an exaggeration to say that the modifications made to the R.E.8 made it "almost a new type", but a good deal of effort was directed towards making it a safer and more manageable aircraft. The first modification was a modest enlargement of the main fin, produced by taking its leading edge

†*The War in the Air*, Vol. III, pp. 351–352.

The Davis-gun R.E.8 in flight over inhospitable country. Although seen here in silhouette only, this photograph gives a clear impression of the gun's enormous length.
(Photo: Imperial War Museum Q67950)

An R.E.8 of a training unit with deep nose cowling, no fairings on the undercarriage V*-struts and no armament.*
(Photo: Imperial War Museum Q67948)

In Mesopotamia one of the R.E.8s of No. 30 Squadron was fitted with a Davis non-recoil gun. The gun was mounted on the starboard side of the fuselage and was apparently intended to be used as a ground-attack weapon; loading was evidently the responsibility of the observer.
(Photo: Imperial War Museum Q67951)

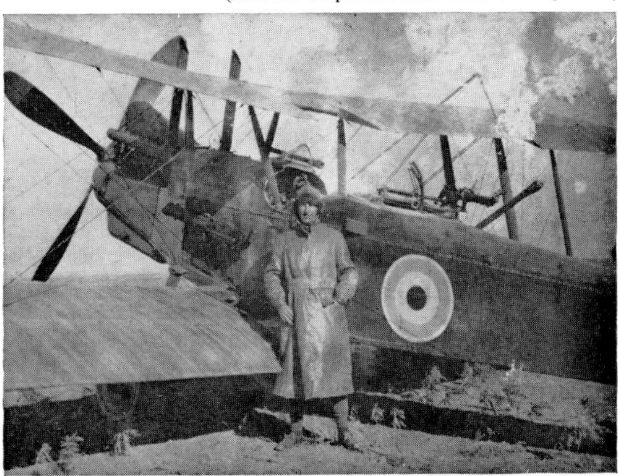

An immaculate R.E.8 of the Aviation Militaire Belge.
(Photo: Jean Noël)

Preserved in the Musée Royal de l'Armée et d'Histoire Militaire in Brussels is this Hispano-Suiza-powered R.E.8. It had been used by the 6me Escadrille *and was brought down by ground fire on 11th August 1918 while being flown by Adjudant Simonet with Lt. Piron as his observer.*

farther forward on the fuselage. This was followed by an increase in the area of the underfin that produced the characteristic outline of the vertical surfaces.

Unfortunately the dates on which these modifications were introduced are not known. Farnborough's efforts did not stop there, however. By 5th May 1917 *A4598* had been fitted with a greatly enlarged fin, 12 sq. ft. in area, and *A4572* with a new type of fin and balanced rudder. At the same time *A3468* was fitted with an enlarged fin similar to that of the B.E.2e.

First flight tests of *A4598* were made on 7th May 1917; *A4572* and *A3468* were tested next day. Other aspects of the R.E.8 were also tested on 8th May: *A4599* was flown with its engine mounted horizontal instead of being tilted rearwards as on the standard aircraft; the first prototype *7996* was also tested with "increased lateral control". The nature of this last modification is not known; nor indeed is the precise form of *7996* itself at that time, for early in February it had been fitted with wings of R.A.F. 18 section. This aerofoil was unusually thin, and it is probable that the wings fitted to *7996* may have been of increased chord in order to obtain the necessary spar depth.

A4598 did not keep its large fin long: on 19th May 1917 it was again inspected, having been fitted with a new type of fin and balanced rudder. At least two types of balanced rudder were tested on 22nd May: *A4598* had a product designed by the R.A.F. drawing office; *A4572*'s balanced rudder had been made by K Dept. of the R.A.F.

It is not known whether there was any connection between *A3468* and the adaptation of a B.E.2e fin evolved by No. 42 Squadron in 1917. A standard B.E.2e fin was bolted to the normal R.E.8 rudder-post, its leading edge faired smoothly up to the top of the rudder-post by a length of 1-in. outside-diameter 22 S.W.G. steel tubing.

As early as 23rd May 1917 an installation of a 200-h.p. R.A.F. 4d engine was made in an R.E.8, *A3406*. The aircraft was flown on that day, and on 12th June it set out for France. It got no farther than Lympne, however, and returned to Farnborough that same day. This R.E.8 was still in use in 1918, by which time it had been fitted with the fin and horn-balanced rudder seen in the illustration on page 5.

In spite of all the work that Farnborough did on the vertical tail surfaces of the R.E.8, the standard service version retained the plain rudder and slightly enlarged upper and lower fins that resulted from the basic modifications. In this form the R.E.8 remained in operational use until the end of the war, the most numerous British reconnaissance two-seater in service. Greatly enlarged fins of slightly varying shapes were fitted to R.E.8s used by training squadrons, however. Despite the variations in profile there can be little doubt that many were made by employing the No. 42 Squadron B.E.2e fin adaptation.

As time went on, modifications of structure and armament were made. In July 1917 Farnborough tested a revised form of undercarriage embodying wooden V-struts. This was standardised for later production aircraft, as was the Constantinesco gun-synchronising mechanism when it became available in sufficient quantities.

By mid-1917 well over 800 R.E.8s had been delivered to the R.F.C. Replacement of the B.E. two-seaters had progressed as R.E.8s became available. No. 21 Squadron re-equipped in February 1917, Nos. 6, 13, 42 and 53 in April, and in the May–June period No. 4, 5, 7, 9, 12, 15 and 16 acquired R.E.8s and No. 52 Squadron reverted to the type. On 23rd February No. 59 Squadron had arrived in France equipped with the type, and No. 63 Squadron arrived with its R.E.8s at Basra in Mesopotamia on 13th August 1917. Last in the field was No. 69 (Australian) Squadron, which arrived in France on 9th September 1917.

The B.E. two-seaters had always been easy prey for the fast and manœuvrable German single-seat fighters, but any hopes that the R.E.8 might bring some

The R.E.9 A4600 *at Farnborough, 24th September 1917, with enlarged upper fin.*
(Photo: Crown copyright)

improvement to the fortunes of the corps reconnaissance squadrons were disappointed. April 1917 was the R.F.C.'s worst month for casualties, and the 13th of that month was a black day for No. 59 Squadron. Six of its R.E.8s set out at 8.15 a.m. to photograph the Drocourt–Quéant switch line; near Vitry they were attacked by Manfred von Richthofen and five of his pilots of *Jasta* 11. All six R.E.8s were shot down at once, *A3190* falling to von Richthofen himself; ten of the twelve pilots and observers were killed.

After Arras the R.E.8s continued their artillery observation, contact and counter-attack patrols and photographic duties through the Battles of Messines, Ypres, Langemarck and Cambrai. Ypres introduced the R.E.8 to night bombing, Cambrai to ground-attack work. Many R.E.8s were shot down, but the enemy did not have things all his own way. On 16th August 1917, two Albatros single-seaters attacked an R.E.8 of No. 7 Squadron over Poelcappelle: one was shot down by the observer; the other dived away. Later that afternoon eight Albatroses attacked another of No. 7's R.E.8s; sixty rounds from the observer's Lewis gun shot down one of the enemy; the others made off without attempting to attack again. Five days later Oberleutnant Eduard Ritter von Dostler, commanding officer of *Jasta* 6, victor in 26 combats and holder of the *Pour le Mérite*, was shot down by the R.E.8 *A4381*, flown by Lts. N. Sharples and M. A. O'Callaghan of No. 7 Squadron.

All the activities required of the R.E.8s were demanded in even greater measure during the German offensive that began on 21st March 1918. But for the failure of the Sunbeam Arab and Hispano-Suiza engine production programmes the R.E.8s would have been replaced in April 1918 by Bristol Fighters with those engines; but as early as August 1917 the Air Board felt obliged to postpone the change until September 1918. In fact the Bristols never materialised and the R.E.8 had to soldier doggedly on, its inadequacies compensated by the determination and gallantry of the men who flew it. At the time of the Armistice the R.E.8 equipped fifteen squadrons of the R.A.F. and one of the Australian Flying Corps in France, two R.A.F. squadrons in Italy, two in Mesopotamia, and four in Palestine.

It may have been the Air Board's decision on the Bristols that led to the Rolls-Royce Eagle being specified in Contract No. A.S.28127, dated 2nd October 1917, as the power unit of 75 R.E.8s (*D4811–D4885*) ordered from D. Napier & Son. But Eagles were scarce and sorely wanted for D.H.4s and Felixstowe flying boats, and none could be spared for the R.E.8s. The aircraft were apparently built as standard R.E.8s, together with *D4886–D4960*, which had also been ordered from Napier, but under Contract No. A.S.35980 dated 15th December 1917.

The Royal Aircraft Factory had pursued a programme of development from the basic R.E.8 design, but surviving records are so confused that it seems doubtful whether the proper sequence of development can now be traced.

An alternative version of the design, designated R.E.8a, had been drawn up as early as October 1916, before production aircraft began to appear. It was designed for the 200-h.p. Hispano-Suiza engine, for which a flat frontal radiator installation was planned; the pilot's Vickers gun was on top of the fuselage, to port of centre, and was installed as on the S.E.5. The airframe was identical with that of the standard R.E.8. In December 1916 *A95* was converted into an R.E.8a and was probably the only specimen of this variant. It was still powered with a Hispano-Suiza engine (No. 27942-100038) on 17th September 1917, when it was reported as an R.E.9. (Yet at that time it was fitted with the lower mainplanes that had belonged to *A4600* at a time when that aircraft was recorded as an R.E.8.) A remarkable feature of *A95* at this time was the use of a T.6296 airscrew with the Hispano-Suiza engine: this was the standard type of airscrew fitted to the R.A.F. 4a engine.

Considerable confusion exists over the R.E.9 and R.T.1 designs. It seems that the Royal Aircraft Factory design staff recognised the need for a stronger wing truss at an early date. Starting on 19th June 1917, *A4600* was flown with B.E.2d wings; on 8th August, still with these mainplanes, it was also flown with elevators of reduced area. A note dated 12th September 1917 in an official inspection record states that *A4600* had been converted to an R.T.1; elsewhere it was recorded as an R.E.9 two days later.

There can be no doubt that the Royal Aircraft Factory had a hand in the design of the R.T.1: so many components were designed for the R.E.9 and R.T.1 jointly that it seems likely that the two types were designed as alternative replacements for the R.E.8. One official A.I.D. publication unequivocally records the R.T.1 as a Royal Aircraft Factory type. Nevertheless the two types differed considerably.

The reference to *A4600* as an R.T.1 is probably a simple confusion between the two, then-new, two-bay developments of the R.E.8; but it is of some interest because the recorded use of this designation thus occurred a full three weeks before the arrival at Farnborough of the first Siddeley-built R.T.1—which was then recorded in Farnborough records as "R.E.9/R.T.1".

The true R.E.9, as delineated in the Royal Aircraft Factory drawings Nos. A17249 and A17250 dated November 1917, consisted of an R.E.8 fuselage fitted with two-bay wings of equal span (38 ft. 3·6 in.) and chord (5 ft. 6 in.); it appears that the R.E.9 and R.T.1 were intended to have the same fin and balanced rudder, respectively 7 sq. ft. and 10·35 sq. ft. in area. These tail surfaces were very similar to one of the designs for a revised fin and balanced rudder for the R.E.8. The design drawings show ailerons appreciably narrower in chord than those of the R.E.8, hinged to

R.E.9 A3561 *with Sunbeam Maori engine, 23rd September 1918.*
(Photo: Crown copyright)

The first Siddeley-built R.T.1, B6625, *with 200-h.p. Hispano-Suiza engine. The pilot's gun was a Lewis above the centre section. The external gravity tank was somewhat similar to that of the early production S.E.5.* (Photo: Crown copyright)

The third Siddeley-built R.T.1, with R.A.F. 4a engine, photographed at Farnborough on 30th October 1917. This photograph provides an interesting comparison with the R.E.9 A4600. (Photo: Crown copyright)

a subsidiary spar a few inches behind the rear spar.

Several R.E.8s were converted to be R.E.9s. Apart from *A95*, the true configuration of which is not known, these were *A3909–A3912*, *A3542*, *A3561* and *A4600*; as noted above, *A4600* was recorded as an R.E.9 on 14th September 1917, and *A3909–A3912* and *A3542* were inspected between 9th October and 2nd November 1917. By 5th December *A3909* had been fitted with a 200-h.p. R.A.F. 4d engine; *A3911* was tested with short-span ailerons on 9th November; *A3542* was flown on 29th December with reduced dihedral.

Perhaps the most interesting modification of the R.E.9 was the fitting of experimental cockpit enclosures to *A3911*; these were tested on 13th March 1918. This aircraft and *A3909* were still flying at the R.A.E. in 1919. In September 1919 *A3542* was fitted with a R.A.F. 4d engine, to which it was intended to fit a variable-pitch airscrew.

Neither *A4600* nor *A3561* had the standard fin and balanced rudder that had been designed for the R.E.9 and R.T.1. On 13th June 1918 *A3561* was submitted for pre-flight inspection, having been fitted with a Sunbeam Maori engine (No. 1/250/19379). The installation was remarkably clumsy and ugly, and the engine gave a good deal of trouble. Severe longitudinal-trim difficulties were experienced with the aircraft itself.

Tests with elevators of different areas and a variable centre of gravity were made on *A3909* from 16th July 1918 onwards.

The R.T.1 aircraft built by the Siddeley-Deasy Motor Car Co. were very different from the R.E.9. Span was 41 ft. 9 in., upper chord 6 ft. 6 in., lower 4 ft. 9 in.; and the gap was reduced to 4 ft. 8½ in. The fuselage was basically that of the R.E.8, but a deeper top decking was fitted. The pilot's armament was a Lewis gun mounted above the centre section. Six aircraft, *B6625–B6630*, were built; they were the last machines of the batch *B6451–B6630*, originally ordered as R.E.8s. The first, *B6625*, arrived at Farnborough on 11th October 1917; it had a 200-h.p. Hispano-Suiza engine with a frontal radiator, the entire installation closely resembling that of the same engine in the S.E.5a. *B6626* and *B6627* were powered by the 140-h.p. R.A.F. 4a; but by 5th December 1917 *B6627* had been fitted with a 200-h.p. R.A.F. 4d. On 9th November 1917 *B6626* and *B6629* were tested with balanced ailerons; in April 1918 *B6629* was subjected to structural tests at the R.A.E. The last R.T.1, *B6630*, had a 200-h.p. Hispano-Suiza with an underslung radiator; it was tested at Martlesham Heath in March 1919.

Neither the R.E.9 nor R.T.1 was adopted for general use, nor were any of the experimental modifications of the R.E.8 introduced. Modified elevators were tested on *B738* and *A4599*; the former aircraft was flown on 31st August 1917 with what Farnborough described as a "small balanced rudder"; on 16th September it was tested with a narrow-chord rudder and elevators. By 11th October it had acquired a 200-h.p. R.A.F. 4d engine; in March 1918 it was fitted with a Rateau turbo-compressor and the R.A.F. variable-pitch airscrew, an enormous air scoop being installed above the engine. In this form *B738* was flown nine times, but on 4th May 1918 the turbine failed at 13,700 ft. and wrecked the engine and supercharger installation beyond repair.

Tests of experimental ailerons were conducted from about September 1917 onwards, when *A4598* was fitted with ailerons having wash-out of incidence. The tests covered ailerons of standard (24-in.) and reduced (16-in.) chord, with incidence washing out by 9 deg. towards the tip, and with chord tapering to only 8 in. at the tip. These last-mentioned surfaces had areas of 13·6 sq. ft. on the upper wings, 7 sq. ft. on the lower.

Of all the allies only Belgium used the R.E.8. Twenty-two were supplied to l'Aviation Militaire Belge in 1917; the type was used by the *6me Escadrille* from July 1917, but later that year most of the Belgian R.E.8s were re-engined with 150-h.p. and 180-h.p. Hispano-Suizas. Replacement of the R.E.8 by the Spad XI began in May 1918.

After the Armistice a few R.E.8s lingered on: in Russia with the R.A.F. Contingent at Archangel, at Basra with No. 6 Squadron from 18th July 1919 until the following year, and in Ireland, where one R.E.8 was on the strength of No. 141 Squadron in 1919. Some were flown at the R.A.E. for a time, notably *B738*, with which tests of variable-pitch airscrews were conducted in 1919. The R.E.9s *A3909* and *A3911* were still flying at Farnborough in 1919.

To all who flew in those days this aircraft was known as the Harry Tate, an ever-present feature of the wartime sky from the spring of 1917 until much too late in 1918. Only two survive. One, *F3556*, hangs in London's Imperial War Museum; the other is in the Musée Royal de l'Armée et d'Histoire Militaire in Brussels.

PRODUCTION

In addition to the two prototypes, 4,430 R.E.8s were ordered under wartime contracts. Of these at least 112 were cancelled or not completed. By the end of 1918 a total of 4,077 R.E.8s had been accepted for service with the R.F.C. and R.A.F.

Royal Aircraft Factory, Farnborough, Hants—7996–7997, A66–A115, A3506–A3530 (*A110–A115* and *A3506–A3530* were not built).

Austin Motor Co. (1914) Ltd., Northfield, Birmingham—A3169–A3268, A4261–A4410, B5851–B5900.

Coventry Ordnance Works, Ltd., Coventry—A4664–A4763, B6631–B6730, C5026–C5045, C5046–C5125, D6701–D6850.

Daimler Co., Ltd., Coventry—A3531–A3680, A4161–A4260, B3401–B3450, B5001–B5150, C2231–C3080, F3548–F3737.

D. Napier & Son, Ltd., Acton, London, W.—A3832–A3931, B2251–B2300, C4551–C4600, D3836–D3910 (cancelled), *D4811–D4885, D4886–D4960, E1101–E1150.*

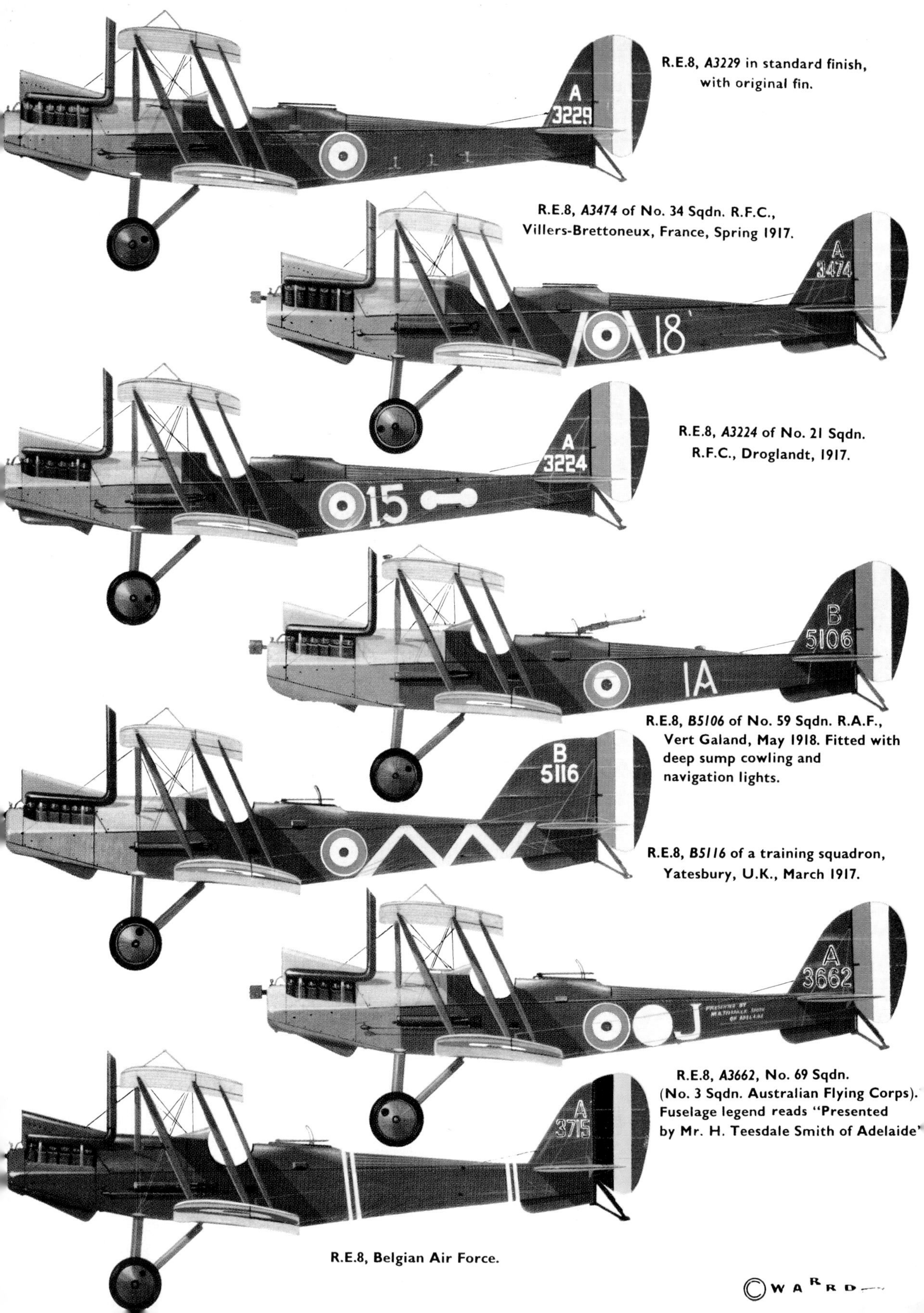

R.E.8, *A3229* in standard finish, with original fin.

R.E.8, *A3474* of No. 34 Sqdn. R.F.C., Villers-Brettoneux, France, Spring 1917.

R.E.8, *A3224* of No. 21 Sqdn. R.F.C., Droglandt, 1917.

R.E.8, *B5106* of No. 59 Sqdn. R.A.F., Vert Galand, May 1918. Fitted with deep sump cowling and navigation lights.

R.E.8, *B5116* of a training squadron, Yatesbury, U.K., March 1917.

R.E.8, *A3662*, No. 69 Sqdn. (No. 3 Sqdn. Australian Flying Corps). Fuselage legend reads "Presented by Mr. H. Teesdale Smith of Adelaide"

R.E.8, Belgian Air Force.

Siddeley-Deasy Motor Car Co., Ltd., Park Side, Coventry—A3405–A3504, A3681–A3830, B6451–B6480, B6481–B6630 (*B6225–B6630* delivered as R.T.1s), *B7681–B7730, E1–E300, E1151–E1250, F1553–F1602, F3246–F3345.*
Standard Motor Co., Ltd., Cash's Lane, Coventry—A4411–A4560, A4564–A4663, D1501–D1600, D4661–D4810, F1665–F1764.
The serial numbers *A6801–A7000* were originally allocated for R.E.8s to be built by the British & Colonial Aeroplane Co., Ltd., but the Bristol company declined the contract and the serials were re-allocated.
A.R.D. rebuilds included the following: *B737, B738, B742, B750, B765, B814, B821, B832, B836, B845, B853, B7808, B7893, B7917, B8884–B8887, B8900, D4980, D4998, F5879, F5897, F5902, F5909, F6016, F6018, F6044, F6049, F6050, F6277, H6843, H7018, H7022–H7027, H7033, H7038, H7042, H7055, H7057, H7139, H7262, H7265.*

Examples of R.E.8s used by operational squadrons:
No. 4 Sqn.: C2411.
No. 4(A) Sqn.: C2491.
No. 5 Sqn.: B7893, F1679, F6044.
No. 6 Sqn.: A3198, A3849, A4270, A4316, B5013, H7038.
No. 7 Sqn.: A4381.
No. 9 Sqn.: A4366 (Aircraft 21), *F6049.*
No. 12 Sqn.: A3631, B832, B6512, C2559, E270, F5909.
No. 13 Sqn.: B5070.
No. 14 Sqn.: B6604.
No. 15 Sqn.: B742, B836 (15), *B2276* (13), *B3412, H7018.*
No. 16 Sqn.: A3196 (14), *A3839* (16), *B5010* (17), *B5028* (15), *C5048* (25), *D4688.*
No. 21 Sqn.: A3224 (15), *A4351* (B).
No. 30 Sqn.: A4352, A4357.
No. 34 Sqn.: A3474, E130.
No. 52 Sqn.: A81, A87, A3489, A3868, A4417 (15), *C2341.*
No. 53 Sqn.: A3538, C2548, C2901, D6801, F5897, H7033.
No. 59 Sqn.: A3190, B5106 ("IA").
No. 63 Sqn.: A4346.
No. 69 Sqn.: A3662 (J), *A4397* (D), *B7917, F6016* (K), *H7042* (J).
Headquarters Communication Squadron, R.A.F.: B6573, C4560, C4579.
R.A.F. Contingent, Archangel: D4960, D6792.

SERVICE USE

Wartime

Western Front: R.F.C./R.A.F. Squadrons Nos. 4, 4(A), 5, 6, 7, 9, 12, 13, 15, 16, 21, 34, 42, 52, 53, 59; No. 69 (Australian) Sqn., R.F.C., later No. 3 Sqn., Australian Flying Corps; HQ Communication Sqn.; one R.E.8 with No. 56 Sqn., R.F.C., March 1918. L'Aviation Militaire Belge: 6me Escadrille.
Italy: R.F.C./R.A.F. Sqns. Nos. 34 and 42.
Palestine: R.F.C./R.A.F. Sqns. Nos. 14, 113, 142; No. 67 (Australian) Sqn., R.F.C.
Mesopotamia: R.F.C./R.A.F. Sqns. Nos. 30 and 63.

The R.E.8 B738 *with supercharged R.A.F. 4d engine, R.A.F. variable-pitch airscrew and balanced rudder similar to that of* A3406. *The tall figure immediately to the right of the airscrew is Lt. Harold Elliott who was then in charge of the Engines Flight at Farnborough and flew as flight observer in this aircraft and in the Maori-powered R.E.9* A3561.

Home Defence: R.F.C. Sqns. Nos. 50, 76 and 77.

Post-war

Russia: R.A.F. Contingent, Archangel.
Mesopotamia: No. 6 Sqn., R.A.F., Basra.
Ireland: One R.E.8 with No. 141 Sqn., R.A.F.

SPECIFICATION

Power: *R.E.8*—140-h.p. R.A.F. 4a, 200-h.p. R.A.F. 4d, 150-h.p. Hispano-Suiza, 180-h.p. Hispano-Suiza. *R.E.8a*—200-h.p. Hispano-Suiza.

Dimensions: Span (upper) 42 ft. 7 in., (lower) 32 ft. 7½ in.; length (R.E.8) 27 ft. 10½ in., (R.E.8a) 27 ft. 7 in.; height 11 ft. 4½ in.; chord 5 ft. 6 in.; gap 5 ft. 6 in.; stagger 2 ft.; dihedral 3 deg. 30 min.; incidence 4 deg.; span of tail 14 ft.; wheel track 5 ft. 9¾ in.; types 700 × 100 mm.; airscrew diameter (T.6296) 9 ft. 9 in.

Areas: Wings 377·5 sq. ft.; ailerons, each upper 21 sq. ft., each lower 11·5 sq. ft., total 65 sq. ft.; tailplane 24 sq. ft.; elevators 22 sq. ft.; fin originally 5 sq. ft., later 6·75 sq. ft.; rudder 9·5 sq. ft.

Armament: One fixed 0·303-in. Vickers machine gun with Vickers-Challenger interrupter gear or Constantinesco C.C. synchronising mechanism, Hyland Type C loading handle, and Aldis and ring-and-bead sights. The bomb load could consist of two 112-lb. or four 65-lb. bombs, or a combination of (e.g.) one 112-lb. and four 25-lb. Cooper bombs; the bomb racks were under the fuselage and lower wings. C.F.S. 4b bomb sight.

WEIGHTS AND PERFORMANCE

Aircraft	**7996**	**A4716**		**R.E.9**	**R.E.9 A3561**	**R.T.1 B6626**	**R.T.1 B6630**
Engine	R.A.F. 4a	R.A.F. 4a		R.A.F. 4a	Maori	R.A.F. 4a	200-h.p. Hispano-Suiza
Bomb load	Nil	Nil	Two 112-lb.	Nil	Nil	Nil	Nil
Weights (lb.):							
Empty	1,622	—	1,803	—	—	1,773	1,803
Military load	232	185	351	—	—	185	185
Crew	360	360	360	—	—	360	360
Fuel and oil	378	—	355	—	—	272	359
Loaded	2,592	2,678	2,869	2,800	—	2,590	2,707
Max. speed (m.p.h.):							
at 6,500 ft.	99	102	98	—	—	101	—
at 10,000 ft.	93	96·5	92·5	—	—	98·5	108
Climb to:	m. s.	m. s.	m. s.	m. s.	m. s.	m. s.	m. s.
5,000 ft.	8 10	11 25	— —	11 20	6 45	7 45	— —
6,500 ft.	11 40	15 50	21 0	— —	— —	10 30	10 35
7,000 ft.	13 0	— —	— —	— —	10 15	— —	— —
10,000 ft.	22 0	29 5	39 50	35 40	— —	19 10	18 30
Service ceiling (ft.)	13,500	13,500	11,000	13,000	—	16,000	18,000
Endurance (hrs.)	4¼	—	—	—	—	—	—

Printed by Hills & Lacy Ltd., London and Watford, England. U.S. 2nd Class Mailing Rates applied for.

PROFILE PUBLICATIONS

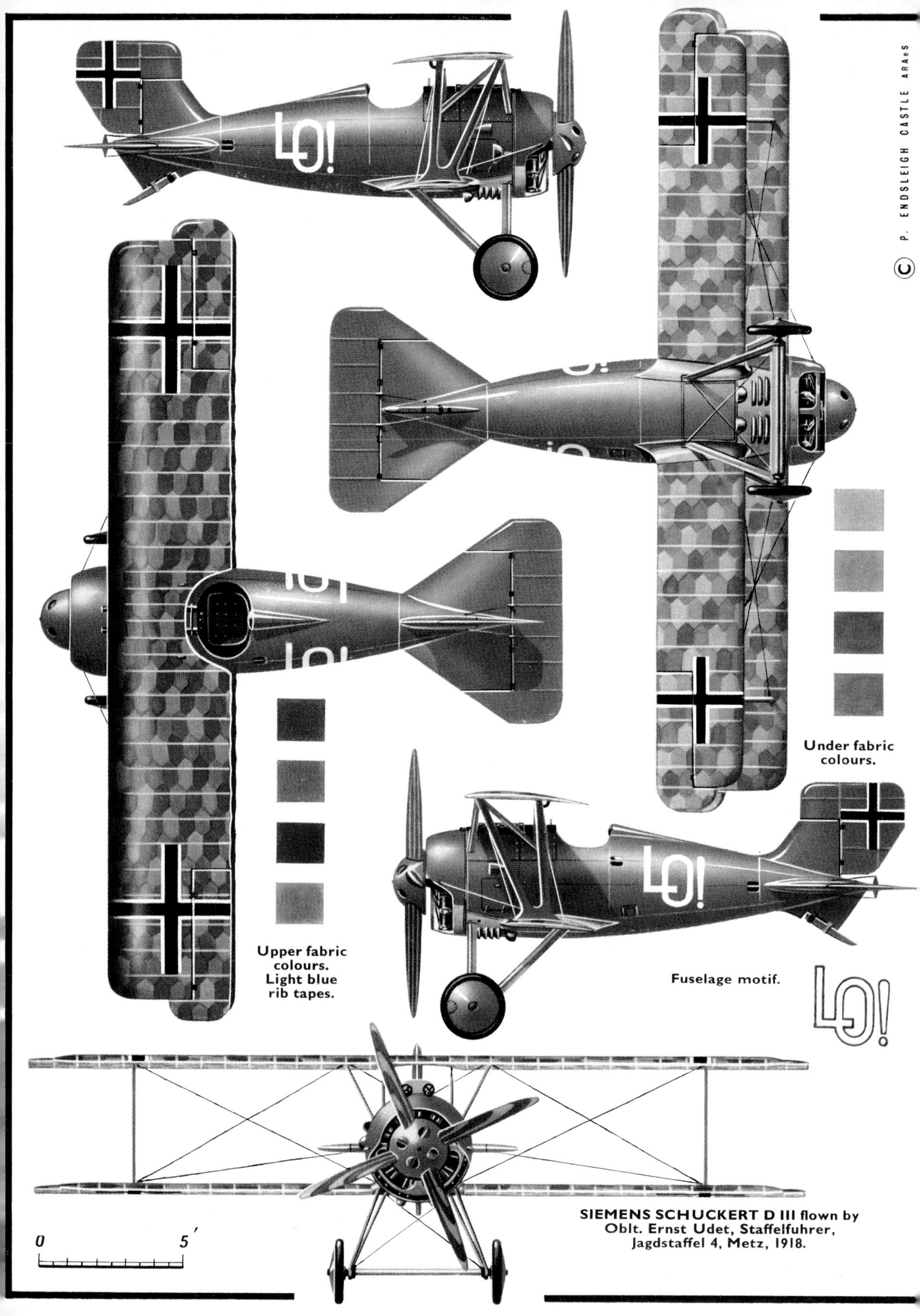

SIEMENS SCHUCKERT D III flown by Oblt. Ernst Udet, Staffelfuhrer, Jagdstaffel 4, Metz, 1918.

The Siemens Schuckert D III & IV

by Peter L. Gray

Rare line-up shot of Jasta *12 in so far as more than one S.S.W. aircraft is depicted.* Left to right: *Fokker D VII, S.S.W. D IV, S.S.W. D IIIs.* (Photo: Alex Imrie)

It was a world of apparent peace. A trio of de Havilland bombing machines clawed their way through the tenuous layer of cloud endeavouring to gain every inch of altitude on this warm morning during the fifth September of the war. Wrapped in the limited visibility of the cloud no signs of hostility existed; no Archie (Flak) barred their easterly flight path; the bitterly contested, war-torn landscape was shrouded from their eyes. They were not deceived into a false sense of security however; every faculty remained alert. Even if the German army was in retreat their air service was still a force to be reckoned with, especially the fighters. The *Jagdstaffeln*, although on restricted fuel supplies, had some excellent fighting aircraft in the new B.M.W.-engined Fokker D VIIs and were in good heart. It was rumoured, too, there were even still better fighters coming into service in the shape of cantilever parasol monoplanes and short, stocky biplanes, powered with huge eleven-cylinder rotary engines, both types being possessed of extreme agility.

Soon there was an increased brightness in the air and in a moment the three bombers had broken through the cloud layer. Saturated in condensation from the cloud they glistened in the brilliance of the early morning sun which glared angrily at their hostile intrusion from the depths of the German Fatherland. As the bombers closed their formation in the now improved visibility, tracers suddenly stabbed with extreme accuracy into the leading machine—a diminutive barrel of a fighter had hurtled up out of the eye of the sun pouring a deadly hail from its twin Spandau machine guns. The de Havilland appeared to stagger: smoke belched from its nose as it slid off, crab-like, to starboard at an ever steepening angle.

Quickly the German fighter pulled up into an impressive Immelmann turn and came roaring back on the right-hand bomber, oblivious to the hail of bullets now vengefully directed at it. Once more the synchronised Spandau guns spoke and an unfortunate gunner collapsed to the floor of his cockpit. Clearly here was an artist; undoubtedly a crack pilot from one of the nearby Marine *Jagdstaffeln*, and flying one of the new rotary-engined biplanes to achieve all this speed and agility at such an altitude. With alacrity the two Allied pilots pushed forward their sticks, eagerly seeking the protective layer of cloud from which they had so recently emerged, while an ominous column of black smoke marked the course of their less fortunate comrades. Certainly this proved to be the case. The machine was one of the new Siemens Schuckert D IVs, several of which had been allocated to the Marine *Jastas*, on an early morning sortie.

Development of the machine had begun almost a year and a half before when the Siemens Schuckert Werke had built three airframes in which to test their new 160-h.p. eleven-cylinder rotary engine, built by the founder Siemens Halske establishment. Originally, Siemens Halske started in 1847, manufacturing telegraphic equipment; it was not until 1873 that the Siemens Schuckert title was adopted on merging with the Nürnberg Schuckert works to form the huge electrical combine. In 1907 the firm made their first entry into the aeronautical sphere when the German General Staff requested the construction of a non-rigid military airship. Between 1909 and 1911 three monoplanes were built, after which aircraft manufacture ceased until 1914 when, due to the urgent need for aeroplanes by the German military forces, the aircraft department was re-opened. It was now directed by Dr. Walter Reichel with Dr. Hugo Natalis, Messrs Forssman, Wolff and the Steffen brothers—Bruno and Franz—as leading assistants.

S.S.W. D IIc D 7551/17. *The long wing span prototype aircraft. First flew in October 1917.* (Photo: P. M. Grosz)

Further view of D 7551/17 *after some modification to cowling. Note retention of* "U" *centre-section struts indicates modification not to full D III standard. First flew in this form 20th December 1917.*

Giant R type *(Riesenflugzeug)* multi - engined machines were designed and built initially and Siemens Schuckert did not enter into the fighter category until 1916, when a few E I and E III monoplanes (much like the Fokker product) were constructed, but which were already obsolescent. About this time several captured French Nieuports were made available to the Albatros, Euler and S.S.W. firms with the idea that the best characteristics of the type be incorporated into a German design as a quick means of obtaining a possibly superior machine. The eventual Siemens production was almost a carbon copy of the Nieuport 17, the only visible differences being in the engine installation, the spinnered propeller and the tailskid. This type was designated D I and accepted for production on 25th November 1916 when 150 machines were ordered. Completed airframes were held up due to slow production of the Siemens Halske engines, and a subsequent order in March 1917 for another hundred aircraft was cancelled, as it was found that by mid-1917 its performance was not up to the standard then required.

A NEW ENGINE

Engineers at the Siemens-Halske works of the combine had designed a radical eleven-cylinder, geared rotary engine based on the experience gained with their smaller nine-cylinder engine. In normal rotary engines the crankshaft was a stationary component around which the crankcase and cylinders revolved at some 1,200 to 1,500 r.p.m. In the Siemens engine the crankshaft revolved in one direction at 900 r.p.m. while the crankcase and cylinders rotated in the opposite direction, also at 900 r.p.m. This achieved a virtual engine speed of some 1,800 for an airscrew speed of only 900 r.p.m.; the obvious main advantage was in increased airscrew efficiency, there were, however, disadvantages in the system. Being a bigger and more powerful engine than its 110-h.p. forebear, the 160-h.p. S.H. III (as it was designated) tended to run a lot hotter and this effect was accentuated by the slow speed at which the cylinders rotated, with consequent reduction in the amount of air cooling obtained. These conditions were further aggravated by the lack

From this three-quarter rear view of D 7551/17 *it will be seen that the tailplane shape differed from eventual production aircraft.*

of a good grade of castor oil (the universal lubricant for rotary engines) available to the Germans, with the result that there occurred a degree of piston seizure after only several hours running. The most encouraging feature of the engine was that, due to the high compression ratio, it maintained its power at very high altitude and for this reason its development was continued. The engine was fitted with twin magnetos and speed was governed by a proper throttle control, sensitive down to about 350 r.p.m. This was a considerable advance over most rotaries of the period which ran flat out and were only partially controlled by a "blip switch" which cut the spark altogether for as long as depressed, or by a control which cut the spark to certain cylinders, which system (in the Gnôme Monos) had a serious attendant fire hazard. Another advantage in the Siemens engine, over standard rotaries, was that a considerable degree of reciprocation was achieved in the opposite rotation of the cylinder and crankshaft masses which accordingly reduced the gyroscopic forces.

A NEW FIGHTER

To take advantage of this powerful 160-h.p. engine a more original and advanced fighter was conceived in the Siemens Schuckert drawing office. Most of the original design work came from Dipl. Ing. Harald Wolff—who had been appointed chief designer after the death of Ing. Steffen—ably assisted by his deputy, Dipl. Ing. Glöckner and a somewhat younger engineer named Hauck.

Three pre-production airframes were built during the spring of 1917 and designated D II (*D 3501/16*), D IIa (*D 3500/16*) and D IIb (*D 3502/16*), the intention being that they would serve mainly as flying test-beds for the S-H III engine. However, due to teething troubles no engines reached the Siemens Schuckert works until June of that year, with consequent delay in flight testing. When the completed prototypes did appear they were seen to be small, stocky, barrel-like machines of extremely aggressive demeanour and the test programme was implemented forthwith. A spectacular performance was achieved with the D IIb during August when 5,000 m. (16,400 ft.) was attained in 15½ minutes and 7,000 m. (22,965 ft.) in 35½ minutes, the result of which ensured an order for three more development aircraft. These were designated D IIc short (*D 7550/17 kurz*), D IIc long (*D 7551/17 lang*) and D IIe (*D 7553/17*) but the order was subject to the proviso that an improvement in the level speed should be attained over the initial three prototypes which, although able to climb like lifts were not notoriously fast when flying straight and level. On completion of the second three prototypes during October 1917 they were re-designated D III and within a few weeks a pre-production order for twenty aircraft was placed, followed by a further order for thirty more in February 1918.

Prototype D III D 7552/17 *at Adlershof D Types competition in January 1918.* (Photo: Alex Imrie)

D IV prototype D 7554/17. *This was originally* D 7551/17 *airframe which crashed at Adlershof in January 1918 and was rebuilt to D IV standards. Machine was yet again rebuilt after above crash with shorter span wings; it was re-designated D IVa.* (Photo: Egon Krueger)

S.S.W. D III D 1620/18, *aircraft is of second production series batch.* (Photo: Egon Krueger)

Stubby proportions of D IV are accentuated in this three-quarter rear view of D 3082/18. (Photo: Egon Krueger)

The two D IIc machines differed in wing arrangement, *7550/17* was built with a span of 8·5 m. (27 ft. 10¾ in.) and an area of 19·4 sq. m. (209 sq. ft.); *7551/17* spanned 9·0 m. (29 ft. 6⅜ in.) but with reduced chord on the upper wing the area grossed only 18·02 sq. m. (195 sq. ft.). This airframe was subsequently modified to become the first D IV production prototype. The D IIe, *7553/17*, was built with wings based on dural girder spars, which it was hoped would enable the interplane bracing cables to be dispensed with. "I" struts were the main distinguishing feature from the other prototypes. In the event it was found on air test that the wings were not rigid enough and flexed considerably. Bracing cables were then added but as this completely negatived the original intention this machine was ultimately rebuilt to D IV standards and sent to the Front for operational assessment with *Jagdgeschwader* II in the spring of 1918. Later it was returned to the S.S.W. factory for further modification and a new engine, after which it was once more ferried back to operational service in July.

Deliveries of the first production batch of D IIIs commenced during January 1918 and the airframes differed from the two prototypes in being equipped with four-blade airscrews of reduced diameter which enabled a shorter undercarriage chassis to be fitted. Under construction at the same time were further development machines which had been ordered, i.e. three D IVs and three D Vs. The latter were little more than a two-bay version of the D IVs and as no improvement in performance was obtained the D V was not proceeded with.

OPERATIONAL TRIALS

Forty-one of the first fifty production D IIIs were sent to JG II on the Western Front during April and May for operational trials. Mostly they were channelled to *Jasta* 12 and *Jasta* 15, which units pilots were most appreciative of their new mounts and acclaimed its combination of sensitivity with good flying qualities and rocket-like climb. These aircraft were fitted with the completely circular cowling, and although victories in combat were coming, over-heating and consequent seizure of the Siemens Halske engines began to occur with disconcerting frequency. The engine had not been sufficiently developed yet for operational usage and opponents of the rotary-engined fighter were quick in their endeavour to discredit the D III. However, an extremely objective report on the type was prepared by Hauptmann

An aircraft of the third production batch; D III D 3008/18. *Note at this stage spinner was not punched with cooling louvres.* (Photo: Egon Krueger)

S.S.W. D IV "ex works". Note bright metal panels and lozenge-fabric-covered wings and wheel discs. (Photo: Egon Krueger)

Rudolph Berthold, in Command of JG II, who listed both the defects and the advantages of the D III and put forward constructive opinion for improvement. He concluded:

> "It is an urgent requirement that this fighter be made available for Front Line use as soon as possible, for, after rectification of its present faults, it could become one of the most useful fighters."

The result of this report was that the operational D IIIs were returned to the Siemens Schuckert factory towards the end of May for the installation of improved engines and airframe modification. Incorporation of these improvements was also applied to a third production batch of thirty D IIIs which were on the production line at this time. Most visibly apparent modification was the cutting away of the lower part of the cowling in an attempt to achieve a greater degree of cooling; there was also some alteration to the vertical tail surface profile. These D III aircraft were then returned to operational service later in the year and were used mainly for home defence by *Kestas* (*Kampfeinsitzer-Staffel*) 2, 4b, 5, 6, and 8 over Western Germany, in which a considerable degree of success was achieved.

THE D IV

Meanwhile, after the abandonment of the two-bay D V, all efforts were concentrated on the D IV. A youthful recruit to the S.S.W. design staff, Heinrich Kann, had produced a new wing layout in which the chord and area of the upper wing was considerably reduced. In fact both upper and lower wings were now identical in shape and of no more than one metre chord. Flight tests were encouraging and showed improvement over the D III; maximum speed at 118 m.p.h. showed slight superiority while climb to 6,000 m. (19,685 ft.) in sixteen to seventeen minutes was something akin to spectacular. A production order for the type was placed in March 1918 but it appears the D IV did not become operational until August when the first deliveries were made to *Jastas*

Right and left side of S.S.W. D III cockpit. (Photos: Egon Krueger)

Left: *Obltn. Ernst Udet in his S.S.W. D III with "LO!" motif at Metz 1918.* Right: *Udet with mechanics in front of his red-fuselaged D III. Note cooling louvres, clearly shown in this shot.* (Photos: Alex Imrie)

14 and 22 and to *Marine Luft Feld Jasta*. More were supplied during September and by the end of that month about half-a-dozen *Jastas* had a few of the type on charge. Although eventual production orders totalled 280 machines delivery was comparatively slow and it is fairly certain that no more than about fifty of the type ever saw active service. On 5th October JG I (Richthofen) requested twelve D IVs, to be followed by a further twelve as soon as possible, but it does not seem that they were ever received by this unit.

"A SUPERIOR FIGHTER"

The first D IV to be received by *Jasta* 22 was used by *Staffelführer*, Lt. Lenz: it had been brought in by Lt. Rath who had previously served with *Jasta* 22 before going to Siemens as a works pilot. On 3rd October Lenz reported at length on the D IV and concluded:

"The S.S.W. D IV is without any doubt superior by far to all single-seaters in use at the Front today. This superiority is shown in its climbing and turning ability and particularly in maximum level speeds at altitudes above 4,000 m. Formation flying with the Mercedes Fokker D VII is for this reason impossible, but on the other hand it seems appropriate that a low-flying Fokker section should work with a S.S.W. section flying above it. In this way their superiority can be used to the full and they are still in a position to protect the Fokkers below.

"On 29th September during an operational flight Lt.

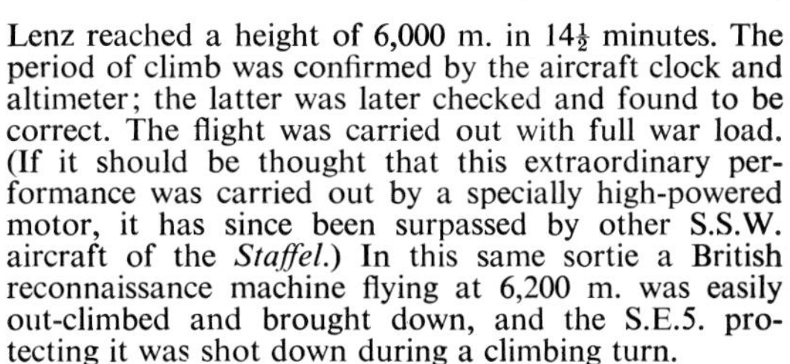

Lenz reached a height of 6,000 m. in 14½ minutes. The period of climb was confirmed by the aircraft clock and altimeter; the latter was later checked and found to be correct. The flight was carried out with full war load. (If it should be thought that this extraordinary performance was carried out by a specially high-powered motor, it has since been surpassed by other S.S.W. aircraft of the *Staffel*.) In this same sortie a British reconnaissance machine flying at 6,200 m. was easily out-climbed and brought down, and the S.E.5. protecting it was shot down during a climbing turn.

"The S.S.W. D IV is an aeroplane which probably gives of its best for only a short period which must be borne in mind during operations. Systematic expenditure of this period by flying when there is low cloud cover, for example, is not the best way of making use of the machine. If skilfully managed it should not be over-taxed. High-flying enemy formations seen approaching from the airfield can be climbed up to and brought down.

"In order to obtain full command of the aircraft, especially for pilots who are unused to rotary motors, a certain number of flights round the airfield are essential. Practically speaking, only advanced pilots should be employed on the Siemens, as its landing speed at first seems considerable. A great advantage is its very short take-off run of only about 60 m. The action of the double ailerons is generally stiffer than experienced with the Fokker D VII; however, the effects are satisfactorily limited. A further adjustment is not recommended lest the feel of the machine suffers."

Ltn. Franz of Marine Land Feld Jasta *with S.S.W. D IV.* (Photo: Egon Krueger)

Nose detail of D III shows initial degree of cowling cut away. (Photo: Egon Krueger)

Note this S.S.W. D III in Allied hands does not have headrest. Attachment to "V" struts is probably a yaw meter. (Photo: Imperial War Museum)

Confirmation of D IV's wayward characteristics when landing. D 3049/18 *overturned by Ltn. Speer.* (Photo: Egon Krueger)

Without exception all who flew the Siemens Schuckert D IV enthused over its fantastic climbing ability but it was an aircraft which was somewhat tricky to land. This difficulty was one of the problems with the D IV, it had to be very precisely landed in a tail down, wheel on, attitude; any attempt to three-point usually resulted in turning upside down. When Siemens machines were handed over to the Allies at Nivelles, after the Armistice, the first three Allied pilots to fly them turned them over on landing and further flying of the type was restricted until an investigation had been carried out. Lt. Greven of *Jasta* 12 stated that the machine had a peculiar oscillation in flight that made aiming difficult, but this may not have been a general characteristic. In a combat report dated 24th October 1918 Major Keith "Grid" Caldwell, C.O. 74 Sqdn. R.A.F. commented that the S.S.W. D IV was very manœuvrable and that although their speed was less than an S.E.5a (which 74 Sqdn. were flying) their climb was very much better and that they were very handy dog-fighting machines. At the second competition for single-seat fighters held at Adlershof in the summer of 1918, Anthony Fokker specially requested to be allowed to fly his parasol monoplane (later to be known as the E V/D VIII) in mock combat against the S.S.W. D IV but even his undoubted skill was not enough to beat the manœuvrability of the Siemens aircraft.

CONSTRUCTION DETAILS

In construction the D III and D IV were fairly conventional. At first a completely circular cowling housed the geared rotary engine which was supported by a front spider mount; later the bottom segment was cut away to afford greater cooling. Eventually the lower half was cut away right up to the centre line. A large, near hemi-spherical, spinner enclosed the coarse pitch four-blade airscrew: on late D III and D IVs this was punched with four louvres between the blade roots to scoop more cooling air on to the crankcase. The fuselage was of circular section throughout, built on four main longerons with transverse bulkheads connected by diagonal formers, to which framework the three-ply covering was pinned, resulting in an extremely rigid structure. Fin and tailplane were built integral with the fuselage and likewise ply-skinned, the fin being asymmetrical in section to counteract torque. The generously horn-

The first true production D IV D 7555/17. (Photo: Alex Imrie)

Ltn. Lenz, Staffelführer, Jasta *22, staunch advocate of the D IV, photographed with his aircraft.* (Photo: Alex Imrie)

balanced rudder and one-piece elevator were of steel tube framing with thin steel sheet ribs and fabric covering.

Although differing in chord, structurally the wings of the D III and D IV were of similar pattern. They were based on two box spars which were spindled out to the required thickness except at strut and compression member locations where they were left solid. All wing spar fittings were designed to go round the spars to avoid weakness attendant on piercing. Ribs were of 1·5 mm. three-ply with pine cap strips and were secured in place with glued wooden blocks. The upper wing was a one-piece structure, the lower in port and starboard panels. Overhung, horn-balanced ailerons, of steel tube framework, were located at all four wing tips and were actuated by torque tubes running through the wings. Centre-section struts of "N" format, springing from the upper longerons, secured the upper wing while the lower panels were attached direct to securing points on the lower longerons, the joint being neatly faired into the fuselage. The "V" pattern interplane struts were fashioned from spruce, hollowed for lightness and fabric-wrapped for strength and to obviate splintering. The wing cellule was diagonally braced with stranded steel cables while a drag wire ran from the cowling to the lower interplane strut junction. An interesting, and unusual feature of the D IV wing cellule was that the port side was some four inches longer than the starboard to offset the considerable torque.

An orthodox "V" type undercarriage chassis was fitted. The main struts were of circular section steel tube and were faired over with sheet aluminium to give a streamline section. The structure was held together with a steel tube spreader bar behind the axle and diagonally cable braced in the plane of the rear struts. The axle was secured to the apices of the "V" struts by steel coil spring shock absorbers. A strong ash tailskin was secured to an integrally-built, ply-covered, under-fin—of triangular shape in the D III but of increased area and with a right angle trailing edge in the D IV.

A singular circumstance pertaining to the S.S.W. D IV was that, unaccountably, production did not cease with the Armistice but continued until about mid-1919. Eventually the majority of the airframes were destroyed in accordance with the terms of the

The last—and much modified—D IV. Used for high-altitude research by Albatros firm. Destroyed in Berlin Museum during W.W.I air raid. (Photo: Egon Krueger)

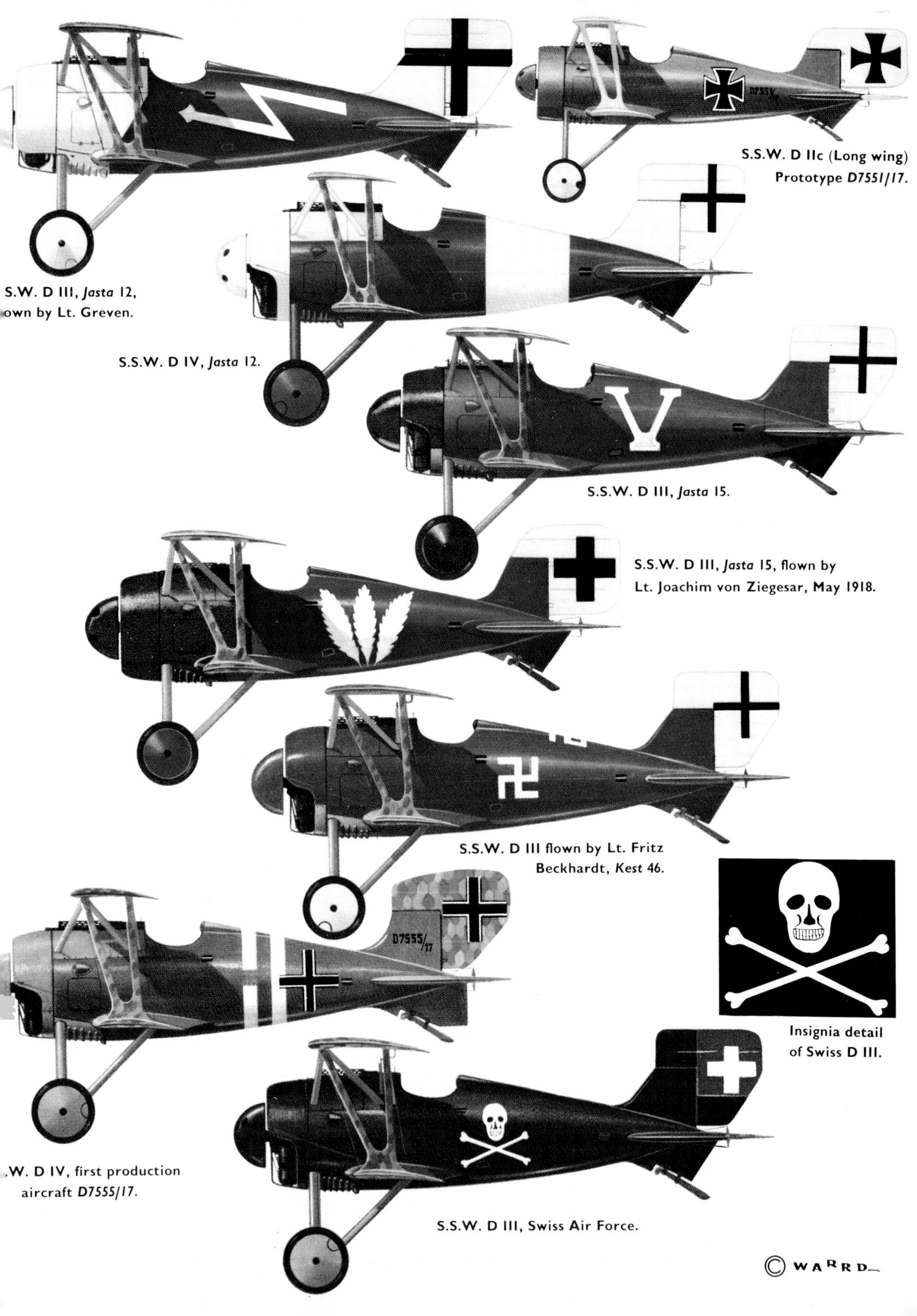

S.S.W. D IIc (Long wing) Prototype *D7551/17.*

.S.W. D III, *Jasta* 12, own by Lt. Greven.

S.S.W. D IV, *Jasta* 12.

S.S.W. D III, *Jasta* 15.

S.S.W. D III, *Jasta* 15, flown by Lt. Joachim von Ziegesar, May 1918.

S.S.W. D III flown by Lt. Fritz Beckhardt, *Kest* 46.

Insignia detail of Swiss D III.

.W. D IV, first production aircraft *D7555/17.*

S.S.W. D III, Swiss Air Force.

S.S.W. D III with skull motif, interned by Swiss authorities and marked with their own National Insignia.
(Photo: P. M. Grosz via Alex Imrie)

Treaty although one D IV was retained at Adlershof and existed—albeit much modified by Albatros—until 1926.

The assistance of Alex Imrie on the colour reference material and Egon Krueger and Peter Grosz, who loaned so much helpful material, is sincerely appreciated.

Serial Number batches: Protos—3500–3502/16, 7550–7555/17.
D III—8340–8359/17, 1600–1629/18, 3007–3026/18, 3037–3046/18.
D IV—3027–3036/18, 3047–3056/18, 3060–3096/18, 6150–6184/18, 9000–9015/18, 9017–9020/18, 9022–9029/18, 11500–11502/18.
Allocation of D IIIs, where known:
Jagdgeschwader II (Js 12, 13, 15 and 19) 8346–8359/17, 1600–1608/18, 1610–1619/18, 1624/18.
Jagdgeschwader III (Js 2 (Boelcke), 26, 27 and 36) 8340–8345/17.
Kest 2—3015–3017/18, 3019–3020/18.
Kest 4b—8342/17, 8346/17, 8348–8349/17, 8351/17, 8357/17, 1604/18, 1611–12/18, 1626–1628/18, 3009/18, 3013/18, 3021–3022/18, 3043–3044/18, 3046/18.
Kest 5—8344/17, 8353/17, 8355–8356/17, 8358–8359/17, 1607/18, 1618/18, 1620/18, 1623/18, 1625/18, 3040/18.

SPECIFICATION

Manufacturer: Siemens-Schuckert Werke G.m.b.H., Siemenstaadt, Berlin and Nürnberg.

Powerplant: 160-h.p. Siemens Halske Sh III and 200-h.p. Sh IIIa. (Some of the later Sh IIIa engines developed as much as 240 h.p.).

Dimensions: D III—Span 8·43 m. (27 ft. 7⅞ in.). Length 5·7 m. (18 ft. 8½ in.). Height 2·8 m. (9 ft. 2¼ in.). Area 18·82 sq. m. (203·5 sq. ft.). D IV—Span 8·35 m. (27 ft. 4¾ in.). Length 5·7 m. (18 ft. 8½ in.). Height 2·72 m. (8 ft. 11 in.). Area 15·12 sq. m. (163·25 sq. ft.).

Weights: D III—Empty 534 k.g. (1,175 lb.). Loaded 725 k.g. (1,595 lb.). D IV—Empty 540 k.g. (1,190 lb.). Loaded 735 k.g. (1,620 lb.).

Performance: D III—Maximum speed c.a. 180 km. hr. (112·5 m.p.h.). Climb 1,000 m. (3,280 ft.) in 1·75 min. 2,000 m. (6,560 ft.) in 3·75 min. 3,000 m. (9,840 ft.) in 6 min. 4,000 m. (13,120 ft.) in 9 min. 5,000 m. (16,400 ft.) in 13 min. 6,000 m. (19,680 ft.) in 20 min. *N.B.* In September 1918 at Adlershof a D III fitted with a Rhemag-built Sh IIIa climbed 8,100 m. (26,575 ft.) in 36 min. D IV—Maximum speed c.a. 190 km. hr. (118·75 m.p.h.). Climb 1,000 m. in 1·9 min. 2,000 m. in 3·7 min. 3,000 m. in 6·4 min. 4,000 m. in 9·1 min. 5,000 m. in 12·1 min. 6,000 m. in 15·5 min. Ceiling approx. 8,000 m. (26,240 ft.), both types.

Duration: Approximately 2 hours.

Armament: Twin synchronised Spandau machine guns.

Kest 6—8347/17, 1600–1602/18, 1619/18, 3037/18, 3041/18, 3045/18.
Kest 8—8345/17, 8354/17, 1605–1606/18, 3007–3008/18, 3010/18, 3012/18,
Z.A.K. 3—1609/18.
Jastaschule I—3018/18, 3038/18.
Marine Landflieger Abt.—3039/18.
From 16th March 1918 to 18th May 1918 the first two batches of D IIIs were issued to Jagdeschwadern II and III. They were soon returned to the factory for modification and many were later reissued to the Kest (Kampfeinsitzer Staffeln), for Home Defence from 22nd July 1918 to 6th September 1918.
Allocation of D IVs, where known (date of issue, where known, also shown):
Jasta 14—3027/18 (23rd Aug. 1918), 3030–3031/18 (23rd Aug. 1918), 3033/18, 3047/18, 3050/18, 3052/18, 6150/18, 6154/18, 6166/18 (28th Oct. 1918), 6172–6174/18 (5th Nov. 1918).
Jasta 22—3035/18 (30th Aug. 1918), 3055/18, 3064–3065/18, 3069–3070/18, 3074/18, 3078/18, 3081/18 (9th Oct. 1918).
Jagd. II—(Jastas 12, 13, 15 and 19, individual allocation not indicated). 3036/18 (25th Oct. 1918), 3063/18, 3077/18 (17th Oct. 1918), 3082–3083/18, 6151/18 (2nd Nov. 1918), 6152/18 (25th Oct. 1918), 6158–6160/18 (31st Oct. 1918), 6161/18 (2nd Nov. 1918), 6163/18 (4th Nov. 1918), 6164/18 (2nd Nov. 1918), 6165/18 (31st Oct. 1918), 6167/18 (31st Oct. 1918), 6168/18 (4th Nov. 1918), 6170/18 (2nd Nov. 1918).
Z.A.K. 5—3080/18 (16th Oct. 1918), 6162/18 (8th Nov. 1918).
Marine Landfeld Jastas—3034/18, 3048/18, 3051/18, 3053–3054/18, 3056/18, 3062/18, 3072/18.
Marine Landflieger Abt.—3036/18, 3088/18.
Flieger Abt. 431—3087/18, 6178/18.

Fuselage of S.S.W. D III D 8356/17, *of* Kest 5, *which landed in Switzerland. Elaborate monogram surmounted by crown to be noted—unfortunately not identified.*
(Photo: P. M. Grosz via Alex Imrie)

PRINTED IN ENGLAND © Profile Publications Ltd., P.O. Box 26, 1a North Street, Leatherhead, Surrey, England.
Printed by Hills & Lacy Ltd., London and Watford, England. U.S. 2nd Class Mailing Rates applied for.

PROFILE PUBLICATIONS

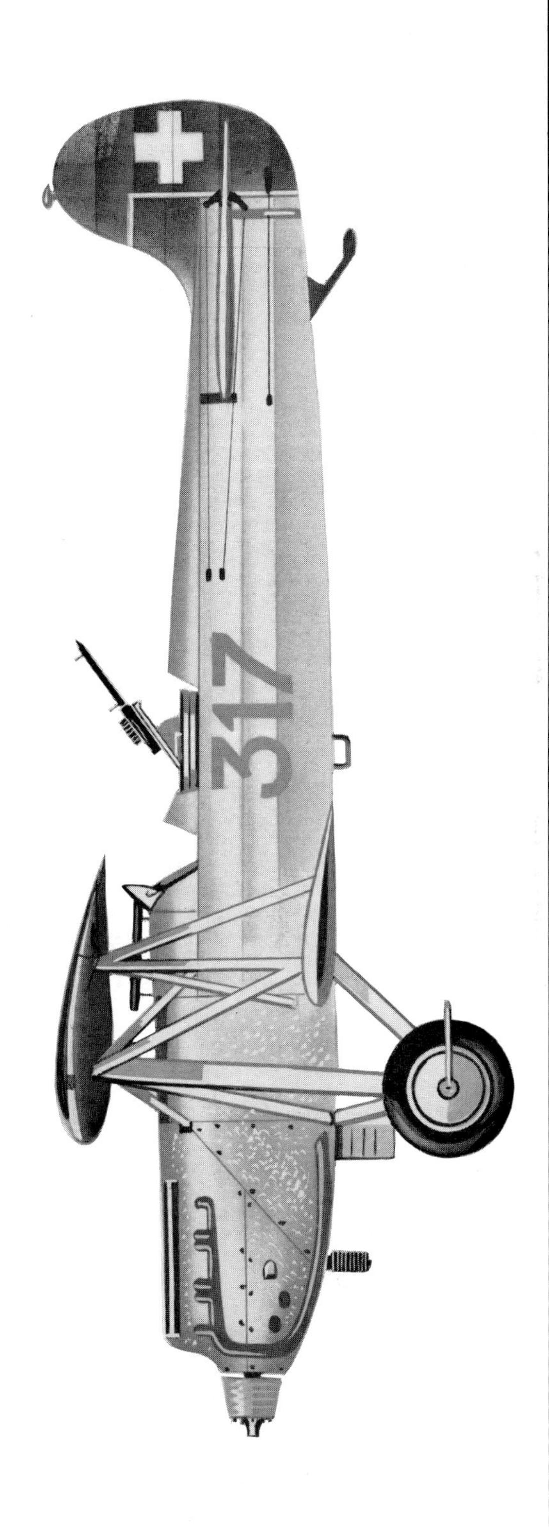

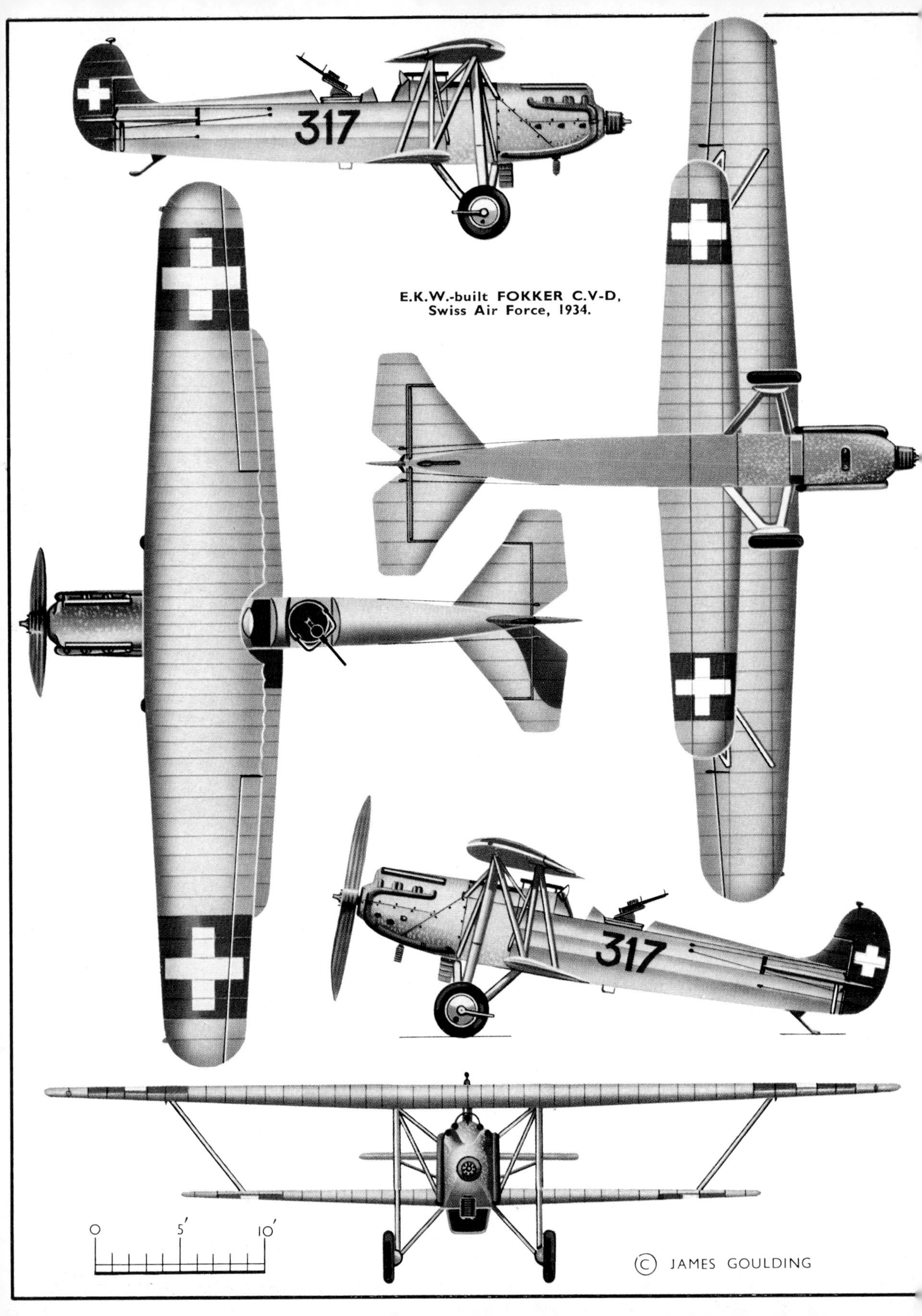
317
E.K.W.-built FOKKER C.V-D,
Swiss Air Force, 1934.
317
0
5'
10'
© JAMES GOULDING

The Fokker C V

by G. H. Kamphuis

A patrol of Swedish C.V-Es in flight over typical Scandinavian terrain. Six C.V-Es were purchased from Fokker in 1928, and forty-five were licence-built by the Swedish State Aircraft factory. (Photo: Fokker)

In 1924, a new reconnaissance aircraft design appeared from the offices of Anthony Fokker's team; as the logical successor to his earlier C.IV, it bore the designation Fokker C.V, and the first prototype flew in May 1924. From this beginning grew one of the most popular and progressive reconnaissance types of the pre-war years, and one of the most widely-acclaimed designs ever to join the Fokker "stable". Accepted as a "standard" by several foreign air forces and widely built abroad under licence, the C.V became the most-used of all Fokker's military designs, in several operational rôles.

A cantilever-wing two-seat biplane of fabric-skinned tubular-construction fuselage, the C.V was basically identical to the earlier C.IV, with a fined-down fuselage and fuel-tanks installed in the upper wing. During design, Fokker wished to evolve a machine which would meet a wide variety of military requirements with maximum efficiency; and this aim was achieved by the novel measure of designing and producing several different sets of wings, which could be changed in less than one hour. Great emphasis was also placed on interchangeability of power plant, and engines ranging in power from 250 h.p. to 500 h.p. could be mounted or changed in about an hour by a skilled team. This scheme gave the C.V the ability to serve as a tactical or strategic reconnaissance machine or a light bomber, according to the needs of the moment.

Over the period of its early use, three distinct variants of the C.V appeared, designated C.V-A, -B and -C respectively. Wing areas were 37·5 sq. m., 40·8 sq. m., and 46·1 sq. m. The performance figures of these versions were obviously dependent on the power plant installed, which included engines by Lorraine-Dietrich, BMW, and Hispano-Suiza. The C.V-A was a tactical reconnaissance type with one or two fixed and two ring-mounted machine guns. Besides the Dutch Army Air Corps, several foreign air arms purchased examples of this type. The Bolivian Air Force acquired a batch of C.V-Cs and operated them in the reconnaissance and light bombing rôles; these machines were fitted with 600-h.p. Hispano-Suiza engines. Among the interesting modifications of the basic design produced at this time was an American version with a small cockpit and side-panels, and an experimental floatplane version which was built in

BMW-engined Fokker C.V-A. (Photo: Fokker)

Hispano-Suiza powerplant installed in a C.V-A; in this case the H.S. 51 II engine is shown.

A civil C.V registered in the Netherlands. (Photo: Fokker)

Two of the original machines ordered by Denmark in 1926.

Holland in 1925. Experiments were carried out with shock-absorbers incorporated in the float-struts, but these were short-lived. In Holland the floatplane project was never developed with any success; the aircraft manifesting a tendency to stand on its nose during landing. More successful was the Swedish floatplane modification, designated S-6H. with a new rudder and enlarged, strengthened undercarriage members with streamlined struts from the undercarriage to the underside of the upper wing.

The next version of the design to appear was the C.V-D, differing from the previous variants in that it featured tapering wings, as opposed to the straight wings and extended ailerons of the first three versions. The C.V-D and -E sub-types were sesquiplanes, needing only two sets of wings to cover the whole range of military requirements. They were also suitable as reconnaissance fighters and as training machines. The two types could be distinguished easily by their strut layout, the -D having "V" interplane struts and the -E having "N"-struts. From January 1926 onwards, the C.V was only delivered with -D or -E type wings, of an area of 28·8 sq. m. and 39·3 sq. m. respectively. The standardisation of fuselage allowed the installation of all-liquid or air-cooled engines in the 350 h.p. to 650 h.p. range; these included the Hispano-Suiza, Napier, Lorraine-Dietrich 400 and 450 h.p., Rolls-Royce F.10, BMW Va and VI, Jupiter, Hornet, Wasp, and Armstrong Siddeley Jaguar. These latter versions were in particular demand in large numbers by Denmark, Hungary, Finland, Sweden, Norway, Italy and Switzerland, and widely built under licence. Finally in 1934 a rejuvenated variant of the C.V-E was produced, powered by a 730-h.p. Bristol Pegasus IIM-2 with Townend ring.

DUTCH MILITARY USE

Logically, the designation C.VI would appertain to the next design in Fokker's series of reconnaissance machines, but in fact this designation refers to a type in the C.V-D group. The Soesterberg establishment of the Dutch Army Air Corps ordered the type, which was simply a C.V-D powered by the 350-h.p. Hispano-Suiza liquid-cooled engine or the Armstrong Siddeley Jaguar (Star) fourteen-cylinder air-cooled radial

C.VI (C.V-D) operated by the Dutch Army Air Corps, with 350-h.p. Hispano-Suiza engine. The machine illustrated is the second in the original order batch. (Photo: Fokker)

The surviving Swedish-built C.V-E, finished in the dubious markings of F.3, seen here in flight during a demonstration. The aircraft is maintained by the Malmen aviation museum. (Photo: Royal Netherlands Air Force)

Dutch Army Air Corps C.V with Rolls-Royce Kestrel engine and ring-mounted machine gun in rear cockpit. Originally a Hispano-powered C.V-D, this machine was re-engined with the rest of its batch in 1936.
(Photo: Rolls-Royce Ltd.)

engine. Besides the two fuel tanks normally installed in the lower wing, a third tank was placed asymmetrically in the upper wing. In all, the Army Air Corps (known as the Air Division at that time) received sixty-seven of these machines, and constructed two further aircraft in the Army workshops. (It was in one of these machines that Lt. J. Schott won the *Coupe Echard* during the International Aerial Alpine Meeting at Zürich in August 1927. The success of the type in this and other events had a most favourable effect on export sales.) The first aircraft delivered to the *Luchtvaartafdeling* was a C.VI registered 591. Numbers 590–618 were powered by the 350-h.p. Hispano-Suiza, and numbers 519 and 520 were fitted with the 380-h.p. Jaguar. Besides these thirty-one machines Fokkers delivered two extra fuselages, for which wings were purchased later, these machines carrying the registration 621 and 622. In 1936 the whole batch was re-engined with the 450-h.p. Rolls-Royce Kestrel and on the same occasion the undercarriage was modified, being moved forward and fitted with brakes. The twenty-six C.V-Ds ordered in June 1927 were powered by the 450-h.p. Hispano-Suiza power plant, and the undercarriages fitted with balloon tyres. Nineteen of this latter batch were still in service in the autumn of 1934 and were re-numbered 623–641 after re-engining with the Rolls-Royce Kestrel. The remainder of the L.V.A. machines were numbered 642–651, although number 651 was re-marked 655 in August 1928 to avoid duplication; the three-seater strategic reconnaissance type C.VIII also carried the registration 651.

Six C.V-Ws, basically C.V-Cs with float undercarriages, were delivered to the Dutch Naval Air Service in 1925. The variant was not a success, and there were many landing accidents.
(Photo: Royal Netherlands Navy)

The Dutch Naval Air Service also used the type; in 1925 six C.V-Cs were delivered, registered Z-1 to Z-6, with float undercarriages. The constant difficulties experienced with this installation resulted in the re-fitting of wheel undercarriages. A second batch numbered Z-7 to Z-24 comprised C.V-Es with conventional wheel undercarriages. The Netherlands Indies Air Division operated twenty C.V-Es powered by the Napier Lion engine, and officially designated FC. Ve-400, this denoting F for Fokker, C.V-E, and the 400-h.p. rating of the power plant.

When the Germans attacked Holland on 10th May 1940, thirty-four machines still served with the Second Air Regiment of the L.V.A. They flew several operational missions during the brief but fierce fighting of the next few days; and the Third Reconnaissance Group, operating twelve of these fifteen-year-old

Rear view of a C.V-A with the 420-h.p. Liberty engine. Interchangeability of powerplant was a major feature of this type.

Views of the C.V-Es supplied to the Dutch Naval Air Service. Z-1 appears to be a conventional landplane which received its registration code after the write-off of one of the six floatplanes originally supplied to the naval air element.
(Photos: Royal Netherlands Navy)

sesquiplanes, particularly distinguished itself. The unit was based on Ruigenhoek; five C.Vs were lost during attacks on Valkenburg and Ypenburg airfields after their capture by the enemy, attacks which destroyed several German transports with bombs and machine gun fire. Fourteen of the original thirty-four machines survived when the Netherlands capitulated on 14th May; the greater part of those which had been lost were destroyed on the ground by German raids.

Ski-equipped C.V-D of the Norwegian Army Air Corps. The type saw combat service in Norway during the German invasion of 1940.
(Photo: Fokker)

LICENCE PRODUCTION

Denmark. Five C.V-Bs, powered by the Lorraine-Dietrich 12Db.A engine of 400 h.p. and registered R-1 to R-5 were delivered to Copenhagen in 1926. The Danish aviation workshops at Tojhugvoerkslaederne subsequently produced thirteen examples of the type, registered R-6 to R-16. A sample C.V-E, registered R-21, arrived in July 1933; this version was also licence-built in Denmark, thirty aircraft being constructed and registered R-22 to R-52. By 1940 only ten aircraft were still in service with the Danish Aviation Troops. Two, registered R-23 and R-42, were flown by the *Luftwaffe* with the codes 3W+NO and 3W+OD, and the latter machine was returned to Denmark in April 1947, having miraculously survived the war.

Twenty other C.Vs found by the Germans in the hangars of various Danish airfields were renovated, and actually sent to Russia in 1943; their fate is not recorded. Another highlight of the C.V's career with the Danes was the peace-time exploit of Captain Botved, who in March–June 1926 flew from Copenhagen to Tokyo in a C.V. His flight took him east via the former British East Indies and back via Siberia; his return flight of 10,395 km. was accomplished in seventy-two flying hours.

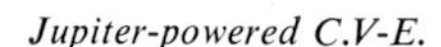

Jupiter-powered C.V-E.

"Fokker C.VI" development of the basic C.V-D, powered by a 380-h.p. Jaguar engine. (Photo: Royal Netherlands Air Force)

Finnish C.V-E equipped with 730-h.p. Bristol Pegasus. This is a Fokker-built machine; several of this version were built in Finland at the State Aircraft Factory at Tampere. (Photo: Fokker)

Swiss-built C.V-E No. 321, with a 475-h.p. Lorraine-Dietrich engine. (Photo: Fokker)

Swedish C.V-E (S-6B) with ski undercarriage. (Photo: Fokker)

One of three Jupiter-C.V-Ds purchased by Switzerland in 1927. (Photo: Fokker)

Finland. The Finnish air ministry purchased several C.Vs, but the exact numbers bought and those built under licence are not recorded. The first machine purchased was a C.V-E delivered in 1927, powered by a Jupiter (Star) air-cooled engine. When the improved C.V-E with the 730-h.p. Bristol Pegasus IIM-2 engine appeared in 1934, several were bought and more were constructed in the State Aircraft Factory at Tampere. In winter, the Fokkers were fitted with ski undercarriages, as was the normal Finnish procedure.

Hungary. Peace treaties did not allow of the existence of a Hungarian Air Force after W.W.I; but prompted by obvious necessity a secret air arm was founded in 1922. Towards the end of the 1920s, nine C.V-Ds and -Es were purchased; and the former type was later manufactured in quantity by the Weiss (Manfred) Aircraft Factory under licence. They were the backbone of the secret Hungarian Air Force for more than a decade, beginning their service in 1927 with bomber, reconnaissance and training units. Weiss modified the basic design in the early 1930s, producing the "Budapest I" light bomber, and the "Budapest II" reconnaissance machine. Grounded on account of their age in 1937–38, the Fokkers were pulled hastily out of retirement when the international situation grew more threatening in late 1938, and loaded with guns, bombs, wireless and camera equipment to a dangerous extent; even if the pilot coaxed his overweight machine into the air there was a good chance of undercarriage failure on landing. They were in service in the spring of 1939 when the Hungarian Army entered Carpatho-Ruthenia, and served with training units to an even later date. The *Solyom*, last of the C.V-D developments in Hungary, even saw service as a short-range reconnaissance type on the Russian Front in 1941.

Italy. *Officine Terroviarie Meridionale*, a subsidiary of the Romeo automobile organisation, constructed a number of C.V-Es, under the designation Ro.1, at

Fokker-built C.V supplied to Denmark, with Bristol Pegasus powerplant.

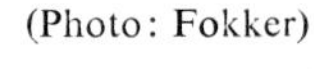
(Photo: Fokker)

Danish C.V-E with Jupiter VI engine. The code R-2 appears to be a re-issue; the original R-2 was powered by a Lorraine Dietrich engine, and was a C.V-B of the first order batch.

their Naples plant. These were operated in Tripoli and Italian Somaliland as well as internally; they were powered by licence-built Jupiter engines. Ernesto Breda's Milan factory also constructed some examples of the type. Several record-breaking flights were carried out in the Italian-built version, including the formation flight from Naples to Tripoli in October 1927. In April 1928 a formation of nine machines led by Major Bitossi flew from Rome to Mogadiscio in Somaliland, a distance of more than 10,000 km., and the first occasion on which Italian aircraft arrived for service in this colony under their own power.

Norway. The Norwegian Defence Programme of 1927 called for the expansion of the Army Air Corps (*Haerens Flyväben*) and it was the C.V-E which was chosen for the bomber elements. Initially five machines were purchased from Holland, bearing non-consecutive registration numbers between 301 and 309, and all powered by the 450-h.p. Jupiter VIA. At the same time licence rights were taken out by the *Haerens Flyvemaskin Fabrik* plant at Keller, near Lillestrom. At first the Norwegian-built aircraft were powered by Jupiter engines but later in the production programme they were modified to take the 575-h.p. Panther II, while some machines were fitted with D-style wings and B.M.W. engines. The Fokkers formed an important part of the Norwegian Air Corps strength between 1930 and 1940, and when Germany invaded Norway on 9th April 1940 some forty machines were in service, registered between 301 and 393. On 14th April, a formation from the Sixth (Bomber) Wing, each aircraft carrying three 50 kg. bombs, attacked

Danish-built machine with modified cowl-ring and gun mounting in rear cockpit. (Photo: Fokker)

Hispano-powered C.Vs of the L.V.A.; note differing styles of code numbers. (Photo: Royal Netherlands Air Force)

eleven Junkers Ju 52s in the area of the Harting Lake, and destroyed all but one as they landed. During the final stages of resistance on 9th June, the surviving aircraft flew to Finland. A small number of these were later purchased and used for target-towing by the Swedish firm *Svensk Flugtjänst*; one, originally registered 349, was handed back to the Royal Norwegian Air Force in 1949 bearing the registration SE-ALS, and has since been restored in its 1940 markings and flown at displays.

Sweden. Two Fokker C.V-Ds were purchased by the Swedish Government from the manufacturer in 1927 and were registered S.1 and S.2. In Swedish service they were initially designated J-3 and later S-6A. A year later Fokker delivered six C.V-Es, registered S.3 to S.8, and these also operated under the designation J-3 for a short period, later taking the designation S.6. It was in one of these machines that Lt. H. E. Lundborg saved the life of General Nobile on 24th June 1928 after the latter failed in his attempted North Pole journey in the airship *Italia.* In 1929 the Swedish State Aircraft Factory started the licence-production of the C.V-E. Powered by Jupiter engines and registered 90 to 96, they carried the designations J-3 and S-6. The next production run numbered thirty-nine machines, three of which were exported to Finland in 1939–40.

Thirty-four Fokker C.Vs were still in L.V.A. service when the German invasion of 1940 began, and saw action in the reconnaissance and light-bombing rôles. These photographs show machines of the Second Air Regiment at the time of the invasion.

One of the Swedish-built machines, registered 386, survives and is to be seen in the air museum at Malmen.

(continued on page 12)

Kriegstechnische Abteilung *of Thun, Switzerland, developed this Hispano-powered variant of the C.V-E, designated C.35. Note "splinter" camouflage.*

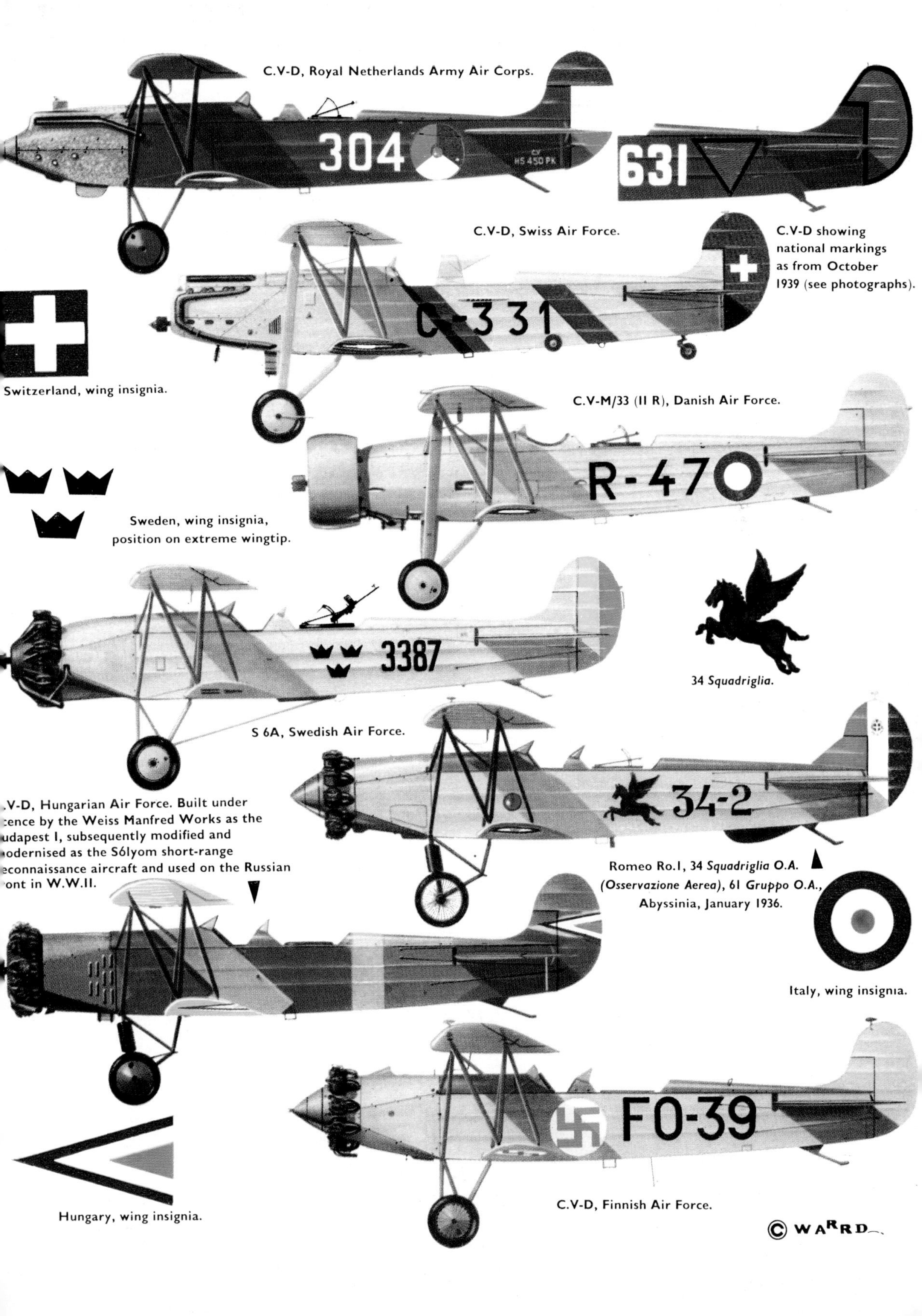

C.V-D, Royal Netherlands Army Air Corps.

C.V-D, Swiss Air Force.

C.V-D showing national markings as from October 1939 (see photographs).

Switzerland, wing insignia.

C.V-M/33 (II R), Danish Air Force.

Sweden, wing insignia, position on extreme wingtip.

34 *Squadriglia*.

S 6A, Swedish Air Force.

.V-D, Hungarian Air Force. Built under :ence by the Weiss Manfred Works as the udapest I, subsequently modified and odernised as the Sólyom short-range econnaissance aircraft and used on the Russian ont in W.W.II.

Romeo Ro.1, 34 *Squadriglia O.A. (Osservazione Aerea)*, 61 *Gruppo O.A.*, Abyssinia, January 1936.

Italy, wing insignia.

Hungary, wing insignia.

C.V-D, Finnish Air Force.

The Ro. 1 was the Italian-built variant of the basic C.V-E, powered by a licence-built Jupiter engine. Here are shown machines of the 38° Squadriglia O.A. *in flight over Ethiopia in the spring of 1936.* (Photo: G. Cattaneo)

Switzerland. This country purchased three Jupiter-C.V-Ds in 1927, registered 821–823. Four years later three C.V-Es registered 302–304 were delivered and in 1933 it was decided to have fifty of these machines licence-built by E.K.W. at Thun and by Dornier at Altenrhein. These were registered 305 and 311–359. One year later another eight -Es were built, numbered 801–808, and were used as target tugs. The type remained in service until W.W.II, and reached a peak operational strength of sixty machines. One Swiss-built C.V also survives.

FOKKER C.V DEVELOPMENTS

Type	Year	Engine	Description
C.V-A	1924	420-h.p. Packard "Liberty"	Two-seat reconnaissance biplane for tactical purposes.
C.V-B	1924–25	250-h.p. BMW IV 450-h.p. Lorr.-Dietrich 450-h.p. Hispano-Suiza	Two-seat reconnaissance biplane. B-wing of 40·8 sq. m.
C.V-C	1925	500-h.p. Hispano-Suiza 51	Two-seat reconnaissance and light bomber. (Bolivian Air Force.)
C.V-C b	1925	400-h.p. Lorr.-Dietrich	Two-seat observation biplane for Netherlands Navy.
C.V-D	1925–27	400-h.p. A.S. "Jaguar" C5 450-h.p. Hispano-Suiza 650-h.p. RR "Kestrel"	Two-seat fighter/reconnaissance sesquiplane.
C.V-E	1925–27	475-h.p. Lorr.-Dietrich 450-h.p. Hispano-Suiza 450-h.p. N. "Lion"	Two-seat reconnaissance/light bomber sesquiplane. Two-seat observation sesquiplane.
	1934	730-h.p. Bristol "Pegasus" IIM-2	Modernised version for reconnaissance and light bomber. (Ski-version also built.)
C.V-W	1925	420-h.p. Packard "Liberty" 500-h.p. Hispano-Suiza 51	Seaplane version of the C.V-C: also with 500-h.p. Hispano-Suiza 51.
C.VI	1925 —	350-h.p. Hispano-Suiza Rolls-Royce	Two-seat light observation sesquiplane version of the C.V-D. U.S. modifications with cabin windows. (Pacific Aera-Bob & Eddie.)

SPECIFICATIONS	C.V-D 520 h.p. Hispano-Suiza	C.V-D 610 h.p. Jupiter VI	C.V-E 450 h.p. Lorraine Dietrich	C.V-E 450 h.p. Napier	C.V with 450 h.p. Hispano-Suiza engine		
					Normal	Small	Large
Span	12·5 m.	12·5 m.	15·3 m.	15·3 m.	13·332 m.	12·036 m.	14·628 m.
Length	9·53 m.	9·46 m.	9·13 m.	9·25 m.	9·25 m.	9·25 m.	9·35 m.
Height	3·3 m.	3·3 m.	3·38 m.	3·38 m.	3·31 m.	3·29 m.	3·38 m.
Wing area ...	28·8 sq. m.	28·8 sq. m.	39·3 sq. m.	39·3 sq. m.	40·7 sq. m.	36·5 sq. m.	46 sq. m.
Weight empty ...	1,315 kgs.	1,125 kgs.	1,390 kgs.	1,420 kgs.	1,430 kgs.	1,380 kgs.	1,480 kgs.
Useful load ...	600 kgs.	600 kgs.	1,000 kgs.	800 kgs.	800 kgs.	600 kgs.	1,000 kgs.
Weight loaded ...	1,915 kgs.	1,725 kgs.	2,390 kgs.	2,220 kgs.	2,230 kgs.	1,980 kgs.	2,480 kgs.
Wing loading ...	66 kg./sq. m.	60 kg./sq. m.	61 kg./sq. m.	56·5 kg./sq. m.	55 kg./sq. m.	54 kg./sq. m.	54 kg./sq. m.
Power loading ...	3 kgs./h.p.	2·8 kgs./h.p.	5 kgs./h.p.	4·4 kgs./h.p.	4·9 kgs./h.p.	4·4 kgs./h.p.	5·5 kgs./h.p.
Speed max. ...	225 km.h.p.	245 km.h.p.	222 km.h.p.	230 km.h.p.	220 km.h.p.	230 km.h.p.	210 km.h.p.
Speed min. ...	95 km.p.h.	90 km.p.h.	95 km.p.h.	90 km.p.h.	—	—	—
Climb to 1,000 m.	2 mins.	1·9 mins.	3·9 mins.	2·8 mins.	—	—	—
Climb to 2,000 m.	4·3 mins.	4·2 mins.	8·9 mins.	6 mins.	—	—	—
Climb to 3,000 m.	7·2 mins.	7 mins.	15·7 mins.	10·2 mins.	10 mins.	8·5 mins.	12 mins.
Climb to 4,000 m.	10·7 mins.	10·5 mins.	26·2 mins.	15·7 mins.	—	—	—
Climb to 5,000 m.	16·5 mins.	15·5 mins.	—	23·8 mins.	25 mins.	20 mins.	32 mins.
Climb to 6,000 m.	26 mins.	23·6 mins.	—	38 mins.	—	—	—
Ceiling	7,000 m.	7,300 m.	5,400 m.	7,000 m.	6,200 m.	6,600 m.	5,800 m.

ARMAMENT POSSIBILITIES

C.V-D (two-seater fighter). Two fixed guns firing forward and twin guns on a flexible mounting over the back cockpit.
C.V-D (artillery co-operation). One fixed gun firing forward and one gun on a flexible mounting over the back cockpit. Wireless apparatus.
C.V-D and -E (reconnaissance). One fixed gun firing forward and twin guns on a flexible mounting over the back cockpit.
C.V-E (day bomber). One fixed gun firing forward and one gun on a flexible mounting over the back cockpit. Bomb-racks.

PRINTED IN ENGLAND © Profile Publications Ltd., P.O. Box 26, 1a North Street, Leatherhead, Surrey, England.
Printed by Hills & Lacy Ltd., London and Watford, England. U.S. 2nd Class Mailing Rates applied for.

PROFILE
PUBLICATIONS

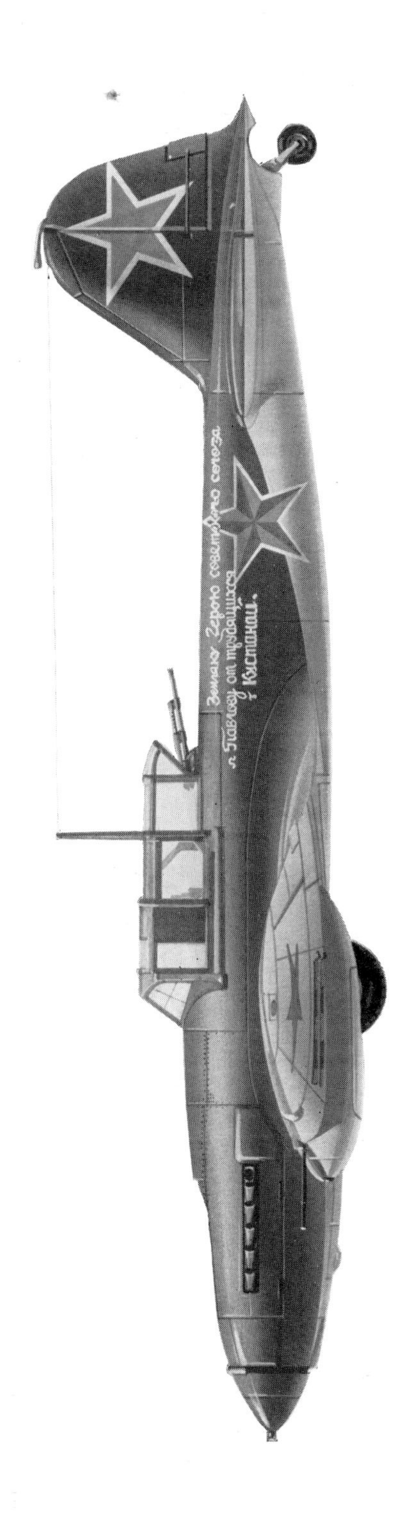

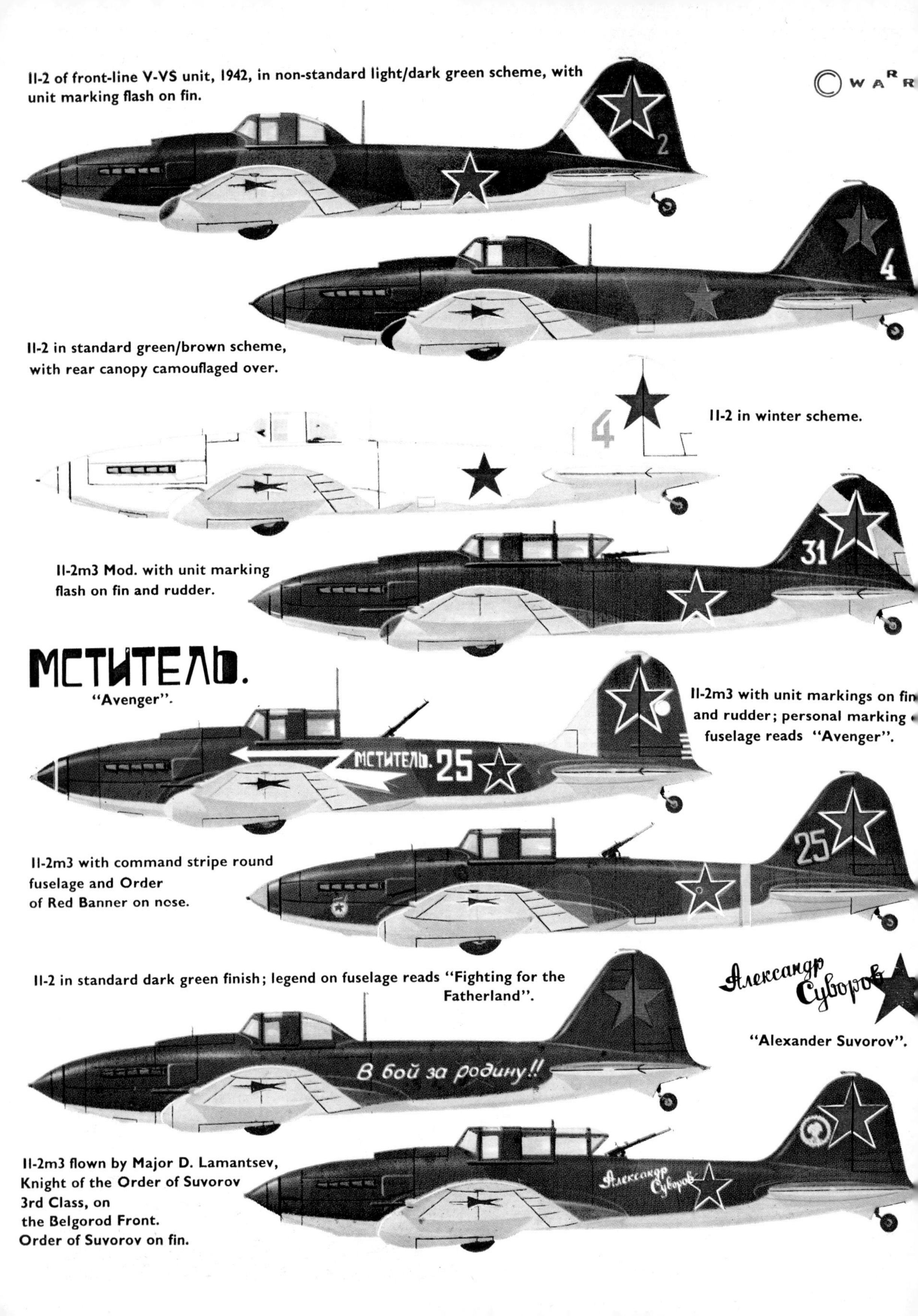

Il-2 of front-line V-VS unit, 1942, in non-standard light/dark green scheme, with unit marking flash on fin.

Il-2 in standard green/brown scheme, with rear canopy camouflaged over.

Il-2 in winter scheme.

Il-2m3 Mod. with unit marking flash on fin and rudder.

"Avenger".

Il-2m3 with unit markings on fin and rudder; personal marking on fuselage reads "Avenger".

Il-2m3 with command stripe round fuselage and Order of Red Banner on nose.

Il-2 in standard dark green finish; legend on fuselage reads "Fighting for the Fatherland".

"Alexander Suvorov".

Il-2m3 flown by Major D. Lamantsev, Knight of the Order of Suvorov 3rd Class, on the Belgorod Front. Order of Suvorov on fin.

A flight of Il-2s silhouetted against the dawn. Although immediately successful, the design did not really come into its own until the appearance of the Il-2m3 two-seater. (Photo: Imperial War Museum)

It is an established fact of aviation history that all major classes of military aircraft employed by the combatant powers of W.W.II had their roots in the experience gained during W.W.I. By the end of hostilities in 1919, the needs of the air forces had crystallised into recognised patterns that were to hold good, in the most part, for more than twenty-five years thereafter. It does not often happen that after the state of the art has developed along established lines for many years, an entirely new requirement is formulated; new, not from the point of view of quality, but in its fundamentals. The principal example of this phenomenon to appear during W.W.II was the requirement for a specialised ground-attack aircraft, fast and agile at low level; heavily armed with a variety of weapons which would make it the scourge of infantry, artillery, armour, installations and shipping alike; capable of operating in close support of the ground forces from front-line positions; capable of absorbing the savage ground fire which is the constant lot of the low-level strike machine; and capable, to some extent, of defending itself against enemy interceptors with a reasonable chance of success. The Germans attempted to fill this need with the Henschel Hs 129 (see *Profile* No. 69); but although it proved itself capable of carrying an astonishing variety of sophisticated weapons, the Henschel was never free of the fundamental faults of powerplant selection which hampered it from its first appearance in action. There can be no doubt that the outstanding all-purpose ground-attack aircraft of W.W.II was Sergei Ilyushin's Il-2, known to the world by the sobriquet of *Shturmovik*.

Large, rugged, and with tremendous destructive capacity, the Il-2 was simple and cheap to produce, even crude by Western standards. It was an aircraft which earned the unwavering trust and confidence of its crews; and many V-VS (Soviet Air Force) personnel survived unscathed the severest combat damage to their aircraft, thanks to the armour-plate "bath" which protected the *Shturmovik*'s engine and cockpit. (*Shturmovik* is a general designation for all ground-attack types, and its application to the Il-2 particularly is comparable to the use of the name *Stuka* for the Junkers Ju 87.) The best operating altitude, at the most favourable engine rating, was little over 2,000 ft.; and the majority of Il-2 sorties were flown at between 30 and 150 ft., and as often as not the target would be caught in a *horizontal* storm of rockets and cannon shells! Capable of delivering a large volume of bombs, rockets and shells from minimum altitude; almost invariably returning to base with huge rents and holes in the wings and tail surfaces, but never in the cockpit or cowling; appearing over land and sea, on all fronts to which the Soviet forces were committed; the Il-2 had no counterpart anywhere in the world. To its pilots it was known and loved simply as *Ilyusha*, surely the first time a whole class of fighting aeroplanes have given birth to a new name for a girl! To the soldiers below it was the "Flying Tank", "Hunchback", and "Flying Infantryman"—surely the highest praise of all, as any ex-infantry soldier will appreciate. The German army called it *Schwarz Tod*—"Black Death".

DESIGN AND DEVELOPMENT

In the Soviet Union the attempts to produce a specialised ground-attack machine began in the year 1930, when such well-known designers as Grigorovich, Porohovshchikov and Kocherygin attempted to build machines fulfilling several apparently contradictory requirements. There had to be good low-level performance, heavy armament to deal with targets such as pill-boxes, tanks and trains, and good armour protection. The machine would also have to be manœuvrable, of comparable speed to contemporary fighters (fighter escort would not be practicable on low-level sorties of the type envisaged, and the *Shturmoviki* would thus be self-reliant for defence) and in addition should not be too large.

Rare photograph of the original CKB 57 prototype, which was test-flown by V. Kokkinaki late in 1939.

An Il-2 captured by German forces. (Photo: H. J. Nowarra)

Between 1930 and 1933 Grigorovich designed two such aircraft, the Tsh-1 and Tsh-2. They were good machines by contemporary standards, but failed because of the lack of a sufficiently powerful engine. The first significant design to appear was S. V. Ilyushin's CKB 55 two-seater prototype, designed during 1938 by Ilyushin's team at the Central Design Bureau. Following Russian procedure, a design contest was held for a ground-attack machine, and Ilyushin's CKB 55 was pitted against the Su-6 of Pavel Sukhoi. Despite certain advantages of the Sukhoi design, Ilyushin won the contest when his competitor failed to meet the deadline. Development continued, and the type was named in *Voyenno Vozdushnye Sily* as the B Sh -2 (for *Bronirovannyi Shturmovik*, Armoured Assault Aircraft).

The prototype of the CKB 57, the true prototype for the single-seater Il-2, was flown in trials late in 1939 by the famous test pilot V. Kokkinaki, and it immediately became obvious that it was underpowered. The 1,370-h.p. AM 35 engine was insufficient to give life to more than four tons of airframe and armour. Re-engined with the 1,680-h.p. AM 38, however, the CKB 57 displayed considerably improved characteristics when test-flown in a new series of trials in October of 1940.

The main features of the CKB 57 included the forward fuselage, built as an armour shell with panels varying between 5 mm. and 12 mm. thickness. The aft fuselage was a wooden monocoque, and the tail unit was of metal construction with dural skinning. Armament comprised two Shkas 7·62-mm. machine guns, two Shvak 20-mm. cannons, rails for eight 82-mm. RS 82 rockets, and a bomb capacity of about

Wartime photograph of Sergei V. Ilyushin in V-VS uniform.

Production line of Il-2m3s in a Siberian plant, 1942.

Il-2 running up on a front-line airstrip; Poland, July 1944. (Photo: courtesy Skrzydlata Polska)

400 kg. (881 lb.). Level speed reached 470 km./h. (292 m.p.h.) and operating altitude was 2,000 m. (6,500 ft.).

Passing its State Trials in March 1941, the machine went into mass production as the Il-2, and 249 were built before the German invasion of that summer. These were immediately delivered to front-line units, and, operating in small numbers against the advancing German columns, provided some of the few localised Russian successes of that disastrous year. Production costs were cut thirty-eight per cent during the first year and the numbers quickly increased; but the rapid advance of the German forces forced the evacuation of plants at Moscow and other industrial centres in European Russia to safer areas in the Urals and to hurriedly-erected factories in Siberia. The period of evacuation, during the hard winter of 1941, was not wasted time, however. Further development studies were carried out with a view to simplifying and speeding production techniques, and only two months after the evacuation Il-2s were once more reaching the front. By this time criticisms of the aircraft were making themselves felt; there was no active rear armament, and this was proving hazardous during a period of almost total German air superiority over the front. The 20-mm. cannons were not very effective against the new German armoured vehicles; and the aircraft was rather difficult to handle. Although the Il-2 continued in full production, and the numbers supplied to the squadrons doubled between summer 1942 and summer 1943, it was obvious that modifications would have to be effected.

THE TWO-SEATER APPEARS

A conference held in the spring of 1942 between the design team and representatives of the combat pilots formulated the final requirements for the "new look" Il-2. The most obvious change was the re-design of the cockpit to provide accommodation for a rear gunner; and the armour-plate "bath" was lengthened accordingly. Armament was improved by the addition of a

Il-2m3 donated in the name of Lena Asarenkova in memory of her father after his death in action; the inscription may be translated as "From little Lena, for Papa". Azarenkov commanded a squadron of the 237th Assault Regiment, V-VS, at the time of his death.

BS 12·7-mm. machine gun in the rear cockpit (sometimes replaced by a UBT weapon of similar calibre) and by the substitution of high muzzle velocity VJa 23-mm. cannons for the Shvaks. Engine power was boosted by the adjustment of the compression ratio, providing the new AM 38 F powerplant with 1,750 h.p. All these changes were introduced to production Il-2s, and some single-seater machines with all other modifications incorporated flew under the designation Il-2M.

From August 1942 the front-line squadrons received the new two-seat Il-2m3 ("model 3"); and despite the addition of a second crew position, the better aerodynamic silhouette of the longer cockpit enabled the Il-2m3 to achieve a top speed of 404 km./h. (251 m.p.h.). A parallel development was the Il-2U trainer, with reduced armament and the controls fully duplicated in the second cockpit.

In 1943 the armament of the Il-2m3 was strengthened yet again, the VJa cannons giving place to

Underwing racks are clearly visible in this view of an Il-2m3 in flight. (Photo: courtesy Skrzydlata Polska)

Il-2m3 of Polish 1st Mixed Air Corps taking off, Germany, March 1945

long-barrelled N-37 (or 11 P 37) weapons, of 37-mm. calibre and improved armour penetration ability. Optional devices which also appeared during this period included containers for 200 small bombs of the PTAB 2,5-1,5 class; and the DAG 10 grenade launcher, a rather strange mechanism which ejected infantry grenades on small parachutes in the path of pursuing fighters. The Il-2m3(Modified) saw action in any numbers for the first time during the Kursk Salient battles of June–July 1943, which is now judged to have been the greatest tank battle in history. Like its near-counterpart, the Henschel Hs 129, the *Shturmovik* distinguished itself during these actions, and caused huge losses in vehicles to the German *Panzer* Divisions and self-propelled artillery units. Even the new Pz.Kw.VI Tiger tank fell easy prey to the 37-mm. cannon of the Il-2.

During the above-mentioned armament changes, considerable structural alterations were introduced. As already stated, early-model Il-2s had wooden rear fuselage structure, and some even had wooden tail surfaces. The Il-2m3(Basic) retained the wooden rear fuselage, with all-metal wings and tail surfaces. Il-2m3(Mod.)s appearing in 1944 were of all-metal construction throughout, and the gunners' back and front plates were replaced by an integral rear bulkhead for the armour "bath".

Later additions to the armoury included the occasional replacement of the RS 82 rockets by RS 132 projectiles of 132-mm. calibre, equipped with either hollow charge or "blockbuster" warheads for use against buildings and installations. Internal wing bomb racks could carry between 400 and 600 kg. (881 and 1,321 lb.); and with the AM 38 F engine the aircraft could take off from a rough grass airstrip with

Ground crew removing camouflage from a V-VS Il-2m3 based in Poland, 1944. (Photo: courtesy Skrzydlata Polska)

Polish Air Force Il-2m3s; note underwing detail.

full load. Some models were modified to carry a single 53-cm. torpedo below the fuselage, and others carried a single reconnaissance camera behind the gunner's cockpit. (It should be noted that all these modifications were carried out on standard production models without any firm change in designation, and distinguishing between the different sub-types of Il-2m3 is sometimes almost impossible for current researchers.)

The final "modification" was really a complete re-design, seeing expression in the Il-10, which carried the NATO code-name "Beast" after its encounters in the Korean War. With new wings, a different silhouette, new armament, new undercarriage, new engine (2,000-h.p. AM 42), the Il-10 was generally too late to see widespread war service. By the time it had its major baptism of fire in Korea, the Il-10 was no longer an effective weapon of air warfare; in the age of the Sabre and the Meteor, the *Shturmovik* was a flying coffin rather than a flying tank.

THE IL-2 DESCRIBED

All versions, from the CKB 57 to the Il-2m3(Mod.) were constructed in similar fashion, as follows:

The aircraft was a cantilever, low-wing, single-engined monoplane powered by a liquid-cooled 12 (Vee) cylinder A. Mikulin engine. The focal point of all versions was the forward fuselage, which, from the nose to the rear of the cockpit, was pressed as a one-piece armour bath with integrally-pressed engine bearers and cooler nest. Both single-seat and two-seat variants had the rear of the bath closed with a 13-mm. armour plate; the canopy was constructed of armour-glass and 8-mm. steel plates, with a 55–65-mm. armour-glass windscreen; and the oil cooler beneath

Views of the Il-2m3 preserved at the Polish Armed Forces Museum at Warsaw: note the extremely heavily armoured cockpit. The great crew and engine protection afforded by the Ilyushin's construction led to its being christened "The Flying Tank" by wartime crews, and one of the outstanding features of its operational career was its ability to absorb considerable combat damage.

the fuselage was protected by 8-mm. sheets. In the Il-2, the armour weight totalled approximately 700 kg. (1,542 lb.), and about 950 kg. (2,092 lb.) in the Il-2m3. The forward fuselage had no construction members; the armour bath itself served as the skeleton, a great design achievement which allowed considerable weight-saving (as well as greater protection) in comparison with a conventional structure to which armour had to be added. No calibre below 20 mm. could pierce this armour shell, and even 20 mm. often failed to penetrate if the interceptor's range and deflection were not perfect; a hard condition to fill when attempting to hit a relatively small aircraft jinking and swerving through obstacles at 400 km./h. (248 m.p.h.) thirty feet above the ground.

The following distinctions may be drawn between the main variants:

CKB 57. Wooden monocoque rear fuselage, wings and tail surfaces of metal construction, metal-skinned. Main undercarriage members retractable, fixed tail wheel. Rear part of cockpit canopy was covered with steel plates. *Armament:* Two Shkas 7·62-mm. machine guns, two Shvak 20-mm. cannon, eight 82-mm. *Raketny Snaryad* rocket projectiles or 500/600 kg. (1,101/1,321 lb.) bomb load in wing chambers. *Engine:* Twelve-cylinder liquid-cooled (60° Vee) AM 38 engine of 46·8 litre working volume. Cylinder bore 160 mm. (6·3 in.), stroke 190 mm. (7·6 in.), compression ratio 6·8, used with 95 octane fuel. Take-off power 1,600 h.p. at 2,150 r.p.m. and fuel consumption of 305 gram/h.p./hour. Emergency power 1,550 h.p. at 2,150 r.p.m. and 2,000 m. (6,500 ft.) altitude, fuel consumption 285 gram/h.p./hour. Cruising power 1,410 h.p. at 2,150 r.p.m., fuel consumption 270 gram/h.p./hour. Weight to power ratio ·54 kg./h.p. (1·2 lb./h.p.).

(continued on page 10)

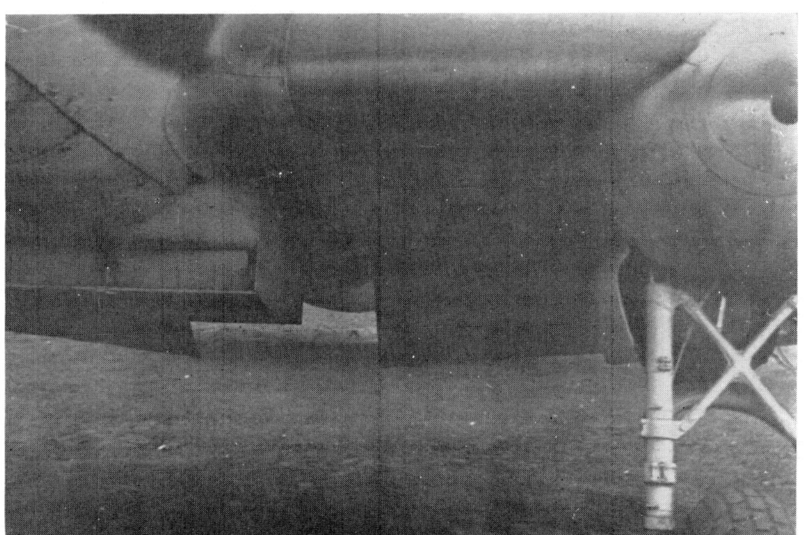

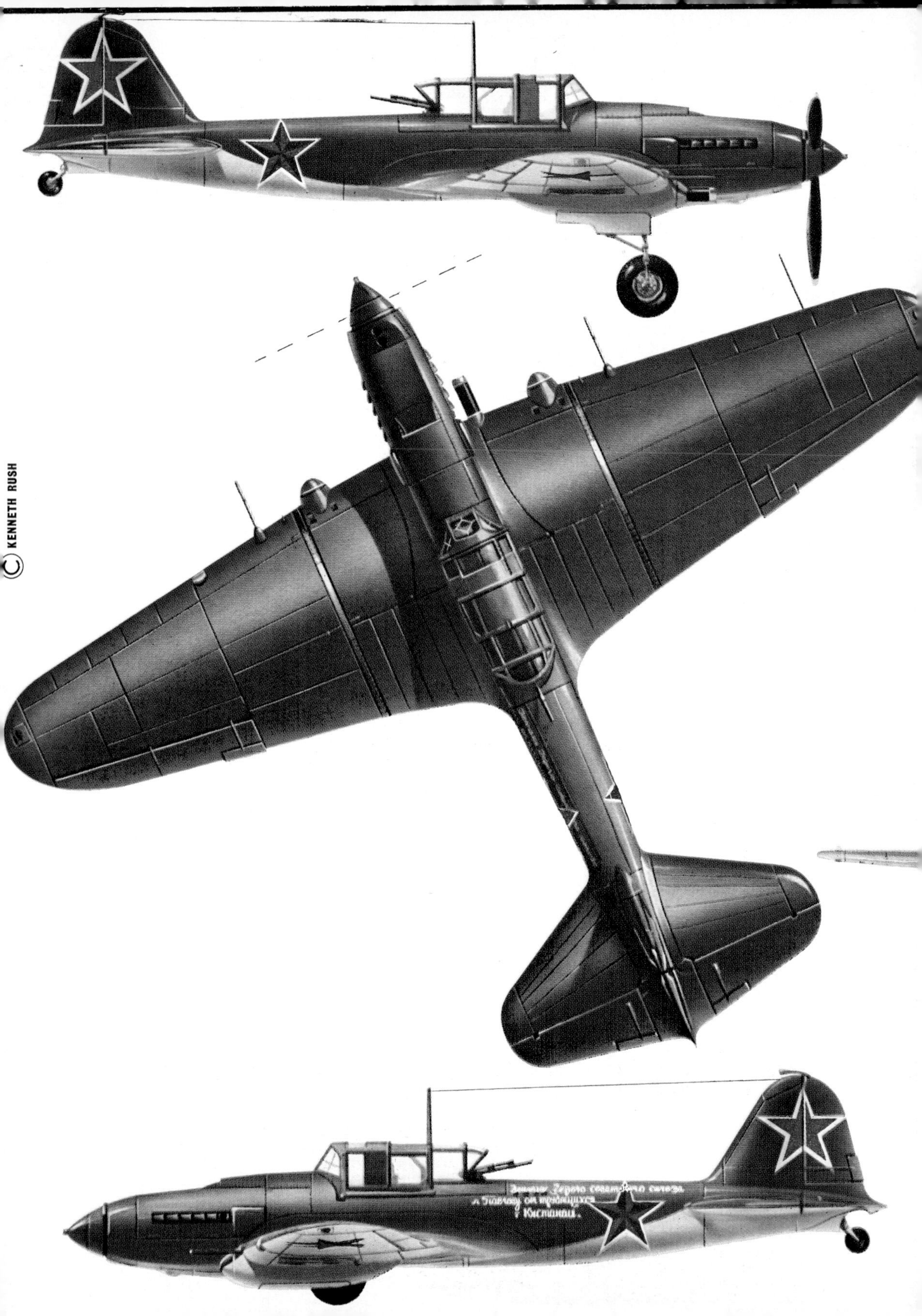
© KENNETH RUSH

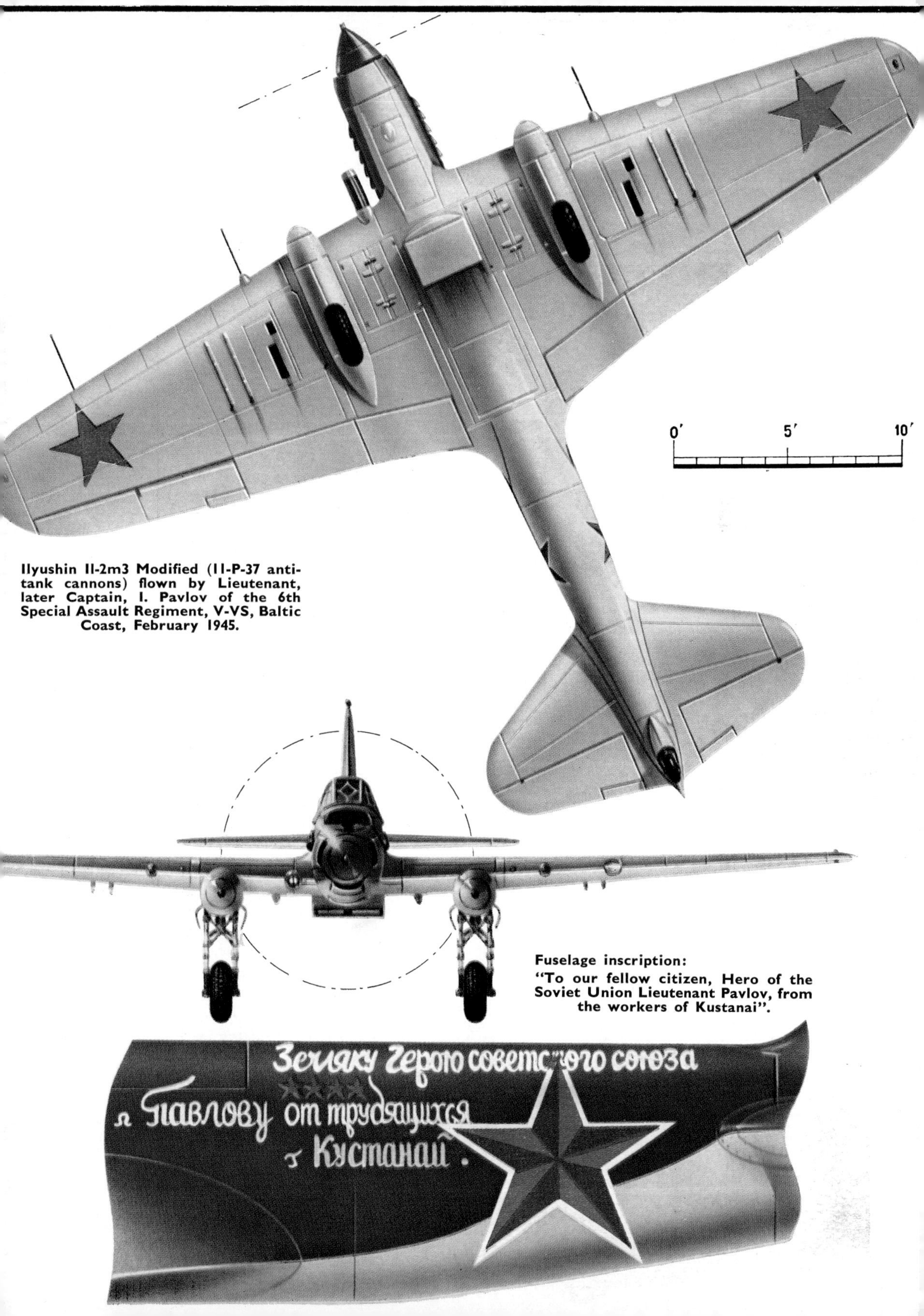

Ilyushin Il-2m3 Modified (11-P-37 anti-tank cannons) flown by Lieutenant, later Captain, I. Pavlov of the 6th Special Assault Regiment, V-VS, Baltic Coast, February 1945.

Fuselage inscription:
"To our fellow citizen, Hero of the Soviet Union Lieutenant Pavlov, from the workers of Kustanai".

Hero of the Soviet Union Major Kitayev poses on the wing of his Il-2m3. This pilot flew with the 3rd Squadron, 3rd Polish Assault Regiment. On the original negative it is possible to distinguish guide lines marked on the windscreen as a form of artificial horizon and an indication of dive angles, after the fashion employed by the Luftwaffe *on Junkers Ju 87s.*

Il-2 Basic. Rear fuselage wooden monocoque, containing radio equipment, oxygen bottles, battery, pneumatic bottle and flap actuation system. Centre fuselage and wing centre section built as integral unit. Wings and tail surfaces of mixed construction; inner wing wood, outer wing all metal, fin and stabilisers wood (all-metal on late production models), control surfaces fabric covered. Metal flaps of the "crocodile" type, pneumatically operated with two-stage movement. Rudder and elevators actuated by push rods, ailerons by control cables. Undercarriage retractable into underwing fairings, wheels partially exposed when fully retracted. Double undercarriage legs with oleo-pneumatic shock absorbers. Fixed tail wheel with small fairing. AM 38 engine driving metal three-blade variable pitch propeller. *Armament:* Two 7·62-mm. Shkas machine guns, two 20-mm. Shvak cannons, four RS 82 rockets or 400 kg. (881 lb.) bomb load. *Dimensions:* Span 14·6 m. (48 ft. ½ in.), length 11·6 m. (38 ft. ½ in.), height 3·4 m. (11 ft. 1½ in.), wing area 38·5 sq. m. (414·4 sq. ft.). *Weights:* Empty 3,800 kg. (8,370 lb.), loaded 5,340 kg. (11,762 lb.). *Performance:* Max. speed 450 km./h. (279 m.p.h.), cruising speed 350 km./h. (223 m.p.h.), ceiling 4,000–7,500 m. (13,100–24,600 ft.), range 600–750 km. (375–469 miles).

Il-2 M. All data except powerplant and armament similar to above. Two VJa 23-mm. cannon replaced the Shvak weapons. Eight rails for RS 82 or 25 kg. (55 lb.), 132-mm. RS 132 projectiles. AM 38 F engine with compression ratio of 6·0, take-off power 1,700 h.p. at 2,350 r.p.m. and fuel consumption of 325 gram /h.p./hour, emergency power 1,550 h.p. at 2,150 r.p.m. at 200 m. (655 ft.) altitude with fuel consumption of 285 gram/h.p./hour, cruise power 1,410 h.p. at 2,150 r.p.m. and 3,000 m. (980 ft.) altitude, fuel consumption 270 gram/h.p./hour.

Il-2 Model 3. Slightly modified AM 38 F engine with stroke increased by 6·7 mm. to 196·7 mm. This caused some increase in fuel consumption (to 325 gram/h.p./hour) but gave smoother engine control and increased mechanical efficiency. Take-off power rose to 1,770 h.p. The addition of the rear cockpit and elongation of the armoured compartment caused some increase in empty weight, but other minor structural changes allowed some cuts in all-up weight and total weight only rose by about 100 kg. (220 lb.). The airframe was of entirely metal construction. The dimensions were identical to the Il-2 basic model. *Weights:* Empty 4,360 kg. (9,604 lb.), loaded 5,510 kg. (12,136 lb.). *Performance:* Ceiling fell to 6,000 m. (19,500 ft.), range remained at 600 km. (375 m.) but max. speed fell to 404 km./h. (251 m.p.h.). *Armament:* Two VJa 23-mm. cannon, two Shkas 7·62-mm. machine guns, one 12·7 mm. BS machine gun in rear cockpit, DAG 10 grenade launcher, eight RS 82 or RS 132 projectiles or 600 kg. (1,321 lb.) bomb load.

Il-2 Model 3 Modified. All data as above, except for the substitution of N-37 or P 37 anti-tank cannons for the VJa weapons; and the addition in 1943 of PTAB 2,5-1,5 hollow-charge anti-tank bombs of 2·5 kg. (5·5 lb.) weight, a full load comprising 200 of these weapons.

Il-2T. Soviet Naval Aviation model differing only in that it had racks below the fuselage centre section for

A group of Il-2m3s and La-5s in Czechoslovakia, 1944; in the foreground, an Li-2, licence-built version of the C-47. (Photo: courtesy Skrzydlata Polska)

one 533-mm. torpedo of a class designed for launching at extremely low altitudes.

Il-2U. Two-seat trainer conversion produced initially in the Naval Aviation workshops under the leadership of Engineer-Colonel Sidorov. Armament reduced to two VJa cannon and two RS 82 or 600 kg. (1,321 lb.) bomb load.

SHTURMOVIKI IN SERVICE

There were three main types of approach used by Il-2 units in combat. In open country and against targets such as vehicles, emplacements and attacking infantry the aircraft would make its attack run at between fifteen and thirty feet above the ground releasing its weapons and firing fixed armament horizontally. Pin-point targets such as individual buildings in a town or pill-boxes would be bombed and strafed from the conventional dive-bombing angle, which was extremely steep in the case of the Il-2. The third and best-known tactic was the so-called Circle of Death. The *Shturmoviki* would cross the front-line to one side of the target area, then circle and attack from the rear in a shallow dive, line astern. After recovery each aircraft would repeat the circle and attack again, and repeatedly, until all ammunition was expended. The beauty of this method was that for some fifteen to thirty minutes the enemy had at least one aircraft overhead and were under fire for the whole period. The effectiveness of the Circle of Death was demonstrated at Kursk; massed use of the Il-2 caused the German 9th *Panzer* Div. to lose seventy tanks in twenty minutes, on the 7th July 1943. Two hours of continuous attack cost the 3rd *Panzer* Div. 270 tanks and nearly 2,000 casualties; four hours saw the virtual extinction of the 17th *Panzer* Div. as an effective unit, with 240 vehicles destroyed out of a strength of approximately 300.

A high level of combat readiness was maintained by V-VS ground-attack units; in two years the 9th Mixed Air Corps, led by General Z. Tolstikov, made over 8,300 combat sorties. In a single day's fighting round Moldava an Assault Division carried out over 500 sorties. In his four years of combat a typical pilot, C. Briuhanov, carried out 140 combat missions, destroyed forty tanks, three self-propelled guns, one train, 152 transport vehicles, twenty mortar emplacements, and thirty-four anti-aircraft nests. Briuhanov was killed in May 1945, within sight of victory. Many *Shturmovik* pilots were Heroes of the Soviet Union; Double Gold Stars were worn by T. Biegieldinov, Mylnikov, Aleksienko, and Musa Gardieyev. Single Stars were awarded to an even larger number, among them Captain I. Pavlov of the 6th Special Assault

Briefing before a flight beside a Polish Air Force Il-2m3 in 1947.

Regiment, Captain Diakonov and Captain Yeldyshev of the 9th Mixed Air Corps, Guards Colonel Bielousov and Guards Major Chochlatshov of Maj.-General Tokariov's 6th Assault Corps. Senior Lieutenant Nikitin, Major Pavlenko and Captain Nikolayev of General Kamanin's 5th Assault Corps also earned this decoration, as did Grigorij Sivkov of the Hungarian V-VS Group and Major Kitayev of the 3rd Squadron, 3rd Polish Assault Regiment.

As far as is known, no entirely female-manned unit of Il-2s operated. However, the aircraft often carried mixed crews. Probably the most famous woman Il-2 pilot was Senior Lt. Anna Yegorova, who was Navigation Leader of her regiment. After 260 missions, and two awards of the Red Ensign order, Yegorova was shot down and captured during a strafing mission in Poland, her gunner E. Nasarkina being killed. She was liberated from Küstrin camp after the war, desperately ill from the brutal treatment she had received, but alive. She had in the meantime been awarded the Gold Star posthumously.

It is hard to pick examples from the fund of anecdotes connected with the "Flying Infantryman's"

Loose formation of Il-2m3s over the ruined outskirts of Berlin in May 1945. The apparent distortion of the outline of the vertical tail surfaces is caused by the unit marking code, involving the painting of the leading edge white.

Hero of the Soviet Union Lt. I. Pavlov, of the 6th Special Assault Regiment, photographed with his aircraft on the Baltic Coast in 1945. Inscription reads "To our fellow citizen, Hero of the Soviet Union Lieutenant I. Pavlov, from the workers of Kustanai". Kustanai was Pavlov's home town. Note also the unusual style of the fuselage star.

service; but the following may be taken as representative. Aircraft of the 9th Mixed Air Corps used steel grappling-hooks on long cables to tear up German field telephone lines in Rumania immediately before a Russian attack; predictably, the Germans began to use large numbers of liaison vehicles which were massacred by waiting Il-2s.

The surrender ultimatum was dropped to the German Army Group South Ukraine from an Il-2. It was accepted.

Il-2s were often used for personal transport under more or less pressing combat conditions; one man could be accommodated lying in the rear of the gunner's compartment, and the crews of crash-landed aircraft were on many occasions picked up and taken safely home in the undercarriage fairings, strapped to the extended undercarriage legs.

In Korea in 1945 an Ilyushin pilot, Lt. Yanko, was killed when he deliberately rammed the control point of a Japanese-held harbour installation in his damaged aircraft. Senior Lt. Koratevitch and Lt. Bykov were posthumously awarded the Gold Star for their sacrifice and courage in ramming a German escort vessel in the Baltic on 19th November 1943.

Rear gunner of Il-2m3 manning the super-heavy 12·7 mm. BS machine gun.

Lt. V. Knishnik saved a hard-pressed comrade when during a combat with Bf 109s in 1944 he rammed the fin and cockpit of one of the enemy fighters with his port wing-tip. The Bf 109 crashed.

In 1942 Hero of the Soviet Union S. Kuzniecov was returning from a recce mission near Kalinin when his flight was attacked by Messerschmitts and his Il-2 shot down. When one German fighter landed on a level strip of ground nearby to collect souvenirs of his "kill" and walked over to the crashed Ilyushin, Kuzniecov left his hiding place, sprinted to the Messerschmitt, took off and returned to his base after near-death at the hands of Russian fighters. His luck ran out in 1944 over Poland, when anti-aircraft fire

Il-2m3 control column and firing buttons.
(Photo: courtesy Skrzydlata Polska)

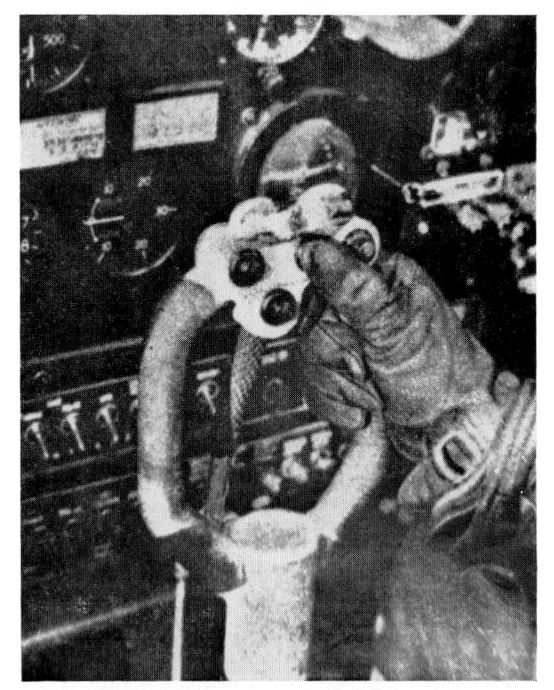

Above: *Chocks away! An Ilyushin with colourful decoration on the undercarriage fairings.* (Photo: Imperial War Museum)

Below: Shturmovik *photographed at Prostejov in Czechoslovakia in 1945.* (Photo: Zdenek Titz)

Below: *Characteristically, this crashed Il-2 has broken in two behind the cockpit; the fuselage centre-section remains relatively undamaged despite severe punishment to the other sections of the aircraft.* (Photo: H. J. Nowarra)

Lutfwaffe *officers and N.C.O.s examine a wrecked Il-2; they are apparently flak-artillery personnel.* (Photos: Der Adler)

blinded him. He succeeded in doing a wheels-up landing despite his wounds; but he never saw again.

Many Il-2s were presentation aircraft, bearing inscriptions appropriate to the donators of the machine. One unusual incident occurred after a squadron commander in the 237th Assault Regiment was killed in action flying an Il-2m3. His seven-year-old daughter, Lena, sent her savings from pocket-money of about 100 Roubles (a few shillings, about one U.S. dollar) to Generalissimo Stalin with the request that the money be used to buy a new *Shturmovik* for her father's comrades to avenge him. The letter was received, and Lena was sent a message of gratitude signed by the Soviet leader; and a new Il-2m3 of her father's old unit was inscribed "From little Lena, for Papa". The cynical may regard this story as unlikely; but a photograph of the aircraft concerned appears in this *Profile*.

A final anecdote concerns what is believed to be the only occasion on which U.S. and Soviet aircraft flew together on a combat mission. On 9th May 1945 two squadrons of Il-2m3(Mod.)s, led by Major Platonov of the 951st Assault Regiment, rendezvoused with four P-38 Lightnings of the U.S.A.F. over St. Pölten in Austria and together they strafed and destroyed a German road column, with one Ilyushin unit providing top cover and beating off an attempt at interception by a section of Fw 190s.

In conclusion, the opinions of two famous men on the Il-2; Eddie Rickenbacker, American W.W.I ace, was shown a demonstration of the *Shturmovik's* abilities and recorded the view that it was the best

Ground-crew arming a Shturmovik; *note underwing rocket racks and access panels under the nose.* (Photo: Imperial War Museum)

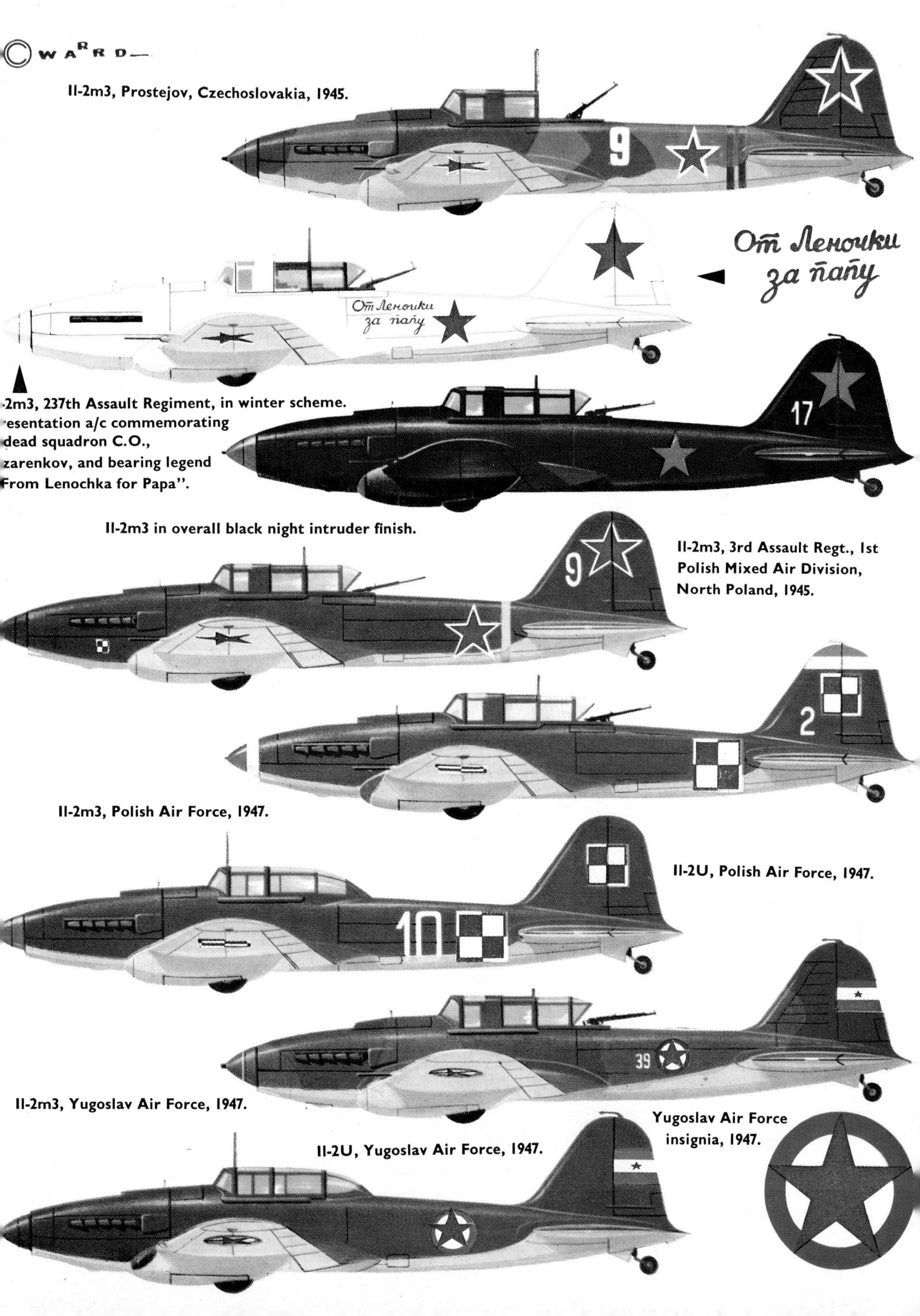

Il-2m3, Prostejov, Czechoslovakia, 1945.

·2m3, 237th Assault Regiment, in winter scheme.
·esentation a/c commemorating
dead squadron C.O.,
zarenkov, and bearing legend
From Lenochka for Papa".

Il-2m3 in overall black night intruder finish.

Il-2m3, 3rd Assault Regt., 1st Polish Mixed Air Division, North Poland, 1945.

Il-2m3, Polish Air Force, 1947.

Il-2U, Polish Air Force, 1947.

Il-2m3, Yugoslav Air Force, 1947.

Il-2U, Yugoslav Air Force, 1947.

Yugoslav Air Force insignia, 1947.

Crash-landed Il-2m3; the pilot was a holder of the Order of the Red Banner, as shown by the nose marking. (Photo: Seeley)

aircraft of its type in the world; that his country had never produced anything in the same class of machine; that as the only truly armoured aircraft in the world it should form part of the equipment of every army and every air force.

The part played by the rugged "Flying Infantryman" in Russia's victory is summed up in the words of Stalin to the manufacturers: "Our Army needs the Il-2 as much as it needs bread, as much as it needs the air it breathes."

SOVIET AIR FORCE UNITS

One of the most important features in the career of the Il-2 was its use in large numbers. Ilyushin-equipped units comprised the following sub-divisions. The largest tactical unit was the Air Assault Corps, which contained two Divisions each of three Regiments. Each Regiment had three Squadrons and each Squadron two *Zveno*s or Flights of four or five aircraft. Thus an Assault Corps had some 200 aircraft; and the basic combat formation was the *Zveno*. Each Regiment had some thirty combat aircraft and two Il-2U trainers, plus a few liaison machines, usually Po-2s.

The average bomb load of a four-machine *Zveno* was 1·6 tons, and for short-range missions up to 2·4 tons could be carried. In action, one Regiment, with six *Zveno*s each carrying out three sorties daily could deliver 43·2 tons of bombs, apart from rockets and cannon-fire.

Almost all operations described above were carried out over land, but the Soviet naval air element used the type for torpedo dropping as mentioned earlier, and the V-VS carried out many anti-shipping sorties. On one occasion Maj. Kitayev of the 3rd Polish Assault Regiment and his wingman, flying Il-2m3s, attacked and sank a 6,000-ton German transport ship; this was the exploit which won Kitayev his Gold Star.

The first foreign Ilyushin unit was the 1st Polish Mixed Air Division's 3rd Regiment. The Division was formed in 1943 with one fighter Regiment, one light bomber Regiment, and the 3rd Regiment with thirty-two Il-2m3s. They first saw action near Warsaw on 23rd September 1944, and ended the war at Metlow airfield near Berlin. The Polish air element was expanded into the 1st Polish Mixed Air Corps, comprising a Division of fighters, another of bombers, and an Assault Division of Il-2m3s, one hundred aircraft strong. This unit operated over the Oder-Nysa river line and ended the war west of Berlin on 9th May 1945. The 1st Czech Mixed Air Division's 3rd Assault Regiment also saw action during 1944–45.

One of the Il-2s lost during the great German advances of 1941. Note absence of star on vertical tail surfaces, an early marking style. In the background, an I-16.

PRINTED IN ENGLAND © Profile Publications Ltd., P.O. Box 26, 1a North Street, Leatherhead, Surrey, England.
Printed by Hills & Lacy Ltd., London and Watford, England. U.S. 2nd Class Mailing Rates applied for.

PROFILE
PUBLICATIONS

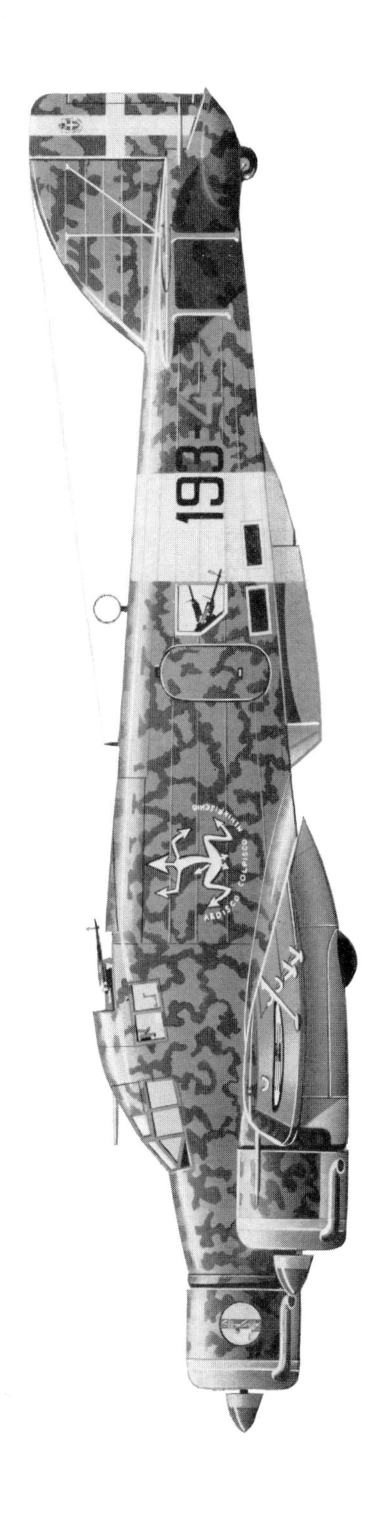

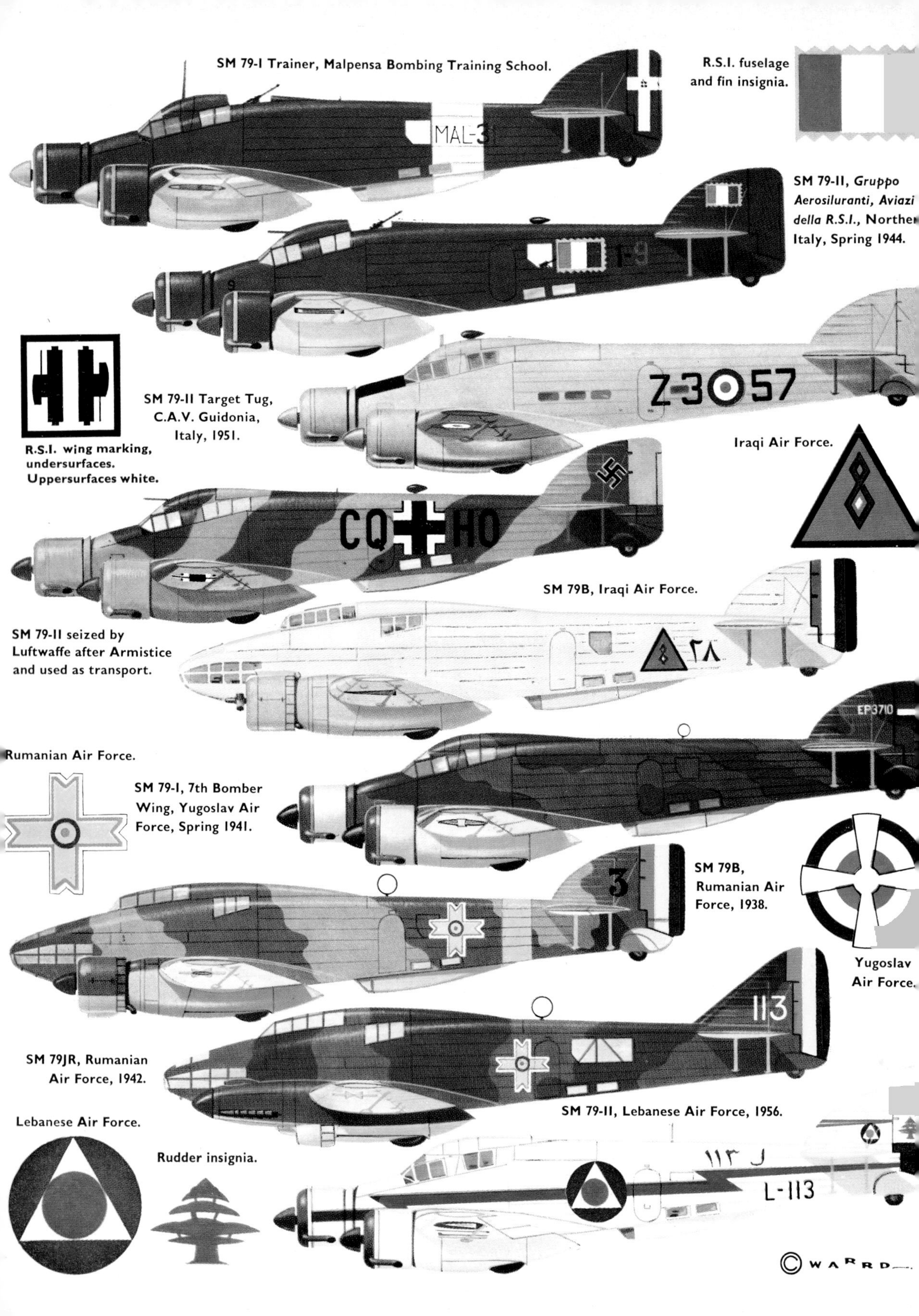

SM 79-I Trainer, Malpensa Bombing Training School.

R.S.I. fuselage and fin insignia.

SM 79-II, *Gruppo Aerosiluranti, Aviazi della R.S.I.*, Norther Italy, Spring 1944.

SM 79-II Target Tug, C.A.V. Guidonia, Italy, 1951.

R.S.I. wing marking, undersurfaces. Uppersurfaces white.

Iraqi Air Force.

SM 79B, Iraqi Air Force.

SM 79-II seized by Luftwaffe after Armistice and used as transport.

Rumanian Air Force.

SM 79-I, 7th Bomber Wing, Yugoslav Air Force, Spring 1941.

SM 79B, Rumanian Air Force, 1938.

Yugoslav Air Force.

SM 79JR, Rumanian Air Force, 1942.

SM 79-II, Lebanese Air Force, 1956.

Lebanese Air Force.

Rudder insignia.

The Savoia Marchetti S.M.79

by Giorgio Apostolo

A pair of S.M.79s of the 10° Squadriglia flying over the Libyan desert. (Photo: R. Ward Collection)

Shortly after sundown in the evening of 15th August 1940 there appeared low over the waters of Alexandria harbour two formations of S.M.79 *Sparviero* torpedo-bombers — their target British warships anchored in the port. No damage, however, resulted from this raid, the torpedoes fouling the shallow mudbanks in the harbour.

Unsuccessful though this attack proved to be, it was significant as being the first action in W.W.II by these Italian torpedo-bombers—extremely efficient aircraft and considered by many as among the most successful land-based torpedo-bombers of the war. To the Italian nation the *Sparviero* was as the Spitfire was to the British, or the Mustang to America. Its name was to become associated with many of Italy's most honoured wartime pilots, Faggioni, Marini, Buscaglia, Di Bella, Cagna, Aramu and Aichner, while the achievements of *Sparviero*-equipped squadrons are almost legendary.

Designed by Alessandro Marchetti and developed from the S.M.81, the S.M.79 began its career in 1934 as an eight-passenger commercial airliner intended for the MacRobertson England–Australia air race. However, the prototype was completed too late to participate, its first flight taking place at Cameri airport (Novara) in October 1934. The three-engine configuration was selected principally for reasons of flight safety—in those years when passengers had not yet learned to complain of vibration from a fuselage-mounted central engine!

As thus stated, the S.M.79 commenced life as a civil aircraft, the full designation being S.M.79P (P for passenger). The first prototype, *I-MAGO*, with exceptionally sleek contours and continuous panoramic windows, was powered by three 610-h.p. Piaggio P.IX *Stella* RC2 nine-cylinder radial engines driving three-blade SIAI Marchetti metal airscrews until it received its Certificate of Airworthiness on 20th July 1935. During the early trials, flown by chief test pilot Com. Bacula, the S.M.79P achieved a maximum speed of 220 m.p.h. at sea level with a normal payload of 2,515 lb., and on 14th June 1935 *I-MAGO* flew from Milan to Rome in 1 hr. 10 min., at an average speed of 254 m.p.h.

Shortly afterwards the engines were replaced by three 750-h.p. Alfa Romeo 125 RC35 (distinguished by larger, smoother cowlings), with a consequent improvement in performance. Within a year of its first flight, on 24th September 1935, with Colonel Biseo at the controls, the S.M.79P established world records for 1,000-km. and 2,000-km. closed circuits with 1,100-, 2,200- and 4,400-lb. payloads at an average speed of 242 m.p.h. (380·952 km./h.).

The limits of the airframe had not however been reached and the following year *I-MAGO* was re-engined with the new 780-h.p. Alfa Romeo 126 RC34, going on to better its own records by achieving an average speed of 260·9 m.p.h. over the 1,000-km. closed circuit with a 4,400-lb. payload.

At this point development of the fast three-engine aircraft took a decisive turn, for the high performance now obtained suggested to the military authorities that a bomber conversion could usefully be achieved. It was averred that the addition of two or three machine guns would render the aircraft virtually invulnerable.

The second prototype was therefore completed as a bomber from the outset, but did not differ materially in structure from its civil predecessor. The central engine posed some problems for forward defence and bomb aiming, and this was overcome by adding a faired ventral nacelle for the bomb-aimer and a gun for undertail defence. A fixed forward-firing gun was also added in a fairing over the pilot's cabin, and in

The S.M.79P prototype after the installation of Alfa Romeo 125 RC 35 engines. (Photo: R. Ward Collection)

A Junkers Jumo-powered S.M.79JR of the Rumanian Air Force; licence production of this variant was carried out by Industria Aeronautica Romana *at their Bucharest plant.* (Photo: R. Ward Collection)

the aft section of this dorsal fairing there was an open position for a flexible gun mounting to cater for upper rear defence. All the guns were the well-known 12·7-mm. Breda-SAFAT weapons, and the dorsal gunner's fairing gave rise to the sobriquet *il Gobbo* (the hunchback), a nickname which persisted even after adoption of the official designation *Sparviero* (Sparrow).

As development of the military aircraft continued as the S.M.79, that of the commercial design emerged as the S.M.83 in 1937.

THE S.M.79 DESCRIBED

The S.M.79 used a conventional structure for its day. The wooden three-spar wing was built as a single unit with only 1° 30′ dihedral, the seventy-two ribs being entirely plywood covered. The whole trailing edge outboard of the engines was hinged, the inboard sections being camber-changing flaps, and the outboard section both as ailerons and flaps. Automatic Handley-Page slots were incorporated in the wing leading edges to enhance low-speed lateral stability.

Ten fuel tanks, together containing 5,622 lb. of fuel, were positioned between the wing spars and two further auxiliary tanks could be installed in the rear of the engine nacelles. All the tanks were interconnected with a central system to transfer fuel between tanks, together with a standby manual pump and jettison system. The oil system consisted of three circuits, each engine being provided with its own hydraulic reservoir.

The spacious fuselage was a welded steel-tube structure; the forward section was duralumin and plywood covered, and the rear fuselage skinned with ply and fabric. Two large emergency exit panels were located in the top of the forward fuselage.

A fireproof bulkhead was located between the fuselage engine and the flight deck which accommodated pilot and co-pilot side-by-side with dual controls, 9·5-mm. armour back plates were provided for these two crew members.

Aft of the pilots, in a separate compartment, were positioned the radio operator (with R.A.30 transmitter, A.R.5 receiver and P.63N radio-compass) and flight engineer with engine instrument panel, fuel system and emergency controls.

The bomb bay was located in the fuselage centre section, aft of which was the bomb-aimer's gondola. This crew member was provided with duplicated rudder controls, basic flight instruments, Jozza bombsight, bomb releases and automatic camera. For photographic missions the equipment also included a Robot camera and a second planimetric camera.

Bomb-load of the S.M.79 amounted to a total of 1,000 kg. (2,200 lb.), comprising two 1,100-lb. bombs. Alternative overloads might, however, consist of five 550-lb. or twelve 220-lb. bombs, all carried vertically due to the confined space within the bomb bay.

Armament was four machine guns: the forward-firing Breda-SAFAT 12·7-mm. gun with 350 rounds was operated by the pilot. A similar gun on a flexible mounting was located under a sliding panel at the rear of the dorsal fairing with 500 rounds, and a third Breda on a flexible mounting in the rear of the ventral gondola for tail defence. Production aircraft also carried a 7·7-mm. Lewis gun on a sliding mount in the rear fuselage for beam defence on either side.

The vertical and horizontal tail surfaces were steel tube structures with fabric covering, the rudder and elevators being aerodynamically and statically balanced.

The engines in the initial production version for the

Left: *One of the five S.M.79C racing machines, which achieved great success in the 1937 Istres–Damascus–Paris race. In the background, the fuselage of the first prototype is just visible under the centre cowling of the S.M.79C.* Right: *An S.M.79B in civil markings.* (Photos: R. Ward Collection)

One of four S.M.79Bs acquired for the Iraqi Air Force in 1938; powered by Fiat A.80 engines, these machines were eventually destroyed during the anti-British rising in 1941. (Photo: R. Ward Collection)

An unusual modification of the S.M.79B, featuring twin fin and rudder layout. (Photo: R. Ward Collection)

Regia Aeronautica were three Alfa Romeo 126 RC34 nine-cylinder air-cooled radial engines giving 780 h.p. for take-off and rated at 750 h.p. at 11,150 feet. The wing-mounted engines incorporated drives to the two Marelli GR-800 generators which provided power for the electrical system which also included two batteries.

The main undercarriage retracted into the wing engine nacelles, these N.A.C.A. nacelles being fabricated in three sections of which the forward section constituted the outer surface of the engine exhaust manifold.

Performance of the initial production S.M.79s included a maximum speed of 267 m.p.h. at 13,100 feet, and 224 m.p.h. at sea level. Cruising speed was 228 m.p.h. at 10,000 feet and 233 m.p.h. at 19,700 feet. On the climb, 3,300 feet was reached in 3 min. 28 sec., and 16,400 feet in 19 min. 45 sec. Service ceiling was 21,320 feet. With a 2,755 lb. overload of bombs and cruising at 211 m.p.h. at 16,400 feet, the S.M.79 had a range of 1,180 statute miles, or 2,050 statute miles without bomb load.

COMMERCIAL EXPLOITS

Apart from the subsequent development of the civil S.M.83, considerable effort was spent on commercial development of the S.M.79 as well.

Two principal commercial variants were evolved, both intended for prestige participation in international flights, the S.M.79C (C for *corsa* or race) and the S.M.79T (T for *Transatlantico*), both without military equipment and ventral gondola. Sixteen such special aircraft were prepared in 1937, the standard Alfa 126 engines being replaced by 1,000-h.p. Piaggio P.XI RC40 fourteen-cylinder radials. Eleven were S.M.79Ts, fitted with increased tankage for transatlantic flights, and the remaining five (S.M.79C) were modified to participate in international air races.

These special variants amassed a fine record of outstanding flights, the best results being the first three positions achieved in the 1937 Istres–Damascus–Paris.

One of the Yugoslavian Air Force S.M.79Is, probably photographed after its transfer to the Croatian Air Force in 1941. (Photo: R. Ward Collection)

A machine of the 192° Squadriglia *in flight; note mass-balance horns and tail bracing.* (Photo: A.S.C.)

Originally this race, organised by France, had been intended to include French, American, British and Italian aircraft flying from Paris to New York, but when it was apparent that the American entries would not be ready in time to participate, the course was changed to Istres–Damascus–Paris, a total distance of 3,863 miles with a single stop at Damascus. France started as favourites with four entries, including the Caudron Typhon—specially prepared for the race. Britain entered with a D.H.88 Comet, the pale blue *G-ACSS* "The Orphan", flown by A. E. Clouston and George Nelson. Italy dominated the field with five S.M.79Cs and three Fiat B.R.20s.

The race proved a walk-over for the S.M.79s, for while the Italian crews covered the first leg to Damascus at about 260 m.p.h., the Comet averaged 217 m.p.h. and the best French aircraft only managed 186 m.p.h. On the return flight, the first S.M.79C (flown by Cupini and Paradisi) won at an average speed of 218 m.p.h. with a total time of 17 hours 35 minutes; second place was taken by the S.M.79C flown by Maggiore Fiori and Ten. Luchini (217 m.p.h., 17 hours 57 minutes), and third by the S.M.79C flown by Col. Biseo, Ten. Col. Mori and Ten. Bruno Mussolini (213 m.p.h., 18 hours 4 minutes). The D.H.88 was fourth.

In November 1937 an S.M.79, flown by Capt. Luchini and Capt. Tivegna, established a new world record over 1,000 km., carrying 1,100-lb. payload at 249 m.p.h.

Magnificent confirmation of the S.M.79s distance-flying performance was provided early in 1938 when three aircraft of the 12th Bomber Group, "*Sorci Verdi*" (green mice) made a fast long-distance flight between Rome and Rio de Janeiro. The three aircraft were squadron machines modified to S.M.79T standard by the addition of increased fuel tankage, and were flown by Col. Attilio Biseo and Maj. Amedeo Paradisi (*I-BISE*), Maj. Nino Moscatelli and Capt. Gori-Castellani (*I-MONI*) and Lt. Bruno Mussolini and Lt. Renato Mancinelli (*I-BRUN*). Taking-off from Guidonia on 24th January 1938 and flying *via* Dakar, the leaders covered the entire 6,116 miles at an average speed of 251 m.p.h. in a total flying time of 24 hours 20 minutes. The first leg from Rome to Dakar was flown at an average speed of 266 m.p.h., suggesting a top speed of over 280 m.p.h. Major Moscatelli's aircraft suffered airscrew failure shortly after take-off at Dakar, but continued on two engines to Natal at an average speed of 192 m.p.h. and joined the other two aircraft at Rio on the following day. Bruno Mussolini's aircraft was presented as a gift to the Brazilian Government at the end of the flight.

Throughout 1937 and 1938 S.M.79s undertook numerous other record-breaking flights, gaining no less than twenty-six international records. On 8th July 1937 Biseo and Mussolini, flying a Piaggio P.XI RC40-powered aircraft, established a new record at 262 m.p.h. on the Rome/Fiumicino–Livorno–Orbetello 1,000 km. closed circuit with 1,100-, 2,200- and 4,400-lb. payloads; this performance was then bettered by Bacula and De Ambrosis at 268 m.p.h. and then 273 m.p.h.

Meanwhile Luchini and Tirregna set up a new 1,000 km. record with 5,000-lb. payload at a speed of 249 m.p.h., and another crew, Tisei and Rondi, flew the same distance with a 10,000-lb. payload at 198 m.p.h. Then, covering a 2,000-km. course, Bacula and

A formation of 52° Squadriglia *S.M.79s display pre-war* Regia Aeronautica *camouflage and markings.* (Photo: Col. Cesar Milani)

Aviacion del Tercio *S.M.79 over the Spanish coast. This machine displays one of the variations of the "chicken" emblem employed by one of the Italian Legion units.*
(Photo: R. Ward Collection)

De Ambrosis achieved 261 m.p.h. with 2,200- and 4,400-lb. payloads.

Most of these records again fell to S.M.79 pilots in 1938 when Tondi averaged 286·4 m.p.h. over 1,000 km. with 1,100- and 2,200-lb. payloads, and Bacula and De Ambrosis managed 273·4 m.p.h. with a 2,200-lb. payload over 2,000 km. Finally Colonel Tondi achieved 287 m.p.h. on the 500 km. and 1,000 km. courses, and 293 m.p.h. with 4,400-lb. payload over 1,000 km.

The second prototype S.M.79, built from the outset as a bomber, seen here in its military livery. (Photo: via the author)

OPERATIONAL DEBUT OVER SPAIN

While these successful efforts by Italy to gain international prestige in the air were progressing, experience of a more tortuous nature was being gained in the skies over Spain. From the outbreak of the Civil War in July 1936 until the end of hostilities in March 1939, Italy supplied more than 730 aircraft to the *Aviacion del Tercio*, including three bomber types: the S.M.81, the S.M.79 and Fiat B.R.20s.

After the initial supply of S.M.81s at the outbreak of war in 1936, more modern equipment followed in 1937 and provided the *Regia Aeronautica* with operational experience with its latest equipment, including the S.M.79-I. The new bomber had entered service with 8° and 111mo *Stormi Bombardamento Veloce* (fast bomber groups) and these units were sent to Spain where they participated in extensive operations over the Republican lines and contributed materially to the neutralising of the Government fleet in port. Operating as four groups in Spain as the 27th and 28th, named *Falchi delle Baleari* (Hawks of Baleares), and the 29th and 30th *Sparvieri* (Sparrows), the S.M.79-Is with two groups of S.M.81s carried out 5,318 bombing sorties during which they delivered 11,850 tons of bombs and scored 224 hits on Government ships. In particular the *Falchi* (joined for a short time by the 12th *Sorci Verdi* Group), operating from the Balearic Islands, carried out raids against Government shipping refuelling in the Mediterranean ports, often being called upon to make three sorties per day.

While the older S.M.81 performed much of the tactical and ground-support commitment, usually with fighter escort or cover, the S.M.79-I really achieved its reputation for long-range strategic raids and patrols without fighter escort.

The first S.M.79s purchased (at a cost of two million pesetas each) by the Nationalists arrived at the beginning of April 1937 at San Juan (Palma, Mallorca) and commenced operations forthwith in the Brunete area under the initial command of Major Aramu, and later under Colonel Cupini. Thence they transferred to Tallada, Seville, and to Soria to take part in operations on the Bilbao front. By the end of the year all four Groups were operational with twenty-five aircraft each, having lost only four aircraft.

During the Civil War several significant operations were undertaken by *Sparvieros*. Following doubts that the S.M.79 was suitable for night operations, the Chief of Staff, Generale Valle, carried out a night raid over Barcelona on 1st January 1938, flying 124 miles to deliver 1,763 lb. of bombs without difficulty to

(continued on page 10)

Compare the camouflage of this Aviacion del Tercio *machine with that displayed in the photograph at the head of this page. This aircraft served with the 28°* Gruppo *"Hawks of the Balearics", a unit which saw considerable service over Spain's eastern seaboard and contributed materially to the neutralisation of the Republican fleet.* (Photo: Dolling via Seeley)

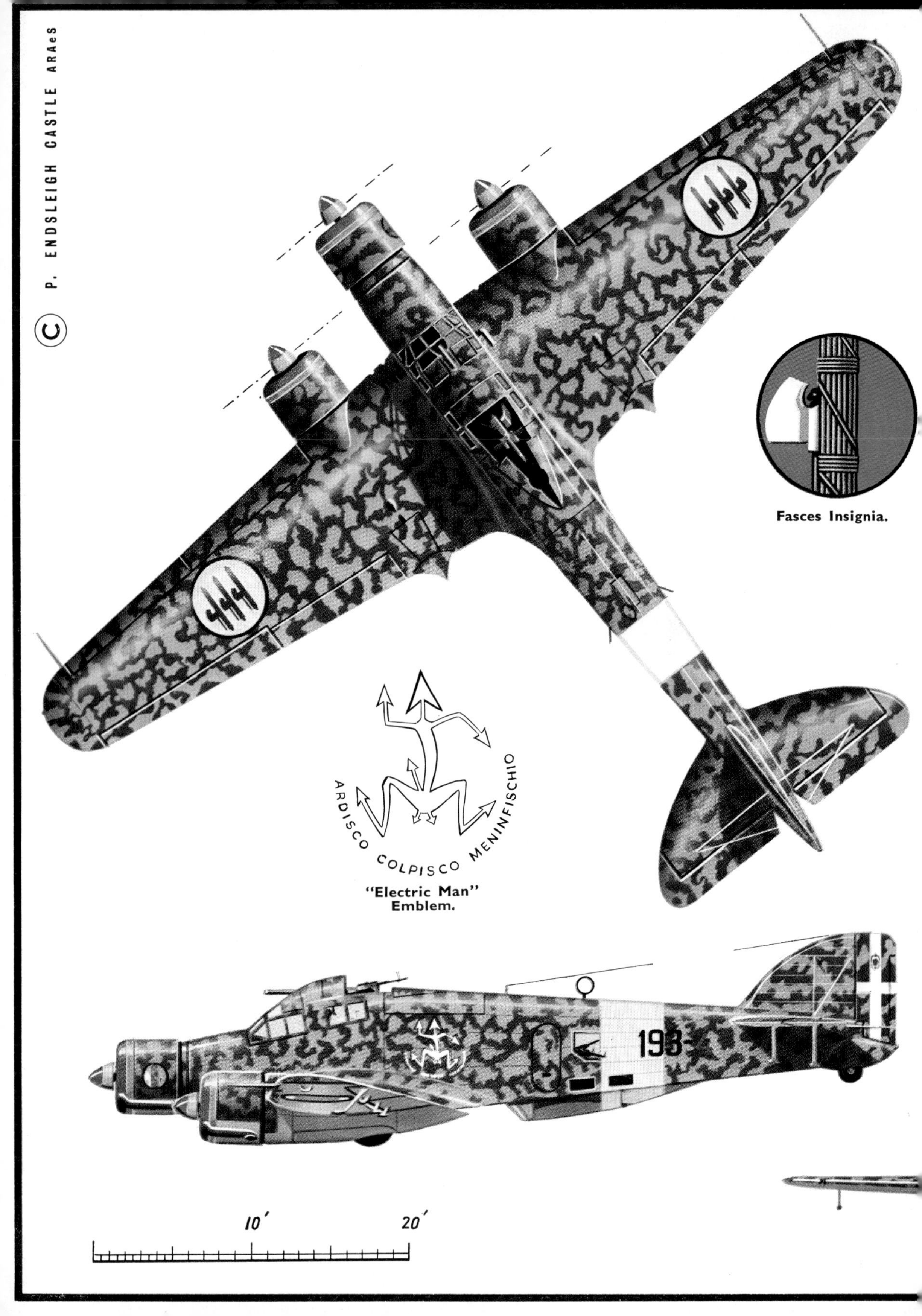

Fasces Insignia.

"Electric Man" Emblem.

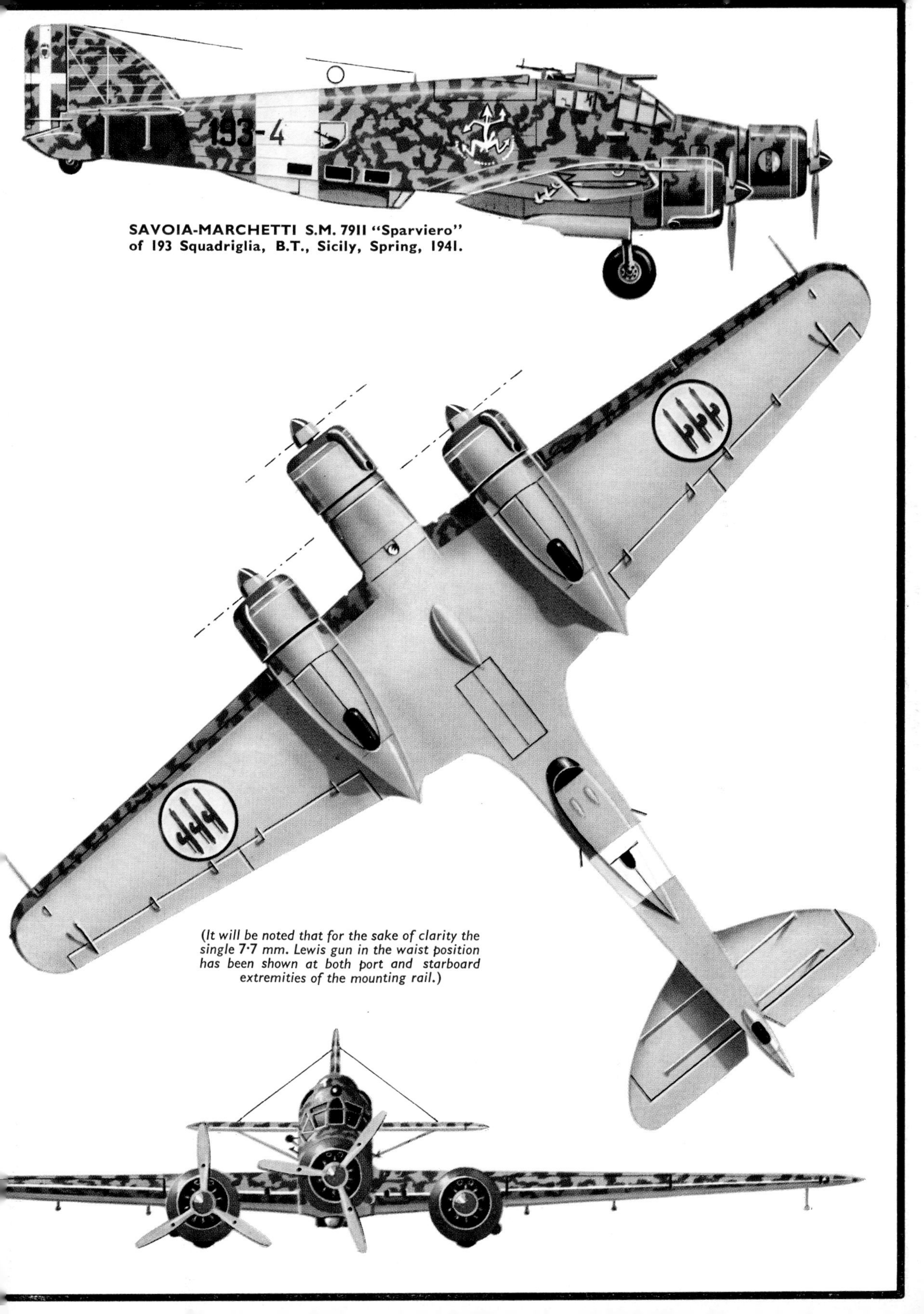

SAVOIA-MARCHETTI S.M. 79II "Sparviero" of 193 Squadriglia, B.T., Sicily, Spring, 1941.

(It will be noted that for the sake of clarity the single 7·7 mm. Lewis gun in the waist position has been shown at both port and starboard extremities of the mounting rail.)

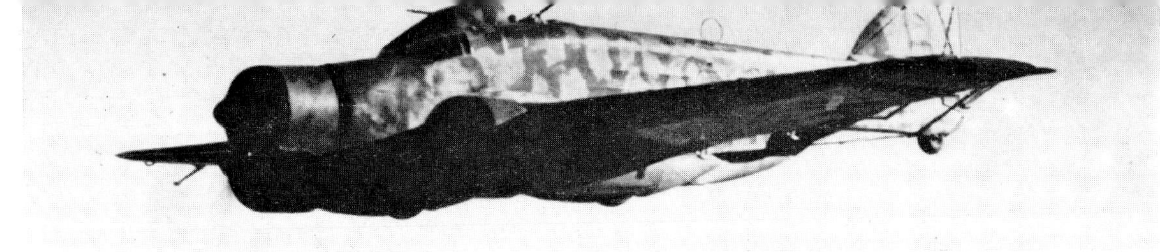

Another view of an Italian Legion Sparviero *over Spain. The Republican air arm was inferior in numbers and equipment to the "volunteer" units of the Nationalist force, and German and Italian bombers operated with little fear of successful interception.* (Photo: Col. Cesar Milani)

dispel such doubts. Exactly one month later a single S.M.79 destroyed the important power station at Seira. On the other hand, a more humane operation was the air supply of 66,000 lb. of bread delivered by S.M.79s to the starving populations of Madrid and Barcelona at the beginning of October 1938.

After the end of hostilities in March 1939, the Spanish Government took over eighty S.M.79s, including those that had been flown by the *Aviación Legionaria*, and these aircraft formed the bulk of the modern Spanish Air Force for many years to come, some aircraft surviving until relatively recent times.

TWO ENGINES

As already remarked, the choice of the three-engine configuration was the outcome of commercial safety considerations, sentiments agreed by the *Regia Aeronautica* who foresaw an increased likelihood of safe return to base from bombing missions with one engine shot up. At the speeds expected from the S.M.79, however, frontal attacks by fighters were discounted by the *Regia Aeronautica*, and the fixed forward-firing gun was considered adequate defence.

Notwithstanding these arguments, most other air-forces of the world still considered nose armament essential and almost universally accepted the conventional twin engine layout. To recognise these potential requirements, Savoia Marchetti therefore pursued the design of the twin-engine S.M.79B.

The S.M.79B differed from the standard aircraft in having an entirely redesigned nose, accommodating the bomb aimer and a single movable 12·7-mm. Breda-SAFAT machine gun. By lengthening the "hunch-back", the single pilot now sat higher and farther forward.

The prototype S.M.79B, originally powered by two 1,030-h.p. FIAT A.80 RC41 18-cylinder two-row radial engines, first appeared in 1936 and attained a speed of 255 m.p.h. at 15,000 feet and 225 m.p.h. at sea level. It was extensively demonstrated to foreign air forces, including those of Argentina, Belgium, Brazil, China, Czechoslovakia, Finland, Iraq, Rumania, Russia, Spain, Turkey and Yugoslavia. It was during participation in a competition held in Argentina to decide on future medium bomber equipment for that country that the S.M.79B's manœuvrability was questioned. The Italian demonstration pilot promptly took off, executed four loops and won the contest! Strategic considerations, however, superseded the result and doubts that spares would be forthcoming in the event of a European war led to an order for thirty-five Martin 139-W bombers being placed.

The same year, Iraq ordered four S.M.79Bs to be delivered in 1938, these aircraft being powered by 1,000-h.p. FIAT A.80 engines. All were finally destroyed during the anti-British insurgency in Iraq

Two Sparvieri *seen from below display their distinctive tail contours and the black-on-white underwing* fasces *marking.* (Photo: R. Ward Collection)

Sparvieri *of the 254°* Squadriglia, *with 78°* Squadriglia *C.T. Fiat C.R.42s in close escort formation, possibly photographed during operations over French airfields in Tunisia in mid-June 1940.* (Photo: via the author)

Rare photograph of an S.M.79 taken over by the Luftwaffe. *Although the aircraft was undoubtedly used for second-line duties, it will be observed that the armament is still mounted.*
(Photo: via R. C. Seeley)

during 1941. Brazil took delivery of three S.M. 79Bs powered by 930-h.p. Alfa Romeo 128 RC18 radial engines.

Perhaps the most widespread use of the S.M.79B was with the Rumanian Air Force. Twenty-four aircraft were purchased in 1938 powered by 1,000-h.p. Gnôme–Rhône K.14 Mistral-Major engines, but so successful did these prove that, with the expansion of that air force in hand, a further twenty-four aircraft were acquired. This latter batch was powered by 1,220-h.p. Junkers Jumo 211Da 12-cylinder liquid-cooled in-line engines. At the same time a licence to build this version, designated S.M.79-JR, was acquired for the *Industria Aeronautica Romana* works at Bucharest. Performance of the JR-version included a maximum speed of 276 m.p.h. at 16,400 feet (compared with 255 m.p.h. at 15,100 feet on the Fiat A.80-powered version). Climb to 10,000 feet occupied 8 min. 40 sec., and the service ceiling was 24,260 feet. Weight empty was 15,860 lb., loaded 23,790 lb. These aircraft were extensively flown on operations by Rumanian forces on the Russian front, while the earlier S.M.79Bs were relegated to transport duties.

While on the subject of exported S.M.79s, it should be recorded here that Yugoslavia preferred the three-engined design, acquiring forty-five standard S.M.79-I tri-motor bombers. These equipped the 7th Bombing Wing and the 81st Independent Bombing Group but most were destroyed in the 1941 hostilities with Germany and Italy, the few survivors being transferred to the Croatian Air Force.

WORLD WAR II

Having demonstrated considerable success with the *Aviación Legionaria*, the *Sparviero* assumed first-line status with the *Regia Aeronautica* bomber squadrons. The CRDA Cant Z.1007 was as yet still under development and the Fiat B.R.20 was approaching obsolescence. Furthermore trials had been commenced at Gorizia in 1937 to demonstrate the S.M.79's ability to launch torpedoes. A special rack, offset from the aircraft centreline, was fitted to carry a 450-mm. naval torpedo with 375-lb. warhead—aimed by a newly developed launching sight. It is worth mentioning here that Italy led the world in air-launched torpedo fusing, so much so that the *Luftwaffe* later came to adopt Italian torpedoes. When ultimately German torpedo-bomber units (equipped with He 111s) underwent attack training at the school established at Grosseto, many of the techniques used had been evolved by the *Aerosiluranti*.

Following very successful trials with the single torpedo installation, it was decided in March 1938 to

Experimental installation of two torpedoes; trials at Gorizia in the spring of 1938 proved that the dual installation caused a marked deterioration in the Sparviero's *performance.*
(Photo: R. Ward Collection)

institute a new programme with dual torpedo installation at Gorizia, the trials commencing in August that year. Due to the marked depreciation in performance with two torpedoes, it was decided to fit more powerful engines first applying the 860-h.p. Alfa Romeo 128 RC18 (this became the prototype of the S.M.84 bomber and was experimentally fitted with twin fins and rudders), and then the 1,000-h.p. Piaggio P.XI RC40. The latter formed the basis of the production S.M.79-II which entered series manufacture in October 1939, built under licence by Aeronautica Macchi and Officine Meccaniche Reggiane and with a few components supplied by Aeronautica Umbra and Aeronautica Sannita. Most aircraft were powered by the Piaggio engines but a few had 1,350-h.p. Alfa Romeo 135 RC32 18-cylinder engines and, later, 1,000-h.p. Fiat A.80 RC41 radials.

Two types of torpedo were employed, one with a 375-lb. warhead, produced by Silurificio Whitehead of Fiume, and the other a 352-lb. head by Silurificio Italiano of Naples. Both were of 450-mm. calibre and were normally launched from a height of about 320 feet at 185 m.p.h. Later, in December 1941, a 440-lb. warhead was adopted as standard and came to be supplied to the *Luftwaffe* as well.

By 1939 eleven *Stormi*, each comprising four *Squadriglie*, deployed a total of 389 aircraft, based in Italy, Albania and the Aegean Islands. When Italy entered the war on 10th June 1940 the number of *Stormi* had increased to fourteen, established with 594 S.M.79s, of which 403 were combat ready. Thus the

Sparviero equipped almost two-thirds of the *Regia Aeronautica* which fielded a first-line strength of 975 aircraft. On that 10th June the *Sparviero* units were deployed as follows:

8° *Stormo* B.T.	Villacidro, Sardinia.
9° *Stormo*	Viterbo, Italy.
10° *Stormo*	Benina, Libya.
11° *Stormo*	Comiso, Sicily.
12° *Stormo*	Ciampino and Orvieto, Italy.
14° *Stormo*	El Adem, Libya.
15° *Stormo*	Castel Benito, Libya.
30° *Stormo*	Sciacca, Sicily.
32° *Stormo*	Decimomannu, Sardinia.
33° *Stormo*	Bir el Bhera, Libya.
34° *Stormo*	Catania, Sicily.
36° *Stormo*	Castelvetrano, Sicily.
41° *Stormo*	Gela, Sicily.
46° *Stormo*	Pisa, Italy.

First action by S.M.79 bombers in W.W.II—during the short-lived campaign against France—was an attack by nine S.M.79s of the 9° *Stormo* and ten of the 46° on 13th–14th June 1940 against French ships off the Riviera coast. *Sparvieri* of the 3rd Division of *III Squadra* in central Italy operated against France and Corsica, those of *Aeronautica della Sardegna* over Corsica, Algeria and Tunisia, and those of *II Squadra* (i.e. 3rd Division, 11°, 34° and 41° *Stormi*, and 11th Brigade, 30° and 36° *Stormi*), over Algeria and Tunisia. The *Sparvieri* of *Aeronautica della Libia*—amounting to a total of 103 aircraft—were active only over Tunisia, and involved aircraft of 10° and 33° *Stormi* and some from 15° *Stormo*.

When war broke out against Greece on 28th October 1940, Albanian-based S.M.79s—104° and 105° *Gruppi* with two squadrons each—were joined by S.M.79s of 92° *Gruppo* and 281° *Squadriglia* of the *Aerosiluranti* based on the Aegean Islands. Throughout this campaign, which lasted until 22nd April 1941, these Italian bomber groups were engaged in particularly intense operations with precious little respite.

Fought simultaneously with the campaign in Greece, operations against Yugoslavia (6th April until 17th April) involved a total of thirty S.M.79s from the Albanian groups, while the Yugoslavs themselves operated an initial total of forty-two similar machines.

Although the airborne invasion of Crete (20th–31st May 1941) was undertaken principally by *Luftwaffe* units, S.M.79s of the Aegean *Aerosiluranti* joined in with attacks against Allied shipping. These comprised the 92° *Gruppo*, which had been based at Gadurrà since before the outbreak of war, and the 281° *Squadriglia*, which had arrived at Rodi from Italy on 20th March 1941.

An S.M.79II in its classic rôle—low-level torpedo attack. The Italian Aerosiluranti *or torpedo-bombing units led the world in equipment and technique.* (Photo: R. Ward Collection)

In the early weeks of the North African campaign four *Stormi*, with a total of 125 aircraft, were deployed in Libya; these included the 15° *Stormo* with thirty-five *Sparvieri* and eight S.M.81s at Castel Benito, and 33° *Stormo* at Bir el Bhera with thirty-one *Sparvieri*. Facing Egypt were the 10° *Stormo* with thirty S.M.79s at Benina, and 14° *Stormo* with twelve S.M.79s and nine S.M.81s at El Adem. From the outset these units operated against enemy targets at Mersa Matruh, Halfaya, Sollum and Sidi Barrani. They were joined during the first Italian offensive by *Sparvieri* of the 27° *Gruppo*. Such was the rate of attrition during those early months that by the end of the second British offensive the total Italian strength in this theatre remained at only 125 aircraft.

Use of the S.M.79 in East Africa was interesting in that this aircraft probably represented the most modern aircraft in the theatre on either side. On the Italian side, the bomber strength consisted of eighty-four obsolete Caproni 133s, forty-two S.M.81s and twelve S.M.79s—opposing a sizable but utterly heterogeneous hotch-potch of Bombays, Valentias, Wellesleys, Vincents, Battles, Hart Variants and Londons. However, such was the importance attached to the S.M.79 that reinforcement of the East African front was undertaken by air direct from Italy—with a single refuelling stop at Cupra oasis in Libya. For the operations against British Somaliland in August 1940 the Italian forces were supported by eighty-five aircraft, including eleven S.M.79s of the 44° *Gruppo* based at Addis Ababa.*

Reinforcements reached the Italian forces in East Africa from time to time, so that by the time of the British offensive in January 1941 five *Squadriglie*, with a total of twenty-eight S.M.79s, were available for operations.

**Records of No. 223 (Bomber) Squadron, R.A.F., indicate that during the morning of 18th August 1940 five Wellesleys of that squadron attacked Addis Ababa, destroying or seriously damaging four S.M.79s.*

Transport version of the Sparviero *operated by the Co-Belligerent Air Force after the 1943 Armistice.* (Photo: R. Ward Collection)

The single off-set torpedo installation more usually carried by the Aerosiluranti, *seen here on an S.M.79III. Note absence of ventral gondola, lengthened airscrew hubs, extended exhaust manifolds, and the forward-firing 20-mm. cannon above the cockpit. Produced in small numbers only, the S.M. 79III was operated in the Mediterranean by Capt. Faggioni's torpedo - bombing Group.* (Photo: via the author)

MARITIME OPERATIONS AND THE MEDITERRANEAN

The *Sparviero* did not take part in the operations of the *Corpo Aero Italiano* in Northern Europe against England, and was used only on a limited scale on the Balkan fronts. It was in the Mediterranean theatre itself that the S.M.79's major rôle lay, and for three years achieved outstanding success in operations against merchant convoys, naval vessels of all sizes and the island fortress of Malta. Among the Allied destroyers sunk by *Sparvieri* were H.M.S. *Husky*, *Jaguar*, *Kujavik II*, *Legion* and *Southwall*, and considerable damage was caused to the battleship *Malaya*, and the aircraft carriers *Indomitable*, *Victorious* and *Eagle*.*

The original operations against Malta and Allied shipping in the Sicilian Channel were carried out by S.M.79s of the 30° *Stormo* and 279° *Squadriglia*, later supplemented by units of the *Luftwaffe's X Fliegerkorps*, the 10° *Stormo* with S.M.79s and the 9° *Stormo* with Cant Z.1007-IIs. At the end of 1941 *Fliegerkorps II* was also transferred to Sicily from the Russian front, by which time fourteen Allied ships had been sunk by air attack, and at least sixty others damaged.

On the North African mainland, the first torpedo-bomber group formed was the 131° *Stormo Autonomo*, established on 25th March 1942 with the 279° *Squadriglia* (which had moved from Catania to the Aegean and now to Benghazi) and 284° *Squadriglia*, which had arrived in North Africa direct from Italy and remained until disbanded in November 1942. The next unit formed, the 133° *Stormo Autonomo*, in April 1942, included the 174° *Squadriglia* (at Benghazi) and 175° at Castel Benito. During the campaign which led up to the Battle of El Alamein, the Italian air force units supporting the Axis advance operated a total of thirty-four *Sparvieri* and twenty-five Cant Z.1007s, together with several groups of Fiat CR.42s, Macchi M.C.200 and 202s. During the subsequent retreat all these units were withdrawn through Derna, Benghazi and Misurata, so that eventually only one *Squadriglia* of *Sparvieri* was left in North Africa—this a special unit, *Aviazione Sahariana*, at Hun in Central Tripolitania.

Undoubtedly the most interesting chapters in the life of the *Sparviero* were those of the great naval operations involving the British attempts to pass convoys to Malta. In the last and most famous sailing—Operation "Pedestal"—fourteen vital merchant ships sailed under a heavy naval escort which included battleships, cruisers, destroyers and the aircraft carriers *Victorious*, *Indomitable* and *Eagle*. Against this convoy, which left Gibraltar on 10th August 1942, were ranged seventy-four *Sparvieri* (sixty belonging to 32° *Stormo*, which had been moved from Gioia del Colle to Villacidro, Sardinia, and 105° from Pisa to Decimomannu, Sardinia, plus fourteen S.M.79s of the 132° which had moved from Gerbini to the island of Pantelleria). In the face of these and other heavy forces which gave the convoy no moment of respite, the British ships managed to reach Malta—albeit at a cost of nine merchantmen, a carrier, two cruisers, a destroyer and eighteen defending aircraft.

During this phase of the war the most outstanding unit was unquestionably the 132° *Gruppo*, commanded by Captain Buscaglia, with two *Squadriglie*, the 278° at Castelvetrano and 281° at Gerbini, both in Sicily. Between June and August 1942 numerous daylight missions were flown against British vessels, resulting in direct hits being scored on the carrier H.M.S. *Argus*, the battleship H.M.S. *Malaya* and several other heavy ships. With this unit also operated the 130° *Gruppo* (280° and 283° *Squadriglie*), whose pilots included such famous names as Melley, Cimicchi and Di Bella.

As the naval struggle entered its final phase in the Mediterranean in November 1942, the *Regia Aeronautica* could muster 112 *Sparvieri* serviceable out of an established strength of 163. These aircraft were deployed as follows:

Formations	*Established Aircraft*	*Serviceable Aircraft*
2 Torpedo-Bomber Groups (Sardinia)	30	18
1 Torpedo-Bomber Group (Sicily)	18	16
1 Bomber Recce. Group (Sicily)	28	16
2 Torpedo-Bomber Groups (N. Africa)	39	28

**Though earlier accounts seem to suggest that H.M.S.* Eagle *succumbed to air attacks by S.M.79s, recent data collation indicates that the ship was in fact sunk by a German submarine.*

Torpedo-armed S.M.79III of the R.S.I. Air Force, the Fascist element who continued operations against the Allies after the Armistice. Just visible under the nose of the machine in the foreground is the distinctive fuselage insignia of the R.S.I. on the second aircraft. (Photo: via the author)

Formations	*Established Aircraft*	*Serviceable Aircraft*
1 Torpedo-Bomber Group (Aegean Islands)	11	9
1 Torpedo-Bomber Group (N. Italy)	16	9
2 Bomber and Torpedo-Bomber Groups (Central Italy)	21	16

It can be seen from these figures that most emphasis was being placed upon torpedo-bombers, as the air/sea battles had confirmed that better results resulted from air-launched torpedo and dive-bombing attacks than from level bombing. Though new aircraft *were* being developed to replace the S.M.79, they were not ready before the end of the war and, in order to increase the effectiveness of the S.M.79, great efforts were made to boost the supply of improved torpedoes. Up-rating of the Alfa 128 engines was effected at the end of 1941, and a system of ethyl injection was introduced to provide 30 m.p.h. extra in speed for short bursts. As their lives lengthened, and as the number of overhauls and repairs mounted, so the S.M.79s came to be regarded as less important in the first-line strength of the *Regia Aeronautica*. Between the closing months of 1942 and mid-1943 the lack of spare parts seriously reduced the number of serviceable S.M.79s in almost all areas, a state of affairs graphically demonstrated by the Order of Battle on the eve of the Allied invasion of Sicily, 10th July 1943:

Unit	*Location*	*Established Aircraft*	*Serviceable Aircraft*
132° *Gruppo* (Torpedo-Bomber)	Gorizia	5	Nil
Raggruppamento Siluranti	Pisa and Siena	44	15
130° *Gruppo*	Littoria	9	2
205° *Squadriglia*	Milis, Sardinia	4	4
279° *Squadriglia*	Gerbini, Sicily	4	1
104° *Gruppo*	Aegean Islands	11	5

Nevertheless operations by S.M.79s continued almost up to the end of the war in Italy. When, on 8th September 1943, Italy capitulated, most of the available *Sparvieri* were concentrated in the metropolitan area, sixty-one aircraft being on the strength of the 3° *Squadra Aerea*, the thirty-six serviceable aircraft deployed on airfields at Siena, Pisa, Littoria and Capodichino. From this force, twenty-two S.M.79s—mostly from the 41°, 104°, 131° and 132° *Gruppi*—reached the Allied lines to form part of the Italian Co-Belligerent Air Force, serving as bombers, torpedo-bombers and transports. However, only four of the twenty-two were in fact combat serviceable and the 41° *Gruppo*, with 204° and 205° *Squadriglie*, was re-formed at Milis in Sardinia, and the 132° *Gruppo Autonomo*, with 246°, 253° and 281° *Squadriglie*, was re-formed at Leece, near Brindisi.

Some Italian crews and aircraft were, however, unable to join the Allies, being deployed well within the area occupied by German forces. When a new Italian air force, that of the Repubblica Sociale Italiana, was formed, a new variant of the *Sparviero* was introduced into service, and the older aircraft were modified up to the new standard.

Above: *A formation of S.M.79Is of the Italian Legion silhouetted against the evening sky over Spain.* (Photo: Col. Cesar Milani.) Below: *A* Sparviero *of the* Regia Aeronautica *running up. Note intricate detail of nose* fasces. (Photo: via the author)

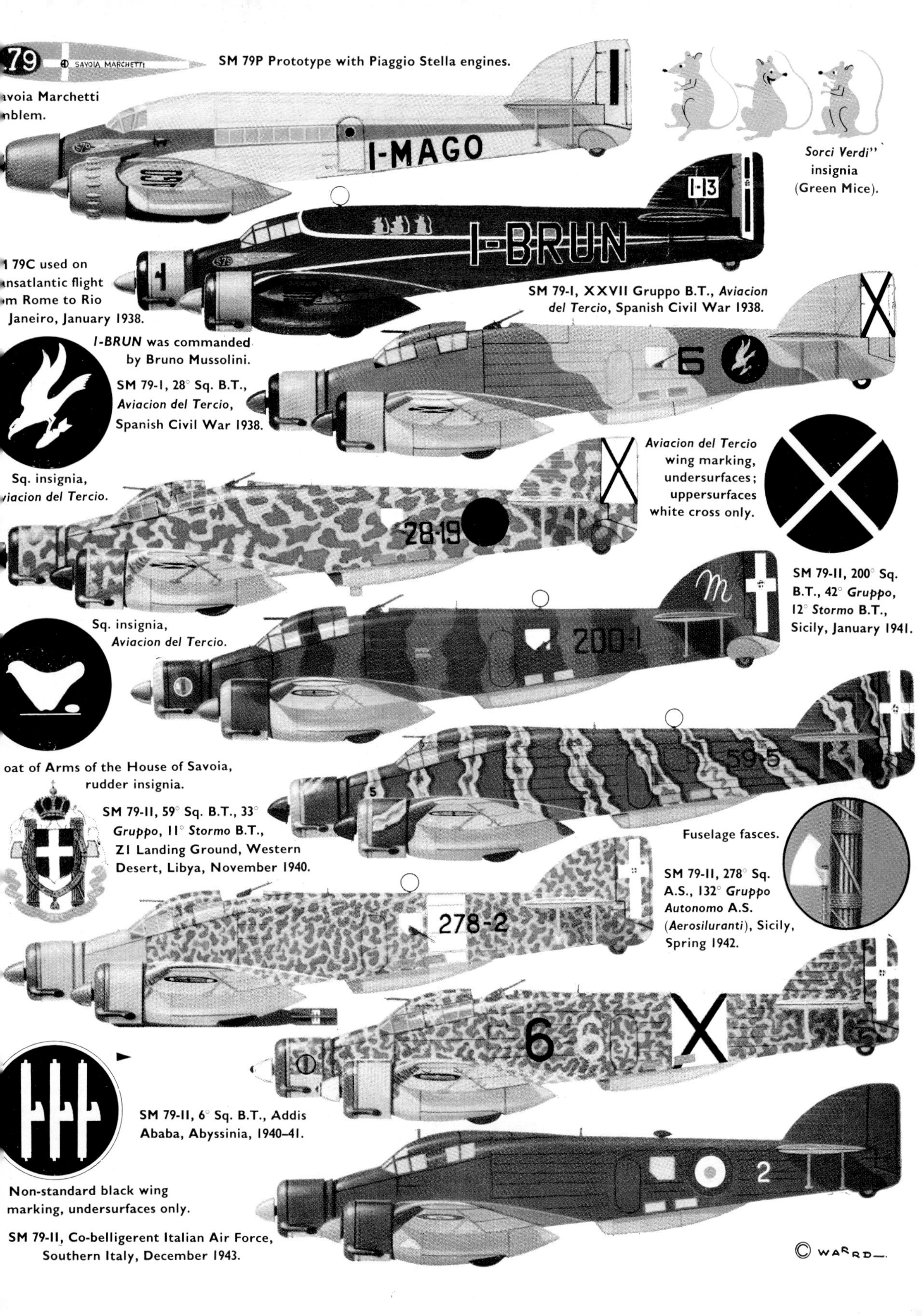

79
SAVOIA MARCHETTI
SM 79P Prototype with Piaggio Stella engines.
avoia Marchetti
nblem.
I-MAGO
Sorci Verdi"
insignia
(Green Mice).
I-13
I-BRUN
1 79C used on
nsatlantic flight
m Rome to Rio
Janeiro, January 1938.
SM 79-I, XXVII Gruppo B.T., Aviacion del Tercio, Spanish Civil War 1938.
I-BRUN was commanded by Bruno Mussolini.
SM 79-I, 28° Sq. B.T., Aviacion del Tercio, Spanish Civil War 1938.
6
Aviacion del Tercio wing marking, undersurfaces; uppersurfaces white cross only.
Sq. insignia,
viacion del Tercio.
28-19
SM 79-II, 200° Sq. B.T., 42° Gruppo, 12° Stormo B.T., Sicily, January 1941.
200-1
Sq. insignia, Aviacion del Tercio.
oat of Arms of the House of Savoia, rudder insignia.
59 5
SM 79-II, 59° Sq. B.T., 33° Gruppo, 11° Stormo B.T., Z1 Landing Ground, Western Desert, Libya, November 1940.
Fuselage fasces.
SM 79-II, 278° Sq. A.S., 132° Gruppo Autonomo A.S. (Aerosiluranti), Sicily, Spring 1942.
278-2
6 6
SM 79-II, 6° Sq. B.T., Addis Ababa, Abyssinia, 1940–41.
Non-standard black wing marking, undersurfaces only.
2
SM 79-II, Co-belligerent Italian Air Force, Southern Italy, December 1943.
© WARD

Post-war Italian Air Force S.M.79. (Photo: via R. C. Seeley)

The new version, the S.M.79-III (sometimes referred to as the S.579), was produced in relatively small numbers in northern Italy, and was in effect a generally cleaned-up modernisation of the familiar *Sparviero*. The ventral gondola was removed, improved airscrews with lengthened hub cylinders were fitted, the exhaust manifold pipes were extended, new and improved radio was installed, and the forward-firing machine gun was replaced by a 20-mm. cannon.

Equipping a *Gruppo Aerosiluranti* led by Captain Faggioni, these S.M.79-IIIs carried out widespread attacks against Allied shipping in the Mediterranean. Captain Faggioni met his death, however, in a shipping strike at Nettuno, after which the group was led by Major Marini. Perhaps this officer's most outstanding attack was the night raid on Gibraltar on 4th–5th June 1944.

The *Sparviero* had, in its time, been employed in a number of rôles. It was used for strategic reconnaissance and, towards the end of the fighting in North Africa, for close support duties; but undoubtedly one of its most bizarre tasks was that of emulating a radio-guided bomb!

After the British capital ships had turned back after escorting the "Pedestal" convoy towards Malta, they hove to off the Algerian coast and at once became the target for this singular S.M.79. Devised by Generale Ferdinando Raffaelli, this aircraft was filled with explosive and piloted off the ground by a pilot who subsequently baled out as soon as the *Sparviero* had assumed its pre-determined course. An attendant aircraft, a Cant Z.1007-II, then assumed control and guided it towards the British fleet by radio. Although a fault developed in the radio, which caused the S.M.79 to crash on the slopes of Mount Klenchela on the Algerian mainland, Generale Raffaelli was encouraged to develop a cheap, expendable guided flying bomb, a project that resulted in the manufacture of the A.R., a simple wooden monoplane powered by a 1,000-h.p. Fiat A.80 radial, built by Aeronautica Ambrosini and flight-tested in June 1943.

After the end of the war in Europe, all the remaining S.M.79s were transferred to the transport rôle, being taken on by the *Corrieri Aerei Militari*, pending the resumption of regular commercial services. Thereafter a few survivors were employed for communications, training and target drone duties until 1952. Three S.M.79s were sold to the Lebanon in 1950 and, registered *L-111*, *L-112* and *L-113*, were still in regular use by the Lebanese Air Force as transports in 1959.

A total of 1,330 *Sparvieri* was built between 1934 and 1944, perhaps small by comparison with Allied production figures, yet these aircraft nevertheless represented almost twenty per cent of the total Italian production effort of this period. It won unstinted praise from its crews for its excellent handling qualities and—perhaps of more significance—achieved undenied respect from its adversaries.

SPECIFICATION

(Data from Technical Manual C.A.289 of the Ministero dell 'Aeronautica, issued 1940, applicable to production series 15 aircraft in the serial blocks MM22546–MM22565, and MM23838–MM23877.)

Powerplant: Three Alfa Romeo 126 RC 34, double row, nine-cylinder engines rated at 750 h.p. at 2,300 r.p.m. at 11,000 ft. Three-blade constant speed Savoia Marchetti propellers.

Dimensions: Wing span 69 ft. 6 in.; length 53 ft. $1\frac{3}{4}$ in.; height 13 ft. $5\frac{1}{2}$ in.; wing area 656·6 sq. ft.

Weights: Empty, 15,310 lb.; loaded, 23,643 lb.; normal useful load, 8,333 lb. Wing loading, 4·29 lb./sq. ft.; power loading, 9·85 kg./h.p.; specific power, 36·5.

Performance:

Max. speed at:	Sea level =	223 m.p.h.	at 2,060 r.p.m.
	3,280 ft. =	227 m.p.h.	at 2,100 r.p.m.
	6,560 ft. =	238 m.p.h.	at 2,170 r.p.m.
	9,840 ft. =	251 m.p.h.	at 2,260 r.p.m.
	13,120 ft. =	267 m.p.h.	at 2,395 r.p.m.
	16,400 ft. =	261 m.p.h.	at 2,320 r.p.m.
	19,680 ft. =	252 m.p.h.	at 2,240 r.p.m.
Cruising speed at:	9,840 ft. =	227 m.p.h.	at 2,070 r.p.m.
	13,120 ft. =	230 m.p.h.	at 2,070 r.p.m.
	16,400 ft. =	231 m.p.h.	at 2,070 r.p.m.
	19,680 ft. =	232 m.p.h	at 2,070 r.p.m.
Climb to:	3,280 ft. =	3 min. 8 sec.	
	6,560 ft. =	5 min. 58 sec.	
	9,840 ft. =	9 min. 15 sec.	
	13,120 ft. =	13 min. 15 sec.	
	16,400 ft. =	19 min. 45 sec.	
	18,045 ft. =	24 min. 21 sec.	

Service ceiling, 21,325 ft.; maximum range at 16,400 ft., and 211 m.p.h., 2,050 miles; stalling speed, 80 m.p.h.; take-off run, 897 ft.; landing run, with brakes, 1,148 ft.; landing run, without brakes, 1,640 ft.

PRINTED IN ENGLAND © Profile Publications Ltd., P.O. Box 26, 1a North Street, Leatherhead, Surrey, England.
Printed by Hills & Lacy Ltd., London and Watford, England. U.S. 2nd Class Mailing Rates applied for.

PROFILE PUBLICATIONS

Chance Vought F8A-H Crusader

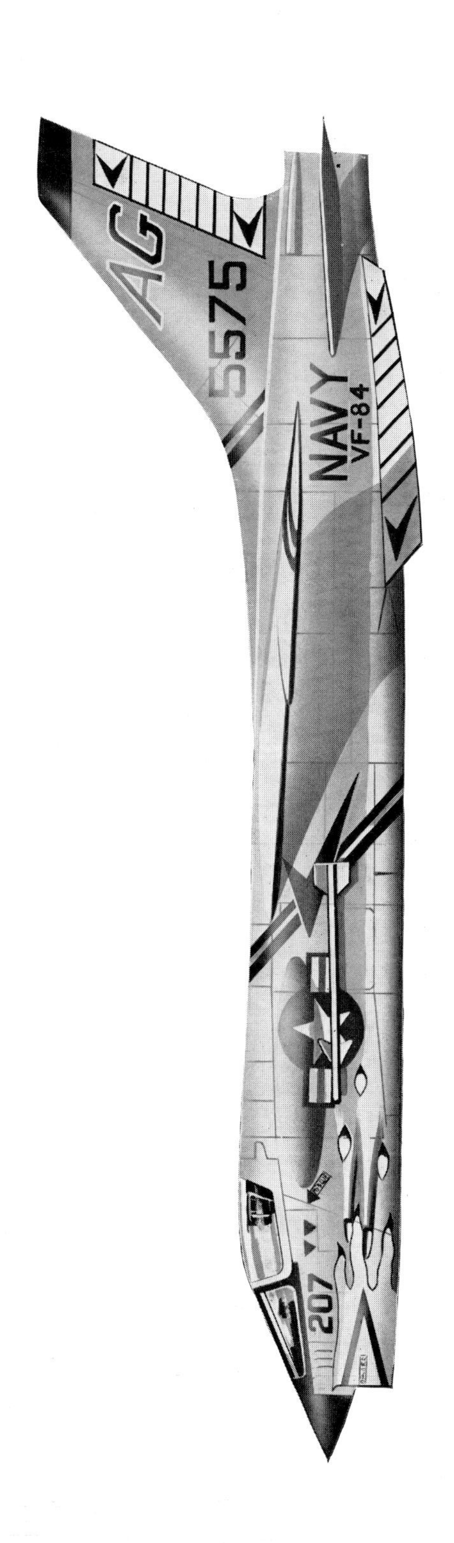

NUMBER [illegible]
TWO SHILLINGS

CHANCE VOUGHT F8U-2 CRUSADER, 145575, of U.S. Navy fighter Squadron VF-84.

The Chance Vought F-8A–E Crusader

by Gerhard Joos

Two F-8Es of VF-11; Bu. Nos. 149161 *and* 149205. (Photo: U.S. Navy)

In September 1952 the U.S. Navy stated the requirements for a new supersonic day fighter concept, and eight aircraft manufacturers took part in the competition for the contract. The specification called for an aircraft which seemed almost impossible to build by the technical standards of that time. Besides the usual characteristics of a naval plane—rugged structure, folding wings, simplicity in handling and maintenance, resistance to open-sea weather conditions—a maximum speed of more than Mach 1 and a landing speed of about 100 knots was required. It took the Chance Vought engineers five months to prepare the basic calculations, as a result of which the Navy in May 1953 announced this company as being the winner; Chance Vought was then a member of United Aircraft Corporation but became independent soon after their design was approved. By doing so the new company staked their whole existence on the new design, but it was supported by the Navy, and today it is evident that neither partner has reasons to regret his decision.

When Chance Vought presented the first details of their new design it was clear that here was a revolutionary aircraft which should take the Navy a significant step forward and which would see a brilliant service career. On 29th June 1953 Chance Vought received an assignment to build two prototypes which were designated XF8U-1, and in February 1955 the first prototype was ready for its initial flight. This took place at Edwards Air Force Base, where it lifted off the dry lake early in the morning on 25th March, only 21 months after design work was started. It exceeded Mach 1 during this 52-minute flight, which was quite an achievement at that time, proving thereby that it was the first shipboard fighter aircraft capable of flying faster than the speed of sound in level flight. The prototype was powered by the Pratt & Whitney J57-P-11 turbojet developing 9,700 lb. static thrust and 14,800 lb. with afterburning.

Exactly 67 months later, on 25th October 1960, this aircraft, Bu. No. *138899*, made its last landing at Washington National Airport, where it was presented to the Smithsonian Air Museum.

During those 67 months the Crusader, as it was named, had achieved an outstanding Service record for a carrier-based jet fighter aircraft: the Navy and Chance Vought had been awarded the Collier Trophy "for conception, design and development of the first carrier-based fighter capable of speeds exceeding 1,000 miles per hour". The Crusader set the first national speed record in excess of 1,000 miles per hour to win for the U.S. Navy its first Thompson Trophy. It was the first aeroplane to span the United States faster than the speed of sound. It also won the first Certificate of Merit ever awarded by the Bureau of Aeronautics.

THE CRUSADER DESCRIBED

Many innovations were introduced with the Crusader in order to meet the demands of the specification. The most unusual feature, however, was the hydraulically operated variable incidence wing. When designing the Crusader the engineers were faced with the problem of finding a compromise between a high maximum speed and the ability of the aircraft to operate from the restricted space of a carrier deck, with good visibility during the approach. This was finally achieved by an astonishingly simple method: for take-off and landing the whole wing, pivoted on the rear spar, is raised 7 degrees by a hydraulic self-locking actuator, thus giving the wing a very high angle of incidence and thereby reducing the approach speed but keeping the fuselage in a near horizontal attitude, providing excellent visibility for the pilot. In addition to the variable incidence wing the ailerons and the whole leading edge are lowered automatically through an interconnection by 25 degrees to increase effective camber and consequently reduce approach and lift-off speeds even further. When the wing is raised the centre section protrudes into the slipstream, thereby acting as a large speed brake.

The wing itself has a sweepback of 42 degrees at one-quarter chordline and a total area of 350 sq. ft., the thickness/chord ratio is approximately five per cent, and anhedral to improve lateral stability is five degrees. The outer wings are hydraulically folded

The first prototype, XF8U-1, Bu. No. 138899, now on permanent display at the Smithsonian Air Museum. (Photo: Chance Vought)

vertically upward for carrier stowage and carry no control surfaces but still have the drooping leading edge, providing the so-called "saw-tooth", a chordwise extension to decrease instability when approaching the stall and to minimise the pitch-up tendency at high speeds. The inboard ailerons are fully hydraulically powered and have proved capable of providing sufficient control even at speeds below the original design minimum. Inboard of the ailerons (sometimes also called flaperons because of their drooping to provide extra lift) are small landing flaps extending about 5 degrees more than the ailerons. The wing unit is of multi-spar structure and forms an integral fuel tank, with the exception of the outer folding portions.

Titanium was used wherever possible. The rear fuselage around the afterburner is constructed of this as well as a large part of the central structure. Also magnesium alloy is used for about 25 per cent of fuselage and wing skins.

The fuselage is composed of the electronic section in the nose, followed by the cockpit area and armament bay. Fuselage fuel tanks are located around the forward engine bay and in the centre section, which also carries the wing unit. Below the fuel tanks are the bays for the main landing gear which could be kept unusually short due to the variable incidence wing. It is also of special lightweight structure and designed to absorb landings of up to 20·5 ft./sec. It is forward-retracting. The steerable nosewheel is rear-retracting into the fuselage. The rear portion of the fuselage contains the engine and afterburner, an extremely large fin and the all-flying tail plane, mounted low with slight dihedral. This is machined from solid metal. All control surfaces have fully duplicated hydraulic power systems. A Marquard-built ram air turbine mounted on a hinged panel on the starboard fuselage side can be extended into the slipstream to provide emergency hydraulic and electric power should the normal systems fail. In the fuselage bottom below the horizontal fin is the sting-type arrester hook which retracts flush with the fuselage. A new lightweight ejection seat was devised but has been replaced by fully automatic Martin-Baker F-5 seats, now installed in all Crusader models.

With wing and fuselage tanks, early Crusaders carried the amazing total of about 1,165 Imp. gallons, giving a maximum endurance of more than three hours. All models of the Crusader are equipped with an in-flight refuelling probe which the Navy made obligatory in September 1955. It is installed in the left forward fuselage and faired over with an elliptical blister except in the reconnaissance version, where it retracts entirely into the fuselage structure.

Four 20 mm. MK-12 Colt cannons are also faired

Two F-8As, 143739 *and* 143764, *of VF-142 over Miramar Naval Air Station. This unit was among the first to receive the new fighter.* (Photo: U.S. Navy)

in, two on either side of the fuselage just below the cockpit, with 144 rounds per cannon. Additional destructive power is given by a retractable rocket pack housing 32 × 2·75-in. "Mighty Mouse" rockets installed in the fuselage bottom in combination with the hydraulically operated dive brake (which retracts automatically when the wing is raised). On the fuselage sides, above and behind the cannon fairing, the Crusader carries launching rails for three types of Sidewinder missiles, primary armament for interception missions. Initially one missile could be carried on each rail but these have been modified on more advanced versions to take two Sidewinders. On early versions no provision was made to carry underwing stores.

QUICK PROGRESS

The extraordinary speed which marked the design of the prototypes was maintained for testing and evaluating the Crusader. The flight of the first production aircraft followed in remarkably short order on 30th September 1955, only six months after the first prototype took to the air. By April 1956 the Crusader had completed its carrier qualification trials aboard the U.S.S. *Forrestal*, and on 28th December 1956 the U.S. Navy accepted its first F8U-1, thanks to the fact that production models could be kept virtually identical to the prototype. F8U-1s were powered by the J57-P-4A engine, which delivered 10,200 lb. dry thrust and 16,000 lb. with afterburning.

Rapid development was also aided by the extensive use of a flight simulator which duplicated the full-scale control system of the Crusader, thus permitting early investigations of flight characteristics and development of a reliable control system and the power servo mechanism long before the "X-1" made its first flight.

(It should be stated here that by the end of 1962 the U.S. Defence Department changed its aircraft designation system, whereby the F8U Crusader was redesignated F-8. In the following text therefore the old designation will be given in brackets, otherwise only the new designation will be used.)

Starting in March 1957, F-8As (F8U-1) started to flow off the Dallas production line at a rate of eight aircraft per month. After 318 aircraft of this version—a pure day fighter—had been built a new model was introduced, designated F-8B (F8U-1E). The first aircraft (*145318*, a converted F8U-1) flew on 3rd September 1958 and was equipped with a new radar scanner, externally distinguishable by the larger plastic nose cone. The improved electronic equipment gave it limited all-weather capability. Like the F-8A it carried Sidewinders, cannon armament and 2·75-in. rockets. 130 F-8Bs were built.

Late in 1958, a new and more powerful version, the

Cdr. R. W. Windsor in the record-breaking F-8A before take-off for the 1,000 m.p.h. speed run which won the Thompson Trophy.

F-8B, 145450, *with the enlarged nose-cone, landing at CV's Dallas, Texas airfield.*

An F-8C, 146941, *of VMF-33 during launching by steam catapult from U.S.S.* Forrestal*; this photo was taken during the carrier qualification trials in the Atlantic.*

F-8C 145573 *during take-off.* (Photo: Chance Vought)

F-8E 149159 *with underwing bomb load and Zuni rockets on the fuselage stations.*

F-8C (F8U-2) completed its Navy Preliminary Programme. It was powered by a J57-P-16 engine providing 10,700 lb. static thrust and 16,900 lb. with afterburning. Also further improvements were made with the radar and fire control equipment. Externally it was distinguishable from its predecessors by the addition of two small air intakes on top of the tail cone for afterburner cooling and two ventral fins under the tail section for increased directional stability. Also the wing span was reduced by 6 in. to 35 ft. 2 in. The first prototype took the air in December 1957, this being merely F-8A (Bu. No. *140447*) with the new engine, followed by a second (Bu. No. *140448*) resembling more closely the new version in January 1958; the first true production F-8C flew on 20th August 1958. Performance was quite impressive, with a rate of climb of more than 25,000 ft./min. initially and a maximum speed of Mach 1·7, which was a limitation due to stability characteristics. During the test programme, however, it has been pushed up close to Mach 2. The last F-8C was delivered on 20th September 1960, bringing the total number built to 187.

The fourth Crusader version to see fleet service was the F-8D (F8U-2N), which was basically a direct development of the F-8C; numerous changes, both external and internal, had been incorporated in the new plane, such as improved electronic equipment, a company developed push-button autopilot which performs many of the pilot's routine tasks allowing him to concentrate more on his mission, and a more powerful engine, the J57-P-20, with increased afterburning thrust of 18,000 lb. Basic cannon armament was retained. The rocket pack, however, was deleted to provide space for increased fuel capacity (being now 1,348 gallons), but with the new Y-shaped missile rack

F-8D, 147921, *of VF-32, photographed here without fuselage Sidewinder racks.*

four Sidewinders could now be carried instead of the previous two. 152 F-8Ds were built by January 1962 when the last aircraft was completed. The first F-8D made its debut on 16th February 1960, with the first production aircraft delivered only three and a half months later, on 1st June.

Beginning in October 1960, early models already in service were returned to Chance Vought for modernisation. Under a $9·5 m. contract many of the improvements of the latest models were incorporated into these aircraft bringing them to a higher degree of efficiency.

Continuous development of the Crusader led to a new variant, the F-8E (F8U-2NE). The prototype flew initially on 30th June 1961, and introduced a considerable modification programme. A new and even larger search and fire control radar gave it improved all-weather capability and another innovation was the introduction of two underwing bomb attachment pylons for the ground-attack rôle, which can be removed rapidly permitting the aircraft to perform

F-8E 150854 *with 2,000-lb. bombs underwing.*

An RF-8A reconnaissance aircraft, No. 144622, *of Navy Squadron VFP-62. The machine is seen here in the landing pattern over the U.S.S.* Forrestal, *with arrester hook extended.* (Photo: U.S. Navy)

interceptor missions. The larger scanner necessitated an enlarged and slightly extended nose cone (increasing the overall length by 3 inches) which is surmounted by the housing for the Sidewinder infra-red scanner. Additional electronic equipment for control of AGM-12 Bullpup missiles is installed in a hump in the wing centre section. Besides the Bullpups the F-8E can carry a wide range of bombs, or wing pods containing 30 Zuni rockets each, within a total gross weight of 34,000 lb. The underwing pylons became standard on all current F-8Es after proving trials were held on U.S.S. *Forrestal* in 1963, since early production aircraft did not feature attack capability. A total of 286 F-8Es were built.

RECONNAISSANCE CRUSADERS

Simultaneously with the F-8A a reconnaissance version, the RF-8A (F8U-1P) was developed. This version has the lower half of the forward fuselage squared off to enable the installation of three trimetrogen cameras and two vertical cameras for vertical, forward and side oblique photography. Photo-flash bombs for night photography can be carried internally whereas cannon armament, the rocket pack and fire control system are omitted. The upper fuselage was area-ruled to compensate for the increase in cross section which resulted in a slight "hump". Also the "blister" on the port fuselage side was eliminated since the air-refuelling boom retracts flush with the fuselage. The first Recce-Crusader flew initially on 17th December 1957 and production ceased in early 1960 after 144 aeroplanes had been built.

In 1963 five RF-8As were fitted with ventral fins and strengthened wings. In 1964 a conversion programme for more RF-8As was initiated under a new contract. This programme included modernisation of 53 RF-8As which were returned to the company for modifications such as strengthened wings, addition of wing pylons and ventral fins, fuselage structural reinforcements, and a new moulded harness electrical system. A new navigation system and provision for improved cameras are also incorporated. After modification these Crusaders continued their service career as the RF-8G.

One extremely promising tandem two-seat training version was built by modifying a single-seat F-8A, which incidentally was the seventy-fourth production aircraft which also served as prototype for the F-8E (Bu. No. *143710*). This aircraft, the TF-8A (F8U-1T), was fitted with a new forward fuselage which had a second cockpit, raised by some fifteen inches to provide the instructor with adequate visibility. Behind the front MB-ejection seat a wind-blast protection shield was installed to protect the rear seat occupant in case of canopy loss or ejection at high speed. Equipment formerly located behind the pilot's cockpit was moved to an area in the fuselage and access to all equipment was made possible through hinged or removable doors in the outer skin. Two cannons, some ammunition boxes and the rocket pack were removed from the

The sole two-seater Crusader trainer made ready for launching on the port catapult of the U.S.S. Independence. *Note "Dual Control" fin emblem.*

trainer version but provision to carry four Sidewinders was retained. Electronic equipment remained the same as for the F-8E and provision was made for additional installation of electronic navigation and weapon control systems. Powerplant was a J57-P-20 engine de-rated to match the performance of the F-8A's engine. Low-pressure tyres for rough field operations and a drag parachute to reduce landing distance were also installed. The first flight was made on 6th February 1962.

Although the TF-8A was developed under a Navy contract it did not go into production due to a cut-back in the 1964 U.S. Fiscal Budget. After evaluation by the U.S.N. it was flown to Europe and offered in England to both services for attack and interception rôles as well as for training purposes. This led to a specification after which a new British version was projected. This specification was based on the trainer version using the second cockpit for an observer. It was to be powered with a Rolls-Royce Spey by-pass engine providing about 12,000 lb. st. thrust and 20,000 lb. with re-heat. All the advantages of this engine would have given the British Crusader a considerable boost-up in performance and an increased range of more than twenty per cent. For the wings the system of the French Crusader including B.L.C. was proposed. The project, which reached the stage of detail design, was dropped however in favour of the Spey-powered Phantom.

Some other Crusader variants were also projected but did not reach production status. These included the F8U-3 Crusader III, sometimes also called Super-Crusader, but this was virtually a new aircraft with only very little resemblance to the Crusader. Five aircraft were built but only three reached flight test stage and were later turned over to N.A.S.A. The project was cancelled in favour of the McDonnell Phantom.

The sixth production F-8A was used for boundary-layer control trials which reduced the stalling speed by some ten knots. This, however, was not adopted by the U.S. Navy since the Crusader could comfortably operate from existing carriers, but the trials provided invaluable information for development of the latest Crusader version for the French Navy.

AÉRONAVALE CRUSADERS

When the *Aéronavale* was looking for a replacement for its ageing Aquilons the choice fell on the F-8E primarily due to the relatively low initial cost,

An F-8E in flight with the French Matra R-530 missile on the fuselage pylon.

A reconnaissance Crusader of VMCJ-2, 145623, *with retro-fitted ventral fins.*

Another view of the TF-8A trainer, pictured here at the U.S. Navy Test Pilot School. (Photo: Joseph G. Handelman, D.D.S.)

although slower approach speeds for the smaller French carriers were demanded. There the experience gained earlier with boundary-layer control tests paid off.

The drooping leading edges of the French Crusaders, designated F-8E (FN), were split into two sections over the full span, to be lowered 35 degrees for the front section and 8·9 degrees for the rear section, giving the inner leading edge a total droop of almost 44 degrees, nearly double the amount of camber of the American Crusader wing. The leading edges of the outer folding wing portions deflect 35 and 20 degrees respectively compared to 27 degrees on the original wing. The amount of extension of the ailerons

Left: *Detail view of extended in-flight refuelling probe which is standard on the Crusader.* Right: *Major (now Colonel) John Herschel Glenn, U.S.M.C., during his transcontinental record flight from Los Angeles to New York in RF-8A Bu. No.* 144608.

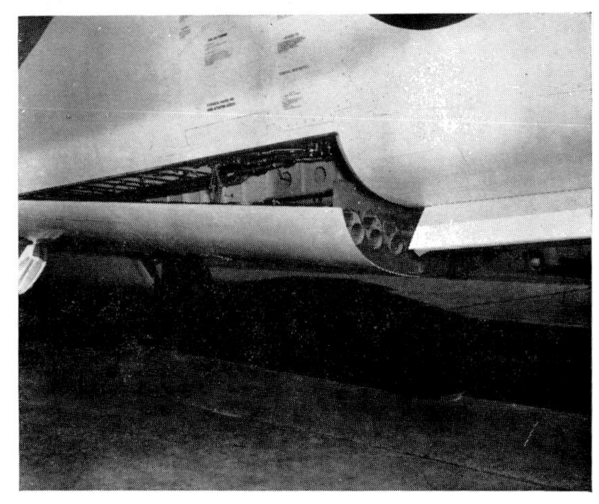

Left: *This photograph of an F-8A on the flight deck of the U.S.S.* Saratoga *gives a good view of the knife-edge air intake. Note also the retractable step and the gun-camera window in the side of the plastic nose-cone; later versions had this installation repositioned on the underside of the cone.* (Photo: Chance Vought.) Right: *Detail view of the "Mighty Mouse" 2·75 in. rocket pack installed in the F-8A, B, C, and D variants.*

and flaps is also doubled to 40 degrees. In addition, air from the engine's high-pressure compressor is led through nozzles in the wing and blown over the flaps to prevent separation of the boundary layer at low speeds. The wing incidence has been reduced by two degrees and the tail plane has been somewhat enlarged. The approach speed of the F-8E (FN) has been reduced thereby by some fifteen knots. These modifications were tested in an F-8D (Bu. No. *147036*), which flew initially on 27th February 1964 after conversion, but this aircraft crashed on 11th April 1964; the first production aircraft for the French Navy was used to complete the flight test programme, making its maiden flight on 26th June 1964. The F-8E (FN) is a multi-mission fighter and retains the standard cannon armament, but for interception missions provision has been made to carry the French MATRA R.530 air-to-air missile on the fuselage racks, although Side-winders can also be used.

The French Navy has purchased 42 Crusaders, assigned to their carriers *Clémenceau* and *Foch* with the reformed *Flottilles* 12F and 14F which were equipped previously with another famous Chance Vought product, the F4U-7 Corsair. Each unit is operating twelve aircraft.

Initial flight tests were held aboard U.S.S. *Shangri-la* by U.S. and French Navy pilots. Then the aircraft were shipped on board the carriers *Arromanches* and *Foch* to the French Naval Base at Lann-Bihoué, whence some aircraft were despatched to the carrier *Clémenceau* in the Mediterranean for carrier trials; these were again made by three French and two American Navy pilots and successfully completed on 9th May 1965. These included tests on the effect of catapulting and arresting on operationally rail-launched MATRA missiles. The modifications applied to the F-8E (FN) permit landings at a nominal sink rate of 11 ft./sec. and arrested landings with less than 3·5 Gs, both lower rates than possible with the U.S. versions of the F-8.

HIGHLIGHTS

The story of the LTV-Crusader (as it was named after Chance Vought joined the Ling-Temco-Vought group in late 1963) would be incomplete if tribute were not made to some of the highlights which have marked its outstanding Service life. On 21st August 1956 a standard production F-8A, piloted by Commander R. W. Windsor, U.S.N., flew over a 15 kilometre course at China Lake, California, to set a new national speed record of 1,015·428 miles per hour. The previous record was set by an F-100 C with 822·135 miles per hour. For this achievement Cdr. Windsor received the Thompson Trophy.

On 6th June 1957 came another "first". Two Crusaders flown by U.S.N. pilots Capt. G. Robert

Crusader F-8E nose and tail detail.

The first production F-8E (FN) which was used to complete the test programme.

Dosé and Lieutenant-Commander Paul Miller, Jr., lifted off the flight deck of U.S.S. *Bon Homme Richard* in the Pacific, refuelled in flight and landed after three hours and 28 minutes on the deck of U.S.S. *Saratoga* off Florida, thereby setting a new but unofficial speed record for a cross-country flight. It was also the first ocean-to-ocean flight between carriers in history.

Five weeks later, on 16th July 1957, an attempt was made to capture the coast-to-coast speed record from California to New York. Two Crusaders fresh from the production lines were set aside for "Operation Bullet", an F-8A and an RF-8A. The pilots were Lt. Charles Demmler, U.S.N., and the now famous astronaut, Lt.-Col. (then a Marine Major) John Glenn. Lt. Demmler unfortunately damaged his refuelling probe when attempting a refuelling rendezvous over Albuquerque, New Mexico, and had to land, but Glenn carried on to land at Floyd Bennet field, N.Y., setting a new record of three hours, 23 minutes and eight and four-tenths seconds, and this despite three refuelling contacts with AJ-2 Savage tankers which had to be made at 25,000 ft. at 350 m.p.h. His average speed was 725·55 m.p.h., equivalent to Mach 1·1 at 35,000 feet. During his flight Glenn had his cameras working at set periods and took a continuous photographic coverage of the terrain along his route. For this flight he received the Distinguished Flying Cross.

On 17th December of the same year the Collier Trophy, one of America's highest tributes, was awarded to the company and the Navy for their notable contributions to the science of aeronautics with the Crusader. In March 1958 the first Certificate of Merit ever awarded to an aircraft manufacturer by the Navy's Bureau of Aeronautics was presented to Chance Vought for the Crusader design, development and production.

Crusaders were very active during the Lebanon Crisis in 1958, when VF-32 flying from U.S.S. *Saratoga* accumulated 533 flying hours in July and 762 hours during 23 days in August.

During the Cuba Crisis in 1962 RF-8As were primarily involved with low-altitude reconnaissance, thereby bringing the evidence of communist missile bases established in Cuba which led to the Soviet "back-down". U.S.N. reconnaissance squadron VFP-62 and Marine squadron VMCJ-2 received Presidential Commendations and a number of pilots were awarded Distinguished Flying Crosses for their missions over Cuba.

A Navy Reserve pilot flying a Crusader stayed in the air for three hours and 40 minutes without refuelling, quite a remarkable time for a single-engined supersonic fighter on internal fuel only.

The most unusual story, however, came from Naples, Italy, where in August 1960 a Navy pilot took off in a Crusader from the Capodichino runway and climbed to about 5,000 ft. without noticing anything abnormal. He found, however, that an excessive amount of forward stick pressure was necessary to complete the level-off. Looking around for the cause he noticed that his wings were still folded up in carrier fashion. He then coolly decided to check the flight characteristics of this unusual configuration. So he kept on flying while dumping excessive fuel, and after 24 minutes he came in for a fast but uneventful landing. The speed—including final approach!—was kept at about 200 kts. After landing the pilot reported that no special handling difficulties were encountered during his flight. It is believed that this is the first case where an aeroplane took off, flew, and landed safely with upturned wings. Earlier similar events usually resulted in crashes.

SUMMARY

Although early F-8 variants are already phased out of operational use and the F-8Es are gradually being replaced by the F-4 Phantom on the larger carriers at the time these words are written, Crusaders play an important part in the Vietnam conflict where they are used in all rôles; the type will certainly continue to see operational life for some years to come. The U.S.

Left: 147036, *the modified F-8D used as a test bed for the French Crusader programme.* Right: *The "double-droop" of the F-8E (FN) can be clearly seen in this view of the 22nd production machine of the batch.* (Photo: É. C. Armées)

VF-211.

VF-62.

VF-103.

F-8E Crusader, VF-11.

VF-11.

Project Bullet.

VMF-312 early scheme.

F-8E Crusader, commanding officer VMF-312.

VF-11.

F-8E Crusader, commanding officer VMF-312, late markings.

MF-232.

VF-132.

C.O.VMF-122.

F-8E Crusader, VMF-122.

VMF-122.

MF-251.

VU-2.

F-8A Crusader target tug, VU-5.

VF-162.

VF-51.

VF-174.

VF-191 standard scheme.

3E Crusader, VF-84, U.S.S. *Independence*. A/c of commanding officer, Air Group 8.

VF-191.

ervice test .A.T.C.

F-8E Crusader, commanding officer VF-191, U.S.S. *Bon Homme Richard*.

RF-8A Crusader, VFP-63, U.S.S. *Coral Sea*.

N.A.T.C.

Head-on view of an Aéronavale F-8E (FN). (Photo: É. C. Armées)

Navy will continue to operate Crusaders as first-line equipment on their smaller Essex-class carriers, which have some difficulty in handling the Phantom. This applies especially to the reconnaissance model, the RF-8G, which has just been modified to bring it to a modern standard and which without doubt will be extensively used for tactical reconnaissance for the next few years. The French Navy, presently in the process of bringing their Crusader squadrons to operational status, will use them into the early 1970s at least.

At the climax of its brilliant career about half of the U.S. Navy and Marine Corps squadrons used the Crusader which hence formed the backbone of U.S. naval aviation for some years. The many successes achieved by the F-8 and the total number of 1,261 built are proving the outstanding qualities of this aircraft which has earned its first-line place in aviation history beyond any possible doubt.

SPECIFICATION

Dimensions: Wing span 35 ft. 2 in.; length 54 ft. 5¾ in.; height 15 ft. 9 in.; wing area 350 sq. ft.

Powerplant: One Pratt & Whitney J57-P-20 turbojet rated at 10,700 lb. static thrust and 18,000 lb. with afterburning.

Armament: Four 20-mm. MK-12 Colt cannon with 144 rounds per gun and four AIM-9 Sidewinder I infra-red homing air-to-air missiles (for intercept missions), twelve 250-lb. bombs, eight 500-lb. bombs or four 1,000-lb. bombs plus eight Zuni air-to-surface missiles, or two AGM-12A or AGM-12B Bullpup air-to-surface missiles (for attack missions).

Weights: Fully loaded without external stores 28,000 lb., max. overload 34,000 lb.

Performance: Max. speed 1,120 m.p.h. at 40,000 ft. (Mach 1·7); climb to 57,000 ft., 6 minutes; service ceiling 59,000 ft.; combat radius 600 miles; max. range 1,400 miles at 560 m.p.h. at 36,000 ft. (Mach 0·85).

SERIAL NUMBERS

Designation	Bureau Number	Total
XF8U-1	138899 & 138890	2
*F-8A (F8U-1)	140444–140448	5
	141336–141362	37
	142408–142415	8
	143677–143821	145
	144427–145415	123
		318
†F-8B (F8U-1E)	145416–145545	130
RF-8A (F8U-1P)	141363	1
	144607–144625	19
	145604–145647	44
	146822–146901	80
		144
F-8C (F8U-2)	145546–145603	88
	146928–147034	129
		187
F-8D (F8U-2N)	147035–147072	38
	148627–148710	114
		152
‡F-8E (§F8U-2NE)	149134–149227	94
	150284–150355 (6)	72
	150654–150683	30
	150843–150932	90
		286
F-8E (FN)	151732–151773	42
‖RF-8G		53

Notes:

*F8U aircraft received the F-8 designation on 22nd October 1962.

†F8U-1 aircraft with AN/APS-67 radar redesignated F8U-1E on 25th June 1959.

‡First aircraft to carry F-8E designation upon delivery was the 142nd F-8E BU. No. 150331.

§F8U-2N aircraft with AN/APQ-94 radar redesignated F8U-2NE 25th June 1959.

‖Fifty-three RF-8A modernised with ventral fins, new reconnaissance gear, engine and wing pylons.

PRINTED IN ENGLAND © Profile Publications Ltd., P.O. Box 26, 1a North Street, Leatherhead, Surrey, England.
Printed by Hills & Lacy Ltd., London and Watford, England. U.S. 2nd Class Mailing Rates applied for.

PROFILE PUBLICATIONS

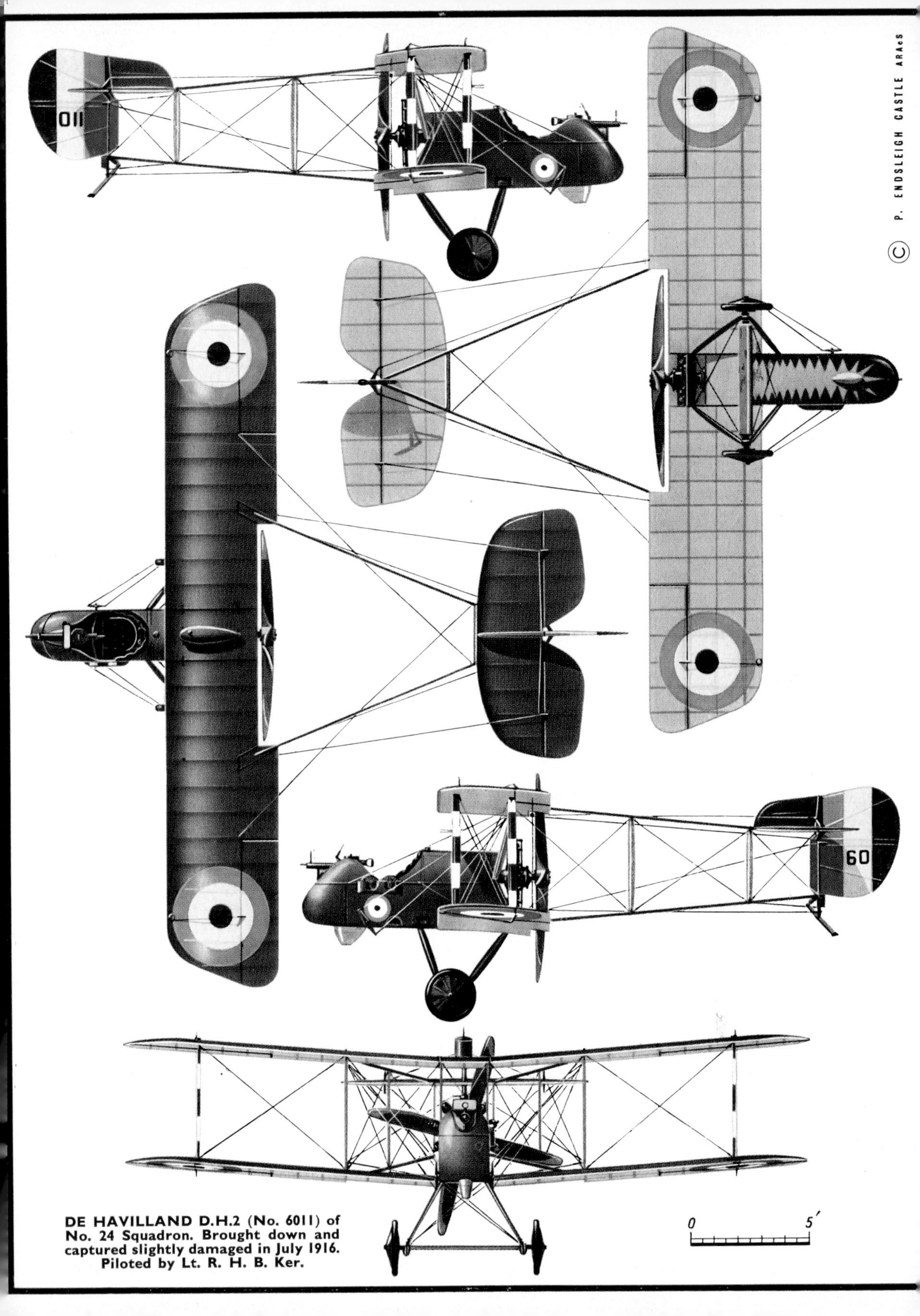

DE HAVILLAND D.H.2 (No. 6011) of No. 24 Squadron. Brought down and captured slightly damaged in July 1916. Piloted by Lt. R. H. B. Ker.

The de Havilland D.H.2

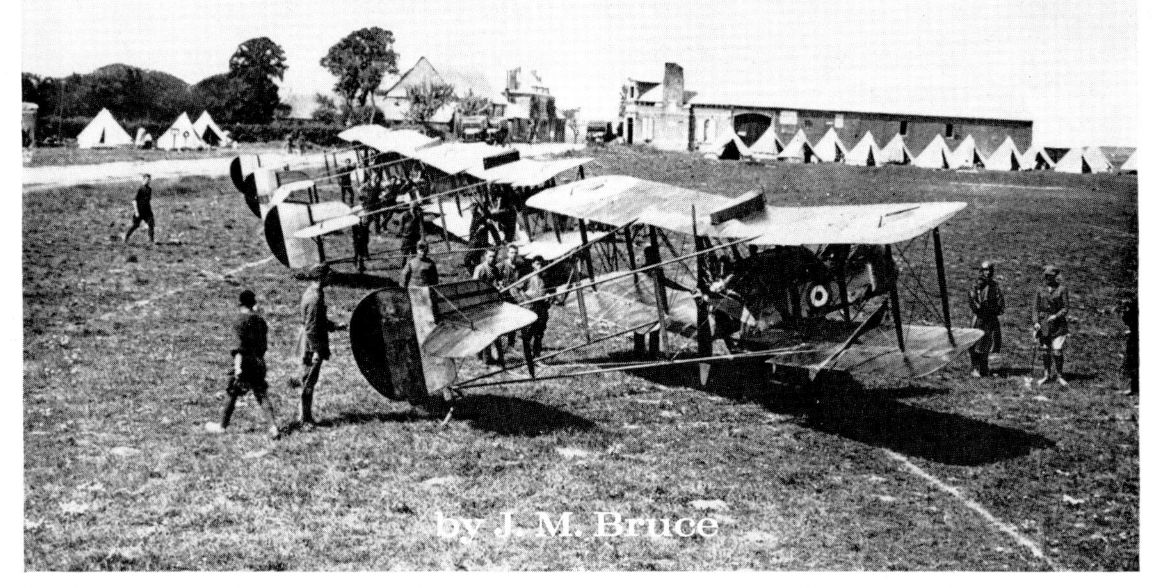

by J. M. Bruce

Four D.H.2s on the aerodrome of the Fourth Army Aircraft Park at Beauval, 1916. (Photo: Imperial War Museum Q11897)

When war broke out in August 1914 few aircraft designers were more widely experienced than Geoffrey de Havilland. After the success of the second biplane that he had himself designed and built in 1910 he joined the small staff of His Majesty's Balloon Factory at South Farnborough as designer and test pilot. His aircraft was purchased by the War Office for £400 and was given the official designation Farman Experimental No. 1, or F.E.1. It thus initiated the first British official system of aircraft nomenclature and was the first of the "Factory" aeroplane series, for by successive changes of title H. M. Balloon Factory became the Army Aircraft Factory in April 1911 and the Royal Aircraft Factory a year later.

For three and a half years Geoffrey de Havilland worked at Farnborough. During that time he worked on the designs of the S.E.1, B.E.1, B.E.2, F.E.2 and, possibly the most significant of all, the B.S.1. This last was a sleek single-seat tractor biplane powered by a 100-h.p. Gnôme rotary engine. Its designation signified Bleriot Scout No. 1; its speed, recorded in April 1913 as 91·4 m.p.h., made it the fastest British aircraft of its day and one of the fastest aeroplanes in existence. Historically the B.S.1 is of the greatest importance for it was the first high-speed single-seat scout in the world, the first expression of a formula that was to produce generations of single-seat fighters in later years.

The Royal Aircraft Factory was also early in the field of aircraft armament. The original F.E.2 was a somewhat refined development of de Havilland's F.E.1, having a sketchy nacelle with a Maxim machine gun on a movable mounting in the prow. A completely revised design was built, again designated F.E.2, but crashed and was destroyed on 23rd February 1914.

A further redesign produced the F.E.2a, a three-bay pusher biplane powered by the 100-h.p. Green engine. The Green was subsequently replaced by the 120-h.p. Austro-Daimler (Beardmore-built) and twelve F.E.2a's in all were built. Several saw operational service with No. 6 Squadron, R.F.C., in 1915.

It is unlikely that Geoffrey de Havilland had much, if anything, to do with the design of the F.E.2a, for he had left the Royal Aircraft Factory to join the Aircraft Manufacturing Co. Ltd. in June 1914. His first design for his new firm was to the same formula as the F.E.2a, and was a two-seat pusher biplane powered by a 70-h.p. Renault engine and capable of carrying a single machine gun in the front cockpit.

The Airco two-seater was given the designation D.H.1. It inaugurated a series of great D.H. designs that ran in unbroken sequence during Sir Geoffrey de Havilland's lifetime. The D.H.1 and F.E.2a were almost precisely contemporary: the Airco two-seater appeared in January 1915, and the first F.E.2a made its first flight on the 26th of that month. Although 100 D.H.1s were ordered, most being delivered as D.H.1As with the 120-h.p. Beardmore engine, the type saw little operational service and later official orders were for the F.E.2b, the production version of the F.E.2a.

It will probably never be known whether Geoffrey de Havilland had learned anything about the pre-war experiments with machine gun synchronising mechanisms conducted by Raymond Saulnier in Paris (see *Profile* No. 38, page 4). Had he known about these it is just possible that the D.H.2 might have been a tractor biplane stemming from the B.S.1/S.E.2 design rather than a pusher that was more or less a scaled-down D.H.1.

In early 1915, however, no kind of synchronising mechanism was available to Allied aircraft designers, the Saulnier gear having been abandoned. Indeed, at that early stage of the war, attempts to fit machine

This three-quarter rear view of the prototype shows that only the port side of the forward decking was cut away to accommodate the gun-mounting. At this time there was no national marking on the upper surface of the wings.

The wings of No. 4732 *being transported from the scene of its crash. This rare photograph shows that the prototype D.H.2 had, by the time of its operational service, acquired an unusual national marking: a single roundel, centrally placed above the centre section.* (Photo: Alex Imrie)

No. 4732 *down on the German side of the lines. Tricolor stripes and the serial number had been painted on the rudder by this time.* (Photo: Alex Imrie)

guns to aircraft were remarkably diverse, and it must have seemed that only an aircraft of pusher configuration offered a reasonable hope of allowing consistently effective use to be made of a gun.

Although the D.H.2 was to enjoy considerable success against the Fokker monoplane, it was not designed specifically as a counter weapon to the enemy type. The first prototype D.H.2 was completed in the early summer of 1915, at just about the time when the first few Fokkers were reaching the front. It was a compact little two-bay biplane powered by a 100-h.p. Gnôme Monosoupape rotary engine. The wooden airframe was wire-braced and, with the exception of the nacelle nose and top decking, fabric-covered. Ailerons were fitted to upper and lower wings; there was no spanwise balance cable, the upper ailerons being spring loaded in order to ensure their return to the neutral position when the controls were centred.

The armament consisted of a single Lewis gun, for which at that time only the 47-round ammunition drum existed. On the prototype D.H.2 the gun was carried on a bracket mounting the vertical shaft of which was attached to the outside of the nacelle on the port side and was faired over by a piece of sheet aluminium. The upper part of the nacelle nose fairing was cut away on the port side to accommodate the gun.

This prototype D.H.2 was given the official serial number *4732*. When its manufacturer's trials were over it was sent to France for operational evaluation on 26th July 1915. Perhaps as a foretaste of what lay in store for D.H.2 squadrons its engine (No. 30045/B.1c) was changed immediately on arrival in France; the replacement Monosoupape was No. 4475/B.152. The D.H.2 was attached to No. 5 Squadron, R.F.C. (its presence on the strength of that unit on 31st July 1915 was officially recorded), but its career was brief. It was reported missing on 9th August 1915; the Germans subsequently dropped a message stating that

The first prototype D.H.2 shortly after completion, with bracket gun-mounting on the port side of the fuselage only. (Photo: Real Photographs Co., Ltd.)

its pilot, Captain R. Maxwell-Pike, had died of wounds. When No. *4732* came down behind the German lines it overturned on landing; nevertheless it was substantially intact and presented the enemy at the earliest possible moment with a specimen of the latest British military aircraft. The reason for No. *4732*'s downfall is not known. In a statement made on 21st June 1916 to the Judicial Committee of Inquiry into the administration and command of the R.F.C. the late C. G. Grey said: "In July last year Mr. de Havilland produced a single-seater scout with the engine—a 100-h.p. Gnôme—behind. That first went to the front on August 15th [*sic*] last. Unfortunately that machine was shot down by the Germans almost the first day it arrived." As Mr. Grey was wrong in the date he quoted he may also have been wrong in saying that No. *4732* was shot down: the aircraft may have merely been an early victim of the unreliability of the Monosoupape engine, its pilot's death the result of injuries rather than wounds.

In spite of this early acquisition of a D.H.2 it seemed to take the Germans a remarkably long time to establish the type's identity. In their eyes all British pushers were "Vickers" aircraft (a not inconsiderable compliment to the sturdy Vickers F.B.5), and in contemporary German documents the D.H.2 was usually described as a "Vickers single-seater". Several sound specimens of production D.H.2s fell into German hands in 1916 and official recognition drawings, correctly titled, were produced for the use of the German pilots and observers of the time; nevertheless uncertainty persisted into 1917, when the German journal *Flugsport* published a detailed description of a captured F.E.8 but described it throughout as a D.H.2.

Despite the premature end to the career of the prototype, the D.H.2 was ordered in quantity from the Aircraft Manufacturing Co. Deliveries of the production aircraft began late in 1915; according to *The War in the Air*, Vol. II, page 159, a few single examples were flying in France before the end of 1915. These may have been some of the few D.H.2s that were with Squadrons Nos. 11 and 18. The latter unit acquired No. *5919* on 9th January 1916, No. *5916* ten days later. On 11th January No. *5920* joined No. 5 Squadron.

The production D.H.2s were substantially similar to the prototype. All major components were unaltered,

Four aspects of No. 5943, *a production D.H.2 of the first batch. These aircraft had longer ailerons than those of the prototype, and the gravity tank was, originally at least, mounted under the port upper mainplane.*
(Photos: *(top)* "*Flight International*"; *(remainder)* K. M. Molson)

Side elevation of production-type D.H.2.
(Photo: Crown copyright)

the only significant changes being in the gun mounting and fuel system. The Lewis gun was carried on a central mounting that enabled it to be traversed, elevated or depressed and had a considerable range of movement. To accommodate this new arrangement the top of the nacelle nose fairing was redesigned: it was now symmetrical and had a central slot in which the gun lay when fully lowered. A quaint feature of the installation was the mounting of the windscreen on the gun itself.

A gravity tank was added to the fuel system. Its position varied: on some D.H.2s it was mounted centrally on top of the centre section; on others it was either above or below the port upper mainplane.

On 1st September 1915, No. 24 Squadron was formed at Hounslow; on the 28th, command of the new unit was taken over by Captain L. G. Hawker, V.C., D.S.O. The squadron had to work up to operational strength and efficiency before going overseas, and was responsible for three Home Defence night-flying stations at Wimbledon, Sutton's Farm and Hainault Farm. No. 24 Squadron had to be content with an ill-assorted collection of Curtiss, Avro, Caudron and Farman two-seaters, a Bristol Scout and a few Martinsyde S.1s.

The squadron had been selected as the first to be equipped with the D.H.2. The first of the little pushers to be delivered to No. 24 arrived on 10th January 1916, and by the time the unit left for France on 7th February it had received a total of twelve D.H.2s. On 10th February No. 24 Squadron arrived at Bertangles, a time which, in the words of the squadron's historian, was "fraught with great possibilities". The Fokker monoplanes were then at the zenith of their influence: on 7th February the escort detailed to protect a single reconnaissance B.E.2c of No. 12 Squadron consisted of three other B.E.2c's, four F.E.2b's, four R.E.7s and one Bristol Scout. "The reconnaissance was not made," says the official history, "but there could be no more significant tribute to the supremacy of the Fokker than is implied in this order for twelve pilots to escort one reconnaissance aeroplane."

No. 24 Squadron spent their first few weeks in France in gaining experience of their aircraft and their area of operations. Early casualties were caused by spinning. In early 1916 spinning was not properly understood; it was regarded as a catastrophic situation to be avoided, for at that time there was no accepted and understood recovery action. In his book, *Hawker, V.C.*, Lt.-Col. Tyrrel Hawker tells how his brother, Major L. G. Hawker, V.C., D.S.O., deliberately spun a D.H.2 repeatedly to demonstrate to his pilots that the aircraft could be brought under control readily and effectively. This was in mid-February 1916, six months before Captain F. W. Goodden deliberately spun an F.E.8 at Farnborough and recovered successfully. It seems extraordinary that Major Hawker's feat was not recorded in the official history of No. 24 Squadron. Following a reference to the D.H.2's proneness to spinning the history says:

> Lieutenant Cowan did much to inspire confidence by the facility with which he handled his machine. He was the first pilot really to "stunt" this machine, and gradually the Squadron gained complete assurance.

Armament was a problem on the D.H.2. The original gun mounting was useless in combat; for the gun itself only the standard 47-round ammunition drums were available and magazines had to be

This photograph of the cockpit of a D.H.2 shows the nature of the gun mounting and the method of elevating the weapon.
(Photo: K. M. Molson)

changed frequently. Second Lieutenants D. M. Tidmarsh and A. M. Wilkinson were the first members of No. 24 Squadron to fit two Lewis guns to their D.H.2s, presumably as fixed weapons firing straight ahead, but it seems that this modification was officially frowned upon and the twin guns had to be removed.

Apparently authority also disapproved of early attempts to dispense with the movable mounting and use the single Lewis as a fixed gun. The trouble with the original mounting was that it was too movable: the pilots of No. 24 Squadron referred to it as the "wobbly mounting". Major Lanoe G. Hawker's experience in dealing with higher authorities who must have been surpassingly obtuse, even by the standards of the 1914–18 war, is recounted thus in *Hawker, V.C.*:

> The official gun mounting, as already mentioned, was quite impracticable; the pilot could not fly in one direction with one hand, and aim and fire his gun in another direction with the other hand; when elevated, the gun got in the way of the joystick. Lanoe first tried clamping down the muzzle of the gun in the straight-forward position; this was at once forbidden by higher authority; the gun on a Nieuport Scout could be fired upwards successfully; so it must be with the D.H.2, regardless of the fact that the relative positions of the pilot and of the gun were quite different. Orders were orders, and even though the pilot of a D.H.2 could not aim his gun upwards, and obviously he could not put his head upside down between his knees to do so, the gun must be free to fire upwards. Lance partly got over the difficulty by making a spring clip with a catch to hold the muzzle down, but enabling it to be released if required; it did not hold the gun as rigidly nor as securely as when clamped, but it was the best compromise possible with red tape.

It has been said repeatedly that the D.H.2's gun was ultimately fixed and the aircraft flown as a conventional fixed-gun fighter. It is uncertain whether the fixing of the gun went beyond Hawker's spring clip device, and it is difficult to determine the time when the general practice of flying the D.H.2 as a fixed-gun fighter began. In a combat report dated as late as 10th October 1916 Major Hawker wrote:

> A Nieuport-type H.A. came overhead without seeing us, so turning I raised the mounting and fired a few ineffectual shots as the mounting was very wobbly.

On this D.H.2 the windscreen was mounted on the rear of the Lewis gun, which is seen partly elevated.
(Photo: Ministry of Defence)

Later that month his squadron orders included detailed instructions for elevating the gun to fire upwards at enemy aircraft that were able to remain above the D.H.2.

A form of double ammunition drum was evolved by Major Hawker and Air Mechanic W. L. French, but it is not known whether there was any relationship between it and the standard 97-round drum, the earlier development of which has been attributed to the armoury section of No. 18 Squadron in December 1915.

No. 24 Squadron had its first engagement with the enemy on 19th March 1916, and the first victory came on 2nd April, when 2nd Lt. D. M. Tidmarsh shot down an enemy aircraft near Bapaume. The D.H.2's first major test occurred on 25th April, when a reconnaissance B.E.2c of No. 15 Squadron was escorted by four other B.E.2c's and three of No. 24's D.H.2s. The formation was attacked by a group of Fokker monoplanes, but the D.H.2s quickly proved themselves to be superior to their opponents, beat off the attack and drove down one of the Fokkers.

Once the D.H.2 had been proved capable of defeating the Fokker its pilots attacked the German fighter unhesitatingly. On 20th July 1916 four D.H.2s (Nos. *5924*, *5992*, *6010* and *7842*) of "B" Flight, No. 24

A D.H.2 of the second production batch. (Photo: Real Photographs Co., Ltd.)

A four-blade airscrew was ultimately standardised for the D.H.2, as seen here on No. 5923.
(Photo: Imperial War Museum MH 3372)

Squadron, attacked a mixed formation of five L.V.G. two-seaters, three L.F.G. Roland C IIs and three Fokkers over Bapaume. The D.H.2 pilots were Captain R. E. A. W. Hughes-Chamberlain, Lt. C. M. B. Chapman, 2nd Lt. H. C. Evans and 2nd Lt. A. E. McKay. Chapman shot a Fokker down in flames, McKay accounted for a Roland, and at least one other enemy aircraft fell to Hughes-Chamberlain; two others were driven down and the others dispersed. Even longer odds were accepted by the D.H.2 pilots: on 15th September 1916 three of No. 24 Squadron attacked a formation of seventeen German aircraft near Morval, shot down two and scattered the remainder.

Imbued with the offensive spirit of its commanding officer, No. 24 Squadron continued to fly the D.H.2 with panache and distinction until its long-overdue replacement by the D.H.5. In 774 combats between 8th April 1916 and 25th May 1917 the D.H.2s of Hawker's Squadron destroyed or captured forty-four enemy aircraft, forced seventeen to land in their own lines, and drove down many others.

These achievements were not easily won. The D.H.2 was never very fast; in particular it was slow in a dive and could be left behind by many contemporary types. Its Monosoupape engine was not reliable, even by the standards of 1916: mechanical failure could have fatal consequences, for it was not unknown for the engine to shed cylinders: at best this caused violent vibration until the engine could be stopped, at worst the ejected cylinder severed a tailboom and the aircraft broke up. In No. 24 Squadron Lt. A. E. Glew and Captain D. Wilson were victims of this failing of the Monosoupape.

A D.H.2 pilot and his gun.
(Photo: Imperial War Museum Q7237)

The shortcomings of the early 100-h.p. Gnôme Monosoupape may have prompted the trial installation of a 110-h.p. Le Rhône in at least one D.H.2, which was tested at Central Flying School. The recorded performance figures suggest that climbing performance with the Le Rhône was poorer than with the Monosoupape, which remained the standard engine.

Two other D.H.2 squadrons took the field in France in 1916. No. 29 Squadron arrived on 25th March, No. 32 on 28th May, and fought with the same skill and gallantry as the pilots of No. 24 Squadron. No. 29 Squadron had had an unfortunate start. Of ten D.H.2s that left Gosport for France six were forced down by a sudden snowstorm before crossing the Channel. Four of the aircraft were damaged and two of the pilots injured.

Captain L. P. Aizlewood of No. 32 Squadron had reason to be grateful for the sturdy construction of the D.H.2 on 9th September 1916. He and two other members of his squadron attacked five enemy aircraft over Thiepval. Aizlewood dived to within twenty yards of his victim before opening fire and flew into the tail unit of the German aircraft; his D.H.2's undercarriage was wrecked, its airscrew shattered and its tailbooms damaged; nevertheless Aizlewood brought his aircraft down without injury to himself. His opponent crashed near Miraumont.

Some two months earlier Aizlewood's commanding officer, Major L. W. B. Rees, had fought the action for which he was awarded the Victoria Cross. On 1st July 1916 Rees, flying No. *6015*, came upon a formation of ten German two-seaters bound on a bombing mission across the British lines. He had at first thought they were British aircraft returning from a sortie but attacked without hesitation when he identified them. His attacks made one of the enemy dive homewards and drove a second down; the formation broke up, only three holding their course. Major Rees kept up his attack and, although wounded in the leg, obliged the enemy leader to abandon the raid entirely.

On 3rd August 1916 Flight Sergeant J. T. B. McCudden was posted to No. 29 Squadron, R.F.C. This move introduced to single-seat fighters a man who was to become one of the greatest fighting pilots of the war. McCudden had been flying F.E.2d's with No. 20 Squadron, and in his book *Five Years in the R.F.C.* he wrote:

> I was allotted machine No. *5985*, which had already done about eighty hours flying. The same evening as I arrived in [No. 29] Squadron I went up to have some practice on my machine. I found it very nice and light after flying the heavy F.E. . . .
>
> The D.H.2 was a very cold little machine, as the pilot had to sit in a small nacelle with the engine a long way back, and so of course he got no warmth from it at all.

McCudden's first victory occurred on 6th September 1916, when he shot down a German two-seater over Gheluve. In his description of a combat on 8th September he indicated clearly that the gun on his D.H.2 could be elevated.

A distinguished fighting career was almost prematurely terminated on 9th November 1916. In a hard-fought combat in the morning McCudden's D.H.2 sustained twenty-four hits: "My tailplane was a mass of torn fabric, and various wires were hanging, having been cut by bullets." That afternoon he tried a loop on a D.H.2 but changed his mind just before becoming inverted; he pushed the stick forward and, with the sudden change of curvature, the spare ammunition drums shot upwards and rearwards. They struck the airscrew, breaking three of its four blades.

> I now found that I wanted full right rudder to keep the machine straight and discovered, on looking round, that the lower right-hand tail boom had been cut clean in two by one of the flying propeller blades, and all that was holding my tail on was a diagonal 10-cwt. tail-boom bracing wire.

Flying views of D.H.2s are rare. Although somewhat lacking in sharpness, this photograph conveys some impression of the airborne appearance of an aircraft with clear-doped wings; the outline of the upper roundels can be seen through the translucent fabric. (Photo: H. F. Cowley)

McCudden managed to bring his severely damaged D.H.2 down to a successful landing.

With the appearance of the fast and well armed Albatros D I and D II in the autumn of 1916 the D.H.2 was outclassed. Nevertheless, re-equipment of the D.H.2 squadrons was long delayed, and their combats became grimmer and more dogged as 1916 ended and 1917 came. By then Lanoe Hawker was gone, killed in combat with Manfred von Richthofen on 23rd November 1916. Despite the considerable

Subject of the five-aspect colour plate on page 2, No. 6011 *of No. 24 Squadron is here seen in German hands. It was brought down by a two-seater of* Kampfgeschwader 1. *By the time of the Battle of the Somme the D.H.2s of No. 24 Squadron had been given a coat of khaki dope on all upper surfaces. The squadron also had its individual marking of red and white bands on the outer interplane struts and used the khaki dope to provide a "saw-tooth" effect on the underside of the nacelle.* (Photo: Egon Krueger)

superiority in speed and armament of von Richthofen's Albatros D II, Hawker, flying No. *5964*, gave the Rittmeister no easy victory. No one had done more than Hawker to make the D.H.2 a useful weapon; his death, at the time when the D.H.2's decline had begun, was one of the war's cruellest ironies.

Replacement of the D.H.2 began in March 1917, when No. 29 Squadron was re-equipped with Nieuport 17s. On 1st May No. 24 Squadron's first D.H.5 arrived, but the little pushers did not finally disappear from operational service in France until June was well advanced.

The R.N.A.S. had been interested in the D.H.2. An aircraft that had originally been ordered for the R.F.C. was transferred to the R.N.A.S.; it was renumbered to become No. *8725*. It was at the R.N.A.S. unit at Hendon in May 1916 and was flown by Flight Commander Harry Busteed on the 26th of that month. Apparently it was subjected to speed tests on the following day. The R.N.A.S. did not adopt the D.H.2, possibly because the Sopwith Pup and triplane were then in prospect.

No Home Defence unit was equipped with the D.H.2; two examples of the type went to H.D. units in 1917, but its performance was inadequate for Zeppelin hunting. Nevertheless, one D.H.2 participated in the destruction of the Zeppelin airship L.48 on 17th June 1917. Flown by Captain R. H. M. S. Saundby, it was from the armament experimental station at Orfordness. Saundby attacked the airship at the same time as Lt. L. P. Watkins of No. 37 Squadron, to whom the destruction of the L.48 was credited.

After the D.H.2's withdrawal from operational use in France small numbers of the type continued in service in Palestine and Macedonia. By the end of May 1917 two D.H.2s were with the Fifth Wing, R.F.C., which at that time consisted of Squadrons Nos. 14 and 67 (Australian) and operated in Palestine. On 27th October 1917 three were on the strength of No. 111 Squadron at Deir el Balah. In that month one D.H.2 was sent to join "X" Flight at Aqaba; this was a special detachment, independent, self-contained, and under the direct control of R.F.C. Headquarters in Egypt, that had been formed on 9th September 1917 for permanent attachment to the Arab forces. Such warlike acts as the Palestine D.H.2s may have committed seem to have been considered of insufficient importance to merit a place in the official history.

In Macedonia No. 47 Squadron, R.F.C., had a few D.H.2s in the spring of 1917. Two of these were allocated to the composite R.F.C./R.N.A.S. fighting squadron that was created in March of that year to combat the German bombing unit *Kampfgeschwader I*, then based at Hudova. No. 47 Squadron still had D.H.2s on its strength in September 1917.

It is not now possible to be certain when the D.H.2 finally disappeared from service. Official statistics indicate that one went to France in 1918 but its mission can scarcely have been an operational one. Possibly the last in official use was *A2569*, which was flown for experimental purposes at the Royal Aircraft Factory. This D.H.2's last recorded flight at Farnborough was made on 20th March 1918, when the aircraft was employed to test Tampier controls, presumably of the carburettor.

(continued on page 12)

Another D.H.2 that fell intact into German hands. This was an aircraft of the second production batch, but its squadron is unknown. Note the fairing piece blanking off the front of the slot in the nacelle and the gravity tank above the port upper mainplane.
(Photo: Egon Krueger)

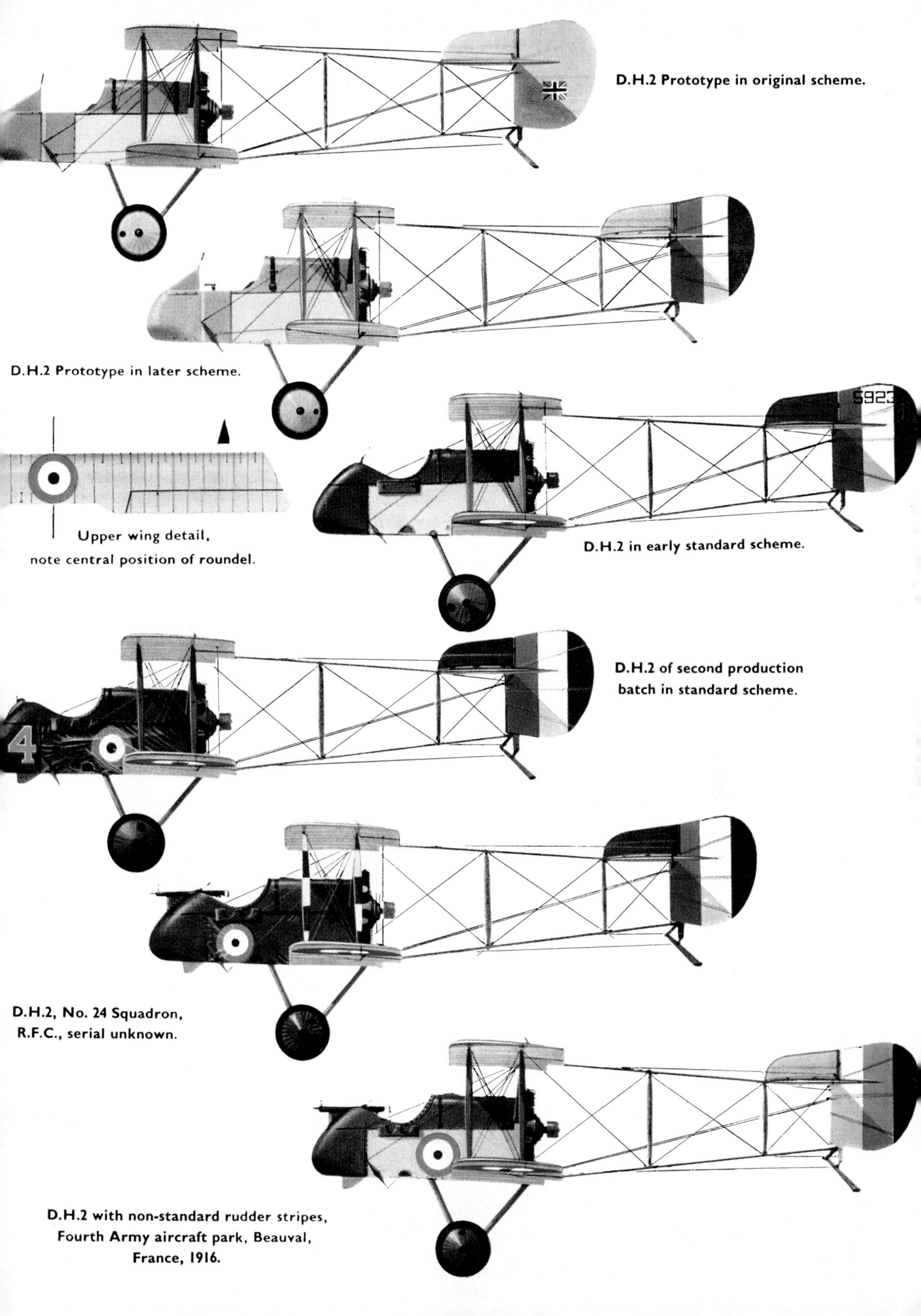

D.H.2 Prototype in original scheme.

D.H.2 Prototype in later scheme.

Upper wing detail, note central position of roundel.

D.H.2 in early standard scheme.

D.H.2 of second production batch in standard scheme.

D.H.2, No. 24 Squadron, R.F.C., serial unknown.

D.H.2 with non-standard rudder stripes, Fourth Army aircraft park, Beauval, France, 1916.

A D.H.2 and a Vickers F.B.19 Mk. II, believed to be with No. 14 Squadron, Palestine. (Photo: R. C. Bowyer)

By any standards the D.H.2's service was remarkable. It had an undistinguished performance, its armament was inadequate and inefficiently installed, yet it was in its day a weapon to be reckoned with. It played a major part in defeating the Fokker monoplane and in maintaining British aerial supremacy above the battlefields of the Somme.

SPECIFICATION

Power: 100-h.p. Gnôme Monosoupape; 110-h.p. Le Rhône 9J.
Dimensions: Span 28 ft. 3 in., length 25 ft. 2½ in., height 9 ft. 6½ in., chord 4 ft. 9 in., gap 4 ft. 9 in., stagger nil, dihedral 4 deg., incidence 3 deg., span of tail 10 ft. 3 in., wheel track 5 ft. 9¾ in., airscrew diameter (Integral D.G.70, two blades) 8 ft. 2½ in.
Areas: Wings, upper 128 sq. ft., lower 121 sq. ft., total 249 sq. ft.; ailerons each 14 sq. ft., total 56 sq. ft.; tailplane 20·6 sq. ft., elevators 13·5 sq. ft.; fin 2·7 sq. ft., rudder 11 sq. ft.
Armament: One 0·303-in. Lewis machine gun on movable mounting; a few experimental installations of two Lewis guns made in No. 24 Squadron.

PRODUCTION

It is difficult to be certain how many D.H.2s were built. The following serial numbers were allotted for D.H.2s ordered from the Aircraft Manufacturing Co., Ltd., Hendon, London, N.W.: *4732–4734, 5916–6015, 7842–7941, 8725, A2533–A2632, A4764–A4813, A4988–A5087.*
The D.H.2 No. *8725* supplied to the R.N.A.S. was a renumbered R.F.C. aircraft. Additionally, *B8824* was an A.R.D. rebuild.

SERVICE USE

France: R.F.C. Squadrons Nos. 5, 11, 18, 24, 29 and 32.
Palestine: Fifth Wing (possibly No. 14 Sqn.) R.F.C.; No. 111 Sqn., R.F.C.; "X" Flight at Aqaba.
Macedonia: "A" Flight of No. 47 Squadron, R.F.C.; R.F.C./R.N.A.S. Composite Fighting Squadron.
Training: No. 6 Reserve Squadron, Catterick; No. 10 Reserve Squadron, Joyce Green; No. 15 Reserve Squadron, Doncaster; No. 22 Training Squadron, Abu Qir, Egypt.

Examples of D.H.2s used by R.F.C. units:
No. 5 Sqn.—4732, 5920.
No. 18 Sqn.—5916, 5919.
No. 24 Sqn.—5924, 5925, 5964, 5989, 5991, 5992, 5998, 6007, 6008, 6010, 6011, 7842, 7884, 7909, 7918, 7930, A2541, A2544, A2554, A2563, A2564, A2581, A2592, A2594, A2606, A2607, A5007, A5018.
No. 29 Sqn.—5985, 7927, A2571.
No. 32 Sqn.—5986, 6015.
No. 47 Sqn.—A2584, A4770, A4771, A4776.
No. 6 Reserve Sqn.—7912, 7913.
No. 10 Reserve Sqn.—7866, 7867, A2550, A2559, A2560, A4798.
No. 15 Reserve Sqn.—A2633.
No. 22 Training Sqn.—A2585, A2618, A4778.

WEIGHTS AND PERFORMANCE

Engine	Monosoupape	Le Rhône
Weights (lb.):		
Empty	943	1,004
Military load	80	80
Pilot	180	180
Fuel and oil	238	283
Loaded	1,441	1,547
Max. speed (m.p.h.) at:		
Ground level	93	92
5,000 ft.	90	85
11,000 ft.	73·5	72
Climb to:	m. s.	m. s.
6,000 ft.	11 0	12 0
10,000 ft.	24 45	31 0
Service ceiling (ft.) ...	14,000	—
Endurance (hours) ...	2¾	3

The author acknowledges gratefully the contributions made to this Profile by Bruce Robertson.

PRINTED IN ENGLAND © Profile Publications Ltd., P.O. Box 26, 1a North Street, Leatherhead, Surrey, England.
Printed by Hills & Lacy Ltd., London and Watford England. U.S. 2nd Class Mailing Rates applied for.

PROFILE PUBLICATIONS

The Grumman F3F Series

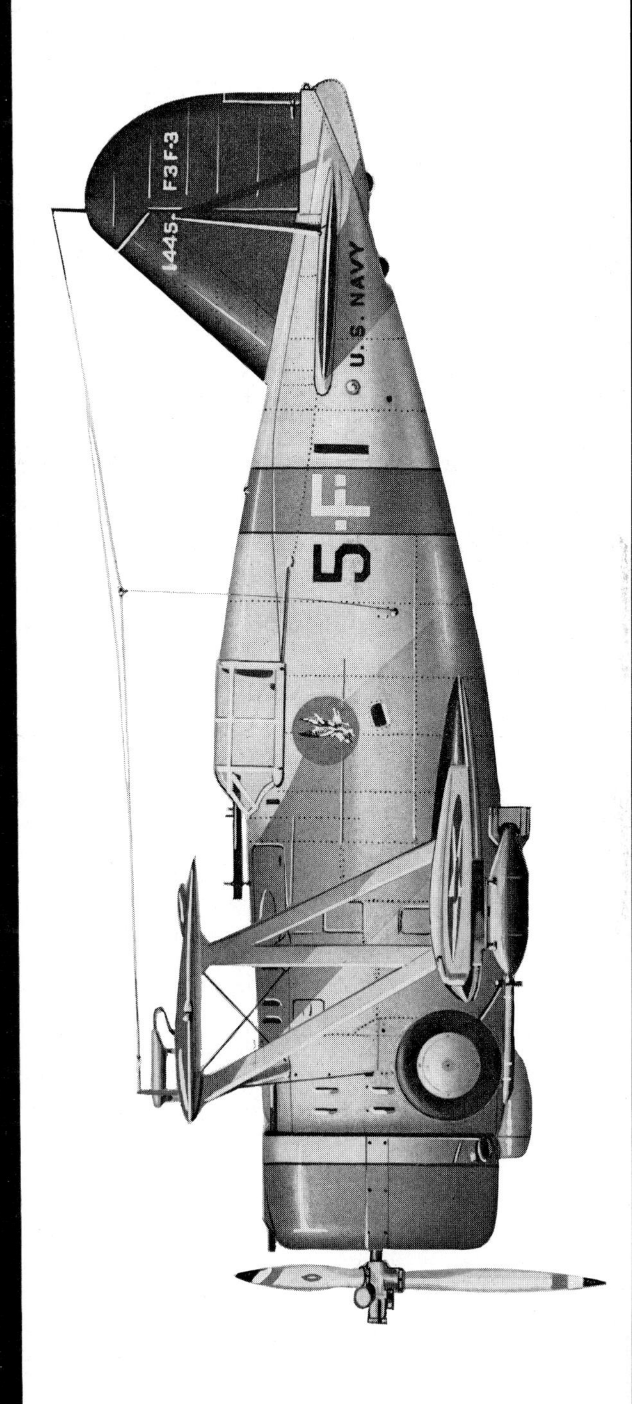

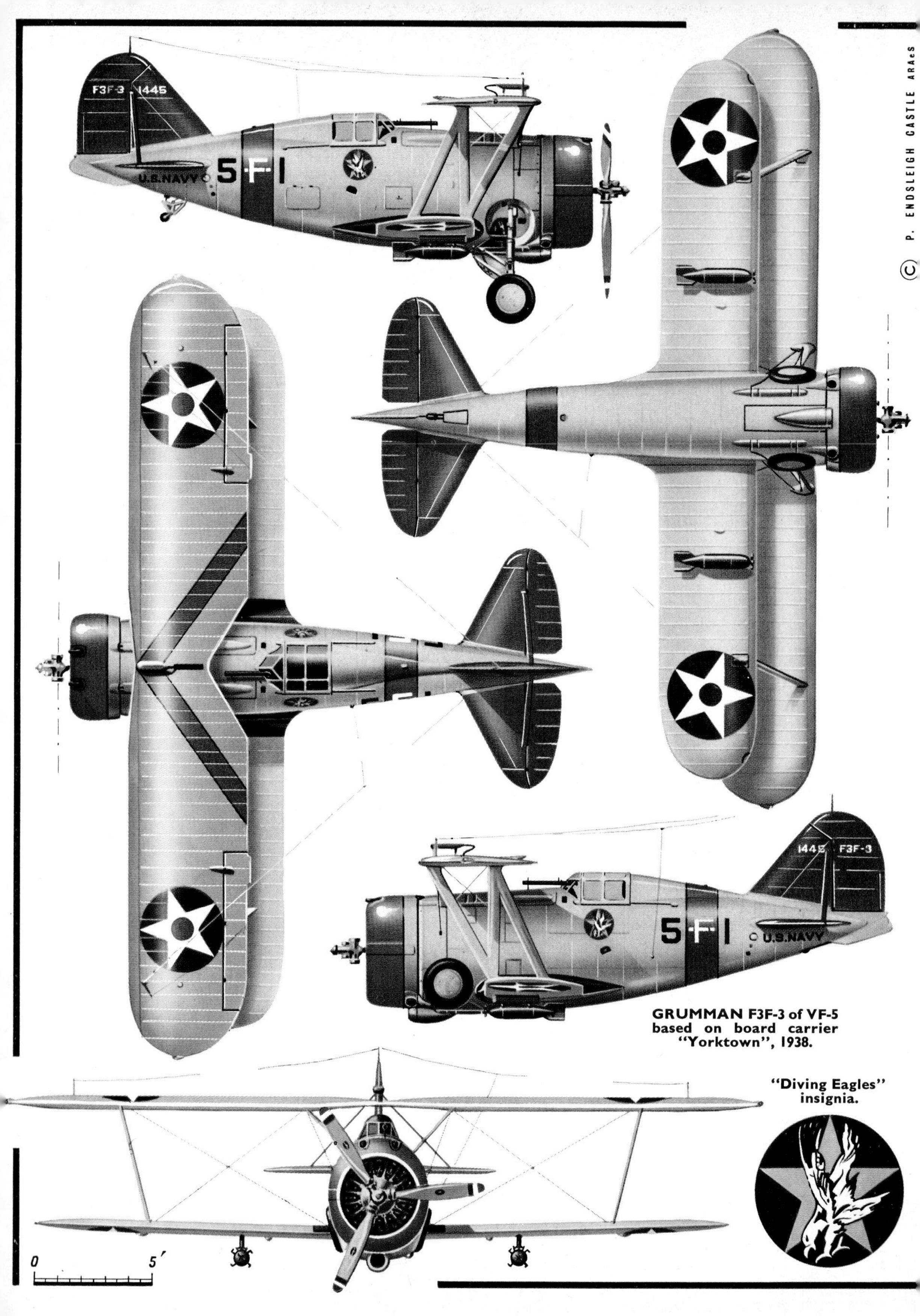

GRUMMAN F3F-3 of VF-5 based on board carrier "Yorktown", 1938.

"Diving Eagles" insignia.

The Grumman F3F Series

by Lt. Cdr. Benton Reams, U.S.N.

F3F-1 (0235) *landing on U.S.S.* Ranger, *22nd March 1938; note fully extended landing gear and arrester hook. This machine had an earlier tour as 6-F-6 before being overhauled in San Diego; later it served with VF-7, becoming VF-72 at Miami.*
(Photo: U.S.N. Archives 80-CF-54854-2)

Horsepower was the key to speed with the Grumman F3F series aircraft as they crested the high water mark of the biplane fighter in the United States Navy. No monoplanes were aboard carriers when they joined the fleet, but only one biplane, the Curtiss SBC, remained when the F3Fs departed. These little Grummans were "sweet" flyers and still draw a wistful look in the eye of their former pilots upon recall of the joyful ease of handling them in the air.

The F3F series was in combat squadron service from early 1936 with VF-5B until VMF-211 turned in its last few in late 1941. They replaced Boeing F4B-4s and two-seater Grumman FF-1s, served alongside the smaller Grumman F2F-1s and were in turn superceded by the Brewster F2As and more Grummans—the F4F series. Earlier F2Fs had started the trend toward single-seat Grumman biplane fighters. Two squadrons' worth (eighteen operating plus nine spares for each) were procured for 1935 delivery. However, before the first production F2F-1 was accepted, Grumman design 11 was sold to the Navy Bureau of Aeronautics as the XF3F-1. The 15th October 1934 was the date on a $75,850 contract for design, test and construction for one aeroplane to be powered by a Pratt & Whitney Twin Wasp Jnr. engine. This aircraft, before acceptance for Navy testing was actually three separate airframes built to the same Bureau and Grumman shop numbers. The first XF3F-1 flew on 20th March 1935. It made three flights that day, including a one hour run at full power. On the 22nd March flight testing was resumed. Navy pilots made two short flights then after lunch Grumman's test pilot, Jimmy Collins, began the required series of ten dives to demonstrate the strength of the XF3F-1. Nine of the dives were completed successfully in five flights with no hint of trouble. Designed to demonstrate an eight to nine "g" recovery, the tenth dive was commenced from about 18,000 ft. At 8,000 feet, a very abrupt pull-out was made; wings and engine flew off the aircraft while the fuselage came down in a flat spin carrying Collins to his death. This pull-out was recorded on the smoked slide of the accelerometer as being between eleven and fifteen "g"—well beyond the design strength of the aircraft. A second prototype was immediately started, incorporated minor modifications, and first flew on 9th May.

During the mid 1930s, experimental Naval aircraft, after preliminary manufacturer's flight tests, were normally delivered by air to the U.S. Naval Air Station at Anacostia in the south-east section of Washington, D.C. After passing a specified sequence of demonstration flights by the contractor, the plane was then turned over to the Navy for service acceptance trials. This rugged series of flight tests was conducted under the direction of the Board of Inspection and Survey mostly at Anacostia, but with the diving, bombing and spinning demonstrations and trials at the nearby Naval Proving Ground, Dahlgren, Virginia. Carrier suitability, lighting and night visibility tests were conducted on the arrested landing platform at Norfolk, Virginia, until the new platform at the Naval Aircraft Factory (N.A.F.), Philadelphia, Pennsylvania went into operation in July 1937.

Thus, in accordance with the contract, the second XF3F-1 was delivered to Anacostia on 13th May 1935. Four days later during the contractor's required ten-turn right-hand spin demonstration, pilot Lee Gehlbach was forced to jump when the plane would not recover from a flat spin. The third XF3F-1 was immediately built using undamaged components of its predecessor and was delivered to Anacostia on 20th June. Modifications to overcome problems en-

XF3F-1 (9727) *after installation of R-1535-84 engine. This aircraft served at Anacostia until mid-1941 when it was sent to Miami for use as a fighter trainer.*
(Photo: Bowers' Collection)

countered with spinning prevented preliminary acceptance and the start of Navy trials until 10th July. Then a high priority permitted rapid progress so that the XF3F-1 design could be accepted for service use on 1st August. A contract for fifty-four production models, incorporating recommended trial board changes, was signed three weeks later. Navy trials, including 150 flying hours Accelerated Service Test continued to 9th March 1936. Following these, XF3F-1 (*9727*) was assigned to Anacostia for utility purposes. It remained in service until early 1943, but became a training plane late in its career.

DEVELOPMENT CONTINUES

Before the first production F3F-1 was completed, a new Grumman biplane fighter was ordered for testing. This was design 16 known as the XF4F-1. It got through the mock-up stage but no further. Grumman aerodynamic studies resulted in a proposal for putting a larger engine in the F3F to give predicted performance almost equivalent to the XF4F-1 and at the same time suggested a monoplane design using still more powerful engines then under development. This evidently caused some head scratching in the Bureau of Aeronautics. The result was cancellation of the biplane design and re-ordering the XF4F-2 as monoplane design 18 on the same contract. A new contract resulted for the XF3F-2 with a Wright Cyclone G engine. For record purposes the latter contract formality was dated 28th July 1936 which was the day after delivery of XF3F-2 (*0452*) to Anacostia.* This was about the mid point in time of the F3F-1 production, so the XF3F-2 received a later shop number (C/N) than the F3F-1s. Teething troubles with the new carburation system in the engine delayed service acceptance of the engine as well as flight tests on the aircraft. Eight months elapsed before the 23rd March 1937 production contract award to Grumman for eighty-one F3F-2 fighter aircraft. The first production article arrived in Anacostia on 27th July 1937 but was not accepted for service use until 4th November 1937. Carburettor, oil cooling and cockpit carbon monoxide problems delayed acceptance, but the handling characteristics were reported as excellent both at high and low speeds and in all plane attitudes. (In fact the flight test report had this to say: "The F3F-2 was found to be the most satisfactory single-place fighter developed for the Navy to date, taking into account all the factors of manœuvrability, performance, maintainability and reliability.")

**The contract date is the date the papers are signed by the manufacturer. Clarifying fine points could add weeks to processing time and thus give a misleading indication as to the actual start of work.*

F3F-1 (0237) *as 6-F-8 from VF-6B. Crashed 21st October 1936 in a night landing at San Diego, the first F3F to be stricken from service.* (Photo: Larkins' Collection)

F3F-1 (0256) *as leader of second section of VMF-2. Note Marine insignia under cockpit and ·50 calibre blast tube visible over cowling.* (Photo: Bowers' Collection)

0220 *of VF-4—the "Red Rippers"—with "E" rating for dive bombing. Note that the F3F-1 did not have access step on port side; cf. photographs of F3F-2.* (Photo: Bowers' Collection)

F3F-1 (0259); *note "Felix" emblem and "E" for machine gunnery; white tail identifies a machine from* Saratoga.
(Photo: Larkins' Collection)

7-F-7 with the black-painted tail of U.S.S. Wasp *aircraft, and chrome yellow paint carried under the leading edge of the wing to prevent airflow disturbance at division line. This machine, F3F-1* (0262), *carries neutrality patrol star, and a Mk. XLIII bomb rack under starboard wing.*
(Photo: U.S. Navy)

One F3F-2 is of especial interest. *1031* was routinely delivered to Anacostia on 4th April 1938. It had been allocated for U.S. Naval Air Station, Norfolk, Virginia as a spare for VF-6, but was first utilised for tests at Anacostia when its assignment was changed and it was sent back to the factory in May for installation of wind tunnel test fittings. There were brief tests with various propellers at Anacostia while waiting for the full-scale N.A.C.A. wind tunnel at Langley Field, Virginia. Here it followed the XF4F-2 into the test chamber so that areas of possible speed improvement could be determined. Following another month at Anacostia it went to Grumman where an upper wing with split landing flaps was installed. Trials with these flaps did not sufficiently impress the Navy so F3F-2 (*1031*) was returned to the manufacturer for completion of its conversion. It was re-delivered as XF3F-3 (*1031*) on 19th October 1938 with several speed-boosting improvements including a newly designed wing leading edge and a different engine cowling. The most noticeable change was a curved plastic windshield similar to that on the modified XF4F-2.

The last F3F-1, 0264, *was stationed at Anacostia until December 1938 for comparative test flying; later flew with VF-4, VF-3 and VF-71.* (Photo: Bowers' Collection)

F3F-2 (0986) *factory fresh at Bethpage, Long Island, before delivery to VF-6. Note louvre above leading edge of stabiliser designed to reduce CO content in cockpit.*
(Photo: Bowers' Collection)

F3F-2 after U.S.S. Enterprise *shake-down cruise to Rio de Janeiro. This machine (*0983, *the last F3F to be stricken) displays bombing "E" and markings of second section leader of VF-6 "Comets".* (Photo: Bowers' Collection)

Fiscal year 1938 (1st July 1937–30th June 1938) saw the Naval fighter monoplane competition between Brewster's XF2A-1 (*0453*), Seversky's NF-1 (Civil Registration *NX1254*) and Grumman XF4F-2 (*0383*). Had quick delivery of quantities of winning aircraft been possible, there probably would have been no product F3F-3s. Brewster's design won the competition but the company could not promise quick delivery. The Navy needed one squadron of fighters in a hurry to replace ageing F2F-1s. Grumman's XF4F-2 had failed the competition mainly because of engine troubles but their proposal to improve the F3F-2 with prompt delivery of twenty-seven fighters won them a contract on 21st June 1938. The money was allocated, then after sufficient testing of F3F-2 (*1031*), the new configuration was released for production on 22nd September 1938. Initial delivery was in December with the final acceptance being made on 11th May 1939. This final aircraft was F3F-3 (*1470*), the last of 164 of the F3F series and the last new biplane fighter aircraft accepted by the U.S. Navy. The series had begun its flying career in the Navy with the acceptance of the XF3F-1 in July 1935. Flying days ended just prior to the end of November 1943 when the last active F3F-2 (*0983*) was stricken from the records of serviceable aircraft.

SERVICE ASSIGNMENTS

Grumman F3Fs were flown by all U.S. Navy and U.S. Marine Corps fighter squadrons active from 1936 to

F3F-2 (0994) *as initially assigned. VMF-2 placed insignia on tail rather than fuselage, VMF-1 did not reproduce squadron insignia on aircraft.* (Photo: Bowers' Collection)

F3F-3 (1463) *assigned to Anacostia; landing light under port wing was common to all but the first XF3F-1. F3F-3 cowling was faired around exhaust stacks in contrast to the F3F-2's cutout.* (Photo: U.S. Navy)

1940. The first green-tailed F3F-1s (*0212–0230*) went to VF-5B assigned to the U.S.S. *Ranger* (*CV-4*) just prior to commencement of the annual training cruise. They arrived in San Diego, California in time to replace nine FF-1s and nine F2F-1s then serving with the "Red Rippers". In June, when the fleet returned from Panama, VF-6B on U.S.S. *Saratoga* (CV-3) turned in its Boeing F4B-4s in exchange for white-tailed F3F-1s (*0230-0247*).* Before the end of October this "Felix the Cat" squadron suffered one fatality in two "strike" and two "overhaul" crashes. This caused a review of the design, a temporary limiting to six "g" and a decision to static test one aircraft to destruction. 5-F-2 (*0213*) was flown to N.A.F. for extensive tests until it was stricken in April 1938. These tests proved the desirability of stiffening the upper wing beam and the aileron bell cranks. These changes were retrofitted to service F3F-1s as well as incorporated into later production models. Use of the F3Fs by the U.S. Marine Corps began in January 1937 when F3F-1s *0251* and *0254* to *0258* joined VF-4M of Aircraft Two, Fleet Marine Force, based at San Diego. Here they served with F2F-1s until the new F3F-2s replaced them both.

Fiscal year 1938 Naval Aeronautic Organisation changed the numbering system for aircraft squadrons. Effective 1st July 1937 the suffixes (B for Battle Force, M for Marine, etc.) were dropped and all carrier-based air groups were assigned numbers corresponding to the hull number of the parent carrier. Thus VF-5B on *Ranger* became VF-4 while VF-6B on *Saratoga* became VF-3. Squadrons in the Marine Corps Air Groups were numbered to correspond to the parent division—but with letters included to indicate Marines and to avoid confusion with Navy squadrons. VF-4M became VMF-2.

The December 1937 to May 1938 delivery of F3F-2s produced somewhat of a jumble of Bureau number assignments. On 1st December VF-6, scheduled for the U.S.S. *Enterprise* (CV-6) at Norfolk, first received *0968* and *0969* with their blue tail surfaces. VMF-2 was issued the next twelve (*0970–0981*) beginning 13th December. These two outfits were brought up to complement before VMF-1, based at Quantico, Virginia, replaced F4B-4s beginning 1st March 1938. Initial assignments of operating aircraft follow: VF-6—*0968–0969*, *0982–0991*, *0998–1003;* VMF-2—*0970–0981*, *0992–0997;* VMF-1—*1009–1026* (remainder as spares).

*0230 *was originally assigned as a cruise spare for VF-5B from 20th April to 9th June. On 11th June it was accepted by VF-6B.*

F3F-2 (0995) *in W.W.II warpaint, with tail lettering reduced from three-inch to one-inch characters.* 0995 *was assigned to both Corpus Christi and Jacksonville in 1942 before being stricken off in January 1943.* (Photo: Bowers' Collection)

Above: *Al Williams'* NR1050 *Gulfhawk II; highly polished chrome struts combined with brilliant orange finish and blue and white trim to produce an extremely colourful aeroplane. In contrast to other F3F types, the span was 28 ft. 6 in., and the machine had improved spin characteristics.* (Photo: Besecker Collection). Below: NC1051 *Gulfhawk III is less well known than the single-seater; this G-32 design had split flaps on upper wing.* (Photo: Grumman)

Grumman company hack and demonstrator. The upper wing of this G-32A design was flown on F3F-2 (1031) *before conversion to show landing performance with flaps.* (Photo: Grumman)

With this outfitting all regular Navy and Marine fighting squadrons had Grumman single-seater equipment. As flying hours accumulated and accidents required replacement or overhaul, these initial postings changed. Marine Air Group One proved the exception by keeping all its original allocation until they were replaced *en masse*, while the remaining fifty-four were used interchangeably by several squadrons. The bulk of the F3F-3s were assigned to VF-5 replacing red-tailed F2F-1s on 18th May 1939 when the U.S.S. *Yorktown* (CV-5) arrived in San Diego from the east coast. During the next several months overhaul schedules were hard pressed to keep up with the increased flying hours by all squadrons. Also, a new fighter squadron, VF-7, was formed at Norfolk on 1st July 1939 for the U.S.S. *Wasp* (CV-7). Thus we should not be surprised to learn of the assignment of F3Fs of different dash numbers to the various squadrons. VF-5 operated F3F-2s (*0986*, *0990*, *0993* and *1037*) for several months alongside its F3F-3s. VF-4, VF-6 and VMF-2 each flew F3F-3s with their other aircraft. In a similar manner, VF-2 on U.S.S. *Lexington* (CV-2) flew F3F-1s (*0219* and *0243*) in mid-1939 with its yellow-tailed F2F-1s.When VF-3 turned in half of its F3F-1s for Brewster F2A-1s in December 1939 the former went to VF-7 and received the black tail colour assigned to *Wasp*.

PHASE-OUT

As biplanes gradually gave way to monoplanes, the colourful F3Fs were retired to training duty. However, they were still in service when the bright pre-war colours were lost to the early non-specular grey finish in early 1941. Actually, VF-71 (ex VB-7*) and VF-72 (ex VF-7*) turned in the last F3F-1s from combat squadron use on 10th February 1941. By April 1941, when *Yorktown* left Hawaii for the east coast and the Neutrality Patrol, Air Group Five's aircraft were victims of the overall light grey paint. When VF-5's last F3F-2 and F3F-3 were turned in on 20th June 1941 the "Striking Eagles" were the last carrier-based fighter squadron to switch to monoplanes. The Marines, however, still had F3Fs. VMF-1 and VMF-2 were respectively re-numbered VMF-111 and VMF-211 on 1st July 1941. By this date VMF-111 had almost completed transition to F4F-3As and retired its last F3F-2 on 28th July. When VMF-211 in Hawaii turned in thirteen F3F-2s on 10th October 1941 all the fighter squadrons were equipped with monoplanes and the Grumman F3Fs were earmarked for fighter-trained usage. F3F-1s served at Norfolk and Miami, Florida. The F3F-2s were principally at Miami and Corpus Christi, Texas, while the F3F-3s were mostly at Corpus Christi. As they became unserviceable or were replaced by modern service types in the training squadrons, they were stricken for ground use in the Naval Technical Training Schools. None apparently survived the rigours of assembly and disassembly in the mechanics' and artisans' training classes.

**Redesignated effective 15th October 1940.*

F3F-3 (1463) *in slow roll, showing wing plan; formation lights just outboard of star insignia. Photographed 7th April 1939 at Anacostia.* (Photo: U.S.N. Archives 464996)

Left: *F3F-1* (0220) *prior to 30th March 1936 delivery.* (V. J. Berinati Collection). Right: *F3F-1* (0231) *before delivery, with red upper cowl half, white tail.* 0230 *marked for 6-F-1 had gone earlier as cruise spare for VF-5B.* (Photo: Grumman)

Left: *F3F-2* (1003) *was the last "Comet" in the initial allocation;* 0999 *and* 1003 *were only two of initial batch to serve full 24-month tour with VF-6 before overhaul.* (Photo: Larkins' Collection). Right: *F3F-2* (1008) *originally assigned as spare, with Mk. III camera gun on top wing and incomplete paint scheme indicating that extra machines were operated by the squadrons.*

F3F-1 (0252) *on 17th January 1939 shortly after overhaul at San Diego; red chevron, cowling and section leader's band on C.O.'s aircraft, and small section light in centre stripe on turtle-back.* (Photo: U.S.N. Archives 7366)

INDIVIDUAL MISCELLANEOUS ASSIGNMENTS

F3F-1 (*0219*) holds the record for the number of different fighter squadron tours starting with VF-5B becoming VF-4, VF-3, VF-2, VF-7 and VF-71. VMF-2 was the only squadron to fly all models of the F3F and had F2Fs as well. F3F-2 (*0986*) flying with VF-6 had the least number of hours. It suffered a low-altitude engine stoppage on 1st February 1938 and was forced to a rough wheels-up salt water landing in Hampton Roads, Virginia. Salvage difficulties kept it submerged for seventeen days. It was stricken with only ten and a half hours' flying time, and was replaced by F3F-2 (*1006*) factory-painted as 6-F-6. F3F-1 (*0248*), F3F-2 (*1033*) and F3F-3 (*1466*) had successive staff tours with the Flag Unit of Commander, Aircraft Battle Force, United States Fleet while F3F-3 (*1464*) served with the Fleet Tactical Unit helping develop aircraft tactics in 1939 and 1940. F3F3s (*1462* and *1463*) were the only ones of the entire F3F production series to serve without assignment to a combat squadron during their careers. The record for the most flying hours will remain unknown unless the logs for the individual aircraft can be located. Perhaps even then it will evade us since unnecessary paperwork details understandably were often overlooked following Pearl Harbour.

ENGINES

The Pratt & Whitney Twin Wasp Jr. engine was the powerplant for the Grumman F2Fs and F3F-1s and scheduled for an alternative to the Wright XR-1670-2 for the XF4F-1. This engine was a 14-cylinder twin-row radial known in service as the R-1535—the 1535 indicating the cubic inches of displacement. Dash numbers, such as R-1535-72 and R-1535-84 indicated various modifications of the basic engine. The -72 was a direct-drive, single-stage supercharged plant used in the F2F-1s and initially in the XF3F-1. But P. & W. was able to offer an improved engine for the later production models. Thus the R-1535-84s in the F3F-1s had automatic valve lubrication, a dynamic damper to overcome torsional vibration and provisions for hydraulic propeller pitch control. The latter enabled a two-bladed Hamilton Standard propeller to replace a mechanically controlled Lycoming Smith propeller on the XF3F-1. The torsional vibration problem was the most troublesome feature of the earlier -72 engine since cruising operation between 1,350 and 1,750 r.p.m. was restricted. The cure was a relatively heavy dynamic damper and this with the other improvements made the -84 almost 40 pounds heavier than the -72. To evaluate the effect of this extra weight, the third XF3F-1 was initially delivered with a lead-filled pipe around the front of the crankcase. This shows clearly in some photographs and serves to differentiate between the second and third XF3F-1s before the latter received its R-1535-84 or the Anacostia markings beneath the cockpit. The last twenty-three F3F-1s had factory-installed Coffman cartridge starters. The first thirty-one had the modification made in the field after removal of the hand inertia starter. This marked the first usage of the "shotgun shell" type starter in U.S. naval fighter aircraft, but certainly was not an unexpected development as engines became larger.

A Grumman letter to the Bureau of Aeronautics on 3rd June 1936 proposed replacing the P. & W. engine with a new Wright Cyclone R-1820-G5 in the fifty-fourth F3F-1. Greatly improved performance was promised with a three-blade constant-speed propeller nine feet in diameter. Grumman evaluated this combination for a maximum speed of 260 m.p.h. at 12,000 ft. against 226 m.p.h. for the F3F-1 and 256 m.p.h. estimated by the Navy for the proposed XF4F-1. Most interesting too was the 35,000 ft. service ceiling that could be made possible by the two-speed supercharger in the Wright. As we have seen, this resulted in the contract for the XF3F-2 (*0452*) powered with the XR-1820-22. This nine-cylinder single-row direct drive Cyclone was still under test by the Navy at the Aeronautical Engine laboratory in Philadelphia. The Wright was heavier than the P. & W. engine but did not affect the balance of the aeroplane since its centre of gravity was farther aft. The ease of the substitution of Cyclone for Twin

F3F-1 (0251) *as aircraft of VF-4M squadron leader, with markings in use January to June 1937. This machine was damaged beyond repair in crash on 26th August 1937 and stricken with 265 hours flight time.* (Photo: Smithsonian Institution Neg. A1013)

F3F-2 (1041) *from VMF-1 coming in to land at the 1938 National Air Races, with pilot's seat cranked up and stabiliser cranked down; compare oleo leg extension with ground photos. Note bomb racks on opposite sides to usual arrangement. A small after carrier approach light is just visible between A and R of MARINES; comparison of photos points out the smaller bulge over the ·30 calibre weapon than over the starboard gun.* (Photo: Jim Tenety)

Wasp Jr. permitted the great similarity in fuselage and wing construction in the F3Fs. The -2 and -3 models used the same basic engine and were so nearly alike that Grumman built them both to design number 19. The basic design was offered for export as G-37 but none were sold. A close look at the biplane specifications will reveal that the structures for *all* F3Fs were very much alike. In fact the XF3F-2 (*0452*), in an overhaul and conversion ending 11th April 1938, became a standard F3F-1 and eventually had tours with VF-3 and VF-4.

CONSTRUCTION

In a 1936 letter to the Bureau of Aeronautics, Captain John H. Towers, U.S.N. then commanding the Naval Air Station, San Diego, pointed out that the Grumman wing spars were easily repaired by bolting on replacement end sections and that the monocoque fuselage also lent itself to economical repair since replacement plates could easily be cut and drilled. The engine mount was welded tubular steel bolted to the aluminium alloy fuselage. There were four main longitudinal stringers and a series of bulkheads between various sections. Special flotation bags and inflating gases were not used in the F3Fs. Instead watertight compartments were built into the lower fuselage and the upper wing forward of the front spar. With these spaces intact the plane would float at about a forty-five degree nose-down attitude. Caution had to be used in towing a floating plane however. The recommended procedure was to tow tail first using the arresting hook or the cross tube built in for lifting the tail. At least one sinking was due to improper handling. F3F-1 (*0241*) operating with VF-3 was forced down and made a full stall, wheels-up landing in a smooth sea alongside *Saratoga.* A line was fastened to the propeller hub and the plane towed by a launch toward the ship's crane, but sank before it could be recovered. However, the flotation design most often worked happily. One pilot talked to the recovery team with his radio while perched astride his ditched Grumman. Only his feet got wet.

The wings and movable tail surfaces were fabric covered over metal frames, while the vertical fin and horizontal stabiliser were all metal.

The upper wing spanned 32 ft. with a 5 ft. chord while the lower wing dimensions were 29 ft. 6 in. and 4 ft. respectively. Ailerons were only on the upper wing. The gap at the wing root was just over 5ft. but decreased toward the tip because of a two-degree dihedral in the lower wing with none in the upper wing. The stagger at the leading edge of the lower wing was 31 $\frac{1}{16}$ in., wing area 260·6 square ft. and the airfoil shape on all F3F wings was the N.A.C.A. "CYH". Brewster built the F3F-1 and F3F-2 wings on sub-contracts from Grumman. But by the time the F3F-3s came along Brewsters were busy with their

Second production F3F-2 (0968) *before delivery on 29th November 1937 to VF-6—"Fighting Six". The tail is "true blue", indicating CV-6 U.S.S.* Enterprise. (Photo: Grumman 6194 for Bu.Aer. Archives 72-AC-18B-9)

F3F-1 (0239), *squadron leader's aircraft of VF-3, with "Felix the Cat" emblem and the* Saratoga*'s white tail. The pilot is Lt.-Cdr. Cooper.* (Photo: courtesy Fred C. Dickey, Jr.)

F2A-1s. Grumman turned to Kirkham Engineering and Manufacturing Corporation in Farmingdale, Long Island, New York near the main plant. This company had been doing basic machine work for Grumman for a long time and took the F3F-3 wings as its first wing building sub-contract. Extensive machine tool facilities were set up, but initial production was slow. Introduction of the F3F-3 to the Fleet was delayed, but as Kirkham gained experience with wings, they became an invaluable asset to later Grumman production records. These later wings also differed slightly from earlier models by virtue of a re-designed leading edge to provide smoother airflow. As for length, the F3F-1 was 23 ft. 3½ in. while the others were 23 ft. 1⅝ in. long. With the tail on the ground the height over the upper wing was 8 ft. 6 in., but with the thrust line horizontal, the height over the tail was approximately 10 ft. 6 in. These heights do not include the propeller or the demountable radio antenna stub masts on wings or tail. All the F3Fs, and later F4Fs too, had manually operated landing gear constructed of steel tubing. Retraction took about thirty-two turns of a hand crank and twelve seconds' time. The wheels could be lowered in eight seconds but many a scraped knuckle resulted if the operator carelessly let go of the handle. The chain drive mechanism had positive stops and locks when in the up or down position. Bendix oleo struts took the shock of landing. All models had hydraulic brakes and 26 in. by 6 in. tyres. The tail wheel was also retractable and could be locked to trail aft while in flight. This position was used for field landings but the wheel was left free to swivel on carrier landings in case the arresting wire was caught off centreline. These Grummans had a wheels-up landing characteristic on grass surfaces that usually resulted in a nose over and damaged vertical tail surfaces. Their behaviour in wheels-up water landings was much better. The horizontal stabiliser had a 10 ft. assymetrical span and was also adjustable by a hand crank from the cockpit. This provided the ability to make a three-point landing in any condition of power or loading.

USEFUL LOAD

As defined by the Navy, the useful load consisted of pilot (200 lb. allowed), armament, fuel and oil, radio and miscellaneous equipment. The F3Fs were fitted for two synchronised Browning machine guns firing through the propeller. A ·50 calibre M-2 or M-1921 gun with 200 rounds was carried on the starboard side with a ·30 calibre M-2 and 500 rounds to port. Beneath each lower wing was a Mark XLI bomb rack for one 110-lb. bomb or alternatively a Mark XLIII training bomb rack with small practice bombs. A Very pistol was carried accessible to the pilot for signalling purposes. The F3F-1s had a 75-U.S. gal. main fuel tank and a 35-gal. auxiliary tank. Because of increased fuel consumption of the more powerful Cyclone engines the production F3F-2 and -3 carried 130 gal. in an 83/47 combination. In each of the aircraft a 20-gal. reserve supply was provided by a standpipe arrangement in the main tank. Oil capacity was 9½ gal. plus foaming space. The radio receiver and transmitter weighed approximately sixty-six pounds and when the antennaes were rigged the maximum speeds were reduced about one knot. A radio direction finder loop was built into the pilot's head rest, behind which was stowed the life raft. The breathing oxygen, emergency rations and first-aid kit comprised the remaining major items of useful load. An electrically operated Mark III gun camera was often carried on top of the upper wing.

During certain spinning trials after the second XF3F-1 spun in at Dahlgren, the F3Fs carried a spin recovery parachute temporarily replacing the arresting hook. Use of this chute was tried by Grumman prior to delivery of the third XF3F-1. In actual Navy trials, the chute was apparently deployed only on one occasion during the Production Inspection Trials of F3F-2 (*0967*). Because of the poor spin recovery characteristics, voluntary spinning of all F3Fs was prohibited. This was the only restriction on manœuvring the aircraft, except that limiting engine r.p.m. could not be exceeded. But with the excellent handling qualities at low speeds a spin could not be entered inadvertently by an experienced pilot. The controls at all speeds were "light, adequate and effective". Very little stick force was required to recover from a high-speed dive and pilots were cautioned not to overstress the aircraft in a heavy-handed pull-out. The calculated terminal velocity was 415 m.p.h. and there was no restriction on terminal velocity dives. All the F3Fs were initially designed for 9 "g" in manœuvres, however the F3F-1 production models were restricted to 8·44 "g" since they were heavier than the prototype. Later models were allowed the full 9 "g". Take-off distance into a 25-knot wind normally found in carrier operation was about 200 ft. for the F3F-1 and 125 ft. for later models. The planes lifted off at 50-55 knots i.a.s. and normally landed at 60-65 knots i.a.s. Performance and weight figures from Navy trials are given on page 12. The maximum speeds are with the engines operated at rated conditions at critical altitude. In most cases, the engines were slightly more powerful and higher speeds could be attained. But in the end, performance was the primary criterion and the monoplane proved superior. During the trials of F3F-2 (*0967*) at Anacostia the experimental monoplanes were also present. A prophetic statement from the trial report clearly shows the situation in the spring of 1938: "The aeroplane was found to be highly manœuvrable, surpassing in this regard any other aeroplane that has been submitted for trials. In manœuvring in combat with two experimental fighter monoplanes*

* *XF2-1 and NF-1.*

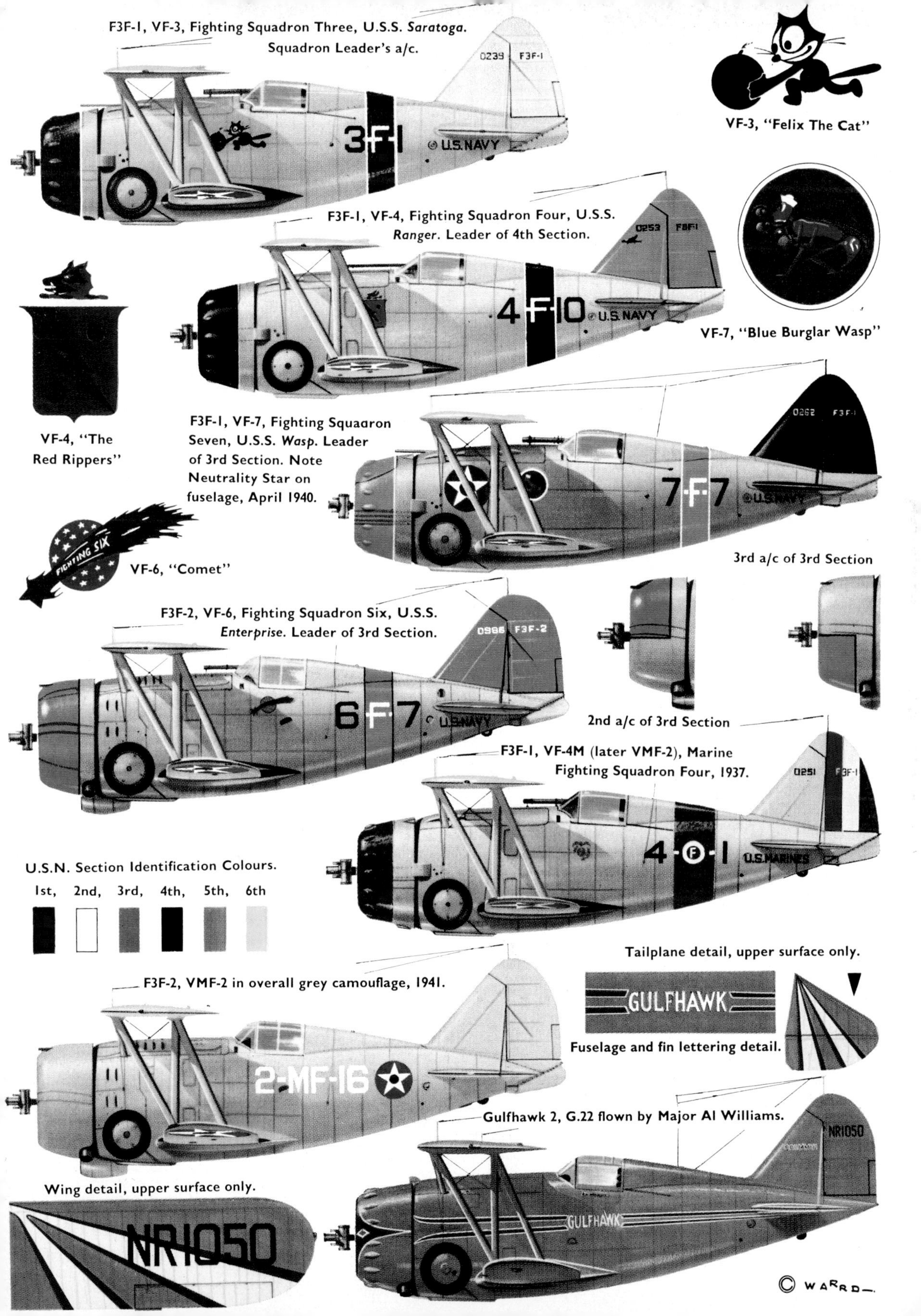
F3F-1, VF-3, Fighting Squadron Three, U.S.S. Saratoga. Squadron Leader's a/c.
0239 F3F-1
3-F-1
U.S. NAVY
VF-3, "Felix The Cat"
F3F-1, VF-4, Fighting Squadron Four, U.S.S. Ranger. Leader of 4th Section.
0253 F3F-1
4-F-10
U.S. NAVY
VF-7, "Blue Burglar Wasp"
VF-4, "The Red Rippers"
F3F-1, VF-7, Fighting Squadron Seven, U.S.S. Wasp. Leader of 3rd Section. Note Neutrality Star on fuselage, April 1940.
0262 F3F-1
7-F-7
U.S. NAVY
FIGHTING SIX
VF-6, "Comet"
3rd a/c of 3rd Section
F3F-2, VF-6, Fighting Squadron Six, U.S.S. Enterprise. Leader of 3rd Section.
0986 F3F-2
6-F-7
U.S. NAVY
2nd a/c of 3rd Section
F3F-1, VF-4M (later VMF-2), Marine Fighting Squadron Four, 1937.
0251 F3F-1
4-F-1
U.S. MARINES
U.S.N. Section Identification Colours.
1st, 2nd, 3rd, 4th, 5th, 6th
Tailplane detail, upper surface only.
GULFHAWK
Fuselage and fin lettering detail.
F3F-2, VMF-2 in overall grey camouflage, 1941.
2-MF-16
Gulfhawk 2, G.22 flown by Major Al Williams.
NR1050
GULFHAWK
Wing detail, upper surface only.
NR1050
© WARD

F3F-2 and F3F-3 aircraft in a formation flight from the Miami advanced training base, on 8th January 1942. No. 91 is F3F-3 (1456), *formerly a section leader's aircraft of VF-5. The tails and cowlings are of various colours.* (Photo: U.S.N. Archives 80-G-10553)

the results were such to indicate that the only chance of success with a monoplane against the F3F-2 would be to get in an effective shot on the first approach and then leave the vicinity. Otherwise, the F3F-2 has an almost insurmountable advantage due to its higher manœuvrability."

CIVILIAN EDITIONS

Two of the three Grumman F3F types built for civilian use still exist. The first, the famous "Gulfhawk II" was built to Grumman design 22 and delivered to Major Al Williams at Roosevelt Field in December 1936. It was licensed as *NR 1050*. The fuselage was approximately the same as the F3F, but the wings were more nearly like the earlier F2F-1s. It had a Wright Cyclone R-1820-G1 engine similar to the F3F-2 installation, but was especially equipped for inverted flying which was one of Major Williams' specialities. He used the plane for aerobatic demonstrations throughout the United States and on a 1938 tour of Europe. During W.W.II the Grumman Gulfhawk kept its brilliant colours and made demonstration flights at various service aviation training schools to inspire fighter pilots to precision airmanship. On 11th October 1948 Gulfhawk II made its final flight at Washington National Airport before being presented to the National Air Museum.

Other civilian Grummans, both two-seaters, followed the F3F-2s off the production line. The first was Gulfhawk III, a G-32 design and registered as *NC 1051*. The engine was a 1,000-h.p. Wright R-1820-G2 very similar to that used in the Navy fighters. Its near sister, the G-32A was built for Grumman's own use and originally registered as *NC 1326* with a 775-h.p. R-1820-F52. In November 1942 both aircraft became U.S.A.A.C. utility cargo planes under the C-103 (later UC-103) designation. Gulfhawk III was U.S.A.A.C. serial number *42-97044*. It later crashed in the southern Florida Everglades and has not been brought out. The ex-company hack became *42-97045* and served with its sister ship ferrying V.I.P.s from Bolling Field, Washington, D.C. until May 1943 when they became fighter-type trainers for ferry pilots in Miami. This latter aircraft has had several owners since being sold as surplus in 1945 and has borne several colourful paint jobs. Post-war registration was as *NC 46110* and later as *N7F* in which guise it simulates a Navy F3F-2 in full pre-war colours. Thus one example of the little Grummans remains in flying condition to remind us of the last and best of the Navy biplane fighters.

Author's note: *Grateful thanks are given to those who helped with pictures and information and especially to Hal Andrews and Grant Daly for their invaluable assistance with reference materials.*

DELIVERY DATES AND SHOP NUMBERS

Aircraft (Bureau Number)	Grumman Shop Number	Design Number	Date of Delivery
XF3F-1 (*9727*)	257	11	see text
F3F-1 (*0211–0264*)	271 to 324 incl.	11	29– 1–36 18– 9–36
XF3F-2 (*0452*)	354	19	27– 7–36
F3F-2 (*0967–1047*)	365 to 445 incl.	19	17– 7–37 11– 5–38
XF3F-3 (*1031*) (Conversion)	429	19	19–10–38
F3F-3 (*1444–1470*)	478 to 504 incl.	19	16–12–38 10– 5–39
Gulfhawk II	355	22	6–12–36
Gulfhawk III	446	32	6– 5–38
NC-1326	447	32A	1– 7–38

NAVY ENGINE CHARACTERISTICS

Navy Model ...	R-1535-72	R-1535-84	XR-1820-22	R-1820-22
Mfg. Model...	R-1535-A2	R-1535-A3	R-1820-G25	R-1820-G5
Ratings: b.h.p./r.p.m./alt. in ft.				
Take-off (Critical Altitude)...	650/2200/SL*	700/2250/SL	1000/2100/SL	950/2200/SL
(Low Blower) ...	650/2200/7500	650/2200/7500	850/2100/ to 5800	850/2100/ to 600
(Hi Blower) ...	one speed	one speed	820/2100/12000	750/2100/15200
Limiting r.p.m. ...	3,100	3,100	—	2,730
Comp. Ratio ...	6·75 : 1	6·75 : 1	6·4 : 1	6·45 : 1
Diameter × Length (in.) ...	$43\frac{7}{8} \times 48\frac{3}{8}$	$44\frac{1}{8} \times 43\frac{3}{8}$	$53\frac{3}{4} \times 43\frac{1}{8}$	$54\frac{1}{4} \times 48\frac{1}{8}$
Dry Weight (lb.) ...	920	959	1,080	1,098
Impeller (Supercharger Blower):				
Diameter (in.) ...	$6\frac{7}{8}$	$6\frac{7}{8}$	11	11
Gear Ratio ...	12 : 1	12 : 1	7·14 : 1 & 10 : 1	7·14 : 1 & 10 : 1

Above ratings based on 87 octane aviation gasoline—all these engines direct drive.
*R-1535-72 later service rated 700/2200/SL for take-off.

PERFORMANCE OF NAVAL F3F SERIES AIRCRAFT

Model	XF3F-1	F3F-1	XF3F-2	F3F-2	XF3F-3	F3F-3
Maximum Speed (m.p.h.) ... (Rated power at critical altitude)	226	231	255	256	263·5	261·5
Minimum Speed (m.p.h.) ... (Without power at sea level)	64·5	65·5	66·2	69	68	68
Service Ceiling (ft.) ...	29,500	29,500	33,100	32,400	33,100	33,200
Critical Altitude of Engine (ft.) ...	7,500	7,500	12,000	15,200	15,200	15,200
Rate Climb SL (f.p.m.) ...	—	1,900	—	2,800	—	2,750
At Critical Altitude (f.p.m.)...	1,750	1,900	—	2,200	2,100	2,100
Full Load Weight as fighter (lb.) ...	4,100	4,116	4,300	4,448	4,529	4,615

PRINTED IN ENGLAND © Profile Publications Ltd., P.O. Box 26, 1a North Street, Leatherhead, Surrey, England.
Printed by Hills & Lacy Ltd., London and Watford, England. U.S 2nd Class Mailing Rates applied for.

PROFILE
PUBLICATIONS

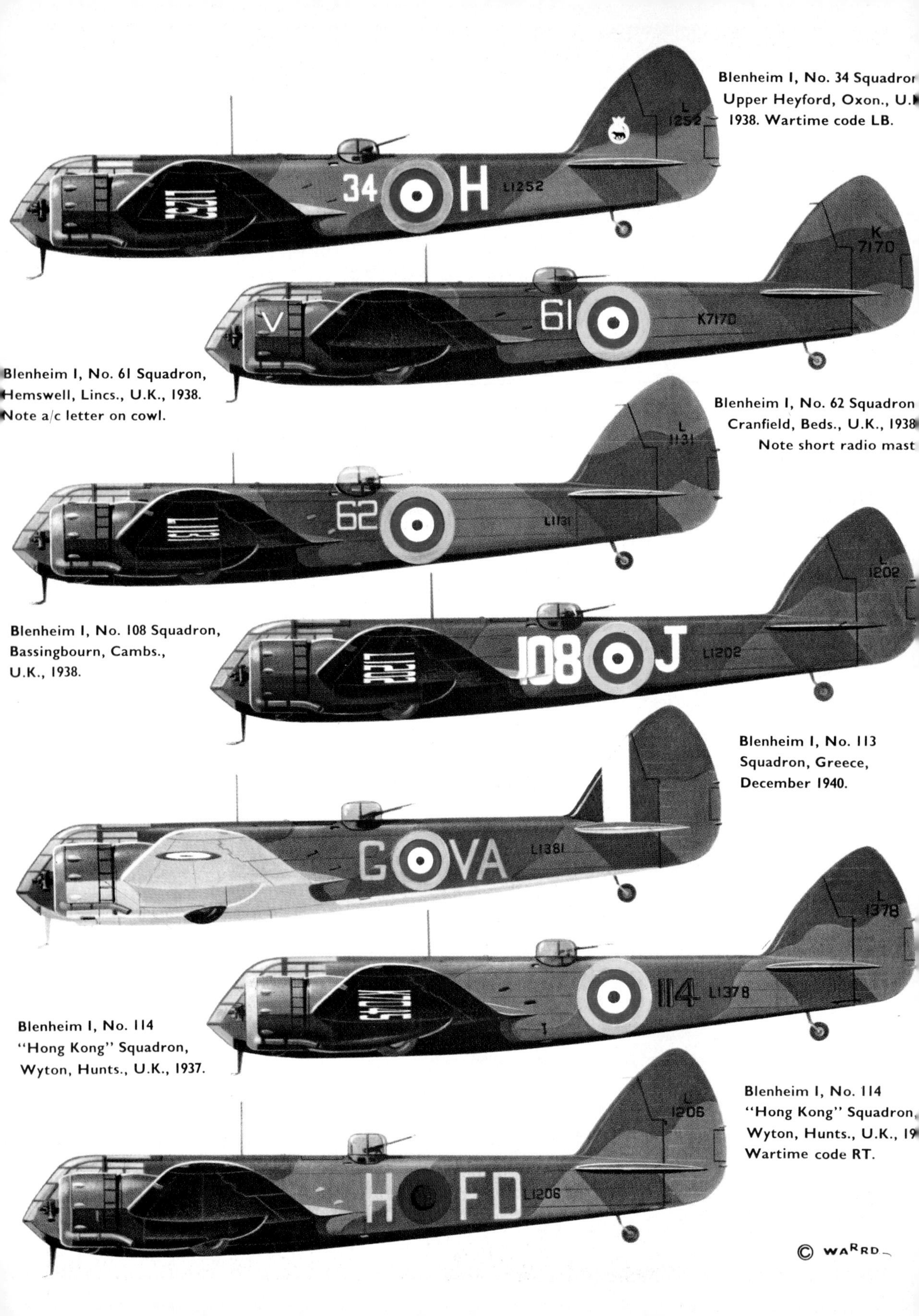

Blenheim I, No. 34 Squadron
Upper Heyford, Oxon., U.K.
1938. Wartime code LB.

Blenheim I, No. 61 Squadron,
Hemswell, Lincs., U.K., 1938.
Note a/c letter on cowl.

Blenheim I, No. 62 Squadron
Cranfield, Beds., U.K., 1938
Note short radio mast

Blenheim I, No. 108 Squadron,
Bassingbourn, Cambs.,
U.K., 1938.

Blenheim I, No. 113
Squadron, Greece,
December 1940.

Blenheim I, No. 114
"Hong Kong" Squadron,
Wyton, Hunts., U.K., 1937.

Blenheim I, No. 114
"Hong Kong" Squadron,
Wyton, Hunts., U.K., 19
Wartime code RT.

The Bristol Blenheim I

by Philip J. R. Moyes

Blenheim IF L1426 *of No. 25 Squadron in 1939 before the outbreak of war.*

In July, 1933, Frank Barnwell, the Bristol Aeroplane Company's chief designer, drafted a small twin-engined low-wing cabin monoplane (Type 135) for six passengers and two pilots, intended for Bristol Aquila sleeve-valve air-cooled radial engines. The design was brought to the attention of Lord Rothermere, the newspaper proprietor, who had previously declared his intention of having built for him "the fastest commercial aeroplane in Europe, if not the world". He wanted this for his private use, to encourage prominent firms and businessmen to make proper use of civil aviation and, not least, to show the Air Ministry how their existing fighters might be no match for a fast transport used as a bomber.

Lord Rothermere asked Bristols for full particulars of the Type 135 within one week, and on 3rd March 1934, Barnwell quoted an estimated top speed for a version with Mercury engines instead of Aquilas of 240 m.p.h. at 6,500 ft. with moderate supercharging. At the end of March, Lord Rothermere placed an order for the Mercury-powered aircraft stating that he would pay the estimated cost of £18,500 in two instalments, half immediately and half in a year's time provided the aircraft was flying by then. The first instalment was not in fact paid until June which gave Bristols two months longer in which to have the machine flying.

The prototype of Lord Rothermere's aircraft, Type 142, made its first flight on 12th April 1935 at Filton, and by the following June it had aroused such great

Type 142 at Filton. It first flew with four-bladed fixed-pitch wooden airscrews but is here seen after being fitted with three-blader Hamilton-Standards.

"Britain First" photographed in 1936 and serialled K7557 *after presentation to the Air Council.* (Photo: "Flight")

interest in Air Ministry circles on account of its high performance—top speed of 307 m.p.h. was faster than that of any contemporary R.A.F. fighter in service—that Lord Rothermere generously presented it to the nation for full evaluation as a potential bomber, having already named it "Britain First"; in July it received the serial number *K7557*.

As early as 9th July a design conference was held at the Air Ministry's request and the question of converting the Type 142 into a medium bomber discussed with Bristols. The outcome of this conference was the issue of Specification 28/35 which Bristols met with the Type 142M Blenheim I. One of the alterations on the bomber (which did not officially become the Blenheim Mark I until about May 1936) was the raising of the wing to mid position to make room for a bomb bay in the fuselage below the wing spars. A Browning gun and a bomb-aimer's position were provided in the nose and provision made for a semi-retractable gun turret in the dorsal position.

INTO R.A.F. SERVICE

The Air Ministry ordered Blenheims "straight off the drawing board" as part of the Expansion Programme. The initial contract for 150 was placed in September, 1935, and the first of these, *K7033*, did in fact serve as the prototype, making its maiden flight at Filton on 25th June 1936. Deliveries of production aircraft to squadrons began in March, 1937, the first going to No. 114 Squadron, Wyton. The unit's first machine (*K7036*) apparently suffered a landing mishap immediately on arrival at Wyton and was a complete write-off. From July 1936 onwards additional contracts were signed for Blenheim Is (including some for export) and before production switched to the Mark IV in 1939, a total of 1,280 Mk. Is had been built including 250 by A. V. Roe at Chadderton and 336 by Rootes Securities at Speke.

At the time of "Munich" the Blenheim I equipped

Blenheim I prototype at Filton in June 1936, and (below) *same aircraft in markings for the Hendon Display of late June 1936.*

Right: *Blenheims in production at Filton in 1938. A total of 694 Mk. Is was built by Bristol, including some for export.*

Below: *No. 114 Squadron's first Blenheim (*K7036*, fourth production aircraft) wrecked on delivery to the squadron at Wyton when the pilot applied brakes too hard, causing it to turn over on to its back, 10th March 1937.*

sixteen R.A.F. bomber squadrons at home and for the record these were disposed as follows:

	Squadron	*Station*
All in No. 1 Group	21	Eastchurch
	34	Upper Heyford
	57	Upper Heyford
	90	Bicester
	101	Bicester
	107	Harwell
All in No. 2 Group	62	Cranfield
	82	Cranfield
	104	Bassingbourn
	108	Bassingbourn
	114	Wyton
	139	Wyton
All in No. 5 Group	44	Waddington
	110	Waddington
	61	Hemswell
	144	Hemswell

Blenheims of No. 114 Squadron in 1937. (Photo: "Flight")

Third production Blenheim, K7035, *of No. 114 Squadron (code letters "FD") at Wyton, early 1939.*

Blenheims K7078 *"J" and* K7070 *"G" of No. 139 Squadron at Wyton, October 1937.*

On 13th January 1938, the Blenheim I entered squadron service overseas—with No. 30 Squadron at Habbaniya, Iraq—and early in 1939 the first Blenheim Is reached India.

When war came in September, 1939, Blenheim Is equipped only two bomber squadrons at home (having been superseded by the Mk. IV) but overseas it equipped eleven squadrons in Egypt, Aden, Iraq, India and Singapore. Seven home-based fighter squadrons, previously equipped with biplanes, had converted—or were in the process of converting—to Blenheim IF fighters, adapted from the standard bomber by the addition of four Brownings in a gun-pack under the bomb cell; the gun-packs were made by the Southern Railway workshops.

The Blenheim IF soon proved itself by costly experience totally inadequate as a day-fighter over western Europe, but because its fuselage was roomy enough to take an extra operator and new scientific apparatus it was chosen to pioneer the technique of airborne radar-guided night interception. The claim of having made the first "kill" by means of airborne radar equipment (A.I. Mk. III) was chalked up by a Blenheim IF of the Fighter Interception Unit at Ford on 2nd/3rd July, 1940. Blenheim IFs served through-

K7133 *of No. 44 Squadron, May 1938.* (Photo: "Flight")

A Blenheim of No. 60 Squadron in the Far East.

Above: *Blenheim* L1131 *o, No. 62 Squadron, early 1938.* (Photo: "The Aeroplane")

Left: K7037 *of No. 90 Squadron pictured at Bicester during the Annual Air Exercises, August 1938.* (Photo: "The Aeroplane")

Mk. IF L8372 *of No. 29 Squadron during a pre-war air exercise.* (Photo: "The Aeroplane")

out the "blitz" of 1940–41 and some details of their activities about this time were given in Roderick Chisholm's book *Cover of Darkness*, C. F. Rawnsley and Robert Wright's book *Night Fighter*, and Bob Braham's book *Scramble*.

In 1940 one Blenheim I (*L1348*) underwent a series of modifications in an attempt to improve its performance for photographic reconnaissance. Its dorsal turret was removed, nose and wingtips specially faired, Rotol constant-speed airscrews fitted, bomb doors and other joints carefully taped over, and its standard camouflage finish replaced by a well-primed low-drag finish. However, the results (which reportedly included an increase in speed at 8,000 ft. from 274 m.p.h. to 296 m.p.h.) did not warrant further development.

To get back to the Blenheim I bomber squadrons. As already stated, two of these were based in the U.K. at the outbreak of war—Nos. 18 and 57 Squadrons. Both were then in No. 1 (Bomber) Group but soon afterwards they were transferred to No. 6 (Training) Group and thence to the Air Component of the British Expeditionary Force in France for strategical reconnaissance duties. In France they operated with their Blenheim Is until the spring of 1940 but by the time of the German break-through in May they had re-equipped with Blenheim IVs.

Following Italy's entry into the war at midnight on 10th June 1940, Blenheim Is struck the R.A.F.'s first blow against the Italians in North Africa: twenty-six aircraft of Nos. 45, 55 and 113 Squadrons from Egypt made a bombing and strafing attack at dawn on El Adem airfield, No. 55 apparently leading; three Blenheims failed to return. A second attack was delivered later in the day and in all eighteen enemy aircraft were destroyed or damaged on the ground. Total tonnage of bombs dropped in these two attacks was 416 forty-pounders, 524 twenty-pounders and 2,080 four-pound incendiaries. Blenheim Is continued to operate in the Middle East until 1941, and during the ill-starred campaign in Greece one of the squad-

Mk. IF L1233 *ZK-I of No. 25 Sqdn. during the "phoney war".* (Photo: "The Aeroplane")

Fighter Blenheims of No. 29 Squadron, Digby, photographed on 11th January 1940.

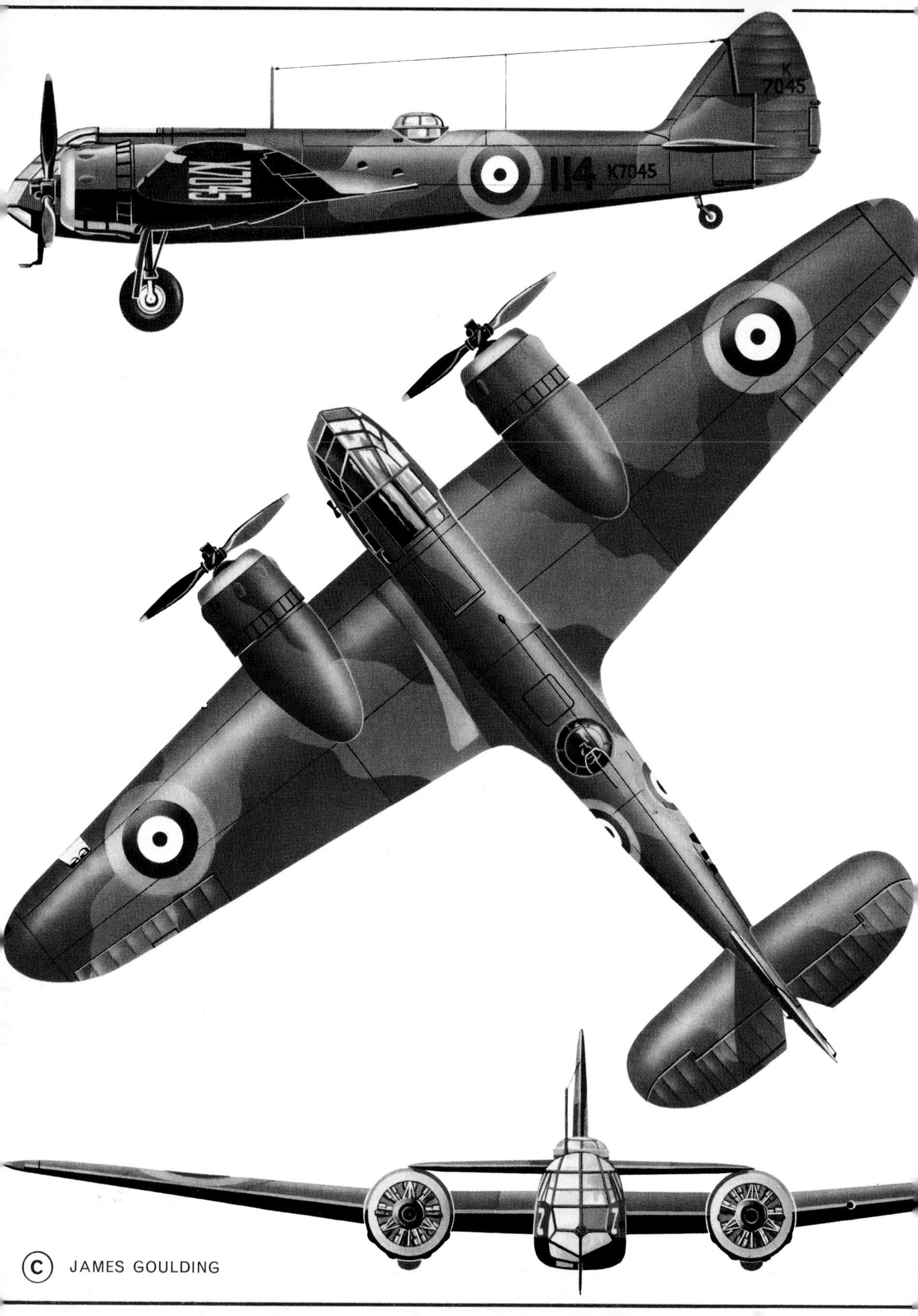
K
7045
114 K7045
K7045

BRISTOL BLENHEIM I, K7045, of No. 114 (B) Squadron. Normally based at Wyton, this aircraft was one of a formation of Blenheims that attacked the Set-piece at the Royal Air Force Display at Hendon in June 1937.

*Mk. IFs of No. 604 (County of Middlesex) Squadron (*L6788 *and* L6762 *nearest camera) at Northolt 6th April, 1940.*

rons (No. 30) operated as a "mixed" unit with bomber and fighter versions. Blenheim Is were subsequently involved in another bitter struggle against appalling odds—the defence of Malaya and Singapore, at the time of the Japanese invasion. Again both bomber and fighter versions were used and, as was the case in Greece, the squadrons were decimated.

For the record, here is the Order of Battle of the Blenheim I Squadrons in (i) Middle East Command at the time of Italy's entry into the war, and (ii) Far East Command at the time of Pearl Harbour:

MIDDLE EAST COMMAND

10th June, 1940

No. 30 (B) Sqdn.	Ismailia (Egypt)	No. 250 Wing of No. 202 Group
No. 55 (B) Sqdn.	Fuka (Egypt)	
No. 113 (B) Sqdn.	Ma'aten Bagush (Egypt)	
No. 45 (B) Sqdn.	Fuka (Egypt)	No. 253 Wing of No. 202 Group
No. 211 (B) Sqdn.	Daba (Egypt)	
No. 8 (B) Sqdn.	Khormaksar (Aden) (2 Flts. Blenheims and 1 Flt. Vincents)	
No. 11 (B) Sqdn.	Sheikh Othman (Aden)	
No. 39 (B) Sqdn.	Sheikh Othman (Aden)	
No. 84 (B) Sqdn.	Shaibah (Iraq)	

FAR EAST COMMAND

7th December, 1941

No. 27 (F) Sqdn.	Sungei Patani (Malaya) 12 a/c on charge.
No. 60 (B) Sqdn.	Mingaladon (Burma) 4 a/c. Detachment, including 8 a/c, at Kuantan (Malaya) for bombing practice. Sqdn. was retained in Malaya on start of war with Japan.
No. 62 (B) Sqdn.	Alor Star (Malaya), 11 a/c on charge.

Mk. IF L1336 *WR-E of No. 248 Sqdn. at Northolt in 1940.*
(Photo: Imperial War Museum)

Mk. IF of No. 614 (County of Glamorgan) Sqdn. with A.I. Mk. III radar.

Blenheim I L6670 *of No. 211 Sqdn. landing at a Greek airfield after a raid on Italian positions in Albania, late 1940.*
(Photo: Imperial War Museum)

Blenheim Is—including L6667—*of No. 62 Squadron on an airfield in Singapore, late 1940. Note Buffalo a/c.* (Photo: Imp. War Mus.)

Above: *Some Finnish Air Force Blenheims at Filton in 1937 prior to delivery.*

Right: *First Finnish Air Force Blenheim* (BL104) *on skis in 1938.*

BLENHEIMS IN FOREIGN COLOURS

Several batches of Blenheim Is were exported, the first foreign customer being Finland who, between June, 1937, and July, 1938, took delivery of eighteen aircraft modified to carry Swedish and American bombs. Early in 1940 during the Russo-Finnish "Winter War" these aircraft were reinforced by twenty-four Blenheim IVs from R.A.F. stocks but too late to prevent Finland's capitulation. Meanwhile Finland had acquired, in April, 1938, a licence to manufacture the Blenheim I in the new Government Aircraft Factory at Tampere, but none were completed until 1941. Production at Tampere continued until the final armistice in September, 1944, by which time a total of 55 Blenheim Is had been built.

The Yugoslav Government bought two Blenheim Is (delivered in November, 1937, with British civil registrations *G-AFCE* and *G-AFCF*) and also acquired a licence to manufacture fifty more. Yugoslav Blenheims were built by Ikarus A.D. at Zemun and the "first-off" flew in March, 1939, just ten months after receiving drawings; sixteen had been completed and twenty-four more were well advanced in the spring of 1941 when Germany invaded the Balkans and Yugoslav patriots sabotaged the Zemun factory to prevent its use against the Allies. Shortly before this twenty Blenheim Is (bearing civil markings *YU-BAA* to *YU-BAT*) were diverted from the R.A.F. to Yugoslavia to supplement those being built locally, some being equipped as fighters with two 20-mm. cannon firing forwards. Royal Yugoslav Air Force Blenheims, serving with the 1st and 8th Bomber regiments fought valiantly during the German onslaught and those few that survived were incorporated in the Croat Air Force.

Another country that purchased Blenheim Is was

One of the two Blenheims supplied to Yugoslavia in the spring of 1938.

Part of the initial batch of twelve Turkish Blenheims, photographed in 1938.

Two views of Blenheim I L1348 *unarmed, lightened and cleaned-up for high-speed P.R. rôle; Staverton, 1940. Note clipped wing.*

Turkey; but, unlike Finland and Yugoslavia she did not undertake licence production of the type. Turkey was actually the second foreign country to order Blenheims and her first two machines were despatched by sea in October, 1937, being joined between March and June, 1938, by ten more flown out with British civil registrations *G-AFFP* to *G-AFFZ*; a second batch of twelve already ordered was increased to eighteen (*G-AFLA* to *G-AFLS*) and were flown out between November, 1938, and February, 1939.

In November, 1939, thirteen Avro-built Blenheim Is were supplied to Rumania in a diplomatic gamble to persuade her to join the Allies, but a year later she joined the Axis, her Blenheims—like those of Finland—subsequently being used against the Russians.

COCKPIT AND HANDLING NOTES

The Blenheim held the distinction of being the aircraft for which the Central Flying School first developed its "twin technique" and probably the verbal "cockpit drill" system as well. With the former, C.F.S. taught the novice to hold a twin low down after take-off, to gain single-engine safety speed quickly, and to disregard initial gain of height. Likewise the trainee was taught to recite the mnemonic "H.T.M.P.F.G." before take-off—or, more explicitly, "Hydraulics, Trim, Mixture, Pitch, Flaps and Gills", to save himself from fatal absent-mindedness.

Not only had the pilot to select hydraulic power, but the plunger could be operated incorrectly—with the result that subsequent "wheels-up" selection by the pilot was of no avail for his previous error had simply provided a perhaps non-existent rear-gunner with plenty of hydraulic power!

The "office" of the Blenheim I.

A gaggle of Blenheims from No. 13 O.T.U.

Being a contortionist would have helped any Blenheim pilot—some knobs and switches were behind his left elbow and the hydraulic service controls (appropriately resembling Victorian lavatory handles) were below and on the right. The addition of a safety catch to the undercarriage lever resulted in some pilots, used only to the previous type, just about pulling the floor out of the cabin in their abortive attempts to move the lever.

According to "Indicator"* of *Flight*, in an article published in that magazine in 1945, the Mark I was the nicest of all the Blenheims, with its low all-up weight and its vast expanse of forward and downward view. "Getting into the Blenheim", he wrote, "was always something of an affair and one soon learned not to attempt to do it while weighed down with a parachute. An assistant put this in the seat while the driver, hatted, gloved and inter-commed, clambered on to the port wing—slippery if wet—and through the roof hatch, letting himself down gently so that, even if the direction was poor, he did not damage his nether garments on the various pointed items surrounding the seat. It was peculiar at first, too, to find that the wings and ailerons were more or less invisible behind the engine cowlings—a disadvantage which was handsomely outweighed in the sight of the amateur by the most unusual way in which the landscape could be seen crawling along through the transparent floor of the nose. . . .

"As for flying characteristics, the Blenheim must have been very easy, since in the early days of the war we were poured more or less straight in from the cockpits of our Moths and found no particular difficulties facing us at all."

**Pseudonym of H. A. Taylor, wartime ferry and test pilot and currently Air Transport Editor of* Flight International.

BLENHEIM MK. I PRODUCTION FOR R.A.F.

Bristol-built

K7033–K7182 (150 a/c), (*K7034–K7036*, *K7041–K7042* and *K7167* fitted with dual control. *K7072* variously modified).
L1097–L1546 (450 a/c), (*L1483*, *L1485*, *L1488*, *L1489* and *L1497* sold to Turkey in 1939. *L1222* modified to become sole example of Mk. II. *L1242* experimentally fitted with tricycle (fixed nose-wheel) undercarriage. *L1348* eventually lightened and cleaned-up for high-speed P.R. rôle. *L1424* was prototype Mk. IF).
L4817–L4834, *L4903–L4934* (50 a/c), (*L4821*, *L4824*, *L4826* and *L4828* sold to Turkey in 1939. *L4822* had dual control).

Avro-built

L6594–L6843 (250 a/c), (*L6594* sometime fitted experimentally with downward-firing 37-mm. C.O.W gun, *L6764–L6773* to Finland; *L6696–L6708* to Rumania; *L6813*, *L6814*, *L6817–L6834* to Yugoslavia).

Rootes-built

L8362–L8407, *L8433–L8482*, *L8500–L8549*, *L8597–L8632*, *L8652–L8701*, *L8714–L8731* (250 a/c). (*L8384–L8385* to Royal Hellenic Air Force, *L8603–L8608*, *L8619–L8620*, *L8622–L8630*, *L8632*, *L8652–L8654* to Rumanian Air Force).
L9170–L9218, *L9237–L9273*. (86 a/c, built as Mk. I and then modified to Mk. IV standard). *L9195–L9203* sold direct to Finland in January 1940.

Blenheim L1222 *modified to Mk. II with long-range tanks and external bomb-load, at Filton, September 1938.*

BLENHEIM MK. I PRODUCTION FOR EXPORT
(All Bristol-built)

Finland: *BL104–BL121* (12 a/c).
Turkey: *2501–2512* (2 +G-AFFP-G-AFFZ) (12 a/c) and G-AFLA-G-AFLS later *397–408*, *385–390* (18 a/c).
Yugoslavia: G-AFCE and G-AFCF (2 a/c).

SQUADRON ALLOCATIONS

Home Bomber: Nos. 18, 21, 34, 44, 57, 61, 62, 82, 90, 101, 104, 107, 108, 110, 114, 139 and 144. Home Fighter: Nos. 17, 23, 25, 29, 64, 68, 92, 145, 222, 248, 600, 601 and 604. Overseas Bomber: Nos. 8, 11, 30, 34, 39, 45, 55, 60 (also had some Blenheim IFs), 62, 84, 113 and 211. Overseas Fighter: Nos. 27, 30 and 203.

Mk. I L6655 *believed photographed in Aden before the war. Potted Service history of this aircraft was as follows: initially to No. 9 M.U.; to Thorney Island, March 1939; to Aden, July 1939; struck off charge in Middle East, September 1943.*

Below: *Two views of Blenheim I* K7072 *after modification to Type 149 Bolingbroke I prototype by lengthening of nose, Filton, October 1937. Nose was subsequently re-designed.*

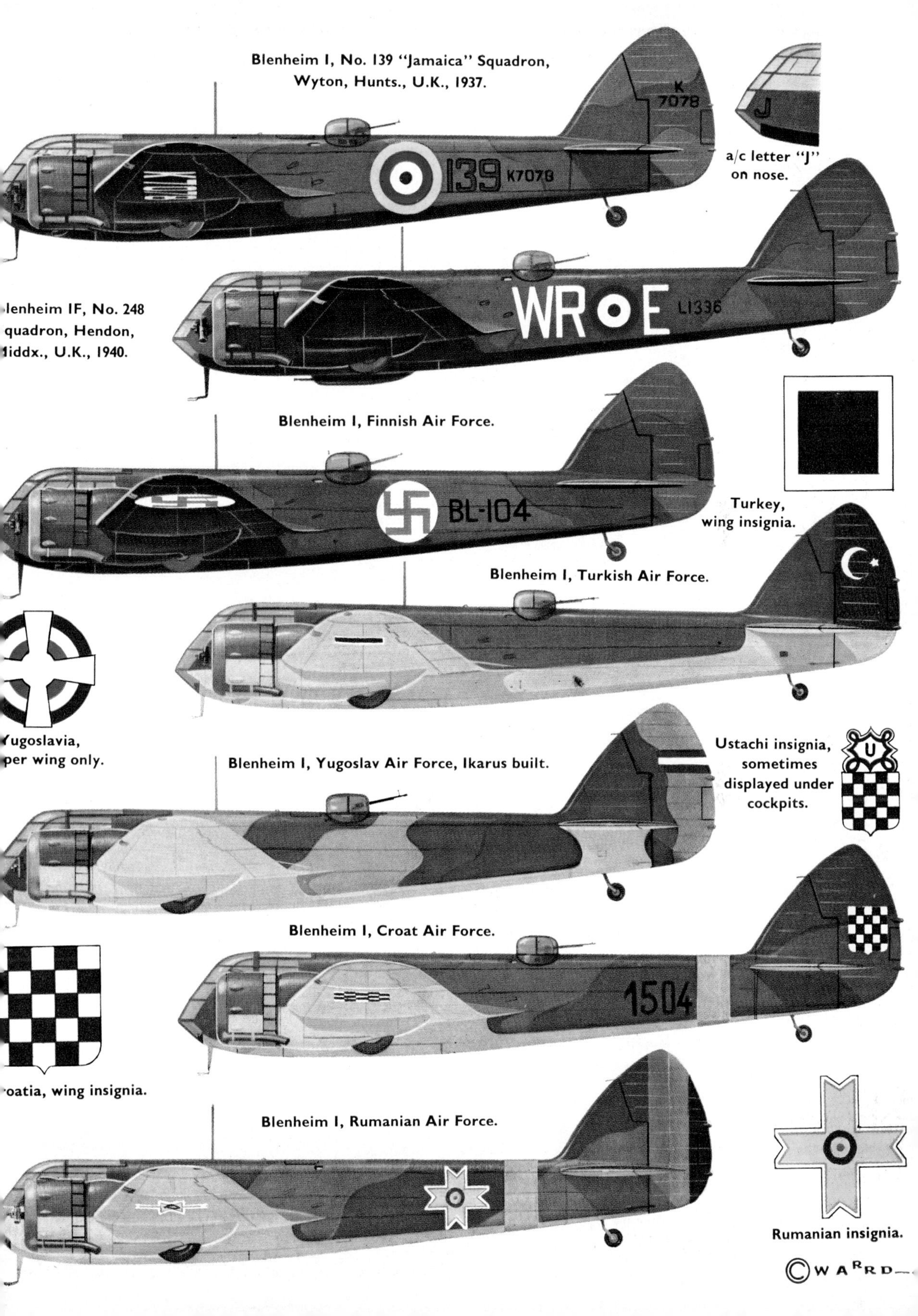
Blenheim I, No. 139 "Jamaica" Squadron,
Wyton, Hunts., U.K., 1937.
K
7078
J
a/c letter "J"
on nose.
139
K7078
lenheim IF, No. 248
quadron, Hendon,
liddx., U.K., 1940.
WR
E
L1336
Blenheim I, Finnish Air Force.
BL-104
Turkey,
wing insignia.
Blenheim I, Turkish Air Force.
'ugoslavia,
per wing only.
Blenheim I, Yugoslav Air Force, Ikarus built.
Ustachi insignia,
sometimes
displayed under
cockpits.
U
Blenheim I, Croat Air Force.
1504
oatia, wing insignia.
Blenheim I, Rumanian Air Force.
Rumanian insignia.
©WARD

SPECIFICATION OF BLENHEIM MK. I

Type: Twin-engined high-performance medium bomber.
Wings: Mid-wing cantilever monoplane. In three sections. Centre-section bolted and riveted to fuselage. Outer sections tapered in chord and thickness. Spars built up of two heavy high-tensile steel flanges and a light single-plate Alclad web between them. Web reinforced with vertical stringers. Ribs made from Alclad sheet, with flanged edges and lipped lightening holes. Alclad stressed-skin covering riveted to flanges of spars and ribs. Bristol-Frise mass-balanced ailerons and split trailing-edge flaps. Flaps of Alclad sheet, with flanged ribs. Ailerons metal-framed and covered with fabric. Small trimming-tabs in ailerons adjustable on the ground.
Fuselage: In three sections. Light alloy monocoque, built up of formers and open-section stringers, with Alclad skin riveted to the flanges of the formers and stringers.
Tail Unit: Cantilever monoplane type. Tail-plane and fin of all-metal construction, similar to the wings. Elevators and rudder metal-framed and covered with fabric. Fixed tail-plane, with servo-strips for fore-and-aft trimming. Servo-tab in rudder. Elevators and rudder aerodynamicaly and statically balanced.
Undercarriage: Retractable type. Each unit retracted backward by a Bristol hydraulic-jack, which broke the knee-jointed radius-rods. Auxiliary hand-pump for emergency operation. Full indication and warning devices, comprising visible, audible and mechanical signals. Intermediate-pressure tyres and pneumatic differentially-controlled wheel-brakes.
Powerplant: Two 840-h.p. Bristol "Mercury" VIII nine-cylinder radial air-cooled engines. Mountings of steel-tube, with standard Bristol duralumin mounting ring with split segment at the bottom to facilitate rapid removal of engines without disturbing carburettors. Long-chord cowling rings with leading-edge exhaust-collectors and trailing-edge controllable gills. Three-bladed controllable-pitch airscrews. Two fuel tanks (140 Imp. gallons each) in centre-section. Oil tanks (9½ Imp. gallons each) in engine nacelles. Hand and electric engine-starters.
Accommodation: Pilot's seat in nose, on port side, with navigator's seat alongside. A sliding and folding seat ahead of the navigator's seat for use when bomb-aiming. Dual controls could be fitted. Fixed and sliding window panels and transparent sliding roof. In centre-section of fuselage was the internal bomb stowage, with side panels and spring-loaded doors. Aft of the wing was the rear gun-turret mounted midway along the top of the fuselage. Normal crew consisted of pilot, bomb-aimer-navigator and wireless-operator-gunner.
Armament: One forward-firing ·303-in. Browning machine gun in the port wing and one ·303-in. Vickers "K" gas-operated gun in a Bristol semi-retractable hydraulically-operated gun-turret. A 1,000-lb. bomb load carried internally in a bomb-cell under the centre-section. A hand-winch for loading was operated from inside the fuselage.
Equipment: Lighting, radio, photographic and navigation equipment, oxygen apparatus, stowage for parachutes, clothing, etc.
Dimensions: Span 56 ft. 4 in. Length 39 ft. 9 in. Clearance height (tail down) 9 ft. 10 in. Span of tailplane 16 ft. 8 in. Maximum depth of fuselage 5 ft. 6 in. Maximum width of fuselage 4 ft. 4 in. Diameter of airscrews 10 ft. 6 in. Wing area 469 sq. ft.
Weights: Weight empty 8,100 lb. Full load (including 278 gallons of fuel and 17 gallons of oil) 4,400 lb. Weight loaded 12,500 lb.
Performance: Maximum speed at sea level 240 m.p.h. Speed at 5,000 ft. 254 m.p.h. Speed at 10,000 ft. 269 m.p.h. Speed at 15,000 ft. 285 m.p.h. Speed at 20,000 ft. 277 m.p.h. Climb to 5,000 ft. 3·7 min. Climb to 10,000 ft. 7·2 min. Climb to 15,000 ft. 11·5 min. Climb to 20,000 ft. 17·5 min. Service ceiling 27,280 ft. Estimated range at 220 m.p.h. with full load 1,125 miles. Take-off run 296 yd. Landing run (with brakes) 364 yd. Landing speed 50 m.p.h.

The writer acknowledges his indebtedness to the researches of C. H. (Chris) Barnes, author of Bristol Aircraft Since 1910 *(Putnam).*

Left: *A Blenheim which was used at Shoeburyness for statistical investigation of effect of shell bursts on an aircraft. (As this goes to press, a Bristol design of recent times, Type 188, is also at Shoeburyness and suffering a similar fate.)*

Below: *Blenheims of No. 90 Squadron at Bicester, November 1938.* (Photo: "Flight")

PRINTED IN ENGLAND © Profile Publications Ltd., P.O. Box 26, 1a North Street, Leatherhead, Surrey, England.
Printed by Hills & Lacy Ltd., London and Watford, England. U.S. 2nd Class Mailing Rates applied for.

PROFILE PUBLICATIONS

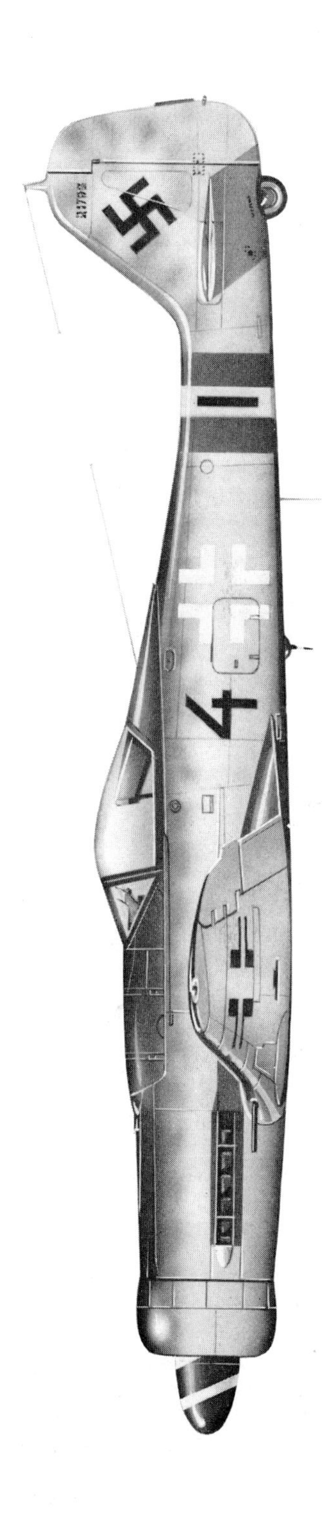

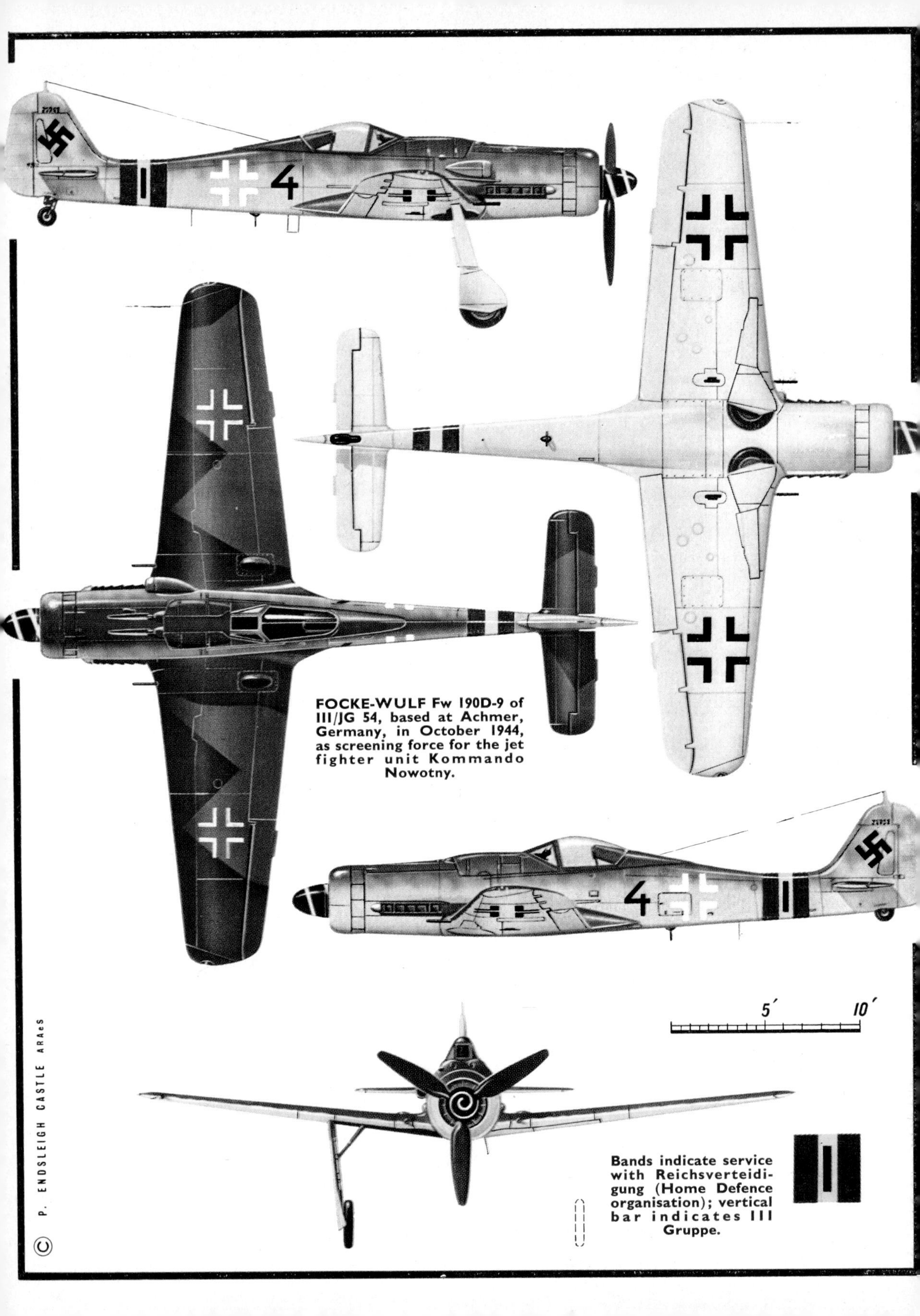

FOCKE-WULF Fw 190D-9 of III/JG 54, based at Achmer, Germany, in October 1944, as screening force for the jet fighter unit Kommando Nowotny.

Bands indicate service with Reichsverteidigung (Home Defence organisation); vertical bar indicates III Gruppe.

The Focke-Wulf Fw190D/Ta 152 Series

by J. Richard Smith

The Focke-Wulf Ta 152C-0/R11 (W.Nr.0007) coded C I + X M. This machine was powered by a DB 603 L engine and had the standard wing of the Fw 190A-8. (Photo: H. J. Nowarra)

Following the startling success that accompanied the appearance of the Focke Wulf Fw 190 A-1 over the English Channel in the late spring of 1941 (see *Profile* No. 3, *The Focke-Wulf Fw 190 A*) work was intensified on several high altitude versions of the basic design. The first variant, designated Fw 190 B, was equipped with a B.M.W. 801 radial, but differed from the A series in having a turbo-supercharger and pressurised cabin. Only a few aircraft were built, and the design was soon replaced by the Fw 190 C series. This last was powered by a 1,750-h.p. Daimler Benz DB 603 A in-line engine with turbo-supercharger, the first prototype for which was the Fw 190 V 13 (Werke Nr. 0036) "SK+JS". This was followed by a second aircraft, the Fw 190 V 18 (W.Nr.0040) "CF+OY" which differed in having a four-bladed V.D.M. airscrew and turbo-supercharger—the machine being dubbed "Kangaroo" because of the large under-fuselage fairing which this installation necessitated.

The second and third genuine prototypes for the Fw 190 C (the V 18 being an interim variant) were the V 29 (W.Nr.0054) "CF+KS" and V 30 (W.Nr.0055) "CF+KT" both of which were fitted with the DB 603 G engine. Both the Fw 190 V 31 (W.Nr.0056) "GH+KU" and the V 32 (W.Nr.0057) "GH+KV" were fitted with larger wings and tail surfaces, but the former crashed on 29th April 1943. The last prototype was the Fw 190 V 33 (W.Nr.0058) "GH+KW" which carried an armament of two engine-mounted 13 mm. MG 131 machine guns and two wing-mounted 20 mm. MG 151/20 cannon. However, the Fw 190 C-1 was finally abandoned both because of the poor performance of the Hirth 9-2281 turbo-supercharger and the success of the Jumo 213 powered Fw 190 D series.

The third of the high altitude projects based on the original Focke Wulf Fw 190 design was the Junkers Jumo 213 powered Fw 190 D. The machine was to be based on the standard Fw 190 A-8 airframe, but the fuselage was to be lengthened to accommodate the 1,750-h.p. Jumo 213 A twelve-cylinder, liquid-cooled, in-line engine, and the tail fin and rudder were to be enlarged to compensate for the increased length. The first prototype for the D series was the Fw 190 V 17 (W.Nr.0039) which was converted from a standard A-O during the winter of 1941–42. This machine was later again re-built as the V 17/U1 making its initial flight in May 1944 from Langenhagen airfield as prototype for the Fw 190 D-9 production model. Five further Fw 190 A-Os were converted as D series prototypes, these being designated Fw 190 V 20, V 21, V 22, V 23, and V 25.

A small pre-production batch of Fw 190 D-0s were completed, these being conversions of standard production Fw 190 A-7 airframes. These machines were similar to the A-7, the Jumo 213 engine being installed as a "power egg" although a compensating section was added to the rear fuselage. Armament was carried in the shape of four wing-mounted 20 mm. MG 151/20 cannon and two 13 mm. MG 131 machine guns mounted above the engine cowling. The pre-production aircraft were followed by a small production batch of Fw 190 D-1s; this model differing in having increased vertical tail surfaces.

The first major production model was the Fw 190 D-9. This was intended to replace the Fw 190 A-8 in service, hence there being no D-2 to D-8 designations. In the event, however, two further A series aircraft were built, designated A-9 and A-10. The first prototype of the Fw 190 D-9 was, as mentioned earlier, the Fw 190 V 17/U1. This had a 1,776-h.p. Junkers Jumo 213 A-1 engine with MW-50 water-methanol injection, which boosted power to 2,240 h.p. and gave the aircraft a maximum speed of 426 m.p.h. The second prototype for the D-9 was the Fw 190 V 53 (W.Nr.170003) which followed in less than a month, this having two further 20 mm. MG 151/20 cannons in the wings in addition to the two MG

The Fw 190V-32/U1, a modification of the old V-32, was a forerunner of the Fw 190C. The machine was unarmed, and power was provided by a DB 603 G engine.
(Photo: H. J. Nowarra)

Fw 190V-13 (W.Nr.0036) coded S K + J S, was the first prototype of the proposed Fw 190C series; the engine was a 1,750-h.p. DB 603 A. (Photo: H. J. Nowarra)

151/20 and two MG 131 machine guns.

The third prototype, the Fw 190 V 54 (W.Nr. 174024) was completed in July 1944 but both this and the V 53 were destroyed in a bombing raid. The Fw 190 D-9 entered production in August 1944, and the Focke Wulf factories at Bremen, Johannisthal/Berlin and Sorau/Silesia and was sub-contracted by Agos at Oscherleben, Arados at Brandenburg and Warnemünde and Fieselers at Kassel. The initial production batch (W.Nr.210001 onwards) had a flat topped canopy, later machines sporting a bulged "Galland" hood. (Not to be confused with the clear-view "Galland" canopy employed by late Bf 109G and K variants.) W.Nr.210009 was delivered to Junkers for engine trials. Several other variants of the Fw 190 D-9 were projected including the D-9/R 11 bad weather fighter with PKS 12 directional controls, FuG 16 Za, FuG 25 a and FuG 125 radio equipment. The Fw 190 D-10 was similar to the D-9 but the two 13 mm. machine guns mounted above the engine cowling were replaced by a single 30 mm. MK 108 cannon firing through the spinner.

The next production model was the Fw 190 D-11 ground attack machine of which seven prototypes were completed. The first of these, the Fw 190 V 55 (W.Nr.170923) was powered by a Jumo 213 F-1 engine with three-stage turbo-supercharger and MW-50 injection. This machine had the standard armament of two 20 mm. MG 151/20 and two 13 mm. MG 131 guns, but the second D-11 series aircraft (the Fw 190 V 56—W.Nr.170924) and all subsequent prototypes except the V 60 had the fuselage-mounted MG 131s replaced by two outboard wing-mounted 30 mm. MK 108 cannon. The Fw 190 V 57 (W.Nr. 170926) was re-built from an A-8 and the V 58 (W.Nr.170933) and V 59 (W.Nr.350156) were both similar. The Fw 190 V 60 (W.Nr.350157) was again similar but had no armament, and the V 61 (W.Nr. 350158) was delivered to Junkers Moternwerke for engine trials.

Several conversion packs were provided for the Fw 190 D-11 including the D-11/R5 with TSA 2D bomb-aiming device and eight 110-lb. bombs, the /R11 with FuG 125 D/F radio, the /R21 similar to the R11 without MW-50 injection and the /R25 with additional fuel capacity. The next production model was the Fw D-12 which differed in having a 30 mm. MK 108 cannon firing through the spinner and increased armour protection around the engine. The prototypes for the D-12 were the Fw 190 V 63 (W.Nr. 350165), V 64 (W.Nr.350166) and V 65 (W.Nr. 350167)—all re-built A-8s. The Fw 190 D-12/R5, D-12/R11, D-12/R20, D-12/R21 and D-12/R25 were similar to the D-11/R series. The Fw 190 D-13 had a Jumo 213 EB engine and the engine-mounted 30 mm. MK 108 cannon replaced by a 20 mm. MG 151/20. Two prototypes were converted from Fw 190 A-8s, designated the Fw 190 V 62 (W.Nr.732053) and V 71

Second prototype for the operational D-9 and D-10 series was the Fw 190V-53 (W.Nr.170003). Note the distinctive engine cowling and propeller unit, with paddle-bladed airscrew. (Photo: H. J. Nowarra)

(W.Nr.732054) and the standard R series conversion packs were to be provided. Only two prototypes of the Fw 190 D-14 were completed, the V 76 (W.Nr. 210040) and V 77 (210043). The D-14 and the generally similar D-15 were to have employed the DB 603 A and EB engines respectively, but were developed into the Ta 152 series.

Many designs based on the Fw 190 D airframe were projected. Most were to utilise the increased power provided by new engines such as the 2,400-h.p. B.M.W. 802 eighteen cylinder radial, the 3,900-h.p. B.M.W. 803 twenty-eight cylinder radial, the 2,660-h.p. DB 609 sixteen cylinder in-line, the 2,020-h.p. DB 614 twenty-four cylinder in-line and the 2,400-h.p. DB 623 twelve cylinder in-line. Another project was for the machine to carry a torpedo, and others included provision for advanced weapon installations.

CONSTRUCTION OF THE Fw 190 D SERIES

The wings comprised an all metal structure with two main spars. The front spar was continuous through the fuselage and the rear was constructed in two sections, attached at either side of the fuselage by pin joints. The spars were built up of flanged plate, reinforced inboard of the ailerons by "L" section extrusions and progressively thickened cap strips to form "I" section members. Outboard of the ailerons the spars had integral flanges. The wing ribs were of flanged plate, the "Z" section stringers were placed span-wise, and the stressed skin was constructed of heavy gauge light alloy. The wing ribs were divided along the centre line to enable the wing to be built in two shells, upper and lower. The front spar was cranked inwards near the wing roots to avoid the wheel wells. Light alloy Frise-type ailerons with fabric covering were fitted and the split trailing edge flaps operated electrically and depressed 10° for take-off and 60° for landing.

The fuselage was an all metal structure, the forward section to the rear of the cockpit having four longerons and a horizontal partition dividing the cockpit from the petrol tank. The rear section of the fuselage was a conventional monocoque structure with light alloy traverse frames and twenty-one "Z" section stringers intersecting but not attached to the frames. The whole was covered with light alloy stressed skin. The power

An early production Fw 190D-9, with 300-litre drop tank under the centre-section. (Photo: H. J. Nowarra)

Three-quarter rear view of a D-9 with 300-litre drop tank. Absence of unit markings on a machine finished in standard camouflage and national insignia probably indicates a production aircraft undergoing manufacturer's tests prior to delivery to the Luftwaffe. (Photo: H. J. Nowarra)

plant comprised a Junkers Jumo 213 A-1 twelve cylinder, liquid-cooled, inverted Vee in-line engine with a maximum take-off power of 1,776 h.p. at 3,250 r.p.m. at sea level. This could be increased to 2,240 h.p. by using water-methanol injection (MW-50). Maximum emergency power in level flight was 1,600 h.p. at 3,250 r.p.m. at 18,000 ft. Armament comprised twin fixed synchronised 13 mm. Rheinemetall-Borsig MG 131 machine guns with 475 r.p.g. mounted above the engine cowling and twin fixed synchronised 20 mm. Mauser MG 151/20 cannon with 250 r.p.g. mounted in the wing roots.

The tail unit comprised an all-metal tailplane continuous through the fuselage and adjustable for incidence. The all-metal stressed skin fin was integral with the fuselage. The control surfaces were of light alloy structure with fabric covering. The undercarriage was of the inward retracting type, the main

An Fw 190D-9, white 15, almost certainly of JG 26, photographed on a forward airstrip during the spring of 1945, after capture. A P-47 is just visible behind the cockpit. (Photo: R. C. Seeley Collection)

wheels being housed ahead of the front spar when raised. The tailwheel was semi-retractable and was interconnected with the main wheels to synchronise retraction, this being achieved by electrical means. The airscrew was of the three-bladed V.D.M. VS 111 constant speed type with metal blades.

THE "DORA 9" ENTERS SERVICE

The Fw 190 D-9 or "Dora 9" as it was nicknamed, proved an immediate success when it entered service with the Luftwaffe's *Jagdflieger* in the late summer of 1944. One of the first *Gruppen* to equip with the fighter was III./JG 54 "Grünherz" under Hptm. Robert "Bazi" Weiss (*Ritterkreuz*) which received its new machines in September 1944. After re-equipment had been completed, III./JG 54 moved to its operational bases at Hesepe and Achmer near the Dutch border. It was on these airfields that *Kommando Nowotny*, the first unit to be equipped with the revolutionary jet fighter, the Me 262, was based. The Messerschmitt fighter was most vulnerable when taking-off and landing and it was for this reason that III./JG 54 was based in the area, to cover the jets during these manœuvres. On 8th November 1944 *Kommando Nowotny* lost three of its pilots including the *Kommandoführer*, Major Nowotny (holder of the Knight's Cross with Oak Leaves, Swords and Diamonds and credited with 258 air victories), who was shot down by a formation of P-51 Mustangs near Bramsche. The death of its founder resulted in *Kommando Nowotny* being withdrawn from operations to form the nucleus of the first jet fighter wing, *Jagdgeschwader* 7.

The next *Jagdgruppe* to equip with the "Dora 9" was II./JG 26 "Schlageter" under Major Karl Borris which was based at Handrup, north-west of Osnabruck. It may serve to give the reader some insight into *Luftwaffe* fighter operations at this time to quote from I./JG 26's war diary from the time of its re-equipment with the Fw 190 D-9 in October 1944 until the end of the year.

12th October 1944
Take-off between 10.28 and 10.30 hours from Handrup near Furstenau by twenty-two Focke Wulf 190 Ds. At 11.50 hours, the German fighters were intercepted by U.S.A.A.F. P-51 Mustangs and P-47 Thunderbolts while flying near Hannover at 22,000 ft. No bombers were intercepted. The Fw 190s landed at Dortmund, Hildesheim, Hannover/Langenhagen and Oldenburg.

16th to 23rd October 1944
No operations because of impossible ground conditions.

Cockpit interior of the D-9, showing pilot's seat, control column, rudder pedals and port instrument console.
(Photo: H. J. Nowarra)

8th November 1944
Generaloberst Stumpf from Luftflotte Reich visited I./JG 26 at their base at Furstenau.

27th November 1944
In the morning, an abortive sortie by four Fw 190s. New aircraft arrive during the morning to increase *Gruppe* strength to sixty-nine Fw 190s.

3rd December 1944
At 11.00 hours, Major Borris, the Kommandeur of I./JG 26 took off with twenty-three Fw 190s. Four aircraft returned with engine failures. Lt. Gunther's *Staffel* intercepted R.A.F. Typhoons and shot down three.

5th December 1944
At 09.25 hours, twenty-nine Fw 190s took-off under Oblt. Heckmann, between 10.05 and 10.15 hours they were attacked by a low flight of P-47 Thunderbolts engaged in strafing attacks in the Luttice area. Oblt. Gunther shot down a P-47. At 13.15 hours, Major Borris led Fw 190s to intercept some straggling U.S.A.A.F. B-17 Fortresses. Borris shot down a B-17 and his machines were down at Handrup by 13.45 hours. A sortie of nine Fw 190s took-off at 14.30

Left: *Cowling detail of the "Dora 9". Note the bulged fairings over the two 13-mm. MG 131 machine guns in the upper cowling, and details of exhaust stack and intake.* Right: *Another view of the D-9's cowling, looking to the rear. Note panel and canopy details.*

This captured D-9 was tested in America with the Foreign Evaluation number FE-121. The camouflage and markings were applied in the U.S.A.; this machine is now in storage for the Smithsonian Institution in Washington. (Photo: Imperial War Museum)

hours, engaged in combat with P-47s with no result, landed at 16.01 hours.

10th December 1944
At 14.50 hours, Oblt. Heckmann led nineteen Fw 190s in a dogfight with U.S.A.A.F. fighters. One P-47 and one P-51 were brought down.

18th December 1944
Total complement of I./JG 26 is fifty-two Fw 190 A-8s and twenty-eight Fw 190 D-9s.

23rd December 1944
At 11.14 hours a sortie by 2 and 3 *Staffeln* of I./JG 26 with twenty-eight Fw 190s led by Ofw. Schwarz took off. Two enemy aircraft shot down.

24th December 1944
Between 11.14 and 11.20 hours, eighteen Fw. 190s took-off to intercept a force of eighty to ninety B-17 Fortresses with fighter escort. One P-38 Lightning and an army Auster were shot down.

25th December 1944
At 10.57 hours seven Fw 190s took-off and engaged in dogfights with P-51 Mustangs. At 14.20 hours there was another alert and combats ensued with P-51s, but there was no result.

26th December 1944
At 10.18, Oblt. Hartigs led a sortie of fifteen Fw 190s from 1 and 4 *Staffeln*. Dogfights with P-51 Mustangs—one shot down by Ofw. Schwarz.

31st December 1944
14.35 hours. Precautions are made for the "Operation Herrman", the attack on Allied airfields planned for New Year's Day, 1945.

On 10th December 1944, the four *Staffeln* (9, 10, 11 and 12) of III./JG 54 had no less than sixty-nine Fw 190 D-9s on hand but this total fluctuated considerably with the fortunes of the *Gruppe*. On Christmas Day 1944, III./JG 54 transferred from Varrelbusch between Achmer and Oldenburg and was put under the control of Oberst Josef Priller's *Jagdgeschwader* 26. Four days later the *Gruppe* suffered its blackest day when its Kommandeur, Hauptmann "Bazi" Weiss and five other *Jagdflieger* were shot down and killed during a battle with a large R.A.F. Spitfire formation. Here it is interesting to note the losses suffered by other *Jadgruppen* during this period.

JG 26 with Fw 190 A-8s and D-9s lost eighteen pilots killed during the period 18th—26th December 1944.

JG 27 with Bf 109 G-6s, G-10s and G-14s lost forty-five pilots during 17th and 29th December 1944.

Left: *The 1,770-h.p. Junkers Jumo 213A-1 liquid-cooled engine which powered the Fw 190D-9.* Right: *The Jumo 213A-1, with cowling fitted, on the Focke-Wulf production line.*

Side view of Ta 152H-0 (W.Nr.0003) which was captured and tested first in Britain and later in the U.S.A. Fake Luftwaffe *markings have been added over the R.A.F. roundels and the Foreign Evaluation number FE-112 applied on the tail and under the wings.*
(Photo: John W. Caler Collection)

III./JG 3 with Bf 109 G-14s lost seventeen pilots killed during 17th and 29th December 1944.

IV./JG 54 with Fw 190 A-8s lost twenty-three pilots killed during the same period.

Weiss was temporarily replaced as *Gruppen* Kommandeur of III./JG 54 by Oblt. Hans Dortenmann, but on 25th February 1945 the unit was redesignated IV./JG 26 and put under the command of Major Hans Klemm. The *Gruppe* then comprised three *Staffeln:* 13./JG 26 under Lt. Crump with eight pilots, 14./JG 26 under Oblt. Dortenmann with eleven pilots and 15./JG 26 under Oblt. Heilmann (author of *Alert in the West*) with nine pilots. JG 26 now comprised four *Gruppen*, all, with the exception of III *Gruppe* which had a few Bf 109 G-14s and K-4s equipped with the Fw 190 D-9. *Jagdgeschwader* 2 "Richtofen" were also equipped with the Fw 190 D-9 and the type had begun to enter service with JG 301, one of the special Reich defence units.

These *Gruppen* all took part in "Operation Herrmann" the mass attack by most of the Luftwaffe's remaining fighter aircraft on Allied airfields in Holland, Belgium and northern France. This was virtually the last fling of the Luftwaffe's piston-engined fighter formations as stocks of fuel rapidly declined following systematic Allied bombing of German refineries, and priority was given to the units equipped with jet aircraft. A small amount of fuel was made available to conventionally powered fighter formations, but this was of little use. In April 1945, *Jagdgeschwader* 6 "Horst Wessel" under Major Gerhard Barkhorn based at Sorau/Silesia was re-equipped with no less than 150 brand new Fw 190 D-9s from the nearby Focke Wulf factory. However, through lack of fuel, the *Geschwader* was only able to mount standing patrols of four aircraft!

THE Fw 190 BECOMES THE Ta 152

In 1944, the *Reichluftfahrtministerium* decided to institute a policy of naming the designer in all new aircraft designations. In the event only two designers, Dipl. Ing. Kalkert of the Gothaer Waggonfabrik A.G., and Dipl. Ing. Kurt Tank of the Focke Wulf Flugzeugbau G.m.b.H., received this honour. Thus, further variants of the Fw 190 series were to be designated Ta 152 and Ta 153. The latter was a much advanced high altitude project with a high aspect ratio wing, a DB 603 engine and four-bladed airscrew. Several development aircraft were built including the Fw 190 V 32/U1 (W.Nr.0057) and the V 33/U1 (W.Nr.0058) but the design was abandoned as it was felt that by the time the aircraft had been tooled up for production, the advanced jet fighter the Ta 183 would be ready to leave the assembly lines.

The Ta 152 was a much less radical modification of the Fw 190 D series and could be produced with little or no disruption of the production machinery. The Ta 152 A-1 was generally similar to the Fw 190 D-9, but was to have had four 20 mm. MG 151/20 cannon and FuG 24 radio in place of the FuG 16 ZY.

The Ta 152C-0/R/11 pictured on page 3 of this Profile, *an all-weather fighter version of the pre-production C series. This view probably captures the distinctive lines of the later Focke-Wulf fighters better than any other existing photograph.*
(Photo: Imperial War Museum)

Two views of the V-30/U1 (W.Nr.0055) coded G H + K T, which served as prototype for the Ta 152H-0. This machine crashed at Langenhagen on 13th August 1944.
(Photos: Imperial War Museum)

This view of a pre-production Ta 152H-0 shows to advantage the high aspect ratio wings of this high-altitude interceptor. (Photo: H. J. Nowarra)

Ta 152H-0 (W.Nr.0003) at Langenhagen airfield in 1945, in its original German markings. (Photo: H. J. Nowarra)

Nose of the Ta 152V-20 (W.Nr.110020) one of the three prototypes of the Ta 152B-5/R11 all-weather fighter. (Photo: H. J. Nowarra)

The Ta 152 A-2 was similar and like its predecessor, remained in the project stage. The Ta 152 B series was similar to the A but was equipped with an engine-mounted 30 mm. MK 108 cannon and GM-1 power boosting. Five sub-series were proposed of which the Ta 152 B-1 and B-2 remained projects only, the B-3 was a ground support aircraft, the B-4 was a heavy fighter of which two versions, the B-4/R1 and B-4/R2 were built. The Ta 152 B-5, for which the modified Fw 190 V 53 and V 68 (W.Nr.170003) were prototypes, had a Jumo 213 E engine and an armament of three 30 mm. MK 103 cannon. An all-weather version of this last model was also projected, designated Ta 152 B-5/R11, for which the Ta 152 V 19 (W.Nr.110019), V 20 (W.Nr.110020) and V 21 (W.Nr.110021) were forerunners.

The second major production version (the Ta 152 H being the first as will be explained later) was the Ta 152 C. The twenty-first prototype of the Fw 190 was modified under the designation Fw 190 V 21/U1 as the forerunner of the Ta 152 C-0. This aircraft differed mainly from the earlier models in having a 1,800-h.p. Daimler Benz DB 603 E engine mounted in a longer fuselage giving the aircraft a maximum speed of 448 m.p.h. with the aid of GM-1. Other prototypes for the C series were the Ta 152 V 6 (W.Nr.110006), the Ta 152 V 7 (W.Nr.110007) with all weather equipment, the Ta 152 V 8 (W.Nr.110008) with EZ 42 gunsight and the Ta 152 V 15 which was never completed. Conversion packs for the Ta 152 C-1 included the /R11 for a bad weather fighter, the /R14 with ETC 504 bomb-racks and the /R31 with increased GM-1 capacity. The Ta 152 C-2 had different radio equipment and the Ta 152 C-3 featured a MK 103 cannon in place of the engine-mounted MK 108. Prototypes included the Ta 152 V 16 (W.Nr.110016), the V 17 (W.Nr.110017), the V 27 (W.Nr.150030) and the V 28 (W.Nr.150031). The projected Ta 152 C-4 was to have carried 210-mm. WGr 21 rocket tubes, the Ta 152 V 22, V 23 and V 24 being ordered as prototypes, but never completed.

The Ta 152 E was a special photo-reconnaissance version of the Ta 152 C, powered by a Jumo 213 E engine. The Ta 152 E-1 carried a vertically-mounted Rb 20/30, 50/30 or 75/30 camera, the Ta 152 V 9 (W.Nr.110009) and V 14 (W.Nr.110014) acting as prototypes. The Ta 152 E-1/R1 had an obliquely mounted camera and the Ta 152 E-2 was a specialised high altitude version of the E-1 with the wing of the H series. One prototype only, the Ta 152 V 26 W.Nr. 110021) was completed.

Although the previously described variants were given earlier designations, the first aircraft to enter service was the Ta 152 H high-altitude machine. This actually followed the Fw 190 G rather than the Ta 152 E and was provided with the Jumo 213 engine of the Fw 190 D series. The first prototype for the Ta 152 H-0 was the Fw 190 V18/U2 (W.Nr.0040) which was

Another view of 0003 in the United States. The machine is still intact. (Photo: H. J. Nowarra)

Captured Ta 152H-1 photographed at the Farnborough display of enemy aircraft held in October/November 1945. (Photo: Imperial War Museum)

Captured Fw 190As, Ds, Fs and Gs on a German airfield at the end of the European war. Note the varying styles of marking. (Photo: Gruppe 66 Archiv)

re-built from the V 18/U2. The wing of the Ta 152 H spanned 47 ft. 6¾ ins. and was of high-aspect ratio, numerous lateral stringers reinforcing the wing structure. The Fw 190 V 18/U2 crashed on 8th October 1944 on one of its early test flights, but was followed shortly afterwards by the Fw 190 V 20 (W.Nr.0042) which although having the Jumo 213 A engine and standard armament, retained the standard wing of the Fw 190 D.

The first Ta 152 H prototype with full equipment was the V 29/U1 (W.Nr.0054) "GH+KS" which had long span wings and a pressurised cabin. Armament comprised an engine-mounted 30 mm. MK 108 and two wing-mounted 20 mm. MG 151/20 cannons. The Fw 190 V 30/U1 (W.Nr.0055) "GH+KT" was similar but all armament was removed. The last Ta 152 H-0 prototype was the Fw 190 V 32 /U1 (W.Nr.0057) which was powered by a Jumo 213 F engine. This was later re-built as the Fw 190 V 32/U2 with Jumo 213 E engine and the MK 213 cannon (a special rapid-firing 20 mm. weapon).

The Ta 152 H-0, although given a pre-production designation, was virtually a production machine. A small number of Ta 152 H-0s were delivered in the spring of 1945 to the *Geschwader Stab* of JG 301, which as already mentioned, was equipped with the Fw 190 D-9. JG 301, like III./JG 54 previously, were engaged in the protection of the Me 262 fighter bases. Some idea of the startling increase in performance of the Ta 152 over previous Luftwaffe fighters can be gained by the following incident. Late in 1944, Kurt Tank, himself no mean pilot, was flying a Ta 152 H between Langenhagen and Cottbus when he was "bounced" by a section of P-51 D Mustangs. Tank operated the control for the MW-50 water-methanol injection and the machine leapt forward leaving the startled Americans far behind.

Several Rusatz conversion packs were designed for the Ta 152 H series including the /R11 all-weather fighter, the /R21, similar but with no GM-1 power boosting and the /R31 with GM-1 but no MW-50. The first production model proper was the Ta 152 H-1, which differed from the H-0 solely in having increased fuel capacity. The only prototype was the Ta 152 V 26 (W.Nr.110026) although another prototype, designated V 25 had been built only to be dismantled. The projected Ta 152 H-2 was similar but had FuG 15 radio equipment in place of FuG 16 ZY. The Ta 152 H-10 was a reconnaissance variant with an Rb 20/30, Rb 50/30 or Rb 75/30 camera to replace the Ta 152 E-1.

The prototype for the Fw 190D-11 was the V-56 (W.Nr.170924). Visible in this rear view are the small horns protruding above the inner wings, indicating undercarriage position. (Photo: H. J. Nowarra)

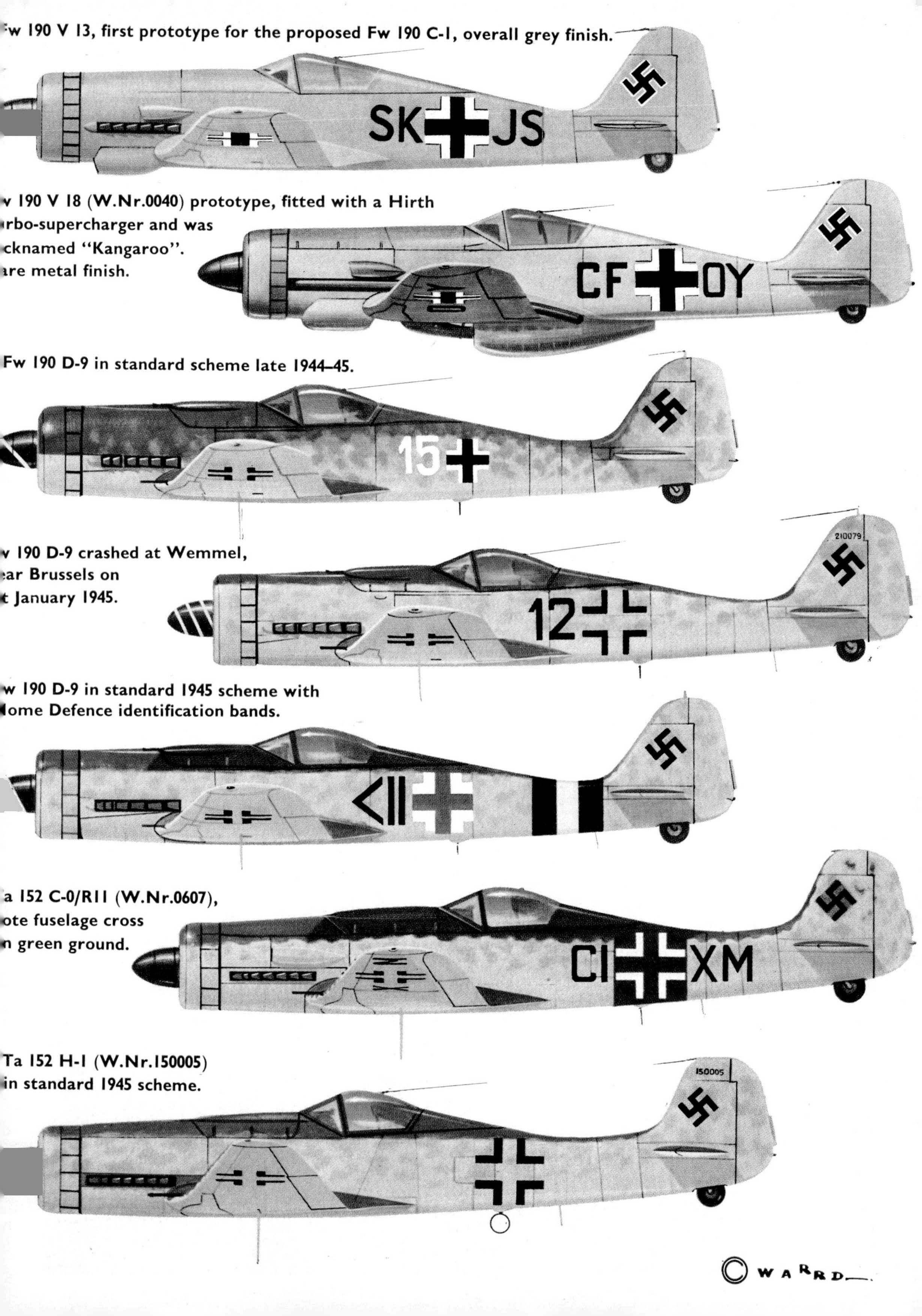

·w 190 V 13, first prototype for the proposed Fw 190 C-1, overall grey finish.

·v 190 V 18 (W.Nr.0040) prototype, fitted with a Hirth
ırbo-supercharger and was
ıcknamed "Kangaroo".
ıre metal finish.

Fw 190 D-9 in standard scheme late 1944–45.

·v 190 D-9 crashed at Wemmel,
ıar Brussels on
t January 1945.

·w 190 D-9 in standard 1945 scheme with
Iome Defence identification bands.

·a 152 C-0/R11 (W.Nr.0607),
ote fuselage cross
n green ground.

Ta 152 H-1 (W.Nr.150005)
in standard 1945 scheme.

Photographic proof that the Ta 152H was issued to front-line units. This line-up of aircraft shows application of fuselage bands in red and yellow (second aircraft from right) and code numbers (fourth aircraft, red "2"). The machines almost certainly operated with the Staff Flight of JG 301. (Photo: Dolling via Seeley)

Final projected variants of the Ta 152 included the long-range R series with provision for extra fuel and the Ta 152 S-1 tandem two-seat conversion trainer similar in many respects to the Fw 190 A-8/U1. Other projects included the use of the 2,200-h.p. Jumo 222 A/B or 3,000-h.p. Jumo 222 E/F engine. The Ta 152 C was also to be modified to tow a Gotha P.57 glider bomb. This was a simple glider type vehicle spanning 15 ft. 6 in. which was to be towed above and behind this aircraft.

After the war, several "long-nose" Focke Wulfs were captured and tested in the United States by the Foreign Evaluation unit at Freeman Field. These included a Ta 152 H-0 (FE-112) and two Fw 190 D-9s (FE-118 and FE 121). The former was originally test flown in the British Isles together with a Ta 152 H-1 (W.Nr.150168) which was given the Air Ministry number 11.

The author would thank the officials of Gruppe 66 *for the assistance given during the preparation of this* Profile.
Acknowledgement is made of the invaluable collaboration of Ian Primmer, Esq., without whose aid the article could not have been written.

Two views of the best-known operational Fw 190D; variously identified in the past, this machine is almost certainly the D-9 of a Staff Major flying with JG 26, photographed at Rhein-Main in 1945. Note Reichsverteidigung *fuselage bands.* (Photos: Swisher via Seeley)

A camouflaged "longnose" photographed in 1945. (Photo: Olmsted via Seeley)

SPECIFICATIONS

FOCKE WULF Fw 190 D-9

Dimensions: Span 34 ft. 5⅜ in. Length 33 ft. 5¼ in. Height 11 ft. 0¼ in. Wing Area 196·979 sq. ft.
Powerplant: One Junkers Jumo 213 A-1 twelve-cylinder, inverted Vee, liquid-cooled in-line engine rated at 1,776 h.p. for take-off and 1,200 h.p. for continuous running. This could be increased to 2,240 h.p. with the addition of MW-50 water-methanol injection.
Armament: Two 20 mm. MG 151/20 cannon with 250 r.p.g. mounted in the wing roots and two 13 mm. MG 131 machine guns mounted above the engine cowling with 475 r.p.g.
Weights: Empty 7,694 lb. Loaded 9,480 lb.
Performance: Maximum speed (with MW-50) 357 m.p.h. at sea level, 397 m.p.h. at 10,820 ft., 426 m.p.h. at 21,653 ft. and 397 m.p.h. at 32,810 ft. Climb to 6,560 ft. was 2·1 min.; to 13,120 ft. was 4·5 min.; to 19,685 ft. was 7·1 min.; and to 32,810 ft. was 16·8 min. Normal range was 520 miles at 18,500 ft.

FOCKE WULF Ta 152 C-3

Dimensions: Span 36 ft. 1 in. Length 35 ft. 5½ in. Height 13 ft. 0 in. Wing area 216 sq. ft.
Powerplant: One Daimler Benz DB 603 L twelve-cylinder, inverted Vee, liquid-cooled in-line engine rated at 2,100 h.p. for take-off.
Armament: One 30 mm. MK 103 cannon firing through the spinner and four 20 mm. MG 151/20 cannon in the wings.
Weights: Empty 9,058 lb. Loaded 11,025 lb. Maximum loaded 12,125 lb.
Performance: Maximum speed 339 m.p.h. at sea level, 350 m.p.h. with MW-50, 439 m.p.h. at 37,000 ft., 463 m.p.h. with MW-50. Service ceiling 40,350 ft.

FOCKE WULF Ta 152 H-1

Dimensions: Span 47 ft. 6¾ in. Length 35 ft. 5½ in. Height 13 ft. 0 in. Wing area 252·95 sq. ft.
Powerplant: One Junkers Jumo 213 E/B twelve-cylinder, inverted Vee, liquid-cooled in-line engine rated at 1,880 h.p. at sea level and 2,250 h.p. with MW-50 water-methanol injection.
Armament: One 30 mm. MK 108 cannon firing through the spinner and two 20 mm. MG 151/20 cannon in the wing roots.
Weights: Loaded 10,472 lb. Maximum loaded 11,508 lb.
Performance: Maximum speed 431 m.p.h. at 35,000 ft; 465 m.p.h. at 30,000 ft. with MW-50 and 472 m.p.h. at 41,000 ft. with GM-1 and MW-50. Normal range 745 miles at 372 m.p.h. at 32,800 ft. Service ceiling 48,560 ft.

PRINTED IN ENGLAND © Profile Publications Ltd., P.O. Box 26, 1a North Street, Leatherhead, Surrey, England.
Printed by Hills & Lacy Ltd., London and Watford, England. U.S. 2nd Class Mailing Rates applied for.

PROFILE
PUBLICATIONS

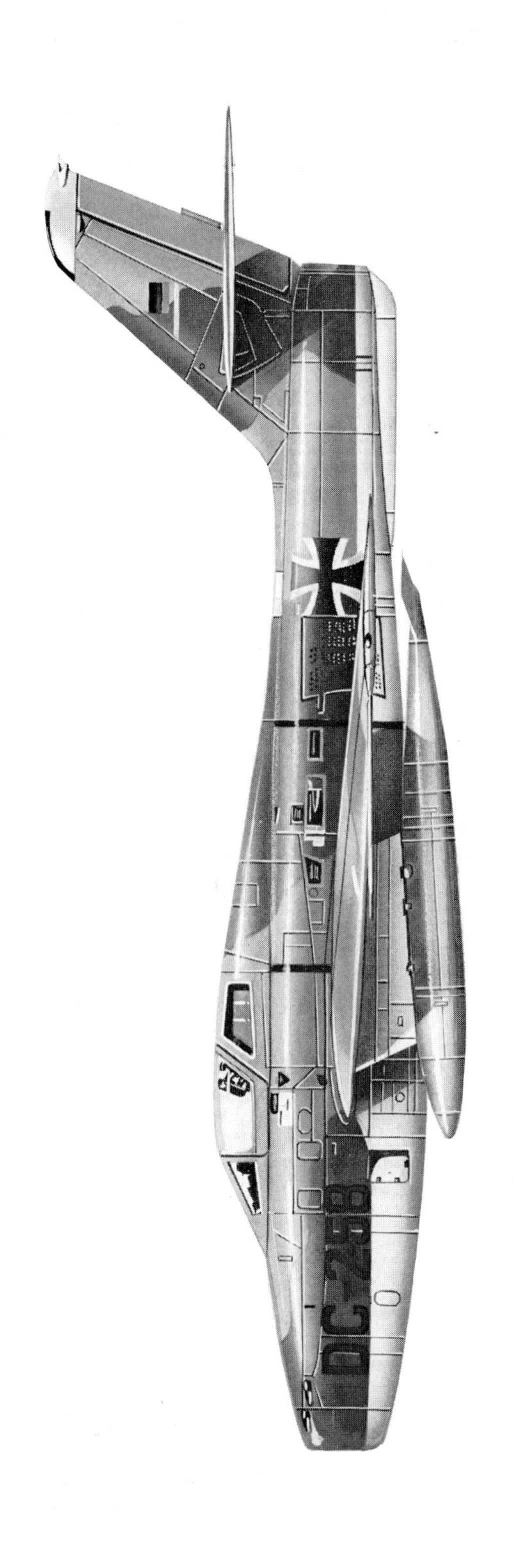

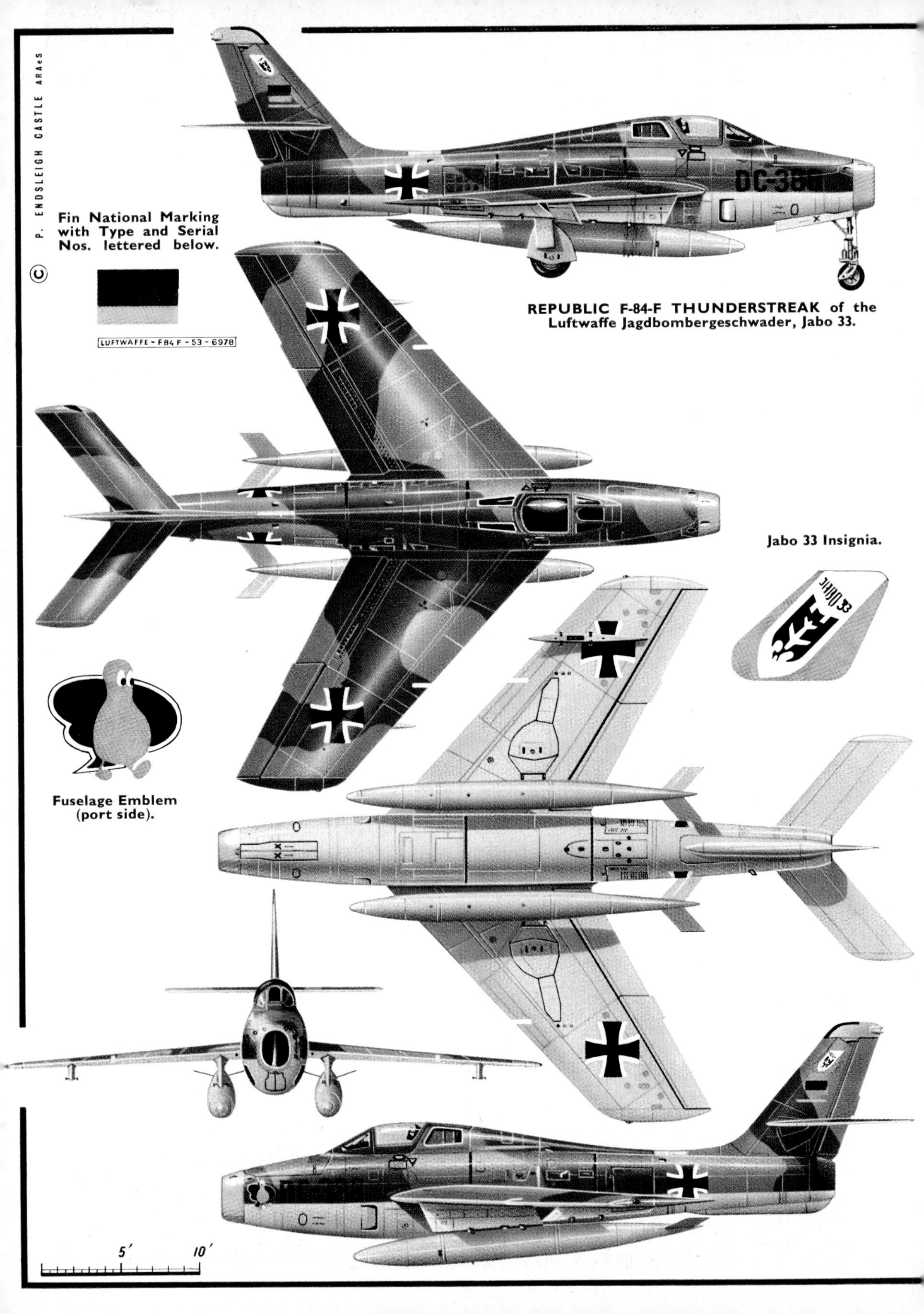
© P. ENDSLEIGH CASTLE ARAeS
Fin National Marking with Type and Serial Nos. lettered below.
LUFTWAFFE - F84 F - 53 - 6978
DC-386
REPUBLIC F-84-F THUNDERSTREAK of the Luftwaffe Jagdbombergeschwader, Jabo 33.
Jabo 33 Insignia.
Fuselage Emblem (port side).
5′
10′

The Republic F-84F Thunderstreak

by Ray Wagner

An F-84F of the Luftwaffe's Jagdbombergeschwader *32.* (Photo: Gerhard Joos)

Long a familiar sight in Western European skies, the Republic F-84F has been used by the air forces of seven nations, and is descended from the first American jet fighter of the post-war generation.

When design of the F-84 series began in November 1944, the first innovation was the use of an axial-flow turbojet, General Electric's J-35 (then TG-180). This engine allowed use of the first nose-air intake on an American jet, with straight-through air flow to the tailpipe, and less fuel consumption than the centrifugal engines of earlier jet fighters, like the F-80. The small diameter of the axial-flow unit permitted a streamlined low-drag fuselage whose maximum width was set by powerplant width, and whose vertical dimension was determined by cockpit height.

Since range, as well as high speed, was a consideration, wing shape had to forgo a thin profile and low aspect ratio in favour of a ratio of 5·10 and an airfoil section thick enough to contain fuel tanks and landing gears. The critical Mach number of this straight conventional wing was considerably below that of the fuselage, and was the primary limitation of performance on early F-84 models.

Three prototypes, designated XP-84, were built with General Electric J35-GE-7 turbojets of 3,750 lb. thrust, but this engine was turned over to Allison for mass production. The first XP-84 was completed in December 1945 and flown from Republic's factory in Farmingdale, New York, to Muroc Air Force Base, California, aboard the Boeing XC-97 transport.

On 28th February 1946 the first flight was made at Muroc by Major William A. Lien. The second prototype was prepared for a record attempt and attained 611 m.p.h. on 7th September 1946; a U.S. speed record, but not high enough to exceed the world's record then held by a Gloster Meteor F.4.

An initial production contract for 100 aircraft had been approved in January 1946, and the first fifteen were completed by April 1947 as YP-84As with Allison J35-A-15 jets, and assigned to the Muroc and Wright-Patterson bases for tests and pilot familiarisation. The remaining eighty-five were completed as P-84Bs from June 1947 to February 1948 with such additions for service operations as an ejector seat, radio compass, and new M-3 guns to replace the six M-2 guns of war-time use.

Most of these aircraft went to the first Air Force unit operational with Republic jets, the 14th Fighter Group at Dow Field, which used the P-84B from November 1947 until the group's inactivation in October 1949. Performance of the P-84B provides a benchmark for measuring progress to the F-84F. Top

As the first Republic jet in service, the P-84B-1 introduced the axial-flow powerplant and the speed brake below the cockpit. (Photo: Bowers' Collection)

Bomb-carrying and long-range capabilities appeared with the F-84E-1. (Photo: Republic)

speed was 587 m.p.h. at 4,000 ft., at 13,465 lb. combat weight, and 786 gallons of fuel in fuselage; wing and wingtip tanks permitted a range of 1,282 miles at 416 m.p.h. Climb was 4,210 ft. the first minute, and service ceiling was 40,750 ft.

New orders made in June 1947 added 141 more P-84Bs and 191 P-84Cs. These models added a ground attack capability, beginning with the P-84B-20, with eight five-inch, 140-lb. rockets on retractable launches under the wing, outboard of the landing gear.

Republic's deliveries of Thunderjets reached one a day during 1948, as the F-84C used the new "F" instead of "P" designation and replaced the J35-A-15 with the J35-A-13's simpler fuel system. Improved maintenance features were introduced on the F-84D, of which 154 had been ordered. The pitot tube was shifted from the tail fin to the nose duct air divider, a mechanical landing gear retraction system replaced the older hydraulic one, the fuel system winterised, and a hinged gun deck cover was provided. The F-84C and F-84D were similar to the B model in appearance and performance, aside from a slight reduction in climb due to about 400 lb. more weight.

At this point, the Republic Thunderjet's performance had been far surpassed by the F-86A Sabre, with its swept-wing and J-47 engine. But a new Thunderjet, the F-84E, was designed with range and ground attack capability unmatched by any contemporary jet type, and a contract for 409 was approved in December 1948.

The first F-84E, *49-2022*, flown on 18th May 1949, had the 4,900-lb. thrust J35-A-17, more fuel, and a longer, roomier cockpit with the new Sperry radar-ranging gunsight. The fuselage length was increased from 37 ft. 5 in. to 38 ft. 6 in. Fuel load including two 230-gallon tip tanks was 912 gallons, giving a 1,485 mile range. Two more 230-gallon tanks could be carried on inboard pylons for a total of 1,372 gallons and ferry range of 1,950 miles. Gross weight had increased from 19,689 lb. in the B to 22,463 lb. in the E.

Top speed of the early F-84E was 613 m.p.h. at sea level with 14,720 lb. combat weight, climb was 6,061 feet the first minute, and service ceiling of 43,220 feet. More important than its capabilities as a long-range escort fighter, was the F-84E's ground attack potential. Two 1,000-lb. bombs, or two 1,200-lb., 11·75 inch "Tiny Tim" rockets could replace the inboard drop tanks. For short ranges, an array of thirty-two five-inch rockets could be carried below the wings. More strength was added to the wing structure, and serviceability improved with 180 access doors, quick-disconnect on all electrical cables, and other improvements.

The F-84E was the model that equipped most of the six U.S.A.F. wings using Thunderjets when the Korean War began, and it was first taken into combat on 7th December 1950 by the 27th Fighter-Escort Group. In Korea, Republic's fighter was an immediate success as in ground support missions, but fighter missions flown to escort B-29 bombers proved the straight-wing F-84E too slow to match the swept-wing MIG-15.

SWEPT WING VERSION

A swept-wing version of the F-84 had been planned late in 1949 to raise its speed to F-86 levels, while retaining, and even increasing, its superior ground attack capabilities. The last, and 409th, aircraft of the F84E contract was selected as the swept-wing, YF-84F prototype.

Construction of the aircraft, *49-2430*, took 167 days from the date the company's experimental shop received the first engineering drawing until the prototype was taxied under its own power. The aircraft was then dismantled and flown to Muroc from Farmingdale aboard a Boeing C-97 and Fairchild C-82.

On 3rd June 1950 Republic Director of Flight Otto P. Hass took the prototype for its first flight. At that time it was designated YF-96A because of its extensive design changes, but on 9th August the designation reverted back to the original YF-84F.

Essentially, the fuselage was that of the preceding F-84Es, including the pilot's canopy and the speed brake underneath the fuselage. The tail was swept back, and an entirely new wing, swept back 40 degrees at the ¼-chord line, was used. Instead of the 260 sq. ft. area and 36 ft. 5 in. span of the older models, the YF-84F had 325 sq. ft. of area and 33 ft. 7 in. span. The airfoil was 10% NACA 64A010 section, with maximum thickness at 45% chord. Wing cathedral, or droop, was 3 degrees, 30 seconds.

Powered by an Allison J35-A-25 of 5,200-lb. thrust, the YF-84F weight was 12,150 lb. empty and 23,230 lb. gross, and could carry 1,505 gallons of fuel. Performance included a top speed of 693 m.p.h. at sea level, a range of 1,716 miles at 514 m.p.h., a 38,300 ft. service ceiling, and climb to 35,000 ft. required 14·8 minutes.

Briefly designated YF-46A, the swept-wing prototype 49-2430 *is seen here with external load.* (Photo: Republic)

The prototype after being rebuilt with the British Sapphire engine. (Photo: Republic)

The first production F-84F-1-RE with new canopy. (Photo: Republic)

F-84F-20-RE with all four drop tanks. (Photo: Roger Besecker)

NEW ENGINE

Although a letter contract for production was received in July 1950, much development work would remain before the old straight-wing types could be actually replaced on the production line. Although the speed already pressed even the aircraft limitation extended by the swept-wings, more power was badly needed to improve take-off, climb, and high altitude performance. For this purpose, examples of the Armstrong-Siddeley Sapphire axial-flow jet engines of 7,200-lb. thrust were ordered from Britain, and arrangements were made to have the Sapphire produced in the U.S.A. under licence by Curtiss-Wright as the J65.

Use of the larger engine required re-design of the fuselage to increase depth by seven inches, and enlargement of the nose intake to elliptical shape. The prototype was flown for the first time with an imported Sapphire on 14th February 1951.

Two pre-production YF-84F prototypes, *51-1344* and *51-1345*, with Sapphire engines were built by Republic in 1951. The second was completed with wing root air intakes, leaving the nose with a solid cover. Another innovation was the reinforced canopy with a flat-front windshield, instead of the earlier V-front.

The wing root intakes resulted in thrust losses, and were not adopted for production fighters, but they did permit a roving camera nose for a reconnaissance version. The next version to appear was a pre-production YRF-84F, *51-1828*, flown in February 1952, which had the wing root ducts and canopy of its predecessor, but added a nose large enough to accommodate six cameras.

Another innovation planned for production aircraft was the use of heavy press forgings in the wing structure. As it turned out, the only forge press in the country suitable was tied up by the B-47 programme, and a breakdown in the press further aggravated the situation. The wing structure had to be re-designed to utilise existing tools and facilities.

The original production schedule for F-84Fs prepared in August 1950, called for the first deliveries of the production version by the autumn of 1951. As early as July 1951 the contractor advised the Air Force that the contract schedule would have to be set back due to serious delays in the production of wing forgings and the engines. These delays were the result of quantity procurement made at a time when the F-84F was thought of as a further development of the F-84E already being successfully produced, instead of as an almost entirely new aircraft with a brand-new engine.

In the meantime production continued on a straight-wing Thunderjet. After completion of the first YF-84F, Republic delivered 145 F-84E-20, followed by 130 F-84E-25 and 160 F-84E-30 ordered after the Korean War began, and fitted with new tail pipes for added thrust. These brought their top speed to 619 m.p.h. at sea level and 543 m.p.h. at 35,000 ft., and the F-84E production total to 843. They were used in Korea by the 27th, 49th, 116th, and 136th Fighter Wings, and in 1951 became the first American jets exported to NATO allies Belgium and France.

The last F-84E-30 in June 1951 was followed by the first F-84G-1, with the 5,600-lb. thrust J35-A-29, provision for air-to-air refuelling, and reinforced canopy. The Gs were a straight-wing interim model intended to fill the production gap until the F was ready in quantity. Delays in getting the swept-wing model into production were so time-consuming that the G became the most widely produced F-84 model, with 3,025 built. Not until the last day of the Korean War, 27th July 1953, was the last F-84G delivered,

Contrast the first F-84F-1 with the line-up of F-84G-11 Thunderjets. (Photo: Republic)

In-flight refuelling of an F-84F-25 by a KB-29 tanker. (Photo: Republic)

bringing the straight-wing Thunderjet total to 4,457. At that time, straight-wing F-84Gs were being used by fourteen U.S.A.F. Wings and ten other air forces.

QUANTITY PRODUCTION

At last, quantity delivery of the swept-wing could begin. The first production F-84F-1-RE, *51-1346*, was flown on 22nd November 1952. Ten were built with early U.S.-built Wright J25-W-1 turbojets, but the F-84F-5-RE had the 7,220-lb. thrust J65-W-3 standardised for production aircraft, or the equivalent Buick-built J65-B-3, and deliveries began in quantity in the latter part of 1953.

Production F-84Fs were named Thunderstreaks, and had several important improvements over earlier models. The cockpit canopy, previously a sliding bubble type, now was a hinged arm, upward-swinging type that raised the part of the enclosure above the pilot. For normal exits it is pushed up to open, but in emergencies the cover is released from the plane to allow seat ejection. This canopy was stronger, easier to install, and better sealed than the sliding cover.

Although previous models had a single, unperforated speed brake on the fuselage bottom, the F-84F had two perforated panels on the fuselage sides just behind the wing trailing edge. They can be opened at any speed up to the maximum dive speed without large trim changes or excessive buffeting.

Another innovation on the swept-wing model was the leading-edge wing-slats to improve airflow characteristics. Control tabs were removed from the ailerons in favour of an irreversible power-boosted control system. The swept-back tail on the first 275 production ships was the conventional stabiliser and elevator, but by the end of 1953, the first F-84F-25, *51-1621*, appeared with the one-piece surface in which the entire horizontal area was used for control and trim. More positive control was obtained from this so-called "all-flying", or all-movable tail.

Six ·50 calibre M-3 guns with 1,800 rounds of ammunition are mounted in the same way on the F-84F as on previous models, with four on the gun deck ahead of the cockpit, and one in each wing root. Wing-tip tanks are impractical on swept wings, but the inboard pylons can accommodate two 450-gallon drop tanks or two 2,000-lb. bombs. Use of the two outboard pylons permitted the full load of 6,000 lb. of bombs or a combination of rockets.

The most destructive weapon carried by the Thunderstreak was a Mk. 6 nuclear store, carried under the port wing. In order to escape a blast greater than the one at Hiroshima, the F-84F had to deliver the weapon by a low-altitude bombing system (LABS). This device selects the right moment to release the bomb during a loop, after which the aircraft escapes with a turn.

Weighing 13,645 lb. empty, the F-84F-25, or AP-23M-3, as it was known on company records, had a normal gross weight of 25,226 lb. Performance included a top speed of 685 m.p.h. at sea level and 608 m.p.h. at 35,000 ft., at a combat weight of 18,700 lb. Climb was 7,000 ft. in one minute, and 35,000 ft. in 7·8 minutes. Service ceiling at full load was 36,150 ft., and combat ceiling at combat weight was 42,250 ft. Stalling speed was 151 m.p.h., and the Thunderjet was known for long take-off runs. Normal combat radius was 850 miles, and when the Thunderstreak had its full load of 1,758 gallons and take-off weight of 27,000 lb. a ferry range of 2,314 miles. An MB-2 autopilot and TACAN radio-navigation equipment aided the pilot on long flights.

Intercontinental ranges were obtained through use of inflight refuelling. The first Republic jets to use this method were F-84Es fitted for the British probe and drogue system. Boeing's flying boom system was adopted for standard air force use and the F-84G had its refuelling receptacle in the port wing's leading edge. In the F-84F, the receptacle is aft of the leading-edge

Red stars on a Thunderstreak! But only for its rôle as a "MiG-15" in the film "Jet Attack"; photo taken at Tucson in May 1959. (Photo: Richard Camm)

Kansas-built F-84F-35-GK taking off. (Photo: Republic)

Thunderstreak in the livery of T.A.C. and the Virginia Air National Guard. (Photo: Roger Besecker)

The URF-84F prototype 51-1828, *with sliding canopy.* (Photo: Bowers' Collection)

The YF-84J in flight. (Photo: Republic)

The bizarre-looking XF-84H. (Photo: Republic)

area, with a single-piece rear-hinged door, which when opened extends the nozzle up into the airstream.

In March 1955, the F-84F-50 appeared with the J65-W-7 (or J65-B-7) or 7,800 lb. thrust. While airframe limitations prevented improvement of low level speed, the added power increased climb to 7,400 ft. the first minute, and combat ceiling to 44,850 ft.

Production of the Thunderstreak at Farmingdale accelerated with the aid of subcontractors like Kaiser Metal Products, building the aft fuselage and empennage in Bristol, Pennyslvania, Servel building wings in Evansville, Indiana, and Goodyear Aircraft building the cockpit windshield, canopy, and turtle deck.

A second source of production was established by a contract approved in June 1952, in which General Motors built Thunderstreaks in the Kansas City factory once used by North American to build B-25 Mitchells in W.W.II. General Motors built 599 Thunderstreaks, known as F-84F-GK when built in Kansas.

Production at the Farmingdale home plant reached a total of 2,112 F-84F Thunderstreaks, with the last F-84F-75-RE delivered in August 1957. This last version had a new fairing under the fuselage for the braking chute, a device also retrospectively fitted to earlier models. The 16-ft. diameter parachute trailed 35-ft. behind the wing, reducing stopping distance from 3,400 to 2,400 ft.

The U.S.A.F. had the F-84F in service with twelve Wings in June 1955. Six of these were attached to the Strategic Air Command to escort and support bomber operations, but as the day of slow-moving formations of propeller-driven bombers had ended, S.A.C. relinquished its fighter units to Tactical Air Command. All F-84Fs were then operated by T.A.C. as ground-support fighter-bombers.

Gradually, the F-84F was replaced in front-line service by the F-100, and given to Air National Guard units. In 1961, however, it was called back into front-line active duty with the Berlin Crisis. The 141st Tactical Fighter Squadron from McGuire Air Force Base, the 163rd T.F.S. from Fort Wayne, Indiana, and the 166th T.F.S. from Columbus, Ohio, were Air National Guard F-84 squadrons deployed to Europe, while re-activated U.S.A.F. units received F-84Fs.

The F-84F was used by T.A.C.'s 12th, 15th, and 366th Tactical Fighter Wings until their replacement by F-4Cs in 1964–65. In 1965, eight Air National Guard Squadrons still used the F-84F.

THE NATO THUNDERSTREAKS

When the F-84F was chosen to replace the straight-wing Thunderjet as the standard fighter-bomber for North Atlantic Treaty Organisation forces, new and more colourful markings appeared on the flanks. Of 2,711 Thunderstreaks built, 1,301 were dispatched to Europe for allied nations.

France received its first Thunderstreaks in 1955 with the re-equipment of French Tactical Air Command's *Escadres:* the 1st, 3rd, 4th, 6th, and 11th. These became the first, and so far the only, F-84Fs to enter combat.

The occasion was the Suez Crisis of 1956, when France and England collaborated with Israel against Egypt. On 23rd October 1956, thirty-six Thunderstreaks from the 1st *Escadre* at St. Dizier flew to the Israeli base at Lydda, and about the same time more F-84Fs from the 3rd *Escadre* moved from Rheims to Akrotiri on Cyprus.

Painted with black and yellow "invasion" stripes for instant recognition*, the French fighters at Lydda were to support the Israeli force that invaded Sinai on 29th October. After direct attacks began on 1st November on Egyptian air fields by the Cyprus-based units, twenty Egyptian Il-28 jet bombers fled to Luxor, where they were destroyed on the ground by the Lydda-based pilots. Meeting only negligible

**The Israel-based fighters appeared to have had their French marking temporarily covered by Israeli markings for political reasons.*

The Tactical Air Command insignia is displayed on the tail of this F-84F-35-RE. (Photo: Roger Besecker)

Fine study of the fourth RF-84F Thunderflash. (Photo: Republic)

resistance from the Egyptian Air Force, operations against hostile air bases were concluded on 6th November, and only one F-84F, with its pilot, was lost.

Belgium began receiving F-84Fs in August 1955, and by the following year the 2nd and 10th Fighter-bomber Wings had replaced their Thunderjets with the Thunderstreaks. The six tactical fighter-bomber squadrons of the Netherlands Air Force, Nos. 311 to 316 inclusive, standardised on F-84Fs in 1956. That year also saw the Italian Air Force equip three Air Brigades (as U.S. Wing) with F-84Fs, *Aerobrigata* 5a, 51, and 51a.

It was the revived German Air Force that received the F-84F in largest numbers. Thunderstreaks began arriving in November 1956, the first combat aircraft received by the new *Luftwaffe* since W.W.II. An operational training unit, *Waffenschule* 30, was formed to familiarise German pilots with the aircraft. On 20th June 1958 the first German fighter-bomber wing, *Jabo** G.31, and became operational, four more, *Jabo* G.32, 34, 35, and 36 were soon added.

The Germans continued to utilise the F-84F until the F-104G became available, the type which has also replaced most of the Belgium and Dutch Thunderstreaks. Some of the ex-*Luftwaffe* aircraft have gone to Greece and Turkey, who operated until 1965 six squadrons each of F-84Fs.

THE RF-84F THUNDERFLASH

A fast photo-reconnaissance jet was required by the Air Force to replace its ageing RF-80s, and the third YF-84F, with its wing root air intakes, offered a potential camera arrangement with only small thrust losses.

Forty-one RF versions were ordered in a contract approved in June 1952, and the first was completed in February 1952 as a pre-production prototype, the YRF-84F, *51-1828*, had wing root inlets, a new nose enlarged to accommodate cameras, four 50-calibre wing guns, and a reinforced sliding canopy. Later, dual fences were added to each wing.

Deliveries of production RF-84F Thunderflashes began in March 1954, with the first RF-84F-1, *51-1829*, displaying the same upward hinging canopy of the F-84Fs. The 363rd Tactical Reconnaissance Wing of T.A.C., at Shaw AFB, South Carolina was the first operational with the RF-84. Early blocks used the Wright J65-W-3, or its Buick counterpart, but the J65-W-7 of 7,800-lb. thrust was introduced on the RF-84F-20 in June 1955. Equipment included four 50-calibre wing guns with 400 rounds, and six cameras of various types in the nose.

With a full fuel load of 1,475 gallons, including two 450-gallon drop tanks, the RF-84F-20 weighed 25,390 lb. at take-off. At a combat weight of 20,091 lb. top speed ranged from 629 m.p.h. at sea level to 582 m.p.h. at 35,000 ft. Climb was 5,820 ft. the first minute, and service ceiling 36,300 ft. Combat radius was 840 miles, and ferry range 1,800 miles.

By June 1956 four U.S.A.F. reconnaissance wings were fitted with RF-84Fs. Although they were replaced in front-line units by McDonnell RF-101s, the F-84Fs served seven Air National Guard Squadrons through 1965.

**For* Jagdbombergeschwader.

Two stages in the remarkable FICON project, which increased the reconnaissance range of the F-84F to almost 5,000 miles. The mother plane is an RB-36F. (Photos: Republic)

Of 715 RF-84F Thunderflashes built at Farmingdale by January 1958, 386 were sent overseas as part of the Mutual Aid programme, and were more widely distributed than their fighter counterparts. They equipped two *Geschwader*, *Aufkl.* G51 and 52, of the *Luftwaffe*, the French Air Forces' 33rd *Escadre*, Belgium's 42*eme Escadrille*, the Netherlands' No. 306 Squadron, Denmark's No. 724 Squadron, Norway's No. 717 Squadron, and the 3a *Aerobrigata* in Italy. The Greek, Turkish, and Chinese Nationalist air arms also had one squadron of RF-84Fs each.

FICON AIRCRAFT

The FICON (FIghter CONveyor) project was begun originally as a way to extend the range of fighter planes by teaming the F-84 with the giant Convair B-36 bomber. Development of small nuclear bombs and the RF version added new possibilities, with the photo-reconnaissance mission being the one chosen for actual service.

An F-84E was chosen for the original experiments, making the first contact flight on 9th January 1952 and the first complete cycle of retrieve, retraction, and launch on 23rd April 1952. In 1953 the experiments entered a new phase when the original YF-84F prototype was fitted with a probe ahead of the cockpit. This probe engaged an H-shaped cradle lowered from the bomb bay of the RB-36F-1 mother plane. The fighter's horizontal tailplane was bent downwards.

During the latch-on the probe operated by engaging a latch in the yoke's crotch, the yoke then was lowered over the fighter to engage hooks in the fuselage, providing a three-point suspension for lifting the F-84F into the larger plane's bomb bay.

As the system proved out, twenty-five RF-84Fs were modified by Republic to RF-84K FICON configuration with nose probe and downward tailplane. They were used by the 91st Strategic Reconnaissance Squadron, Malmastrom AFB, Great Falls, Montana, working with GRB-36 mother ships operated from Spokane, Washington. The conveyor system increased the radius of the jets from 840 miles to nearly 5,000 miles, but was abandoned in the spring of 1956 when the B-36 was phased out of service. Perhaps appearance in service that year of the U-2 presented another way of deep penetration reconnaissance.

Michigan Air National Guard RF-84F-15-RE.
(Photo: David W. Menard)

F-84F 52-7143 *of the 3rd Sqdn., 2nd Wing,* Aviation Belge Militaire, *based at Florennes.* (Photo: David W. Menard)

RF-84F of Belgium's 42nd Recce. Sqdn.
(Photo: David W. Menard)

Luftwaffe *F-84F in early natural metal finish; compare this* Jabo *G33 aircraft with the painting on page 2 of this* Profile.
(Photo: David W. Menard)

Red-tailed RF-84F (*ex*-53-7689A) *of* Luftwaffe Aufklarung *51 photographed at Wethersfield, England, in May 1960.*
(Photo: G. J. Letzter)

Thunderstreaks of the Italian 5th Aerobrigata *bear the "Archer" emblem carried by Macchi fighters in W.W.II.* (Photo: G. Apostolo)

SPECIAL MODIFICATIONS

The 88th and 89th F-84F-25 were completed with the General Electric YJ73-GE-7 of 8,920 lb. thrust and designated YF-84J. First flown 7th May 1954, YF-84J, *51-1708*, had a deeper fuselage and nose scoop.

Although designated XF-84H, Republic's turbo-prop fighter used few F-84F components and was an entirely new aircraft designed in 1952 around the Allison XT-40-A-1 delivering 5,332 h.p. to an Aero-products three-bladed supersonic propeller and 1,296-lb. thrust out of the tailpipe. Two prototypes were built to a separate contract, with the first, *51-1759*, flying on 22nd July 1955, with a Tee tail anti-torque fin. Due to the numerous mechanical difficulties with the experimental engine, the second prototype was not flown.

AIR NATIONAL GUARD UNITS WITH F-84Fs

Squadron	Wing	Base
112 T.F.S.	122 T.F.W.	Toledo, Ohio
113 T.F.S.	122 T.F.W.	Terre Haute, Ill.
149 T.F.S.	108 T.F.W.	Richmond, Va.
162 T.F.S.	121 T.F.W.	Springfield, Ohio
163 T.F.S.	122 T.F.W.	Fort Wayne, Ohio
164 T.F.S.	121 T.F.W.	Mansfield, Ohio
169 T.F.S.	131 T.F.W.	Peoria, Ill.
170 T.F.S.	131 T.F.W.	Springfield, Ill.

AIR NATIONAL GUARD UNITS WITH RF-84Fs

Squadron	Wing	Base
106 T.R.S.	117 T.R.W.	Birmingham, Ala.
107 T.R.S.	127 T.R.W.	Detroit, Mich.
153 T.R.S.	117 T.R.W.	Meridan, Miss.
160 T.R.S.	117 T.R.W.	Montgomery, Ala.
171 T.R.S.	127 T.R.W.	Detroit, Mich.
173 T.R.S.	127 T.R.W.	Lincoln, Neb.
184 T.R.S.	117 T.R.W.	Fort Smith, Ark.

REPUBLIC F-84F SERIAL NUMBERS

No. A/C	Type	Contract	U.S.A.F. Serials
1	YF-84F-RE	AF22053	*49-2430*
2	YF-84F-RE	14803	*51-1344* to *51-1345*
10	F-84F-1-RE	14803	*51-1346* to *51-1355*
25	F-84F-5	14803	*51-1356* to *51-1380*
50	F-84F-10	14803	*51-1381* to *51-1430*
80	F-84F-15	14803	*51-1431* to *51-1510*
110	F-84F-20	14803	*51-1511* to *51-1620*
87	F-84F-25	14803	*51-1621* to *51-1707*
2	YF-84J	14803	*51-1708* to *51-1705*
51	F-84F-25	14803	*51-1710* to *51-1769*
67	F-84F-30	14803	*51-1761* to *51-1820*
10	F-84F-1-GK	18503	*51-9311* to *51-9327*
25	F-84F-5-GK	18503	*51-9321* to *51-9330*
21	F-84F-10-GK	18503	*51-9336* to *51-9356*
43	F-84F-25-GK	18503	*51-9357* to *51-9409*
45	F-84F-30-GK	18503	*51-9410* to *51-8454*
49	F-84F-35-GK	18503	*51-9455* to *51-9503*
44	F-84F-40-GK	18503	*51-9504* to *51-9547*
2	XF-84H	20501	*51-17059* to *51-17060*
28	F-84F-35-CRF	14803	*51-17061* to *51-17088*
68	F-84F-30-RE	6704	*52-6355* to *52-6422*
97	F-84F-35-RE	6704	*52-6423* to *52-6519*
3	F-84F-35-GE	AF6704	*52-6520* to *52-6522*
120	F-84F-40-GE	AF6704	*52-6523* to *52-6642*
170	F-84F-45	AF6704	*52-6643* to *52-6812*
95	F-84F-50	AF6704	*52-6813* to *52-6907*
100	F-84F-55	AF6704	*52-6908* to *52-7007*
10	F-84F-56	AF6704	*52-7008* to *52-7017*
32	F-84F-35	AF6704	*52-7018* to *52-7049*
40	F-84F-40	AF6704	*52-7050* to *52-7089*
25	F-84F-45	AF6704	*52-7090* to *52-7114*
12	F-84F-46	AF6704	*52-7119* to *52-7126*
65	F-84F-51	AF6704	*52-7127* to *52-7191*
37	F-84F-56-RE	AF6704	*52-7192* to *52-7228*
68	F-84F-41-KC	18503	*52-8767* to *52-8834*
148	F-84F-46-KC	18503	*52-8835* to *52-8982*
146	F-84F-51-KC	18503	*52-8983* to *52-9128*
29	F-84F-56-RE	6704	*52-10510* to *52-10538*
184	F-84F-61-RE	22316	*52-6532* to *52-6715*
120	F-84F-66-RE	22316	*52-6716* to *52-6835*
120	F-84F-71-RE	22316	*52-6836* to *52-6955*
275	F-84F-75-RE	22316	*52-6956* to *52-7230*

RF-84F SERIAL NUMBERS

No. A/C	Model	Con-tract	Date	U.S.A.F. Serials
1	YRF-84F	14810	6–12–51	*51-1828*
40	RF-84F	14810	6–12–51	*51-1829* to *51-1868*
90	RF-84F	14810	31–8–51	*51-1869* to *51-1958*
48	RF-84F-RE	14810	12–6–51	*51-11250* to *51-11297*
63	RF-84F-RE	14810	25–9–51	*51-16996* to *51-17058*
5	RF-84F-21	6581	28–6–52	*52-7229* to *52-7233*
2	RF-84F-20	6581	28–6–52	*52-7234* to *52-7235*
8	RF-84F-21	6581	28–6–52	*52-7236* to *52-7243*
35	RF-84F-20	6581	28–6–52	*52-7244* to *52-7276*
8	RF-84F-26	6581	28–6–52	*52-7279* to *52-7286*
9	RF-84F-25	6581	28–6–52	*52-7287* to *52-7295*
12	RF-84F-26	6581	28–6–52	*52-7296* to *52-7307*

Planview detail of 6th Aerobrigata *F-84F.*

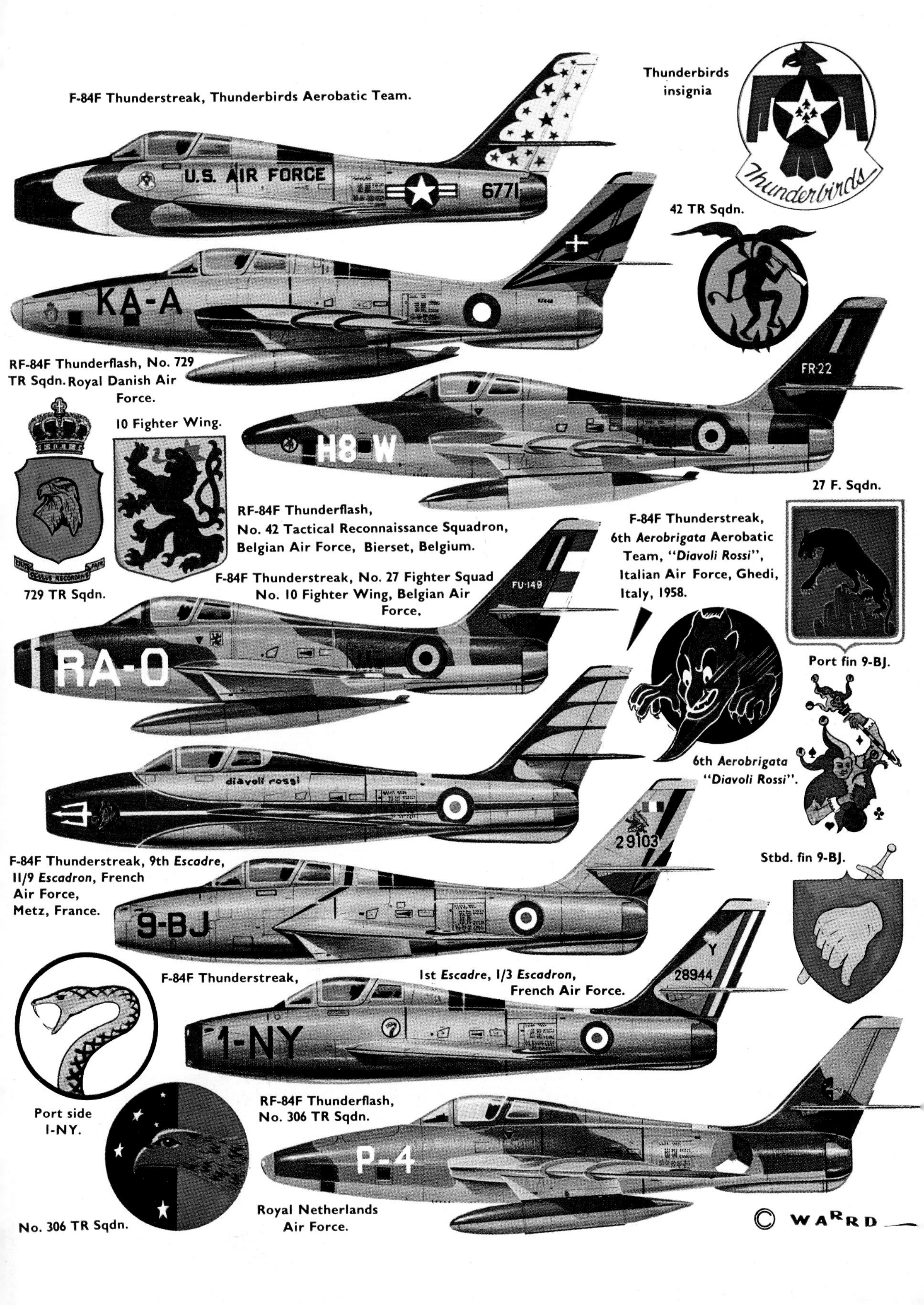

F-84F Thunderstreak, Thunderbirds Aerobatic Team.
U.S. AIR FORCE
6771
Thunderbirds insignia
Thunderbirds
42 TR Sqdn.
KA-A
RF-84F Thunderflash, No. 729 TR Sqdn. Royal Danish Air Force.
FR-22
H8 W
10 Fighter Wing.
729 TR Sqdn.
RF-84F Thunderflash, No. 42 Tactical Reconnaissance Squadron, Belgian Air Force, Bierset, Belgium.
27 F. Sqdn.
F-84F Thunderstreak, 6th Aerobrigata Aerobatic Team, "Diavoli Rossi", Italian Air Force, Ghedi, Italy, 1958.
F-84F Thunderstreak, No. 27 Fighter Squad No. 10 Fighter Wing, Belgian Air Force.
FU-149
RA-O
Port fin 9-BJ.
diavoli rossi
6th Aerobrigata "Diavoli Rossi".
29103
F-84F Thunderstreak, 9th Escadre, II/9 Escadron, French Air Force, Metz, France.
9-BJ
Stbd. fin 9-BJ.
Y
28944
F-84F Thunderstreak, 1st Escadre, 1/3 Escadron, French Air Force.
1-NY
Port side 1-NY.
RF-84F Thunderflash, No. 306 TR Sqdn.
P-4
No. 306 TR Sqdn.
Royal Netherlands Air Force.
© WARRD

Belgian Thunderflash over the Channel. (Photo: AVI. BEM.)

RF-84F SERIAL NUMBERS *continued*

11	RF-84F-25	6581	28–6–52	*52-7308* to *52-7318*
21	RF-84F-26	6581	28–6–52	*52-7319* to *52-7339*
12	RF-84F-25	6581	28–6–52	*52-7340* to *52-7351*
3	RF-84F-26	6581	28–6–52	*52-7352* to *52-7354*
23	RF-84F-25	6581	28–6–52	*52-7355* to *52-7377*
8	RF-84F-30-RE	AF6581	28–6–52	*52-7378* to *52-7385*
20	RF-84F-31	AF6581	28–6–52	*52-7386* to *52-7405*
27	RF-84F-30	AF6581	28–6–52	*52-7406* to *52-7432*
40	RF-84F-31	AF6581	28–6–52	*52-7433* to *52-7472*
1	RF-84F-35	AF6581	28–6–52	*52-7473*
2	RF-84F-36	AF6581	28–6–52	*52-7474* to *52-7475*
50	RF-84F-36	AF6581	28–6–52	*52-8717* to *52-8766*
12	RF-84F-35-RE	22315	3–4–53	*53-7521* to *53-7532*
9	RF-84F-36	22315	3–4–53	*53-7533* to *53-7541*
17	RF-84F-35	22315	3–4–53	*53-7542* to *53-7558*
32	RF-84F-36	22315	3–4–53	*53-7559* to *53-7590*
26	RF-84F-35	22315	3–4–53	*53-7591* to *53-7616*
17	RF-84F-35	22315	3–4–53	*53-7617* to *53-7633*
7	RF-84F-35	22315	3–4–53	*53-7634* to *53-7640*
57	RF-84F-36	22315	3–4–53	*53-7641* to *53-7697*

F-84F of Jagdbombergeschwader *32 at altitude, photographed by a brother pilot.* (Photo: Gerhard Joos)

Jabo *G34 machine carrying yellow drop tanks. Note* Geschwader *emblem on nose.* (Photo: Gerhard Joos)

SPECIFICATION
(Data selected from the Official Standard Aircraft Characteristics Charts dated 2nd September 1958)

	F-84F-25	F-84F-50	RF-84F-20
Span	33·6 ft.	33·6 ft.	33·6 ft.
Length	43·4 ft.	43·4 ft.	47·5 ft.
Height	15 ft.	15 ft.	15 ft.
Wing area	325 sq. ft.	325 sq. ft.	325 sq. ft.
Powerplant	J65-W-3	J65-W-7	J65-W-7
Thrust	7,220 lb.	7,800 lb.	7,800 lb.
Weight: Empty	13,645 lb.	13,645 lb.	14,014 lb.
Take-off	25,226 lb.	25,226 lb.	25,390 lb.
Ferry...	27,000 lb.	27,000 lb.	27,000 lb.
Combat	18,700 lb.	18,700 lb.	20,091 lb.
Fuel: Normal	1,479 gal.	1,479 gal.	1,475 gal.
Maximum	1,758 gal.	1,758 gal.	—
Speed: Top at sea level (5,000 ft. on RF-84F)	658 m.p.h. (595 knots)	658 m.p.h. (595 knots)	629 m.p.h. (547 knots)
Top at 35,000 ft.	608 m.p.h. (528 knots)	612 m.p.h. (532 knots)	582 m.p.h. (506 knots)
Cruising	539 m.p.h.	539 m.p.h.	542 m.p.h.
Stalling	151 m.p.h.	151 m.p.h.	166 m.p.h.
Ceiling: Service	36,150 ft.	37,500 ft.	36,500 ft.
Combat	42,250 ft.	44,850 ft.	—
Climb, minutes...	7,000 ft./1 min.	7,400 ft./1 min.	5,820 ft./1 min.
	35,000 ft./7·8 min.	35,000 ft./7·2 min.	35,000 ft./11·6 min.
Combat radius	860 miles	856 miles	840 miles
Ferry range	2,314 miles	2,343 miles	1,800 miles

PRINTED IN ENGLAND © Profile Publications Ltd., P.O. Box 26, 1a North Street, Leatherhead, Surrey, England.
Printed by Hills & Lacy Ltd., London and Watford, England. U.S. 2nd Class Mailing Rates applied for.

PROFILE PUBLICATIONS

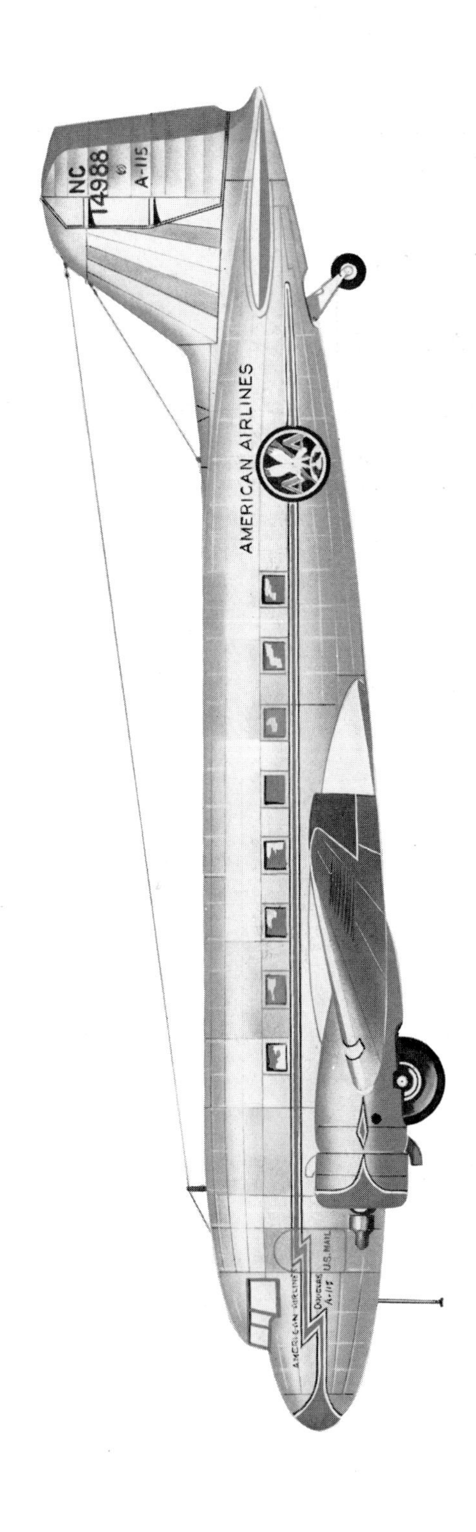

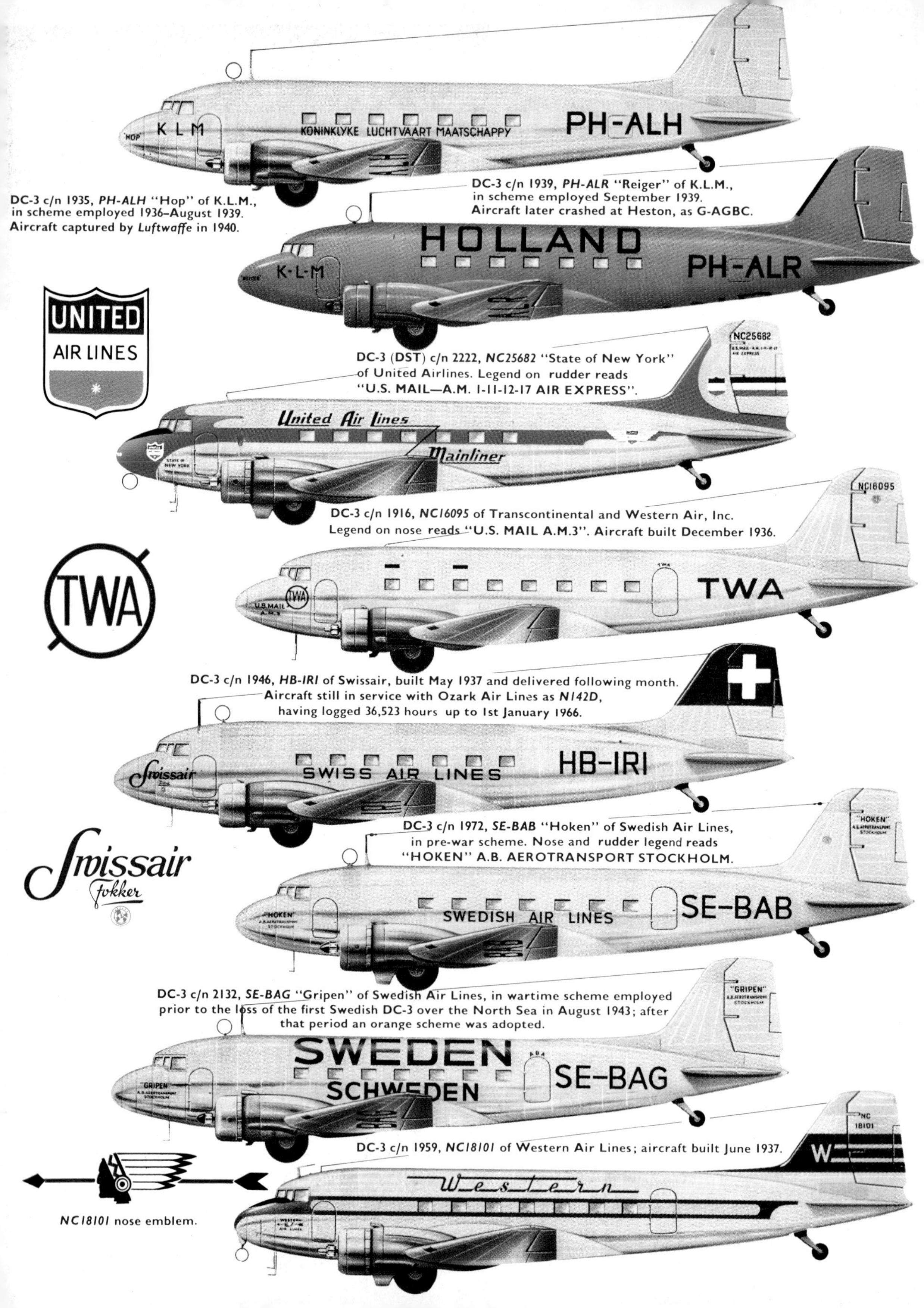

DC-3 c/n 1935, *PH-ALH* "Hop" of K.L.M., in scheme employed 1936–August 1939. Aircraft captured by *Luftwaffe* in 1940.

DC-3 c/n 1939, *PH-ALR* "Reiger" of K.L.M., in scheme employed September 1939. Aircraft later crashed at Heston, as G-AGBC.

DC-3 (DST) c/n 2222, *NC25682* "State of New York" of United Airlines. Legend on rudder reads "U.S. MAIL—A.M. 1-11-12-17 AIR EXPRESS".

DC-3 c/n 1916, *NC16095* of Transcontinental and Western Air, Inc. Legend on nose reads "U.S. MAIL A.M.3". Aircraft built December 1936.

DC-3 c/n 1946, *HB-IRI* of Swissair, built May 1937 and delivered following month. Aircraft still in service with Ozark Air Lines as *N142D*, having logged 36,523 hours up to 1st January 1966.

DC-3 c/n 1972, *SE-BAB* "Hoken" of Swedish Air Lines, in pre-war scheme. Nose and rudder legend reads "HOKEN" A.B. AEROTRANSPORT STOCKHOLM.

DC-3 c/n 2132, *SE-BAG* "Gripen" of Swedish Air Lines, in wartime scheme employed prior to the loss of the first Swedish DC-3 over the North Sea in August 1943; after that period an orange scheme was adopted.

DC-3 c/n 1959, *NC18101* of Western Air Lines; aircraft built June 1937.

NC18101 nose emblem.

Douglas DC-3-G102-277B, c/n 2198, NC21793 of American Airlines in flight. This machine was completed at Santa Monica on 24th February 1940.
(Photo: American Airlines)

The Douglas DC-3

by Arthur Pearcy

As its design implies, the DC-3 was the third commercial model developed by the Douglas Aircraft Company. A couple of years earlier in 1933, Douglas, then a comparatively small manufacturer specialising in torpedo and observation aircraft for the American armed forces, had bid successfully for a new passenger aircraft ordered by Transcontinental & Western Airlines. Known as the DC-1 in the earliest model, and as the DC-2 after it went into quantity production, this first Douglas entry into the transport field revolutionised the industry.

However, the DC-2 was not alone. In 1932 Boeing had introduced the first really modern airliner, the 247. Of all-metal construction, this advanced twin-engined monoplane carried ten passengers and a crew of two at a top speed of nearly 180 m.p.h. The new airlines were not slow to realise its tremendous capabilities and United Air Lines invested $4,000,000 on a fleet of no less than sixty of these machines.

Jack Frye, vice-president of T.W.A. a newly formed airline operating noisy Ford and Fokker tri-motors, visualised the present and future needs of T.W.A. and wrote to his friend Donald Douglas with a specification for a new transport aircraft. This historic letter formed the birth certificate of the DC-1, forerunner of the famous DC-3.

With the introduction of the Boeing 247 and DC-2 fierce competition raged in air transport. Among the operators who were losing heavily to their better equipped competitors was American Airlines, whose slow old Curtis Condors were flying almost empty, despite the attraction of the sleeper berths with which they were fitted. From the date of its formation on 13th May 1934 to the end of that year, the company had lost over one million dollars flying its fourteen passenger Condors, twelve passenger Fokkers and a variety of smaller aircraft—most of them empty—over their 4,000 odd miles of route.

But as good as the DC-2 was, American decided it wanted something better. They wanted to retain their luxury sleeper traffic, and the DC-2 was just too narrow to accommodate a comfortable berth. One summer afternoon in 1935, President C. R. Smith, telephoned Donald Douglas from Chicago. What American wanted, specifically, was a larger, more comfortable plane which could lure the luxury trade.

Douglas already had more DC-2 orders than he could handle, so was reluctant to take on any new headaches, but eventually he was persuaded to try. American agreed to buy twenty of them, with an option of twenty more, at a price of $110,000 each. In those days the aviation business was so run that this $2,000,000 plus contract was accepted over the phone by Douglas, with nothing on paper until months after the first aircraft had been delivered.

With Fred Stineman of Douglas as project chief, engineers from the airline and manufacturer worked together for the rest of 1935 on the designs for the new transport. William Littlewood, American Airlines chief engineer, spent most of his time at the Douglas plant, and the success of the design owes much to his co-operation. It was known then as the Douglas Sleeper Transport, or DST, and incorporated a number of ideas borrowed from the Pullman Company, of railway fame. The initial layout had seven upper and seven lower berths, with a separate private cabin up front for honeymoon couples. The wider fuselage was combined with the nose, undercarriage and wings of the DC-2, using larger wing-tips to extend the span from 85 to 95 ft., since the gross weight had gone up to 24,000 lb. The length was increased from 62 to 65½ ft. It was powered by two 900-h.p. Wright Cyclone engines giving a cruising speed of 180 m.p.h., the increased power being matched by larger tail surfaces. The new aircraft could carry a useful payload of 9,000 lb. and a gross weight of 25,000 lb.

It was realised that by taking out the berths they could make room for a third row of seats, two on one

The Douglas DC-3/DST production line at Santa Monica in September 1936. Deliveries averaged six aircraft per month.
(Photo: Douglas)

Mainliner "San Francisco"—DC-3A c/n 1903 on final approach at Oakland Airport, California, 1940. (Photo: William T. Larkins)

side of the aisle and one on the other, instead of just the two rows in the DST dayplane Boeing 247 and DC-2. The 50 per cent increase in payload, from 14 to 21 passengers, could comfortably be lifted by the bigger engines, yet its operating cost would be only 3 per cent higher than that of the DC-2. Thus was born the DC-3, the most successful transport aircraft ever built, and the first to carry enough passengers comfortably and at low enough fares to allow air transport to really develop.

FIRST FLIGHT AND INTO SERVICE

The logbook for the prototype machine, registered X14988, type DST, serial No. *1494*, begins with an entry on 14th December 1935 recording a three-hour run up on each of the Cyclone engines. On 16th December the run up was repeated and on 17th December, after each engine had been run up for 30 minutes by Crewchief Woolfolk, the aircraft taxied out at Clover Field, now Santa Monica, and took off at 3 p.m. Touchdown was at 4.40 p.m just as it was getting dusk. The pilot was Carl A. Cover who had flown the DC-1 on its maiden flight. He was accompanied by engineers Fred Stineman and Frank Collbohm. Everything went smoothly.

17th December 1935 incidentally, was the thirty-second anniversary of the Wright Brothers historic "First Flight".

Carrying the livery of American Airlines, the aircraft was retained by Douglas for test flying before being handed over to the airline on 11th July 1936 as *NC14988* "Flagship Texas".

The DC-3 was not only bigger than the DC-2 but also much easier and safer to fly. The automatic pilot, then only recently developed by the Sperry Gyroscope Company, was installed as standard equipment. Two sets of instruments were installed in the cockpit, each independent of the other; if one set went unserviceable the other was there for an emergency. Because the airlines were beginning to go in for night flights, special lights to illuminate the instrument panel were designed. So excellent was the design that the basic specifications for the aircraft were never changed—a rare thing in aviation. The DC-3 was an immediate success.

The first American Airlines DC-3 went into service on 7th June 1936 on the non-stop New York to Chicago route. Orders poured in from other U.S. and foreign airlines. The speed with which the airline industry converted to DC-3s seemed limited only by the rate at which Douglas could produce them at Santa Monica.

The first DC-3, c/n 1494, carried out development flying as X14988. *It is seen here at its birthplace, Santa Monica, California, during 1935.* (Photo: William T. Larkins)

The first DC-3 in full airline livery, as NC14988 *of American Airlines, in June 1936.* (Photo: Douglas No. 9621)

"Flagship Airfreighter"—American Airlines' NC16002, *c/n 1496, in war paint. Note pennant above cabin.* (Photo: American Airlines via J. F. Dial)

Not only was the DC-3 larger, faster, and more luxurious than any previous aircraft, but it was also more economical to operate. Costs per seat-mile were about a third less than those of its predecessor, the DC-2. Standardisation on the DC-3 reduced maintenance and other costs and boosted safety records.

Within a few months of the DC-3s introduction into scheduled service the president of United Air Lines, W. A. Patterson, was forced to admit that the days of their Boeing 247s were numbered. The new DC-3 was knocking 60 minutes off the journey time, making money as fast as the 247s lost it. United purchased a new fleet of DC-3s powered by Pratt & Whitney engines, the first going into service on 30th

American Airlines NC16013, *c/n 1551, was named "Flagship Virginia"; she is seen here seconds after take-off.* (Photo: American Airlines via J. F. Dial)

June 1937. It was not long before the airline again had figures on the profit side of their ledger.

Three years to the day, on Wednesday 1st July 1936, after the DC-1 had made its first flight, the DC-3 received recognition as the "outstanding twin-engined commercial transport plane". Those were the words that President Roosevelt read from the citation when he presented Donald W. Douglas with the Collier Trophy at the White House. "This airplane," the script recounted, "by reason of its high speed, economy, and quiet passenger comfort, has been generally adopted by transport lines throughout the United States. Its merit has been further recognised by its adoption abroad, and its influence on foreign design is already apparent. In making this award, recognition is given to the technical and production personnel of the Douglas organisation."

There was even more pleasing news. That same day an American Airlines DC-3 "Flagship", had flown non-stop from Newark to Chicago and return, 1,472 miles in just over eight hours, and the airline announced it would begin non-stop service between the two cities that very week.

The public liked the DC-3's luxury and her club-lounge atmosphere, including such innovations as electric razors; meals served on tables with silverware, real china, and linen; and air conditioning at terminals and aloft.

Air traffic more than doubled in the two years after the opening of the DC-3 service, taking the airlines a long step forward on the road to solvency. C. R. Smith president of American Airlines speaking at a businessmen's gathering in New York City said, "The DC-3 freed the airlines from complete dependence upon government mail pay. It was the first airplane that could make money just by hauling passengers."

Tail of Transcontinental and Western Air Inc's NC17312 *"Sky-sleeper". The aircraft, c/n 1922, was built in February 1937.* (Photo: via R. W. Harrison)

The first DC-3 in Europe; c/n 1590, built in 1936, and flown as PH-ALI *by K.L.M. This aircraft was shot down in 1943 when bearing the registration* G-AGBB. (Photo: K.L.M.)

At Santa Monica orders for the DC-3 were flowing in. United Air Lines ordered more of the version with Pratt & Whitney Twin Wasp engines, this being designated DC-3A, and by December 1941 had a fleet of 39 DC-3As and 15 DSTs.

Eastern Air Lines had acquired its first two DC-3s in 1936. The following year it retired five of its Lockheed Electras and purchased eight new DC-3s. Air traffic was so great during 1938 that Eastern had to lease four DC-3s from United Air Lines for use during the peak winter season. By 1941 a fleet of 35 aircraft were in regular use with this airline, all DC-3s.

In August 1939 Braniff announced the purchase of four new 21-passenger DC-3 airliners at a cost of approximately $100,000 each. The first DC-3 "Super B-liner", as they were called, was received by Braniff in Oklahoma City, and was put into regular scheduled service between Dallas and Amarillo on 3rd February 1940. By July 1940 Braniff had retired its Lockheed Electra and was operating 30 daily flights with DC-2 and DC-3 aircraft. By 1938 the 350th aircraft had been delivered.

Progress with air transport was being felt elsewhere. In South America Panagra (Pan American Grace Airways) replaced its slow and noisy Ford tri-motors, Panair do Brasil with its large Sikorsky S.42 flying boats reverted to land planes, whilst the Electras and Lodestars of Linea Aeropostal Venezolana (L.A.V.) disappeared in a huge modernisation programme. All chose the now familiar DC-3. Even

Maker's plate of the second DC-3 built, a DST model c/n 1495, built 4th June 1936. Actual plate now held by William T. Larkins.

United Air Lines' NC18105 "*State of Ohio*" *in flight, a DST built mid-1937.* (Photo: U.A.L.)

the Boeing 247Ds of Compania Mexicana de Aviacion (C.M.A.) were gradually replaced with the DC-3.

1936 was an important year for Australian National Airways, for in June they introduced the first Douglas aircraft into the country after exerting considerable pressure on the government to remove the ban on American aircraft imports. Four DC-3s made their appearance in December 1937. *VH-UZJ/VH-UZK* c/n 2002/3 and *VH-ABR/VH-ABC* c/n 2029/30.

By 1938 the DC-3 was carrying 95 per cent of all commercial air lines traffic in the U.S.A. alone, and was in service with 30 foreign air lines throughout the world. By 1939, 90 per cent of the world's airline business was being flown in DC-3s.

EARLY TROUBLES

There were crashes. In December 1936 came the first fatal accident to a Douglas transport. A brand new United Air Lines DC-3 was coming in for a landing at San Francisco airport, when it plunged into the bay and all on board were drowned. The weather was clear at the time, the aircraft was on its correct approach path, and was commanded by one of United's best pilots. The aircraft was salvaged from the sea bed and it was found that the co-pilot's microphone had dropped on to the floor and jammed the controls, so that they had been unable to pull out of their glide.

In 1937, the airlines had a rough year, weather being exceptionally bad all over the U.S.A. American Airlines lost a "Flagship" shortly after the airline inaugurated its DC-3 service and United Air Lines lost another in the Rocky Mountain region. Eddie Rickenbacker was almost killed in the first fatal accident involving a DC-3 of the Eastern Air Line "Great Silver Fleet". And there were others, but the aircraft themselves were exonerated in the investigations, and there were no indications of structural failures. The safety record which the DC-3s established even converted insurance companies to selling policies to air travellers while pilots for the first time could get insurance, without paying added risk premiums. In 1939, the Scheduled Airlines of the U.S.A. received the Collier Trophy for flying seventeen months without a single fatality.

There have been numerous instances, when DC-3s continued to fly even after aerial collisions or damage received whilst on the ground.

During the summer of 1941 a DC-3, one of the fleet of six operated by the China National Aviation Corporation, on a flight from Hong Kong to Chungking, made a forced landing at Suifu because of a Japanese air raid. Five Jap bombers spotted and strafed the helpless aircraft. When the smoke had cleared away the right wing was blasted off and there were more than fifty holes in the fuselage. Captain H. L. Woods, the pilot, called Hong Kong asking that a new wing be flown out. The only wing available was that from a DC-2 which was five feet shorter and designed to carry several thousand pounds less weight than a DC-3 wing.

In Hong Kong, C.N.A.C. maintenance men bolted the wing under the fuselage of another DC-2 and flew it 900 miles to the airport at Suifu, where they attached it to Wood's DC-3. The aircraft looked a little lopsided, but it took off and flew beautifully after the necessary aileron trim tab adjustment. It was christened the DC-2½.

There was the bird strike hazard. On 20th October 1941 American Airlines "Flagship Erie" *NC25663* c/n 2207 hit a flock of wild geese and crashed at New

Left: *An unlucky landfall; DC-3 c/n 2036*, PH-ASK "*Kemphaan*" *of K.L.M., displays the orange scheme adopted in September 1939 as it rests on the runway at Norway's Oslo-Fornebou airport. In the background is a Heinkel He 111P of the* Luftwaffe; *the Douglas was caught on the ground on the first day of the German invasion, and later pressed into* Luftwaffe *service as* NA + LB. (Photo: Schmetz via Seeley.) Right: *One of three C-49Bs (ex-DC-3, c/n 4095) built during early 1941 seen at San Francisco in August of that year.* (Photo: William T. Larkins)

London, Ontario, killing all seventeen passengers and crew of three. The DC-3 had been delivered to the airline on 21st March 1940 and had logged 3,868 hours.

LICENCE TO BUILD

Licence to manufacture the DC-3 outside the U.S.A. was granted to the Dutch Fokker company, but they never went into production. Instead Fokker became the Douglas agent in Europe, and so handled all the DC-3s which were shipped over from the U.S.A. to the ports at Rotterdam and Cherbourg. After final assembly the aircraft were delivered to the airlines; these included K.L.M. in Holland, A.B.A. in Sweden and many other of the European operators of the DC-3. Sales were so good that Fokkers held a pool of DC-3s, and it will be noted from the production lists that they purchased five out of the first 100 aircraft to be produced. The purchase price of a DC-3 was then approximately £30,000 or $115,000.

Nakajima in Japan also obtained a licence to manufacture the DC-3, and on 30th September 1938 the assembly of the first aircraft was completed at Haneda Airport for Dai-Nippon Airways.

A third licensee was the State Aircraft Plant in the U.S.S.R. who not only bought large quantities of jigs and tools from the U.S.A., but purchased a total of eighteen DC-3s from Santa Monica between November 1936 and March 1939. These were delivered by Douglas in the name "North Eastern" and "Excello", both of which were represented by Amtorg the pre-war purchasing agency. There is considerable reason to believe that the "Airlines" were paper organisations of the Russian Government. The first aircraft was c/n 1589 registered *NC14995* in the U.S.A. with Excello, followed by a block of eleven delivered between May and August of 1938 and concluded with a block of six, the last of which was delivered in March 1939. Of the eighteen DC-3s, two were delivered disassembled, ostensibly for use as spare parts.

The State Aircraft Plant's leading aviation expert, Boris Lisunov, spent two years studying with the Douglas Company at Santa Monica, before returning to Russia to supervise production. Small scale production did not commence until 1940, but it is believed that by the summer of 1941 about thirty to forty aircraft per month were being produced in Russia. Designated the PS-84 and later the Lisunov Li-2 the aircraft was for use by Aeroflot the Russian State airline.

EUROPEAN OPERATORS

Under the leadership of its first managing director, Albert Plesman, Holland's K.L.M. began to consider the impressive developments in air transport being made by the American West Coast manufacturer, Donald Douglas. This resulted in their combined entry with Douglas for the England to Australia race, and as a direct sequel, their order for DC-2 and later DC-3 aircraft, thus opening the way for a major invasion of Europe by Douglas.

From this time K.L.M. set the pace in Europe, and two years later, in 1936, an initial order was placed for eleven DC-3s with thirteen more to follow. Thus K.L.M. became the first European operator of the type.

K.L.M. operated DC-3s on the European network (twenty-one-passenger version) from 1936 onwards and on the Amsterdam to Djakarta service (eleven-passenger version) from 1937 to 1942.

In Northern Europe Aktiebolaget Aerotransport (A.B.A.) of Sweden became the second airline in Europe to introduce the DC-3, an indication that Sweden was taking its place among the leading airline countries.

A.B.A. took delivery of its first DC-3 in July 1937 (*SE-BAA* c/n 1947 "Ornen"), the second and third being delivered in September (*SE-BAB* c/n 1972 "Hoken" *SE-BAC* c/n 1975 "Falken"). A fourth DC-3 (*SE-BAF* c/n 2133 "Gladan") was delivered in November 1939, and a fifth (*SE-BAG* c/n 2132 "Gripen" ex *HB-IRU*) was bought from Swissair in May 1940.

Ceskoslovenska Latecka Spolecnost (C.L.S.) joined the Douglas ranks, purchasing both DC-2s and DC-3s to supplement its ex-K.L.M. Fokker aircraft. DC-3s included *OK-AIH* c/n 1973, *OK-AIE* c/n 2023, *OK-AIF* c/n 2024 and *OK-AIG* c/n 2095.

On 26th March 1931 two Swiss companies, Balair and Ad Astra combined to form Schweizerische Luftverkehr (Swissair). In 1932 Swissair followed K.L.M. with the purchase of the DC-2 and later the DC-3. The first two DC-3s (*HB-IRA* c/n 1945 *HB-IRI* c/n 1946) were delivered in June 1937 followed by a third aircraft (*HB-IRO* c/n 2054) in February 1938. Two more (*HB-IRU* c/n 2132 *HB-IRE* c/n 2121) were delivered in July 1939.

During 1935 Air France purchased a DC-2 from Douglas, and their one and only DC-3 (*F-ARQJ* c/n 2122) was registered on 2nd April 1939.

In January 1939 the components of Sabena's first Douglas DC-3 (*OO-AUH* c/n 2093) arrived by sea in packing cases, and was assembled in Belgium by Fokker. The second DC-3 (*OO-AUI* c/n 2094) arrived during the same month.

The arrival of these aircraft opened a new chapter in the history of Belgian aviation. Unfortunately, however, the chapter was interrupted by the outbreak of war on 10th May 1940 and the company's European services were then paralysed.

Other European operators of the DC-3 included Polskie Linie Lotnicze (L.O.T.) in Poland, Linile Aeriene Romaue Exploatate cu Statul (L.A.R.E.S.) in Hungary and Magyar Legiforgalmi (M.A.L.E.R.T.) also in Hungary. Several DC-3s were in the process of being shipped from the U.S.A. to Europe when hostilities commenced in September 1939.

Left: NX33606 *(later* NC33606*) c/n 4806 "Maunoloa" of Hawaiian Airlines at Oakland, California, 27th August 1941. Rare photo of a C-48,* 41-7681, *c/n 3256, carrying two-star General insignia, probably of Technical Training Command. This aircraft, originally built for T.W.A., was photographed at Oakland during November 1941.* (Photos: William T. Larkins)

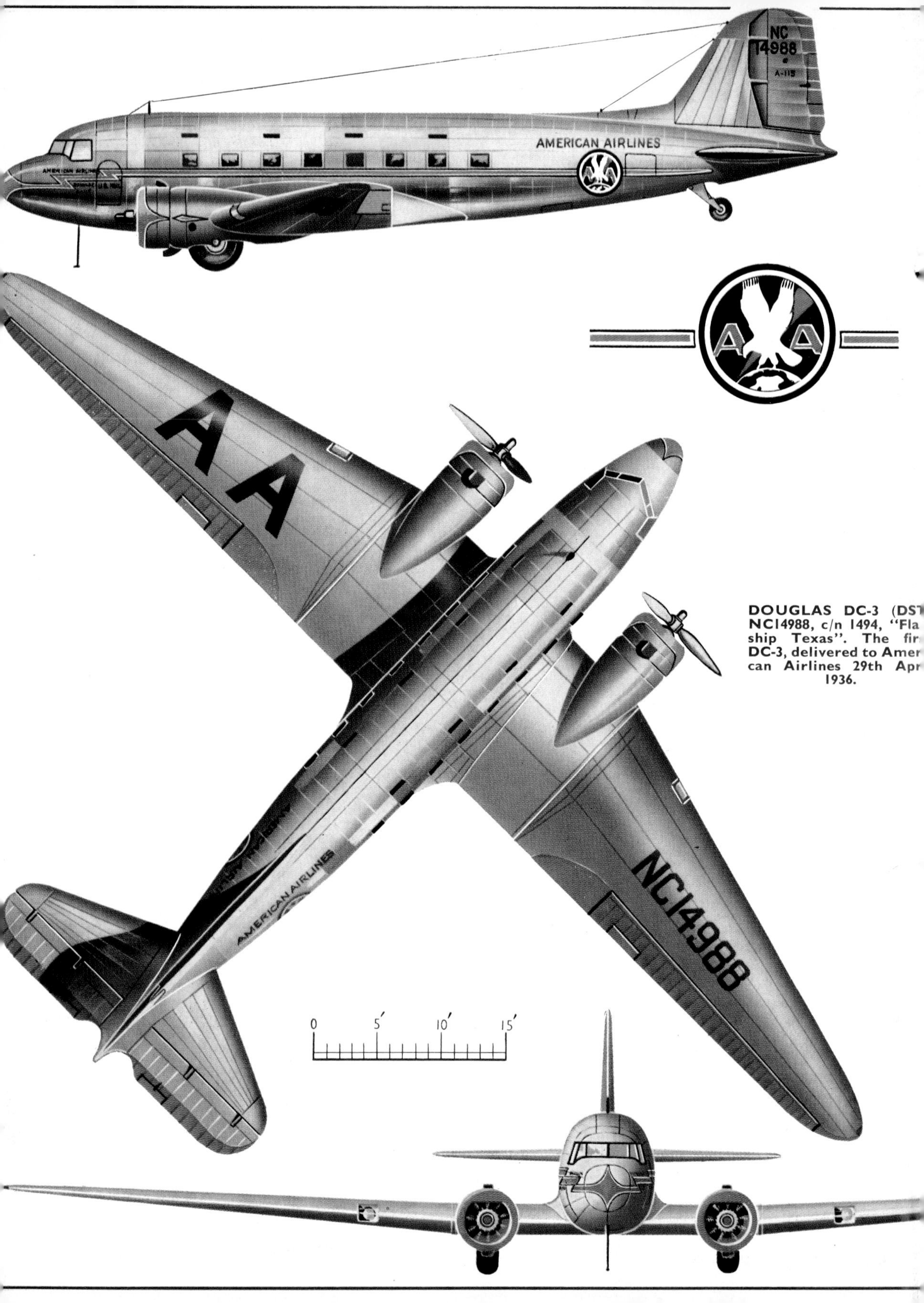

DOUGLAS DC-3 (DST NC14988, c/n 1494, "Fla ship Texas". The fir DC-3, delivered to Amer can Airlines 29th Apr 1936.

NC
14988
A-115
AMERICAN AIRLINES
AA
NC14988
AMERICAN AIRLINES
U.S.MAIL
FLAGSHIP TEXAS
AMERICAN AIRLINES
DOUGLAS
A-115
U.S.MAIL

K.L.M. FLEET

Reg.	c/n	Name	Del. date	Remarks
PH-ALI	1590	"Ibis"	21.9.36	
PH-ALH	1935	"Hop"	18.3.37	
PH-ALN	1936	"Nandoe"	23.3.37	to Far East as *PK-ALN* 1.6.40
PH-ALO	1937	"Oehoe"	27.3.37	to Far East as *PK-ALO* 1.6.40
PH-ALR	1939	"Reiger"	8.4.37	
PH-ALS	1940	"Specht"	1.4.37	crashed in Indonesia 6.10.37
PH-ALT	1941	"Torenvalk"	10.4.37	to Far East as *PK-AFW* 2.6.40
PH-ALU	1942	"Uil"	15.4.37	
PH-ALV	1943	"Valk"	23.4.37	
PH-ALW	1944	"Wielewaal"	25.4.37	to Far East as *K-ALW* 1.6.40
PH-ALP	1965	"Pelikaan"	25.8.37	to Far East as *PK-AFV* 2.6.40
PH-ARB	1980	"Buizerd"	27.8.37	
PH-ARE	1981	"Emoe"	28.8.37	to Far East as *PK-AFZ* 2.6.40
PH-ARG	1982	"Gier"	1.9.37	to Far East as *PK-ARG* 1.6.40
PH-ARW	2019	"Wulp"	23.2.38	
PH-ARX	2020	"Xema"	9.3.38	
PH-ARY	2021	"Ijsvogel"	18.3.38	crashed Schiphol 14.11.38
PH-ARZ	2022	"Zilverreiger"	2.4.38	
PH-ASK	2036	"Kemphaan"	21.4.38	
PH-ASM	2042	"Mees"	21.7.38	
PH-ASP	2109	"Patrijs"	10.3.39	
PH-ASR	2110	"Roek"	10.3.39	
PH-AST	2111	"Tapuit"	10.3.39	
PH-AXH	2147	"Havik" registered to K.L.M. 17.12.39 but never delivered; sold to United Air Lines during April 1940 as *NC25675*.		

WAR CLOUDS

In September 1939 just when the whole world was about to be covered by an inter-connecting air transport system, the nations divided themselves again in hostilities. By 1941 every great trading and commercial country was involved in active military operations, or was under the complete domination of the Axis Powers. The few neutral nations such as Sweden and Switzerland lived an uneasy life between the belligerents. Swissair retained two DC-3s in flying condition for occasional flights undertaken on behalf of the International Red Cross, and put the rest of its fleet in storage.

All the European services of K.L.M. were stopped on 23rd August 1939 except those to Scandinavia, Belgium and London. The Scandinavian service closed down on 9th April 1940, the Belgium on 18th April and finally on 10th May 1940 all European services were terminated and the Germans occupied the Netherlands. On that fatal day four K.L.M. DC-3s were destroyed by German Air Force bombing at Schiphol Airport—*PH-ALU*, *PH-ARX*, *PH-ASP* and *PH-AST*. A further four were captured intact by the German Air Force when they reached Schiphol and Amsterdam on 16th May these being impressed into service with the *Luftwaffe*—*PH-ALH* (*PC+EA*), *PH-ALV* (*NA+LC*), *PH-ASM* (*NA+LB*) and *PH-ASR* (*VE+RR*).

Nothing daunted, K.L.M. joined the Allied cause and with four remaining DC-3s fled their stricken country to set up a base at Whitchurch Airport, Bristol. Here the aircraft were allocated British registrations—*G-AGBB* (*PH-ALI*) 25th July 1940, *G-AGBC* (*PH-ALR*) 5th August 1940, *G-AGBD* (*PH-ARB*) 29th July 1940, and *G-AGBI* (*PH-ARW*) 17th August 1940. They opened a service between Bristol and Lisbon in August 1940, but their fleet was reduced by half after *G-AGBC* had to be withdrawn on 21st September after an accident at Heston, followed by the destruction of *G-AGBI* during a German air attack on Whitchurch on 24th November 1940.

On the opening of hostilities, the Sabena fleet left Belgium for the United Kingdom, and were put under requisition and used for military missions over France. On 23rd May 1940—Sabena's seventeenth birthday—the company suffered a grievous war loss, when two Savoia Marchetti's and DC-3 *OO-AUI* were shot down at Merville, France. Two members of the crew were killed and several others wounded.

Later the remaining Sabena aircraft were authorised to proceed to Belgian Africa, and they left the U.K. with an intermediate stop in Algeria. On 27th August 1940 four Savoia Marchetti aircraft were seized by the French Vichy Government authorities at Oran, and handed over to the Italians; at Algiers two more Savoia Marchetti aircraft and the remaining DC-3 *OO-AUH* suffered the same fate.

The Swedish airline, A.B.A., tried to maintain its pre-war services with its DC-3 aircraft, and the routes to Moscow, Berlin and London were all kept going under difficulties. For these flights the aircraft were clearly marked with "SWEDEN" in large letters on both sides and under the fuselage.

It is believed that when the Germans overran Czechoslovakia in 1938 the complete DC-3 fleet of C.L.S. was taken over by Tschechiche Luftverkehs Gesellschaft as three DC-3s were later registered with Deutsche Luft Hansa (D.L.H.). *D-AAIE* (*OK-AIE*), *D-AAIF* (*OK-AIF*), and *D-AAIG* (*OK-AIG*).

By as early as July 1940 it is reported that D.L.H. had added at least two ex-K.L.M. DC-3s to its fleet, these being *D-AOFS* (*PH-ASK*) and *D-ABUG* (*PH-ALH*) which the *Luftwaffe* had captured during the invasion of the Netherlands. They had also included six K.L.M. DC-2 aircraft in their haul from Schiphol, which after a period of service with the *Luftwaffe* found their way into the D.L.H. fleet.

It is rumoured that the *Luftwaffe* experienced servicing difficulties with the DC-2s and DC-3s; lack of spare parts led them to provide for interchangeability of certain critical items, as for example—landing gear tyres and wheels were made interchangeable between the Douglas DC-3, DC-2 models, and the Heinkel He.III bomber. Through neutral sources D.L.H. kept their Douglas aircraft

Left: *The first Swissair DC-3, c/n 1945, at Zurich, Dubendorf, shortly after delivery in June 1937. Still in service with Ozark as* N141D, *this veteran has logged 38,574 hours up to 1st January 1966.* (Photo: Swissair.) *The only DC-3 delivered to Air France before the outbreak of war; c/n 2122, built in April 1939, photographed at Santa Monica in its French registration.* (Photo: Douglas)

SE-BAA "*Ornen*" *after and before application of wartime identification markings.* (Photos: *The Aeroplane*, Swedish Air Lines)

modified with all changes recommended by the manufacturer and Civil Aeronautics Board during the war. This was accomplished by contracting for overhaul and other repair work with concerns operating from a neutral country. Through this source replacement parts and other information pertaining to this design were made available.

D.L.H. were not lacking experience of the Douglas type, as during the early part of 1936 they obtained a DC-2 from Fokkers for use in various tests at their airfield Staaken near Berlin.

INTO UNIFORM

Early Army Air Corps attempts to develop transport aircraft had produced no satisfactory model, and so inevitably they turned to civilian types already in production. The early standby, and indeed the most dependable aircraft within its capacity was the Douglas DC-3 known alternately, according to its special modifications, as the C-47 and the C-53. Long successful in civilian passenger service the twin-engined DC-3 had many features ill-suited to the convenient handling of bulky freight, and its payload was too light for the new tasks. But it was flyable under almost any conditions, was easily maintained, and, above all it was in production.

Air Transport Command borrowed heavily from the civil airlines, which during the 1930s had grown into a large enterprise and an increasingly significant part of the transportation services on which the country depended. From the airlines came experienced executives who were commissioned for key posts of command in the development of a military transport service and veteran pilots who became pioneers of distant military air routes.

Not until the fall of France in the summer of 1940 did the aircraft programme in the U.S.A. include substantial orders for transport aircraft. The Air Corps ordered 545 C-47s in September 1940, and in the following June an order was placed for just under a hundred C-53s, the Army's passenger version of the DC-3. Contracts were signed in September 1941 for fifty more C-53s and for an additional seventy C-47s. Each of these aircraft had been designed originally for passenger service on civilian airways.

All plans for the development of a transport system were dominated by the scarcity of transport aircraft. Transport production still had to compete with that of combat types, which enjoyed, initially

at least, an overriding priority. Although a substantial number of C-47s and C-53s had been ordered, none of these had been delivered at the time of the Pearl Harbour attack. The number of medium range transports belonging to the Army Air Corps on 7th December 1941 was so small that the forty to fifty twin-engined C-32s, C-33s and C-39s, all military DC-2s, belonging to the 50th Transport Wing represented very near the full total. Only in the equipment of the civil airlines did the U.S.A. possess an immediate supply of additional transport aircraft.

A first step towards mobilising the resources of the airlines was taken on 13th December 1941, when the President signed an executive order directing the Secretary of War to take possession of any part of any civil aviation system required for the war effort.

As the War Department reached right and left for whatever aircraft might be immediately available, the Army Air Corps enlarged its procurement programme. Fortunately it had made a heavy commitment to the DC-3 before Pearl Harbour, and fortunately the prime consideration of the speed with which the manufacturer could make deliveries led to additional orders. However, the DC-3 was not considered to be an ideal military transport, as it had been designed for civil passenger service.

The DC-3 was a low wing monoplane whose fuselage stood so high off the ground that loading from an ordinary truck platform was impractical. Also the door was narrow and the flooring lacked the strength to support heavy cargo. A larger door, reinforced flooring, special loading equipment, and other improvisations were devised for the C-47. Fortunately most of the design work on the military version had already been completed when the first orders were placed, in 1940, for large numbers of C-47s.

By this time, the Santa Monica factory was already committed to the production of other types, and the C-47 was in consequence produced in a new Douglas plant at Long Beach. The engines of the initial

Detail of American Airlines livery displayed by DC-3 c/n 1557.
(Photo: via R. W. Harrison)

version were 1,200-h.p. Pratt & Whitney R-1830-92 engines, whereas most of the commercial DC-3s had Wright Cyclones. The airline interior gave way to utility bucket type seats along the cabin walls and the permissible operating weight increased from 25,000 to 29,300 lb. in the C-47.

Long Beach built 953 C-47s and then changed to the C-47A, which differed significantly only in having a 24 V. electrical system.

The airlines in December 1941 were operating nearly 300 DC-3s, and already a substantial number had been commandeered by Air Transport Command for military service as C-48s, C-49s, C-50s, C-51 and C-52s. Many of these aircraft retained their airline interiors and were used as staff transports.

The Army Air Corps at Wright Field had done static tests with a military DC-2 during 1935, the aircraft finally breaking up under loads three times its design limitations. At this time the cargo version of the commercial DC-3 was taking shape at Santa Monica and naturally the Army Air Corps were interested. Government defence expenditure was centred on bombers, fighters and training types, leaving very little for transport aircraft. It is believed that one or two of the airline DC-3s were purchased from a special fund for generals' aircraft, a possible example being the ex-Eastern Air Line C-49B used by Lt. Gen. Krueger for travelling between San Antonio, Texas, and Lake Charles, Louisiana.

The Naval Air Transport Service ordered 30 versions of the commercial DC-3 on 16th September 1940. These were designated R4D-1 and were powered by Pratt & Whitney R-1830-92 engines, but were not delivered until a later date. However, two R4D-2s were delivered during 1941 and were allocated to the Naval Air Stations at Pensacola—Buaer *No. 4708*, and Anacostia—Buaer *No. 4707* c/n 4097.

In Australia the R.A.A.F. were operating ten DC-2 aircraft, and with the outbreak of hostilities in 1939 took over the four DC-3s operated by A.N.A. These were used for a short period by No. 8 Squadron for the training of wireless operators and were given R.A.A.F. insignia—*VH-UZJ* became *A30-1*, *VH-UZK A30-2*, *VH-ABR A30-3*, and *VH-ABC A30-4*. The first two were returned to A.N.A. during 1940.

During 1941 the British Purchasing Commission in the U.S.A. bought a number of surplus DC-3s from American Airlines and T.W.A. for use by the R.A.F. in the India and Middle East theatres of war. They were dismantled and shipped as deck cargo to the Maintenance Units in the Middle East. Two DC-3s from American Airlines, *NC33653* c/n 4116 and *NC33655* c/n 4118, which had been delivered to the airline on 5th May 1941, were sold to the purchasing commission on 9th July. They were allocated the R.A.F. serial *MA925* and *MA943*, having flown 317 and 376 hours respectively. Others included *MA928* and *MA929*, whilst a batch of six were allocated *LR230* to *LR235*.

On 7th December 1941 the Japanese attacked Pearl Harbour. One of the casualties was a DC-3 *NC33606* of Hawaiian Airlines which was shot up by the attacking aircraft.

One week later most of the American Airlines DC-3 fleet were ordered to fly to a secret rendezvous—there had been a threat that the Axis Powers were moving to take over radio stations and other installations in South America.

In the Far East a K.L.M. DC-3 *PK-ALN* was destroyed by the Japanese at Medon Airport, Indonesia, on 28th December 1941.

This was just the beginning for the DC-3, for it was during the war that this famous aircraft, the "workhorse of the air", made an imperishable name for itself.

The author gratefully acknowledges the valuable assistance given by Messrs. William T. Larkins and Crosby Maynard, plus the Douglas Aircraft Company and the many airlines in the preparation of this Profile.

Left: *Rare wartime photograph of Swedish Air Lines* SE-BAG "*Gripen*" *(Griffon) showing identification markings carried for the courier flights to Britain.* SWEDEN *was also painted in large characters under the fuselage.* (Photo: Swedish Air Lines.) Right: *Pan American's* NC28305, *c/n 4085, photographed at San José, Costa Rica, in 1941.* (Photo: P.A.A.)

Douglas DC-3 (Pre-1942)

SANTA MONICA PLANT PRODUCTION

The pre-1942 Santa Monica civilian production line included 19 DSTs with Wright SGR-1820-G2 engines, 19 DSTs with Pratt & Whitney SB3G engines, and a total of 417 DC-3s, making a total of 455 machines produced. The construction blocks are listed below in detail.

Constructors numbers	*Type*	*Total*	*Constructors numbers*	*Type*	*Total*	*Constructors numbers*	*Type*	*Total*	*Constructors numbers*	*Type*	*Total*
1494 to 1500	DST	7	1951 to 1960	DST	10	1985 to 2000	DC-3	16	4080 to 4148	DC-3	69
1545 to 1557	DC-3	13	1961	DC-3	1	2002 to 2036	DC-3	35	4174	DC-3	1
1588 to 1590	DC-3	3	1962 to 1965	DST	4	2054 to 2056	DC-3	3	4177	DC-3	1
1900 to 1921	DC-3	22	1966 to 1970	DST/DC-3	5	2093 to 2094	DC-3	2	4179 to 4184	DC-3	5
1922 to 1924	DST/DC-3	3	1971 to 1975	DC-3	5	2102 to 2111	DC-3	10	4800 to 4816	DC-3	17
1925 to 1929	DC-3	5	1976 to 1977	DST	2	2118 to 2149	DC-3	32		Grand total	455
1930 to 1934	DST/DC-3	5	1978 to 1982	DC-3	5	2165 to 2272	DC-3	108			
1935 to 1949	DC-3	15	1983 to 1984	DST	2	3251 to 3299	DC-3	49			

Quite a number of the latter production aircraft were allocated to airlines and given a civilian registration, but taken over by the Army Air Corps and given a military designation. This was during 1941. Production of the DST/DC-3 commenced during the latter part of 1935.

DOUGLAS DC-3 MODEL DESIGNATIONS

U.S. ARMY AIR CORPS MODELS

Model		*Description*
DC-3-253	C-41,	one only *38-502*, c/n 2053 similar to C-39 (DC-2)—P. & W. R-1830-21 engines.
DC-3-253A	C-41A,	one only *40-70*, c/n 2145 commercial DC-3, plush interior for 23 passengers, P. & W. R-1830-21 engines.
DC-3-360	C-47-DL,	953 built at Long Beach plant including *41-7722/7866* c/n 4200/4374 (includes 30 Navy R4Ds in c/ns); *41-18337/18699* c/n 4375 onwards, *41-38564/38763* c/n 6000/6222 but serials not running consecutively, militarised DC-3, cargo and troop carrier, P. & W. R-1830-92 engines.
DC-3-377	C-48,	one only *41-7681* c/n 3256, originally built for United Air Lines as *NC25612*, but turned over to Army Air Corps, 21 seats, P. & W. R-1830-82 engines.
DC-3-368	C-48A,	three built *41-7682/4* c/n 4146/8, commercial DC-3, staff transport with P. & W. R-1830-51 engines.
DC-3-384	C-49,	six built *41-7685/7689* c/n 3270/4, originally for T.W.A. with 24-passenger interior and Wright Cyclone R-1820-71 engines.
DC-3-385	C-49A,	one only *41-7690* c/n 3282, originally for Delta, 21 passengers door on left, Wright Cyclone R-1820-71 engines.
DC-3-386	C-49C,	two built *41-7715* c/n 4814, *41-7721* c/n 4815, originally for Delta, DC-3 trooper with side seats, Wright Cyclone R-1820-71 engines.
DC-3-387	C-49B,	three built *41-7691/3* c/n 4094/6, originally for Eastern, commercial DC-3, 21 passengers, door on right side, Wright Cyclone R-1820-71 engines.
DC-3-389	C-49D,	five built *41-7716/7720* c/n 4141/5, originally for Eastern, DC-3 trooper with side seats, Wright Cyclone R-1820-71 engines.
DC-3-390	C-51,	one only *41-7702* c/n 3289, originally for Colonial as *NC34962*, right-hand door, Wright Cyclone R-1820-83 engines.
DC-3-391	C-50C,	one only *41-7695* c/n 4083, originally for Penn-Central, commercial DC-3, 21 passengers, left-hand door, Wright Cyclone R-1820-79 engines.
DC-3-392	C-50D,	four built *41-7696* c/n 4084, *41-7709* c/n 4131, *41-7712* c/n 4134, *41-7713* c/n 4135, originally for Penn-Central, left-hand door, as C-53, Wright Cyclone R-1820-79 engines.
DC-3-394	C-52A.	one only *41-7714*, c/n 4813, originally for Western Air Lines as *NC19387*, DC-3 trooper, right-hand door, P. & W. R-1830-51 engines.
DC-3-395	C-52B,	two built *41-7706/7* c/n 4127/8, originally for United Air Lines, as *C-52*, *C-52A*, right-hand door, P. & W. R-1830-51 engines.
DC-3-396	C-50,	four built *41-7697/7700* c/n 4119/4122, originally built for American Airlines (c/n 4122, *NC33662* but never taken up) commercial DC-3, 21 passengers, right-hand door, Wright Cyclone R-1820-85 engines.
DC-3-397	C-50B,	three built *41-7703/5* c/n 4109/4111, originally for Braniff, commercial DC-3, left-hand door, Wright Cyclone R-1820-81 engines.
DC-3-398	C-52,	one only *41-7708* c/n 4112, originally for United Air Lines, DC-3 trooper, right-hand door, P. & W. R-1830-51 engines.
DC-3-401	C-50A,	two built *41-7710/11* c/n 4804/5, originally for American Airlines but taken over on production line, c/n 4805 allocated *NC33628* but never taken up, as *C-53*, right-hand door, Wright Cyclone R-1820-85 engines.
DC-3-402	C-52C,	one only *41-7701* c/n 4136, originally for Eastern, trooper with left-hand door, P. & W. R-1830-51 engines.
DC-3-405	C-53,	219 built including *41-20045/6* c/n 4816/7, *41-20051* c/n 4821, *41-20053* c/n 4823, *41-20060/20136* c/n 4830/4906. Troop transpor with P. & W. R-1830-92 engines, 28 passengers, side seats, as Navy R4D-3.

Note: All but C-47-DL produced at Santa Monica plant—symbol "DO" allocated to this plant.

Douglas DC-3 (Pre-1942)

U.S. AIRLINE FLEET LIST 1939/41

American Airlines Inc. (Cyclone powered)

Reg.	*c/n*	*Date built*	*Reg.*	*c/n*	*Date built*	*Reg.*	*c/n*	*Date built*
NC15575	4109	6-41	*NC17332*	1918	2-37	*NC21797*	2201	2-40
NC15577	4805	7-41	*NC17333*	1919	2-37	*NC21798*	2202	2-40
NC15579	4122	6-41	*NC17334*	1920	2-37	*NC21799*	2203	3-40
NC15580	4134	8-41	*NC17335*	1921	3-37	*NC25629*	2249	3-40
NC15590	2244	7-40	*NC17336*	1961	6-37	*NC25658*	2204	7-40
NC15592	2248	7-40	*NC17337*	1962	6-37	*NC25660*	2205	3-40
NC16002	1496	6-36	*NC17338*	1963	7-37	*NC25661*	2206	3-40
NC16003	1497	6-36	*NC17339*	1964	7-37	*NC25664*	2208	3-40
NC16004	1498	6-36	*NC17340*	2140	5-39	*NC25665*	2209	3-40
NC16006	1500	7-36	*NC18141*	2137	5-39	*NC25670*	2210	3-40
NC16007	1549	8-36	*NC18142*	2138	5-39	*NC25671*	2211	3-40
NC16009	1545	8-36	*NC18143*	2139	5-39	*NC25672*	2212	3-40
NC16011	1547	9-36	*NC19922*	4135	8-41	*NC25673*	2213	5-40
NC16012	1548	9-36	*NC21745*	2103	2-39	*NC25676*	2214	5-40
NC16013	1551	9-36	*NC21746*	2104	2-39	*NC25684*	2215	5-40
NC16015	1553	10-36	*NC21747*	2105	2-39	*NC25685*	2216	5-40
NC16016	1554	10-36	*NC21748*	2106	2-39	*NC28325*	2263	5-40
NC16018	1556	10-36	*NC21749*	2107	2-39	*NC28350*	2264	8-40
NC16019	1557	10-36	*NC21752*	2165	8-39	*NC33651*	4115	8-40
NC16030	1546	8-36	*NC21768*	2167	8-39	*NC33654*	4117	5-41
NC16096	2136	5-39	*NC21794*	2199	2-40	*NC33656*	4802	5-41
NC17331	1917	2-37	*NC21795*	2200	2-40	*NC21793*	2198	5-41

The first R4D-2, 4707, *c/n 4097, based on U.S.N.A.S.* Anacostia *and photographed at San Francisco in November 1941.*
(Photo: William T. Larkins)

Still serving the U.S.A.F. at Air National Guard H.Q. is this C-53, 41-20088, *c/n 4858. Note door on starboard side of fuselage.* (Photo: A.P. Library)

Braniff Airways Inc. (Cyclone powered)

Reg.	c/n	Date built	Reg.	c/n	Date built	Reg.	c/n	Date built
NC21773	2179	12-39	NC25668	2241	6-40	NC28362	4106	6-41
NC21775	2181	12-39	NC25669	2242	6-40	NC28363	4107	6-41
NC21776	2182	12-39	NC25693	2266	9-40	NC28364	4108	6-41
NC25667	2240	6-40						

Chicago & Southern Airlines Inc. (Cyclone powered)

NC25625	2218	4-40	NC25627	2220	4-40	NC25628	2221	3-40
NC25626	2219	4-40						

Continental Airlines Inc. (Twin Wasp powered)

NC15565	4849	12-41

Delta Air Corporation (Cyclone powered)

NC28340	3277	11-40	NC28342	3279	12-40	NC28344	3281	12-40
NC28341	3278	12-40	NC28343	2267	12-40	NC28345	2224	2-40

Eastern Air Lines (Cyclone powered)

NC15596	2247	9-40	NC21728	2144	8-39	NC28382	4090	2-41
NC15597	2257	9-40	NC21729	2141	6-39	NC28384	4092	2-41
NC15598	2258	9-40	NC21743	2102	2-39	NC28385	4093	2-41
NC15599	2259	9-40	NC21744	2108	6-40	NC28391	2268	10-40
NC18120	1996	10-37	NC25646	2234	6-40	NC28392	2269	10-40
NC18121	1997	10-37	NC25647	2235	6-40	NC33631	4137	9-41
NC18124	2000	12-37	NC25648	2236	6-40	NC33632	4138	9-41
NC19963	2260	9-40	NC25650	2225	2-40	NC33633	4139	9-41
NC19968	3252	10-40	NC25651	2226	2-40	NC33634	4140	9-41
NC19969	3253	10-40	NC28381	4089	1-41	NC33643	4129	6-41
NC19970	3254	10-40						

Northeast Airlines Inc. (Cyclone powered)

NC28323	2253	7-40	NC28324	2254	8-40

Northwest Airlines Inc. (Twin Wasp powered)

NC21711	2123	4-39	NC21777	2146	8-39	NC33324	1954	7-37
NC21713	2125	4-39	NC25608	2183	1-40	NC33326	4127	7-41
NC21715	2130	6-39	NC25609	2184	1-40	NC33327	4128	7-41
NC21716	2131	6-39	NC25610	2185	1-40			

Pennsylvania-Central Airlines Inc. (Cyclone powered)

NC21781	2169	11-39	NC21786	4131	7-41	NC25689	4099	4-41
NC21782	2170	11-39	NC21787	2186	5-40	NC25691	2256	9-40
NC21783	2171	11-39	NC33677	4132	3-41	NC25696	4082	3-41
NC21784	2172	12-39	NC21788	4110	6-41	NC25695	4081	3-41
NC21785	2173	12-39	NC21790	2189	5-40	NC33678	4133	7-41

Transcontinental & Western Air Inc. (Cyclone powered)

NC1941	3266	12-40	NC15589	2243	6-40	NC18949	2013	12-37
NC1942	3267	12-40	NC15591	2245	7-40	NC18950	2014	12-37
NC1943	3268	12-40	NC16095	1916	12-36	NC18952	2016	12-37
NC1944	3269	1-41	NC17312	1922	2-37	NC18953	2027	1-38
NC1945	3294	2-41	NC17314	1924	5-37	NC18954	2028	1-38
NC1947	3296	2-41	NC17318	1933	6-37	NC19974	2250	7-40
NC1948	3298	3-41	NC17320	1966	8-37	NC28321	2252	7-40
NC1949	3299	3-41	NC17321	1967	8-37	NC28393	3251	10-40
NC14931	2118	3-39	NC17323	1969	8-37	NC33623	3288	6-41
NC14932	2119	3-39	NC17324	1970	8-37	NC38943	3280	12-40
NC14933	2120	4-39						

United Air Lines Inc. (Twin Wasp powered)

NC18938	2004	2-38	NC25617	3261	11-40	NC16063	1903	12-36
NC18939	2005	3-38	NC25618	3262	11-40	NC16065	1905	1-37
NC18940	2006	3-38	NC25620	3264	11-40	NC16067	1907	1-37
NC18941	2007	4-38	NC25621	2227	5-40	NC16068	1908	1-37
NC18942	2008	4-38	NC25622	2270	9-40	NC16069	1909	1-37
NC18943	2010	4-38	NC25675	2147	10-39	NC16070	1910	11-36
NC18944	2017	4-38	NC25677	2174	1-40	NC16071	1911	11-36
NC18945	2018	4-38	NC25679	2176	1-40	NC16087	1926	1-37
NC19948	3287	5-41	NC25680	2177	2-40	NC16088	1927	2-37
NC19964	2265	8-40	NC25681	2221	4-40	NC16089	1928	3-37
NC25611	3255	11-40	NC28379	3283	3-41	NC18103	1951	7-37 DST
NC25613	3257	11-40	NC33641	4113	4-41	NC18105	1953	7-37
NC25614	3258	11-40	NC15586	4112	7-41	NC18111	1983	8-37

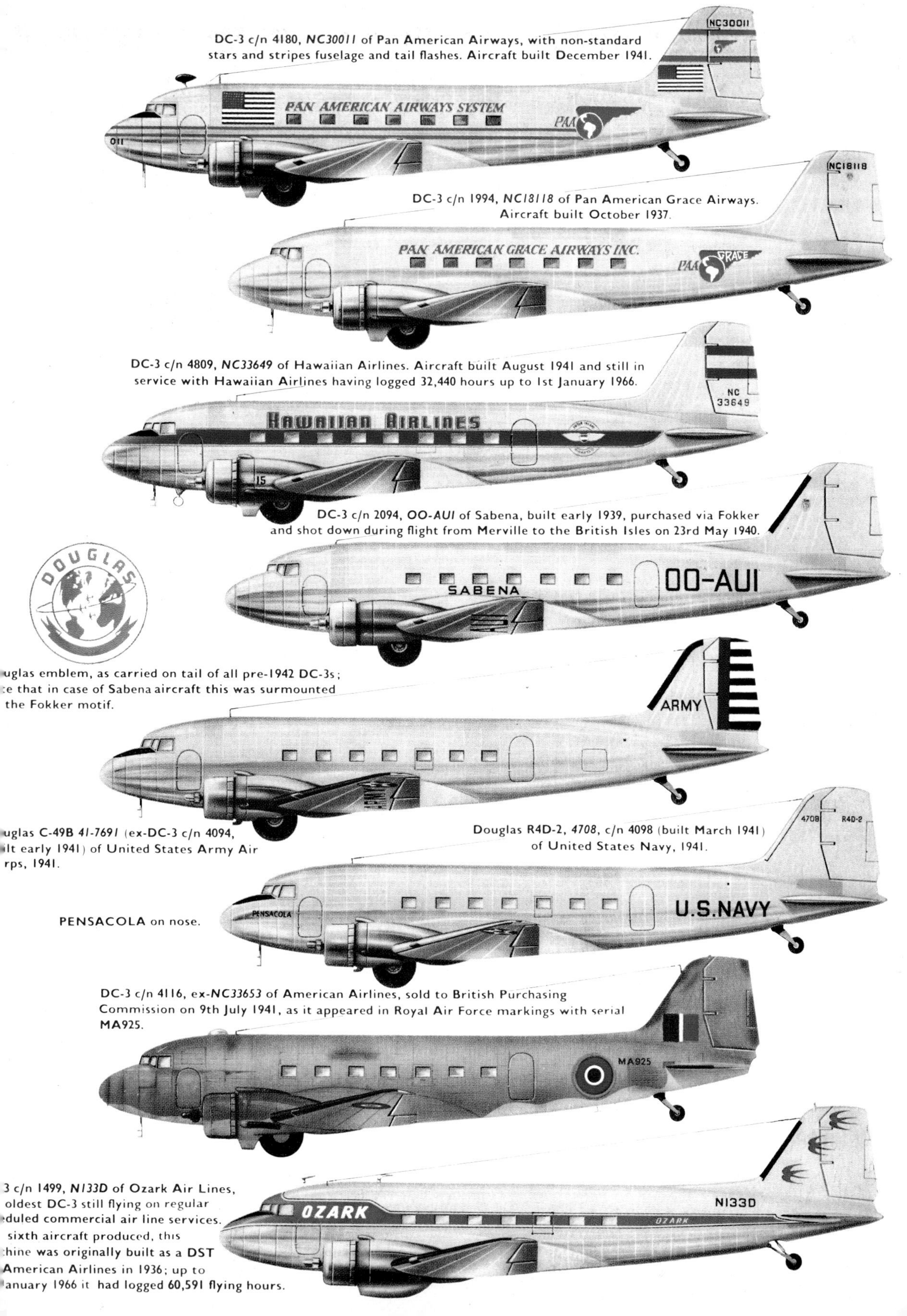

DC-3 c/n 4180, *NC30011* of Pan American Airways, with non-standard stars and stripes fuselage and tail flashes. Aircraft built December 1941.

DC-3 c/n 1994, *NC18118* of Pan American Grace Airways. Aircraft built October 1937.

DC-3 c/n 4809, *NC33649* of Hawaiian Airlines. Aircraft built August 1941 and still in service with Hawaiian Airlines having logged 32,440 hours up to 1st January 1966.

DC-3 c/n 2094, *OO-AUI* of Sabena, built early 1939, purchased via Fokker and shot down during flight from Merville to the British Isles on 23rd May 1940.

uglas emblem, as carried on tail of all pre-1942 DC-3s; :e that in case of Sabena aircraft this was surmounted the Fokker motif.

uglas C-49B *41-7691* (ex-DC-3 c/n 4094, ılt early 1941) of United States Army Air rps, 1941.

Douglas R4D-2, *4708*, c/n 4098 (built March 1941) of United States Navy, 1941.

PENSACOLA on nose.

DC-3 c/n 4116, ex-*NC33653* of American Airlines, sold to British Purchasing Commission on 9th July 1941, as it appeared in Royal Air Force markings with serial MA925.

3 c/n 1499, *N133D* of Ozark Air Lines, oldest DC-3 still flying on regular eduled commercial air line services. sixth aircraft produced, this chine was originally built as a DST American Airlines in 1936; up to anuary 1966 it had logged 60,591 flying hours.